Studies of Economic Growth in Industrialized Countries

French Economic Growth

Studies of Economic Growth in
Industrialized Countries

MOSES ABRAMOVITZ & SIMON KUZNETS, EDITORS

French Economic Growth

J.-J. Carré, P. Dubois, and E. Malinvaud

TRANSLATED FROM THE FRENCH BY JOHN P. HATFIELD

Stanford University Press, Stanford, California   1975

Originally published in French under the title
*La Croissance française: Un Essai d'analyse économique
causale de l'après-guerre,* © Editions du Seuil, 1972

Stanford University Press, Stanford, California
London: Oxford University Press
© 1975 by the Board of Trustees of the
Leland Stanford Junior University
Printed in the United States of America
ISBN 0-8047-0878-9   LC 74-82775

Preface

The study on which this book is based was undertaken in 1963 and carried out intermittently over seven years. It presents certain ideas that we have reached through a consideration of the economic growth experienced in France since the end of World War II.

The first impetus for this work came to us from Professors M. Abramovitz and S. Kuznets and from the Social Science Research Council, who encouraged parallel research on growth in seven industrial countries: Germany, Great Britain, the United States, France, Italy, Japan, and Sweden. We had the pleasure of meeting the authors of the studies on these other countries twice, in London in January 1964 and at Saltsjöbaden, Sweden, in July 1965. Although no systematic coordination of these studies has been attempted, we satisfied ourselves during these two meetings that we were pursuing similar goals and were following the same methods.

As our study was taking shape, it was the subject of numerous papers and discussions at the Institut National de la Statistique et des Etudes Economiques (INSEE) within the framework of the research conferences of the Ecole Pratique des Hautes Etudes. We benefited from the advice and suggestions of persons too numerous to mention. But among those to whom we must especially express our gratitude are MM. L. Blanc, R. Froment, C. Gruson, J. Mayer, C. Prou, J. Ripert, L. A. Vincent, J. Ullmo, and Y. Younès. Above all, our friend P. Berthet, now dead before his time, contributed to this project at its outset and through all of its subsequent stages. May our work meet the high standards of quality he always set. Finally, by numerous suggestions Professor M. Abramovitz helped us improve the first rough drafts of this book.

Our study does not, of course, commit either the organizations to which we belong or the many people who have helped us. But it is inspired to a great extent by what we have learned from both.

Contents

Abbreviations   xvii

Introduction   1

PART ONE. PHYSICAL SOURCES OF GROWTH

1. Production   11

   Outline of nineteenth-century economic history, 11. Postwar growth
   in the context of historical evolution, 16. Developments in the main
   sectors, 27.

2. Human Resources   35

   Growth of total population, 36. Employment, 46. The search for a measure of quality of the working population, 68. Conclusion: the evolution
   of total labor resources, 75.

3. Labor Productivity   77

   Trends in labor productivity in the economy as a whole, 78. Changes
   in the labor force, and in activity rates, by industry groups, 87. Labor
   productivity by industries, 95.

4. Investment   104

   Gross fixed capital formation, 1946–69, 105. The investment ratio, 113.

5. The Growth of Capital   122

   The measurement of capital, 122. Estimates for the postwar period,
   125. Postwar growth of capital, 140. Growth of productive capital over
   the first half of the century, 147. Capital assets per person employed,
   and postwar capital-output ratios, 152.

6. The Industrial Structure   158

   Has the rate of migration between sectors increased? 158. The structure
   of industry, 161. Changes in agriculture, 170. Trade and services, 173.

7. Total Factor Productivity and Technological Progress   177

   Total productivity, 178. Quality of labor and capital, 191. Effects of
   intersector transfers, 197. The residual and technological progress, 208.
   Provisional conclusions, 219.

PART TWO. A SEARCH FOR CAUSES

8. Aggregate Demand   225

Measurement of the pressure of demand, 226. The generation of
demand, 241. The effect of demand on growth, 256.

9. Investment and Savings   267

Demand for investment, 269. The supply of savings, 285.

10. The Role of Finance   306

Internal sources, 307. The role of outside resources, 321. The financing
of different categories of enterprises, 336. Conclusion, 342.

11. Economic Stability: Problems and Policies   345

Causes of inflation, 345. Domestic effects of inflation, 362. Foreign
balance, 370. Regulation of the economy, 379.

12. Foreign Trade and the Growth of Productivity   393

The expansion of foreign trade, 393. Structural causes of the growth
of foreign trade, 402. Effects on productivity, 407.

13. Competition, Mobility, and the Price System   417

The situation in the early 1950's, 419. The labor market, 421. Labor
mobility, 431. The capital market, 437. Controls over products, 439.
Prices and social costs, 443. Agreements and competition, 449. Action
on regional development, 453.

14. Planning and Economic Information   458

National Plan forecasts and the behavior of firms, 459. National planning and economic policy, 473. Development of economic and technological information, 489. Conclusion: the role of national planning
and economic information in growth, 493.

Conclusions   495

Appendixes   509

A. Estimation of indexes of production over the long term, 1896–1963,
509. B. The method for determining the contributions of various factors
to change in the aggregate labor force participation rate, 520. C. Estimation of gross fixed capital formation since the war, 522. D. Fixed
capital formation, 1896–1938, 525. E. Effects of the decline in the age
of capital, 532. F. Effects on growth of transfers of factors from one
sector to another, 536. G. The self-financing ratio and the growth rate
of investment, 540. H. Sociological factors in growth, 542.

Appendix Tables   546

Index   571

Figures

1.1 The Growth of French Production, 1900–1965   25

1.2 Agricultural Production in 90 French *Départements,* Including Alsace-Lorraine, 1892–1964   29

2.1 Distribution of Population by Sex and Age as of January 1, 1962   44

2.2 Female Labor Force Participation Rates by Age-Groups   50

3.1 Labor Productivity per Man-Hour, 1913–38 and 1938–65   80

3.2 Labor Productivity per Man-Year, 1913–38 and 1938–65   80

3.3 The Growth of Production and Production per Man-Hour in Industry, 1950–69   85

3.4 Production per Man-Hour, 1896–1966, for Sectors with Accelerated Productivity after 1929   98

3.5 Production per Man-Hour, 1896–1966, for Sectors with Retardation in Productivity after 1929   98

4.1 Investment by Principal Use Categories, 1949–66   107

4.2 Productive Investment in Plant and Equipment and Construction, 1949–66   110

4.3 Productive Investment in Two Groups of Sectors, 1949–65   110

4.4 Gross Investment in Fixed Capital as a Percentage of Gross Domestic Production, Current and Constant Prices, 1949–66   115

4.5 Gross Investment in Fixed Capital as a Percentage of Gross Domestic Production, 1896–1966   116

5.1 Estimated Growth of Capital Stock by Principal Category, 1949–66   145

5.2 Steam Power in Industry, 1896–1938   148

8.1 Total Output of Cast Iron, 1896–1968   233

8.2 Gross Value Added in Industry, 1949–69   240

11.1 Consumer Price Indexes, 1950–69   347

12.1 Industrial Production and Transportation as a Function of the "Corrected" Labor Force in Various Countries, 1869–1955   410

13.1 Changes in the Guaranteed Minimum All-Occupations Wage,
     the Consumer Price Index, and the Index of Hourly Wage
     Rates, 1950–69   423
13.2 Geographical Mobility of Workers, 1876–1962   432
 D.1 Relative Value of Investment and Issues of Corporate Securities,
     1896–1938   531

Tables

TEXT TABLES

1.1 Growth Rates of French Production, 1896–1969   21
1.2 Growth Rates of Production in France and Selected Other
    Countries, 1896–1963   23
1.3 French Gross Domestic Production, 1896–1969   24
1.4 Indexes of Production, 1946–49   26
1.5 Gross Domestic Product and Industrial Production, 1947–69   27
1.6 The Growth of Real Value Added by Sector, 1949–69   30
1.7 The Growth of Industrial Production by Industry, 1896–1963   31
1.8 The Growth of Construction, Transportation, and Services,
    1896–1963   33
2.1 Components of Peacetime Population Growth, 1896–1968   41
2.2 Population, 1851–1968   41
2.3 Population Growth in the Principal Western Countries, 1850–1965   42
2.4 Sex and Age Structure of the Population, 1896–1968   43
2.5 Increase in the Total and Working-Age Population, 1896–1969   45
2.6 Labor Force Participation Rates for Males, by Age, 1901–68   47
2.7 Contributions of Age Structure and of Participation Rates by
    Age to the Change in the Overall Labor Force Participation
    Rates of Males and Females, 1901–68   49
2.8 Contributions of the Age-Sex Structure and of Participation
    Rates by Age and Sex to the Change in the Overall Labor
    Force Participation Rate, 1901–68   55
2.9 Components of the Working Population, 1896–1969   58
2.10 Proportion of Unemployed to Working Population, 1896–1969   58
2.11 Workers Outside the Productive Sectors, 1954–68   59
2.12 Changes in Hours Worked per Year, 1896–1969   61
2.13 Working Population by School-Leaving Age, 1901–68   67
2.14 Effect of Changes in Sex and Age Structure on the Quality
     of the Working Population, 1901–68   71

2.15 Coefficients of Quality of the Working Population by
      School-Leaving Age   73

2.16 Effect of Changes in Level of Education on the Quality of
      the Working Population, 1901–68   73

2.17 The Overall Growth of Labor Resources, 1896–1969   74

2.18 The Growth of the Working Population in the Principal
      Western Countries, 1896–1962   76

3.1 The Growth of Labor Productivity, 1896–1969   79

3.2 The Growth of Labor Productivity in the Principal Western
     Countries, 1896–1963   83

3.3 National Income per Man-Hour in the Principal Western
     Countries, 1950–62   86

3.4 Size of the Labor Force by Sector, 1896–1968   88

3.5 Manpower by Sector, 1913–63   90

3.6 Structure of the Labor Force by Major Industrial Divisions,
     1896–1968   91

3.7 Indexes of Annual Hours by Sector, 1913–63   92

3.8 Indexes of Total Man-Hours Worked by Sector, 1913–63   93

3.9 Indexes of Output per Man-Hour by Sector, 1896–1963   97

3.10 Growth Rates of Output per Man-Hour by Sector, 1896–1963   99

3.11 Growth Rates of Productivity by Industry over Three Cycles,
      1951–69   101

4.1 Investment, 1946–49   106

4.2 Investment by Principal Use Categories, 1949–66   109

4.3 Investment in Building and Public Works as a Percentage
     of Total Productive Investment in 1956 Prices, 1949–65   109

4.4 Heavy and Light Investment, 1949–65   112

4.5 Investment in Gross Fixed Capital as a Percentage of Gross
     Domestic Production, 1949–69   114

4.6 Investment in Gross Fixed Capital, 1896–1963   117

4.7 Investment in Gross Fixed Capital as a Percentage of Gross
     National Product, Selected Countries, 1900–1960   120

4.8 Investment in Plant and Equipment as a Percentage of Gross
     National Product, Selected Countries, 1900–1960   121

5.1 Fixed Reproducible Capital by Sector, 1956: Estimates from
     Different Sources   129

5.2 Depreciation Rates in Relation to Net Capital Stock and
     Service Life, 1956   130

5.3 Number and Capital Value of Housing Units by Category in
     Cities of Over 50,000 Inhabitants, 1962   136

5.4 Number and Capital Value of Housing Units Classified by
     Age, 1962   137

5.5 Investment and Capital Stock in Housing, 1949–66   138

5.6 Net Capital Stock by Principal Category of Capital, 1949–66   140

5.7 Distribution of Net Reproducible Capital by Category, 1949–63   141

5.8 Range of Uncertainty in Estimates of Capital Growth, 1949–63   143

5.9 Estimated Growth Rates of Capital by Principal Category, 1949–66   146

5.10 Growth Rates of Capital Stock by Sector in Three Cycles, 1951–69   146

5.11 Power Available to Producing Establishments by Sector, 1906–31   149

5.12 Industrial Motive Power in Selected Countries, 1906–31   150

5.13 Comparison of Two Estimates of French Capital Stock, 1913 and 1954   151

5.14 Growth of Fixed Reproducible Capital in Three Countries   152

5.15 Capital-Output Ratios by Sector, in France and England, 1949–63   153

5.16 Aggregate Capital-Output Ratios, 1949–66   154

5.17 Net Fixed Capital per Worker by Sector, 1949–63   155

5.18 Growth Rates of Capital per Worker by Major Sector, France and Germany, 1949–63   156

5.19 Growth Rates of Capital per Man-Hour by Sector During Three Cycles, 1951–69   157

6.1 Distribution of the Industrial Labor Force by Size of Establishment, 1906–66   162

6.2 Distribution of the Labor Force by Size of Establishment in Establishments Employing More than Ten Persons, 1906–66   164

6.3 Distribution of the Labor Force in Selected Industries by Size of Establishment in Establishments Employing More than Ten Persons, 1906–62   164

6.4 Distribution of the Industrial Labor Force by Size of Establishment in Selected Countries, 1961–63   166

6.5 Concentration of Firms Assessed on the Basis of Real Profits in Selected Industries, 1955 and 1964   169

6.6 Size Distribution of Agricultural Holdings of More than One Hectare, 1892–1967   171

6.7 Distribution of the Labor Force in Commerce by Size of Establishment, 1906–66   174

6.8 Distribution of the Labor Force in Commerce by Size of Establishment in Establishments Employing More than Ten Persons, 1906–66   175

7.1 Total Productivity in France and Its Components, 1913–66   182

7.2 Growth Rates of Total Productivity in Three Countries, 1913–63   184

7.3 Growth Rates of Total Productivity in Selected Countries, 1950–62   185

7.4 Shares of Labor and Capital in Value Added by Sector, 1956   187

7.5 Growth Rates of Total Productivity by Sector, 1951–69   189

7.6 Various Calculations of Increases in Total Productivity and
the Effect of Capital Renewal, 1951–66   195

7.7 Earnings of Labor and Capital by Sector, 1956 and 1962   199

7.8 Corrections for the Index of Total Productivity Resulting
from Labor Movements Out of Agriculture, 1963   206

7.9 Contributions of Sources to the Growth of French Production,
1951–69   209

7.10 The Growth of the Labor Force in Certain Socio-occupational
Categories, 1954–68   215

7.11 Engineers and Technicians in the Manufacturing Industries
in Selected Countries, 1960–62   215

8.1 Number of Unemployed per 1,000 Employees, 1896–1968   231

8.2 Growth Rates of the Various Components of Demand, 1938–63   243

8.3 Estimates of Autonomous Demand, 1896–1938   246

8.4 External Causes of Changes in Demand, 1938–63   250

8.5 Influence of Demand Pressure on Labor Supply, 1949–66   260

9.1 Weighted Index of British Industrial Wages, 1831–1907   270

9.2 Costs of Capital Equipment and Labor Compared, 1949–66   283

9.3 Savings Rates in Selected Periods, 1896–1969   286

9.4 Net Domestic Savings Rates in Selected Countries, 1956–64   287

9.5 The Structure of Savings, 1949–66   288

9.6 Capital Transactions of Households, 1951–69   296

9.7 Data for the Study of Savings by French Corporations, 1949–66 298

9.8 Profit Margins in French Firms, 1951–64   300

9.9 Average Profit Margins of All Firms in Selected Sectors,
1956–67 and 1962–63   301

10.1 Changes in Self-Financing Ratios of Firms by Three
Definitions, 1949–67   310

10.2 Assets and Liabilities of Firms, Excluding Housing, 1953–66 316

10.3 Debt Ratios of Firms, Excluding Housing, 1953–66   318

10.4 The Effect of Price Increases on Indebtedness Ratio, 1953–66 320

10.5 Increases in the Supply of Financing, Gross Domestic
Production, and Gross Capital Formation, 1954–64   322

10.6 Representative Savings Ratios, 1954–64   323

10.7 Distribution of External Funds by Category of User, 1949–67 326

10.8 Distribution of Financial Resources Between the Public and
Private Sectors, 1956–66   328

10.9 Sources and Uses of Firms' Funds, 1954–64   330

10.10 Financing Ratios of Firms, 1953–67   333

10.11 Stock and Bond Issues, 1896–1964   334

10.12 Proportion of Gross Savings and External Finance, by Category
of Enterprise, 1956–66   337

10.13 Stock and Bond Issues by Private Corporations, 1950–66   340

10.14 New Medium- and Long-Term Credits for Capital Equipment
to Private Firms, 1956–66   341

11.1 Changes in Energy Prices, 1947–67   365

11.2 Price Indexes of Gross National Product in Six Countries, 1950–66   371

11.3 Principal Components of Balance of Payments Between France
and Other Countries, 1949–67   374

11.4 Indexes of Trade with Countries Outside the Franc Zone, 1953–67   375

11.5 Comparison of Projected and Actual Growth Rates, 1954–67   386

12.1 The Growth of Foreign Trade and Production, 1896–1969   395

12.2 The Growth of Production and Foreign Trade of Industrial
Products, 1896–1963   396

12.3 The Growth of Foreign Trade, 1951–69   399

12.4 The Growth of Foreign Trade and Production in Selected
Industry Groups, 1951–66   401

12.5 Trade in Semi-Manufactured and Manufactured Products,
1959 and 1968   401

12.6 The Growth of Trade by Area of Origin and Destination, 1959–68   405

12.7 Trade with EEC Countries as a Proportion of French Foreign
Trade, 1913–68   405

12.8 Imports of EEC Countries from Inside and Outside the EEC,
1953–63   407

12.9 Production and the Labor Force in Industry and Transportation
in Various Countries, 1869–1955   411

12.10 The Growth of Industrial Production in Four Countries, 1953–62   412

13.1 Hourly Wage Rates and Changes in Employment by Industry
Group, 1949–63   427

13.2 Changes in Hourly Earnings and Employment by
Industry Group, 1949–63   429

13.3 Annual Migration Rates in France and the United States, 1963   434

13.4 Proportion of Population Moving to a Different Commune
Between 1954 and 1968   435

13.5 Mobility Coefficient of Wage Earners, 1947–68   437

13.6 Prices of Energy Products, 1949–69   445

14.1 Forecasts and Outcomes of Four National Plans, 1952–70   463

14.2 Production Forecasts and Outcomes for the Third Plan, 1957–61   465

14.3 Production Forecasts and Outcomes for the Fourth Plan, 1959–65   466

14.4 Knowledge of Forecasts of the Fifth Plan by Industrial Firms,
January 1967   467

14.5 The Use of Forecasts by Industrial Firms, January 1967   468

14.6 Background Services for Decision Making Within Industrial
Firms, January 1967   469

14.7 The Influence of Plan Forecasts on Industrial Firms, January 1967   470

14.8 Effects on Economic Growth Attributable to Government
Economic Planning   474

14.9 The Structure of Gross Fixed Capital Formation, by Functions
      and Decision Centers, 1959   476
14.10 The Growth of Investment by Government Agencies, 1955–65   479

TABLES IN APPENDIXES A–E

A.1 Production by Sector in Key Years, 1896–1963   511
A.2 Proportional Distribution of Value Added at Factor Cost, 1949–63 517
A.3 Weighting Coefficients by Sector, 1896–1963   518
A.4 Aggregate Indexes of Production, 1896–1963   519
C.1 Production Figures for Construction and Public Works, 1949–56   524
D.1 Indexes of Investment in the Mechanical and Electrical
     Industries, 1896–1938   526
D.2 Unit Values Adopted for Indexes of the Volume of Imports
     and Exports   527
D.3 Indexes of Overall Investment, 1896–1938   528
E.1 Age Structure of Gross Productive Capital, 1881–1965   534

APPENDIX TABLES

 1 Gross Value Added by Sector, 1949–66   546
 2 Population of France, 1851–1968   548
 3 Factors of Population Change in France, 1896–1968   548
 4 Annual Changes in Various Categories of Workers, 1949–66   549
 5 Working Population by Economic Activity, 1949–66   550
 6 Indexes of Working Population by Economic Activity, 1949–66   552
 7 Indexes of Annual Hours Worked per Worker by Sector, 1949–66   554
 8 Indexes of Total Annual Labor Input by Sector, 1949–66   556
 9 Indexes of Production per Worker by Sector, 1949–66   558
10 Indexes of Production per Man-Hour by Sector, 1949–66   560
11 Investments by Sector, 1949–65   562
12 Fixed Reproducible Capital by Sector, 1949–66   564
13 Financing of Firms, 1953–67   566
14 Comparative Changes in Self-Financing Ratios of Firms,
    Including and Excluding Housing, 1949–66   568

Abbreviations

BIPE	Bureau d'Information et de Prévision Economique
BNCI	Banque Nationale pour le Commerce et l'Industrie
CEPREL	Centre d'Etude et de Prévision Economique à Long Terme
CETA	Centres d'Etudes Techniques Agricoles
CGP	Commissariat Général du Plan
CNJA	Centre National des Jeunes Agriculteurs
CREDOC	Centre de Recherches et de Documentation sur la Consommation
DATAR	Délégation à l'Aménagement du Territoire et à l'Action Régionale
DGRST	Délégation Générale à la Recherche Scientifique et Technique
ECA	Economic Cooperation Administration
ECSC	European Coal and Steel Community
EDC	European Defense Community
EEC	European Economic Community
EPU	European Payments Union (Marshall Plan)
ERP	European Recovery Program
FDES	Fonds de Développement Economique et Social
GATT	General Agreement on Tariffs and Trade
GEPEI	Groupe d'Etudes Prospectives sur les Echanges Internationaux
HLM	*habitations à loyers modérés* (low rental apartments built by public housing offices)
IBRD	International Bank for Reconstruction and Development
IEDES	Institut d'Etude du Développement Economique et Social
INED	Institut National d'Etudes Démographiques
INSEAD	Institut Européen d'Administration des Entreprises
INSEE	Institut National de la Statistique et des Etudes Economiques
ISEA	Institut de Science Economique Appliquée
JAC	Jeunesse Agricole Chrétienne
NATO	North Atlantic Treaty Organization
OECD	Organization for Economic Cooperation and Development
OEEC	Organization for European Economic Cooperation
SAEI	Service des Affaires Economiques et Internationales
SATEC	Société d'Aide Technique et de Coopération

SEDES	Société d'Etude du Développement Economique et Social
SEEF	Service d'Etudes Economiques et Financières
SGF	Statistique Générale de la France
SMIG	*salaire minimum interprofessionnel garanti* (guaranteed minimum all-occupations wage)
SNCF	Société Nationale des Chemins de Fer
VAT	Value-added tax

French Economic Growth

Introduction

Every Frenchman who has lived through the recent postwar period has had personal experience of the economic expansion of our country. Because this growth was so rapid, no one could deny it or be unaware of it. In the 50 years between the Universal Exhibition of 1889 and the beginning of World War II, the annual volume of production in France roughly doubled. Economic growth during that half-century could remain partly unnoticed by the public at large, for it was slow. In the 20 years between 1946 and 1966, in contrast, the volume of production increased by a factor of three. There are few today who cannot bear witness to the improvement in our material well-being over the course of this period. This expansion was accompanied by a profound transformation in French society. It permitted France to surpass such an old industrial leader as Great Britain and to narrow the gap between itself and the United States.

The causes, however, have been little analyzed. The scale of growth had not been foreseen. Not even the most optimistic had dared to hope after the war that the pace of growth in France could be maintained for so long at such a high level. Even today, explanations for this major phenomenon are in some cases imprecise and in others obviously incorrect or merely partial. The causes of economic growth are always complex. An objective observer discovers them only with difficulty. He may prefer not to commit himself to an answer before all the data can be collected for a detailed study and for the 25 years since the war to be placed in the context of history, in relation not only to the distant past but also to the decades ahead. In a man of science this may be prudent wisdom, but it becomes blindness for a man of action: he must make immediate decisions and foresee future economic development if he wishes a clear picture of the consequences of his actions. Unavoidable forecasting of this kind will be sound to the extent that it rests on a good understanding of past events. Every deliberate decision thus depends implicitly or explicitly on analysis of the causes of past expansion. He who tries to place present-day economic policies on a firm footing must first interpret contemporary growth.

We undertook our research in order to improve the objective basis for forecasts now being made and to break down in greater detail the analysis of facts that historians will turn to for a long time to come. Our ultimate goal was of course to understand the origins of postwar French economic growth. But this must be done in stages. Moreover, history, even when restricted to economic phenomena, is too complex and too empirical to lend itself to any complete explanation. Our objective, therefore, has been more modest. We have tried to bring out by systematic analysis the factors that have played a positive or negative role in the progress achieved over the last 25 years. We have tried to assess the weight of each of these factors and the changes they have brought about in the economy's long-term trends. Our work was both stimulated and given additional motivation by the fact that analogous research was being undertaken simultaneously in several countries. We have been able to use the provisional results gained by our colleagues abroad to throw light on our studies. Although our presentation does not turn on international comparisons, we have been able to make use of them for a number of important points.[1]

The reader will not find here a monistic thesis on the cause of present-day growth, but rather a number of partial explanations that complement one another. Our research makes us doubt whether one can ever trace the phenomenon it deals with back to one simple cause. Our analytical method doubtless is weighted against any grand synthesis, since it divides up reality and examines each of its aspects in turn. But if the various theses suggested do not pass this test, we may rightly question their force.

It may be rewarding to recall here how the sciences have moved forward. In physics, then in chemistry, and recently in biology, mankind

---

[1] Concurrently with the country studies, of which ours is one, related research was undertaken by Professor E. Denison on a systematic comparison of growth in eight European countries and the United States, restricted to physical factors and to the postwar period. His study, published before ours, is an important source for contemporary economic history. (See E. F. Denison, assisted by J. P. Poullier, *Why Growth Rates Differ: Postwar Experience in Nine Western Countries*; Washington, D.C., 1967.) Thanks to the author's kindness, we were able to use a preliminary draft of his text in the course of our own research. This has provided authoritative backing for our own international comparisons.

at first set out to find a single explanation of the complex facts it was observing. But the different general theories and the different explanatory systems put forward at the dawn of these sciences were contradicted by detailed analysis, and had to be abandoned. The syntheses that bore fruit came later and looked very different from first conceptions. Today they are useful in organizing our understanding of phenomena rather than in providing a definite key. We have little doubt that knowledge of economic evolution must pass through stages analogous to those in other areas of science, and that to construct general explanatory systems is today likely to be an empty exercise.

Clearly our research must have a historial dimension. Contemporary developments have meaning in relation to the past, either through continuation or by contrast. This is particularly true in France, whose position at the end of World War II was quite untypical, a fact poorly understood at the time. Moreover, certain important factors in recent growth had their origin between the wars, and even earlier. Of course, historical description alone does not explain developments, but it may reveal the first links in the causal chain. It suggests directions in which research in greater depth can be fruitful, and is too often neglected by those who judge the contemporary scene.

We have taken the year 1896 as the starting point for our historical studies. The 25 years since World War II have thus been placed within a 70-year period roughly equivalent to a human life span. The choice of such a distant reference point is justified by the large-scale disturbances experienced by the French economy between the two wars. The period 1920–39 does not provide an adequate basis for comparison, since economic growth during those years was affected by too many accidental circumstances: reconstruction was barely complete in 1927, when the Poincaré stabilization was effected; from 1930 on, France felt the backlash of the world crisis; the recovery that took place elsewhere from 1934 on was hampered in France by blundering economic policies and far-reaching social reforms. In order to relate the postwar years to historical trends, one must therefore consider a fairly long period before 1914.

The year 1896 has a double reason to be taken as a base. From the point of view of economics, it represents the turning point in the long-term trend of prices. Except for a slight increase during the 1870 war, wholesale prices had fallen almost continually from 1856 to 1896, at an average rate of 1.6 percent a year. From 1896 to 1913, however, they rose at an average annual rate of up to 2.2 percent. This turnabout in price trend was accompanied by a certain increase in the growth of

French output. From the point of view of statistics also, 1896 is a good base. In that year the first of a new series of quinquennial demographic censuses was carried out, all conceived and analyzed by a common method. Given the paucity of statistical information on early periods, this homogeneity in sources relating to the total population and the work force is highly valuable in our view. We have made use, moreover, of the work of L. A. Vincent, who also took 1896 as his starting year.

Our method is quantitative as well as analytical and historical. In most cases, the interest lies not in knowing whether a particular factor was at work but in evaluating its effects. Since growth has multiple causes, only a quantitative study can rank them in order of relative magnitude and distinguish those that predominate. Only a quantitative study provides the material necessary for forecasts of further growth. The course we have followed is therefore to measure the different phenomena involved, and then to seek their explanation by moving back successively through each causal channel. This distinguishes our work from other studies of economic growth over the same period. Our stress on explanatory analysis separates our work from those studies devoted to a pure description of the facts as well as from those organized around a single central thesis acting as a guideline for examining economic development. In particular, the influential book published by C. Gruson has a different aim from ours.[2] It traces the chief themes of economic policy and shows how the French gradually improved their understanding of how to control the economy. This aspect must play a part in our study, but we have not allowed it any special weight.

Our analysis is not limited to physical factors, e.g. to research on the respective roles of increases in the volume of labor, improvements in education or technical training, accumulation of capital, organization of the productive system, or technical progress. We have tried to work further back through the causal links and to explain the reasons for level of activity, scale of investment, structural changes, and technical progress. To this end we have tried to take advantage of the most diverse models developed by economic science for each particular phenomenon. We have thus deliberately avoided circumscribing our field.

The obvious and numerous gaps in our measurements of the different growth factors and in our explanation need justification. The scope and accuracy of our measurements have been seriously limited by the avail-

---

[2] C. Gruson, *Origine et espoirs de la planification française* (Paris, 1968).

ability of French statistical data. Here we must distinguish the postwar years from earlier periods. Since 1949 the tools of statistical reporting have been gradually built up so as to cover almost every economic phenomenon. In some cases the accuracy achieved leaves much to be desired, and some important data are missing for the first ten postwar years. Nevertheless the National Accounts and the statistics on which they are based provide us with a systematic description of economic activity.

By contrast, there is a serious lack of basic information on the first 40 years of this century. For our purposes the lack of direct data on a large part of production, on income, and on savings has caused great difficulty. Fortunately, we have had available certain long-term estimates, particularly those compiled by A. Sauvy and L. A. Vincent on the bases of the existing data. Thanks to them, certain overall phenomena can be traced, imprecisely, of course, since the missing statistics have been replaced by measurements that are indirect, but nonetheless more or less accurate. Moreover, the historic background established in the prewar part of the study is of some use, even if the picture it gives is not so sharp as that for the main period. A substantial share of our attention has nevertheless had to be devoted to statistical description. On the one hand, we have had to establish in many cases homogeneous series on the basis of available data. To achieve comparability between series and at some points also to improve our analysis, we have revised some estimates and filled some gaps. On the other hand, we have made original estimates of certain values that the present statistics and National Accounts do not cover. For example, we present series on physical capital not previously estimated for the recent period.[3] So that others may use them, we have reproduced the statistical series we compiled and describe our methods of measurement. This interrupts our text somewhat, although we have relegated the main tables and the longer methodological notes to an appendix. Although our analytic discussion is concerned with developments up to very recent years, we have restricted our more detailed statistical research to the period ending in 1966. To reconcile all our series with the new estimates in the National Accounts would have required work that did not seem justified. Only for the most important comparisons have we shown the latest years, particularly 1969, and in those cases we have ensured comparability with our own series.

[3] After our work was finished, new series of productive capital were drawn up by J. Mairesse. They are dealt with in Chapter 5.

Our work is necessarily incomplete in its interpretations. A comprehensive causal analysis of contemporary growth is impossible, since its origins are too numerous, too remote, and too deeply buried to be fully discovered. Our training has led us to stress economic causes; and the reader may well be surprised not to see more importance given to political and sociological analyses. This feature of our work shows that no research is ever finished. If this represents a weakness, we hope other researchers will correct it. Even in purely economic analysis we have not plumbed to great depth. On many points more profound research would be useful; for example, investment is an important link in every growth model. A complete study would look upstream for the distant sources of developments in investment and look downstream for their effects on the rate of growth. We have of course dealt with both these questions and have suggested various appropriate measurements. But our findings should be compared with the more detailed econometric studies based on major research works; these we have not been able to undertake. We hope that our study will lead others to carry out research in greater depth on some of the more important topics, and later we hope to go on to sectoral studies, each limited to a particular phenomenon that may lead to more exact and rigorously based conclusions than those we present here.

Our study falls fairly naturally into two parts. In the first part we examine mainly the effect of developments that may have influenced the physical factors of production: labor and material capital. In the second part we seek to explain changes in those factors or in residual productivity, that is, in that portion of the growth rate of output not attributable to growth in the physical factors.

The first part begins with a description of the growth of production itself. The contribution of the work force is the subject of Chapter 2, and labor productivity that of Chapter 3. We describe the changing scale of investment in Chapter 4, and in the following chapter present estimates of capital resources. We then examine the changes in the structure of the productive system. The first part ends with a chapter evaluating the contribution of each of the physical factors to the growth rate of production and thus showing the increase in residual productivity.

The second part begins with an examination of the stimulus of demand on the productive system. We then study the causes of investment, considering in succession the propensity of firms to invest and the formation of savings. A separate chapter deals with the effects of financial factors on capital formation. Another concerns inflation and short-term economic regulation. We then investigate what role may have been played in French growth by the freeing of foreign trade. Next we examine changes in the price system by which the various factors are ruled. Finally we consider the role of the French National Plan and of changes in the institutions concerned with French economic policy. The concluding chapter tries to draw together the analyses of particular causes into a consistent whole.

PART ONE

Physical Sources of Growth

CHAPTER ONE

Production

Our study of French economic growth must begin by examining the rate at which production increased. It will be useful to proceed from two different viewpoints: the overall economy, whose growth can be measured by an aggregate, and the main sectors[1] that make up the productive system. The second and third parts of this chapter each adopt one of these viewpoints. The first part is devoted to a short summary of progress during the nineteenth century.

OUTLINE OF NINETEENTH-CENTURY ECONOMIC HISTORY

We shall study contemporary economic growth in the context of the long period of the past 70 years. Nevertheless, a brief reminder of earlier economic history may serve as a background. After the Revolutionary and Napoleonic periods, France experienced an era of sustained economic growth in the nineteenth century whose many aspects have often been described. Recent studies by Marczewski, Markovitch, and Toutain give various measurements of this phenomenon.[2] Thus, from 1820 to 1930 agricultural production doubled, whereas the total output of industry and small craftsmen multiplied by more than ten.

In itself such an expansion seems impressive. Nevertheless, by comparison with that of other countries, French growth was relatively moderate. In 1820 France was first in the world in output for the "secondary sector," which includes industry and craftsmen. It was ahead of Great Britain—with a much greater population, to be sure, and already despite

---

[1] The French term *branche* has been translated variously as "sector," or "industry group," or sometimes "individual industry."

[2] J. Marczewski, "Le Produit physique de l'économie française. Comparaison avec la Grande Bretagne," *Cahiers de l'ISEA* (Institut de Science Economique Appliquée), series A.F., no. 4 (1965). See also J. Marczewski, *Introduction à l'histoire quantitative* (Geneva, 1965). The studies by Toutain and Markovitch are published in *Cahiers de l'ISEA*, series A.F., nos. 1–7 (1961–66).

a certain lag in the development of industry, strictly speaking. A century later, the United States, Germany, and Great Britain were clearly ahead of France. Undoubtedly this loss of France's predominance was due, to some extent, to the demographic expansion of the other countries. Whereas the French population grew by a third, Britain's multiplied by three, Germany's by more than two despite the reduction of its land area, and the United States' by thirteen. A comparison of growth rates of national product per capita also showed a slower increase in France than in other countries.

In the century between 1830 and 1930, the rate of growth in France was on the average about 1.1 percent per annum, whereas in Germany it was about 1.4 percent, and in the United States some 1.6 percent.[3] Great Britain had an output per head, considerably higher than that of France throughout the nineteenth century, but a comparable growth rate. In the first 30 years of the twentieth century, expansion was slower in Britain than in France. But this fact was not enough to change France's relative position. The picture that emerges is thus of France experiencing rapid growth but benefiting less than other countries from the Industrial Revolution. This lag has been exhaustively discussed by historians, who have often looked for an explanation based on statistics that were shown later to have considerably underestimated the country's rate of growth. We do not attempt to draw a conclusion from these discussions; however, we present a brief sketch describing the main features of French development during the nineteenth century and the beginning of the twentieth century.[4] Three periods can be distinguished fairly easily: the expansion from 1820 to around 1870, the retardation from 1870 to 1896, and the resumption of growth from 1896 to 1930.

The 50 years of expansion between 1820 and 1870 were in fact interrupted by the economic depression and political crisis of the years 1845–50. But over the long term this interruption was minor. The half-century is marked by almost continual progress in agriculture and industry, in the course of which urbanization increased rapidly. At the beginning of the nineteenth century, agriculture had not yet achieved the same rate of progress in France as in Britain. However, farming methods were gradually becoming modernized. Up until 1870 there was a slow trans-

---

[3] Approximate estimates for Germany are based on the results supplied to us by our colleagues of the German team, and for the United States on those supplied by M. Abramovitz and P. David.

[4] Complete references and a lively discussion of the subject can be found in Charles P. Kindelberger, *Economic Growth in France and Britain, 1851–1950* (Cambridge, Mass., 1964). Other useful references are the articles by J. Marczewski, already cited, and R. E. Cameron, "Profit, croissance et stagnation en France au XIXe siècle," *Economie appliquée*, April–September, 1967.

formation: new crops were introduced, such as sugar beets, lime and fertilizers began to be used, the sickle was replaced by the scythe, etc. Production was rising at an average rate of about 1 percent per annum. Nevertheless, the sociological structure of agriculture remained stable. The property and succession laws introduced by the Revolution enabled small farms to be kept up; moreover, these small farms were able to take advantage of the progress as much as the larger farms.

It is difficult to know, on the basis of information now available, if there was a large-scale movement of the agricultural working population toward industry in this period.[5] On the one hand, an undeniable process of urbanization can be observed. The big towns developed fairly slowly up to 1850, but thereafter at a rapid rate. The population of Paris and Lyon, for example, doubled between 1851 and 1876. The smaller towns were also developing, since the number of *communes* (the smallest French administrative territorial divisions) with over 10,000 inhabitants increased roughly by 60 percent between 1836 and 1872.

On the other hand, the few data directly related to the farming population do not give the impression of a substantial exodus. These figures are provided by five population censuses, dating only from 1856. They are affected by the return to France of Savoie and then by the loss of Alsace-Lorraine, and are based on replies to questions that may have been poorly understood. Nevertheless, they suggest that the agricultural population living in French territory as of 1871 changed little between 1856 and 1876. The total population grew in that period by 5 percent; consequently, the agricultural proportion moved from nearly 54 percent to around 51.5 percent. Over the same period the proportion of the total population living in *communes* of fewer than 21,000 inhabitants fell from 74 to 67 percent. These statistics, in brief, give the impression that urbanization affected chiefly the nonagricultural population of the rural *communes* rather than farmers. Nevertheless, the proportion of the working population in agriculture must have fallen slowly, probably from a little under 60 percent in 1820 to around 52 percent in 1870.

The 50 years from 1820 to 1870 also saw rapid development of industry and transportation, stimulated by newly trained engineers and enterprising bankers, i.e. by the first group of men trained in the high-level technical institutions set up by Napoleon I. The gross output of industry and craftsmen grew at an average annual rate of 2.3 percent, although the work force in this sector increased slowly. The growth of industry itself was of course much faster. The progress of mechanization, al-

[5] The data quoted are taken from *Annuaire statistique de la France, Résumé rétrospectif 1966.*

though behind that in Britain, led to the formation of large-scale under-takings. The building of canals and railroads dates for practical purposes from this period. This was also the time when French engineers and businessmen had the greatest influence on Western Europe, in the development of which they took an active part. Under the Second Empire investment abroad began to become sizable.

The decrease in the French rate of growth between 1870 and 1896 was due not so much to defeat in the 1870 war as to a serious setback in agriculture. There were a series of bad crops and part of France's vineyards was destroyed by phylloxera. Above all, however, French products were forced to meet an inflow of foreign goods that the development of communications had made competitive—American wheat, tropical commodities, frozen meat from the Argentine, etc. The farmers' purchasing power fell markedly, and the exodus from the countryside began. The proportion of the male work force employed in agriculture fell from 52 percent in 1872 to 44 percent in 1896. In an economy still largely agricultural, as France's was in 1870, this slump naturally had repercussions on industry by reducing its domestic outlets. The increase in real income of the nonagricultural sector did not compensate for this fall in demand, since a high proportion of savings was devoted to investment abroad. Economic policy tried to redress the situation, but it did so clumsily.

The Freycinet Plan, covering the years 1878 to 1882, led to a massive increase in public expenditure on communications and school buildings and stimulated a sharp revival in industry. But it was both too large in scale for the years in question and too short-lived: too large, because it gave rise to a rapid increase in imports and without doubt hampered the development of French exports, which had been increasing during the previous decades; too short-lived, because when it ended it led to a deep recession, which was accompanied by large-scale bankruptcies and reached its lowest point in 1886. To solve agriculture's difficulties, a protectionist policy was adopted. Increases in customs tariffs were made from 1881 on, crowned by the Méline Law, which came into force in 1892. Imports then fell, and the balance of trade was reestablished.

But, it would appear, the depressions preceding and following the boom of 1878–82, as well as the adoption of protectionist policies, significantly reduced the dynamism of French industry. Despite the substantial input of labor from the farms, the rate of growth of industrial and craftsman output probably did not exceed 1.6 percent per annum on the average between 1870 and 1896. With agricultural output practically stationary, total income grew by not more than around 0.8 percent per annum. Yet during this period industrial output grew rapidly in Germany and the United States. In 1870 pig iron production in Germany was equal to that in France, and in the United States it was higher by 30 percent; in 1896 Germany and the United States had about 2.4 and 3.8 times the output of France. In 1869 estimated consumption of raw cotton in Germany was one-third that of France; in 1896 it was more than twice as great. Between these same years, estimated raw cotton consumption in the United States grew from less than twice that of France to about four times.[6] The estimated consumption of wool grew slowly: in 1870 in Germany it was barely more than half, and in the United States barely 60 percent, of French consumption, whereas by 1896 Germany's lag had fallen to 20 percent, and the United States had caught up with France.

Although the French slowdown in the last third of the nineteenth century was partly provoked by the slump in agriculture—and without doubt aggravated by economic policy—did it also stem from earlier weaknesses in our institutions? We cannot of course make any pronouncement on this point, but our feeling is that this period, more than any other, deserves the attention of economic historians.

From 1896 French output again began to grow at a faster rate. According to our estimates, which do not seem to differ much from those of Marczewski, agricultural production increased by an average of 0.5 percent per year between 1896 and 1929, and industrial production by 2.5 percent. Total output per capita grew faster than in the other major countries, apart from the United States. The work force in agriculture fell at a rate of about 0.7 percent per year, and in industry it increased at the same rate. Simultaneously, an increasing concentration can be seen both in agriculture and in industry. From 1892 to 1929 the proportion of total agricultural area covered by holdings of over ten hectares grew from 74 to 78 percent. From 1906 to 1931 the proportion of the industrial work force employed in establishments of over ten persons rose from 42 to 66 percent, and in establishments of over 500 persons from 12 to 22 percent.

Doubtless the acceleration experienced in the last years of the nineteenth century was triggered by an extremely favorable international economic situation. The development of Germany and Belgium stimulated a rapid surge in French exports and helped effect fundamental changes in French industry. This expansion might well have been short-lived. Yet after a slowdown from 1901 to 1906, it accelerated right up to World War I and again from 1920 to 1929. The delaying factors at work in the last third of the nineteenth century no longer seemed to be

[6] Statistics extracted from *Annuaire statistique de la France*, 1913, and M. G. Mulhall, *A Dictionary of Statistics* (London, 1899).

felt. This brings us, therefore, to the start of a new phase of French economic development, and it is with this phase that our study is concerned.

POSTWAR GROWTH IN THE CONTEXT OF
HISTORICAL EVOLUTION

Rates of Growth

The large scope of expansion over the past 20 years is well known. What is less well known is how the growth rates now achieved compare with those of the past and the relationship between present-day French output and its long-term trend. This discrepancy can be explained by the lack of basic data, as well as by the limited number of comprehensive studies. But to start with, we must set the scene by a credible description of the growth in output from the beginning of the century, without concealing the uncertainties inherent in this description.

Statistical difficulties. Statistical data on output are relatively numerous and complete for recent periods, but extremely rare for the first 40 years of the century. We must reconstitute the early development of production from a very restricted body of directly observed results. The best source for long-term studies would be a series of industrial and agricultural censuses carried out at regular intervals, and going back some time into the past. Most other countries have such a basis for research. In France, unfortunately, censuses of production in the twentieth century were not carried out before very recent times. The first agricultural census was made in 1955 and the first industrial census in 1962. This gap would not be too serious if results were available for the distant past as well as for recent years from sufficiently numerous and complete surveys on various types of production. We could then reconstitute a fairly accurate picture of growth in each sector. But the information we have is far too scarce. The annual agricultural statistics established by totaling the information supplied by the communal commissions cover only vegetable crops. Estimates by the Ministry of Agriculture covering various principal animal products exist only for widely separated years for which there were "major inequities," that is, 1892 and 1929 in the period we are concerned with. Such inquiries were made annually only from 1933. As well as being scarce, these agricultural statistics are not very accurate, since they stem from estimates rather than from direct observation.[7]

[7] See *Les Statistiques agricoles en France et dans divers pays étrangers* (Paris, 1950).

Statistics of industrial production in the early periods are also very limited. They cover chiefly extractive industries under the control of the Bureau of Mines, that part of metallurgy covered by the Iron and Steel Federation, and some of the main industries—electricity, building materials, fertilizers, shipbuilding, etc. But there is no direct measurement for such important sectors as textiles and metalworking industries. Their output can be studied only through the apparent consumption of raw materials: raw textile products or metals. Between the wars, more complete statistics were gradually developed by the trade organizations. But the major part of output is covered for only the last 20 years or so. This lack of certainty in the basic data makes reconstruction of industry indexes for earlier periods difficult, but not impossible. A careful examination of existing information leads to results that enable postwar growth to be compared broadly with earlier trends. We have available on this subject studies by L. A. Vincent, who made estimates of the gross domestic product for a number of earlier years:[8] 1896, 1913, 1924, 1928, 1929, 1930, and 1938. We use this reliable work and reconcile it with the data in the National Accounts, which are used for the most recent years. We have made some changes in Vincent's estimates in order to improve comparability with recent series. These are explained in Appendix A.

The uncertainty affecting statistical knowledge of growth has been brought out by the revision of the National Accounts for the most recent years. Having changed its estimating methods, the Institut National de la Statistique et des Etudes Economiques in 1968 modified many results for the period 1959–66. In particular, the average annual growth rate of the gross domestic product in the period was increased from 5.8 to 6.4 percent. This increase is above the margin of error we should like for many of our analyses.

The main change has been to start from basic data on firms' activities rather than on output classified by product. Previously the primary source for estimates was the statistics collected by trade organizations or the authorities relating to the output of different products. More recently the National Accounts data have been recalculated from statistics

[8] L. A. Vincent, "Evolution de la Production Intérieure brute en France de 1896 à 1938, méthode et premiers résultats," *Etudes et conjoncture*, November 1962. See also his "Population active, production et productivité dans 21 branches de l'économie française (1896–1962)," *Etudes et conjoncture*, February 1965. We had the benefit of frequent discussions with M. Vincent during the drafting of our study. In particular, he kept us informed of successive improvements in his estimates. Our text takes account of the results he presented in 1969. For this reason our figures differ from those published in the two references mentioned.

of the firms' accounts that were supplied to the tax authority. The data by products contain gaps because of the very basis on which they are organized, since in principle it would be necessary for each firm to reply to as many trade organization questionnaires as it has products. The inevitable gaps are particularly frequent for new products and also for new lines undertaken by each firm; in a period of rapid development this can lead to underestimation of growth. Although the new series come closer to reality, in this book we shall use only series estimated from data on products, since this is the only estimating principle possible for the years before 1956. For the comparisons we want to make, a systematic error that probably has acted in a constant manner over time is better than a mixture that would be biased in favor of more recent years.[9] We must stress, however, that even for recent years our estimates are somewhat imprecise. This can be particularly serious in comparisons between countries that have different methods of evaluation and publish results affected by systematic errors that are presumably different.

Conceptual difficulties. In addition to statistical gaps, aggregative comparisons between widely separated periods must be, to some extent, conventional. Since we make frequent use of growth rates, we must from the start stress the conceptual difficulties of defining these rates. The difficulties appear at two stages of analysis: first, when one attempts to designate by an aggregate all the very different output of one year, and second, when a number is chosen to represent the average growth of this aggregate over a period that covers one or several decades.

Any measure of this aggregate presupposes, on the one hand, that the list of activities to be regarded as productive has been chosen, and, on the other hand, that a system of weights has been specified for combining different products. From both points of view we have referred to certain rules in use in the National Accounts.[10] We have therefore treated as productive those activities that entail the provision of goods or the supply of services that enter into the market economy. To these

---

[9] It should be noted that the series used in this study contain some remaining discrepancies, since the results for 1956 to 1959 are based on data by firms. The period is a short one, however, and we can evaluate the resulting bias: the average annual growth rate of the gross domestic product by volume for those three years increased from 3.5 to 4.1 percent if data by firms are substituted for data by products. For details of the revision, see "Les Comptes de la nation de l'année 1962," *Etudes et conjoncture*, August-September, 1963, pp. 744–45. For the volume of output, compare *Annuaire statistique*, 1961, p. 355, with *Etudes et conjoncture*, December 1963, p. 1141.

[10] For a detailed examination of these rules see, for example, INSEE, *Initiation à la comptabilité nationale*, 3d ed. (Paris, 1964), especially chaps. 1 and 6.

we have added, as is usual, agricultural products consumed on the farm. Our measurements therefore omit activities within the home and services provided by individuals to each other without payment. To the extent that changes in patterns of life may have radically altered the relative importance of these household activities or services, our results may lead to error. Equally, the fact may be controversial that we have considered as final all goods and services acquired by households, since urbanization has made inevitable the consumption of certain goods or the employment of certain services that are useless in a rural society (in particular urban transport). Nevertheless, it should be remembered that France was already heavily urbanized at the beginning of the century, and that patterns of living have changed only slowly. On reflection, uncertainties about exactly where to draw the line around the area of production do not seem likely to seriously affect our results.

To combine in one single aggregate measure the basic data on various goods and services, we use prices as weights, believing that they measure the relative importance of units of products. If the outputs of two different periods are compared, the same prices must of course be used in calculating the aggregate in each.[11] But the choice of prices can influence the result of the comparison. Applying the selling prices of the earlier period defines a Laspeyres index, and using those of the later period gives a Paasche index. Experience has shown that the former has almost always been higher than the latter. In order, however, to base ourselves on a measure that we could a priori consider neutral, we have in most cases used a Fisher index, which is the geometric mean of the two former indexes. But this choice does not entirely free our aggregative comparisons from arbitrariness (the results in Appendix A based on the Laspeyres and Paasche indexes illustrate the impact of this arbitrary factor). In the same context, certain conceptual difficulties remain, which we will not discuss here, of the precise methods used to determine the weights in the calculations of aggregates representing final output.

Last, even if we had a series available showing year-by-year variations in an aggregate that measured total output perfectly, we should still ask what definitions of growth rates would represent the trends that interest us for a study of growth. Short-term fluctuations mean that results can differ quite significantly according to the definition adopted. A priori, one can think of one or another of the following four methods: (1) Re-

---

[11] This can be arranged by comparing two widely separated periods by means of an intervening one. This is the principle of "linked indexes," which we have used for long-term comparisons.

place an annual series having somewhat erratic variations by a series calculated as close to it as possible but regular in movement (for example, by a series growing at a constant rate over particular long periods chosen in advance). (2) Smooth the annual series by a mechanical process, e.g. by calculating a moving average over a given number of successive years (for example, five or ten years). (3) Identify years showing analogous short-term situations (for example, business cycle peaks); then, ignoring intervening years, calculate the average annual growth rate between those selected. (4) Select particular years for historic or statistical reasons but with clearly defined economic characteristics; operate as above, bearing in mind the direction of systematic errors that may be entailed.

None of these methods is perfect, as would appear from a detailed examination of each. The fourth is obviously the least satisfactory and likely to produce the largest systematic errors. It is nevertheless the one we have followed, both because the detailed statistical estimates we have used were not made annually and because two major wars and a prolonged depression made the other three methods just as uncertain in practice.

Of the six years we have selected for calculating long-term average growth rates, 1929 and 1963 had an undoubtedly favorable economic position. The year 1913 was marked by a temporary slowdown but followed a period of high prosperity. It can therefore also be considered a year of great prosperity. (In the case of gross domestic product, if 1912 were taken instead of 1913, this would increase the average annual growth rate over the preceding 16 years by 0.1 percent and reduce that for the following 17 years by an equal amount.)

The years 1896–97 mark the end of a long period of relatively depressed activity. The French economy's productive capacity was clearly partially unused. From 1897 to 1900 growth was rapid. It follows that the average rates calculated for the periods 1896–1913 and 1896–1929 somewhat overestimate the long-term trend (to substitute 1900 for 1896 would reduce the average annual growth rate of gross domestic product in those two periods by 0.3 percent and 0.1 percent respectively).

The business cycle position in 1938 and 1949 is difficult to define, since comparisons with adjacent years matter less than the very special nature of growth during the period in which these two years fall. The Great Depression had brought industrial development to a stop in France as elsewhere and recovery had not really developed by 1938. Postwar growth was already well under way by 1949, but the level of output was still only slightly above that of 1929, so there was great room for improvement. Although 1938 and 1949 are only mediocre benchmarks for

TABLE 1.1
Growth Rates of French Production, 1896–1969
(Percent per year)

Period	Industry	Gross domestic production	Gross national product
1896–1913	2.4%	1.9%	1.8%
1913–29	2.6	1.7	1.5
1929–38	–1.1	–0.4	–0.3
1938–49	0.8	0.9	1.1
1949–63	5.3	5.0	4.6
1949–69	5.3	5.0	4.7
1896–1929	2.6	1.8	1.7
1929–63	2.2	2.2	2.1
1929–69	2.7	2.6	2.5

Source: See Appendix A.

studying long-term trends, adjacent years clearly would not be better. Accordingly, we must be satisfied with them.

Results. The estimates we have finally adopted give the growth rates shown in Table 1.1 for three aggregates: industrial output, gross domestic product[12] (covering all sectors considered in France as productive), and gross national product (covering productive sectors and also various services). Of the five periods shown in the first part of Table 1.1, 1949 to 1963 had a particularly high growth rate for gross domestic production—5 percent per year—whereas the rate had not reached 2 percent in any of the other periods. This rate of growth was maintained thereafter, since on the basis of the estimating methods discussed, gross domestic production rose at an average of 5.1 percent per year between 1963 and 1969. The post–World War II period therefore stands out as altogether exceptional.

The high rate of recent growth may seem natural in view of the ground lost in the two previous periods. The volume of French output in fact fell in the 1930's and during the war, so that in 1946 it was 20 percent below the level reached 17 years earlier. If over those 17 years output had increased at the same rate as achieved on the average from 1896 to 1913, or from 1913 to 1929, the level in 1946 would have been two-thirds higher than in fact it was. To put recent growth in the context of earlier years, it is probably advisable to consider not only the rate between 1949 and 1969, but also the average annual rate over a longer period, such as 1929 to 1963, and then to compare this with

[12] As explained in Appendix A, the results of long-period comparisons differ slightly from those in the National Accounts covering the last 20 years. But the divergences are very small.

70351

growth between 1896 and 1929. The second part of Table 1.1 makes this comparison possible.

The growth of total French output seems to have been faster from 1929 to 1963 than from 1896 to 1929. In particular, if we allow for the extension of growth from 1963 on, present-day levels seem definitely higher than those that would have resulted from a continuation of growth after 1929 at the same average rate as in the first 30 years of the century. But this result does not seem due to industrial production. If our estimates are right, output grew at roughly the same rate from 1896 to 1929 as from 1929 to 1969. (The special position of 1896 cannot introduce of itself, over such long periods, a marked bias in the average annual rates.) The increase in total growth rate must be explained by the acceleration observed in agriculture and services.

These results relating to total production would not be particularly revealing if they were not confirmed by an examination of rates of change in output per person. In Chapters 2 and 3 we discuss changes in population, in the work force, and in productivity. However, we note that output per head (calculated on the total of "productive sectors" —*des branches productives*) was 1.6 percent per year from 1896 to 1929 and 2.2 percent per year from 1929 to 1969.

This phenomenon is not of course peculiar to France. In the three other major European countries—Germany, Italy, and Great Britain— output per capita increased between 1929 and 1963 at a much faster rate than in the first 30 years of the century. The difference in fact was significantly higher than in France. By contrast, in the United States output per person grew faster than elsewhere before 1929, but its lead over Europe does not seem to have increased between 1929 and 1963.

Table 1.2, which provides the statistical basis for this conclusion, also compares French rates of growth with those of four other large industrial countries. In the last 20 years, the rate of development varied greatly between countries. France holds a middle position, with growth rates lower than those of Germany and Italy but markedly higher than those of the United Kingdom and the United States. On the other hand, since the beginning of the century, output per capita increased at broadly the same rate in every country except Great Britain. From 1896 to 1963 the figure was multiplied by about 3 in France, Germany, and Italy, by 3.5 in the United States, and by 2 in the United Kingdom.

To study French economic growth, it is not enough to look at widely separated key years. We need also to form a picture of the changing pattern of growth, by looking at shorter-term movements within the prewar periods. To this end, it would be useful to have available annual

TABLE 1.2
Growth Rates of Production in France and Selected
Other Countries, 1896–1963
(Percent per year)

Period	France	Germany[a]	United States	Italy	United Kingdom
Total output:[b]					
1896–1929	1.7%	–	4.2%	2.1%	1.0%
1929–63	2.1	–	3.0	2.7	2.1
1949–63	4.6	7.8%	3.8	5.8	2.6
Output per inhabitant:					
1896–1929	1.5	1.3	2.1	1.3	0.5
1929–63	1.7	2.1	1.7	2.0	1.6
1949–63	3.7	6.1	2.1	5.1	2.1

Source: National Studies of the Social Science Research Council Project.

[a]Actual German territory at each period; 1950–62 for the last period. Figures for total output for the first two periods are rendered insignificant by territorial changes.

[b]Concept close to that of gross national product; in the case of France, total output (sectors classified as productive plus others).

series comparable with those for the latest period. However, we have not been able to carry out the detailed statistical studies necessary for annual estimates. analogous to those shown earlier for the particular years 1896, 1913, 1929, and 1938. We have, therefore, simply reconciled our estimates with the annual series given to us by L. A. Vincent for the between-war years and with those published by Alfred Sauvy[13] for the years 1901–13. For 1896–1901 we have used available indexes of industrial and agricultural production and some statistics of the main products.[14] The results are shown in Table 1.3 and Figure 1.1.

As we shall show in the second part of this study, the series established in this way greatly exaggerates short-term fluctuations in the years before 1929. Accordingly, the contrast between the apparent irregularity of the periods 1896–1913 and 1920–29 and the regularity of the movement in the period 1946–69 should be ignored and attention paid only to growth rates. Figure 1.1 shows fast expansion from 1946 to 1969. Such rapid growth over 20 years has no precedent in France's economic history since the beginning of the century, and probably not before. Growth rates were also high after World War I, but they slowed down much sooner, apparently even before the impact of the world economic slump. Our index shows an average growth rate of over 7 percent per year between 1920 and 1924 and of 3 percent from 1924 to 1929. But

[13] Cf. *Rapports du conseil économique*, session of March 23, 1954, Paris.

[14] See, in particular, *Indices généraux du mouvement économique de la France de 1901 à 1931* (Paris, 1932), and *Production agricole et consommation alimentaire de la France de 1892 à 1939* (Paris, 1944).

TABLE 1.3
French Gross Domestic Production, 1896–1969
(1929 = 100)

Year	Index of production	Year	Index of production	Year	Index of production
1896	55	1920	65	1946	80
1897	54	1921	64	1947	87
1898	57	1922	74	1948	100
1899	60	1923	78	1949	107
1900	61	1924	86	1950	115
1901	59	1925	87	1951	122
1902	59	1926	88	1952	125
1903	61	1927	87	1953	129
1904	64	1928	92	1954	136
1905	63	1929	100	1955	143
1906	64	1930	97	1956	151
1907	65	1931	93	1957	161
1908	66	1932	89	1958	165
1909	67	1933	93	1959	171
1910	67	1934	93	1960	184
1911	70	1935	90	1961	192
1912	76	1936	91	1962	206
1913	76	1937	96	1963	218
		1938	96	1964	230
		1939	100	1965	240
				1966	253
				1967	265
				1968	276
				1969	295

Source: Appendix A and annual estimates by L. A. Vincent; also A. Sauvy in *Rapports du conseil économique*, session of March 23, 1954, Paris.

Figure 1.1 also shows the substantial setback between 1930 and 1940. The trend established from the beginning of the century was not caught up with and overtaken until the period 1955–60. In brief, the speed of recent growth is an entirely new phenomenon that needs explaining.

Postwar Growth Phases

For the detailed analyses that follow, we must look at the patterns of short-term growth over the past 25 years. We do not propose to give a causal interpretation but only a description, in order to emphasize the years between which comparisons need not take account of short-term fluctuations.[15] The National Accounts series begins in 1949, but an order of magnitude of growth for 1945 can be obtained from the indexes

[15] For a detailed descriptive study of recent short-term fluctuations, see P. Herzog, "Comparaison des périodes d'inflation et de récession de l'économie française entre 1950 et 1965," *Etudes et conjoncture*, March 1967.

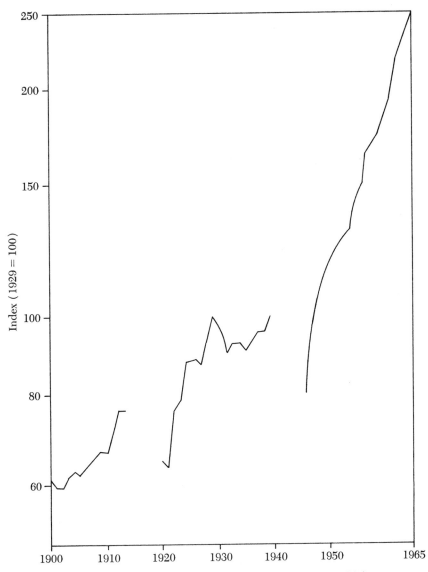

Fig. 1.1. The growth of French production, 1900–1965.

TABLE 1.4

Indexes of Production, Major Industrial Divisions, 1946–49

(1938 = 100)

Sector	1946	1947	1948	1949	Index 1949 (1946=100)
Agriculture	83	85.5	91.5	99	119
Industry	77	87	103	109.5	142.5
Services and building	91	99	109	115	126
Total	81	89	102	109	134

Note: Indexes are taken from the studies of M. Gavanier, "Le Revenu national de la France: production et disponibilités nationales en 1938 et de 1946 à 1949," *Statistiques et études financières,* supplément finances françaises, no. 20, 1953. The indexes for sectors exclude taxes, whereas the total index includes indirect taxes, making it more comparable with the movement of gross domestic production after 1949. The overall index is not the weighted average of the sector indexes.

of agriculture and industry given by Gavanier, as shown in Table 1.4. In the light of Table 1.4 and the National Accounts from 1949, postwar growth can be divided into four periods: 1945–51, reconstruction and restarting of the economy; 1951–57, first postwar cycle; 1957–63, second postwar cycle; and 1963–69, third postwar cycle.

The rapid growth rates of the postwar years (on the order of 10 percent in 1947 and 13 percent in 1948, followed by 7.5 percent per year in 1949 and 1950) can be explained by the combined effect of the gradual return to work of prisoners and veterans and the reconditioning of industrial plant, much of which had not been really affected by bombing or destruction during the Liberation. The 1938 level was rapidly regained, although that year, it is true, was not the highest prewar. In this first period, growth was concentrated on the production of energy and capital goods rather than on household consumption, and it was accompanied by a gradual return to normal economic conditions: the official allocation of industrial products ended in April 1949, and food rationing in January 1950; foreign trade gradually revived, although substantial protection of home industry was maintained.

The term "cycle" used to designate the three following periods should not mislead: we do not believe that French growth is necessarily cyclical, causing periods of substantial slowdown roughly every six years. We have simply observed some analogy between developments from 1951 to 1957, from 1957 to 1963, and from 1963 to 1969. In all cases there was a spurt of growth leading (in 1951, 1957, and 1963) to disturbing inflation, followed by deflationary action by the government to stabilize prices, then a decrease in growth for one or two years, and finally a revival at a rate of 5 to 6 percent a year, stimulated to some degree by government measures. We should note, moreover, that the

TABLE 1.5
Gross Domestic Production and Industrial Production, 1947–69
(Previous year = 100)

Year	Gross domestic production	Industry	Year	Gross domestic production	Industry
1947	109.9	113.4	1958	102.6	103.8
1948	113.2	118.0	1959	103.0	102.2
1949	107.5	106.5	1960	107.9	108.7
			1961	104.6	105.0
1950	107.9	108.7	1962	106.9	106.0
1951	106.4	109.6	1963	105.6	106.0
1952	102.3	102.0	1964	106.2	105.9
1953	103.1	102.4	1965	104.1	103.5
1954	105.4	104.7	1966	105.0	106.2
1955	106.0	106.0	1967	104.4	103.3
1956	105.1	109.1	1968	104.2	104.5
1957	106.3	105.8	1969	107.0	109.0

Source: Figures for 1947–49 are from Table 1.4; figures for 1950–69 are from French National Accounts.

annual indexes relate to the average position each year and partially mask the short-term fluctuations: the lowest point of output in the slow-down of 1952–53 was reached around the end of 1952, in that of 1958–59 toward the end of 1958, and in that of 1964–65 at the beginning of 1965. The cycle that began with the Stabilization Plan in the autumn of 1963 has a rather special form. Revival began in 1965, but was stopped at the end of 1966 by the joint effect of prudent economic policy and the repercussions of the depression in Germany. On the other hand, a strong boom in output, and in economic activity generally, followed the events of spring 1968.

Year-by-year growth rates of gross domestic product and of real value added for all industrial sectors together are shown in Table 1.5, which summarizes postwar developments. In our detailed analysis we have not taken account of the early years of reconstruction, which are obviously unrepresentative. For that reason, in order to eliminate the effect of short-term fluctuations, in most cases we have concentrated on the four years of high output: 1951, 1957, 1963, and 1969.

DEVELOPMENTS IN THE MAIN SECTORS

A number of points can be made on growth in the main sectors (*branches*) of production to throw light on the overall description just made and to confirm the characteristics of postwar development. Production grew much faster after 1945 than it had grown from the beginning of the century, except in some industries that began between the two wars. The same phases of growth can be found in each sector. Finally, in each case a comparison of the two main periods 1896–1929 and 1929–63 leads to the same conclusions. It is probably not essential for our research into the causes of growth to break sectors down in great detail; moreover, we should soon run out of data, especially for the earlier periods. We have therefore confined ourselves to a 17-sector division of the economy, following the National Accounts publications.[16] This breakdown is used systematically in the first part of our study, and as often as necessary or possible in the second. We shall now consider in turn agriculture, industry, and the services.

Agricultural Output

Farm output is very sensitive to weather, and shows irregular movements, as is well illustrated in Figure 1.2: it is not unusual for output to increase or decrease by over 10 percent from one year to another. In the long run, however, accelerated growth can be observed, particularly after World War II; thus the annual average increase was over 3 percent after 1945, although it had been only 1 percent in the previous periods. This undeniable acceleration occurred on a cultivated area that hardly changed over the period. It is due, without doubt, to a more systematic use of fertilizers, the consumption of which grew at more than 7 percent per year, and of cattle feed, which increased at 5.5 percent and made a more rational type of breeding possible. In addition, it is probable that farm mechanization, which had been on a small scale before the war, has led to more suitable cultivation of the soil and has raised yields. It should be recalled that, whereas there were about one million tractors in the country in 1964, the figure in 1949 was only 95,000, and had exceeded half a million by 1957. By contrast with other industries, agriculture was not affected by the 1930 depression. On the other hand, the two world wars brought output to a very low level, where it remained for a particularly long time after 1920: output corrected for weather did not regain the 1913 level (itself only average) until 1930. World War II reduced output less: recovery was rapid from 1946 on, and the 1938 level was regained by 1949. Thus, for agriculture the change in growth rate is marked and cannot be considered as simply making up lost ground because of war and depression. The case of industry as a whole is different.

---

[16] These sector headings are repeated in each table, as, for example, in Table 1.6. Their precise postwar definition is given in "Méthodes de la comptabilité nationale," *Etudes et conjoncture*, March 1966, pp. 208–10, 96–143. The regroupings for years before the war fit fairly closely into these definitions.

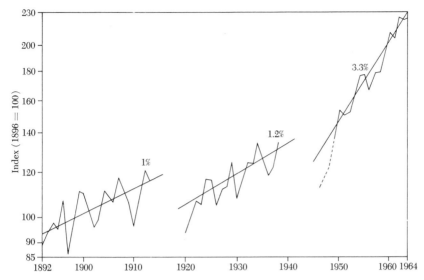

Fig. 1.2. Agricultural production in 90 French *départements*, including Alsace-Lorraine, 1892–1964.

Industrial Production

We shall first outline postwar industrial development as shown in the National Accounts. We shall then compare this with growth over longer periods, and assess how much ground was lost during the depression and World War II.

Development of production since 1949. Value added in industry[17] grew by an average of 5.6 percent per year, and at broadly the same rate over the three cycles we have considered when taken as a whole, but it varied somewhat in particular industrial sectors (see Table 1.6).[18] The level of aggregation of the National Accounts masks certain phenomena, such as a slowing down of coal output, compensated within industry 03 by increased gas distribution. Similarly, the differing growth rates of the various mechanical and electrical industries are averaged out in classification 09. Nevertheless, the significant postwar results show through; they concern the rate of development of each industry,

[17] See classifications 02 to 12 in Appendix A tables, which included extractive industries, electricity production, and agricultural and food industries, but excluded building and public works.

[18] The results for the period 1963–69 proceed from estimates on a 1962 base, which were corrected roughly to ensure consistency with the rest of the table. (The correction of the growth rates was based on a comparison of estimates with 1959 and 1962 bases for the period from 1959 to 1966.)

TABLE 1.6

The Growth of Real Value Added by Sector [branche], *1949–69*

(Percent per year)

Sector	1949–1966	1951–1957	1957–1963	1963–1969	Gross value added, 1956 *(000 francs)*
01. Agriculture and forestry	2.9%	2.4%	2.8%	1.9%	17,883
02. Processed foods and farm products	3.6	3.3	2.2	5.0	13,289
03. Solid mineral fuels and gas	1.6	1.9	0.3	1.5	2,961
04. Electricity, water, and kindred products	9.5	8.0	9.3	7.5	2,193
05. Petroleum, natural gas, and oil products	10.1	7.0	10.0	10.1	5,846
06. Building materials and glass	6.2	5.6	5.2	7.9	2,678
07. Iron mining and metallurgy	4.8	5.9	3.5	5.3	3,686
08. Nonferrous minerals and metals	7.9	7.0	7.2	6.3	904
09. Mechanical and electrical industries	6.1	5.7	6.4	5.0[a]	20,950
10. Chemicals and rubber	8.0	7.2	7.9	8.2	5,688
11. Textiles, clothing, and leather	4.0	4.0	3.4	0.8	11,356
12. Wood, paper, and miscellaneous industries	5.0	4.4	4.7	4.2[b]	7,897
02–12. Industry	5.6	5.0	5.3	5.4	77,448
13. Building and public works	6.5	6.3	6.3	7.2	12,607
14. Transportation and communications	5.0	4.7	4.8	4.5	10,612
16. Services other than housing	5.2	4.9	4.9	5.6	19,933
19. Trade	4.8	5.2	4.9	4.5	20,774
Gross domestic production	5.2	4.7	5.1	5.1	166,480
Gross national product	4.9	4.3	4.9	4.9	191,300

Source: National Accounts.
  [a]Latest estimate, 7.2 percent per year.
  [b]Latest estimate, 6.2 percent per year.

and the sensitivity of each to the three main periods of economic slow-down. The industries can be divided into three groups, according to their ranking in relation to the average.

Growth was fast and continuous in all the energy industries except for coal, and in chemicals and nonferrous metals (mainly aluminum). Average annual growth rates from 1949 to 1966 were 10.1 percent (petroleum and natural gas refining and distribution), 9.5 percent (electricity production and distribution), 8 percent (chemicals), and 7.9 percent (nonferrous minerals and metals). These rates are of the same order of magnitude in the three cycles, but some short-term movements must be noted—the temporary drop in the oil industry after the Suez crisis (by nearly 6 percent from 1956 to 1957), and a speeding-up of chemical output. Beginning in 1960, French nonferrous metals producers tended to invest abroad, and the growth of home output slowed.

In certain sectors postwar growth was slow. Coal output rose slightly

TABLE 1.7
The Growth of Industrial Production by Sector, 1896–1963
(Percent per year)

Sector	1896–1913	1913–1929	1929–1938	1938–1949	1949–1963	1896–1929	1929–1963
Processed foods and food products	1.4%	2.1%	0.3%	0.0%	3.6%	1.7%	1.6%
Solid mineral fuels and gas	2.2	2.2	-0.8	1.7	1.4	2.2	0.8
Electricity and water	8.9	12.9	3.3	2.2	9.9	10.8	7.1
Petroleum and oil products	–	–	19.6	5.5	10.5	–	11.2
Building materials	2.4	2.5	-5.0	1.0	5.6	2.4	1.2
Metallurgy	6.5	4.0	-4.5	3.5	5.4	5.2	2.1
Mechanical and electrical industries	4.5	4.4	-8.9	1.4	6.3	4.4	2.2
Chemicals	5.9	7.5	0.9	2.7	7.9	6.7	4.3
Textiles, clothing, and leather	1.4	0.8	-1.4	-1.0	4.6	1.1	1.2
Miscellaneous	2.5	2.4	1.9	0.3	5.1	2.5	2.7

Source: Appendix A.

until 1960, and then began to drop. The average annual increase of solid mineral fuels and gas as a whole was less than 2 percent for the whole period 1949–66. Growth in textiles, clothing, and leather was below the figure for all industry, especially after 1963. The particular characteristics of each of the three cycles led to certain differences. For example, annual growth of iron mining and metallurgy was rapid during the first cycle, when heavy industry was given special incentives, then slowed down from 6 to 4 percent, and later increased slightly again.

Comparison with earlier growth. Table 1.7 shows the average growth of industrial output in the five periods already considered for the analysis of overall results. It was consistently faster postwar than earlier. Nevertheless, in the two periods covering the years 1929–49, growth was slow and in many cases negative. Later fast rates can be explained partly by that lengthy stagnation. Table 1.7 gives an impression of some continuity in the growth of output from 1896 to 1929, with the ground lost during World War I being regained in the 1920's. To facilitate direct comparison between present-day figures and those in 1929, the last two columns of Table 1.7 show average annual growth rates achieved in the different industries over the two long periods 1896–1929 and 1929–63. In almost every industry, output seems to have increased on the average more slowly between 1929 and 1963 than between 1896 and 1929. This conclusion, however, has only limited significance.[19]

[19] The economic situation in the first year of the period 1896–1929 was far less favorable than in 1929. As we have seen, however, this cannot greatly affect average growth rates over a 33-year period.

To interpret this movement properly, we must first take account of changes in the total population and the labor force as well as in working hours. This topic is examined in the next two chapters. However, it can be mentioned here that between 1896 and 1929 the French labor force grew by around 5 percent, whereas from 1929 to 1963 it fell by 6 percent. Second, it should be noted that the drop in growth rates between the periods 1896–1929 and 1929–63 was particularly marked in the four sectors whose average annual rates in the first period had exceeded 4 percent: electricity, metallurgy, mechanical and electrical industries, and chemicals. These were then relatively new industries with rapid technical progress, which had not yet established a leading place in the French economy. Among them they employed only 16 percent of the industrial work force in 1896 and 30 percent in 1929. The high growth rates achieved between those years were therefore mainly the result of the rapid increase in demand experienced by new products in their early stages.

Building, Transportation, and Services

Average postwar growth of this group was similar to that of gross domestic product. Building increased faster, and the services taken as a whole slightly less fast (see the last section of Table 1.6). By comparison with earlier periods, the last 20 years stand out for the rapid expansion of building, transportation, and services (see Table 1.8). However, contrary to what we have noted for industry, comparison between the two long periods 1896–1929 and 1929–63 shows an acceleration in trade and services other than housing. Output of trade, if taken as proportional to the volume of all products traded,[20] probably grew by about 60 percent between 1896 and 1929 and by 100 percent from 1929 to 1963, two periods of almost the same length. The difference between the two rates of growth is too high to be explained by estimating errors. The index for other services is particularly unreliable. It covers activities where there is no direct measure of output in the earlier periods (hotels, restaurants, entertainment, personal services, laundry, medical and legal services, etc.). Mostly, estimates are based on variations in the work force in each of these occupations, and on some hypotheses about likely developments in labor productivity. Despite the

[20] In fact, our figures for the period 1949–63 are based on direct estimates of value added at constant prices. They allow for a slight increase in the scale of intermediate consumption in distribution and therefore lead to an index for this sector a little lower than that for the volume of products flowing through distributive channels. According to L. A. Vincent, the latter was about 218 in 1963 (1949 = 100), whereas our figure is 197.

TABLE 1.8

The Growth of Construction, Transportation, and Services, 1896–1963

(Percent per year)

Sector	1896–1913	1913–1929	1929–1938	1938–1949	1949–1963	1896–1929	1929–1963
Building and public works	2.0%	1.4%	–5.8%	3.8%	4.8%	1.7%	1.6%
Transportation and communications	3.6	3.0	–1.7	2.7	5.1	3.3	2.5
Trade	1.5	1.4	0.3	–0.2	5.0	1.4	2.1
Housing services	1.6	1.6	0.7	–0.8	3.4	1.6	1.4
Other services	2.0	1.1	1.5	1.2	5.1	1.6	1.9
Financial institutions[a]	3.1	3.1	–3.1	0.9	2.2	3.1	0.4
Domestic service[a]	–0.5	–1.5	–1.1	–2.2	–2.1	–1.0	–1.9
Government[a]	0.9	–1.8	2.6	3.0	2.4	–0.4	2.6

Source: Appendix A.

[a]Indexes based on man-hours of employment.

low accuracy of the indexes, the increase in growth rate of these services can be assumed to be correct, since it can undoubtedly be explained by two factors: a quickening in leisure-time spending and the rapid spread of health services over the past 20 years.

In brief, France, like some of the other European countries, has experienced rapid although not entirely regular growth since World War II. To set it in the context of earlier growth, two approaches can be followed. The first compares average annual growth rates over the fairly continuous periods of expansion between 1896 and 1963 (with the immediate postwar years excluded), i.e. 1906–13, 1922–29, and 1949–69. Gross domestic product increased in those periods by 2.5 percent, 4.4 percent, and 5.0 percent per year, respectively. The period 1949–69 then appears exceptional, not so much in its rate of growth as in its duration; such a rate over a long period like this had never before been observed. This seems to be evidence of a qualitative change in the structural factors underlying economic growth. The second approach considers as one the whole period from 1896 to the present, treating the two world wars and the Great Depression as merely temporary interruptions in long-term trends already under way since the recovery that occurred at the beginning of the century. The post–World War II expansion then can be seen as following upon 20 years in which output hardly exceeded its 1929 level. In this long-term context, today's levels are scarcely above those that would have resulted from a continuation of the movement observed between 1896 and 1929. From this viewpoint, in the last 25 years France has done little more than catch up with the ground lost between 1929 and 1945.

Developments in the ten years from 1970 to 1980 will remove the ambiguity. If the present rate of expansion continues, it will lead to an increasingly distinct improvement on pre-depression trends. Growth would then represent a lasting acceleration of French development. In order to define the outlook for future growth, it is important to establish how much truth is contained in each of the two views of postwar expansion. This question will be considered again in later parts of our study, particularly in Chapters 3 and 7. At this stage it is only possible to say that acceleration seems to have been most pronounced in agriculture and services; most of the individual sectors had already experienced high rates in the first 30 years of the century.

We must now analyze French economic growth in detail, concentrating first on the factors of production, and particularly on the most important one, labor.

CHAPTER TWO

Human Resources

The main purpose of this chapter is to describe the development of overall labor resources within the French economy since 1896 and to reveal the underlying sociodemographic factors. The first part describes and explains the growth of total population and its age and sex structure, which of course affect the structure of the labor force. The second part examines the development of the latter in relation to social and demographic factors, the rate of utilization of manpower, and the level of education, which plays an important part in the quality of the work force. The third part of the chapter presents the methods and results of a study into ways of measuring this quality. In conclusion, Table 2.17 summarizes the growth of labor input in the economy over the period considered.

Our approach in this chapter, and more generally in this part of the study, emphasizes the dependence of output on labor resources treated as a factor of production, and their dependence in turn on the growth of total population. The relationship between demographic factors and long-term economic growth is obviously more complex. For example, an increase in total population can stimulate demand, or the number of children per family can influence the intensity of work done by heads of households. Some relationships, however, pull in the opposite direction from the one studied; e.g. those between the rate of expansion on the one hand and the behavior of different sectors on the other—or between the rate of immigration and the pressure of demand on growth. Such links are examined in the second part of this study, in Chapter 8, where we consider the role of demand in growth. Again, to change the context, birthrates and the emphasis on education depend to a certain extent on economic growth. These points are mentioned in the following discussion.

GROWTH OF TOTAL POPULATION

We shall examine first the factors affecting total population—births and deaths and migratory movements—and then its overall growth and the resulting changes in sex and age structure.[1]

Natural Population Increase

From "Malthusianism" to the revival of the birthrate. Over most of the nineteenth century and the beginning of the twentieth, the French birthrate was very low in comparison with that of other Western countries.[2] From 1851 to 1860, the gross rate had fallen to 26 per thousand, whereas in European countries for which relevant statistics are available it was between 30 and 38 per thousand. In Germany in that period it was still as high as 35 per thousand, and in Great Britain 34 per thousand. Between 1901 and 1910, the French birthrate was only 20.5, whereas in the other European countries it was still above 25 per thousand (33 in Germany and 27 in Great Britain). Thus the drop in the birthrate, which began in most other European countries in the latter part of the nineteenth century, affected France very early, with a head start of more than half a century. World War I caused a substantial shortfall of births, estimated at 1.5 million, despite a temporary postwar increase in the rate due to marriages and births deferred during the four years of conflict. The fall in the birthrate continued up to World War II. At 18.5 per thousand between 1925 and 1929, it was comparable with that of many other Western countries: e.g. 19 in Germany, 17 in Great Britain, and 20 in the United States. Between 1935 and 1945, however, it fell to 15 per thousand. These very low levels can be explained by the joint effect after 1930 of the small cohorts of 1915–19 reaching child-bearing age, of the depression, and of World War II. The revival of the French birthrate after the war is well known: it averaged 20 per thousand between 1946 and 1954, 18 from 1954 to 1962, and 17.5 from 1962 to 1968.

A study of variations in marriage and fertility rates shows that the course of the birthrate in France was determined largely by changes in attitude toward conception. The gross reproduction rate[3] trended

---

[1] Most of the data used in this section come from *Annuaire statistique rétrospectif de la France* (Paris, 1966). Hereafter referred to as *Annuaire statistique*.

[2] The natural development of France's demography—births and deaths—is known with great precision, thanks to the exhaustive coverage of official records back to very early periods.

[3] The gross reproduction rate in year t is the number R of girls born from a fictitious generation of 100 women, assumed to be unaffected by mortality, and having at every age (between 15 and 50 years) the fertility observed in year t. This is a

downward fairly constantly from the beginning of the nineteenth century to the eve of World War II. The drop was particularly fast from 1875 (around 170 percent) to 1940 (about 100 percent). By contrast, the rate picked up strongly after World War II: between 1950 and 1954 it stood at 135 percent, from 1955 to 1959 at 132 percent, and between 1960 and 1964 at 138 percent. It has fallen in the last few years, however (to 126 percent in 1968).

The change since the war seems to have had its origins in ·the first years of the war itself. This interesting phenomenon has been the subject of numerous studies. M. Febvay[4] has shown that it can be explained chiefly by the increase in couples willing to have two children rather than one and, to a lesser extent, three rather than two. On the other hand, the proportion of young, childless households remained as high after the war as before, and the proportion of families with over three children was almost unchanged. The change in attitudes toward births was thus not widespread. Nor was it definitive, as is shown by the drop in fertility observed since 1964.[5] It is too early, however, to know whether this drop will be lasting or will become more pronounced.

The causes of postwar changes in attitudes toward conception have not been fully elucidated. Several different and complex factors seem to have been at work.[6] Paradoxically, the war—that is to say, the experience of insecurity in a society that until then had built one kind of security upon another—may have helped to lower individual standards of security, and these factors among others determined the extent of birth control. After the war, expansion and full employment created a secure situation favorable to a high birthrate. Family security was strengthened, moreover, and the cost, both real and psychological, of the "marginal" child was reduced by the introduction of social security and by family support measures, such as the Family Code of 1938–39 making family allowances general, substantial postwar increases in these allowances, the establishment in 1946 of prenatal and maternity allowances, and the institution in 1945 of a "family" deduction from the direct

---

better indicator for the study of births than gross birthrate, since, unlike the latter, it depends only on fertility by age and is not a function of the age structure of the population.

[4] See M. Febvay, "Niveau et évolution de la fécondité par catégorie socio-professionnelle en France" (paper presented at the International Congress on Population, Vienna, 1959).

[5] See G. Calot and S. Hémery, "La fécondité diminue depuis quatre ans," *Economie et statistique*, no. 1, May 1969; and S. Hémery and Q. C. Dinh, "La Situation démographique en 1968 et 1969," *INSEE*, Collection D, August 1971.

[6] On this subject see P. Bourdieu and A. Darbel, "La Fin d'un malthusianisme," in the collective work edited as Darras, *Le Partage des bénéfices* (Paris, 1966).

tax-on household income. These measures in themselves reveal a change in official attitudes toward the birthrate and toward planning for the future, which men such as Adolphe Landry and Alfred Sauvy were largely responsible for bringing about. In addition, there seems to have been a change in social standards governing family values and the value placed on children or on their number.

It is worth inquiring whether the surge in the birthrate can be explained partly by a relative improvement in the economic position and income of young adults by comparison with other sectors of the population. Studies by the American economist R. A. Easterlin[7] have led him to conclude that the economic factor accounts to a great extent for the postwar "baby boom" in the United States. Easterlin argues that the improvement in the economic position of young adults in the United States after the war can be explained by the strong demand for labor and a slowing down in the growth of the younger age-groups in the working population (mainly because of the stop to immigration).

No long-term data on income by age-group are available in France. We cannot establish, therefore, whether the economic position of young adults has especially improved since the war. But two comments are in order. First, World War I caused great losses in the young adult age-group. This may have led to an improvement in their postwar economic position, particularly in the case of the middle classes (whose attitudes largely accounted for the rise in the birthrate after World War II), since the large-scale immigration between 1920 and 1930 hardly affected those in that class who were employed. No lasting improvement in the birthrate can be noted after World War I. On the other hand, the young adult age-group changed differently in France than in the United States after World War II. The deficit of births during World War I led to a dip beginning in 1940 in the working population aged 25 to 35.[8] This age-group decreased in 1940–45, hardly changed in 1945–50, and increased after 1950. By 1955 the deficit no longer affected the 25–35 age-group. Thus, the demographic factors behind the improved economic position of young adults after the war, unlike the United States, were lacking in France. Obviously, it is tempting to associate sharp demographic change with the growth of the economy after World War II, and to ask whether these two phenomena, which reveal a new vitality in French society, can be explained at least in part by a combination of common causes. This point will be taken up again in the general conclusion of the study.

[7] "The Baby Boom in Perspective," *American Economic Review*, December 1961.
[8] The age at which couples have a second or third child is in most cases between 25 and 35 years.

Drop in the death rate, and wartime losses. The death rate has fallen considerably in France, as in other countries of Western Europe, since the beginning of the nineteenth century. The gross rate was 24 per thousand in 1851–60, and dropped gradually from about 20 per thousand at the turn of the twentieth century to 17 or 16 per thousand between the wars and 12 per thousand around 1960.[9] Superimposed on this secular drop in the death rate and profoundly affecting the demography of France were the losses sustained in the two world wars: 1.4 million in 1914–18,[10] or 3.5 percent of the population in that period, and 0.6 million in 1939–45. The magnitude of World War I losses gave rise to a "populationist" explanation of the economic stagnation in France after the Great Depression of the 1930's, which gave as its main cause the decimation of the elite by the war. This hypothesis seems to us scarcely justified, or at least overstated.[11]

Excess of births over deaths. Gross birthrates barely exceeded gross death rates from the beginning of the twentieth century (and even from the middle of the nineteenth century) until World War II (see Table 2.1). The natural yearly rate of increase of the French population was therefore extremely low up to 1945: 0.13 percent from 1896 to 1913 and also from 1921 to 1936. The natural change in the total population was in fact downward between 1936 and 1946 (a rate of −0.1 percent per year). After World War II natural growth settled at 0.7 percent, a rate not previously achieved in France for over a hundred years. This development can be explained by a slight acceleration of the decline in the death rate, but chiefly by changes in attitude toward births.

France as a Host Country for Immigration

The statistical sources do not provide exact or complete information on migratory movements in and out of France by direct methods.[12] Up to 1932 there were very few restrictions, and those set up since 1932 were never total. After World War II the ease with which one could

[9] Gross French mortality rates since the beginning of the century have been slightly higher than those observed in many other Western countries. This is due, on the one hand, to the age structure of the French population, which has become older faster than in the other Western countries because the French birthrate fell so early in the nineteenth century, and, on the other hand, to a slightly higher death rate, especially in men.

[10] See Michel Huber, *La Population de la France pendant la guerre* (Paris, 1913).

[11] On this problem, see in particular Alfred Sauvy, *Histoire économique de la France entre les deux guerres* (Paris, 1965), vol. 1, chap. 2. The author draws up a quantitative and qualitative human balance sheet of World War I and then discusses the possible psychosocial consequences of that war.

[12] See Chapter 8 for a study of the links between migratory movements on the one hand and the tightness of the labor market and the pressure of demand on the other.

move across most of France's borders favored illegal immigration. The entry of workers from French-administered overseas territories has always been unrestricted or poorly controlled. Exit by temporary immigrants is not recorded in any way. Consequently, migratory movements must be estimated as a residual, taken as the difference between population growth between two successive censuses, on the one hand, and the excess of births over deaths, on the other (something known very precisely from the registers of births, deaths, and marriages).[13] Such estimates enable us to establish only net apparent immigration; minor errors in successive censuses can cause substantial errors in this figure. In fact, however, the estimates obtained agree fairly well with partial information available from other sources, from which annual series of net immigration between successive censuses can be constructed.

By contrast with many European countries that experienced net emigration at least up to the Great Depression of the 1930's, France has for a long time been a host country for immigration.[14] Over the entire period studied (1896–1966), few Frenchmen left their country to settle abroad, other than in French-administered territories. The slow natural growth of the French population by comparison with that of other countries is of course relevant.

Annual average net immigration was low between 1896 and 1906 (roughly 20,000 persons). It rose to some 30,000 for the years between 1906 and 1911, a period of relatively rapid expansion. In 1911 to 1921 the total figure is estimated at 450,000. Between 1921 and 1931 net immigration reached an average level never subsequently attained again (except for the special case of repatriation from Algeria in 1962): 250,000 per year in 1921–26, and 140,000 in 1926–31, both periods of reconstruction and fast growth.[15] This excess gave way to an average annual deficit of 20,000 during the depression years 1931–36. Net immigration, practically nonexistent between 1936 and 1946, resumed after the war, and continued at a fairly slow rate of some 40,000 persons a year until 1954. After that year, net immigration increased and reached an average of 155,000 persons between 1955 and 1961. On the one hand, this was a period of rapid growth in France, while the total labor

[13] Estimates have also been carried out by more complex methods. See H. Bunle, *Mouvements migratoires entre la France et l'étranger* (Paris, 1943).

[14] The principal sources for our study are Bunle, *Mouvements migratoires*, for the prewar period and various internal official documents and estimates given in *Annuaire statistique* (1966) for the postwar period.

[15] The largest groups of immigrants were Polish, Italian, and Spanish. Most of the immigration occurred during the period 1922–26, being particularly high in 1923, 1924, 1929, and 1930. The 1927 recession was reflected in a net emigration, as immigrants of earlier years returned home. The links between immigration and expansion were very close throughout this period (see Chapter 8).

TABLE 2.1
Components of Peacetime Population Growth, 1896–1968
(Average annual rate per thousand)

Rate	1896–1911	1921–1931	1931–1936	1946–1954	1954–1962	1962–1968
Birthrate	21	19	16	20	18	17.5
Death rate	20	17	15.5	12.5	11.5	11
Rate of natural increase[a]	1	2	0.5	7.5	6.5	6.5
Rate of increase attributable to net immigration	1	5	–0.5	1	4.5	3.5
Overall rate of increase[b]	2	7	0	8.5	11	10

[a]Difference between birth and death rate.
[b]Rate of natural increase plus increase attributable to net immigration.

TABLE 2.2
Population, 1851–1968
(Millions of persons)

Year	Number	Year	Number	Year	Number	Year	Number
1851	35.8	1911	39.6	1931	41.9	1954	43.1
1896	38.6	1921	39.2	1936	41.9	1962	47.0
1901	39.0	1926	40.9	1946	40.3	1968	49.9
1906	39.3						

Source: *Annuaire statistique rétrospectif de la France* (Paris, 1966), pp. 66, 68, 72.
  Note: Figures refer to midyear population in census years, within the borders at each period: 1851, present territory excluding Nice and Savoie; 1896–1911, present territory excluding Alsace-Lorraine. See also Table 2.1 and Appendix Table 2.

force remained stationary. On the other hand, the end of colonization led to some 65,000 persons yearly, on the average, being repatriated between 1955 and 1961. In 1962 repatriation was on a massive scale: 700,000 from Algeria settled in France at the end of the Algerian war. Net immigration continued at an average of roughly 150,000 a year from 1963 to 1969, in spite of the large increase in the labor force due to repatriation, reductions in the armed forces, and the fact that the large age-groups born after the war had reached working age—in spite also of the greater slackness of the labor market from 1964 on.

Stagnation to Fast Climb in the French Population

The overall changes in the total population resulting from the natural and migratory movements just analyzed are shown in Tables 2.1 and 2.2.[16] Between 1896 and 1911 the total population of France grew at an average rate of 0.2 percent yearly. This very low rate is the same as that experienced in the previous half-century. Despite the restoration to

[16] See also Appendix A, Tables A.1 and A.2.

TABLE 2.3
Population Growth in the Principal Western Countries, 1850–1965
(Percent per year)

Period	France	Germany[a]	United States	Italy[b]	United Kingdom
1850–1910	0.2%	0.8%	2.3%	0.5%	1.1%
1910–60	0.3	–	1.4	0.7	0.3
1921–30	0.7	0.5	1.4	0.8	0.5
1930–38	0.1	0.7	0.7	0.8	0.4
1946–50	0.9	2.1	1.8	0.8	0.7
1950–60	0.9	1.1	1.7	0.6	0.4
1960–65	1.4	1.3	1.5	0.8	0.8
1921–38	0.4	0.6	1.1	0.8	0.4
1946–65	1.0	1.4	1.7	0.7	0.6

Principal source: Annuaire statistique rétrospectif de la France (Paris, 1966), pink pages.
[a]Through 1937 the territory included the Saar. After World War II it included only the German Federal Republic.
[b]From 1900 figures are for the present territory.

France of Alsace-Lorraine (1.7 million inhabitants) and a not inconsiderable net immigration (0.45 million), the population of France declined by 400,000 persons between 1911 and 1921 as a result of war losses (1.4 million) and the wartime shortfall of births. Between 1921 and 1931 the population increased at 0.7 percent per year, of which 0.2 percent was the natural increase and 0.5 percent was immigration. The depression led to a drop in fertility, a halt in immigration, and even to the departure of some immigrants who had entered in the previous period. On the other hand, the meager cohorts born between 1915 and 1918, on reaching child-bearing age, lowered the birthrate. The result was complete stagnation of the total population from 1931 to 1936. In World War II, deaths and a shortfall of registered births were both considerable, resulting in a population drop of 1.3 million from 1936 to 1946. All things considered, in the half-century between 1896 and 1946 the population within the present boundaries of France did not grow at all. The post–World War II demographic expansion has no precedent in France over the past hundred years. From 1946 to 1954 the population grew at 0.85 percent per year, mainly through natural increase. From 1954 to 1968 it rose by 1.05 percent, under the effect of a birthrate that stayed relatively high and large-scale immigration of foreign workers and repatriated nationals. In all, the population of France increased far more in the 25 years after World War II than between the mid-nineteenth century and World War I.

Table 2.3 gives the growth of total population in the main Western countries over a century, and shows how France compared with the others. Despite considerable net emigration, population in the other

TABLE 2.4
Sex and Age Structure of the Population, 1896–1968

Year	Proportion of women in population *(percent)*	Age structure of the population *(percent)*					
		Men			Women		
		0–14	15–64	65 & over	0–14	15–64	65 & over
1896	51%	26%	66%	8%	25.5%	65.5%	9%
1911	51	26	66	8	25	66	9
1921	52.5	24	68	8	21.5	68.5	10
1926	52	24	68	8	22	68	10
1936	52	26	65	9	24	65	11
1946	53	23.5	67.5	9	20.5	67	12.5
1962	51.5	28	63	9	25	60.5	14.5
1968	51	26	64	10	24	60.5	15.5

Source: *Annuaire statistique rétrospectif de la France* (Paris, 1966).

countries before World War I increased much faster than in France. Relative growth movements changed somewhat between 1920 and 1930, but stabilized between 1930 and 1940. By contrast, the relative positions altered completely after World War II: French population grew at a faster rate than that of Italy or Great Britain.

Stagnation of Working-Age Population; the "Upsurge of Youth" After the War

The changes in the population's sex and age structure, which determine changes in the population of working age, were determined by four factors: (1) the downward trend in the birthrate up to World War II, which led to an aging of the population, followed by an upturn after the war, which brought the average age down again; (2) the wartime shortfall in births, in 1915–18 and 1933–45; (3) wartime losses, affecting chiefly adult males; these were particularly large in World War I among the age-groups born between 1875 and 1900; and (4) migratory movements that tended to increase the proportion of adults who were of working age.

Table 2.4 and Figure 2.1, the age pyramid of the French population as of January 1, 1962, show the result of the interaction of these different factors on the sex and age structure of the total population. The proportion of women rose during both wars, but fell afterward, chiefly because of migration, which affected primarily men of working age. The relative weight of the 15–64 age-group—that is, of people of working age[17]—

[17] The working population, for all practical purposes, consists of men and women aged 15–64. In 1962, for example, 94 percent of the working population fell between these ages.

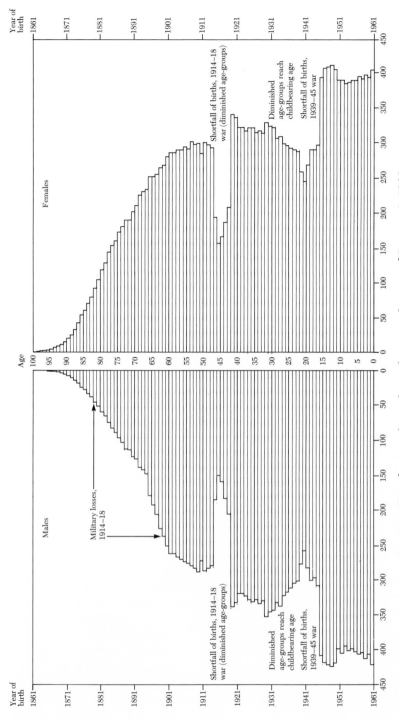

Fig. 2.1. Distribution of population by sex and age as of January 1, 1962.

TABLE 2.5
Increase in the Total and Working-Age Populations, 1896–1969
(Percent per year)

Period	Total population	Population aged 15–64
Long-term increase		
1896–1913	0.2%	0.2%
1913–29	0.2	0.4
1929–38	0.2	–0.4
1938–49	–0.1	0.2
1949–63	1.0	0.5
1896–1929	0.2	0.3
1929–63	0.5	0.2
1896–1963	0.35	0.25
Increase after World War II		
1951–57	0.8	0.1
1957–63	1.3	0.8
1963–69	0.9	0.8

Note: Figures for 1963 include 700,000 persons repatriated from Algeria in 1962.

remained stable between 1896 and 1911. It increased after World War I because of migration and the wartime shortfall in births, then dropped beginning in 1930 as a result of the "hollow" year cohorts entering this age-group. It rose again from 1936 to 1946 because of the fall in the birthrate in the same period. Finally, it dropped from 1946 to 1962, owing partly to the high birthrate and partly to the fact that the small cohorts born between 1933 and 1945 had reached working age. The interplay of these two factors led to highly varied changes in the different age-groups: the total population grew by 15 percent between January 1, 1946 and 1962, i.e. at an average rate of 0.9 percent. Over the same period the population of working age rose by only 6 percent, at a rate of 0.4 percent, whereas the age-group under 15 increased in numbers by 43 percent, at a rate of 2.2 percent. Beginning only in 1962 did the population of working age grow as fast as that of the total population.

The "upsurge of youth"[18] has undoubtedly influenced many factors of economic growth. The rise in the birthrate has made it harder for women to take up employment, but on the other hand it has increased the pressure of demand, stimulated the efforts of family breadwinners, and probably helped to develop a greater concern for expansion and for actively planning for the future. Changes in the age structure of the total population caused the working age-group to develop in a different way from that of the total. Table 2.5 compares the development of each over

[18] *La montée des jeunes*; we owe this expression to Alfred Sauvy.

the periods most relevant to the analysis of economic growth, rather than (as in earlier pages) over those periods appropriate to demographic analysis. Table 2.5 emphasizes in this way the demographic foundations of changes in the supply of manpower.

EMPLOYMENT

The first section below analyzes changes in participation rates by sex and age. This permits us in the second section to account for changes in the total labor force on the basis of sociodemographic factors. The third section deals with the growth of the labor force employed in the productive sectors, with which we are particularly concerned. Changes in working hours are dealt with in section four. Finally, section five studies the rising level of education of the working population, which played a great part in improving its quality. Estimates of the working population shown here are based on population censuses. For the years between, various indicators of employment have been used, which are briefly described in Chapter 3. Figures from the censuses of 1954, 1962, and 1968 have been reproduced unchanged. Those from the 1896 census, however, were clearly underestimates, and have been corrected. So have the figures for the female working population in agriculture from the 1896–1946 censuses, in order to eliminate as far as possible changes in the statistical handling of family helpers. These corrections are explained in Chapter 3 (pp. 87–90).

Rates of Participation and Labor Force Characteristics

Changes in participation rates since the beginning of this century affected chiefly the young, the aged, and women. Because of the uncertainties about the female labor force, we shall begin by examining the first two on the basis of the male work force only. In view of the poor quality of labor data in the 1896 census, the starting point will be 1901.

Drop in the male participation rate for younger and older age-groups. Table 2.6 shows changes in the male participation rate at each census. It illustrates both long-term movements and the influence of the economic situation in particular census years. For example, the consequences of World War I and the Great Depression of the 1930's can be seen clearly. There was a slight but general increase in participation rates in 1911–21, although the 1921 census was carried out at a time when underemployment was relatively high. This postwar high labor participation can be explained by various factors. Considerable war losses affected the male age-groups of working age (those born between 1875 and 1900). In families affected in this way, women usually not in

TABLE 2.6
Labor Force Participation Rates for Males, by Age, 1901–68

Age-group	1901	1906	1911	1921	1926	1931	1936	1946	1954	1962	1968
0–14			8%	9%	7%	3.5%	4.5%	2%	2%	2%	
15–24			86.5	87	86.5	87	81.5	81	81	74.5	64%
Under 25	37%	37%	37	41	41	37	30.5	35.5	31	25.5	25.5
25–54	96	96	96	96.5	96.5	96.5	95.5	96	96	96	96
55–64	88	87	86.5	89	86	85	79	81.5	76.5	76.5	71.5
Over 65	60	60	60	61	55.5	53.5	47.5	48	34.5	25	16
Total	67%	66.5%	67%	70%	69%	68%	64%	66%	62.5%	58.5%	55%

Principal source: Mme L. Cahen, "Evolution de la population en France depuis cent ans, d'après les dénombrements quinquennaux," *Etudes et conjoncture,* May-June, 1953, p. 244. (Some of the figures have been corrected for the reasons given on pp. 87–90.) Ages refer to years completed on January 1 of the year in which the census took place (mostly in March).

employment were forced to work, and older persons had to postpone retirement. In addition, inflation wiped out much of the savings, which in the absence of pension plans were then the main resource of old people, with the result that an increased proportion of old people were obliged to keep working. By contrast, participation rates were slightly lower in all age-groups in 1936 than in 1931 and 1946, pulled down by the difficulty of finding jobs in the depression. If these effects are set aside, what were the long-term trends in male participation rates?[19]

From 1901 to 1911 these rates were stable, except for a slight fall in the upper age-groups. The same is over the whole period for men between 25 and 54: the average rate fluctuated weakly around 96 percent. In the upper age-groups, however, a downward trend began between the wars and accelerated after World War II. It affected particularly the over-65 group (with rates of about 56 percent up to 1926, dropping to 36 percent in 1954 and to 16 percent in 1968), and the 55–64 group (87 percent at the beginning of the century, 85 percent in 1931, 76 percent in 1954, and 71 percent in 1968). This drop seems to be due to a complex combination of factors. There was a fall in the farming population, where a higher proportion of older persons worked than in other groups. More generally, wage earners came to account for a higher proportion of the labor force at the expense of the self-employed and family helpers. The standard of living rose; social attitudes toward working at an advanced age changed: technical progress and more education re-

[19] The low activity rate in the 0–14 age-group in 1931 is also accounted for by the effects of World War I. The only members of the labor force in this group are children not legally bound to attend school, i.e. in 1931 those aged 13 and 14. In that year, their proportion in the groups was unusually low because of the low wartime birthrate.

duced the demand for older workers. Social security benefits were instituted, and pension plans became widespread.

The participation rates of those under 25 also show a downward trend from the early 1930's, becoming particularly steep between 1954 and 1968. For the 15–24 age-group the average rate fell from 81 percent in 1954 to 64 percent in 1968. This drop was chiefly linked to the increase in total time spent at school, a trend that accelerated between the wars and after World War II. This development, itself reflecting an important change in family attitudes, is examined below, together with its consequences for the quality of the labor force.[20]

We have attempted to distinguish the extent to which the overall activity rate of the male population has been influenced by differing rates of participation rather than by changes in the age structure. To this end we have calculated the rate for the years considered if the participation rate in each age-group had been constant at the 1954 level. The results are shown in Table 2.7. In any given year the gap between the observed and the calculated rate illustrates the effect of changes in the participation rate in the different age-groups between that year and 1954. It can be seen that the high overall male participation rate in 1921 follows both from a favorable age structure (with a large 15–64 age-group) and from high rates in each group. The big drop in the rate between 1931 and 1936 (4 percentage points) can be explained by a contrary combination: 2 percentage points are accounted for by a fall in activity rates in each group and 2 by changes in the age structure. The overall rate fell substantially from 1901 to 1968 by 12 percentage points, of which over 10 were due to a reduction among young people and in the older age-groups. The sharp drop overall between 1946 and 1962 (7.5 points) was the result half of a fall in the rate in the lower and higher age-groups and half of structural changes, i.e. of a lowering of the average age of the population as a whole.

Female activity rates. Long-term changes in the female activity rate cannot be studied directly from the figures of participation by age-group available from population censuses. As already mentioned, the numbers of females employed in agriculture from one census to the next are not comparable before 1954. Adjustments we have made in order to obtain a homogeneous series are in some cases very great (ranging up to nearly one million, i.e. 15 percent of the total female labor force), and are overall only, with no age breakdown. Nevertheless, from an analysis of available or calculated data, some conclusions can be drawn on long-

[20] Cf. below, section on Progress in Educational Level of the Population (p. 62), and Search for a Measure of Quality of the Working Population (p. 67).

TABLE 2.7
*Contributions of Age Structure and of Participation Rates by Age
to the Change in the Overall Labor Force Participation
Rates of Males and Females, 1901–68*

Year	Percent observed		Percent calculated from 1954 participation rates		Difference	
	Males	Females	Males	Females	Males	Females
1901	67%	36%	62%	31%	5%	5%
1906	66.5	36	62	31	4.5	5
1911	67	35.5	62	31	5	4.5
1921	70	35.5	63.5	32	6.5	3.5
1926	69	33	64	32	5	1
1931	68	33	64	32	4	1
1936	64	30.5	62	30.5	2	0
1946	66	32	64	32	2	0
1954	62.5	30	62.5	30	0	0
1962	58.5	27.5	60	29	−1.5	−1.5
1968	55	28	60.5	29.5	−5.5	−1.5

term movements in female activity rates. The overall figure, after all adjustments, has moved as shown in Table 2.7. This series shows a downward trend from 1901 to 1962, or more exactly from 1921 to 1931, and then from World War II on. A comparison with the men's rates reveals a faster and earlier drop in the women's figures. Although the absolute reduction from 1901 to 1962 was the same in both cases (8.5 points), the relative reduction was almost twice as large for women. A calculation similar to that for male participation rates enables us to determine the effect, respectively, of changes in the female age structure and changes in the participation rate itself.

The results, given in Table 2.7, show that, of a drop of 8 points in the overall female rate between 1901 and 1968, 6.5 points were due to a fall in the rates in the different age-groups and 1.5 points to changes in the age structure. Between 1901 and 1962 the fall in the women's rate was as large as that in the men's. Since the female rates in all age-groups are lower than the male, a given absolute reduction must be due either to a much higher relative drop among the young and the old or, more likely, to a combination of falling rates in the extreme age-groups and a drop over the period in the participation of women aged 25–54. The gaps show that this took place soon after World War I. After World War II, however, the female 25–54 participation rate seems to have risen from 1946 to 1954, to have stayed roughly constant between 1954 and 1962, and to have increased considerably from 1962 to 1968.

A more precise and detailed analysis of changes in participation rates

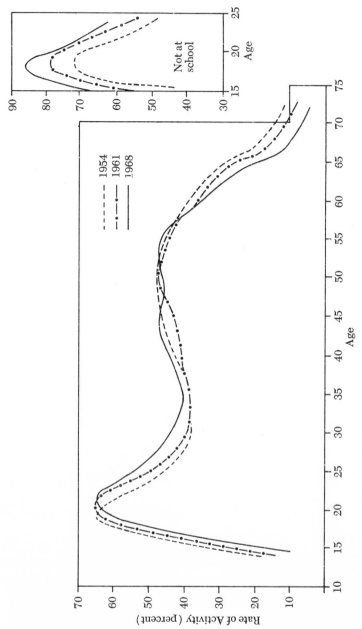

Fig. 2.2. Female labor force participation rates by age-groups.

can be made for the years 1954, 1962, and 1968 because the population censuses carried out in those years are closely comparable.[21] It shows that the drop in the overall female rate between 1954 and 1962 can be explained, as for men entirely, by a combination of changes in the age structure and a fall in the rates for the youngest and oldest age-groups. Among young people, this drop was due to a voluntary lengthening of years at school, and occurred despite an increase in the rate among those not at school. The overall incidence of rate changes between ages 25 and 54 was almost nil; an increase in the 25–30 age-groups offset a fall in the groups over 35 (see Figure 2.2). From 1962 to 1968, however, a sharp rise in the rate for the 25–45 groups compensated for a fall in the two extreme age-groups.

The last two population censuses show insignificant differences in female participation rates between the farming population and others. In 1962, for example, 34.2 percent of women in farming families reported themselves gainfully employed,[22] as compared with 25.9 percent in other families. For this reason, it is of interest to assess quantitatively to what extent the drop in the overall female participation rate observed between 1901 and 1962 can be ascribed to a fall in the proportion of the agricultural population to the whole. This can be calculated from data in the 1962 census, from the 1891 census figures of persons "making their living from agriculture," and from the 1891 and 1901 census data on males employed in farming. It would appear that the proportion of the female population living in farming households changed from 40–45 percent in 1901 to 17 percent in 1962. If activity rates among women in both farm and other households had been constant throughout at 1962 levels, changes in the distribution between those two classes of household would have pulled the overall female participation rate down by about 2 percentage points.

Similar calculations can be made for men, whose participation rate was far higher in farm than in nonfarm households: 63.3 percent and 54.5 percent, respectively. A drop of 2 percentage points in the overall

[21] See, in particular, Michel Praderie, "L'Emploi féminin en 1962 et son évolution depuis 1954," *Etudes et conjoncture*, December 1964. See also the breakdown of changes in the working population between 1954 and 1962, *Annuaire statistique*, 1966, p. 110. For comparisons between 1962 and 1968, see "Résultats préliminaires du recensement de 1968," INSEE, Collection D3; and R. Salais and M. G. Michal, *Economie et statistique*, September 1971.

[22] In households headed by a farmer, an employed farm worker, or a person retired from one of these categories (categories 0.1 and 93 of the social and occupational groups coding).

male activity rate between 1901 and 1962 can be imputed to a fall in the ratio of agricultural to total population. But differences in the participation rates by age-group between men in agricultural and other households in 1962 essentially concern those under 25 and over 54. These differences must therefore be regarded as one of the factors behind the falling trend of male participation rates in the youngest age-groups, and even more so in the oldest. This is not so for women, whose participation rates differed considerably between agricultural and other households in all age-groups, including those between 25 and 45, where the differences averaged 15 points. Thus, 1 to 1.5 percentage points of the drop in the overall female participation rate from 1901 to 1962 can be specifically imputed to the relative decrease in the farming population.

After correcting for this effect, the impact of the change in participation rates by age-group on the overall female rate from 1901 to 1962 can be estimated as 5 percentage points, as compared with 6.5 for men. Thus the drop was 14 percent for women and 10 percent for men. Allowing for the lack of precision in our knowledge of changes in the female population, the difference between the two is not significant, and it can be concluded that between the beginning of the century and the years after World War II the female and male participation rates probably changed in a fairly similar way: the rate fell in the lowest and highest age-groups and was relatively constant at ages 25–54, after correction for the particular effect of the drop in the farming population on the figures for women. This conclusion nevertheless contradicts a widely held view that women in France have been entering employment at an increasing rate over a long period, just as in fact occurred in the Anglo-Saxon countries: Great Britain, the United States, and the Commonwealth. In Great Britain, the overall female activity rate was 25 percent at the beginning of the century, maintained a steady trend until the end of the between-war period, then rose as a result of the war and continued to rise thereafter to 31 percent in 1961.[23] In the United States women's participation in employment grew continually from the beginning of the century: the proportion of working females aged 14 and over rose from 20 percent in 1900 to 23 percent in 1930, 27 percent in 1940, 35 percent in 1960, and 37 percent in 1966.[24] This increase in the United States can be ascribed to the growing importance of tertiary activities,

[23] This information comes from the study by our British colleagues as part of the Social Sciences Research Council joint project.

[24] *Historical Statistics of the United States* and *Statistical Abstract of the United States.*

the reduction in working hours, and the development of spare-time working, as well as to the drop in age at marriage and at starting school.[25]

These differences in rates of development in France and the Anglo-Saxon countries are no doubt largely due to differences in the situation in each country at the starting point: at the beginning of the century the overall female activity rate was 36 percent in France, as against 25 percent in Great Britain and only 14 percent in the United States.[26] The case of Germany, too, is very striking. Its overall female participation rate had reached the relatively high figure of 32 percent at the beginning of the century, and after various fluctuations it stood once again at 32 percent in 1962. Around 1960, then, the rates were fairly close in France, Germany, and the United States, although this overall resemblance masked large differences in the structure of female employment in each country. From 1962 to 1968, however, the overall rate in France increased in a manner comparable with that in Anglo-Saxon countries.

A relevant question, however, is why the factors that increased female participation rates in those countries did not act in a similar way in France. One important difference in the United States was the supply of part-time work, which increased rapidly after World War II. Nothing comparable arose in France until 1968. It is also relevant that in France, in contrast to the United States, neither age at marriage nor average age of mothers at birth of children of any one birth-ranking changed from the beginning of the century.[27] But, above all, female employment in France had somewhat special characteristics in earlier periods. The proportion of women working in industry was particularly high because of the large size of the textiles and clothing sector in relation to industry as a whole, and the very high dependence of these industries on female labor, resulting from the practice of domestic piecework. The decline of

[25] On this subject see, for example, C. D. Long, *The Labor Force Under Changing Income and Employment* (Princeton, N.J., 1958).

[26] These big differences can be accounted for by several factors: the large size of the French agricultural population and the population of women engaged in farm work, the large number of small family businesses in French nonagricultural areas, and the high proportion of wage earners working in France at home at the beginning of the century.

[27] See J. C. Chasteland and R. Pressat, "La Nuptialité des générations françaises depuis un siècle," *Population*, April-June, 1962; and E. Henry, "Fécondité des ménages," *Cahier de l'INED* (Institut National d'Etudes Démographiques), no. 16, p. 47. On the other hand, the increase in the number of children enrolled in nursery schools after World War II (some 25 percent of children around 1950 and 40 percent around 1962) has tended to encourage female participation in the labor force since World War II. Nothing similar, however, seems to have happened over the first half of the century. See *Annuaire statistique*, 1966, p. 132.

these sectors and the gradual disappearance of work at home sharply reduced female employment in these sectors and in industry in general. In 1906 women accounted for 34 percent of the total industrial work force, but only 28 percent in 1931 and 23 percent in 1962. In 1906 female workers in industry totaled 2 million, of which 1.6 million were in textiles and clothing. In 1962 these sectors employed 1 million fewer women, and despite an increase of 0.7 million in the other sectors, females in industry as a whole were 0.3 million fewer than in 1906. The growing proportion of women in the tertiary sector (39 percent in 1906, 40 percent in 1931, 43 percent in 1954, and 46 percent in 1962) and the resulting increase in the female labor force (1.4 million between 1906 and 1962) did not wholly offset the fall in female employment in agriculture and industry; as a result, the overall female employment rate dropped.[28]

The conventional view that female employment in France has been increasing for a long time is due in fact to a "social optical illusion," i.e. extrapolating to the population as a whole developments that affected chiefly the more highly qualified professions, such as doctors and teachers. The makeup and the quality level of women's part in paid employment have in fact completely changed: the proportion of women wage earners has sharply increased,[29] and, more particularly, the number of women in the more highly qualified positions has grown very fast, as the study by Praderie[30] shows for the recent past. In his words, it is likely that "a wage-earning status means a more regular and intensive share in production and often longer working hours than those of family helpers." The effect of these structural changes on growth is taken into account later in our study, both in the examination of the quality of the work force and in the analysis of changes in the structure of production.

[28] On this subject see Mme F. Guelaud-Leridon, "Le Travail des femmes en France," *Cahiers de l'INED*, travaux et documents, no. 42, 1964.

[29] Between 1954 and 1968 the proportion of wage earners in the working population rose from 51.3 to 72.6 percent for women, against an increase from 67.8 to 75.4 percent for men.

[30] "L'Emploi féminin en 1962." In the eight-year period 1954–62 and the six-year period 1962–68, the rates of growth in the female labor force by social and employment categories were as follows:

	1954–62	1962–68
Farmers	−29%	−22%
Farming employees	−44	−36
Employees in industry and trade	−15	−9
Liberal professions and higher management	66	53
Middle management	43	37
Employees	28	31
Blue-collar workers	3	3
Domestic service	1	9

Changes in the Total Labor Force, and Underlying Factors

The changes in the working population (resulting partly from variations in the total population and its sex and age structure and partly from changes in activity rates) are shown in Table 2.8. The labor force grew at the extremely slow average annual rate of 0.15 percent from 1896 to 1931 (0.2 percent between 1896 and 1911, virtually nil from 1911 to 1921, 0.2 percent between 1921 and 1931); as a result, it increased by one million. A peak of 20.5 million was reached in 1931. The labor force then dropped by 1.2 million between 1931 and 1936 (−1.2 percent per year), was almost constant between 1936 and 1946 (0.1 million), and grew at only 0.1 percent per year, i.e. by 0.35 million, from 1946 to 1962. Thus, between 1896 and 1962 the total working population rose by only 0.25 million, which over such a long period amounts to almost complete stagnation. From 1962 on, however, the labor force has been growing again (at an annual rate on the order of 0.6 percent). The overall participation rate was stable at the beginning of the century (51 percent), reached a high point after World War I (52 percent) and then fell regularly, apart from an exceptionally low rate in 1936 (47 percent). From 1946 to 1968 the drop was considerable: 48.5 to 41 percent.

TABLE 2.8

Contributions of the Age-Sex Structure and of Participation Rates by Age and Sex to the Change in the Overall Labor Force Participation Rate, 1901–68

Year	Total working population[a] *(millions)*	Overall activity rate[b] *(percent)*	Difference in rate from 1954	Difference in rate due to:[c] Sex structure of total population	Age structure of total population	Activity rate by sex and age
1896	19.5					
1901	19.6	50.9%	5.2%	0.3%	−	4.9%
1906	19.8	50.9	5.2	0.3	−0.1%	5.0
1911	20.0	51.1	5.4	0.3	0.1	5.0
1921	20.1	51.9	6.2	−0.2	1.5	4.9
1926	20.3	50.4	4.7	−	1.7	3.0
1931	20.5	49.8	4.1	0.1	1.3	2.7
1936	19.3	46.9	1.2	0	−0.1	1.3
1946	19.4	48.4	2.7	−0.2	1.6	1.3
1954	19.6	45.7	−	−	−	−
1962	19.7	42.6	−3.1	0.1	−1.9	−1.3
1968	20.6	41.1	−4.6	0.1	−1.3	−3.4

Note: Figures include Alsace-Lorraine from 1921 on.

[a] As of census dates through 1946; thereafter, as of January 1. Figures include the unemployed and the draft contingent for each year.

[b] Calculated from a statistical total population differing slightly from total population figures used earlier (see Appendix Table 2).

[c] The method applied is described in Appendix B.

These developments are important and should be noted. The break in the parallelism in growth of total population and working population (particularly after World War II) led to a break in the parallelism of productivity (per working man-year) and output per head.

The factors underlying these developments can be analyzed on the basis of the overall population growth just examined, and of Table 2.8, in which changes in the overall participation rate have been imputed to three factors: sex structure and age structure of the total population, and participation rate by sex and age. Between 1896 and 1911 the working population changed along with total population. The structure by sex and age of the total population and participation rates barely changed. Between 1911 and 1921 total population fell slightly, and the overall participation rate increased slightly, owing to a change in the age structure (an increase in the proportion of age-groups covered by the labor force). This led to a very slight increase in the working population. Male participation rates were rising, but female rates were falling (see below); taken as a whole, changes in the rate did not influence movements of total working population. From 1921 to 1931 the total population grew by 0.7 percent per year. Changes in age and sex structure had little influence on the overall participation rate, but there was a marked fall in the female rate, and in the male rate at higher ages. These behavioral changes led to a drop of almost 2 percentage points in the overall rate, so that the labor force increased by only 0.2 percent per year.

From 1931 to 1936 population growth was nil, while the overall participation rate fell by about 3 percentage points, half of which was due to changes in age structure of the population as a whole and half to reductions in participation rates: the result was a drop of about 1.2 million in the labor force. From 1936 to 1946 a fall in the total population was compensated by a rise of 1.5 percentage points in the overall participation rate, ascribable to an increase in the relative size of the age-groups with the highest rates. The male and female rates barely changed, and the working population as a whole was almost stationary. From 1946 to 1962 a total population growth of 0.9 percent per year was accompanied by an increase in the labor force of only 0.1 percent per year. The overall participation rate fell by 6 percentage points; almost half of this was due to a reduction in male and female rates at the lowest and highest ages, and slightly over half was the result of an increase in the proportion of those aged over 64 and under 15 to the population as a whole. The postwar baby boom clearly could not have an effect until the age-groups it had swollen reached working age—from around 1962 on. From 1962 to 1968 the working population began to grow again, but at a slower rate than might have been expected from its age and sex structure, because the participation rates in the extreme age-groups fell faster.

Unemployment—Numbers Employed Inside and Outside of the Productive Sectors

Changes in the labor force relevant to the fluctuations in output dealt with in Chapter 1 are different from the changes in the total labor force, for two reasons. First, not all the working population is employed in the so-called productive sectors, i.e. those whose activity is taken into account in the calculation of gross domestic product. Second, part of the available work force is made up of the unemployed. The working population employed in productive sectors is therefore equal to the difference between the total working population and the number drafted into the armed forces, unemployed, or in occupations outside these sectors, i.e. government, financial institutions, and domestic service. In census data before 1954, the draft was included with the career military under the heading "army." Up to 1946, although this is not wholly satisfactory, draftees were included with government employees.

Table 2.9 shows movements in each of the population categories over the long term. Table 2.10 indicates how the number of unemployed changed in relation to the total labor force over the long term and year by year beginning in 1949.

Unemployment fluctuations are marked by the high level reached in the 1921 recession (540,000 unemployed, or 2.7 percent of the total labor force), and particularly in the Great Depression, when the already high 1931 figure (450,000, or 2.2 percent of the working population) went up to a maximum in 1936 of 860,000 unemployed, or 4.5 percent of the labor force. Apart from those years, unemployment did not exceed 2 percent of the working population. After World War II and until very recent years, it was very low throughout, with a peak in 1954 (310,000 unemployed, or 1.6 percent of the labor force) and a low point in 1957 (160,000). There has been a gradual increase in unemployment since 1964, however, which can be ascribed in part to large age-groups reaching working age.

Numbers employed outside the productive sectors gradually increased, but only slowly, in 1896–1913 and 1921–38. The bulge after each of these periods was due to the increase in the armed forces before the two world wars. From 1913 to 1921, on the contrary, there was a drop in the numbers working outside the productive sectors, linked to the return to peacetime conditions. After World War II, developments were very dif-

TABLE 2.9
Components of the Working Population, 1896–1969
(Thousands of persons)

Year	Total work force	Unemployed	Military draft	Employed out- side productive sectors	Employed in productive sectors
1896	19,490	270	2,120		17,100
1901	19,590	310	2,160		17,120
1906	19,770	240	2,160		17,370
1911	20,030	210	2,230		17,590
1913	20,100	200	2,330		17,570
1921	20,120	540	2,080		17,500
1926	20,290	240	2,000		18,050
1929	20,540	240	2,100		18,200
1931	20,510	450	2,180		17,880
1936	19,310	860	2,300		16,150
1938	19,490	730	2,400		16,360
1946	19,420	130	2,440		16,850
1949	19,500	240	210	2,480	16,570
1951	19,560	230	230	2,520	16,580
1954	19,610	310	310	2,640	16,350
1957	19,880	160	610	2,740	16,370
1962	19,750	230	510	2,910	16,100
1963	20,050	270[a]	410	2,990	16,380
1968	20,600	430	250	3,330	16,590
1969	20,770	360	250	3,410	16,750

Note: Figures include Alsace-Lorraine from 1921. Population is from census figures up to 1946, except for private estimates for 1913, 1929, and 1938. Estimates for annual averages are from 1949, based on census results in 1954, 1962, and 1968, and on various indicators of employment.

[a]Of this figure about 50,000 were repatriates from Algeria who had not yet found work.

TABLE 2.10
Proportion of Unemployed to Working Population, 1896–1969
(Percent)

Year	Proportion of unemployed: To total working popula- tion	To wage- earning popula- tion	Year	Proportion of unemployed: To total working popula- tion	To wage- earning popula- tion	Year	Proportion of unemployed: To total working popula- tion	To wage- earning popula- tion
1896	1.4%		1950	1.4%	2.3%	1960	1.2%	1.8%
1901	1.6		1951	1.2	1.9	1961	1.1	1.6
1906	1.2		1952	1.3	2.0	1962	1.2	1.7
1911	1.0		1953	1.5	2.5	1963	1.4	1.9
1921	2.7		1954	1.6	2.5	1964	1.1	1.5
1926	1.2		1955	1.4	2.3	1965	1.3	1.8
1931	2.2		1956	1.1	1.7	1966	1.4	1.9
1936	4.5		1957	0.8	1.2	1967	1.8	2.4
1946	0.7		1958	0.9	1.4	1968	2.1	2.8
1949	1.2	2.0%	1959	1.3	1.9	1969	1.7	2.3

TABLE 2.11
Workers Outside the Productive Sectors [hors branches], *1954–68*

Employment	Thousands of persons (Yearly average)			Average annual growth rate	
	1954	1962	1968	1954–62	1962–68
Govt. and private administration	1,850	2,140	2,510	1.8%	2.6%
(Military)	(285)	(300)	(250)	0.6	–3.1
(Civil)	(1,565)	(1,840)	(2,260)	2.1	3.5
Financial institutions	200	265	350	3.5	4.7
Domestic service	590	505	470	–2.0	–1.2
Total	2,640	2,910	3,330	1.2%	2.3%

Note: The number of workers excluded military draftees.

ferent: excluding the military draft, the average yearly rate of increase was 1.6 percent from 1949 to 1969.

Table 2.11 makes possible a more precise analysis of the changes between the 1954, 1962, and 1968 censuses. These changes were due mainly to the rapid growth in the numbers employed in civilian government offices. The rise was particularly noticeable in education, and was due to the great increase in school enrollment, resulting partly from the demographic swell of children born just after the war and partly from the increase in average years spent at school. Staff employed by the Ministry of National Education grew from 290,000 in 1954 to 410,000 in 1962, and to 620,000 in 1968. (Just before and after World War I, the corresponding numbers had been 150,000, rising to 185,000 in 1936, and to 230,000 in 1946.) This increase relates to a rapid growth in the services provided by official bodies, a growth not directly included in the calculation of gross domestic product. Nevertheless, it is indirectly and partially taken into account, to the extent that it influences the trend of increases in GDP. For example, the drive for education improved the quality of the labor force even within the postwar period studied, and this was a factor in the growth of GDP.

The work force employed in the productive sectors grew slowly, at an average rate of 0.2 percent yearly, or by about one million persons, between 1896 and 1929, when it reached a peak of 18.2 million. (The rate from 1921 to 1929 was faster than over the period as a whole, 0.5 percent.) From 1929 to 1936, seven years, the numbers employed in these sectors fell by two million—twice the increase over the first 30 years of the century. The figure grew by 200,000 between 1936 and 1938, but over the entire period 1929–38 the work force employed in the productive sectors fell by 10 percent, or approximately 1.7 percent per year.

It then increased by about 500,000 from 1938 to 1946, but thereafter dropped very slowly and almost steadily until 1962. This was due partly to the slow rise in the total working population and partly to the increase in the numbers drafted and those employed outside the productive sectors. Overall, from 1929 to 1962 the work force in these sectors fell by almost 11 percent, or some two million persons. Since 1962 it has been growing again, at around 0.5 percent per year.

Long-Term Reduction of Hours Worked, and Postwar Stability

Changes in average hours worked per person employed since the beginning of the century were in the main the result of general changes in the working week and in the length of annual paid holidays, affecting all industries.[31] There were three great discontinuities: the adoption of the eight-hour day in 1919 and the 40-hour week in 1936, and the increase in hours worked after World War II. See Table 2.12. The eight-hour day—that is, the 48-hour week—was already in force in some firms before World War I. It was the subject of frequent labor demands, and was made generally mandatory by the law of April 23, 1919.

Under the impact of large-scale strikes and factory sit-ins in the spring of 1936, and with the double objective of improving living conditions and fighting unemployment, the 40-hour week became law in June 1936 (and with it two weeks' paid vacations yearly). The regulations spelling out this principle were issued shortly afterward, and the law was in force throughout industry by the end of April 1937. The shortening of hours, so abruptly brought about, was considerable, since before this the average working week had been 44 hours. The situation thus created presented an exceptional characteristic: by comparison, the working week in Britain at that time was about 47 hours.[32] Under the circumstances, it is not surprising that in the years following World War II hours worked were higher than before the war. The effective working week had in fact increased to 42 hours in 1939, under regulations softening the effect of the 1936 legislation. In 1950 it became 44 hours. Nevertheless, the annual average of hours worked by employees was still lower in France than in the other Western European countries.

The yearly total of hours worked did not vary significantly from 1950

---

[31] Nevertheless, structural effects such as those resulting from the drop in the proportion of farmers, and more generally of non–wage earners in the labor force, may have significantly affected the long-term development of average hours worked per employed person. We have not been able to take them into account for lack of data.

[32] On the 40-hour week, see Alfred Sauvy, *Histoire économique de la France entre les deux guerres*, vol. II (1967), pp. 197, 205–7, 241–45, 312–13, 328–30.

TABLE 2.12
Changes in Hours Worked per Year, 1896–1969

Long-term changes, all sectors			Postwar changes, sectors other than farming (1956 = 100)					
Period	Index base 100 at start of each period	Annual average rate of change	Year	Rate	Year	Rate	Year	Rate
1896–1913	95	–0.3%	1949	98.9	1956	100.0	1963	100.6
1913–29	86	–0.9	1950	100.0	1957	100.4	1964	100.2
1929–38	88	–1.4	1951	100.4	1958	100.0	1965	99.9
1938–49	107	0.6	1952	99.8	1959	99.8	1966	100.0
1949–63	99	–	1953	99.8	1960	100.7	1967	99.2
1963–69	98	–0.4	1954	100.7	1961	101.1	1968	98.4
1896–1969	*74*	*–0.4*	1955	100.4	1962	101.6	1969	98.2

Note: The indexes of change before World War II are based on the average of indexes for each sector, weighted by numbers employed; after World War II they are based on the sum for each year of total hours worked in each sector, divided by total number of employees in the sectors. Chapter 3 (pp. 91–92) explains how the sector indexes were obtained.

to 1963, because of the combination of longer paid annual vacations (increasing from two to three weeks between 1954 and 1956, and from three to four weeks[33] between 1962 and 1964), and an increase in weekly hours (increasing in nonfarm sectors from about 44 hours weekly at the beginning of the period to 46 hours in 1963). Over the same period, hours worked were falling in other Western countries. From 1950 to 1962 the annual figure for nonagricultural employees dropped by 6–8 percent in most countries (less in Britain, more in Germany).[34] The starting levels were such, however, that in 1960 average yearly nonagricultural hours worked in France were similar to those elsewhere in Western Europe: very close to the German and United Kingdom figures, slightly higher than the Scandinavian figures, and a little lower than those in the Netherlands and Italy. A fairly high French weekly figure (46 hours) was compensated for by the long paid vacations (three weeks). Hours worked weekly were roughly the same in France, Italy, and West Germany, about one hour higher in the Netherlands, an hour lower in Great Britain, and some two hours lower in the Scandinavian countries. Hours worked yearly were 10 percent higher in France than in the United States, where the weekly figure was 41 hours.[35]

[33] Through the spread of a decision taken by the Renault company.

[34] International comparisons of hours worked after World War II are based on the estimates presented by E. F. Denison in *Why Growth Rates Differ: Postwar Experience in Nine Western Countries* (Washington, D.C., 1967, chap. 6).

[35] Half this difference can be accounted for by differences in the proportion of the population employed part-time in the labor force, and the other half by differences in hours worked by full-time employees.

The unchanged level of hours worked in France per year up to 1963 despite a rapid increase in living standards is a noteworthy phenomenon that cannot be interpreted merely as a "return to normal." Nor apparently can it be explained by the play of institutional factors, such as legislation on overtime pay[36] or the setting of earnings ceilings for social security contributions. Throughout this period there was a discrepancy between the union leaders' goal of shorter working hours and wage earners' behavior, which reflected the wish of individuals to raise their earnings and living standards rather than increase their leisure. Probably this desire was partly stimulated by the nature of the productive system as well as by the authorities. More widely, the postwar scale of work seems to have reflected changes in real values within society, the analysis and explanation of which should be the concern of sociological research. Only from 1963 on was there a downward trend comparable with that in other countries.[37] Fluctuations in the economy between 1946 and 1969 led to changes in hours worked: the weekly figure increased in periods of high growth and dropped slightly in recessions. On the other hand, the increase in paid vacations was achieved in expansionary periods, when wage earners' claims met favorable reception. The paradoxical result was a drop in average annual hours worked in the high growth years 1954–56 and 1963.

Progress in Educational Level of the Population

The working population's level of education continually improved over the period studied, as a result of the drive toward more schooling that developed early in the nineteenth century. We shall outline the main steps at each level of schooling, and then show what the consequences were for raising the educational level of the working population between 1896 and 1969.

Development of full-time schooling. The development of primary schooling dates from the first half of the nineteenth century. The first important law organizing primary education was in 1833. It stipulated that every *commune* had to support a boys' primary school. This provision was extended to girls in *communes* of over 800 inhabitants in 1850 and of over 500 inhabitants in 1867. In 1851 the school enrollment rate was close to 55 percent for children between 6 and 11 years old, 40 percent for those aged 12, and 20 percent for those aged 13.[38] In 1876 the

[36] Overtime paid at time-and-a-quarter for more than 40 hours (and at time-and-a-half for more than 48 hours).

[37] See B. Durieux, "La Baisse de la durée du travail," *Economie et statistique,* no. 15, September 1970.

[38] These figures include both sexes, after removing the effect of absenteeism on the school rates. Statistical estimates of school-enrollment rates by age and the

rates were respectively 60, 50, and 30 percent. Primary schooling became free in 1881 and compulsory from ages 6 to 13 in 1882. These provisions could only be applied gradually, and their effect was to speed up developments already widely under way and bring them to fruition. In 1891 the enrollment rates for all ages between 6 and 11 were close to 90 percent, and in 1901 they reached nearly 100 percent. In 1937, raising the minimum school-leaving age to 14 increased the rate for 13-year-olds; as a result, in 1946 all children of primary-school age were in school.

The progress achieved in school enrollment in the second half of the nineteenth century, and particularly between 1880 and 1900, had a marked effect on the distribution of the working population by age at leaving school. Since working lives were on the order of 50 years, this effect was felt up to the eve of World War II. In addition to the quantitative effects of the increase in average length of schooling, there were qualitative effects that are difficult to measure but certainly significant. The quality of primary education considerably improved under the Third Republic, with the creation of normal schools and the appointment of a body of teachers with better qualifications than the schoolmasters previously hired and paid by the *communes*.

Enrollment rates at ages covered by secondary schooling (14 to 18 inclusive) were very low in 1851—not much above 5 percent for the entire group. The rates about doubled between 1851 and 1876. From 1876 to 1921 there was very little improvement (except for 14-year-olds). The first jump forward was after World War I, when rates began to accelerate continuously, but the advance was by no means complete by 1968: there was a spread of rates between 89 percent for children aged 14 and 31 percent for those aged 18. In order to trace the changes in secondary school enrollment more precisely, we have compared the number of students receiving senior school graduation certificates (*baccalauréats, deuxième partie*) with the total number of students aged 15 to 19. The ratio between these shows that there were marked differences, first between 1926 and 1931, and then between 1936 and 1946. This confirms the acceleration of enrollment rates suggested by the figures of rates by age-groups. There is no complete explanation for the change in attitudes toward secondary schooling between the wars. An important part must have been played by the institution of free secondary education around 1930. But this does not give the complete answer, since

breakdown of age-groups by length of schooling are taken from the studies by M. Debeauvais and P. Maes in the IEDES (Institut d'Etude du Développement Economique et Social) research group for the years 1851, 1876, 1891, 1901, 1921, 1936, 1946, 1954, and 1962. The principal results of their work are published as "Une méthode de calcul du stock d'enseignement," *Population*, May–June, 1968.

statistics show that fee-paying private schooling grew faster over this period than public schooling.

Higher education (of young people aged over 18) increased at a rate similar to that of secondary education. Enrollment rates were still very low in 1921, 2.5 percent at age 19, between 2 and 1 percent at ages 20–22, and under 1 percent at ages above 22. There was a marked improvement between 1921 and 1936, in which latter year the rates were 6 percent at age 19, and between 4 and 2 percent at ages 20–22. The rates increased, by and large, at an accelerating pace from 1936 to 1968. In March 1968 they were 23 percent for people aged 19 on January 1, 1968, and 16 percent for those aged 20. If changes in the ratio between student members and their age-groups are examined at closer intervals than those in the IEDES study, the main acceleration can be seen to have taken place around 1950. This acceleration cannot be explained chiefly by the growth in number of females, which was higher than that of males throughout the period. Since female enrollment rates in higher education had started at a very low level in 1901, female students increased at a far faster rate in the first 30 years of the century than over the next 30 years (from about 1,000 in 1900 to 20,000 in 1920, and to 80,000 in 1960).

Rise in educational level of the working population. The progressive increase in school enrollment led to continual improvement in the level of instruction of the working population as a whole. In order to measure its effect on the quality of labor, we have calculated, for each census year, the structure of the working population by educational level. As an operational definition of the concept of educational level, we have taken the age at leaving full-time schooling. This in fact amounts to taking the total time spent at school, since in France schooling is in most cases continuous; therefore school-leaving age is broadly equal to years at school plus six (excluding time spent at nursery school). We have made no correction for changes in the average number of school hours per week or in length of vacations (which increased from around eight weeks in 1895 in primary and secondary schools to twice that in 1960). We feel that the learning acquired in a year at school has not varied significantly in association with total hours spent in class.[39] No qualitative index of the progress of teaching has been applied to the figures. From the eco-

---

[39] On the other hand, as we said earlier, the IEDES studies corrected the school-enrollment rates for the effect of absenteeism. According to the IEDES estimates, the absentee rate went from 25 percent in 1851 to 20 percent in 1891 and to 10 percent in 1901.

nomic standpoint, the quality of teaching dispensed over a year should be judged by how far it modifies a person's ability to respond to the needs of the economy over his working life. To measure the impact of education on economic growth, it would be desirable to determine co-efficients of quality varying as a function not only of the year in which the teaching was carried out, but also of the year that is being studied from an economic viewpoint. We do not, however, have available methods, or indeed statistical data, that would allow us to take these quality effects validly into account, in spite of the fact that, apart from the improvement after 1880 in the public teaching profession, technical training developed at a faster rate than that of schooling as a whole.

We have defined the different educational levels, i.e. the school-leaving age-groups, on the basis of the observable relationship between school-leaving age and wages received. Generally speaking, wages tend to rise with school-leaving age, but not in a regular way. In places the curve in fact runs flat, presumably because there is some dispersion in the ages at which particular levels of education are reached (for example, the completion of secondary studies and *baccalauréat* certificate), and there is no significant systematic difference in the level of attainment of two persons both of whom have reached a given educational level at different ages or after a different number of years of study. Salary levels related to school-leaving age are known for the year 1963. From an analysis of these and of the average length of primary, secondary, and higher school cycles, we have adopted four age-groups: under 15, 15–18, 19–21, and 22 and above. These categories correspond approximately to the following levels of education: (1) primary cycle, completed or not; (2) secondary cycle, both general and technical, completed or not, and if completed whether or not the student has passed examinations for the general secondary school certificate (*brevet*), the certificate of vocational studies (*certificat d'aptitude professionnelle*), or the certificate of secondary studies (*baccalauréat*); (3) higher cycle not completed; (4) higher cycle completed.

These school-leaving age-groups seem useful for measuring qualitative changes in the working population after World War II. But they are insufficient for the beginning of the period studied, since they make no distinction between workers who had completed, not completed, or even not begun primary schooling. Workers who have not fulfilled the compulsory schooling requirement at the mandatory age are very rare in France today; they represent marginal population categories such as immigrants from underdeveloped countries, children of very poor rural families, or mental defectives. At the beginning of the period, however, there was a considerable increase in the proportion of working population that had enjoyed partial or complete primary schooling. We have therefore distinguished first the illiterates, and second three school-leaving age-groups for children whose studies stopped before age 15: ages 7–9, 10–12, and 13–14 (this last group in fact having completed primary schooling).

The working population can be broken down by school-leaving age-groups on the basis of the available data in two ways: (1) from the results (unfortunately not fully comparable) of the 1954 population census and the inquiry into training and qualifications carried out by the INSEE in 1963, i.e. from data on the distribution of the working population by age and school grade on leaving school at two dates late in the period studied; (2) from school statistics of numbers enrolled and from census figures by sex and age, which allow the school enrollment rate at different periods to be calculated. By interpolation for the different generations, the breakdown of population by age on leaving school can be deduced.

To calculate the breakdown of the working population over the whole period, two hypotheses must be made: that mortality is independent of the level of education, and that the distribution by school-leaving age is the same for persons of a given age whether or not they are in paid employment. Neither of these two hypotheses is rigorously proved. Mortality rates by age are a decreasing function of educational standards. Participation rates by sex and age for older persons and for women rise with the level of education. But the biases introduced in this way seem minor, particularly since, for comparisons over time that we have in mind, they always act in the same direction and therefore do not significantly distort the measurement of relative changes between periods. We have used the work, already referred to, of the IEDES, which is based exclusively on the second method of calculation[40] and which provides for sex breakdowns by school-leaving age for each generation born since 1840. For the years 1901–46 we calculated the figures we needed by applying the male distribution to the male working population break-

[40] Some differences can be noted between the IEDES results and estimates suggested by the 1954 census and the 1963 inquiry. We have not undertaken the lengthy task of reconciling the various statistical data, but have followed the IEDES estimates, which have the great advantage of forming a series constructed by a homogeneous method and covering the entire period studied. This series somewhat overestimates the levels of schooling achieved, particularly since it was calculated without taking account of migratory movements, i.e. of an inflow of workers, on the average, less well educated than the remainder of the working population.

TABLE 2.13
Working Population by School-Leaving Age, 1901–68
(Percent)

School-leaving age	1901	1906	1911	1921	1926	1931	1936	1946	1954	1962	1968
Illiterates	12%	10%	8%	6%	5%	4%	3%	2%	1%	1%	1%
7–9	14	12	10	7	4	3	2	1	1	—	—
10–12	17	15	14	11	10	8	6	4	2	1	1
13–14	40	44	48	54	58	61	64	65	65	61	57
15–18	12	13	14	15	16	17	18	20	23	27	30
19–21	4	4	4	5	5	5	5	5	6	7	7
Over 21	1	2	2	2	2	2	2	3	2	3	4

Note: Figures are based on the male working population for 1901–46 and on the total working population thereafter.

down by ages from the various population censuses. The female employment figures by age seemed too unreliable to be used. Since male employment amounted to two-thirds of total employment, we applied our results to the working population as a whole. For the years 1954–62 we followed the estimates for the total working population provided by Debeauvais and Maes referred to earlier.[41]

We have also estimated directly what proportion of the working population had no schooling (the IEDES study does not distinguish between children never enrolled and those who attended primary school but left before they were 10 years old). For this we have used various statistical sources: statistics of illiterate conscripts, data on married persons who signed the marriage register with a cross, and figures on illiteracy in some census results.

Our results from these various calculations are shown in Table 2.13, which breaks down the working population by school-leaving age at the different population census dates. The proportion of illiterates dropped from 12 percent in 1901 to 6 percent in 1921, and can be regarded as very low after World War II. The proportion whose schooling stopped at the primary stage (leaving age before age 15) fell progressively. Of this category, those who completed primary schooling amounted to 50 percent in 1901, but was close to 100 percent in 1962. The percentage of the working population that pursued studies up to the final secondary school years (leaving age 15–18) gradually increased from 12 percent in 1901 to over 30 percent in 1968. The proportion of persons with higher education (school-leaving age over 18 years) rose continually from 5 percent in 1896 to 11 percent in 1968.

[41] *Population*, May–June, 1968, pp. 432–33.

To assess the contribution of the labor factor to economic growth it is not enough to measure changes in the number of hours worked in the productive sectors. Hours worked can be unequal in quality. They must therefore be weighted by a coefficient of the quality of labor. The productivity of a working hour of course depends on equipment, the allocation of resources in the economy, and the internal organization of firms. The role of these factors will be examined in the following chapters. But productivity depends also on individual factors: age, sex, and educational level, the workers' experience and initiative, the quality of work, etc. The part played by some of these factors can be measured. It is possible, therefore, to apply coefficients to the number of hours worked in the economy to take partially into account the qualitative development of the working population. This third part of the chapter describes the method followed and the results of our calculations.

The Method Followed

Up to the present, work has been done by economists[42] on the measurement of three factors: composition of the working population by sex and age, educational level of persons in the labor force, and variations in work intensity in relation to hours worked. The effect of this third factor can be measured only arbitrarily as yet, although it is certain that the quality of work in each hour falls as the total length of time worked increases: thus the quality was lower at the beginning of the century, with a 60-hour week and no paid vacations. We shall confine ourselves to measuring changes in the quality of work ascribable to the first two factors, while at the same time measuring the quantity of labor supplied in the economy in terms of both numbers of workers and hours worked. This will provide lower and upper limits for estimates allowing for the rising quality of work per hour as the length of time worked decreases.

The method used for evaluating work quality is very simple. We have allotted a weight (i.e. a quality) to each member of the working population as a function of age, sex, and educational level. The qualitative effect of any one of these factors on the structure of the working population is measured by changes in the average weighting of its members,

[42] See, in particular, two studies by E. F. Denison, *The Sources of Economic Growth in the United States and the Alternatives Before Us* (Washington, D.C., 1962) and *Why Growth Rates Differ*.

since the weights appropriate to each category are invariable.[43] The effects of each factor on the quality of the labor force are measured independently, and are assumed to be additive. The weights for a particular factor are taken as proportional to average remuneration of labor at a given moment in time (i.e. to average wages, with the averages defined in relation to the factor in question). The following hypotheses are implied by the use of this method:

1. That statistical differences in labor remuneration at a particular time in relation to different values or forms of the factor considered (sex, age, educational level) approximately measure differences in productivity due to this factor. For this to be true, substitution must be possible between the various labor categories distinguished, and the remuneration of a member of the work force must be statistically equal to his marginal output in the job filled,[44] whether or not he is a wage earner. These conditions are certainly not met rigorously, but it is not unreasonable to suppose that they are met approximately. Moreover, corrections can be made to the gross differences observed where there are good reasons to believe that the scale of remunerations does not accurately reflect that of marginal output.

2. That the weights used can be regarded as invariable over time.[45] This assumes a constant balance between the relative scarcities and utilities of the different categories of labor over the entire period studied. Since the period is long, this assumption is questionable. Changes in the supply structure of the work force in relation to particular factors or changes in the structure of demand for labor due to technical and structural developments in industry, or even the evolution of institutions and attitudes, may in fact have produced changes in the relationships in question. But all these developments are relatively slow, and we can assume that they have not fundamentally altered the scales of marginal output.

3. That each of the factors considered is statistically independent in its action. This condition is not rigorously met, but the effects of interdependences are thought to be slight.

[43] For example, changes in quality of the male working population that can be ascribed to the age structure are measured as follows: let s_i be the weighting for a working male of age i. Let $p_i(t)$ be the proportion of working males of age i in the total male working population in year t (this gives $\Sigma_i p_i(t) = 1$). The change will be measured by variations in $\Sigma_i p_i(t) s_i$.

[44] This position is not necessarily the one in which that person might be most economically efficient, allowing for his aptitudes and the demand for labor. This is for reasons of preference other than economic, imperfect information, or institutional or psycho-sociological rigidities.

[45] Statistical data are not available for checking the validity in this hypothesis.

4. That the different values of average labor remuneration at a given time in specified categories of the labor force as a function of various modalities or values of a particular factor can be ascribed solely to that factor. Where this is not so, it is advisable to correct the results obtained. For example, the length of a person's schooling bears a relationship on the one hand to the cultural level of the family in which he was reared and on the other hand to his innate qualities of intelligence and character. For a given social and family situation, gifted persons on the average pursue studies longer than those not so gifted. For given innate qualities and early schooling, children from low-income families (and particularly from those with low education) are less successful at school, and leave it earlier, than those from the privileged classes of society.[46] The specific effect of innate qualities and family environment should therefore be eliminated from any criterion based on work remuneration as a function of time spent at school.

Finally, it should be noted that changes in the factors considered not only affect the individual quality of the members of the labor force, but also help to modify certain general growth factors. Thus, scientific progress, on which technological progress depends, is linked to the opportunities available in the field of education. These opportunities also play an important part in determining the speed with which innovations spread, or society's ability to carry out institutional and structural changes that influence growth. These effects of educational progress on the allocation and use of resources, on techniques employed, and on general economic organization set in motion complex sociological mechanisms. These are not allowed for in the measurements shown below.

Effects of Changes in Sex and Age Structure of the Labor Force

Sex structure. A comparison of annual average earnings in recent years for wage earners of equal age and equal qualifications or educational level but of different sex shows a negative differential in women's remuneration of about 30 percent. Several factors account for this: average weekly hours worked in employment are lower for women than for men; absenteeism is higher for women; for a given theoretical level of education or qualifications, women have less experience on the job because of interruptions while bearing and bringing up children; in view of the work done in domestic jobs, total time spent working is higher for women than for men wage earners, and hence the intensity of the effort is likely to be smaller; women are discriminated against, either

---

[46] Pierre Bourdieu, "La Transmission de l'héritage culturel," in Darras, *Le Partage des bénéfices* (Paris, 1966).

TABLE 2.14
*Effect of Changes in Sex and Age Structure
on the Quality of the Working Population, 1901–68*
(1954 = 100)

Year	Sex	Age	Year	Sex	Age	Year	Sex	Age
1901	99.9	96.5	1926	100.2	96.5	1954	100.0	100.0
1906	99.8	97.1	1931	100.2	98.3	1962	100.0	101.3
1911	99.9	96.9	1936	100.2	99.3	1968	100.0	102.0
1921	99.8	96.3	1946	100.0	98.3			

Note: The coefficient of efficiency used is 1.0 for men and 0.8 for women.

by being given lower-ranking jobs or by being paid less for the same marginal output. We must remove the effect of differences in weekly hours worked (these are allowed for separately) and of remuneration not following marginal output. These corrections have led us to adopt a coefficient of efficiency of 1.0 for men and 0.8 for women. Table 2.14 applies these coefficients to the sex structure of the total labor force at the various censuses. This shows that the effect of the slight changes in sex distribution on the quality of the working population was negligible.

Age structure. Changes in the age distribution of the female working population before World War II are very poorly documented, chiefly because of uncertainties about the female labor force in agriculture. We have therefore based our estimates on figures for males, which account for two-thirds of the working population, on the assumption that the results can be extrapolated to the labor force as a whole.[47] Two statistical sources for 1962 make possible an analysis of changes in earnings as a function of age: the processed tax declarations by employers of earnings of each employee,[48] and the results of the 1963 INSEE survey of family training and qualifications. This survey enables us to study remuneration by cross-referencing age and educational level. We have therefore been able to remove the factor of average educational level of the labor force, which drops with age, from changes in earnings by age.

In order to establish a scale of efficiency by age-group as a function of age, we have ascribed to workers aged 65 and over lower efficiency than that resulting from a comparison of earnings. We felt, on the one hand, that in French socioeconomic circumstances an "age bonus" is in effect paid to older workers. This impression can be drawn in particular from comparisons with earnings scales in the United States. On the other hand, our statistics cover wage earners only; whereas among those aged

[47] Calculation has been made for each sex between 1954 and 1962. The overall result differs little from the result obtained for males alone.
[48] See *Etudes statistiques* (INSEE), April–June, 1964, pp. 120–24.

65 and over there is a high proportion of nonearners and, it would seem, many with only part-time work. The scale for coefficients of age finally adopted is as follows:

Under 20 years	0.4
20–24	0.7
25–64	1.0
65 and over	0.7[49]

This implies that the efficiency of workers increases rapidly up to age 25, as the qualities of maturity (and particularly experience) take the lead over the qualities of youth (mobility, dynamism, more recently learned knowledge). Thereafter, it remains stable between ages 25 and 64, and drops significantly at the higher age levels. Changes in composition of the working population ascribable to changes in age structure and consistent with this scale are shown in Table 2.14. There were qualitative improvements between 1926 and 1936, and between 1946 and 1968, but a slight deterioration between 1936 and 1946. These differences were due to a combination of several factors: alterations in the age structure of the total population; a fall in participation rates in the lowest and highest age-groups, the effects of which on growth are reduced by allowing for labor quality; and changes in activity rates as a result of depression (1936) or war (1946)—which affected the youngest and oldest workers more than the adult population, and therefore had a smaller impact on labor resources than is implied by figures for total population.

Effects of Rising Educational Levels

The 1963 INSEE inquiry on training and qualifications provides data on level of earnings in relation to school-leaving age. The differentials vary greatly according to age: as age increases, the differentials widen. It is possible, however, to establish one scale of earnings from a combination of all scales by age-groups (based on averages corrected empirically for observed anomalies). This scale can be used in calculations where the only variable is school-leaving age. This method makes it possible to eliminate most of the interaction effect of the two explanatory variables.[50]

[49] This coefficient would have been 0.9 if the downward adjustment mentioned had not been made.

[50] Theoretically it would have been preferable to calculate jointly the effect of changes in the working population according to age structure and school-leaving age by a cross-breakdown of the working population on both counts and by applying different weighting coefficients to each "box" in the breakdown. But the degree of accuracy of available data did not encourage use of such a refined method. For one thing, the 1963 inquiry covered a sample of only 25,000 persons, and the

TABLE 2.15
Coefficients of Quality of the Working Population by School-Leaving Age

Ratio	Illiterates	6–9	10–12	13–14	15–18	19–21	22 and over
Uncorrected ratio				1	1.5	1.9	2.7
Ratio adopted	0.6	0.7	0.8	1	1.3	1.5	2.0

TABLE 2.16
*Effect of Changes in Level of Education
on the Quality of the Working Population, 1901–68*
(1954 = 100)

Year	Index	Year	Index	Year	Index	Year	Index
1901	84.2	1921	90.2	1936	94.7	1962	102.7
1906	85.8	1926	92.1	1946	97.4	1968	104.5
1911	87.7	1931	93.6	1954	100.0		

As already mentioned, differences in earnings by school-leaving age are the result not only of the "schooling factor" but also of other factors correlated with education, e.g. original family background, innate qualities. Some weight must therefore be given to these other factors. Following Denison,[51] we have assumed that two-fifths of the observed differences should be ascribed to other factors. The corrected and uncorrected efficiency ratios by school-leaving age are shown in Table 2.15. They are based on observed data for school-leaving ages exceeding 12 years. For ages below 13, however, for which we would need data going back to the beginning of the century (cf. above), we have adopted a priori assumptions based on scales observed in the United States. Applying coefficients of quality by school-leaving age (Table 2.15) to the breakdown of working population by school-leaving age (Table 2.13) gives the progression shown in Table 2.16. The average increase in quality in the working population linked to the rise in school-leaving age was 0.4 percent per year before World War I; it can be explained by the spread of primary schooling in the second half of the nineteenth century. This continued between the two wars, although at a slackening pace, whereas the increase in secondary and higher schooling had only begun to lift

---

earnings data from a cross-breakdown by age and by school-leaving age show a number of anomalies that can be explained only by errors in sampling or observation. In addition, the estimates of distribution by length of schooling in each generation are subject to considerable uncertainties, as can be seen by comparing the IEDES study based on school statistics and the results of the 1963 inquiry or the 1954 population census.

[51] *The Sources of Economic Growth in the United States* and *Why Growth Rates Differ.*

TABLE 2.17

The Overall Growth of Labor Resources, 1896–1969

(Percent per year)

Period	Total working population	Resources used in productive sectors		Changes in quality of working population			Resources used in productive sectors with effects of quality	
		Man-years	Man-hours	Linked to changes in sex and age structure	Linked to changes in educational level	Total	Man-years	Man-hours
Long-Term Development								
1896–1913	0.2%	0.2%	-0.1%	–	0.4%	0.4%	0.6%	0.3%
1913–29	0.1	0.2	-0.7	–	0.3	0.3	0.5	-0.4
1929–38	-0.5	-1.1	-2.5	0.2%	0.3	0.5	-0.4	-2.0
1938–49	–	0.1	0.7	–	0.3	0.3	0.4	1.0
1949–63	0.15	-0.15	-0.15	0.15	0.35	0.5	0.35	0.35
1896–1929	0.15	0.2	-0.4	–	0.4	0.4	0.6	–
1929–63	-0.1	-0.3	-0.5	0.1	0.3	0.4	0.1	-0.1
1896–1963	–	-0.1	-0.5	0.1	0.35	0.45	0.35	-0.05
Postwar Development								
1951–57	0.2	-0.2	-0.2	0.15	0.3	0.45	0.25	0.25
1957–63	–	-0.1	-0.1	0.15	0.3	0.45	0.35	0.35
1963–69	0.6	0.4	–	0.1	0.35	0.45	0.8	0.4

the quality of the working population further: the increase was 0.3 percent per year, on the average, between 1921 and 1936. After World War II the advance of secondary and higher schooling was the only factor raising the quality of the labor force; the average yearly increase was 0.35 percent from 1946 to 1968. If estimates are made for future years on the basis of the IEDES projections of the working population by educational level,[52] an acceleration to an average of 0.7 percent between 1970 and 1978 becomes apparent. Over the whole period 1901–68, increase in educational level would seem to have helped raise the quality of the labor force by 24 percent, an average annual improvement of 0.35 percent.

CONCLUSION: THE EVOLUTION OF TOTAL LABOR RESOURCES

To sum up, Table 2.17 covers data on the evolution of total labor resources between 1896 and 1969 in the productive sectors, i.e. in those economic activities whose output is included in the official production aggregate (excluding, therefore, employees of central and local government and financial institutions and domestic servants). The years shown within the period 1896–1969 are the most relevant to the goal of our research—that is, to the study of economic growth rather than to demographic analysis, such as in this chapter. We have switched from demographic key years to economic key years by interpolation, and where necessary with the help of ad hoc indicators. We have assumed, moreover, the changes in "quality effects" in the productive sectors, which employ four-fifths of the working population, can be taken as identical to those in the total population.[53] The evolution of labor resources can be measured in man-hours or in man-years. Measurable changes in quality of the labor force can be taken into account or not. The different results of these various approaches are shown in Table 2.17. Table 2.18 gives comparative figures of the growth of the employed labor force in the principal Western countries.

These tables make clear how little the labor resources of the French economy have grown over the whole period studied. From 1896 to 1929 the employed labor force grew at the very slow annual rate of 0.15 percent in France, whereas it increased at nearly 1 percent in the United Kingdom and at 2 percent in the United States. From 1929 to 1963 the

[52] M. Debeauvais and P. Maes, "Une méthode de calcul du stock d'enseignement," *Population*, May–June, 1968.

[53] Minor adjustments have been made, however, for the post–World War II period to the qualitative changes of the labor force by age, in order to allow for the growing size of the military draft, made up of young men aged 20–24.

TABLE 2.18
The Growth of the Working Population in the Principal
Western Countries, 1896–1962
(Percent per year)

Period	France	Germany	United States	Italy[a]	United Kingdom
1896–1913	0.2 %	1.4%[b]	2.6%	0.4%	1.0%
1896–1929	0.15	—	2.0	0.3	0.9[c]
1929–63	–0.1	—	1.2	0.7	0.8
1950–62	0	1.9	1.2	1.2	0.6

Source: National studies of the Social Science Research Council project.

[a]Figures are for the working population regularly employed and living within the present borders. Between 1950 and 1962, the regularly employed group increased from 16.9 to 19.4 million, although the overall work force grew only slightly (from 20.4 to 20.6 million). This increase can be accounted for by a drop in the number of those unemployed (from 1.5 to 0.6 million) and of those employed only occasionally (from 2.0 to 0.6 million).

[b]The years covered are 1895 to 1907.

[c]From figures made homogeneous by correcting for the effect of Southern Ireland's separation from the United Kingdom after World War I.

rise was close to 1 percent in the United States, the United Kingdom, and Italy, while in France there was a slight fall. From 1950 to 1962 the French employed labor force did not change at all, but that in the United Kingdom grew by 0.6 percent, in the United States and Italy by 1.2 percent, and in West Germany by 1.9 percent. In the last two countries much of the substantial increase in employment was linked to the drop in underemployment in the aftermath of World War II, as well as (in the case of West Germany) to the inflow of refugees from East Germany. In France the work force employed in the productive sectors did not grow by more than 2 percent per year in any part of the period studied, except the last few years; in fact, since 1929 it has been on a continuous downward trend. Total hours worked, allowing for the long-term downward trend, fell each year, except in the period just before and just after World War II. The total drop between 1896 and 1963 was 30 percent. However, this was offset by an increase of the same order of magnitude in the quality of the working population. It would seem, therefore, that apart from the latest years, the growth of French output outlined in Chapter 1 must be ascribed entirely to increases in labor productivity. This we shall now examine.

CHAPTER THREE

Labor Productivity

As we stressed in Chapter 1, the postwar acceleration of productivity growth needs explaining at least as much as does the rise in output. If output had grown chiefly as a result of an increase in the labor force, that would be a simple and limited phenomenon. We have seen, however, that this was not the case, since employment in the productive sectors was smaller from 1945 to 1969 than at the beginning of the century, and well below the high point of 1929.

Labor is, of course, only one of the factors of production, and the main cause of the changes we have traced might be the growth of capital. We shall, therefore, pay particular attention to overall factor productivity, which allows for changes in capital used as well as in manpower. The proper question will then be whether the pace of overall productivity has changed significantly, and if so, why. Chapter 7 gives only a very approximate answer to this question for lack of prewar estimates of capital. For this reason we propose to examine here the development of labor productivity, for which relatively precise and detailed analysis is possible. Using the estimates given in Chapters 1 and 2, we can study its movements since 1896, both for the economy as a whole and for the main industries.

The most satisfactory indicator of labor applied is probably the number of hours worked per year by the entire working force. This allows for the size of the work force employed, the length of working week, and the number of weeks worked per year. Some economists, however, question whether the number of persons employed over the long run is not a more accurate and more appropriate indicator: more accurate, because working hours are not known with much precision, particularly for non–wage earners (although variation in working hours is better known than the level); and more to the point, since an absolutely exact indicator should take account of the intensity of effort put into the work, and this may have been inversely proportional to the length of the working days. It is in fact very likely that workers at the beginning of the century, who worked an average of over ten hours a day seven days a week without annual vacations, were more often absent, and organized their work in a more relaxed fashion than workers today.

No indicator can be devised to measure increases in the intensity of effort. It seems difficult to agree, however, that they have entirely made up for the reduction in hours worked. The best measure of labor productivity in the long term probably lies between value added per employed member of the labor force and value added per man-hour. We shall therefore consider both these values, referring to the former as "production per man-year" and to the latter as "production per man-hour." We shall not deal here with changes in the quality of work, for the double reason that change has been very slow and is difficult to determine by individual industries. We shall consider this topic in Chapter 7 in relation to overall productivity. We shall first analyze labor productivity for the economy as a whole and for industry as a whole. The development of the working population and of participation rates by sector will then be reviewed and the growth of productivity in each examined. At both the general and sectoral levels, long-term trends and changes over the past 20 years will be studied in turn.

TRENDS IN LABOR PRODUCTIVITY IN THE
ECONOMY AS A WHOLE

Three questions chiefly engage our attention. How do improvements in productivity since World War II relate to long-term trends? How did labor productivity fluctuate? Can a trend toward deceleration be detected in the growth of this productivity?

The Postwar Period in Relation to Earlier Periods

The growth in productivity since 1949 has been much faster than in any earlier period. The two postwar periods are similar, it is true, in relation to production per man-hour. But acceleration in growth of productivity can be seen clearly from a comparison of the two long periods on either side of 1929. Let us examine these three points in succession.

Overall growth of productivity. By comparison with earlier periods, the growth of labor productivity was rapid after World War II. In all the productive sectors taken together and for both of the indicators we have adopted to measure labor input, productivity increased on the average by over 5 percent per year between 1949 and 1969. In the four other major periods studied, average rates of increase of overall production per man-year and per man-hour did not exceed, respec-

TABLE 3.1
The Growth of Labor Productivity, 1896–1969
(Percent per year)

Sector	1896–1913	1913–1929	1929–1938	1938–1949	1949–1963	1949–1969
Agriculture and forestry:						
Production per worker	1.5%	0.9%	2.1%	1.3%	6.0%	6.0%
Production per man-hour	1.9	1.4	2.5	1.7	6.4	6.4
All industry:						
Production per worker	1.7	2.1	1.0	0.2	5.2	5.3
Production per man-hour	2.0	3.4	2.9	-0.9	5.1	5.3
All productive sectors:						
Production per worker	1.7	1.5	0.8	0.9	5.1	5.0
Production per man-hour	2.0	2.5	2.2	0.3	5.2	5.2
Gross national product:						
Production per worker	1.6	1.4	0.7	0.8	4.5	4.4
Production per man-hour	1.9	2.3	1.9	0.3	4.5	4.6

tively, 2 and 2.5 percent annually. No other 20-year period can be found in France since the beginning of the century, or perhaps even earlier, over which labor productivity grew at such a pace. This is clearly illustrated by Table 3.1, in which we have shown, on the basis of tables analogous to those in earlier chapters, the average annual growth rate of labor productivity for different aggregates and for agriculture.

Production per man-hour increased from 1949 to 1969 by 5.2 percent per year in all productive sectors taken together, and by 5.3 percent in industry proper. The highest earlier growth was from 1913 to 1929: 2.5 percent per year for the whole productive economy and 3.4 percent in Industry proper. Growth was fairly stable for all productive sectors taken together over the three periods covering 1896 to 1938. In industry proper the differences between the periods were greater, but, in general, productivity increased faster than in the whole economy. We emphasized agriculture in Table 3.1 because its postwar record was the most distinctive. Production per man-hour in that sector increased by 6.4 percent, whereas it had never previously exceeded 2.5 percent per year. It should also be stressed that in contrast to the economy as a whole, where productivity scarcely rose from 1938 to 1949, productivity in agriculture improved during that period at the same pace as earlier.

Production per worker changed in a similar way, but of course more slowly before 1949 because of the reduction in hours worked. From 1929 to 1938, production per worker in industry grew by an annual average of only 1 percent, whereas production per man-hour rose by 3 percent. This difference was due to the substantial reduction made by the Pop-

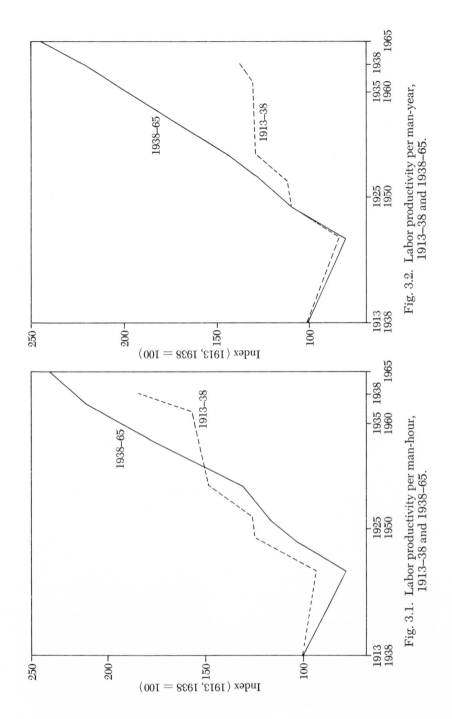

Fig. 3.1. Labor productivity per man-hour, 1913–38 and 1938–65.

Fig. 3.2. Labor productivity per man-year, 1913–38 and 1938–65.

ular Front government in hours worked. (It is worth noting that growth of hourly productivity was not significantly affected by the Great Depression.) Table 3.1 shows figures relating to gross national product. These have been calculated by adding to the labor force, in all the productive sectors together, an estimate of employees of central and local government and of other workers treated as nonproductive in the French National Accounts. At the same time, the gross domestic product was increased by an estimate of the "production" of those categories. The productivity figures for gross national product grew more slowly than those for the productive economy, as a result of the definition used for production in "nonproductive services": the growth of this production was assessed on the basis of the growth in numbers employed, on the assumption that output per man-hour did not change in government offices, financial institutions, and domestic services. The relative differential between the two measures of productivity for the economy as a whole, however, seems to have been of the same order of magnitude in all the periods.

Comparative growth of productivity, 1913–38 and 1938–63. The substantial increases in productivity after 1949 followed a period of near-stagnation between 1938 and 1949. A comparison between 1949–63 and 1913–29, which includes World War I, would therefore not be a fair one. Consequently, it seems appropriate to examine productivity growth more closely during each of these postwar periods. France enjoyed a sharp increase in labor productivity after World War I as well as after World War II, although our main figures do not reveal this because they compare the year 1929 directly with the year 1913. We have not made a detailed study of the intervening years, but statistics for the working population in the census years 1921 and 1926 and the annual production series shown in Table 1.3 (p. 24) enable us to make a rough calculation. From 1921, a recession year, to be sure, to 1929, overall production per man-year and per man-hour seems to have risen by an average of 5.1 percent per year and 5.5 percent, respectively—that is, at rates comparable with those achieved after World War II.

In order to trace developments more clearly from the start of each of the last prewar years, i.e. 1913 and 1938, we have shown together in Figures 3.1 and 3.2 the growth curves of labor productivity for the 25 years 1913–38 (1913 = 100) and for the 28 years 1938–66 (1938 = 100). Figure 3.1 shows production per man-hour, and Figure 3.2 shows production per man-year. Some similarity can be seen in movements over the first 15 years of each period. The rapid increase in labor productivity from 1921 to 1929 after the setback due to World War I can be compared with the increase from 1946 to about 1953. On the other hand, whereas productivity growth was interrupted in the early 1930's, it has continued at a fast pace from 1953 to the present.

Admittedly, the overall picture differs according to whether production per man-hour or production per man-year is considered. Production per man-hour seems to have been depressed considerably more by World War II than by World War I. In fact, although its growth was slowed by the depression, the annual average rate over the 25 years 1913–38 (2.4 percent) was only slightly below that over the 25 years 1938–63 (2.9 percent). Production per man-year fell by some 20 percent between 1913 and 1921, and also between 1938 and 1946. Growth was a little slower in the 1920's than from 1946 to 1955. In the 1930's there was very little increase, whereas over the whole period after World War II the rate of increase was high.

Developments over the two long periods. While bearing in mind the differences in the pace of growth just discussed, we can now examine long-term trends. As in Chapter 1, we shall consider the two periods covering respectively 1896–1929 and 1929–63. The average growth of production per man-hour for the whole productive economy was 2.3 percent per year from 1896 to 1929, and rose to 2.7 percent from 1929 to 1963. The increase in production per man-year accelerated faster: from 1.6 percent per year in the first period to 2.5 percent in the second. From this viewpoint, as from the earlier one considered, it seems undeniable that the growth of labor productivity has speeded up. This acceleration seems to have begun, in fact, well before the end of World War II. The average annual growth of output per man-hour rose progressively: 2.0 percent in 1896–1913, 2.5 percent in 1913–29, 2.2 percent in 1929–38,[1] and 3.0 percent in 1938–63.

The same phenomenon of acceleration during the present century can be seen in the long-term trends of the other industrial countries. Table 3.2 shows that labor productivity grew faster after 1929 than before in Germany, the United States, Italy, and Great Britain, as well as in France, in the case of both production per worker and production per man-hour.[2] The widespread character of this development suggests that the industrial nations benefited in the twentieth century from accelera-

---

[1] On this point it is striking that, if the high rates of the early 1920's are regarded simply as making up lost ground, the economic stagnation of the 1930's was accompanied by only a moderate slowing down of production per man-hour. The halt in production was reflected chiefly in a reduction in employment and in hours worked.

[2] The figures for Italy in Table 3.2 are slightly biased, we believe, because in the absence of estimates for 1929 we have had to use a depression year (1931) as the cutoff point between the two long-term periods. Nevertheless, the increase in growth rates considerably exceeds that attributable to this inadequate choice of cutoff year.

TABLE 3.2
*The Growth of Labor Productivity in the Principal
Western Countries, 1896–1963*
(Percent per year)

Production	France	Germany[a]	United States	Italy[b]	United Kingdom
Overall production per worker:					
1896–1929	1.5%	1.0%	1.8%	1.4%	0.6%
1929–63	2.2	2.4	1.9	2.9	1.3
1949–63	4.4	5.3	2.5	4.9	2.0
Production per man-hour:					
1896–1929	2.1	1.8	2.1		1.1
1929–63	2.4	2.7	2.5		1.3
1949–63	4.5	6.0	2.9		2.1

Source: National studies of the Social Science Research Council project.
Note: Production is measured by an aggregate approximately equal to gross national product.
[a]For Germany, figures are for the territory at each period. Comparisons are slightly distorted because of regional disparities. The last two periods are for 1929–62 and 1950–62.
[b]For Italy, figures are for the present territory. The periods are 1901–31, 1931–61, and 1950–62.

tion in technical progress: the replacement of methods of production by new ones has apparently proceeded at an ever faster pace. At this stage of our study it is premature to draw any conclusions, since we have not yet considered the possible effect of the other factors of production. Moreover, even if we later confirm that technical progress has accelerated, it may be explained at least in part by structural changes in the manner of working of industrial economies. This question must therefore be considered separately in other parts of our study. And finally, it should be noted that at least in France the increase in productivity was less marked in Industry, where the rate was almost the same over the two long-term periods considered.

Productivity After World War II: Fluctuations and Trends

A more detailed study shows how labor productivity over the past 20 years has changed in relation to short-term economic developments, and gives information on end-of-period trends. The comparison between the two postwar periods suggested that the rapid increase in production per man-hour after 1946 may have been due to the fact that the starting point was lower in relation to 1938 than that in 1929 was in relation to 1913. A slowdown in the 1960's might confirm this hypothesis, and would suggest the likelihood of a change in rate. We shall see that, in fact, productivity growth did not tend to slow down.

We shall first measure this growth after the war by using figures for production per man-hour. Changes in production per man-year were fairly similar up to 1965; however, they are clearly less significant for a study of short-term fluctuations, since they do not take into account variations in weekly hours worked. Figure 3.1 shows the general movement of production per man-hour—a rapid overall increase, particularly up to 1951. For all sectors taken together, the annual rise was 6 percent from 1949 to 1951, as against 5 percent from 1951 to 1963. For Industry, the rates were respectively 7 percent and 4.9 percent. Available data on production and the working population between 1946 and 1949 suggest, moreover, that productivity growth was particularly lively between these years. The speed of the increase between 1946 and 1951 can be explained as the joint consequence of a rise in the intensity of labor, the rapid repair of plants that had been only damaged and not destroyed in the war, and the reorganization of economic channels.

During the three cycles bounded by the years 1951, 1957, 1963, and 1969, the productivity of the economy as a whole seems to have grown at a roughly constant rate, rising from an average of 4.9 percent per year in the first six years to 5.1 percent in the next 12. This approximately even pace for production as a whole nevertheless masks quite substantial differences among the principal industrial groups. We return to this point in the third part of this chapter, but examine here the important, special case of productivity in Industry. The possibility of a slowdown in productivity affects this group more than the others. The most outstanding and reliable results concern this group. In addition, productivity measurement is less imprecise in this group than in others; measures of hours worked and annual changes in the work force are more reliable in Industry than in agriculture, the services, and trade. Fluctuations in hourly productivity in Industry are clearly linked to the short-term economic fluctuations examined in Chapter 1. Productivity increased weakly in the years of retardation and very strongly in the years of economic recovery. Thus output per man-hour rose only slightly from 1951 to 1954 and over the years 1957 and 1958. Figure 3.3 shows the year-by-year growth rates of production and productivity, which exhibit both parallel movements and differences. The changes in productivity were less pronounced than those in production, in both boom and recession years. From 1952 to 1954 both productivity and production slowed down together, whereas in 1958 this was not the case. Productivity rose by only 2.5 percent in 1957, whereas production continued to grow at almost 6 percent. By contrast, in 1959, when output rose more slowly (2.2 percent), productivity had recovered to a healthy pace, and grew by almost 5 percent. Despite the small growth of output in 1965 and 1967, productivity continued to increase.

Before studying whether any slowing down of productivity growth

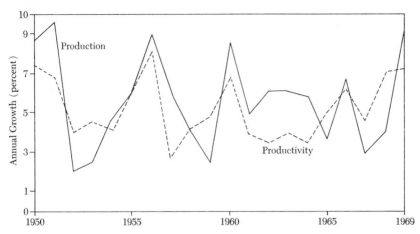

Fig. 3.3. The growth of production and production per man-hour
in Industry, 1950–69.

rates occurred in industry, we should compare the peaks and troughs in
Figure 3.3. Although productivity and production grew at a common
rate in 1956, production had a lead of 2 percentage points in the other
peak years (1951, 1960, and 1969). In a symmetrically opposite way,
productivity increased by almost 4 percent in 1952 and 1953, whereas
production rose by only 2 percent. In 1957 productivity grew by no more
than production did in 1959. Examination of the figure shows no apparent trend toward a slowing down of productivity. After the immediate postwar years, the average annual rate settled at 4.9 percent over
each of the cycles 1951–57 and 1957–63. In the third cycle, 1963–69,
however, it was as high as 5.8 percent. Measured by production per man-
hour, industrial productivity tended in fact to accelerate. For production per man-year, this movement was less marked, but present nevertheless, since in the three cycles the growth rates were 5.0, 4.8, and 5.4
percent, respectively.[3] This productivity increase is not evident when all
the productive sectors are taken as a whole, partly because (if the estimates used here are to be believed) a reverse phenomenon occurred in
trade and services, and partly because the big productivity improvements in agriculture had reduced weight as the relative size of the agricultural work force diminished.

Is a constant rate of productivity growth to the present day characteristic of France alone, or is it also found in the other industrial countries?
A reply to this question must assume that three major difficulties in sta-

[3] See also J.-F. Ponsot and C. Sautter, "La Croissance de la productivité du travail dans l'industrie s'est accélérée dès 1967," *Economie et statistique,* June 1970.

TABLE 3.3
National Income per Man-Hour in the Principal
Western Countries, 1950–62
(Percent per year)

Period	France	Germany	United States	Italy	United Kingdom
Direct comparison between periods:					
1950–55	4.6%	7.1%	2.9%	5.2%	1.4%
1955–62	5.0	4.3	1.9	5.4	2.1
Adjusted rates:					
1950–55	4.4	7.1	2.5	5.1	1.2
1955–62	4.8	4.3	2.3	5.5	2.4

Source: E. F. Denison, assisted by J. P. Poullier, *Why Growth Rates Differ: Postwar Experience in Nine Western Countries* (Washington, D.C., 1967), particularly Tables 21-1 to 21-19.

tistical comparisons have been resolved: those of comparisons between separate periods, separate countries, and separate sources of data (i.e. between figures on production and employment). This is why we have not been able to up-date the calculations shown in Table 3.3. These calculations relate to the periods 1950–55 and 1955–62. They concern both the effective average annual growth rate of labor productivity and also an adjusted rate, regarded as more significant. The nature of the distinction is easy to understand. Let us take the United States as an example.

A direct comparison of productivity growth rates shows a clear slowing down in the United States and a slight acceleration in France. The average annual increases in national income per hour over the two periods were respectively 2.9 and 1.9 percent in the United States and 4.6 and 5.0 percent in France. Denison comments, however, that over such short periods the special features of the boundary years of each period have an important effect. He then identifies two sources of irregularity and makes appropriate corrections. On the one hand, he replaces agricultural production in the years in question by a figure based on the observed trend: this should eliminate weather effects. On the other hand, to allow for variations in the pressure of demand and for related variations in the use made of productive capacity, he makes a correction that we shall describe in Chapter 8. After these two adjustments, the results for the United States change as follows: 2.5 percent instead of 2.9 percent for the first period, and 2.3 percent instead of 1.9 percent for the second. This suggests that a high degree of precision would have to be attributed to the estimates to make a slowing down seem a credible conclusion. (The growth in United States production after 1962 suggests, moreover, that labor productivity has risen sharply since then.)

A comparison of the adjusted rates in Table 3.3 suggests that there was a drop only in the case of Germany. But that country's results for 1950–55 were obviously affected by a reconstruction occurring later than it did elsewhere. The acceleration in the United Kingdom led to a rate low by comparison with the other European countries. The steady pace of productivity change observed in France does not on balance seem exceptional. The conclusions of this overall analysis seem clear. From the beginning of the century, productivity has been growing in France as in most countries. This growth has been much faster since the last war than before it. The change in pace does not seem to be due to the wartime standstill, since it has continued without faltering for 25 years. Analysis by industries will enable us to confirm these findings.

CHANGES IN THE LABOR FORCE, AND IN ACTIVITY
RATES, BY INDUSTRY GROUPS

Since the beginning of the century, the distribution of the French labor force among the different industry groups has undergone considerable change as a result of alterations in the structure of demand and related movements in labor productivity. Census data provide a description of those changes, which we shall study first for the century as a whole, and then for the last 20 years.

The Period 1896–1963

The development of the working population from 1896 to 1963 is shown in Table 3.4. True, the figures in it are subject to a number of uncertainties, which make them somewhat inaccurate.[4] First, most of the years in our study are not census years. We have therefore had to use sometimes tenuous interpolations. For 1938 and 1949 the Ministry of Labor's employment statistics provided a sufficient base for most industry groups. But these figures did not exist in the earlier years. The censuses closest to 1929 were made in 1926 and 1931, before and after the period of high activity that preceded the Great Depression. The 1911 census, which was closest to 1913, was not broken down in the same way as the others, and gave no distribution of the working population by industry groups. The 1913 estimates shown are therefore the result of a somewhat uncertain extrapolation of the figures for 1901 and 1906.[5]

[4] There are slight inconsistencies in the 1949, 1954, 1963, and 1968 results between the figures for long-term changes and those for the postwar periods. These differences, which are very minor, arise from the fact that the part of the study relating to the prewar years was based on a provisional breakdown of the 1954 labor force.

[5] In many cases, for 1913, 1929, and 1938 we have used the extrapolations by L. A. Vincent in "Population active, production et productivité dans 21 branches de l'économie française, 1896–1962," *Etudes et conjoncture*, February 1965.

TABLE 3.4
Size of the Labor Force by Sector, 1896–1968
(Thousands of persons)

Sector	1896	1913	1929	1938	1949	1954	1963	1968
Agriculture and forestry	8,350	7,450	6,600	5,900	5,580	5,030	3,650	2,950
Industry:								
Processed foods and farm products	470	520	550	580	610	610	610	630
Solid mineral fuels and gas	170	240	340	280	310	260	200	150
Electricity and water	10	30	60	70	80	90	100	120
Petroleum and oil products			20	30	40	50	70	80
Building materials	260	290	350	250	240	250	260	290
Metallurgy	80	120	230	200	260	250	290	240
Mechanical and electrical industries	660	870	1,400	1,160	1,450	1,550	2,010	2,050
Chemicals	70	110	210	210	280	310	370	420
Textiles, clothing, and leather	2,790	2,850	2,300	1,800	1,600	1,430	1,200	1,020
Miscellaneous industries	660	730	850	700	740	750	810	850
Total industry	5,170	5,760	6,310	5,280	5,610	5,550	5,920	5,850
Other industry groups:								
Building and public works	830	960	1,120	780	1,020	1,320	1,670	2,000
Transportation and communications	600	750	1,150	1,000	990	910	1,030	1,050
Trade	1,000	1,250	1,500	1,650	1,570	1,650	1,950	2,220
Other services	1,150	1,400	1,520	1,750	1,780	1,870	2,130	2,530
Total of industry groups	17,100	17,570	18,200	16,360	16,550	16,330	16,350	16,600
Financial institutions	60	110	220	200	200	200	270	330
Domestic service	950	930	780	750	620	590	490	490
Government[a]	1,110	1,290	1,100	1,450	1,890	2,130	2,620	2,730
Total employed population	19,220	19,900	20,300	18,760	19,260	19,250	19,730	20,150

[a]Including armed forces draftees.

Second, the nomenclature used in 1896 and 1936 for the industrial breakdown of the labor force differed considerably from that adopted in recent censuses and from that in the National Accounts. Some of the labor force therefore must be divided among industry groups, not without a certain arbitrariness. It might have been possible to reduce this to a minimum by using the most detailed census data, but we have not undertaken such a difficult task. We have used two comparative studies that give series set up on a common basis, although with different classifications from those used here.[6]

Third, the definition of participation in the labor force is always somewhat arbitrary for family helpers. There is reason to believe that different criteria have been adopted in practice in the different censuses. For example, a shopkeeper's wife considered part of the labor force in one case would not have been included if the rules adopted in another case had been strictly followed. In most industry groups, the resulting lack of comparability can be considered negligible by comparison with other causes of uncertainty, but it may well have a great influence on movements in the figures of the agricultural labor force. An examination of sex and age breakdown in agriculture does indeed show some changes that appear manifestly artificial: for example, the number of women per 100 men was 48 in 1896 and 1901, 60 in 1906, 78 in 1921, around 70 in 1926, 1931, and 1936, and 54 in 1954. We have therefore reconstructed a series for the active population in farming on the basis of the number of men aged 25–64 recorded as part of the agricultural labor force. We have assumed that the number of other participants in this labor force stayed at a fairly constant ratio to the number of men, except for two factors that we have allowed for as carefully as possible: the longer time spent at school and the alteration of the demographic structure caused by World War I.

Fourth, the labor force appears to have been considerably underestimated in the 1896 census, the first that applied the rules for recording and analyzing the data followed from 1896 to 1936. The resulting activity rates for men in age-groups 25–34, 35–44, and 45–55 were, respectively, 92, 92, and 93 percent. At the 1901 census, however, these rates were 96, 97, and 95 percent, and they remained the same within 1 percentage point at all the next censuses. On the other hand, an examination of changes in the labor force from 1896 to 1911 reveals discontinuities in certain parts of the working population that cannot be explained,

[6] A. Lucchi, "Evolution de la population active entre 1906 et 1954," *Etudes statistiques*, July–Sept., 1956; and Mme L. Cahen, "Evolution de la population active en France depuis cent ans d'après les dénombrements quinquennaux," *Etudes et conjoncture*, May–June, 1953.

TABLE 3.5
Manpower by Sector, 1913–63
(Indexes)

Sector	1913 1896=100	1929 1913=100	1938 1929=100	1949 1938=100	1963 1949=100
Agriculture and forestry	89	89	90	94	65
Industry:					
Processed foods and farm products	110	106	105	105	100
Solid mineral fuels and gas	140	142	82	112	63
Electricity and water	370	200	120	117	126
Petroleum and oil products			200	130	170
Building materials	112	120	71	98	110
Metallurgy	167	190	87	130	111
Mechanical and electrical industries	132	160	83	125	139
Chemicals	165	193	99	135	135
Textiles, clothing, and leather	102	81	79	89	75
Miscellaneous industries	111	116	82	106	109
Total industry	112	110	84	107	106
Other industry groups:					
Building and public works	116	116	70	131	162
Transportation and communications	125	154	87	99	104
Trade	125	120	110	95	124
Other services	122	109	115	102	120
Total of industry groups	103	104	90	101	99
Financial institutions	180	200	90	100	135
Domestic service	98	85	96	83	79
Government	116	85	132	130	139
Total employed population	104	102	92	103	103

as between 1896 and the other census years. Rather than retain a notoriously underestimated figure for the 1896 labor force, therefore, we have systematically raised it by assuming for that year the same activity rates by sex and age as for 1901. This has led to an overall increase of 560,000 persons, which we have divided among the industry groups after examining the 1901 and 1906 census results, and subsequently those of the 1866 census.[7]

The changes in breakdown of the labor force by industry groups are shown clearly in Table 3.4, and in Tables 3.5 and 3.6 derived from it. The agricultural labor force was 43 percent of the employed working population in 1896, but only 15 percent in 1968. Between the same two years, Industry's share of the working population rose from 31 to 39 per-

[7] As an example, the recorded work force in domestic services was 845,000 in 1896, 945,000 in 1901, and 935,000 in 1906. We have assumed that the 1896 result should be increased by 105,000 persons.

TABLE 3.6
Structure of the Labor Force by Major Industrial Divisions, 1896–1968
(Percent)

Sector	1896	1913	1929	1938	1949	1954	1963	1968
Agriculture	43.4%	37.4%	32.5%	31.4%	29.0%	26.1%	18.5%	14.6%
Industry	31.3	33.8	36.6	32.3	34.5	35.7	38.4	38.9
Bldg. & pub. works alone	(4.3)	(4.8)	(5.5)	(4.2)	(5.3)	(6.9)	(8.5)	(9.9)
Services	25.3	28.8	30.9	36.3	36.5	38.2	43.1	46.5
Productive sectors	(14.3)	(17.1)	(20.5)	(23.5)	(22.4)	(23.0)	(25.8)	(28.9)
Others	(11.0)	(11.7)	(10.4)	(12.8)	(14.1)	(15.2)	(17.3)	(17.6)
Total	100.0%	100.0%	100.0%	100.0%	100.0%	100.0%	100.0%	100.0%

cent (including building and public works) and that of services from 25 to 46 percent. Shifts within Industry have been very diverse. Between 1896 and 1963 the work force in textiles, clothing, and leather fell by 58 percent, whereas that in mechanical and electrical industries was multiplied by three. Apart from the interruption caused by the depression in the 1930's, the changes were fairly regular. As might be expected, the growth of employment was particularly high in the early years of new industries (i.e. chemicals, electricity, petroleum and products). A change can be seen in the trends of solid fuels and of transportation, where the work force had grown rapidly up to 1929.

To trace changes in hours worked in the different industries we have again made use of the estimates of L. A. Vincent.[8] Quite clearly, these changes are not known with accuracy for early periods, or even today for certain industries and non–wage earners. In Industry, trade, and the services, hours worked since 1931 can be followed in a Ministry of Labor survey of establishments of more than 10 employees. For earlier periods, Vincent has used comparisons between hourly and daily earnings recorded for a number of trades in a survey of conciliation boards. He has also allowed for changes in practice and in legislation relating to days worked in a year. A steady decline in hours worked in agriculture seems to be generally accepted as fact. It has been the subject of estimates by P. Coutin,[9] continued by Vincent. The rate of decrease, however, seems to be very poorly documented. We have completed Vincent's estimates with figures for domestic services, for which an arbitrary reduction has been assumed, and for government departments[10] where the

---

[8] See his "Population active," quoted on p. 87.
[9] See *Population*, April–June, 1949, p. 349.
[10] The regulation working week seems to have been 48 hours before World War I;

TABLE 3.7
Indexes of Annual Hours by Sector, 1913–63
(Indexes)

Sector	1913 1896=100	1929 1913=100	1938 1929=100	1949 1938=100	1963 1949=100
Agriculture and forestry	95	92	96	95	94
Industry:					
Processed foods and farm products	96	81	82	110	101
Solid mineral fuels and gas	96	83	89	119	87
Electricity and water	96	82	83	112	91
Petroleum and oil products			84	120	94
Building materials	95	82	84	117	101
Metallurgy	95	84	81	120	98
Mechanical and electrical industries	97	80	82	116	101
Chemicals	93	84	84	113	99
Textiles, clothing, and leather	94	82	82	110	104
Miscellaneous industries	94	80	83	113	103
Total industry	96	82	83	112	101
Other industry groups:					
Building and public works	96	86	82	116	104
Transportation and communications	93	82	84	118	96
Trade	93	82	83	108	101
Other services	95	82	83	110	101
Total of industry groups	95	86	88	107	99
Financial institutions	93	82	83	110	101
Domestic service	94	94	94	94	94
Government[a]	100	87	95	107	100
Total employed population	95	86	89	106	99

[a]Including armed forces draftees.

index follows changes in the regulation working week, which differs significantly from the hours actually worked as a result of numerous tolerances, but in a way impossible to measure.

Table 3.7 shows the figures we have thus adopted. Before World War I, time at work was slowly decreasing. The introduction of the 8-hour day after World War I and the 40-hour week in 1936 accelerated this change. In 1938, hours worked in industry had fallen by one-third below the 1913 level. After World War II, longer hours were worked again, and from 1949 to 1963 there was little change in most industries, since a slight increase in overtime made up for longer vacations. Tables 3.5 and 3.7 present the two types of data necessary for an assessment of changes in labor input, defined as the total number of hours worked by

it was set at 45 hours in 1929, at 40 hours in 1936, and again at 45 hours after the end of World War II. We have assumed that vacation rules did not change since the beginning of the century.

TABLE 3.8
Indexes of Total Man-Hours Worked by Sector, 1913–63
(Indexes)

Sector	1913 1896=100	1929 1913=100	1938 1929=100	1949 1938=100	1963 1949=100
Agriculture and forestry	84	82	87	89	61
Industry:					
Processed foods and farm products	106	86	86	115	101
Solid mineral fuels and gas	135	118	73	133	55
Electricity and water	350	160	99	131	114
Petroleum and oil products			170	160	160
Building materials	106	98	60	115	111
Metallurgy	159	160	70	156	109
Mechanical and electrical industries	128	128	68	145	140
Chemicals	153	162	83	153	133
Textiles, clothing, and leather	96	67	64	98	78
Miscellaneous industries	104	93	68	120	112
Total industry	107	90	70	120	107
Other industry groups:					
Building and public works	111	100	57	152	168
Transportation and communications	116	126	73	117	100
Trade	116	98	91	103	125
Other services	116	89	95	112	121
Total of industry groups	98	89	79	108	98
Financial institutions	167	164	75	110	136
Domestic service	92	79	90	78	74
Government[a]	116	74	126	139	139
Total employed population	99	88	82	109	102

Note: These figures are the product of the corresponding figures in Tables 3.5 and 3.7.

[a]Including armed forces draftees.

the work force of an industrial group, i.e. the total numbers employed multiplied by the length of time at work. Table 3.8 shows the results obtained on this basis.

The relative stability of the total working population, the increase in employment in government and financial institutions, and the shortening of time at work substantially reduced the labor input available to the productive sectors. Total man-hours worked in these sectors fell by 28 percent from 1896 to 1963, chiefly as a result of the rapid drop between 1913 and 1938. The last period, in fact, differs from the prewar years both in the level of labor input and in its rate of change. Labor input in 1963 was 5 percent above that reached in 1938. Between 1949 and 1963 it fell by 2 percent, a far slower annual drop than the 0.9 percent per year observed from 1896 to 1938. There was a very slight increase between 1963 and 1969.

Changes After World War II

The annual series of labor force figures by industry group shown as Appendix Table 5 were calculated from population censuses of 1954, 1962, and 1968, and from various indicators of changes in numbers employed, in particular the quarterly Ministry of Labor surveys of industrial and commercial establishments. Except for the census years, these series are based not only on observations but also on calculations made on certain assumptions, particularly in regard to non–wage earners.[11]

Between 1949 and 1962 there was little change in the total employed labor force. However, the number "outside the productive sectors" increased fairly regularly; the work force employed in the productive industries consequently fell by 500,000 persons. The overall increase in nonproductive services was chiefly the result of an increase in government employees, notably teachers. It will be recalled that this was due both to the steep rise in school-age population and to increases in the length of schooling. After 1962 the total employed labor force grew as a result of workers returning to mainland France from its dependencies, and also because the large postwar birth cohorts began to reach working age. Despite an acceleration of growth in nonproductive services, the employed work force within productive industries increased by 500,-000 persons between 1962 and 1968.

In the 1950's employment increases in the nonfarm groups were due only to a rapid drop in the agricultural working population. This continued at an exceptionally fast, even increasing, rate; between 1949 and 1968 the average rate of fall was 3 percent per year. The farm work force then fell from 5.5 million in 1949 (26.5 percent of the total working population—a very high proportion for a Western country) to 3 million in 1968 (15 percent of the total). This drop in numbers must be related to the rapid increase in farming productivity over the period, although it cannot be stated a priori whether this increase was a cause or an effect of the flight from the land. It is probable, however, that the increase in productivity was stimulated partly by the rapid spread of technical progress in farming and partly by the demand for labor from other sectors of the economy; in other words, by the growth in the other industry groups. This will be dealt with further in Chapter 7.

The growth of the work force in the nonfarm industries concerned not so much the extractive and manufacturing industries (whose num-

[11] See *Etudes et conjoncture*, March–April, 1964.

bers grew by an average of 0.2 percent per year from 1949 to 1968) as it did building and public works, as well as trade and the services. Over the same period, the average annual increase in numbers employed in building and public works was 3.4 percent, in trade 1.8 percent, and in other services 1.6 percent. In the latter two groups there was a clear upward trend. The near-stability in numbers employed in Industry does not apply to each industry separately: in some there was a considerable increase or decrease. For example, in the period 1949–68 in chemicals, and up to 1964 in the mechanical and electrical industries, manpower increased strongly by an average of 2.1 percent and 1.8 percent per year, respectively. In solid mineral fuels and gas, however, manpower fell sharply, by an average of 3.9 percent per year, with a particularly rapid drop after 1959. A substantial reduction in the employed work force also occurred in textiles, clothing, and leather, on the order of 2 percent. In the first of these two cases, the changes in manpower accompanied a drop in production, but in the second case production of textiles rose at a respectable rate.

Annual hours worked varied little in every industry up to 1965. The working week increased by about two hours after 1949 and remained steady in the high output years, but the number of working weeks dropped in the same proportion: a third week of paid vacation, which became mandatory in 1956, was already enjoyed by half the wage earners in 1955, and a fourth paid week spread to the economy as a whole in 1963 and 1964, following the agreement between staff and management in the nationalized Renault factories. Annual hours worked were thus about the same in 1963 as in 1957, with fluctuations of some tenths of percentage points in the years between. Changes in labor input in individual industries in this period were therefore more or less identical with changes in numbers employed, broadly outlined earlier. Appendix Tables 6 and 8 show the slight differences that existed. After 1965, hours worked fell, so that the index for 1969 (1963 = 100) was 98 in most industries. This drop slightly made up for an increase in numbers in the labor force.

LABOR PRODUCTIVITY BY INDUSTRIES

Turning our attention now to estimates of productivity on a disaggregated basis, we shall study each industry separately and seek to answer two questions: Does the acceleration of productivity growth observed in the economy as a whole occur in each industry? Can the rapid postwar increase of productivity be explained by exceptionally rapid development in particular industries? Long-term analysis will enable us to answer the first question, and a detailed study of the postwar period will be made in relation to the second.

Long-Term Trends

An analysis of the industry groups on the basis of Table 3.10 shows a fairly wide diversity of results. The ranking of industries and other activities by growth rates of man-hour production varies from one period to another without apparent reason. The uncertainty of our estimates doubtless explains much of the difference. Nevertheless, over the 70 years taken as a whole, the industries can be grouped in categories according to their pace of productivity increase.

In the first category, output per man-hour grew very fast: it includes the two industries producing new forms of energy—electricity and petroleum—as well as chemicals. The second group comprises industries whose productivity grew by a factor of over 5 in the past 70 years, that is, at least as fast as productivity in the economy as a whole. Textiles are at the head of this group, with a growth coefficient of 7, followed by agriculture, miscellaneous industries, and transportation and communications. The last category gathers together industries where production per man-hour rose at a significantly slower rate than the economy as a whole (with coefficients of between 2.2 and 3.8). In the mechanical and electrical industries, metallurgy, and building materials, the coefficient was close to 4. In the services, processed foods and farm products, and solid mineral fuels and gas, it was at least equal to 3. It was under 2.5 in trade and in building and public works.

As shown in Table 3.9, the different industries did not remain in the same categories throughout the periods considered. From 1896 to 1913, the fastest growth seems to have been in metallurgy, chemicals, and the mechanical and electrical industries. From 1913 to 1929, productivity increased exceptionally fast in electricity supply and almost as fast in chemicals and textiles. It rose very slowly in metallurgy and coal mining. From 1929 to 1938, productivity growth was particularly sharp in the miscellaneous industries, but ceased in metallurgy. The period 1938–49 was marked by a drop in every industry except transportation and communications, petroleum and products, and particularly agriculture, where productivity grew by 20 percent.

In all, the breakdown by long-term trends is quite similar to that of postwar rates of increase. Some exceptions must be noted, however:[12]

[12] The detailed data given here and subsequently have been taken from Vincent, "Population active."

TABLE 3.9
Indexes of Output per Man-Hour by Sector, 1896–1963
(Indexes)

Sector	1913 1896=100	1929 1913=100	1938 1929=100	1949 1938=100	1963 1949=100	1963 1896=i
Agriculture and forestry	137	124	125	121	239	6.4
Industry:						
Processed foods and farm products	119	163	120	87	161	3.2
Solid mineral fuels and gas	107	120	122	90	212	3.0
Electricity and water	120	440	135	97	330	23.0
Petroleum and oil products			300	113	245	–
Building materials	141	151	103	97	191	3.6
Metallurgy	182	116	94	93	207	3.6
Mechanical and electrical industries	164	155	113	81	164	3.8
Chemicals	175	196	130	88	217	8.5
Textiles, clothing, and leather	132	170	138	92	240	6.8
Miscellaneous industries	147	158	173	86	181	6.2
Total industry	140	170	130	91	198	5.7
Other industry groups:						
Building and public works	126	124	105	99	135	2.2
Transportation and communications	157	127	116	115	200	5.3
Trade	110	126	114	95	157	2.4
Services other than housing	122	134	120	102	166	3.3
Total of industry groups	141	148	122	103	202	5.3

(1) Although productivity continued to rise at a far higher rate in electricity than in any other industry, it also grew in farming, textiles, and the oil industry, with annual overall rates close to 7 percent. (2) Labor productivity in solid mineral fuels and gas grew at a fast rate after the war, contrasting with its extremely slow growth in previous periods. The increase in importance of the gas industry, which was particularly well situated to benefit from the technical progress, coincided with considerable reorganization and capital investment in coal mining. (3) Similarly, productivity in metallurgy, which had scarcely risen since 1913, increased by about 5.3 percent per annum between 1949 and 1963, largely because of the development of nonferrous metals. (4) By contrast, the relative position of the chemicals and rubber group worsened, as a result of a slower rise in growth of productivity in rubber, a new industry with fast prewar growth. (5) The miscellaneous group was in a similar position, since productivity had grown rapidly between the

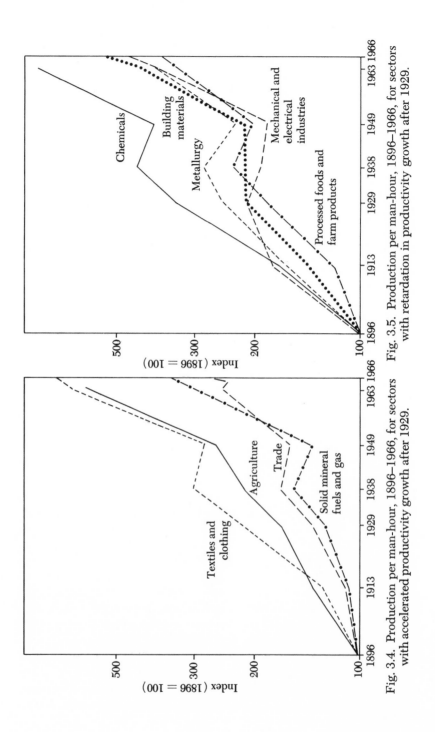

Fig. 3.5. Production per man-hour, 1896–1966, for sectors with retardation in productivity growth after 1929.

Fig. 3.4. Production per man-hour, 1896–1966, for sectors with accelerated productivity growth after 1929.

wars in paper, printing, and publishing but more slowly in the next 20 years.

With these exceptions, therefore, there was some stability in the increases in relative productivity of the different industries. Progress was much faster after the war than before, except for industries such as electricity and petroleum, which were new areas of production. We now examine the different industries more systematically in order to study those with accelerated productivity, already observed in a general way. To this end we can compare either the first two columns of Table 3.10, which show rates of productivity increase in the two major periods 1896–1929 and 1929–63, or the first and third columns, to find which industries had the most marked postwar acceleration. Finally, we turn to Figures 3.4 and 3.5, which present indexes (1896 = 100), on a semilogarithmic scale, of production per man-hour for the years studied. In these figures a straight line represents growth at a constant rate. Figure 3.4 shows those industries in which productivity growth seems to have speeded up, and Figure 3.5 those where it has slowed down.

We need not devote much time to electricity and water or to petro-

TABLE 3.10

Growth Rates of Output per Man-Hour by Sector, 1896–1963

(Percent per year)

Sector	1896–1929	1929–1963	1949–1963
Agriculture and forestry	1.6	3.9	6.4
Industry:			
Processed foods and farm products	2.0	1.6	3.5
Solid mineral fuels and gas	0.8	2.7	5.5
Electricity and water	5.2	4.4	8.9
Petroleum and oil products		6.6	6.8
Building materials	2.4	1.8	4.7
Metallurgy	2.3	1.7	5.3
Mechanical and electrical industries	2.9	1.3	3.6
Chemicals	3.8	2.7	5.7
Textiles, clothing, and leather	2.5	3.2	6.5
Miscellaneous industries	2.6	3.0	4.3
Total industry	2.7	2.6	5.0
Other industry groups:			
Building and public works	1.4	1.0	2.2
Transportation and communications[a]	2.1	3.0	5.1
Trade	1.0	1.6	3.3
Other services	1.5	2.1	3.7
Total of industry groups	2.3	2.8	5.2

[a] As a result of a likely overestimate of the work force in 1929, the productivity growth rate for this industry is probably slightly underestimated for 1896–1929 and overestimated for 1929–63 (see text).

leum and its products, which barely existed at the beginning of the century and in which, in any case, capital equipment matters far more than manpower. We can also leave aside other services, since the production index for this group depends largely on hypotheses about the development of labor productivity. The slowdown implied in Table 3.9 between 1913 and 1929 in the productivity growth of transportation and communications should be treated with some reserve. Further study of the work force in this industry shows that our series exaggerate the increase before 1929 and the decrease from 1929 to 1954.[13] For this reason, we have classified transportation as one of the groups in which labor productivity grew at a broadly constant rate.

In two industries, acceleration is undeniable: agriculture, on the one hand, solid mineral fuels and gas on the other. We have already mentioned the special circumstances of the latter. The rapid increase in productivity of agriculture is one of the chief features of present-day expansion, if only because of the large numbers employed in farming and their reduction to the benefit of the remainder of the economy. We shall discuss again the causes of this productivity increase, and try to measure its effects, in Chapters 6 and 7. A less marked acceleration seems to have taken place in trade, as well as in textiles, clothing, and leather. These employ a large work force, and small firms are particularly frequent. The structure of these two industries is similar to that of agriculture. At the other extreme, the industries in which production per man-hour seems to have grown less fast in 1929–63 than in 1896–1929 are those often considered modern and highly organized, or highly capital-intensive: metallurgy, mechanical and electrical industries, chemicals, processed foods and food products, and building materials and glass. We must note in passing the rather remarkable nature of productivity growth. It seems to contradict the argument that the principal postwar role was played by a few dynamic firms or sectors that triggered the whole of French development. France's growth appears rather as a widespread phenomenon, in which the less highly concentrated sectors played an important part.

To sum up, although labor productivity increased faster in every sector after the war than before, this acceleration seems less general if a prewar year is taken as base (say 1938 or 1929) and if the comparison is made in terms of production per man-hour. A continuation of present rates, if maintained, will bring labor productivity in every industry group above pre-1938 trends. However, this will take quite a few years.

[13] However, this bias does not seem great enough to require a review of our estimates as a whole.

Up to now we have used production per man-hour as a measure of changes in labor productivity by industries. If, instead, we took production per man-year as a basis, our conclusions would need to be changed somewhat. Differences between industries would not alter greatly, but within most industries a slowing down of productivity growth would be observed between 1929 and 1938, and the postwar acceleration would be much more evident. We should find at a less aggregative level results similar to those already observed overall.

The Period 1949–69

We have already compared productivity growth by industries, and Table 3.10 showed average annual rates from 1949 to 1963. We propose here to describe in more detail developments over the three postwar cycles, and to look for any indication of acceleration or retardation. See Table 3.11. Productivity growth was affected by the three short-term economic crises, but more so in 1952–53 than in 1958–59 and 1964–65. The indexes in Appendix Table 10 give annual changes in production per man-hour in each industry. The energy industries and transportation sustained a constant rate up to 1952, but there was little growth in iron mining and metallurgy, the mechanical and electrical industries, and

TABLE 3.11
Growth Rates of Productivity by Industry over Three Cycles, 1951–69
(Output per man-hour; *percent per year*)

Sector	1951–1957	1957–1963	1963–1969
02. Processed foods and farm products	3.4	2.7	4.4
03. Solid mineral fuels and gas	4.9	5.8	7.2
04. Electricity, water, and kindred products	7.4	8.5	6.1
05. Petroleum, natural gas, and oil products	4.6	6.4	9.0
06. Building materials and glass	4.9	4.9	7.2
07. Iron mining and metallurgy	5.6	3.8	9.7
08. Nonferrous minerals and metals	5.1	4.9	5.0
09. Mechanical and electrical industries	3.1	3.7	4.7
10. Chemicals and rubber	5.8	5.8	6.4
11. Textiles, clothing, and leather	6.9	5.8	4.0
12. Wood, paper, and miscellaneous industries	4.2	3.9	3.4
Total industry	4.9	4.9	5.8
13. Building and public works	0.7	3.8	5.5
14. Transportation and communications	5.4	3.7	3.3
16. Services other than housing	3.8	3.8	2.8
19. Trade	3.8	2.7	2.9
Nonagricultural groups	3.9	4.0	4.4
Total productive economy	4.9	5.1	5.1

miscellaneous industries. There was a drop in nonferrous minerals and metals and a stronger one in chemicals. In 1953 productivity resumed an upward movement (but at moderate rates) in all the industries where it had stagnated except mining and metallurgy, but it barely increased in the energy industries and transportation. Only in oil did high increases continue.

After 1957 productivity fell in only a few industries, mainly oil, where the drop can be explained by the unusual situation following the Suez events. Growth was weak, however, in most industries and remained so in 1958 and 1959, with no real recovery until 1960. The special features of 1957 do not prevent comparison of productivity growth over the first two cycles, but they should lead to slightly raised rates in the second period, if trends were maintained. We have already seen that, both in the economy as a whole and in industry, productivity growth rates remained constant over these two periods, but they accelerated later in industry. Over the period as a whole, acceleration can be seen in almost every industry group, the chief exceptions being textiles and clothing, miscellaneous industries, and transportation. The slowdown shown for trade and services is probably not significant, given the uncertainties in the measurement of production and manpower in these industries. For textiles and clothing, comparison can be made of changes in the rates of productivity and of growth (cf. Table 1.6, p. 30). The slowing down of output growth seems to have reacted on productivity growth, which is easy to understand in view of the difficulties of accelerating reductions in manpower.

The chief characteristics of the growth of labor productivity can thus be seen clearly: growth was much faster after the war than in the early part of the century, and has accelerated progressively since 1896; this acceleration affected all industries, and in general those with higher or with lower growth were the same in each period; progress in the less concentrated industries, however, was particularly noteworthy. Up until 1962, productivity growth was accompanied by only slight variations in the level of the employed work force, which after that date, however, grew at 0.6 percent per year. This important change in the supply of labor nevertheless did not lead to a slowing down of productivity change.

We ended Chapter 1 on a note of uncertainty between two interpretations, but already we are reaching a clearer view. We have established that the rate of growth of production was roughly constant in 1896–1929 and 1929–63, but that it became progressively higher over the different periods of fairly continuous expansion. This raised the question whether the explanation of high growth over the past 20 years should be sought in the stagnation of the 1930's and 1940's, or whether it was due to a structural change in the growth factors. The acceleration of productivity growth and its maintenance without any consistent slackening until very recent years support the second hypothesis.

The analysis in Chapter 7 will consider the physical growth factors, and will complete the conclusions reached so far. However, it will not go beyond this in relation to long-term trends. As we stated at the start, we have not been able to reconstruct capital series for the early part of the century, and this will become apparent in the two following chapters, on investment and capital.

CHAPTER FOUR

Investment

The working population and capital are the two main factors of production that we examine in this first part. Whereas considerable demographic data are available, we have made our own estimates in order to outline the development of France's productive capital. This chapter and the next one are therefore largely devoted to a description of the statistical methods adopted and the series obtained.

Before giving our estimates of the value of capital, we shall describe the development of investment: capital is of course the physical factor of production, but its evolution depends on investment. Estimates of investment can be made more directly than those of capital, from data on the production and importing or exporting of goods chiefly intended as capital equipment. We can therefore outline long-term movements of investment, but shall not be able to do so for capital. Moreover, investment not only leads to the accumulation of capital; it is relevant to growth in other ways. It is an element in final demand, and at certain periods it may give fresh impetus or support to the forward movement of the economy. It results from anticipation of future growth, and thus makes concrete the dynamism of business managers and decision makers in the public sector. Investment therefore needs to be studied for its own sake. Chapters 8–10 make use of the descriptions given in this chapter, with the aim of studying effects other than capital increases or the reasons for the development observed.

This chapter is essentially descriptive. It reports first on investments made during the postwar period, and second on the investment carried out since the beginning of the century, as measured by the share of gross fixed capital formation in gross domestic product. Even for overall analysis, it is often necessary to give some detail, in particular on those types of productive investment in which changes in different sectors throw light on the total picture. We shall therefore examine briefly some breakdowns of this type. Some international comparisons, finally, will help us appreciate better the effort invested by France in future growth. The measurement, particularly that of the volume, of investment raises conceptual difficulties to which we shall return in Chapters 5 and 7. The estimates shown here follow the conventions of the French National Accounts, as is usual in this kind of study.

GROSS FIXED CAPITAL FORMATION, 1946–69

Over the period as a whole, the rate of gross fixed capital formation grew by a factor of 4. This overall increase needs more detailed analysis. We shall therefore examine the chief investment categories (productive investment, investment in housing, and public investment), and then discuss changes by products and by industries. Appendix C outlines the methods used and the degree of precision reached. This is only moderate, particularly for the breakdown of investment by industries before 1956, but it is probably acceptable for the broad groups considered here.

Overall Results

To follow the movements in gross fixed capital formation, we shall consider in turn each of the periods examined in the discussion of production. In 1946, investment was high in relation to production. From 1946 to 1951 it grew slowly but continuously. Table 4.1 takes the investment estimates of Gavanier for the years 1946–49 and compares them with changes in output. The first part of Table 4.1, in constant prices, shows the growth in volume of investment. The second part, in current prices, enables us to compare these estimates with those for 1949 in the National Accounts. Since there is reasonably good agreement between the two sets of figures, we have used these results for the early postwar years in order to complete the National Accounts data, which we have followed consistently in later years. It should be pointed out, however, that we have adjusted downward the estimates of output of building and public works, as explained in Appendix C, since those in the National Accounts for 1949 to 1952 did not seem satisfactory. This gives faster growth for those years.

To understand the scale of capital accumulation in the early postwar years, we should make comparisons in terms of 1938 prices, which are far more significant than those in current prices. On this basis, there appears to have been a high rate of investment, reaching 22 percent in 1947 and reflecting the work of reconstruction. Between 1946 and 1951 investment growth averaged 5.2 percent per year. This average rate was the result of a sharp increase of over 12 percent in 1947, near-stag-

TABLE 4.1
Investment, 1946–49
(Million francs)

Category	1946	1947	1948	1949	1949 accounts
In constant 1938 prices:					
Production	3,300	3,580	4,000	4,275	
Investment	695	780	815	815	
Rate of investment	21.1%	21.8%	20.4%	19.0%	
In current prices:					
Production	26,660	35,900	61,900	74,900	*76,270*
Investment	4,060	6,150	12,500	14,050	*13,780*
Rate of investment	15.3%	17.1%	20.2%	18.8%	*17.9%*

Source: M. Gavanier, "Le Revenu national de la France: production et disponibilités nationales en 1938 et de 1946 à 1949," *Statistiques et études financières,* supplément Finances françaises, no. 20, 1953, for the first four columns. The last column is taken from National Accounts figures, as described in Appendix C.

nation in the two following years, and a growth of 3.3 percent in the next two years. As a result, although the economic situation in 1951 was very favorable, the rate of investment fell to the rather modest level of 18 percent.

Over the three following periods, 1951–57, 1957–63, and 1963–69, investment grew at a fairly even, and significantly higher, rate. Growth in the first of these periods averaged 7 percent per year. More specifically, the slowdown in 1952 caused a slight drop in that year, and a slight increase in the year following. But after 1953 investment forged ahead strongly and with some steadiness, at an average annual rate of over 10 percent. In the second period, growth was slightly slower, averaging 6.5 percent per year, but more regular. The 1958 economic slowdown did not reduce investment, which in that year grew by 4.5 percent. The growth rate then rose to 8 percent, and to 10.5 percent in 1961. Over the period 1963–69, investment continued to grow at a sustained rate; average growth was 7 percent per year.[1]

This overall description can be completed by examining the three main categories: (1) productive investment by firms to improve their production plant, raise labor productivity, and increase output (social investment by firms, not directly related to output, particularly in housing, is excluded); (2) investment in housing, both new building and major upkeep of old buildings; and (3) investment by civilian government agencies, most of which concerns capital equipment for schooling and transportation infrastructure—highways, harbors, and canals (we

[1] As explained in Appendix C, our calculations for these last years are considerably less accurate than those in the National Accounts. For the sake of homogeneity with the rest of our study, we have guessed what the official estimates would have been if the methods had not been changed from a base year of 1959 to 1962.

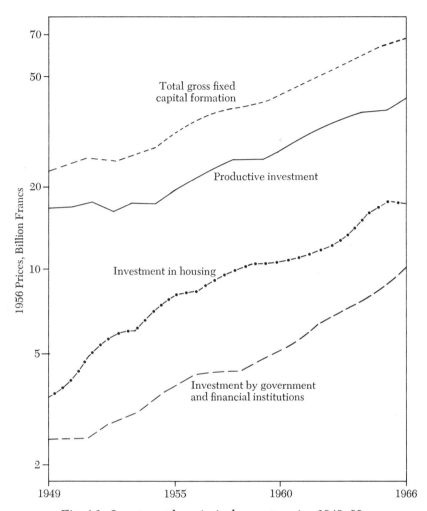

Fig. 4.1. Investment by principal use categories, 1949–66.

should remember that all purchases by the armed forces are considered consumption, and that building and equipping hospitals are treated as productive investment).

As shown in Figure 4.1, each of the three categories developed in a somewhat different way. Index numbers covering the whole postwar period make little sense, and it is helpful for many purposes to distinguish two phases—before 1954 and after. Productive investment, however, moved more or less in line with gross fixed capital formation. Its volume was almost the same in 1954 as in 1949, after slow growth in

1950 and 1951, a drop of 8 percent in 1952, and again a slow increase up to 1954. Thereafter, the rate of rise was sustained at an average of over 8 percent per year, despite a marked slowing down in 1958 and even more in 1959. This acceleration from 1954 was apparently stimulated by the strong need of industrialists to raise capacity and modernize equipment, and perhaps also by the introduction in April 1954 of the value-added tax, which is deductible on investments.[2]

Investment in housing grew rapidly over the whole period up to 1965, and then slowed down. From 1949 to 1955, the average yearly rate was over 15 percent, from 1955 to 1965 it was about 8 percent, and from 1965 to 1969 it was 4 percent. It must be said that immediately after the war the number of housing completions was very low: only 60,600 in 1949 and slightly over 200,000 in 1955. It was not until 1959 that the figure rose above 300,000 completions, a target long regarded as both urgent and attainable.

Finally, investment by government agencies was low and fairly steady from 1949 to 1951, rose by 12 percent yearly until 1956, slowed to 4.7 percent from 1956 to 1960, and then grew at almost 12 percent up to 1967. Here again the low starting level and the pressure of need explain the high growth rates sustained.

Table 4.2 traces the development of each category of investment over the period 1949–66, for which our estimates are in principle homogeneous. Productive investment accounted for the major share of the total, about 63 percent in most years, being particularly high in 1949, 1950, and 1951 (over 70 percent). It was low in 1954, 1959, and 1965, when the growth of productive investment declined while other types of investment continued to grow at a smart pace; economic recessions affect productive investment most.

Developments by Products and by Industries

Over the period as a whole, only two major groups of investment goods can be distinguished with the help of the National Accounts: building and public works, and plant and equipment. This distinction is significant only for productive investment, since building and public works in any case makes up the major share of the other investment categories. In 1949, building and public works accounted for nearly 39 percent of productive investment; this proportion fell sharply until 1954, then

---

[2] The value-added tax, paid by all firms, is calculated as the difference between a tax at a fixed rate on sales and the analogous tax payments included in purchases. For this calculation, fiscal legislation treats as current purchases acquisitions of most capital equipment other than vehicles. Chapter 9 gives further details of the effect of this provision.

TABLE 4.2
Investment by Principal Use Categories, 1949–66
(1956 prices, *million francs*)

Year	Productive investment	Investment in housing	Investment by govt. & financial institutions	Total
1949	16,631	3,530	2,451	22,612
1950	16,958	3,920	2,495	23,373
1951	17,367	5,015	2,524	24,906
1952	15,945	5,635	2,873	24,453
1953	16,432	5,935	3,023	25,390
1954	16,932	7,170	3,478	27,580
1955	19,182	8,115	3,867	31,164
1956	21,284	8,250	4,222	33,756
1957	23,681	9,268	4,323	37,272
1958	24,675	9,893	4,418	38,986
1959	24,889	10,110	4,864	39,863
1960	27,031	10,466	5,074	42,571
1961	30,162	11,158	5,712	47,032
1962	32,479	11,831	6,439	50,749
1963	34,438	13,027	7,101	54,566
1964	36,864	16,063	7,811	60,738
1965	37,630	17,523	8,723	63,876
1966	40,333	17,507	9,955	67,795

TABLE 4.3
Investment in Building and Public Works as a Percentage of Total
Productive Investment in 1956 Prices, 1949–65

Year	Percent	Year	Percent	Year	Percent
1949	38.7%	1955	30.7%	1961	29.4%
1951	34.7	1957	28.7	1963	28.2
1953	34.1	1959	30.6	1965	29.6

steadied at around 30 percent from 1955, as can be seen in Table 4.3.[3] Figure 4.2 shows the movements for the two groups of products divergent over the first five years and thereafter broadly parallel. The situation at the beginning of the period can be accounted for by two facts: in 1949 reconstruction was not complete, and in the subsequent years there was a relative drop in investment, requiring a high proportion of building or public works. It should be noted that the recessions of 1959 and 1965 reduced investments in equipment, whereas building and public works continued to grow—sustained by "heavy" investment.

[3] The steady share of building and public works is in terms of constant price estimates (here on a 1956 basis). But since building costs grew faster than the cost of equipment, the proportion of expenditure on building and public works (in current prices) tended to grow.

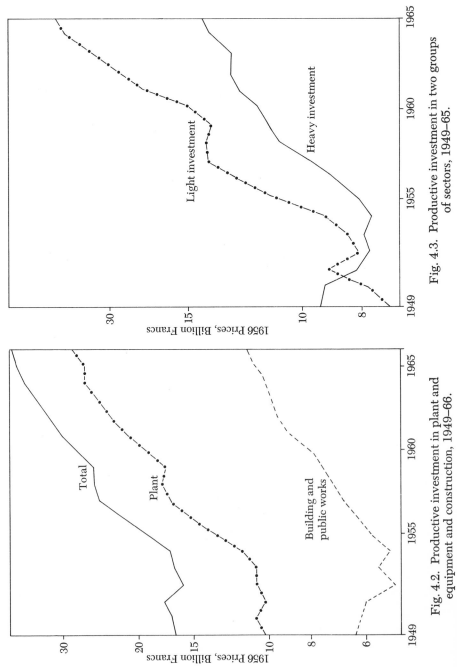

Fig. 4.2. Productive investment in plant and equipment and construction, 1949–66.

Fig. 4.3. Productive investment in two groups of sectors, 1949–65.

The different industries can, in fact, be divided into two classes. The first class comprises energy production (coal, gas, electricity, and petroleum), mining and production of metals, building materials, transportation and communications, all of which require very large investment. In 1956 those industries produced 16 percent of total value added and accounted for over 40 percent of productive investment. We shall use the term "heavy investment" to designate capital formation in this first class of industries. The second class is more heterogeneous; it includes manufacturing and processing industries, farming, building and public works, services, and trade. It relates to industries in which investment is lower in relation to value added and the payoff period in many cases is much shorter. For these industries we shall use the term "light investment."

In the first industry class, dominated by electricity and transportation, the share of building and public works is on the order of 45 percent, whereas in the second it is about 20 percent. From 1949 to 1951 heavy investment dropped by almost 15 percent, whereas other productive investment increased by over 25 percent. This change is enough to account for the drop of 3 of the 4 percentage points in building's share of productive capital formation.

A study of these two classes also clarifies overall movements. In heavy investment, the 1949–51 fall was followed by a long standstill up to 1955. This stagnation was the result of a drop in electricity investment and slow investment growth in transportation and communications. Light investment dropped sharply in 1952, a movement linked to the general slowdown in the economy, but it recovered from 1953 on and thereafter grew at a steady 10 per cent per year up to 1964. In heavy investment the recovery did not come until 1955, and its growth slowed down after 1958: the average annual rate was 9.4 percent from 1955 to 1958, but under 4 percent from 1958 to 1963. Recovery followed thereafter. The fact that the 1959 economic standstill was not felt in heavy investment was due solely to nationally owned undertakings, which were given considerable help in that year to promote the economy's recovery. This effect can be seen particularly well in electricity investment,[4] which rose by 12 percent in 1959, although it remained more or less stationary thereafter until 1962. Light investment, on the contrary, was stable in 1958, and fell slightly in 1959, to regain a growth rate thereafter equal to that in the period 1953–58.

Taken as a whole, light investment followed a course similar to that

[4] See Appendix Table 11, p. 562.

TABLE 4.4
Heavy and Light Investment, 1949–65
(1956 prices, *million francs*)

Year	Heavy investment	Light investment	Total	Year	Heavy investment	Light investment	Total
1949	9,389	7,242	16,631	1958	10,655	14,020	24,675
1950	9,156	7,802	16,958	1959	11,152	13,737	24,889
1951	8,198	9,169	17,367	1960	11,656	15,375	27,031
1952	7,819	8,126	15,945	1961	12,508	17,654	30,162
1953	7,963	8,469	16,432	1962	12,927	19,552	32,479
1954	7,719	9,213	16,932	1963	12,944	21,494	34,438
1955	8,140	11,042	19,182	1964	13,772	23,092	36,864
1956	8,861	12,423	21,284	1965	14,122	23,508	37,630
1957	9,723	13,958	23,681				

of gross domestic product but with wider variations; the 1952 drop and the 1958–59 stagnation were bracketed on either side by periods of rapid increase at rates exceeding 10 percent per year. Heavy investment, on the other hand, by its lack of growth held back the recovery of productive investment as a whole until 1955, but also acted in the opposite direction, moderating the 1958–59 slowdown.

Figure 4.3 and Table 4.4 illustrate the movements just described, and Appendix Table 11 gives the value in 1956 prices of investment in the different industries from 1949 to 1966, showing which contributed most to the growth of capital accumulation in each of the two main investment groups. The development of heavy investment was dominated by movements in two sectors, electricity and transportation, the first of which accounts for almost 20 percent of the total and the second for 28 percent. During the 1954–65 growth period, capital formation increased by some 75 percent in transportation and communications, and by almost 100 percent in electricity. In the other heavy industries, investment grew in inverse proportion to its relative volume; thus the 1965 index numbers on a 1954 base were 390 for the petroleum industries and 300 for building materials. In iron mining and metallurgy there was a rapid increase up to 1962 (index number 290, 1954 = 100), followed by a sharp drop. Finally, because of the gradual fall in output, coal investment dropped regularly after 1953.

Light investment, with development similar to that of gross domestic product, will be studied over each of the first two cycles considered; although the growth profiles were different in each case, the rate from 1951 to 1957 was about the same as from 1957 to 1963, an average of 7.2 percent per year for the first six years, and 7.4 percent for the next six. Similar regularity can be seen in the mechanical and electrical industries, with an average growth of 6.4 percent per year in both periods. In agriculture, textiles, and miscellaneous industries,[5] growth in the second period was much lower than in the first: 1 percent per year as against 9 percent for agriculture, and 5.9 percent per year as against 11.3 percent for textiles and miscellaneous industries. The opposite result can be seen in processed foods and farm products, chemicals, services, and trade. Investment in processed foods and farm products was practically the same in 1956 as in 1951, and thereafter increased at 5.8 percent per year. In chemicals, an annual average growth rate of 5.5 percent in the first period rose to 8.4 percent in the second. Last, in services and trade taken together, investment, which had grown quite sharply over the first cycle by 6 percent per year, increased by almost 11 percent during the second cycle.

To sum up: gross fixed capital formation grew slowly up to 1954 as a result of the high levels reached by heavy investment in the early postwar years and the marked drop from 1950 to 1952. After 1954, light investment grew almost twice as fast as heavy investment (10 percent per year on the average as against 5.5 percent). Investment in housing and by government agencies began at a low level in 1949, to achieve a high and sustained rate over the entire period in the case of housing, and from 1953 on in the case of government agencies.

THE INVESTMENT RATIO

The proportion of gross domestic product devoted to gross fixed capital formation is a good measure of the national economic effort. We shall first examine that proportion in the postwar years, then place it in a longer-term perspective and compare it with the same proportion in other countries.

Developments Since 1946

The rate of investment in production was high in 1949, and higher yet in the years before that. The figures summarized in Table 4.1 represent a share in constant prices of almost 22 percent of gross domestic product in 1947, falling steadily to 19 percent in 1949. The National Accounts estimates, corrected as shown in Appendix C, for the period 1949–52, suggest a share of 19.7 percent in 1949, and a continued drop to 1952, leveling off in 1953 to about 18 percent. The share of productive investment in production seems to have fallen right up to 1954. After 1954 the rate of investment became rapidly stronger and settled at an aver-

---

[5] Sectors 11 and 12 in the National Accounts.

TABLE 4.5
Investment in Gross Fixed Capital as a Percentage
of Gross Domestic Production, 1949–69
(1956 prices)

Category	1949	1952	1954	1957–1960[a]	1963	1966	1969[b]
Total investment	19.7%	17.8%	18.5%	21.2%	22.7%	24.1%	25%
Productive investment	14.6	11.7	11.3	13.4	14.4	14.1	15

[a]Four-year average.
[b]Estimates theoretically comparable with those of preceding years.

age of over 21 percent in 1957–60. Several years after that it had reached 24 percent, surpassing the high 1947 level. The share of productive investment followed a similar course but at far slower rates, settling at around 13.5 percent in 1957–60, and at slightly above 14 percent for several years after, that is to say, at a rate slightly below that in 1949. Although the investment ratio in this period was high in relation to the prewar years, it was thus not consistent. Falling sharply from the war's end to 1954, it then recovered vigorously until recent years, but with a leveling off from 1957 to 1960. Table 4.5 gives shares of gross domestic product in the most representative years, and Figure 4.4 shows movements from 1949 to 1966.

The estimates above, which are in 1956 prices, give a general picture of the proportion of physical production devoted to investment. They can be completed by estimates in current prices that allow better long-term comparisons, especially with prewar years, and they also indicate the scale of financial activity that made this investment possible. Prices of capital goods did not always move parallel with those of other goods, and some significant differences can be observed, especially in the years 1946–53. More particularly, prices of capital goods increased considerably in relation to those of production as a whole from 1950 to 1951 and from 1951 to 1952 (by 7.8 and 5.4 percent, respectively). As a result, an equal investment expenditure in current prices in 1949 and 1951 represents a far lower volume of investment in 1951. This partly explains why, despite a temporary recovery in production, investment growth was so low in 1951. Apart from these earlier years and some oscillations due to short-term economic conditions, particularly in 1957 and 1958, prices of production and investment moved broadly parallel. Consequently, as shown in Figure 4.4, investment at both current and constant prices moved at similar rates.

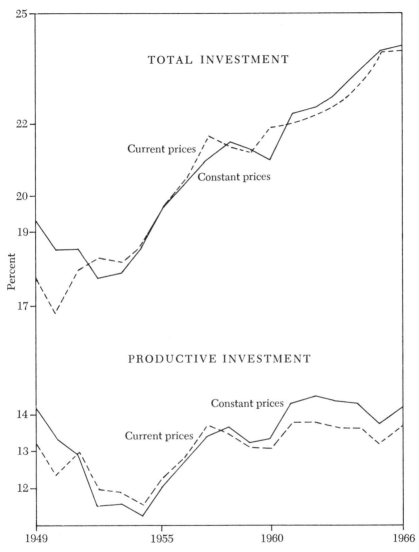

Fig. 4.4. Gross investment in fixed capital as a percentage of gross domestic production, current and constant prices, 1949–66.

Scale of Investment Before World War II

How does the investment effort from about 1950 to 1970 compare with that in the past? This question has some importance for understanding the factors behind the postwar expansion of investment. However, the answer is subject to uncertainties in our statistical knowledge of investment in the first 40 years of the century, uncertainties greater than those relating to movements in production. We cannot hope, therefore, to do more than describe the most obvious developments.

We shall use various annual series we have set up for the periods 1896–1913 and 1922–38. Appendix D describes our estimating methods in sufficient detail, we hope, for the reader to judge the precision of the results discussed below. The most outstanding features of long-term movements in investment seem to be irregular rates of capital formation, high rates from about 1950 to 1970, and a growing proportion taken by investment in plant and equipment. Our series of course measure very imperfectly year-by-year fluctuations in the investment ratio, defined as the proportion of gross domestic product taken by gross fixed capital formation. Nevertheless, Figure 4.5, which presents developments from 1896 to 1966, shows quite significant trends. The investment ratio was 13 percent in 1896, rose to 15 percent in 1900, fell gradually until 1904, rose again and reached almost 16 percent immediately before World War I. From 1922 to 1927 there seems to have been an investment effort

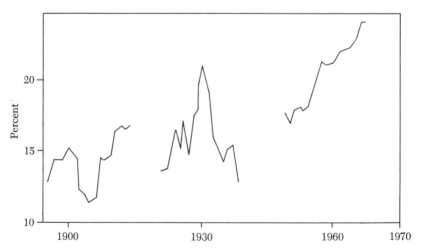

Fig. 4.5. Gross investment in fixed capital as a percentage of gross domestic production, 1896–1966.

TABLE 4.6

Investment in Gross Fixed Capital, 1896–1963

(1913 = 100)

Year	Volume of investment:			Relative value of investment	Investment ratios[a]
	Products of mechanical industries	Building and public works	Total		
1896	37	72	59	59	13.4%
1913	100	100	100	100	16.8
1924	128	100	110	112	16.7
1929	166	124	140	144	18.3
1930	184	135	153	158	20.8
1934	116	90	100	107	14.6
1938	123	75	93	101	13.4
1949	202	120	150	150	17.9
1954	228	156	183	202	18.5
1963	484	288	350	378	22.2

[a]Percent of gross domestic product accounted for by gross fixed capital formation.

comparable with that in the first prewar period. The ratio thereafter rose rapidly to over 20 percent in 1930. It then fell until 1938, when it seems to have been lower than in any other year between the wars.

The period after World War II was marked by a systematically higher investment ratio than before the war except for the three years 1929, 1930, and 1931. Over the whole period 1949–63, the average ratio was over 20 percent, whereas from 1896 to 1913 it was 14.9 percent, and from 1922 to 1938 it was 16.1 percent. This effort, continued over a long period, undoubtedly raised the growth rate of productive capital in France. More particularly, the chief element in the rise of the investment ratio was the rapid increase in capital equipment produced by the mechanical and electrical industries.

According to our estimates, investment in building and public works developed over the long term at a rate little different from that of production. As can be seen from Table 4.6, after World War I, investment fell behind production, but in 1930 it reached a level one-third higher than that of 1913, as did gross domestic product. Investment in building and public works fell considerably from 1930 to 1938, but rose rapidly again after World War II. Over the whole period 1896–1963, it grew fourfold, as did gross domestic product.

Investment in equipment, however, seems to have grown by a factor of 13 between 1896 and 1963. The movements over time are of some interest to trace. In 1896, this type of investment represented 30 percent of gross fixed capital formation, and hardly more than 4 percent of gross domestic product. It increased by about 45 percent from 1896 to 1900, stimulating not only the national production of machinery and equipment but also a rapid increase in their import. Investment in equipment dropped in 1901 and 1902; then there was a slight recovery, which grew stronger after 1906. Over the eight years from 1905 to 1913, the total more than doubled. In this period, as in the preceding investment boom, purchases abroad rose very high. Imports of mechanical equipment, machines, and spare parts, which had stood at almost exactly 50,000 metric tons in 1896, rose to 110,000 metric tons in 1900 and to 210,000 in 1913. We estimate that in 1913 imported equipment accounted for over 40 percent of French investment in products of the mechanical and electrical industries.

After World War I, a major replacement of capital equipment was undertaken, chiefly by means of purchases abroad. In 1922 investment in equipment had broadly the same volume and makeup as in 1913. From 1922 to 1927 there were fluctuations, which, however, are certainly exaggerated by our series; at the same time, purchases of imported equipment fell. The investment boom in 1928, 1929, and 1930 was accompanied by simultaneous growth in production and imports. In 1930 investment in equipment was more than 90 percent higher than in 1913; the proportion of equipment imported in 1930 was only 30 percent, but it stands out as higher than in the years around it. Investment in equipment fell sharply from 1930 to 1932. Between 1933 and 1938 it steadied at a level one-third lower than in 1913. The proportion of imported equipment was by then barely 10 percent, so that before World War II capital formation in goods manufactured by the French mechanical and electrical industries reached about 180 percent of its 1913 level.

In the first few years after World War II, investment regained its 1930 volume, and thereafter developed as described earlier. Imports of equipment and machinery were very high in 1946 and 1947, fell to a relatively low level in 1949, but then rose at a substantially faster rate than French output. Foreign equipment accounted for 15 percent of total equipment investment in 1949, and for 20 percent in 1963. However, the proportion was still much lower than it had been before World War II.

What overall assessment should be made of the French investment effort over the first 70 years of the century? To answer this question we must find a basis for comparison and then refer to experience in other industrial countries. In this field as in others, international comparisons at present are hardly conclusive. Apart from difficulties of concept, our study has met with obstacles arising from variations in the quality of estimates in different countries. The figures in our series are certainly highly approximate, as are those to which we refer for some other countries. Differences observed therefore may well not reflect the true facts.

Nevertheless, we have attempted to compare French investment ratios with those of three countries for which we had sufficiently precise estimates—the United States, Italy, and the United Kingdom. For this comparison we have used the ratio of gross fixed capital formation to gross national product. These ratios have been estimated for each country (and each period) at prices appropriate to that country (and that period). To assess the contribution of capital accumulation to production, it might be preferable to compare ratios calculated from a set of prices common to all the countries, and this might lead to somewhat different conclusions. Thus, after an extremely detailed study of the year 1950, Gilbert and Kravis[6] estimated that on the basis of prices for all goods making up gross national product, with French prices = 100, the price of equipment was about 70 in the United States, 135 in Italy, and 90 in the United Kingdom. Similarly, costs of nonresidential building were 120 in the United States and the United Kingdom and 100 in Italy. Overall, the relative price of investment goods was consequently lower in the United States and higher in Italy than in France, the difference being particularly significant in productive investment. We have no data at all for earlier periods. However, it is thought that at the beginning of the century France's technical lag behind Britain and the United States, and Italy's behind France, caused the relative price of investment goods to be much higher in France than in the two Anglo-Saxon countries, and higher still in Italy.

Table 4.7 shows the ratios calculated for selected years in the period 1900–1960. The French ratios seem consistently higher than the British, but in many cases they are 2 or 3 percentage points below the figures for the United States and Italy. To assess the effect of investment on productivity, it is necessary to allow for differences in the rate of demographic growth in each country. When the population is stable, investment can either replace old equipment or increase the physical capital available to each member of the labor force. When the population is growing, the capital required by each new worker must be provided as needed. A given investment ratio therefore implies the fastest increase in capital per worker in countries whose population is growing most slowly.

In the four countries considered we have tried to eliminate roughly

[6] M. Gilbert and I. Kravis, *An International Comparison of National Products and the Purchasing Power of Currencies* (OEEC; Paris, 1954).

TABLE 4.7
*Investment in Gross Fixed Capital as a Percentage of Gross
National Product, Selected Countries, 1900–1960*

Approximate year	Ratio of gross national product				After correction for growth in the labor force[a]			
	France	United States	Italy	United Kingdom	France	United States	Italy	United Kingdom
1900	14%	18%	10%	9%	13%	10%	9%	6%
1910	16	17	16	6	15	12	14	2
1925	15	18	20	8	14	14	18	4
1929	17	–	19	9	17	–	19	9
1938	12	13	18	10	14	10	–	4
1950	15	18	18	13	15	14	18	10
1960	18	17	23	16	18	13	17	14

Source: National studies of the Social Science Research Council project.
[a]For definition, see text.

the proportion of investment required to provide equipment for new members of the work force. To do so, we have substracted from the investment ratio a figure equal to three times the annual growth rate of the labor force. The correction assumes a capital-output ratio of three. Let K be the volume of capital, Q the volume of output, N the size of the labor force, and I_0 the volume of investment devoted to providing equipment required by the growth of the labor force. If $\Delta N/N$ is that growth per year, to maintain a constant value of capital per worker requires that the ratio $I_0/\Delta N$ be equal to K/N. The ratio I_0/Q is then equal to $K/Q \times \Delta N/N$, i.e. to the product of the capital-output ratio and the growth rate of the labor force. The results corrected in this way are given in the last four columns of Table 4.7. The corrected investment ratio appears higher in France than in the United States in almost every year shown. If, in addition, a correction could be made for differences in relative prices, the ratios would probably be similar in the three countries; in the United Kingdom capital accumulation seems to be exceptionally slow.

Instead of considering investment as a whole, we could look only at investment in equipment, which is motivated in a particularly direct way by the requirements of economic growth. Table 4.8 shows the proportion of gross national product taken by these investments in selected years in France, the United States, and Britain. The results seem similar in the three countries in the later years, but between 1900 and 1938 they were consistently higher in France. This difference in the years before World War II could be explained by the higher relative prices of equipment in France than in the other two countries.

TABLE 4.8

Investment in Plant and Equipment as a Percentage of Gross National Product, Selected Countries, 1900–1960

Approximate year	France	United States	United Kingdom
1900	4.7%	4.3%	4.0%
1910	5.5	3.9	2.6
1925	5.9	5.1	3.6
1929	7.4	4.9	3.7
1938	5.9	5.0	4.4
1950	7.1	7.2	6.8
1960	8.2	—	8.4

Source: National studies of the Social Science Research Council project.

Despite their uncertainty, these few international comparisons seem to show clearly that, allowing for the growth of the labor force, productive investment was relatively high in France by comparison with other countries immediately before World War I and between the wars. Low demographic growth did not necessitate any exceptional effort in this direction. Soon after World War I, building fell behind, and more so after the 1940's. Investment in equipment was high, however, and would seem to have been reflected in rapid growth of French capital equipment, which we shall see was at a low level at the beginning of the century. At the end of Chapter 5 we shall make a few direct comparisons of the volume and growth of productive capital in France and other industrial countries, and shall then spell out in detail the indications given here. The investment effort was substantially higher after the war than before, but this seems to be a feature in most industrial countries.

CHAPTER FIVE

The Growth of Capital

As a result of the investment effort outlined in Chapter 4, the physical capital available to French production increased substantially from the beginning of the century, and faster still from 1949. We shall try to gain an understanding of this feature by means of quantitative measurements, and to this end we shall present a number of new estimates, in particular of national capital and its growth since World War II. In the first part we shall briefly define the concept of capital to be used thereafter. In the longer second part we shall describe our estimating methods and give our results for the last twenty years. In the third part we shall examine these results and show the development of capital both overall and by main groups; this will lead to a consideration of the order of magnitude of our indexes' precision. In the fourth part we shall attempt to compare capital growth rates before and after World War II. And last, in the fifth part we shall compare these rates with those of the labor force and production, and then examine the growth of capital per worker and of the capital-output ratio.

THE MEASUREMENT OF CAPITAL

That the accumulation of capital equipment is a factor in growth has been widely accepted and developed for sometime in the economic literature. It is therefore with some surprise that newcomers to quantitative studies note the many difficulties arising in the measurement of capital and its growth. Without aiming at a systematic discussion, we shall show how we have resolved some of these difficulties. To this end we shall consider first how capital can be estimated at a given moment, and then how its changes can be measured over time.

The physical capital of a community at any given moment comprises all the goods then existing in it. In definitions of capital it is therefore necessary to delimit the list of goods included. It is customary to include only objects produced by man and those natural resources, such as land, that he has appropriated. Other benefits derived from nature are always excluded. We shall follow here a fairly narrow definition, which excludes a great many goods. Since our object is to study growth, we have not tried to assess the value of land in France, since the contribution of that factor to the country's production clearly has not varied (the increase in farm yields is due to the work of man, to fertilizers, to technical progress, etc., and not to the land itself). We have thus confined ourselves to a concept commonly described as *"reproducible* capital." Similarly, we have excluded all stocks of new materials, products in course of manufacture, and finished products, as well as movable goods belonging to households and directly used by them (i.e. all durable consumer goods apart from housing itself. The exclusion of goods held by households is in accordance with the convention in the National Accounts, according to which they are consumed as soon as acquired.

What we shall study is in fact "reproducible fixed capital," which comprises chiefly equipment, vehicles, buildings, and infrastructures belonging to firms, households, and government agencies. We shall distinguish (1) *productive capital,* i.e. equipment, vehicles, and plant used in firms (therefore excluding housing and land owned by firms)—assets in turn subdivided into the 17 productive industry groups already considered in the preceding chapter; (2) *housing;* and (3) *capital of government agencies.*

Since the goods comprising fixed reproducible capital are heterogeneous, a principle must be established for defining aggregates of them. The general rule in the National Accounts is for each good to be multiplied by its price. However, this is not as easy to apply to capital as to current flows of production, consumption, or investment; most old equipment and plant have no market price, since they are not put on the market. This is a familiar difficulty for accountants, who must assess the value attributed to old fixed capital in balance sheets. In principle, our method of estimating, which is identical with that of private accounting, is to amortize new fixed capital over the period of its utilization. However, we have not relied on the firms' own amortization for two reasons: first, we have attempted a continual reassessment of the replacement value of capital goods in order to allow for changes in prices and building costs; second, we have tried to base amortization on effective life rather than follow the rules adopted by tax authorities.

Apart from these two differences, the value of old plant in our aggregates is analogous to that in the firms' balance sheets—replacement value less the sum of amortizations already carried out. (Revaluing has

eliminated the effect of price changes of both amortizations and replacement value.) To define our principal aggregate we shall therefore
use the concept of "*net* capital." This approach can be argued against.
Our objective is a correct appreciation of the effect of capital accumulation on France's productive capacity each year. It might be argued
that a given plant yielding the same use throughout its life should not
be amortized in the context of measuring its productive capacity, but
should be assessed at its entire replacement value until taken out of
service. If all plant had these properties, in place of net capital we
should use "gross capital," in the definition of which amortization does
not occur.

The reason we have adopted the concept of net capital is not so much
one of principle as to make use of the different sources of information
as simply as possible. Net capital, which relates to market value, however fictitious, is a more familiar idea and more frequently used than
gross capital. However, we shall refer to the latter concept frequently
both in our statistical estimates and in our subsequent analyses.

To measure the growth of physical capital, it is not enough to know
what changes have occurred in value; it is necessary also to know how
to remove the effect of price changes, and how to compare plant installed at different dates so as to identify those items to be valued
equally, and therefore allotted the same prices in calculating volume
aggregate. This is a difficult operation, since the goods making up investment vary in value much more between periods than goods making
up most other aggregates. In broad terms, two basic principles can be
contrasted in calculating an aggregate capital figure at constant prices.
By the first principle, two plants—built for example in 1950 and 1960
respectively—can be considered of equal value if they yield broadly
equal service in output terms, with perhaps higher energy consumption
in one making up for somewhat lower capacity in the other. By the second principle, the two plants are treated as of equal value when they
would have had the same price if built in the same year.

As can be imagined, these two principles lead to quite different results. The first allows for every step of progress made in the design of
machinery, vehicles, and equipment. The second treats only those
changes that would have required cost increases in the base year as
quality improvements leading to volume increases (valued at constant
prices). Yet technical development has frequently led to progressive
improvements in the design of plant, i.e. in its fitness for the task, but
has not necessarily raised the cost of producing it.

The normal practice in valuing the nation's capital follows the second principle, which certainly raises many problems in application but less intractable ones than those arising from the first principle. We have not striven for originality, but have followed the second principle, which has the advantage that its capital volume results agree with those usually obtained for investment regarded as use of current production. The quality improvements included in our estimates are therefore the same as those in the National Accounts figures in constant prices. As pointed out, this approach has the added advantage of giving equal weight to the two chief inputs, labor and capital. For both of these, we have first measured quantitative changes in the volume of resources made available to the productive system, and only then assessed quality changes that may have increased the effectiveness of input. (This last point is considered in Chapter 7.)

ESTIMATES FOR THE POSTWAR PERIOD

We have attempted an evaluation of capital with the same breakdown as for investment: productive capital in 17 industry groups, housing capital, and capital of government agencies. The method followed is the same for each group, although the sources in many cases are quite different. It consists of two stages: a direct estimate of gross capital and amortization for a given year, and an annual capital series constructed from series relating to investment.

Productive Capital

The basis for the annual series was an evaluation of capital in 1956. When we made our first estimates, this was the only year for which we had detailed accounts for firms, in particular those providing amortization figures by main industry groups. We have in general brought together four kinds of data: fiscal statistics of net fixed capital, fire insurance valuations, the sum of net investments over the life of plant, and estimates that can be deduced from amortization and from the life of equipment. Finally, we have compared our assessments with those of Matthys for the year 1954.[1] It was not possible, however, to compare sources for every industry, and in many cases there are considerable uncertainties about capital levels. In a first study of this kind it could hardly be otherwise. Nevertheless, we believe that the movements shown by our figures give some indication of the part played by capi-

[1] G. Matthys in Divisia, Dupin, and Roy, *Fortune de la France*, vol. 3 of *A la Recherche du franc perdu* (Paris, 1956).

tal growth. Moreover, we show figures at the start of the third part of this chapter that will enable readers to assess the effect of lack of precision in the level of capital on estimates of its rate of growth.[2]

Agriculture, transportation, and electricity. We shall now describe how we arrived at our estimates of capital by a joint use of different sources of data. First, we shall outline the method followed for three particular industry groups: agriculture, transportation, and electricity. For the first two, we simply used the thorough research by Matthys, and put it on a 1956 basis. For agriculture the value of capital so obtained is close to the estimate suggested by Vincent, who has added together investments over the life of various equipment and subtracted relevant amortization.[3]

There is a particular problem in defining capital in transportation because of the need to distinguish the capital of firms (whether their business is railroads or transportation by road, inland waterways, sea, or air) from the infrastructure (railroad track, highroads, canals, harbor works, and airfields). The French National Accounts treat as "productive investment" in transportation only that by firms. Purchases of equipment and building, e.g. improvements to railroad track, are therefore included, but building and maintenance of roads, harbors, canals, and airfields are excluded, and are treated as investments by government agencies. This approach is convenient for measuring changes year by year, but less so for analyzing long-term growth. The highway infrastructure does not of course serve only road transport operators, but we have felt it less of an error to associate the output of road transportation with this group's total capital than to exclude roads completely. We have therefore included all transportation infrastructure in "productive capital." As a result, there is some lack of homogeneity between the aggregates of investment in this chapter and those in Chapter 4, and also between our estimates and those of other researchers.

---

[2] After this study had gone to the printers, we learned of estimates of productive capital made by J. Mairesse based on new National Accounts figures. These estimates show considerable differences of detail compared with ours, but the order of magnitude is broadly the same. For example, we estimate net productive capital excluding the infrastructure on January 1, 1962, as 248 billion francs in 1956 prices. Mairesse estimates it as 282 billion francs in 1959 prices. His growth rates are higher than ours: +135 percent as against +110 percent for the same aggregate between 1949 and 1966. His detailed results have been published in the INSEE collections *L'Evaluation du capital fixe productif; méthode et résultat* (série C, no. 18–19, comptes et planification; Paris, 1972).

[3] L. A. Vincent, "Productivité et prix relatifs dans 15 branches de l'économie française, 1949–1963," *Etudes et conjoncture*, February 1962. In his Table 10 Vincent simply gives his results, but he has been kind enough to provide us with the investment series on which his estimates are based.

To avoid danger of confusion, we shall in most cases distinguish infrastructure in the tables and calculations from other capital. Thus, in 1956, capital for transportation and communications can be broken down into 56 billion francs for capital of firms and 86.7 billion francs for infrastructure other than railroads.

For electricity, water, and miscellaneous, where electricity supply and transmission account for almost the whole of the sector's capital, Matthys's figures seem to underestimate investment since the war. He shows 6.3 billion francs for the value of capital, whereas total investment from 1949 to 1954 was close to 14 billion. Amortization must of course be deducted, but since life of plant in the sector is exceptionally long, this does not explain the difference. From a breakdown of investment in water and thermal power stations, assuming plant life of 78 and 27 years, respectively, Vincent obtains a capital value of 19.7 billion francs for electricity. We have raised this to 20 billion to allow for the other activities in the industry group as a whole. This estimate broadly agrees with figures suggested in a study by Electricité de France.[4]

Statistical sources for other sectors. For the other sectors, explanations are less simple and the results probably more doubtful. We shall describe the various sources and indicate how they have been used. Net fixed capital figures were first obtained from accounting figures by adding the firms' tax declarations required for assessing their liability on industrial and commerical profits (the so-called B.I.C. statistics, or *bénéfices industriels et commerciaux*). Therefore these are figures by industrial sectors (or groups of firms) rather than by individual industries (groups of establishments), but this disadvantage can be ignored here for most cases. A more serious factor is that in 1956 few accounts had been revalued; capital was therefore entered at purchase price, and since prices increased by a factor of about 30 between 1938 and 1956 and by a factor of 7 between 1945 and 1956, equipment bought before or just after World War II was entered at values bearing no relation to their current levels. This is of course particularly marked in the case of industrial and other buildings, a high proportion of which dated from prewar years, as well as of long-life equipment found in many industries. In particular, as we shall see, over 40 percent of the total stock

---

[4] L. A. Vincent, "Les Progrès de la productivité et leur utilisation à l'Electricité de France de 1952 à 1962," *Etudes et conjoncture*, January 1965. From a careful study, we have assessed amortization in 1956 at 622 million francs; accordingly, we estimate gross capital at 24 billion francs, with a life of about 40 years, and net capital at about 17 billion francs. These figures relate to Electricité de France only. To them must be added, broadly, the capital of the Compagnie Nationale du Rhône and of the electricity plants of the French Coal Board.

of machine tools in 1955 was manufactured before 1935. Another disadvantage of these statistics is that they relate only to companies, and
therefore lead to underestimates in industries with a high proportion of
independent ownership. For both these reasons, accounting figures are
merely a substitute for unavailable estimates of net capital.

In contrast, fire insurance valuations for most industries give a good
approximation of the residual value of plant. They are likely to underestimate the capital value only in industries where a high proportion
of the equipment is unlikely to burn, as in building and public works,
or in those industries where firms are so large that they do not need the
safeguard of insurance. Unfortunately, the data available to us are not
complete; as with the B.I.C. statistics, those for insurance valuations
relate only to companies, and in addition give results covering only
some 55 percent of the companies' total capital. And last, the concept
of insured capital seems to lie between that of gross and net capital:
it is the replacement value of equipment allowing for wear and tear,
but not in general for the time it is likely to remain in use. For the sake
of completeness we should point out that fire insurance valuations include stocks, which we have deducted using an approximate estimate.
We do not know by how much the insurance valuations underestimate
capital in each sector, and have therefore not been able to present an
exhaustive figure. However, we have compared the insurance values and
our best capital estimates for sectors where the statistics are meaningful (columns 2 and 5, Table 5.1).[5] We estimate capital in these sectors
at 70 billion francs, and the fire insurance statistics assess it at 45 billion francs. The ratio of 64 percent between these two estimates is consistent with the suggestion that the statistics cover only some 55 percent
of companies' capital, for we have retained the industries with probably
the best coverage, and in addition insurance values are higher than net
capital as we conceive it.

If the investment series by industries went far enough back, we could
estimate capital from the sum of net investment. This estimating technique, which we shall call the "chronological method," is described as
follows. The net value of capital is estimated by main types and year of
installation. The cost at purchase is given by the figures of annual investment. It is assumed that each capital good is amortized by a constant
annuity, whose ratio to the initial investment is $1/N$ for life N. Thus, an

[5] We have excluded sectors dominated by the nationalized industries, which appear to make little use of insurance; building, public works, and services, where too
high a proportion of the capital belongs to individual entrepreneurs; and agriculture,
where fire insurance covers harvests as well as equipment. The total shown therefore
relates to industry groups 02, 05–12, and 19.

TABLE 5.1
*Fixed Reproducible Capital by Sector, 1956: Estimates
from Different Sources*
(Million francs)

Sector	Accounting figures	Insurance valuations[a]	Matthys's estimates	Chronological method	Net capital estimates adopted
01. Agriculture and forestry			20,000	18,000	20,000
02. Processed foods and farm products	3,140	4,840	7,000[b]	6,000	7,500
03a. Solid mineral fuels	6,430	900	5,500	6,400	8,000
03b. Gas			2,480	2,100	3,000
04. Electricity, water, and kindred products	19,950	360	15,000		20,000
05. Petroleum and oil products	1,680	1,650	2,000	2,800	3,500
06. Building materials and glass	1,140	910	3,000[c]	2,800	3,000
07. Iron mining and metallurgy	3,600			7,200	7,150
08. Nonferrous minerals and metals	450	4,100	6,800	600	850
09. Mechanical and electrical industries	7,450	11,200	20,000	16,000	15,000
10. Chemicals and rubber	3,060	3,400	8,000	5,000	6,000
11. Textiles, clothing, and leather	2,970	7,300	9,000	6,000	8,000
12. Wood, paper, and misc. industries	2,390	5,100	6,400[b]	3,800	6,000
13. Building and public works	3,130	330	4,000[c]	3,200	4,000
14. Transportation and communications[d]	6,670[e]	6,600	142,700 (56,000)		142,700 (56,000)
16. Services other than housing		1,210[a]	19,000	8,500	5,800
19. Trade		6,650[f]		10,000	13,000
Total			270,780		273,500

Source: Figures in column 3 are taken from G. Matthys, in Divisia, Dupin, and Roy, *Fortune de la France,* vol. 3 of *A la Recherche du franc perdu* (Paris, 1956). Column 4 is taken from L. A. Vincent, "Productivité et prix relatifs dans 15 branches de l'économie française, 1949–1963," *Etudes et conjoncture,* February 1962.

[a]Very partial estimate.

[b]Agricultural and food industries and miscellaneous industries are grouped together by Matthys. We have distinguished between them by means of our own estimates.

[c]Actually, Matthys's calculations suggest 7,000 for building and public works and building materials together.

[d]Figures in parentheses in columns 3 and 5 relate to capital of transportation firms. They therefore exclude infrastructure other than railroad track.

[e]Excludes nationally owned undertakings.

[f]Includes stocks.

investment made n years prior to a period considered will be included in the capital figure at $(N - n)/N$ times its value, for all cases where n is less than N. This method provides an incidental estimate of each year's economic amortization, considered as equal to $1/N$ multiplied by the sum of investments made in the N years preceding. Different lives can be used for different construction dates, in particular longer life for plant constructed before the war.

The two chief sources of uncertainty in this method are the assessment

TABLE 5.2
Depreciation Rates in Relation to Net Capital Stock and Service Life, 1956

Sector	Amortization A (million francs)	Life of plant (years)	Gross capital C (million francs)	Net capital K (million francs)	a=K/C (percent)	λ=A/K (percent)
01. Agriculture	1,330	40	53,000	20,000	38%	6.65%
02. Processed foods and farm products	650	23	15,000	7,500	50	8.66
03a. Solid mineral fuels	500	23	11,500	8,000	70	6.25
03b. Gas	190	20	3,800	3,000	79	6.33
04. Electricity, water, and kindred products	810	38	31,000	20,000	65	4.26
05. Petroleum and oil products	300	15	4,500	3,500	78	8.57
06. Building materials and glass	260	20	5,200	3,000	58	8.67
07. Iron mining and metallurgy	625	22	13,800	7,150	52	8.75
08. Nonferrous minerals and metals	75	12	900	850	94	8.83
09. Mechanical and electrical industries	1,500	20	30,000	15,000	50	10.0
10. Chemicals and rubber	590	20	11,800	6,000	50	9.83
11. Textiles, clothing, and leather	620	26	16,000	8,000	50	7.75
12. Wood, paper, and misc. industries	500	20	10,000	6,000	60	8.35
13. Building and public works	580	11	6,400	4,000	63	14.5
14. Transportation and communications:						
Productive	2,300	40	92,000	56,000	61	4.10
Infrastructure	700	200	140,000	86,700	60	0.8
16. Services other than housing	725	20	14,500	5,800	40	12.5
19. Trade	1,300	20	26,000	13,000	50	10.0
Total	13,555	36	485,400	273,500	57%	5.0%

of service lives and the estimates of investments made before 1949. Length of service life of capital plays an important part in this chronological method, but only very approximate information is available to establish its value. A difference of one year in some cases can alter the level of capital by 10 percent, whereas in most cases equipment life is known only to within a few years. Investment statistics must be traced at least ten years back, and this assumes knowledge of the order of magnitude of investments made since 1936. (For buildings and equipment the figures should of course go considerably further back still.) L. A. Vincent has used various estimates and rearrangements of the figures to apply the chronological method in his study, already mentioned, on productivity and relative prices. We should be inclined to work on figures for longer life, but have nevertheless reproduced his results in the fourth column of Table 5.1. The figures supplied by Matthys in *Fortune de la France* are precise and detailed for nationalized industries and government offices but sketchy for Industry, services, and trade. However, since he follows the same estimating method as we do, we have included a column of his estimates in Table 5.1. The figures are not strictly those of Matthys; we first updated his 1954 capital estimates to a 1956 basis by adding net investment for the two intervening years. Then we moved from one industry to another the capital in a given firm that did not relate to the activity of that firm's industry group (chiefly chemical and electrical activities of the coal industry). Finally, for the processing and manufacturing industries we made estimates of net capital from Matthys's figures, which related to gross capital.

Our estimates for 1956. Table 5.1 summarizes the results obtained from these different sources, and compares them with our own. Table 5.2 shows how we reached these results. From the sources used in Table 5.1, we selected a first value for net capital. Then we estimated appropriate equipment life, defined as the ratio of gross capital to amortization, and compared the information with that obtained directly on the probable life of average equipment. When necessary, we then modified our first estimate of net capital accordingly.

The 1956 amortizations, provided by the sector accounts, are based on the amortizations for tax purposes in the B.I.C. statistics, corrected to bring them closer to economic amortization. We cannot easily establish a priori, however, whether they are too low or too high. They seem likely to be too high because equipment life authorized for tax purposes is very short, for example seven years for most machines. In addition, revaluations of the accounting figures to which they apply have been very slight, whereas inflation was very marked from 1949 to 1956. Last, firms do not always take advantage of the short life allowed, particularly when their investment prospects are not good, as could sometimes still be the case in 1956. We therefore retained the depreciation figures in the National Accounts, and used them as a check on the level of capital. To do this we converted net capital to gross capital. The proportion of net to gross fixed capital in the B.I.C. statistics was one possible guide, but the unadjusted figures seemed too low. For example, in the mechanical and electrical industries the proportion is 42 percent, which is probably too low, and can be explained by the amortization facilities granted to firms; we have therefore raised the figure to 50 percent. In the same industry group, a net capital of 20 billion francs (Matthys's estimate) would suggest a gross capital value of 40 billion francs, and a life of 27 years, with amortization worth 1.5 billion francs. This life estimate is almost certainly too high, and has led us to adopt a figure of 15 billion for net capital, i.e. to accept as more probable a life of about 20 years.

Our evaluations of capital are systematically higher than the corresponding accounting figures—more than twice as high in most of the processing and manufacturing industries. This is not surprising in the absence of any revaluation of assets. Our figures are also much higher than the fire insurance valuations: this result seems consistent in general with the partial coverage of the latter statistics. For all industries taken together, our figures for estimate of capital are close to those of Matthys and Vincent.[6] However, our estimate differs from that of Matthys by having a high figure for solid mineral fuels and gas, which accounts for investment since the war. On the other hand, it is considerably lower in the case of mechanical and electrical industries and chemicals, and slightly lower for textiles. Divisia, Dupin, and Roy, the authors of *Fortune de la France*, themselves agree that their estimates for those industry groups are very uncertain, and they give little explanation of their basis. We have seen that their estimates, when compared with the 1956 amortizations, suggest equipment life that is too long.

The values we have adopted are higher for almost all sectors than those arrived at by the chronological method. This is because we have used longer lives than Vincent. Our capital figures for services and trade taken together are about the same as his, but the breakdown between them is very different. Data on these industry groups, however, are more uncertain and scarcer than on any others; our breakdown between services and trade is based on amortization figures, perhaps not the best

[6] If our estimates for electricity and transportation in Table 5.1 are added to those resulting from the chronological method, the total amounts to 261 billion francs, as compared with 273.5 billion.

approach. It is advisable therefore to give more weight to the estimates for these two groups taken together than to each separately.

Developments from 1949 to 1966. Calculations of series for the years 1949–66 are based on the assumption that amortization is a constant proportion of net capital. This assumption would be consistent with the usual rule by which amortization is a regular proportion of gross capital (amortization by *n*ths) if there were a constant ratio of net to gross capital over the whole period in question. This no doubt was not the case, since the scale of investment that was achieved somewhat lowered the average age of equipment. For example, a comparison of investigations into the stock of machine tools in use in 1955 and 1960 suggests that their average age fell from 18 to 16 years in that period.[7] It is true that the proportion less than ten years old was 42 percent in both years, and this may explain why amortization in mechanical and electrical firms was 58 percent of gross fixed assets in both 1956 and 1959. The regulations, however, permitted newly purchased equipment to be written off faster in 1959 than in 1956, and the stability in the balance sheet rates of amortization suggests a slight increase in the true proportion between gross and net assets.

Although asset lives have dropped and the ratio of net to gross capital assets has fallen, the series shown in note 8 below show a slightly higher growth for net capital than for gross capital. However, the discrepancy does not seem great. The order of magnitude of the discrepancy can be determined from the age distribution of machine tools. On the assumption of a 30-year life consistent with the investigations, which suggest a 16 percent scrapping in five years, we estimate the ratio a of net to gross capital as 46 percent in 1955 and 48 percent in 1960.[8] A linear growth might be accepted for this ratio, since $a_t = 46 + 2/5(t - t_0)$, where t is any given year, t_0 is the year 1955, and a is expressed as a percentage.

[7] H. Ournac, *Le Parc des machines-outils dans les industries mécaniques et électriques* (sponsored by the Mechanical and Electrical Machinery Industries, Ministry of Industry, Paris, 1961).

[8] If we assume that purchases of machine tools were negligible between 1940 and 1945 and regular in the other ten-year periods, Table VII in Ournac, *Le Parc des machines-outils dans les industries mécaniques et électriques*, can be made to yield the age distribution in years of machine tools as follows (the last line shows the relevant amortization rate for a 30-year life, and leads to a 54 percent write-off in 1955 and to 52 percent in 1960):

Year	Under 5	5–10	10–20	20–30	Over 30	Total
1955	20.2	22.4	15.8	15.7	25.9	100
1960	24	18	19.8	18.9	19.3	100
Amortization rate	8%	25%	50%	83%	100%	—

If this rule were applied to capital as a whole, assuming a_t to be constant would mean overestimating amortization by a percentage equal to $100/46 \times 2/5(t - t_0)$, or by 10 percent at the end of ten years. The effect on the capital estimates is probably about the same.[9] Although not negligible, this discrepancy would not be very high in relation to total growth of capital assets, which was some 70 percent from 1950 to 1960. The 1956 amortization estimates are based on figures of firms by sector,[10] approximately corrected to an industry group basis. These amortization figures have also been used to check the estimates of capital assets; consequently, the ratio of amortization to net capital that we have used is consistent with the asset lives in the various industries.

If λ is the rate, assumed constant, of annual amortization A on net capital K, for year t we have gross investment J and net investment I:[11]

$$I_t = J_t - A_t \qquad A_t = \lambda K_t$$

And therefore $K_{t+1} = (1 - \lambda)K_t + J_t$.

The year-by-year figures of capital assets are shown in Appendix Table 12. Those for transportation were calculated from the sum of two series: firms' assets, and infrastructure other than railroad track. A functional breakdown of investment by government agencies is available from 1959 only, but it would appear that the proportion for the function of transportation is fairly steady at 20 percent, and we have assumed that this proportion can be applied over the whole period. This rule of thumb would suggest that the capital value of highway infrastructure was virtually static from 1949 to 1956, which agrees quite well with available information: the network of highways was kept in proper condition, but the total mileage of main highways remained constant between 1933 and 1957. Building of superhighways first began in 1957, which explains the subsequent increase in capital value.

Net Value of Existing Housing

Following the same approach as for productive assets, we have estimated housing at a base year, and calculated its changes year by year from investment series. Results of the 1962 demographic census provide not only strictly demographic data but also detailed information on dwellings occupied by households and on "secondary" housing (e.g.

---

[9] If A is amortization, K is net capital, and C is gross capital, we should expect $A_t = \lambda C_t$. Instead, we have $A'_t = \lambda' K_t$. Since $K_t/C_t = a_t = a_0 + a(t - t_0)$, we have $A'_t/A_t = (a_0 + a[t - t_0])/a_0$ for $\lambda = \lambda' a_0$. Hence A_t should be raised by $a(t - t_0)/a_0$.

[10] Les Comptes, vol. 1 of Les Comptes de la nation (Paris, 1960), pp. 142, 255.

[11] I_t and J_t are investments made over the year t, and K_t is net capital halfway through the year t.

vacation cottages). We have accordingly selected 1962 as the base year. We first calculated gross capital assets, and then estimated net assets on the basis of census data on housing age. There are two separate methods of calculation, applying respectively to housing built before and since 1949. In the first case, we multiplied the number of dwellings by an average price. In the second case, we considered it safer to show the sum of investments made after 1949.

Investment in housing, as outlined in Chapter 4, comprises both expenditure on new buildings and major maintenance on old buildings, accounting for about 20 percent of the total figure. We have therefore taken as the gross capital value of postwar housing 80 percent of total housing investment from 1949 to 1961, i.e. 78,700 million francs in 1956 prices. (The small number of dwellings built between 1940 and 1949 are included by this method with the prewar figures.) A unit price for dwellings was calculated by type of housing, taken from a 1959 survey that makes possible a breakdown by housing quality.[12] Although it referred to only a proportion of dwellings, this survey can be used as the basis for an estimate of the entire housing stock. However, since this was an inquiry into maintenance costs, only houses built before the war were included. The figures were further restricted to dwellings in towns of over 50,000 inhabitants, which according to the 1962 census account for slightly over half of total housing:[13]

Dwellings built before 1949	13,600,000
Dwellings covered by the survey	6,640,000
Other dwellings	6,960,000

The inquiry therefore did not cover rural dwellings or housing built before 1940 in towns of under 50,000 inhabitants, and also excluded the 420,000 dwellings built between 1940 and 1948 in town or country.

Table 5.3 gives the breakdown of housing in towns of more than 50,000 inhabitants by the categories defined in the September 1, 1948, rents act, and listed in decreasing order of unit price. The table also shows unit prices estimated and the resulting gross capital values in 1956 prices. Housing assets excluded are largely accounted for by rural dwellings (about 5 million out of 6.96 million), which, according to the survey data, are on the average less well built than town houses: 91 percent are of "solid" construction as against 96.8 percent in the cities, and only 54 percent as against 86 percent are connected to a piped water supply. On the other hand, the average floor area is larger outside cities. We

[12] "Enquête par sondage sur les dépenses d'entretien de la propriété bâtie," *Etudes statistiques*, no. 1, 1959.
[13] *Annuaire statistique de la France*, 1963.

TABLE 5.3
*Number and Capital Value of Housing Units by Category in Cities
of Over 50,000 Inhabitants, 1962*

Housing category	Number (thousands)	Unit price (million francs)	Gross capital value (million francs, 1956 prices)
Luxury and grade I	25	66	1,650
Quality, II:			
Grade A	90	45	4,050
Grade B	720	30	21,600
Grade C	373	25	9,300
Ordinary, III:			
Grade A	3,822	16	61,200
Grade B	1,050	10	10,500
Defective, IV	460	5	2,300
Not reported[a]	100	17	1,700
Total	6,640	17	112,300

[a]For dwellings not reported, the unit price is the average of the other categories.

have therefore allocated to dwellings built before 1949 but not covered by the survey an average price of 15,000 francs, i.e. 10 percent lower than that in Table 5.3.

On all these assumptions the value of gross housing in existence at the beginning of 1962 can be broken down as follows (in million francs at 1956 prices):

Houses built before 1949	217,300
Houses built 1949–61	78,700
Total gross housing assets	296,000

The value of net assets can be deduced from these figures by applying an amortization rule. We have assumed a life of 100 years for dwellings built after 1914, and 150 years for those built between 1870 and 1914. Dwellings built before 1870 have been allowed 20 percent of gross value, to take into account the careful maintenance and sound construction of many still in use. Table 5.4 shows the results. For the evaluation of housing assets in 1954, the authors of *Fortune de la France* showed only 60 percent of net capital value obtained by a method similar to ours, on the basis that maintenance had been insufficient. Because of postwar achievements in this field, however, and the marked drop in the age of dwellings, we have not thought it necessary to discount in this way the net capital figures for 1962.

Annual series of housing value were calculated for gross assets, and then for net investment (equal to changes in net assets) on the assumption that annual amortization was 1 percent of gross assets. The gross

TABLE 5.4
Number and Capital Value of Housing Units
Classified by Age, 1962

Period of construction[a]	Number *(thousands)*	Gross capital value *(million francs)*	Amortization rate *(percent)*	Net capital *(million francs, 1956 prices)*
Principal residences built:				
Before 1870	4,690	75,000	80%	15,000
1871–74	4,280	68,500	50	34,300
1915–39	2,690	42,800	35	27,900
1940–48	420	6,700	20	5,400
Secondary residences built before 1949	1,520	24,300	58	10,200
Total built before 1949	13,600	217,300		92,800
Total built 1949–61	2,740	78,700	5	75,000
Total	16,340	296,000		167,800

[a]The breakdown by age relates to houses used as principal dwellings, as shown in *Annuaire statistique de la France*, 1963. We have assumed that secondary houses built after the war have the same average age as principal houses.

value of pre-1949 dwellings was assumed constant for the whole postwar period; this amounts to assuming that scrapping in that period was negligible. Rebuilding of decayed areas is the sole exception, but this has taken place only recently and does not yet affect any significant number of dwellings. The approximation may slightly overstate the growth of gross assets, but has much less effect on the estimates of net assets. Assets from construction since 1949 are estimated for each year n as the sum of investment in new dwellings built between September 1, 1949, and December 31 of year $n - 1$. Writing down each year's investment by 1 percent of gross assets (average life, 100 years) gives net investment, i.e. annual changes in net assets.

Major maintenance, comprising large-scale repairs such as roof rebuilding, wall strengthening, and outside painting, improves the quality of existing dwellings. For that reason it has been excluded from the investment figure in calculating the gross value of postwar assets, but included in calculating net investment. Because of the recent high level of major maintenance, net assets are growing much faster than the aggregate of housing depreciated simply by age. For example, an estimate of gross value of housing assets in 1954 by the same method as for 1962 would have given a net value of 127 billion francs, whereas our calculations show 114.7 billion—a difference of 12 billion representing major maintenance between these two years. If, as we have assumed, housing in 1962 was so well maintained that the net capital value represents the residual value, 10 percent would have had to be knocked off the net

TABLE 5.5
Investment and Capital Stock in Housing, 1949–66
(1956 prices, *million francs*)

Year	Gross capital stock		Net investment	Net capital stock
	Before 1949	Total		
1949		217,300	1,360	101,870
1950	2,820	220,120	1,720	103,230
1951	5,960	223,260	2,780	104,950
1952	9,970	227,270	2,360	107,730
1953	14,480	231,780	3,620	111,090
1954	19,230	236,530	4,800	114,710
1955	24,960	242,260	5,190	119,510
1956	31,460	248,760	5,760	124,700
1957	38,060	255,360	6,710	130,460
1958	45,470	262,770	7,260	137,170
1959	53,380	270,680	7,400	144,430
1960	61,470	278,770	7,680	151,830
1961	69,850	287,150	8,290	159,510
1962	78,780	296,070	8,870	167,800
1963	88,230	305,530	9,970	176,670
1964	98,640	315,940	12,900	186,640
1965	110,870	328,170	14,240	199,540
1966	124,910	344,210	14,060	213,780

Note: Figures are as of January 1 of each year. Gross capital stock for housing constructed before 1949 has been assumed constant at 217,300 million francs.

value in 1954 to allow for poor maintenance. The authors of *Fortune de la France* had reduced the net value by 40 percent, with no justification. This figure of 40 percent seems totally lacking in credibility if the selling price of buildings is compared to the cost of major repairs. Writing down by 10 percent seems far more satisfactory.

Table 5.5 regroups the figures for gross and net housing assets. The increase in building shows up clearly, since net investment grew tenfold between 1949 and 1964; it must be remembered, however, that the starting level was very low.

Assets of Government Agencies

As mentioned in connection with the estimates of productive capital, our concept of assets of government agencies is not the same as the definition in the French National Accounts. It seems to us more consistent to group transportation infrastructures under productive capital, rather than to impute it to government agencies. In addition, we have assumed that investment by government agencies other than for transportation was equal in each year to 80 percent of the National Accounts figures.

The estimating method followed is similar to that for productive capital, with one exception: the value of assets taken for 1954 is approximately that given in *Fortune de la France*. We have not been able to compare it with other estimates. The breakdown is as follows, in million francs:

Public schools	5,000
Hospitals and rest homes[14]	500
Administrative buildings	14,000
Urban roadways (excluding land)	15,000
Equipment and vehicles	4,200
Total, mid-1954	38,700

The assets in equipment and vehicles are not from *Fortune de la France*. We have estimated them at about 11 percent of total assets in this group, and have based this figure on the average proportion of equipment in the gross fixed capital formation of government offices from 1949 to 1962; allowing for the very different life for equipment and fittings, we have halved this.[15]

Following the rules we have adopted for capital estimates, the value of land is excluded. We have not counted it in the evaluation of urban roadways, nor have we shown the value of parks and public gardens. Broadening somewhat the concept of nonreproducible capital, we have not included public buildings and museum collections (estimated at 5 billion francs in 1954). Their value arises precisely from their unique character, and they are therefore more comparable to natural resources than to reproducible capital.

The National Accounts show 360 million francs for amortization of government assets in 1956; this seems too low. Given the advanced age of the capital stock, the gross assets can be assumed to be roughly twice the net assets, say 80 billion franc of which a little less than 10 percent, say six billion, might be equipment. If we allow a life of 20 years for equipment and 150 years for buildings, we get a total amortization of 300 million francs for equipment and 500 million francs for buildings. These are probably maximum estimates for duration of life, and an amortization of 800 million francs therefore seems a minimum. Our calculation of net capital for each year since 1949 is on this basis, and on the assumption that the ratio of amortization to net capital has been constant at 2 percent. The formula is exactly the same as that used for

[14] The bulk of the health services' assets has been considered productive capital and included under services.

[15] In fact, equipment acquired directly by government agencies is 11 percent of their assets, but at least as much is included in equipment installed by the building and public works sector, and those must also be allowed for.

TABLE 5.6

Net Capital Stock by Principal Category of Capital, 1949–66

(1956 prices, *million francs*)

Year	Productive capital	Housing assets	Government assets	Total capital
1949	227,150	101,870	30,280	359,300
1950	235,660	103,230	31,640	370,530
1951	244,050	104,950	33,000	382,000
1952	251,890	107,730	34,360	393,980
1953	257,130	111,090	35,970	404,190
1954	261,850	114,710	37,670	414,230
1955	266,650	119,510	39,700	425,860
1956	273,500	124,700	42,000	440,200
1957	281,840	130,460	44,540	456,840
1958	291,820	137,170	47,100	476,090
1959	302,020	144,430	49,700	496,150
1960	311,750	151,830	52,590	516,170
1961	322,930	159,510	55,600	538,040
1962	336,080	167,800	59,060	562,940
1963	350,580	176,670	63,030	590,280
1964	367,350	186,640	67,450	621,440
1965	385,280	199,540	72,350	657,170
1966	400,200	213,780	77,880	691,860

Note: Figures are as of January 1 of each year.

the various industry groups. The results, in Table 5.6, show figures for the other main categories (productive capital and housing assets) as well as for total capital.

POSTWAR GROWTH OF CAPITAL

For a proper understanding of the growth of capital, its structure in 1956 should be recalled. In that year, productive capital amounted to 65 percent of the total, but 21 percent of that figure was transportation infrastructure other than railroads. Housing accounted for 25 percent, and government for 10 percent. Under the effect of different growth rates in each of these groups, the structure changed slightly, as shown in Table 5.7. The share of reproducible capital fell as a result of a drop in the proportion of infrastructure assets. The shares of housing and government assets increased substantially. Before analyzing the growth of each group, it seems useful to consider what degree of significance lies in the differences shown by our estimates.

Precision of Our Estimates of Capital Growth

We shall now measure the effect of possible inaccuracies on the estimates of capital assets in 1956, and to that end we shall show that (1) the figures of net investment in each year are fairly insensitive to the

TABLE 5.7
*Distribution of Net Reproducible Capital
by Category, 1949–63*
(1956 prices, *percent*)

Category	1949	1956	1963
Productive capital	66.5%	65%	59.4%
Excluding infrastructure	(41)	(44)	(44.3)
Housing assets	24.7	25	29.9
Government assets	8.8	10	10.7

estimates of capital, (2) the growth rate falls roughly inversely to amendments of the 1956 level of capital, and (3) differences between the growth rates of the various capital groups remain, on the whole, significant.

(1) Net investment depends only slightly on the level of capital assets. We have in the main used the amortization figures in the National Accounts, with only two links between them and net capital—the ratio of net to gross capital and asset life, both somewhat imprecise figures. These coefficients are relevant to an assessment of any possible inaccuracies in the assets level, but they do not affect the amortization values. If the 1956 capital is modified by x percent, the coefficient λ is changed in a proportion such that the 1956 amortization remains constant:

$$A = \lambda K = \frac{\lambda}{100 + x} K(100 + x)$$

The 1956 net investments are not changed, nor therefore is the capital increase in 1957. Accordingly, the formula above remains almost valid for the 1957 amortization. The ratio of the latter to assets is still $100\,\lambda/(100 + x)$, but the 1957 assets change by a proportion of y percent, which is slightly different from x percent, so that $y = 100x(K_{56}/K_{57})$ and amortization is equal to $\lambda/(100 + x) \times K_{57}(100 + y)$.

As an illustration, if the range of accuracy of the capital figures is $x = 10$ percent and if capital growth is 5 percent per year, then $y = 9.5$ percent. Amortization in 1957 will then be $(\lambda/1.10)K_{57} \times 1.095$, or something under 0.5 percent of the previous figure, which does not greatly affect the figures of net investment. We should note that, in any case, investment is affected in the same direction as is the level of capital.

(2) Let us for the moment overlook the fact that net investment has some dependence on the level of capital. If we assume net investment to be constant, the capital growth rate changes because a given increase in assets relates to a different absolute value. If the growth rate is $\Delta K/K$ for the capital figure adopted, with ΔK indicating the annual variation

of K, it would be $100\Delta K/K(100 + x)$ for a capital figure x percent higher in 1956, i.e. growth would be approximately x percent slower.

Let us assume that the total value of productive capital is known to within 10 percent. As we shall see, according to our figures it grew by 20 percent from 1949 to 1956 and by 28 percent from 1956 to 1963. The actual figure, however, may have ranged from 18 to 22 percent in the first period and from 25 to 31 percent in the second. Since net investment is affected in the same direction as capital assets, these ranges somewhat overestimate the possible error in the amount of growth arising from uncertainty in the estimate for capital assets in the base year.

(3) We can indicate how exact the index numbers are that we shall be examining. The level of productive capital assets is known within an error of probably 10 percent. It must be remembered in this context that the figures for energy and transportation assets are largely direct estimates by firms, and a range of uncertainty of 5 percent seems acceptable for them. Since they account for over 50 percent of productive assets, an uncertainty of 10 percent for the whole implies an error of 15 to 20 percent for the assets of the other industry groups, which seems probable for the order of magnitude of maximum error.

We take as another example the electrical and mechanical industries. Their 15 billion francs of assets represent 15 percent of total capital excluding transportation and energy, and there is a considerable difference between our estimate and that of Matthys. We have assumed 20-year life and a ratio a of net to gross capital assets equal to 50 percent. In fact, asset life is likely to be at least 18 years, the average life in 1955 of machine tools, which account for a large share of the equipment in this sector. Their life, however, may be as high as 25 years. The ratio a is likely to vary between 40 percent, as shown in the fiscal statistics (which would be consistent with a life of about 25 years), and 60 percent (which would be consistent with a life of 18 years). Since amortization is 1.5 billion francs, gross assets would be 27 or 37.5 billion francs, according to the asset life assumed. In the former case net assets would be 16.2 billion francs with a equal to 60 percent, and in the latter case 15 billion francs with a equal to 40 percent. If we take a as 50 percent in each case, net assets can be between 13.5 and 18.7 billion francs —that is, 10 percent lower or 25 percent higher than our estimates.

In the estimates of housing assets, the uncertainty results from the average prices assumed for each housing category. A 10 percent range seems the maximum appropriate. And last, the figures for government assets are based on approximations that are themselves fairly uncertain, with perhaps a 10 percent range of error, and the amortization figures

TABLE 5.8

Range of Uncertainty in Estimates of Capital Growth, 1949–63

(Base year = 100)

Category	1949–56			1956–63		
	H^0	H^1	H^2	H^0	H^1	H^2
Productive capital	120	118	122	128	125	131
Housing assets	123	120	126	142	137	147
Government assets	139	134	144	150	144	156

have been estimated as a function of the assets. We have assumed that if the assets were 10 percent higher, we should also have taken amortization as 10 percent higher in order to avoid a life longer than credible. This convention leads to lower asset figures than an assumption of constant amortization would, because for capital growth rates, these two differences are cumulative: higher asset figures are consistent with higher amortization, and if gross investment is unchanged, net investment becomes lower. Since amortization is roughly 25 percent of gross investment, an increase of 10 percent would be consistent with a drop of 3 percent in net investment. Overall, the growth rate of assets would differ by some 13 percentage points.

Table 5.8 summarizes the results of these approximate uncertainties on the growth indexes of the three groups in 1949–56 and 1956–63 in three assumed cases: H^0 representing our estimates, H^1 assets 10 percent higher, and H^2 assets 10 percent lower. The range of uncertainties we have assigned to each estimate is obviously highly subjective. In addition, we must allow for possible errors in the estimates or amortization and in the gross investment series, which are approximate only, particularly for 1949–51. On balance, however, we consider that neither of our two main findings is affected: the growth of capital accelerated after 1956 and there were substantial differences in the rate of increase of various categories.

Rate of Capital Growth

The growth of net assets since the war has been well maintained and fairly regular, with an average of 3.9 percent per year from 1949 to 1956. This rate was slowed down by the standstill in road building between 1949 and 1956 and slow development thereafter: the relevant assets, whose heavy weight has been noted, were completely static up to 1955, with only slow growth subsequently. The other groups grew more steadily, at nearly 5 percent per year. The increase was particularly fast for government assets. The chief factor here was investment in school equipment, made necessary by the considerable swelling of the younger age-groups and the rapid increase in the ratio of school attendance beyond the mandatory age. Although this investment was too small or too late, since for many years classrooms had been overcrowded, it was nevertheless on a substantial scale.

Figure 5.1 shows the acceleration in growth of capital assets after 1956, which should be compared with the sustained revival of investment since 1955. The same results can be seen clearly in Table 5.9 if the two columns relating to successive seven-year periods are compared: the index numbers are higher in the second column than in the first—by some 20 points in the case of housing. Between 1949 and 1956 productive assets other than infrastructure and government assets grew at similar rates, although the housing stock increased a good deal more slowly. After 1956, the growth of housing assets was close to that of productive assets, strictly defined, but remained lower than that of government assets.

The development of productive capital deserves particular attention because of both its high weight in the total and its direct effect on output. According to our estimates, it grew at about 3.4 percent yearly from 1949 through 1951, then at 2.1 percent from 1952 through 1955, again at 3.4 percent from 1956 through 1960, and at 4.4 percent from 1961 through 1965. Overall, from January 1, 1949, to January 1, 1966, the average annual growth rate was 3.4 percent. If we take "net productive assets excluding transportation infrastructure," the rate is 4.7 percent.

The more precise estimates made by J. Mairesse, unpublished at the time of our study, give somewhat different results but show a similar evolution. They relate solely to productive assets excluding transportation infrastructure. Over the whole period 1949–66, they show an average annual growth rate for net capital of 5.1 percent, whereas the figure of 4.4 percent per year applies according to J. Mairesse to gross assets. His figures for gross assets are 3.6 percent per year for 1949–51, 3.0 percent for 1952–55, 4.5 percent for 1956–60, 5.9 percent for 1961–65, and 6.5 percent for 1966–68. The acceleration from the mid-1950's on can be seen in Mairesse's figures in the same way as in ours.

Table 5.10 gives the increase in capital assets in each industry group over the three postwar cycles. In calculating the rates for the last period we have taken account of Mairesse's results for 1966–69 while ensuring consistency with our estimates for the earlier years. In most of the industry groups a speeding up of growth can be seen between the first cycle and the second and between the second cycle and the third. The only important exceptions relate to the heavy industries. A steady slow-

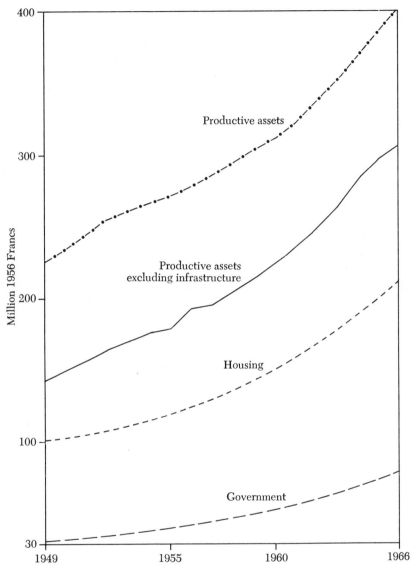

Fig. 5.1. Estimated growth of capital stock by principal category, 1949–66.

TABLE 5.9
Estimated Growth Rates of Capital by Principal Category, 1949–66
(Base year = 100; *percent per year*)

Category	1949–56		1956–63		1949–66	
	Index	Rate	Index	Rate	Index	Rate
Productive capital	120	2.7%	128	3.6%	176	3.4%
Excluding transportation infrastructure	(133)	(4.2)	(141)	(5.0)	(220)	(4.7)
Housing assets	123	3.0	142	5.1	210	4.5
Government assets	139	4.8	150	6.0	260	5.8
Total capital	122	2.9	134	4.3	192	3.9

TABLE 5.10
Growth Rates of Capital Stock by Sector in Three Cycles, 1951–69
(Percent per year)

Sector	1951–57	1957–63	1963–69
01. Agriculture	4.4%	4.9%	6.9%
02. Processed foods and farm products	4.8	3.6	5.8
03. Solid mineral fuels and gas	5.4	3.4	1.4
04. Electricity, water, and kindred products	8.9	6.9	6.3
05. Petroleum, natural gas, and oil products	6.5	11.1	9.0
06. Building materials and glass	2.5	6.4	8.6
07. Iron mining and metallurgy	4.5	8.4	1.7
08. Nonferrous minerals and metals	2.4	7.1	1.0
09. Mechanical and electrical industries	3.9	6.6	6.4
10. Chemicals and rubber	5.0	7.6	6.5
11. Textiles, clothing, and leather	–0.5	2.4	3.8
12. Wood, paper, and misc. industries	1.2	4.0	8.7
Total industry	3.1%	6.0%	5.4%
13. Building and public works	7.7	6.7	9.2
14. Transportation and communications[a]	1.9	3.0	3.9
16. Services other than housing	8.3	9.1	12.1
19. Trade	0.7	3.9	8.6
Total productive economy[b]	2.4%	3.7%	4.7%

Note: Growth is measured from January 1 of the first year of each cycle to January 1 of the last year.
    [a]Excludes transportation infrastructure.
    [b]Includes transportation infrastructure.

ing down of investment occurred in electricity (where, however, it remained very high absolutely), and particularly in coal (where it fell to a low level). After the heavy investment of the late 1950's in metal production, the growth of assets similarly slowed to a modest rate in the 1960's. Allowing for the importance of the heavy industries, the assets of industry as a whole, including the energy sectors, grew a little more slowly in the third cycle than in the second.

All in all, despite their uncertainties, our estimates enable us to conclude that net fixed reproducible capital as a whole grew by about 90 percent from 1949 to 1966, and that productive assets (excluding transportation infrastructure), housing assets, and government assets alike more than doubled over the same period. We shall see that the growth of capital assets also seems to have been high before the war, but undoubtedly the rate was slower.

GROWTH OF PRODUCTIVE CAPITAL OVER THE FIRST HALF OF THE CENTURY

To what extent can the growth of labor productivity, already observed between 1896 and 1938, be explained by successive increases in capital equipment installed? In order to reply to this question in Chapter 7, we must get some feel for the expansion of the productive assets available to the French economy at different periods.

Our study of investment suggests that this expansion must have been rapid, particularly in regard to engines and machinery. But our series excluded the war and postwar years, and we have not attempted to estimate replacements of worn-out plant or the wartime destruction twice suffered by France. We must therefore seek more direct sources of information on the scale of productive equipment installed at different periods. Available data, however, are extremely scarce. We cannot hope to present and analyze series of the volume of assets in those years such as those we prepared for recent years. We shall confine ourselves to examining two partial sources of information: the statistics of motive power installed in industry, and a comparison between two fairly homogeneous assessments of French capital assets, respectively, by C. Colson for 1913 and by Divisia, Dupin, and Roy for 1954.[16]

Annual statistics for motive power show the power of steam engines installed in industry. These figures are somewhat incomplete since they do not apply to small establishments, and above all they are difficult to interpret for our purpose for two reasons: they concern only one form of primary motor (although, to be sure, the main one), and they cover not only industrial and commercial establishments in the true sense but also electric power stations (which have accounted for an increasing share of the whole and which serve domestic as well as industrial consumers).

Nevertheless, the series reproduced in Figure 5.2 shows the wide scale of mechanization achieved in France over the period in question. The

[16] C. Colson, *Cours d'économie politique* (definitive edition; Paris, 1927; book 3); and Divisia, Dupin, and Roy, *Fortune de la France.*

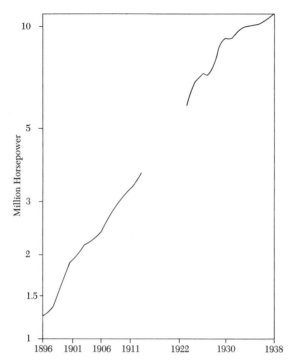

Fig. 5.2. Steam power in industry, 1896–1938.
(Agriculture, mining, and construction and generation
of electricity are included, but not transportation.)

total power of steam engines employed in industry grew at an average
annual rate of 8.7 percent between 1896 and 1901, 4.0 percent from 1901
to 1906, and 6.3 percent from 1906 to 1913. The post–World War I dip
below trend was almost corrected by 1924, so that the increase from
1913 to 1930 was at an average annual rate of 5.5 percent. The rate fell
to 4.0 percent from 1930 to 1933, and virtually to zero from 1933 to 1938.

More complete statistics were prepared before World War II for the
years of the major surveys into motive power: 1906, 1926, and 1931.[17]
Estimates were made in those years of the total useful power in establishments, whether produced by the establishments using it or supplied
by others. Table 5.11 shows the most important of these estimates. It
can be seen that useful power in the different industries (excluding
power stations) grew at an average annual rate of 5.5 percent from 1906
to 1926, and 5.8 percent from 1926 to 1931. A comparison between useful

---

[17] See *Statistiques des forces motrices en 1931* (Paris, 1936).

TABLE 5.11
Power Available to Producing Establishments by Sector, 1906–31
(Thousand kilowatts)

Sector	1906	1926	1931
Fishing, agriculture, and forestry	103	148	162
Extractive industries	260	1,123	1,550
Food industries	351	603	687
Metal industries	488	2,217	3,122
Textiles, clothing, and leather	510	1,056	1,349
Chemical, rubber, and paper industries	245	757	955
Other processing industries	222	734	962
Trade, transportation, etc.	222	421	568
Total[a]	2,401	7,059	9,355
Power stations	262	3,451	4,937

Note: The dates shown are the times of inquiry. Figures exclude locomotion engines.
[a]Excluding power stations.

power and the paid work force in each industry shows that between 1906 and 1931 useful power per wage earner grew by a factor of 2 or 3 in most industries.[18] The slowest progress was made in the food and chemicals industries, which were already relatively highly mechanized in 1906. The fastest increases were in mining and metallurgy and in industries only slightly mechanized at the beginning of the century, such as the timber industries.

How does this increase in motive power available to industry compare with that achieved in other major countries over the same period? Table 5.12 points up some comparisons, which are certainly lacking in precision but sufficient to bring out the orders of magnitude involved. At the beginning of the century, mechanization in French industry lagged behind that of Germany, the United States, and the United Kingdom. In 1907 primary power engines installed in industrial establishments provided an average housepower of 2.2 in the United States, 1.5 in the United Kingdom, and 0.7 in Germany. In 1906 the corresponding figure in France was 0.5.

From 1906 to 1931, industrial mechanization seems to have advanced faster in France than in the United States and the United Kingdom, and at about the same pace as in Germany. In the two Anglo-Saxon industrial nations, power produced direct by industrial establishments grew very slowly over the period; progress in mechanization took the form chiefly of new electric motors, most of which appear to have been fed by energy from outside sources. In France, however, as in Germany, industry continued installing steam and other primary power engines

[18] *Ibid.*

TABLE 5.12
Industrial Motive Power in Selected Countries, 1906–31

Category	France	Germany	U.S.	Italy	United Kingdom[a]
Power of primary engines *(million horsepower):*[b]					
	1906–31	1907–25	1907–30	1911–27	1907–30
Average annual growth rate	14	7	10	15	5
Total power at end of period	12.9	23.7	64.2	5.6	17.8
Power of primary engines per person employed *(horsepower):*[c]					
	1906–31	1907–25	1904–29	1911–27	1907–30
Average annual growth rate	3.2	4.6	0.5	1.7	0.3
Power at end of period	0.90	1.46	2.45	0.48	1.63
Power of electric motors per person employed *(horsepower):*[c]					
	1926–31	1907–25	1914–29	1911–27	1924–30
Average annual growth rate	10.6	11.3	7.9	4.8	5.8
Power at end of period	0.86	0.75	3.94	0.47	1.50

Source: Statistiques des forces motrices en 1931 (Paris, 1956).
[a]Including mines and quarries.
[b]Including power stations.
[c]Excluding power stations.

at the same time that electric motors were being introduced. In 1931, overall France still lagged well behind the United States, but was much closer to the United Kingdom than in 1906.

In brief, on the basis of motive power installed, capital equipment in French industry seems to have grown over the first 30 years of the century at a rate comparable with that in Germany and the United States, but faster than in Britain. The conclusions emerging from our study of rates of investment seem to apply approximately also to industrial steam power, and this would therefore seem for that period an acceptable indication of machinery assets.

We shall now try to compare the estimates of French capital assets in 1913 (by Colson) with those in 1954 (by Divisia, Dupin, and Roy).[19] Whatever its uncertainties, such a comparison may throw new light on our subject. Neither Colson's estimates nor those of Divisia, Dupin, and Roy are very precise. In the crucial group "industry, trade and services," Colson based his figures on an estimate of the market value of plant from assessments made for taxes on real estate. He then multiplied his estimates by a coefficient designed to allow for "movable tool" content. Since, in addition, his breakdown is different from ours, we have had to make some very rough corrections. Our final figure of 30 billion francs required some stretching of Colson's figures, which otherwise implied too fast a growth of capital from 1913 to 1954. For their part, Divisia,

[19] C. Colson, *Cours d'économie politique,* and Divisia, Dupin, and Roy, *Fortune de la France.*

TABLE 5.13
Comparison of Two Estimates of French Capital Stock, 1913 and 1954
(Fixed reproducible capital)

Sector	1913 assets (billion francs)	Index of 1954 prices, 1913=1	1913 assets in 1954 prices (trillion francs)	1954 assets[a] (trillion francs)	Index of volume of assets in 1954, 1913=100
Agriculture	8.6	220	1.9	2.0	105
Industry, trade, and services	30.0	200	6.0	12.5	210
Transportation and communications	40.1	230	9.2	16.6	180
Total productive capital	78.7		17.1	31.1	182
Housing[b]	48.0	250	12.0	14.8	120
Local government	11.0	250	2.7	3.0	110
Total	59.0		14.7	17.8	230
Grand total	137.7		31.8	48.9	154

Source: The 1913 estimates are given in C. Colson, *Cours d'économie politique* (definitive edition; Paris, 1927; book 3). The 1954 estimates are from Divisia, Dupin, and Roy, *A la Recherche du franc perdu:* vol. 3, *Fortune de la France* (Paris, 1956).
[a]The 1954 estimates, from Divisia, Dupin, and Roy, are slightly different from our figures in the analysis of developments from 1949 to 1963.
[b]Divisia, Dupin, and Roy reduced the "net inventory value" of housing in 1954 by 40 percent for lack of maintenance. We have not followed suit, since this reduction is not seriously justified by the authors.

Dupin, and Roy used poor sources in constructing their estimates of plant in industrial and commercial undertakings. Estimates for other groups, shown in Table 5.13, are probably less unreliable. These comparisons, however, can do no more than suggest orders of magnitude. The price indexes we have had to apply to them are based, moreover, on very fragmentary information on some products and some building costs.[20] Of all the volume indexes, the most firmly based is probably that for housing, since we have been able to confirm its accuracy by the fact that, according to the 1962 demographic census, only 30 percent of dwellings standing before 1934 were built later than 1914. (Our index takes account of demolitions from 1913 to 1962, the return of Alsace-Lorraine, and the higher average quality of dwellings built after 1913.) The results, presented in Table 5.13, show an approximate doubling of fixed reproducible capital in industry, transportation, and services over the period considered, and very slow progress under the other headings. These results are comparable with those emerging from the study of investment, which showed a lag in building investment by comparison with that in equipment after 1913. We can compare the volume indexes calculated for France with those

[20] The source for these is Divisia, Dupin, and Roy, *Hausse et dispersion des prix*, vol. 1 of *A la Recherche du franc perdu* (Paris, 1954).

TABLE 5.14
Growth of Fixed Reproducible Capital in Three Countries

Category	France 1954	United States 1953	United Kingdom 1954
Fixed reproducible capital	154	194	158
Housing	120	187	192
Other fixed reproducible capital (excluding housing)	172	215	131
Other fixed reproducible capital per person employed (excluding housing)	180	123	110

Note: The results in this table are very approximate (see text).

over the same period for the United States and Britain (see Table 5.14, in which the figures for the two other countries are based on national studies carried out in conjunction with ours). Any such confrontation is of course highly undependable, since our calculations in the case of France are very unreliable, and a comparison between countries provides additional opportunities for error. (The estimates for France relate to net assets; those for the other countries to gross assets, but this difference is unimportant in indexes covering long periods.) The point, therefore, is not to attempt to supply true statistical results, but to make sure that the approximate comparison available to us does not contradict the qualitative conclusions reached earlier. At any rate, housing assets seem to have increased far less in France than in both the other countries, whereas all other fixed reproducible capital appears to have grown faster in France than in the United Kingdom. If we allow for differences in the development of the working population and calculate an index of the volume of fixed reproducible capital per person employed (excluding housing), we can see a far higher growth in France than in the other two countries.

To sum up, what information we have suggests that France's industrial equipment was relatively undeveloped at the beginning of the century, and grew at a fairly high rate over the first half of the century.

CAPITAL ASSETS PER PERSON EMPLOYED, AND
POSTWAR CAPITAL-OUTPUT RATIOS

Before analyzing, in Chapter 7, the effect of capital increases on the growth of output and productivity, we shall give here two simple overall indicators to show the relative importance of capital equipment in the different industries in three postwar years, using both the "capital-output ratio" (the ratio of net capital to value added) and "capital per person employed" (the ratio of net capital to number of employees).

As shown by Tables 5.15 and 5.17, the values of these two indicators

TABLE 5.15

Capital-Output Ratios by Sector, in France and England, 1949–63

(1956 prices)

Sector	France			United Kingdom 1954
	1949	1956	1963	
01. Agriculture	1.01	1.12	1.24	
02. Processed foods and farm products	0.49	0.56	0.62	1.3
03. Solid mineral fuels and gas	2.40	3.72	4.48	4.0[a]
04. Electricity, water, and kindred products	7.93	9.12	8.05	8.9
05. Petroleum, natural gas, and oil products	0.94	0.60	0.77	5.5
06. Building materials and glass	1.33	1.12	1.15	0.8
07. Iron mining and metallurgy	1.88	1.94	2.40	1.3
08. Nonferrous minerals and metals	1.33	0.94	0.97	1.0
09. Mechanical and electrical industries	0.85	0.72	0.74	0.7
10. Chemicals and rubber	1.15	1.06	0.98	1.4
11. Textiles, clothing, and leather	1.12	0.70	0.63	1.5[b]
12. Wood, paper, and misc. industries	1.02	0.76	0.71	0.9
13. Building and public works	0.23	0.32	0.34	0.4
14. Transportation and communications	17.6	13.4	10.2	3.4
16. Services other than housing	0.25	0.29	0.39	0.8
19. Trade	0.80	0.63	0.60	0.7

Note: The ratio is of net assets to gross value added. For the United Kingdom, value added is gross at factor cost (excluding taxes).

[a]Gas only.

[b]Textiles only.

differ widely from one industry to another (the ranking is broadly the same in both cases). The figures are particularly high for electricity supply and transportation, with assets on the order of 200,000 francs per employee in 1956 and a capital-output ratio of about 10 in the same year. In the "heavy" sectors such as solid mineral fuels and gas, petroleum, mining and metallurgy, and chemicals, the results are also high, except that in the last two the capital-output ratio is not outstanding, by reason of an above-average value added per employee. By contrast, the indicators are at medium levels in the processing and manufacturing industries, services, trade, and agriculture, where assets are on the order of 10,000 francs per employee and the capital-output ratio is about 0.7. Both indicators are low for building and public works.

We have compared the capital-output ratio by industry group with those for Britain in 1954.[21] The chief differences relate to petroleum and transportation, apart from services where international comparisons are always uncertain. A great deal of the difference in the oil figures is explained by high taxation on petroleum products, since the French value-added statistics include indirect taxes, whereas the British do not. The

[21] The British figures are taken from R. Stone, *Capital, Output, and Employment,* vol. 4 of *A Programme for Growth* (Cambridge, 1964).

TABLE 5.16
Aggregate Capital-Output Ratios, 1949–66
(Net reproducible capital in 1956 prices)

Category	1949	1950	1953	1956	1959	1963	1966
Total capital	3.06	2.93	2.85	2.64	2.47	2.47	2.47
Productive capital	1.93	1.86	1.86	1.64	1.61	1.47	1.43

ratio in Britain nevertheless seems to be higher. In the other sector, transportation infrastructure is probably not included in the British figures of capital assets, a fact that goes far toward explaining the differences between the two countries' ratios. For the other sectors, the capital-output ratios are very similar in both cases (the indirect taxes included in the French figures represent in most of the sectors about 20 percent of value added).

The low reliability of the estimates of capital growth allow no clear conclusions to be drawn on variations in the capital-output ratios. Overall, these seem to have fallen, and particularly fast from 1949 to 1956: the same result appears if gross domestic product is compared with either total or productive capital. (See Table 5.16.) The 1949 level seems high, since in the following year the ratios dropped by 4 percent. They then remained steady until 1953, and thereafter fell regularly up to 1956, remained steady until 1959, and later fell again until 1963; since then changes have been small. The overall drop of 20 to 25 percent is too high to be due to the errors that our estimates are sure to contain. This drop gains credence in that it can be largely explained by the particularly slow growth of infrastructure assets in transportation. Moreover, the comparison by industry group of the capital-output ratios in 1949, 1956, and 1963 (see Table 5.15) suggests that the coefficients fell substantially only in transportation and communications—from 17.6 to 10.2 in 14 years. By contrast, the ratio rose substantially in the case of solid mineral fuels and gas. In some of the remaining industries, movement was upward (as in agriculture, mining and metallurgy, and building and public works); in others it was downward (particularly the processing and manufacturing industries and chemicals). But there was no clear trend.

The movements were clearer and also more significant for capital per employee, where there has been a definite increase in every industry. The average annual rate of growth was 3.3 percent in all groups together, and 5.5 percent in Industry. The increase was very sharp—on the order of 9 percent per year—for solid mineral fuels and gas. It was high in electricity—with an average of 8.2 percent per year—in ferrous metals,

TABLE 5.17

Net Fixed Capital per Worker by Sector, 1949–63

Sector	Capital per person employed[a]			Annual average growth rates *(percent)*	
	1949	1956	1963	France 1949–63	United Kingdom 1954–60
01. Agriculture	2.7	4.3	7.6	7.6%	
02. Processed foods and farm products	7.1	11.7	15.0	5.5	3.6%
03. Solid mineral fuels and gas	20.6	45.8	71.3	9.4	5.9[b]
04. Electricity, water, and kindred products	105.6	230.0	319.4	8.2	3.8
05. Petroleum, natural gas, and oil products	59.7	68.2	110.2	4.5	7.4
06. Building materials and glass	11.5	11.7	17.4	3.0	11.2
07. Iron mining and metallurgy	21.1	31.5	49.0	5.8	13.1
08. Nonferrous minerals and metals	23.4	26.6	34.9	2.9	3.6
09. Mechanical and electrical industries	8.15	9.0	11.7	2.7	8[c]
10. Chemicals and rubber	14.6	18.9	27.6	4.9	6.8
11. Textiles, clothing, and leather	5.7	6.0	8.2	2.7	3[c]
12. Wood, paper, and misc. industries	7.7	7.9	9.7	1.6	5[c]
Total of industry	10.5	15.6	22.4	5.5%	
13. Building and public works	2.1	2.8	3.8	4.3	2.7
14. Transportation and communications	121.0	155.2	154.0	1.7	2.5
Excluding infrastructure other than railroads	(48.0)	(60.0)	(65.8)	(2.2)	
16. Services other than housing	2.0	3.1	5.4	7.4	3.7
19. Trade	7.4	7.5	8.6	1.2	3.4
Total of sectors	13.7	16.7	21.5	3.3%	

[a]Thousand francs per person employed (1956 prices).
[b]Gas only.
[c]Approximate figures resulting from consolidation of more detailed data.

mining and metallurgy, in processed foods and farm products, and in chemicals. It was on the order of 3 percent per year in the mechanical and electrical industries and in textiles. It was particularly low—at slightly above 1.5 percent per year—in the wood, paper, and miscellaneous industries, and in transportation and communications.

Comparison with overall results for other countries shows that in France growth of net capital per person employed has been fast but not exceptionally so. According to Denison, from 1950 to 1962 the annual rates were about 5 percent in Germany, Norway, and Denmark, 4.2 percent in France, and lower in the Netherlands (3.9 percent), the United Kingdom (3.5 percent), Italy (3.4 percent), the United States (2.6 percent), and Belgium (2.47 percent).[22]

We have been able to carry out more detailed comparisons with Brit-

[22] Figures relate to net fixed reproducible capital available to undertakings (excluding housing and transportation infrastructure). See E. F. Denison, *Why Growth*

TABLE 5.18
Growth Rates of Capital per Worker by Major Sector,
France and Germany, 1949–63
(Percent per year)

Sector	France 1949–63	Germany 1950–60
Agriculture	7.6%	7.5%
Manufacturing industries[a]	3.9	4.8
Building and public works	4.3	12.2
Electricity, water, and gas	9.2	5.8
Transportation	1.7	1.8
Total of industry[b]	5.5%	5.2%
Total of productive sectors	3.3%	4.3%

[a]For France, industry groups 02 and 06 to 12.
[b]For Germany, manufacturing industries, mines, quarries, and energy.

ain and Germany. For Britain Table 5.17 shows in the last two columns the annual average growth of net capital per person employed from 1954 to 1960, next to rates for France from 1949 to 1963. (Since the period for Britain is very short, the indicators shown may be highly sensitive to short-term economic fluctuations.) Growth seems to have been higher in France than across the Channel in industry groups where the coefficient was rising fast (such as with solid mineral fuels and gas, and electricity). However, growth was substantially lower in France in the processing and manufacturing industries, particularly mechanical and electrical, and in chemicals.

Comparison with Germany leads to the same conclusion—that the growth of capital per employee was lower in France in the processing and manufacturing sectors. See Table 5.18. For industry as a whole, the growth rate was of the same order in both countries (5.2 percent per year in Germany from 1950 to 1960, as against 5.5 percent in France from 1949 to 1963). For electricity, water, and gas, however, the rate was only 5.8 percent in Germany and in Britain, whereas in France it exceeded nine percent. By contrast, in the manufacturing industries, capital per person employed grew at 4.8 percent per year in Germany, and at only about 4 percent in France.

Last, in order to examine the factors affecting variations in labor productivity, Table 5.19 shows estimates of the growth of "capital per man-hour" in the different industry groups. Movements of this degree are measured by an indicator easily obtained by dividing the index of the volume of fixed reproducible capital by the index of man-hours. Table

Rates Differ: Postwar Experience in Nine Western Countries (Washington, D.C., 1967), p. 139.

TABLE 5.19
*Growth Rates of Capital per Man-Hour by Sector
During Three Cycles, 1951–69*
(Percent per year)

Sector	1951–57	1957–63	1963–69
02. Processed foods and farm products	4.9%	4.1%	5.2%
03. Solid mineral fuels and gas	8.4	8.9	7.1
04. Electricity, water, and kindred products	8.3	6.1	4.9
05. Petroleum, natural gas, and oil products	4.1	7.5	7.9
06. Building materials and glass	1.8	6.1	7.9
07. Iron mining and metallurgy	4.2	8.7	6.1
08. Nonferrous minerals and metals	0.5	4.8	0.7
09. Mechanical and electrical industries	1.3	3.9	5.8
10. Chemicals and rubber	3.6	5.5	4.7
11. Textiles, clothing, and leather	2.4	4.8	7.0
12. Wood, paper, and misc. industries	1.0	3.2	7.9
13. Building and public works	2.1	4.2	7.5
14. Transportation and communications	2.6	1.9	2.9
16. Services other than housing	7.2	8.0	9.3
19. Trade	–0.7	1.7	7.0
All productive sectors	2.6%	3.7%	4.7%

Note: Growth is measured from January 1 of the first year of each cycle to January 1 of the last year.

5.19 shows that the substitution of capital for labor has accelerated in most industries, being high in agriculture, energy, and the services over the whole postwar period, but only moderate or even low over the 1951–57 cycle in the other groups. In the 1963–69 cycle, however, it rose at a fast rate all round. The exception in nonferrous metals is not important, and that in transportation can be explained by a change in the composition of this industry—the relative increase in road transport, where capital per person employed is relatively low.

The estimates given in this chapter confirm that the growth of France's productive capital accelerated after World War II. They suggest, however, that this result of its investment drive explains only a small part of the progress achieved in labor productivity. For one thing, mechanization of French industry had proceeded actively since the beginning of the century, and France soon made up much of the lag existing in 1900 in equipment. For another thing, international comparisons from 1950 to 1970 suggest a rate of growth of productive assets in France little different from that in other countries where labor productivity has been less dynamic as in the United Kingdom. We shall take up the whole question again in Chapter 7, where we shall assess the contribution to France's growth made by the development of capital equipment.

CHAPTER SIX

The Industrial Structure

Having studied the two basic factors of production, labor and capital, we shall now look briefly at the structure of the productive system. We shall treat as physical growth factors all changes in organization that increased the efficiency of productive activity over time. We shall inquire whether the rate of such organizational changes increased after the war, or whether it followed trends established since the beginning of the century. The macroeconomic approach appropriate to this study does not allow the technical structure of firms to be examined in detail or in great depth. We must, however, take account of such major changes as are revealed by the available statistics.

To assess how the balance between productive sectors in France has changed, we shall first consider manpower movements, showing the large scale of movements from agriculture into higher-productivity sectors. We shall then discuss whether industrial activity tended to concentrate in increasingly large technical or financial units. We shall examine the structure of agriculture and in passing take a brief look at the acceleration of growth in agricultural productivity. Finally we shall devote a short section to trade and services.

HAS THE RATE OF MIGRATION BETWEEN SECTORS INCREASED?

We have given in Chapter 3 an estimated breakdown of the working population by industry groups (Table 3.4). A glance at these results shows the importance of manpower movements from one industry to another since World War II. Between 1949 and 1968, employment in agriculture fell by 46 percent, and in textiles, clothing, and leather by 36 percent, while in the mechanical and electrical industries it grew by 45 percent and in building and public works it doubled. This, however, is not a new phenomenon. Substantial migration between industries took place in all the preceding periods we have considered. We should therefore investigate not so much the fact of structural change in the working population as the quickening in its rate. Has the increase in the growth rate of production been accompanied by greater movements of labor between sectors than in the past?

In studying this point, we ought to consider migration out of agriculture separately, both because of its size and because of certain special aspects of its probable effects on growth.[1] From our point of view, the best measure of the level of migration from the land is the rate of average annual decrease in the proportion of the total working population employed in agriculture. Despite gaps, the data shown in Chapter 2 make possible an approximation of this rate. The decrease seems to have taken place at an average annual rate of 1 percent per year between 1896 and 1929 (0.9 percent from 1896 to 1913, 1.0 percent from 1913 to 1929). It appears to have stopped completely between 1929 and 1938 (0.0 percent), and from 1938 to 1949 it averaged only 0.5 percent. By contrast, between 1949 and 1968 the annual rate of decrease was 3.3 percent.

The increase in recent years is undeniable. Nevertheless, like the present increase in French output, this acceleration in the rate took place after a 20-year period in which change fell behind earlier trends. It might be tempting therefore to explain the size of recent movements out of agriculture as a kind of "catching up." In fact, however, these movements have been greater than a projection of the trends up to 1929 would predict. Over the 39 years of the period 1929–68, the average annual rate of decrease was 2.0 percent, significantly higher, that is, than the rates recorded up to 1929.

Nevertheless, by comparison with experience in other industrial countries, this average decrease has not been exceptional. On the contrary, the discrepancy lies in the relative slowness of migrations from agriculture into other sectors in prewar France. Between 1851 and 1891 the proportion of the British labor force employed in agriculture dropped from 22 to 11 percent, i.e. at an average annual rate of 1.7 percent. Since then the rate of decrease has stayed at around 1.4 percent per year.[2] In the United States the rate of decrease was 1.8 percent per year between 1889 and 1929, and 2.9 percent between 1929 and 1953.[3]

---

[1] For recent analysis of migration from agriculture, and a good bibliography, see G. Barbichon, "Mutation et migration des agriculteurs," *Revue d'économie politique*, March–April, 1969.

[2] See P. Deane and W. A. Cole, *British Economic Growth, 1688–1959* (London, 1967), Tables 30 and 31.

[3] According to the statistics compiled by M. Abramovitz and P. David for their study on growth in the United States.

Changes in the structure of the working population are also apparent in the nonagricultural sectors. The data in Chapter 3 show the large scale of manpower increases in the mechanical and electrical industries. They also bring out the continuing drop of manpower in textiles and associated industries. But have these changes, in the aggregate, increased since the war?

To answer this question, we need an appropriate composite index. Let n_{it} be the number of workers in industry i in year t, and let N_t be the number of workers in the nonagricultural sectors as a whole. If θ is the year studied subsequent to the year t (for example, 1913, where $t = 1896$), let $n'_{i\theta}$ be the number of workers that industry i would have employed in year θ if the breakdown of the nonagricultural labor force had remained as in year t. By definition

$$(1) \qquad\qquad n'_{i\theta} = \frac{N_\theta}{N_t} \times n_{it}$$

An indicator of the magnitude of structural change is provided by the ratio to N_θ of the sum of the absolute values of the differences between $n'_{i\theta}$ and the observed manpower $n_{i\theta}$, i.e.

$$(2) \qquad\qquad x_\theta = \frac{1}{N_\theta} \sum | n'_{i\theta} - n_{i\theta} |$$

This indicator measures changes in structure between the years t and θ. To compare periods of varying length, it is convenient to refer to the average annual rate of change between year t and year θ, i.e. of the indicator y_θ as defined by

$$(3) \qquad\qquad (1 + y_\theta)^{\theta-t} = 1 + x_\theta$$

Calculations from data in Table 3.4 (p. 88) give the following annual rates of migration for the nonagricultural labor force: 0.5 percent from 1896 to 1913, 1.1 percent from 1913 to 1929, 1.6 percent from 1929 to 1938, 1.0 percent from 1938 to 1949, and 1.1 percent from 1949 to 1963. These results are, however, only moderately exact, because of uncertainties about the distribution of the labor force over the years considered.

It is not surprising to note that the biggest structural changes took place in the years of slump and stagnation from 1929 to 1938. This is accounted for by the exceptionally large drop in the proportion of the labor force in building and public works, and the exceptional increase in the proportion in trade and services. By comparison with the rates for earlier periods, that for the postwar years is not particularly high. We may therefore conclude that there was apparently no speeding up of the changes in the distribution of the working population among non-agricultural industries. We shall look again at workers' migration between sectors in Chapter 13. Its effect as a physical growth factor does not seem to have been different after the war from before, except in the case of movements out of agriculture into other types of work.

THE STRUCTURE OF INDUSTRY

At our present level of statistical analysis, we cannot assess the impact of changes in the internal structure of industrial firms.[4] We can, however, identify three phenomena that may have altered the conditions of industrial productivity: the gradual disappearance of small craftsmen, the increasing concentration of industrial production in ever larger manufacturing units, and the growth potential of very large firms at the expense of the rest.

To study the first two phenomena, we shall use mainly a common statistical source about which some brief comments should be made. We shall retain the breakdown of the working population by numbers of workers per firm. This provides a convenient indicator for comparisons between widely separated years, since it is simple to interpret and not very sensitive to changes in statistical conventions. We shall compare results from the 1906, 1926, 1931, and 1936 population censuses with figures for 1954, 1962, and 1966 from the register on establishments compiled by the INSEE.[5] Both these sets of figures seem to provide fairly complete coverage; their comparability should therefore be high despite some difficulties mentioned below. In studying the prewar census figures, we shall make use of the work by de Ville-Chabrolle and of its updating by Denuc.[6]

Some uncertainty arises in comparing census figures with those from the INSEE register, because in the census businesses are classified by the total number of persons working there, and in the register by the number of paid employees only. The difference is important only for small establishments. Adopting the same convention as other researchers, we have assumed that each establishment contained only one unpaid worker. This amounts to treating as negligible the number of unpaid family helpers. In the 1962 census, these amounted to no more than 12

[4] On this subject, see also M. Didier and E. Malinvaud, "La Concentration de l'industrie s'est-elle accentuée depuis le début du siècle?" *Economie et statistique*, no. 2, 1969.

[5] See *Les Etablissements industriels et commerciaux en France*, 1954 and 1962 (INSEE, Paris, 1956 and 1962).

[6] M. de Ville-Chabrolle, "La Concentration des entreprises en France," *Bulletin de la statistique générale de la France*, April–June, 1933; and J. Denuc, "Structure des entreprises," *Revue d'économie politique*, 1939, pp. 220–70.

percent of the figure for heads of firms and self-employed workers, i.e. 1.2 percent of the industrial labor force. The presence of unpaid family helpers therefore seems unlikely to distort significantly our comparison of the prewar and postwar periods.

Disappearance of Small Craftsmen

To assess the rate at which small craftsmen slowly gave way to modern industry, we consider the proportional distribution of the working population in industry as a whole by the following four categories of business: no employees, 1–4 employees, 5–9 employees, 10 employees and over. Because of the consideration mentioned above, these same groups for the years 1906 to 1936 cover 1 worker, 2–5 workers, 6–10 workers, and over 10 workers. The distribution of the labor force for 1954, 1962, and 1966, shown in Table 6.1, has been deduced from the total number of employees by adding one person for each establishment. This means that the proportion of the group "no employees" is slightly underestimated both before and after the war, whereas that for the group "1–4 employees" is probably very slightly overestimated before the war and underestimated after.

Table 6.1 shows the fast rate at which small craftsmen disappeared over the first half of the century. In 1906, more than 60 percent of the working population in industry was in establishments of under 10 employees. The proportion today is only 20 percent. As far as can be judged, this change was well advanced by 1954; it was bound to slow down in the next 15 years. Table 6.2 shows that the phenomenon could be described in a qualitatively analogous way if we considered the proportion of the labor force working in firms with under 20 employees: the proportion fell from 63 percent 1906 to 31 percent in 1954, and then to 27 percent in 1966.

The figures for 1936 show a reversal of the trend, as a result of the

TABLE 6.1

Distribution of the Industrial Labor Force by Size of Establishment, 1906–66

(Percent)

Number of paid employees by firm[a]	1906	1926	1931	1936	1954	1962	1966
0	27%	14%	12%	17%	6%	5%	4%
1–4	26	21	16	16	13	11	10
5–9	5	6	6	6	6	5	6
10 and over	42	59	66	61	75	79	80

Note: Figures include the extractive industries and building and public works (groups 06 to 08 and 10 to 61 of the INSEE business nomenclature).

[a]See text for definition of groups in years 1906–36.

Great Depression. Whereas the industrial labor force fell from 1931 to 1936, the number of small shops with no paid employees increased. This tendency may have lasted through World War II: it is likely that there were at least as many craftsmen in 1946 as in 1936. There must therefore have been a rapid reduction in their total number immediately after the war, releasing large numbers of skilled workers for the reconstruction of industry.

Concentration of Industrial Establishments

One could in principle think of many ways of measuring the concentration of production in ever larger units. For long-term comparisons we shall be concerned with industrial establishments of more than 10 employees and shall consider their distribution by number of employees. The effect of the general growth in productivity has been to increase the amount of value added in firms with a constant number of employees. However, this fact is not significant here, because what we wish to study is whether the rate of concentration of businesses has accelerated since World War II and whether this has played a particular role in the economic development of this period.

To avoid misunderstanding, we should make it clear that for the moment we are interested only in the concentration of production evidenced at the level of individual establishments. The next section examines what can be termed financial concentration, characterized by large businesses. We refer here to the same statistical data as we used earlier to study the position of small craftsmen. Table 6.2, drawn up on the same lines as Table 6.1, shows the distribution of the working population of industrial establishments by size. The results for 1906 and 1926 refer to number of persons working, those for 1954, 1962, and 1966 to numbers of paid employees. Assuming that each firm included one unpaid worker, we have estimated for 1926, 1931, and 1936 figures that are comparable with those since the war.

Table 6.2 shows a surprisingly constant size distribution between medium and large units. A slight trend toward very large establishments took place between 1906 and 1936. (Note in particular the average number of employees in establishments with over 1,000 employees.) But this trend does not seem to have persisted, or to have resumed after World War II.

These aggregate figures do not seem to conceal much divergence between different sectors of industry. Despite the difficulty of comparing statistics based on very different nomenclatures, we have examined the distribution within a few of the major industrial sectors. Table 6.3 shows

TABLE 6.2

Distribution of the Labor Force by Size of Establishment in Establishments Employing More than Ten Persons, 1906–66

(Percent)

Number of persons by firm	All workers		Paid employees					
	1906	1926	1926	1931	1936	1954	1962	1966
Ave. no. of paid employees in firms employing over 1,000	2,228	2,486	2,486	2,530	2,610	2,180	2,170	2,230
11–20	12%	11%	10%	10%	10%	8%	8%	8%
21–50	16	16	15	15	15	16	15	16
51–100	12	12	12	12	12	12	13	13
101–200	14	13	} 30	30 {	13	14	14	14
201–500	17	16			17	17	18	19
501–1,000	11	10	} 33	33 {	11	12	12	12
Over 1,000	18	22			22	21	20	18

Note: Figures include the extractive industries and building and public works (groups 06 to 08 and 10 to 61 of the INSEE business nomenclature).

TABLE 6.3

Distribution of the Labor Force in Selected Industries by Size of Establishment in Establishments Employing More than Ten Persons, 1906–62

(Percent)

Number of persons by firm[a]	1906	1926	1954	1962
Metallurgy:				
11–100	2%	2%	2%	2%
101–500	18	15	8	10
Over 500	80	83	90	88
Mechanical and electrical industries:				
11–100	33	28	27	27
101–500	28	27	27	29
Over 500	39	45	46	44
Chemicals:[b]				
11–100	35	31	29	28
101–500	33	35	37	38
Over 500	32	34	34	34
Textiles:				
11–100	24	26	29	29
101–500	47	43	44	46
Over 500	29	31	27	25

[a]Working population for the years 1906 and 1926; paid employees for 1954 and 1962.
[b]Including tobacco and fats.

remarkable stability within sectors. Some weak trends can be noted, but as far as can be judged from the figures given, the trend does not seem to have accelerated since the war. Examination of the proportion of establishments employing over 500 persons shows, in three cases out of four, a slight decrease between 1954 and 1962, which contrasts with the increase shown between 1906 and 1926. Further examination of the figures for 1954 and 1962 does not show very significant changes. Whether one examines a larger number of sectors or a breakdown into smaller divisions, especially for large establishments, no particularly significant conclusions can be drawn.[7]

To sum up: postwar French growth took place without substantial change in the degree of concentration of industrial production in effect at the beginning of the century or earlier. This is somewhat surprising, particularly since the present-day concentration of establishments is less advanced in France than in the other major industrial nations.

Table 6.4 compares the French position in 1962 with that of the other Common Market countries, Japan, and the United States. It shows that only in Italy and Japan was industry less concentrated than in France. Establishments with more than 1,000 employees accounted for over 30 percent of all industrial employees in Germany, the United States, and the Netherlands, but for only 21 percent in France. The study from which the figures in Table 6.4 are taken shows that a gap of this order can be found in nearly every industrial sector, and is not due primarily to differences in specialization among industries. It is to be noted also that the degree of concentration of establishments in British industry is similar to that in Germany, and therefore considerably higher than in France.[8]

It is difficult to explain this persistent gap, and the associated low proportion in France of giant establishments with over 1,000 employees. It might suggest a certain inefficiency of French firms, unable to take advantage of the economies provided by large production units. But the gap might also be due to the lag in development of French industry at the end of the nineteenth century, when the relative advantage of large establishments was even greater than now. The fact that, according to

[7] These conclusions seem well established for the postwar period. They are confirmed in the far more detailed study of different industry groups (see, for example, J. Houssiaux and C. Amoy, "L'Evolution de la concentration dans les industries françaises: l'exemple de l'industrie textile," *Revue d'économie politique*, March–April, 1965).

[8] See, in particular, figures quoted by S. Wickham, *Concentration et dimensions* (Paris, 1966).

TABLE 6.4
Distribution of the Industrial Labor Force by Size of Establishment
in Selected Countries, 1961–63
(Percent)

Number employed by firms	France 1962	Germany 1961	Belgium 1963	United States 1963	Italy 1961	Japan 1963	Netherlands 1962
10–49	21%	16%	17%	13%	26%	32%	17%
50–99	12	10	11	10	14	13	24
100–499	34	29	31	32	30	26	15
500–999	12	12	14	13	11	11	13
1,000 and over	21	33	27	32	19	18	31

Source: J. P. Nioche, "Taille des établissements industriels dans sept pays développés," *Collections de l'INSEE*, Entreprises E.1, 1969.
    Note: Figures are for the manufacturing industries (excluding mining, energy, and building and public works).

Table 6.4, Italy and Japan share France's position may lend weight to this second explanation.

Variations in the Concentration of Firms

It would seem that the breakdown of firms by size was less stable than that of establishments. In a broad sense, the long-term developments seem to have been as follows. From the beginning of the century to the 1930 depression, very large firms seemed to grow even larger. Some lessening of this trend appears to have taken place up to the end of World War II. From 1946 to 1955, the earlier trend reappeared, and then was interrupted until 1965. The trend in recent years, almost up to the present day, seems to have involved medium-size firms rather than the very large ones.

There is, however, a dearth of convenient studies for long-term comparison, and we have not ourselves undertaken the laborious statistical research to enable us to measure, with at least some degree of refinement, the trends in very large undertakings. The only available information concerns companies quoted on the Paris Stock Exchange. In an article published in 1939, Denuc studied the distribution of quoted companies by size of authorized capital in 1911 and 1936.[9] We have supplemented these with the results of a quick analysis of figures for 1963. J. Houssiaux has made a careful study of the breakdown in 1912 and 1952.[10]

If we bear in mind that France's national income grew in terms of

[9] Denuc, "Structure des entreprises."
[10] J. Houssiaux, *Le Pouvoir de monopole* (Paris, 1958).

current value by about 6.5 times from 1911 to 1936, and by about 800 times from 1911 to 1963, we can compare the number of companies with an authorized capital of over 5 million francs in 1911, more than 32.5 million francs in 1936, and over 40 million new francs in 1963. The figures were, respectively, about 300 in 1911, 370 in 1936, and 210 in 1963. If we consider the number of companies whose capital exceeded 20 million francs in 1911, 130 million francs in 1936, and 160 million francs in 1963, we see that these were, respectively, 83, 85, and 65.

This comparison, showing a drop between 1936 and 1963 in the number of very large companies quoted, has only limited significance, since the end-of-war nationalization turned a number of companies previously quoted on the stock exchange into nationally owned corporations. Some 15 of these had an official capital exceeding 160 million francs in 1963. If they are added to the quoted companies of the same size, the total number of very large corporations comes close to those in 1911 and 1936.

These results apply to companies as a whole. To concentrate our analysis on the industrial sector, we have taken Houssiaux's figures for gross assets of the largest industrial firms. From 1912 to 1936 the assets of the top 10 grew by a factor of 10.7, and those of the top 50 by 10.4, whereas national income rose by 6.1 times. From 1936 to 1952 the gross assets of the biggest firms did not increase significantly faster than did national income (the growth factor was 52 for the top 10 firms, 48 for the top 50, and 49 for national income).

The analysis of firms should be completed by a study of relationships among companies, since the development of financial links is often considered the most advanced form of concentration. Over the last number of years there has been a marked trend in this direction. We should note, however, that Denuc wrote as early as 1939: "The most remarkable phenomenon in relation to the concentration of production has been the development of groups of companies or links between companies." A reflection of these financial links can be seen in the size of the "portfolio investment and stockholding" items in company balance sheets. Denuc's comparison of the accounts of the chief companies in 1911 and 1936 showed a far faster growth under this item than in the companies' own issued capital. Our examination of particular balance sheets seems to suggest, despite problems of interpretation, a fairly substantial drop in the relative size of companies' stockholding during and immediately after World War II. Developments over the past 15 years would therefore represent a return to a previous state (from 1957 to 1966 stockholding as a proportion of total use of capital in 400 large quoted companies rose from 17 percent to 27 percent).

It should be stressed that these conclusions are fairly tentative. Greater accuracy is possible for postwar years, at least for the period up to 1964, with the help of official statistics on company taxes. Because of the long delay in their publication, we cannot yet note the outcome of the trend that has become apparent in the most recent years. This, however, is not important, since the new development clearly cannot yet have affected growth over the period covered by our study.

The statistics of the accounts of industrial and commercial firms include items taken from business accounts on which tax is assessed on the basis of "real profits." The firms concerned are those with a turnover exceeding a certain figure, called the flat-rate assessment ceiling, plus a number of other firms that have chosen to pay taxes on the basis of real profits, although eligible for the flat-rate assessment. For comparisons of the degree of concentration at different periods, it is important to make sure that the flat-rate assessment ceiling is at comparable levels; otherwise the figures would include a proportion, different in different years, of small firms almost in the category of small craftsmen. This condition is approximately satisfied for the tax years 1955 and 1964 (coinciding with calendar years 1955 and 1964 for most firms). Between these two years, the ceiling grew by a factor of 2.66 (up to 400,000 francs in 1965), whereas the turnover of industry as a whole grew by a factor of about 2.5.

Admittedly, the short-term economic situation was somewhat different in the two years: 1955 was in the phase of balanced expansion of the 1951–57 cycle, and 1964 was at the down-turn point following the 1963 boom. However, this is unlikely to affect the comparison significantly, and we have been able to verify that these same two conclusions can be reached by comparing the figures for 1955 and 1961, when the short-term economic situation was similar, but the flat-rate assessment ceilings were not closely comparable.

A comparison between 1955 and 1964 shows first a drop in the number of undertakings. Table 6.5, column 2, gives index numbers for certain sectors (these were selected both for their importance in the economy and for their relative homogeneity, which is a safeguard against variations in the statistical classification of a number of large companies). The drop in numbers was especially great in light industry and undoubtedly reflects industrial concentration: the average number of persons employed per firm grew in every group except the basic industries (energy, extractive industries, metallurgy). We have already noted that no concentration took place at the level of individual establishments, but the number of establishments per firm increased. This must have been

TABLE 6.5

*Concentration of Firms Assessed on the Basis of Real Profits
in Selected Industries, 1955 and 1964*

(Percent)

Sector[a]	Number of companies in 1964 (1955=100)	Proportion of sales of the top 10% of firms	
		1955	1964
22. Mechanical industries, general[b]	91	77%	69%
26. Automobiles, bicycles	50	83	90
28. Electrical manufacturing	97	86	83
35–36. Chemicals	90	80	79
47. Textile industry	74	75	74
49. Clothing	71	67	63
53. Wood and furniture	83	63	61

[a]Sector numbers refer to the INSEE business nomenclature.
[b]The drop apparent in column 2 may be the result of changes in the classification of metal-processing firms. For groups 19 to 24 as a whole, the number of firms increased by 3 percent from 1955 to 1964. On the other hand, in each one of the metal-processing and manufacturing industries there was a reduction in the proportion of sales of the largest firms.

accompanied by reorganization favoring greater specialization by establishments. Some economies of scale may therefore have been achieved without apparent changes in the concentration of establishments.

Table 6.5 suggests a second conclusion, that the tendency toward greater concentration of firms was more marked in medium-sized firms than in large ones. We have considered available classifications of each sector by amount of turnover, showing within each class the number of firms and their own turnover figures.[11] We then estimated the proportion of turnover achieved by the largest firms—about one-tenth of all firms—in each sector (as found by interpolation on graphs plotting degrees of concentration, which is sufficiently accurate for our purposes). This proportion was slightly lower in 1964 than in 1955 in almost every sector; the only noteworthy exception was "automobiles and bicycles."[12] In other words, the degree of concentration was lower in 1964 than in 1955, but applied to a smaller number of firms; i.e. medium-sized firms had concentrated at a faster rate than very large ones. The wave of concentration since 1965 in the largest French firms is likely of course to reverse the tendency observed earlier. This conclusion is confirmed by the fact that the relative importance of the largest undertakings had been growing in the immediate postwar period, but stayed remarkably steady from 1955 to 1963. The proportion of turnover of the top 10 in-

[11] See, for example, "Les Bénéfices industriels et commerciaux déclarés en 1965," *Statistiques et études financières*, February 1967, pp. 254–72.

[12] Similar results are obtained by taking the proportion of turnover achieved by 20 percent of firms.

dustrial firms rose from 5.8 percent in 1955 to 6.0 percent in 1964, the proportion of the top 50 moved from 14.3 percent to 15.3 percent between the same years.[13]

It is difficult to compare the situation in France with that of the other major industrial countries, even if the comparison is limited to concentration at a particular date, with no attempt to trace movements over time. It is well known, on the one hand, that France has few giant industrial groups comparable with those in the United States, or even in Japan, Germany, the Netherlands, or Britain. On the other hand, apart from this extreme case, the degree of concentration of large firms does not seem any smaller in France than elsewhere.[14]

To sum up this examination of the industrial structure, we have found no sign of acceleration in the changes that can be found over the long term. By contrast, concentration of medium-sized firms in the period 1955–65 must have made possible a substantial degree of reorganization, and may partly explain the growth of productivity.

CHANGES IN AGRICULTURE

We have already observed that the rate of growth of labor productivity in agriculture and the rate of migration from agricultural employment were both substantially higher after the war than before. We can therefore expect a similar acceleration of structural change in agriculture. This was indeed the case. The size of agricultural units can be defined easily and naturally by reference to their area. Another criterion might be value added by agriculture, but apart from certain problems that have already been mentioned in relation to industry, no statistics exist on this basis.

There is a great scarcity of data even on the breakdown of farms by area. The only figures that seem suitable for a comparative analysis are the results of the major agricultural surveys of 1892 and 1929, those of the agricultural census of 1955, and those of the 10 percent samples carried out in 1963 and 1967 with the aim of studying the structure of this sector.[15] The ground rules adopted make the 1929 statistics comparable in principle with those for 1892, and the 1967 and 1963 figures with those for 1955. But it is extremely difficult to compare the results

[13] For more detailed results, see Didier and Malinvaud, "La Concentration de l'industrie s'est-elle accentuée depuis le début du siècle?"

[14] For further information, see the figures given by Wickham, *Concentration et dimensions*; and J. Bain, *International Differences in Industrial Structure* (New Haven, 1966).

[15] See, among others, Statistical Office of the European Community, *Statistique agricole*, no. 10, October 1960; and C. Laurent, "Premiers résultats de l'enquête au dixième sur les structures agricoles en 1963," *Etudes et conjoncture*, June 1965.

TABLE 6.6
Size Distribution of Agricultural Holdings of More Than One Hectare, 1892–1967

Area of holdings[a] (hectares)	Number of holdings (thousands)					Proportion of arable agricultural area (percent)		
	1892[b]	1929	1955	1963	1967	1955	1963	1967
1–5	1,829	1,146	649	454	375	5%	4%	3%
5–10	788	718	477	364	308	11	8	7
10–20	430	593	536	485	413	23	22	20
20–50	335	380	377	394	372	35	37	38
50–100	52	82	75	85	85	16	17	19
Over 100	33	32	20	23	24	10	12	13
Total	3,467	2,951	2,134	1,805	1,577	100%	100%	100%

[a]The area included woods in 1892 and 1929, and "arable agricultural area" in 1955, 1963, and 1967.
[b]Excluding Alsace-Lorraine.

of the two early studies and those relating to the three postwar years. In the former case, areas refer to the total land held including woods, whereas in the latter they relate to "arable agricultural areas," which exclude wooded land.

Table 6.6 nevertheless shows available data for holdings of over one hectare. A clear concentration can be seen over the 12 years 1955–67. The number of holdings fell in the groups of agricultural holdings under 20 hectares, but rose in those with areas of more than 50 hectares.

Over such a short period, these changes show how rapidly the structure of French agriculture is changing. The rate is far faster than in the past. The number of holdings of over one hectare fell by 18 percent between 1892 and 1929 (after correction for the return of Alsace-Lorraine), by 28 percent from 1929 to 1955, and by 25 percent from 1955 to 1967. The annual average rates of change are respectively 0.5, 1.0, and 1.9 percent—an unmistakable acceleration.

Although there was a rapid increase in holdings of 10 to 20 hectares at the beginning of the century, holdings of more than 20 hectares (the portion of total arable agricultural area in France, not counting wooded land) rose from 60 percent in 1955 to 69 percent in 1967. Today's level represents a degree of concentration far higher than that of other countries in the European Economic Community.[16]

There are two possible interpretations of this acceleration of change in French agriculture. According to the first, technical progress in farming over recent decades freed an increased proportion of the farm labor force for nonagricultural employment. According to the second, the

[16] See *Statistiques agricoles de la Communauté économique européenne*, no. 4, 1962.

rapid growth of production in the remainder of the economy raised the demand for manpower, made it easier for young farmers to find employment in industry, and reduced the degree of hidden underemployment in agriculture. The acceleration of structural change in agriculture was due, according to the latter view, to the growth of the French economy, and not to truly autonomous factors. There is a good deal of truth in this second interpretation. In its support, one can note that migration from farm employment between 1954 and 1962 was particularly heavy in regions where demand for labor was heaviest. This is the conclusion reached by Echard, who measured the pressure of demand by the rate of immigration of foreign workers.[17] But industrial growth does not explain all the changes in agriculture, for the acceleration of improved productivity in agriculture predated the rise in the demand for labor in industry. Productivity improved in agriculture at an average annual rate of about 0.5 percent from 1896 to 1929. This rose to 1.0 percent from 1929 to 1938, when unemployment was high, and fell to 0.7 percent during the period 1938–49, when there was a lack of both machinery and fertilizers. The second third of the twentieth century witnessed a real agricultural revolution, which has been vividly described by Gervais, Servolin, and Weil.[18]

Our conclusion seems to be confirmed in a study by Brangeon,[19] who has analyzed changes from 1954 to 1962 in the male farm labor force and in agricultural labor productivity in each of the 21 planning regions. (The productivity figures were obtained by comparing the results for the three consecutive years 1962–64 with those for 1953–55.) If improvements in agricultural productivity were due only to the demand from industry, there should be a clear correlation between the drop in numbers employed in agriculture and the growth of farm productivity. But this is not the case.

Brangeon comments,

Thus Brittany can be seen to have the highest rate of growth in productivity, and yet a lower rate of decline in male labor force than the French average. The Paris region, which has the highest rate of migration from the land, is only eighth in its index of productivity. Alsace, Franche-Comté, and Picardy have rates of decline in the labor force above the national rate, and their indexes of productivity are among the highest. But Provence–Côte d'Azur, Languedoc,

---

[17] P. Echard, "Quelques aspects de l'évolution de la population active masculine agricole de 1946 à 1962," *Cahiers de l'ISEA*, series AG, no. 4, November 1964.

[18] M. Gervais, G. Servolin, and J. Weil, *Une France sans paysans* (Paris, 1965).

[19] J. L. Brangeon, *Comptabilité économique régionale et disparités dans le développement et le progrès de l'agriculture française* (Institut National de la Recherche Agronomique, Station d'Economie Rurale de Rennes), February 1959.

and Lower Normandy, with more rapid rates of progress than the average, are among the regions with the lowest emigration. Limousin, Aquitaine, and Auvergne have some of the lowest indexes of productivity, but a rate of reduction in the labor force close to that for France as a whole.

The magnitude and speed of these changes can be explained partly by a worldwide acceleration in the improvement of farming techniques, and also by France's backwardness in the nineteenth and early twentieth centuries. The inheritance system and protectionist policies that applied over the whole period, except for the very poor years from 1860 to 1881, prevented France from achieving the rapid progress of Britain and northern Europe. The use of fertilizers and machinery spread slowly and late. After World War II the farmers themselves became aware of the lag, and strove to adopt modern production and management techniques. This is shown both by the activity of professional organizations and by the success of the Centres d'études techniques agricoles (CETA) set up by farmers anxious to improve their knowledge and to take better advantage of progress. The rapid growth of productivity was partly due to this desire.

Action by the farmers themselves was complemented by the establishment of integrated agricultural and industrial complexes. A number of industrial firms and cooperatives organized large-scale processing or distribution of certain products (poultry, fruit, etc.). To ensure regular supplies with consistent standards, they persuaded the farmers in a given region to sign production contracts, and then demanded use of the most modern techniques.[20]

TRADE AND SERVICES

The activities grouped under the heading of services cover a wide range. For many of them our statistical sources do not permit long-term comparisons, for the breakdown of firms in the prewar censuses is different from that in the index of establishments. We have therefore confined ourselves to two sectors—transportation and trade (this latter includes the hotel business and liquor sale outlets). The work force of these two sectors accounts for some 80 percent of that in trade and services as a whole.

The same trend can be seen in transportation as in Industry—a drop in the proportion of small establishments, and a fairly stable rate of distribution in medium and large establishments. There does not seem

---

[20] On this new form of agricultural development, see P. Mainié, "Les Nouvelles relations entre l'agriculture et ses transformateurs," *Revue d'économie politique*, March–April, 1969.

TABLE 6.7
Distribution of the Labor Force in Commerce by Size of Establishment, 1906–66
(Percent)

Number of workers per firm	1906	1926	1931	1936	1954	1962	1966
1–5	81%	69%	65%	66%	66%	60%	54%
6–10	6	7	7	7	8	10	10
Over 10	13	24	28	27	26	30	36

Note: Figures include the hotel business, and groups 69 to 81 of the INSEE business nomenclature.

to have been any change in the rate as between prewar and postwar. For example, in transportation other than railroads and urban transport, the proportion of the labor force working in establishments with over nine employees was 39 percent in 1906, 47 percent in 1926, 58 percent in 1954, and 60 percent in 1962.

The structure in trade was rather different. Table 6.7 shows the changes experienced in the size of small establishments. Drawn up on the same basis as Table 6.1, it shows the size of small shops, except that we have allowed here for family helpers, who are too numerous in small trading businesses to be ignored. Since their numbers are available from the population censuses, we have been able to allocate them without great danger of error to the different categories of establishment size in Table 6.7 (although we could not isolate establishments with only one worker without being too arbitrary). After a marked increase in the proportion of medium and big businesses from 1906 to 1931, small businesses seem to have benefited from the Great Depression and the lack of spending power to maintain their relative position until the early 1950's. Their number then dropped rapidly again, and apparently at an accelerating rate in the 1960's. The proportion of persons working in establishments with fewer than six workers fell by 20 percent in the period 1906–31, remained almost steady in 1931–54, and then fell again by 18 percent in 1954–66.

Table 6.8 gives a breakdown of employees in trades and the hotel business with over 10 workers. It shows a clear prewar trend toward concentration, since the proportion of establishments with over 100 workers rose from 28 percent in 1906 to 38 percent in 1926 and to 41 percent in 1936. After the war the trend seems too weak to be significant. The proportion of the work force drawn to the large stores seems to have fallen considerably between 1936 and 1954. The difference is so marked as to suggest that the statistical definitions of retail outlets may have altered. None of the sources available to us, however, gives

TABLE 6.8
Distribution of the Labor Force in Commerce by Size of Establishment in Establishments Employing More than Ten Persons, 1906–66
(Percent)

Number of persons per firm	All workers		Paid employees				
	1906	1926	1931	1936	1954	1962	1966
11–20	33%	24%	22%	22%	27%	27%	26%
21–50	27	25	38	23	31	31	30
51–100	12	13		14	14	16	16
101–200	8	11	12	12	11	11	11
201–500	8	10	10	11	9	8	10
Over 500	12	17	18	18	8	7	7

Note: Figures include the hotel business, and groups 69 to 81 of the INSEE business nomenclature.

any evidence for this,[21] and therefore we take the change shown in the last line of Table 6.8 to be correct.

To sum up: two opposite postwar developments can be observed—an accelerated decline in the number of small businesses, and a postwar decline following a prewar advance in the share of this group taken by the large stores, with no noteworthy change in recent years. The first of these developments, which should be seen in relation to the acceleration in the growth of labor productivity in trade, was probably a result of the demand of Industry for labor, of the development of personal transportation, making small country shops less and less useful, and of changes in marketing methods. It is therefore an effect partly of general economic growth and partly of an autonomous factor of technical progress.

The drop in the relative position of large establishments—assuming, indeed, that this has occurred—is more difficult to interpret. A drop does not necessarily lead to reduction in efficiency, for the economies of scale in these commercial establishments probably do not make big companies more productive than those of medium size.

The developments observed in small businesses are similar, both in manifestations and in causes, to those in agriculture. Small merchants and their family helpers in many cases gave up businesses that seemed

[21] The number of workers in firms with over 100 employees in the group "big stores and textile sales" was 31,000, 84,000, and 85,000 in the 1906, 1926 and 1936 censuses. The register of firms shows 38,000 persons in 1954 and 59,000 in 1962. The number of stores employing more than 1,000 persons seems to have dropped from 18 in 1936 to 9 in 1954, and those employing over 5,000 persons seems to have dropped from 5 to 0.

less and less profitable by comparison with paid employment—and in fact were so because of competition from more modern methods of distribution. Nevertheless, the rate of decline is far smaller in small businesses. From 1954 to 1968 the agricultural labor force was reduced by 2 million persons. The number of owners in industry and trade (including family helpers) fell by 340,000 as a result of reductions in craftsmen and small businesses together. To this should probably be added the reduction in employees of establishments too small to be profitable, but no exact definition is available of these, and their number cannot be large.

The postwar structural changes in France's industrial structure seem, all in all, to have been narrowly localized, apart from long-term trends in the relative growth or shrinkage of particular activities as a result of technical progress. The concentration of industry seems to have been somewhat limited—nonexistent at the level of individual establishments, and, at the level of firms, greater in the medium-sized than in the larger firms. This seems to have led, at the level of financial groupings, to a return to the situation before the Great Depression. In face of these facts, we believe it is difficult to support the theory that the rapid development of modern capitalism toward highly monopolistic forms has played a major part in achieving France's growth. The most striking feature we have found is the accelerated change in agriculture, induced partly by expansion, but also by a real transformation in techniques and attitudes.

Finally, in this chapter we have taken the term "structure" in the relatively narrow sense often given to it by economists. We have not examined changes in legal or institutional structures. Apart from the fact that to study them in many cases would take us out of our field, we have not counted them as "physical factors," and we have put off dealing with some of them until the second part of our study.

CHAPTER SEVEN

Total Factor Productivity and Technological Progress

The growth enjoyed by France since World War II has undoubtedly been accompanied by substantial technological improvement, evidenced by abundant data at the level of individual firms. An economist seeking to assess the effect of this improvement at an aggregative level, however, meets serious difficulties. Some macroeconomic figures can accurately reflect particular aspects of technical development, but none seems to measure its impact directly on the natonal volume of production.

For this reason an indirect approach is frequently adopted, by breaking down the rate of economic growth into a number of elements, each with particular significance—the effect of increases in the labor force, the effect of capital accumulation, etc. Direct measurements are sought for all elements except one; this last element is treated as a "residual" obtained from the difference between the rate of economic growth and the sum of the contributions of the other elements. It reflects particularly the effect of technological progress.

The weakness of this approach is obviously that the "residual" varies according to what other elements are considered in the analysis, and also according to the methods used for estimating each. The residual is certainly an ambiguous measure of the effect of technological progress. In the absence of anything better, however, calculating it imposes a necessary discipline on anyone who wishes to observe reality in this field objectively. In this chapter we shall therefore be mainly concerned with estimating and critically examining the residual, and only seek direct measures of technological improvement at the end. We can also define our aims in another way, as presenting a synthesis of Part One, devoted to the physical factors or sources of growth.

In Chapter 3 we compared changes in production and labor input. With the two measures of labor productivity that we considered, we assessed the extent of French expansion since the war, related it to previous trends, and compared it with experiences in other countries.

Among the numerous causes that can explain improvements in labor productivity, capital accumulation and changes in technical makeup of the productive system undoubtedly play a leading part. In three chapters we examined the role of productive capital and structural changes, without, however, assessing their impact on the growth of production. It will be relevant for us to determine, if only approximately, what share accrues to each of these physical factors, and to ascertain by subtraction the residual that they apparently fail to explain. Such a breakdown is the first step in our explanatory analysis, providing a point of reference against which to plot later research.

Taking the matter from a different viewpoint, we can attempt to find a composite index that will combine as fully as possible the different physical factors—labor, capital, and other—or we can develop indexes of "overall productivity" that will cover all these factors together. How to define such measures is open to discussion. But their use in other countries or for particular sectors has shown that they can shed new and interesting light on the phenomena under analysis.

We shall first examine the indexes of total productivity to be obtained by relating indexes of production and indexes of "total input" covering both labor and capital. Then we shall consider the effect of improvements in the quality of labor and capital. We shall then estimate the probable impact of labor movements from less productive to more productive forms of work. Finally, we shall examine the residual and compare our conclusions with those suggested by the few available direct statistics on technological development. We shall end the chapter with a summary of the more important findings made in the course of this first part of our study.

TOTAL PRODUCTIVITY

The Search for a Composite Index

Labor productivity, the ratio between production and the amount of labor utilized, provides an imperfect means of measuring the development of productivity because it takes no account of faster or slower rates of capital accumulation. The ratio between production and the amount of capital employed, the "productivity of capital," has sometimes been considered as well. This value, which is the exact inverse of the capital-output ratio briefly examined in Chapter 5, does not allow for variations in labor activity; it is therefore itself also imperfect.

The development of a third value has often been suggested, which would lack the defects of the other two and allow simultaneously for changes affecting capital and manpower. With some differences of detail, the solution adopted in every case has been to attempt a definition, as we shall do, of "overall productivity" or "total productivity." This third value is usually defined directly.[1] We shall try to penetrate more deeply into the matter, making use of the concept of "production function." This is not the place to discuss extensively the meaning and limitations of this concept.[2] The use we shall make of it hereafter will make clearer the following brief comments.

The *production function* of a country or an industry over a specified period is the function that determines the volume of output in the country or industry in question over the period considered on the basis of the quantities of particular factors used. Such a function therefore defines how output would have changed if specific changes had been made in the use of these factors. A series of production functions valid for different periods in a given country or industry defines how output would have developed if the quantities of the factors used had changed in certain given patterns. If we knew the production functions appropriate to the situation in France at each period, we could at once determine the proportion of each factor in the growth of production, as well as the residual.

Let us, for example, consider a case in which the only factors are labor and capital. Let us call the quantities of these two factors used in the period t, respectively, N_t and K_t. Let Q_t be the volume of production in the same period. Let us assume that the production function has the following form:

$$(1) \qquad Q_t = q_t N_t{}^a K_t{}^{1-a}$$

where q_t is a series of specified coefficients and α is a number, also specified, between 0 and 1. (We shall make use of a "Cobb-Douglas func-

[1] It is not possible to give a complete bibliography on this subject; accordingly, the reader is referred to L. A. Vincent, *La Mesure de la productivité* (Paris, 1968). The study with the closest methodology to ours is J. W. Kendrick, *Productivity Trends in the United States* (New York, 1961). Vincent advocates, and applies in studies of various sectors, an indicator of overall productivity that takes account of the consumption of each sector in current inputs but does not treat capital as we do. (See in particular his "La Mesure de la productivité à l'échelle de la nation et des branches d'activité," *Etudes et conjoncture*, August 1961. See also the estimates for various sectors in *Etudes et conjoncture*, March and November 1963, March and October 1964, and January 1965.)

[2] Although this is one of the most frequently used and discussed concepts in modern economic theory, we do not know of any text that explains it in a manner appropriate to the needs of historical-econometric studies such as ours. See, however, L. Stoleru, *L'Equilibre et la croissance économique* (Paris, 1969), chap. 15.

tion" of this type in later pages.) The index of production for period t in relation to period 0 is equal to

$$(2) \qquad \frac{Q_t}{Q_0} = \left[\frac{N_t}{N_0}\right]^a \left[\frac{K_t}{K_0}\right]^{1-a} \times \frac{q_t}{q_0}$$

This is the product of the three terms, representing, respectively, the shares attributable to the increase in labor input, the growth of capital and the residual, which have affected the volume of output.[3]

We may also consider that the product of the first two terms, i.e.

$$(3) \qquad \frac{F_t}{F_0} = \left[\frac{N_t}{N_0}\right]^a \left[\frac{K_t}{K_0}\right]^{1-a}$$

represents a composite index of the factors employed (labor and capital) and that

$$(4) \qquad \frac{q_t}{q_0} = \frac{Q_t}{Q_0} \div \frac{F_t}{F_0}$$

is an index of "total factor productivity."[4] Thus, when a is known but not the value of q_t, these operations would permit both a breakdown of the index of production and a calculation of the index of total productivity.

In order to avoid unnecessary complexity in our calculations, we shall argue in this chapter as if functions of the form (1) were fully applicable both to French production as a whole and to each sector considered. As a result, we shall not take account of economies of scale that may arise in particular industries or at the national level, since according to equation (1), if the quantities of the two factors N_t and K_t are doubled, the volume of production is also exactly doubled.

We shall consider economies of scale separately, in order to determine how far they would have affected our results, if allowed for. Up to now such economies have never been measured precisely, and are the subject of guesses rather than of true estimates. Conversely, we shall for the present ignore the services of nonreproducible factors such as land.

In our subsequent calculations of total productivity, we shall choose

---

[3] The Cobb-Douglas function is obviously a favorable special case in which the index of production can be broken down unambiguously. In less simple cases, other conventions—sometimes less natural—must be adopted to define the share of each factor. The informed reader will note that the production function we put forward here excludes any allowance for economies of scale. We shall return to this point later (see p. 211).

[4] We shall use the term *total* productivity to avoid confusion with Vincent's "indexes of *overall* productivity" in *La Mesure de la productivité*.

the value of α in advance, on the basis of a commonly adopted assumption, already discussed in Chapter 2 when we tried to measure changes in the quality of work. We shall assume that the real rate of pay to labor is equal to its marginal productivity, except in certain special cases to be discussed. Following this assumption, we may assess α as labor's share of the value of production, since with function (1) the marginal productivity of labor (a derivative of the relationship between production and N_t) is equal to

$$\alpha \, q_t N_t^{a-1} K_t^{1-a} = \alpha \frac{Q_t}{N_t}$$

If s_t and p_t represent, respectively, the rate of wages and product prices in the period t, the assumption mentioned earlier can be expressed as

$$\frac{s_t}{p_t} = \alpha \frac{Q_t}{N_t}$$

that is,

(5) $$\alpha = \frac{s_t N_t}{p_t Q_t}$$

We can therefore conveniently estimate α from the ratio between the value of labor remuneration and the value of production.[5]

The assumption that labor receives a rate of pay equal to its marginal productivity rests on a double assertion: (*a*) it is of advantage to every undertaking to employ only workers whose marginal productivity is at least equal to the rate of pay; (*b*) because of competition between firms, every worker can find a job in which his earnings will be equal to his marginal productivity. It goes without saying that this assumption is not perfectly fulfilled. But it seems to provide a first approximation, which is valid for the very broad viewpoint we have adopted. We shall study the sensitivity of our results to the values chosen for α, just as we shall question the validity of Cobb-Douglas functions for our purpose.

Total Productivity at the National Level

We shall apply the principle presented above first of all to the data relating to the French economy as a whole. Production, labor, and capi-

---

[5] This demonstration (indeed, like the assumption that overall production is a function only of overall labor and capital inputs) ignores the multiple nature of goods and qualities of labor. Not to use this simplification, however, would greatly complicate the discussion. There is a partial treatment of this problem in the effects of intersector transfers (p. 197).

TABLE 7.1
Total Productivity in France and Its Components, 1913–66
(1956 = 100)

Year	Gross domestic production	Labor input	Net fixed productive capital	Output per man-hour	Total productivity
1913	50	133	53	38	49
1949	70.8	100.5	83.0	70.4	74.4
1950	75.8	101.1	86.2	75.0	78.5
1951	80.7	102.0	89.2	79.1	82.2
1952	82.6	101.0	92.1	81.8	83.9
1953	85.1	100.0	94.0	85.1	86.6
1954	89.8	101.0	95.8	88.9	90.3
1955	95.1	100.5	97.5	94.6	95.4
1956	100.0	100.0	100.0	100.0	100.0
1957	106.4	100.7	103.1	105.7	104.9
1958	109.2	100.0	106.7	109.2	107.2
1959	112.5	98.7	110.4	114.0	110.4
1960	121.5	99.4	114.0	122.2	117.6
1961	127.0	99.6	118.1	127.5	121.3
1962	135.8	100.3	122.8	135.4	127.9
1963	143.3	101.0	128.2	141.9	132.7
1964	152.2	102.1	134.3	149.1	138.1
1965	158.5	101.8	140.9	155.7	142.2
1966	166.6	101.8	146.4	163.6	147.8

tal will be represented, respectively, by gross domestic production, labor input[6] of the total work force in the productive economy, and net fixed productive capital.[7] The indexes given in Chapters 1–5 for the years 1949–66 and for 1913 are repeated in the first three columns of Table 7.1; 1913 is the only distant year for which an estimate of capital, although very uncertain, is available.

To calculate an index of overall productivity, we had to estimate the share of wages; the procedure is described below. It has led us to adopt for α a value of 0.72, which we do not justify in greater detail for the present. By applying formulas (3) and (4), we then obtained the series shown in the last column of Table 7.1. To facilitate comparisons, the next-to-last column shows the index of output per man-hour.

However imprecise, a comparison with 1913 is of some interest. Although the capital index for that year is only approximate, its order of

[6] Man-hours worked in each year by the working population.

[7] Although some readers might prefer a definition of capital that includes stocks, the results of our calculations would be very little altered if the definition of capital were changed in this way. From 1949 to 1959 the ratio of stocks to turnover fell by 13 percent in undertakings taxed on the basis of "real profits." The growth of stocks was thus slower than that of production, but on the same order as that of net fixed capital. We shall return to this point later.

magnitude seems to agree well with the indicators shown in **Chapter 5.** We can therefore relate postwar growth to an earlier point of reference. A comparison on these lines has the same advantage here as in the case of labor productivity, although it is necessarily much less detailed and more uncertain.

From 1913 to 1949, total productivity grew far more slowly than did labor productivity. Over this 36-year period, the average annual growth rate was 1.1 percent for total productivity and 1.8 percent for labor productivity. After World War II the two growth rates remained in the same relative positions, but the gap between them seems to have narrowed. From 1949 to 1966 the average growth rates were 4.1 and 5.1 percent.[8]

An examination of total productivity thus reinforces the conclusions we had reached in our study of labor productivity. Immediately after World War II, productivity in France was relatively low; it was certainly higher than in 1913, but by a proportion that implied a low average growth rate. In the postwar period, on the contrary, growth was very fast. The series of annual indexes of total productivity does not show any marked tendency toward retardation of growth after the war. The average annual rate was 4.1 percent from 1951 to 1957, 4.0 percent from 1957 to 1963, and 3.8 percent from 1963 to 1969. The drop in this composite index is so slight that it is scarcely significant.

All in all, it seems that the change in growth rate of labor productivity between the prewar and postwar periods should not be ascribed mainly to capital accumulation. France's productive capital had increased substantially between 1913 and 1949, and although it grew rapidly over the next 20 years, this does not seem to explain more than a small part of the growth of productivity.

We shall return to these conclusions later. But first we should see how the developments observed in France compare with those in other

---

[8] The growth rate of total productivity varies somewhat according to what estimates are used for coefficient α and for capital. Thus, it could be shown, as we shall see later, the estimates of the share represented by labor remuneration in some cases lead to overestimating α. If a value of 0.65 had been taken for α instead of 0.72, the growth rate of total productivity from 1949 to 1966 would have been 3.9 percent per year instead of 4.1 percent. Conversely, while retaining a value of 0.72 for α, if we had taken as an estimate of capital total net fixed capital (including land) instead of net fixed reproducible capital, the growth rate would have moved from 4.1 to 4.2 percent over the same period. Similarly, using gross capital figures would have slightly raised the estimate of total productivity growth. Although the definitions and estimating methods we used are somewhat arbitrary, this is not a serious problem for the aggregated indicators we are considering, since the phenomenon is clearly too complex to be perfectly pinned down by any one of them.

TABLE 7.2
Growth Rates of Total Productivity in Three
Countries, 1913–63
(Percent per year)

Country	1949–63	1913–49	1913–63
France	3.5%	1.1%	1.8%
United States[a]	2.3	2.0	2.1
United Kingdom	1.2	1.1	1.1

Note: See the text for definitions of the various indexes. The data have been taken from the studies on the United States and the United Kingdom paralleling our study on France.
[a]For the United States, the second period covers the years 1913-53.

countries. Available data are rather incomplete, and we have been able to obtain suitable long-term comparability only with the United Kingdom and the United States.[9]

In order to obtain the results shown in Table 7.2, we applied formulas (3) and (4), taking a value of 0.7 for α, which seems approximately right for all three countries. We took one series each for gross domestic product, for man-hours worked by the total labor force, and for fixed reproducible capital excluding housing. By this approach, total productivity would seem to have grown since 1913 at a rate close to 2 percent per year in the United States and at slightly over 1 percent in the United Kingdom. The high rate achieved in France between 1949 and 1963 seems substantially superior to the rates apparent over the same period in the other two countries. But from 1913 to 1949 the growth of French productivity lagged seriously behind that of the United States. Even over the entire 50-year period 1913–63, France seems to have lost ground in relation to the United States.

For the postwar period, we can make use of Denison's systematic work on nine countries.[10] Table 7.3 shows certain results of his based on definitions and weightings that differ somewhat from ours (thus, the value taken for coefficient α varies for different countries, and is in every case higher than the 0.7 we used in calculating the figures shown in Table 7.2).

The growth rate of total productivity is particularly high in France,

[9] We should note, however, that according to the calculations of H. Gerfin (in the study of economic growth in Germany for this series), total productivity grew in Germany at average annual rates of 1.5 percent from 1851 to 1911, 2.2 percent from 1925 to 1938, and 5.1 percent from 1950 to 1962. But there is no linking between 1911 and 1925 or 1938 and 1950 (estimates presented at the conference on economic growth in industrialized countries in Saltsjöbaden, Sweden, in July 1965).

[10] E. Denison, assisted by J. P. Poullier, *Why Growth Rates Differ* (Washington, D.C., 1967).

TABLE 7.3

Growth Rates of Total Productivity in Selected Countries, 1950–62

(Percent per year)

Country	National income adjusted[a]	Labor input[b]	Net fixed productive capital[c]	Total productivity[d] 1950–62	1950–55	1955–62
France	4.70%	0.08%	4.3%	3.85%	3.7%	4.0%
West Germany	7.26	1.64	6.9	4.63	6.7	3.1
Belgium	3.03	0.32	2.9	2.37	2.3	2.4
Denmark	3.36	0.66	6.0	1.88	0.9	2.7
United States	3.36	0.89	3.8	1.80	1.9	1.8
Italy	5.95	0.63	4.0	4.78	4.8	4.7
Norway	3.47	−0.03	5.1	2.60	2.6	2.6
Netherlands	4.52	0.81	5.0	2.86	3.5	2.4
United Kingdom	2.38	0.43	4.2	1.52	1.3	1.7

Source: E. Denison, *Why Growth Rates Differ* (Washington, D.C., 1967).

[a]Shown in the penultimate line of the odd-numbered tables in Denison, chap. 21.

[b]Number of man-hours, corrected by Denison to remove the effect of work intensification after reductions in time worked.

[c]From Denison, Table 12.2, p. 137.

[d]Calculated from the odd-numbered tables in Denison, chap. 21 (penultimate line minus lines 4, 5, 8).

especially in the second period, 1955–62, when the effect of delays in reconstruction, still being felt in several countries in 1950, was less strong. (We should recall here that Denison introduced two corrections to eliminate short-term variations in agricultural production and in the pressure of demand.) Only two countries, Italy and France, enjoyed an annual growth rate substantially above 3 percent in the second period, and Italy's success can be explained by large labor transfers from agriculture into industry. In several countries where productivity was growing fast in the early 1950's, significant retardation has been experienced since. The French performance would look even better if the recent revision of the National Accounts for 1959 and 1962 were allowed for.

Results by Industry Group

The same calculations of total productivity as we have carried out for the economy as a whole can be undertaken for each of the industries considered in earlier chapters. It is important to determine the value of α for each industry. To this end we must estimate what share of value added was accounted for by the remuneration of labor.

The earnings of labor and capital have been calculated for the year 1956 from sector accounts published in 1960.[11] We have made supplementary estimates only in the case of independent entrepreneurs, that is, the owner-managers of unincorporated enterprises. The National Ac-

[11] *Les Comptes,* vol. 1 of *Les Comptes de la nation* (Paris, 1960).

counts provide the "gross income of owner-managers," which includes both remuneration for work and that for capital invested in their firms. These two kinds of remuneration must be isolated in all sectors where the number of owner-managers is high, that is, in every one except the energy and metal-producing sectors.

Two methods were followed. In the first, we have assumed that the remuneration of each owner-manager was in general equal to average wages in the industry group concerned; then by deduction we obtained the earnings of capital. In the second, we calculated first the earnings of owner-managers' capital by assuming it stood in the same ratio to value added as was the case for corporations; then by deduction we obtained the earnings of labor. We have checked the figure for reliability in relation to the number of persons involved.[12]

We used the second method except in the cases of agriculture and services. It has the advantage of using the numbers of owner-managers only as a check. These numbers are obtained from demographic censuses and are only approximately compatible with income figures from the sector accounts. We have also assumed that the shares of value added, allocated respectively to labor and capital, were the same in the industry groups as in the sectors approximately corresponding to them.

To be precise, the total earnings of labor comprise wages and social security contributions and benefits paid out by corporations and by individually owned unincorporated businesses; they moreover comprise a share of the gross income of the latter. The earnings of capital comprise the residual share of this gross income, along with the interest, dividends, and profit shares paid out by corporations, their direct taxes, and corporate savings.

Table 7.4 gives the result of all these calculations, and in particular the proportion of each industry group's value added, taken by the earnings of labor and capital, respectively. If we retained unchanged the assumption we used in the calculations at the national level, the proportion represented by labor's remuneration would provide the value of α that is necessary for determining the index of total productivity as defined by formulas (3) and (4). But a detailed examination of the results reveals some anomalies that we must take into account.

---

[12] The remuneration of labor per independent member of the labor force (individual owner-managers and their family helpers) appears from this to have amounted in 1956 to 3,300 new francs in agriculture, 21,900 in processed foods and farm products, 18,200 in building materials, 12,800 in the mechanical and electrical industries, 7,300 in textiles and clothing, 6,600 in the wool and miscellaneous industries, 9,500 in building, 7,800 in transportation, 5,400 in trade, and 9,300 in other services.

TABLE 7.4
Shares of Labor and Capital in Value Added by Sector, 1956
(1956 prices, *million francs*)

Sector	Earnings on		Value added[a]	Percent share of earnings on	
	Labor	Capital		Labor	Capital
Agriculture	15,340	3,020	18,360	0.83	0.17
Processed foods and farm products	6,920	3,190	10,110	0.68	0.32
Solid mineral fuels and gas	2,290	1,030	3,320	0.69	0.31
Electricity, water, and kindred products	1,060	1,770	2,830	0.38	0.62
Petroleum and oil products	730	1,475	2,205	0.33	0.67
Building materials and glass	1,640	890	2,530	0.65	0.35
Iron mining and metallurgy	2,070	1,432	3,502	0.59	0.41
Mechanical and electrical industries	13,260	5,120	18,380	0.72	0.28
Chemicals	2,760	1,890	4,650	0.59	0.41
Textiles, clothing, and leather	6,460	2,390	8,850	0.73	0.27
Wood, paper, and misc. industries	4,470	1,800	6,270	0.71	0.29
Building and public works	8,420	2,150	10,570	0.80	0.20
Transportation and communications	8,490	3,780	12,270	0.69	0.31
Services other than housing	11,800	2,280	14,100	0.84	0.16
Trade	11,600	6,340	17,940	0.65	0.35
Total	97,330	38,557	135,887	0.72	0.28

[a]Gross value added at factor cost.

In a further examination of these results in the section on marginal productivity and rates of remuneration (p. 198), we shall see that they imply a very low rate of return on capital in solid mineral fuels, electricity, and transportation. Nationally owned companies predominate in these industries. Their management does not follow exactly the rules of competition that we have assumed to apply, in order to justify the hypothesis that α is equal to labor's share of value added. This should be taken into account in order to improve the estimates of α in those industries.

We can assume that government policy has obliged the nationally owned companies in question to keep their prices below what would ensure a normal return on capital invested.[13] Value added in production is therefore underestimated in the prices charged, and labor's share

[13] This is to some extent confirmed by a study of the Société d'Etudes pour le Développement Economique et Social, *Application d'un modèle de prix de référence à l'économie française* (Paris, 1965). Following chiefly the assumption that factor remuneration is the same in every use, their model leads to prices significantly higher than those in fact obtaining for gas, electricity, and transportation. The price of solid mineral fuels remains at its actual level, but only if imports are substituted for home production. On the other hand, the reference prices of petroleum and oil products are far lower than those obtaining in practice.

overestimated. To obtain a more reliable estimate of α, it seems desirable to raise the remuneration of capital by at least 100 percent in solid mineral fuels and transportation and by 50 percent in electricity. The consequent rates of return are still low (see Table 7.7). They suggest values for α of approximately 0.5 in solid mineral fuels and transportation and 0.3 in electricity, which are the values we shall use here.

By contrast, the return on capital was quite exceptional in 1956 in petroleum and oil products. On National Accounts conventional assumptions, gross output in that industry in 1956 greatly exceeded its level in the years immediately before and after, and the remuneration of capital was abnormally high. We have reduced it by a third, and adopted 0.43 as the value of the coefficient α in that sector. Reexamining the validity of the estimates in Table 7.4 for determining α could of course take us deeper into the subject. The remuneration of capital includes monopoly surpluses, which should be excluded from our calculation. The rates of return on capital shown in Table 7.7 suggest that these surpluses were high in processed foods and farm products, building and public works, and services. We could have considered raising α somewhat in those industries in order partly to eliminate this effect, but have not done so for lack of objective data.

This discussion shows, as expected, that our calculations of total productivity cannot pretend to any great precision, since the weights used are subject to considerable uncertainties. Nevertheless, the results achieved usefully complement those reported earlier on the subject of the productivity of labor.

We have calculated figures for every nonagricultural industry previously considered for each of the three postwar cycles. The results are shown in Table 7.5 in the form of average annual growth rates for 1951–57, 1957–63, and 1963–69. Examining the indexes of labor productivity is of some interest, as can be seen by comparing Table 7.5 with Table 3.11 (p. 101). The growth of total productivity seems slower and less variable between industries than the growth of labor productivity, and the rates in Table 7.5 rarely exceed 5 percent per year. In particular, the capital-intensive industries in which labor productivity grew very fast do not stand out consistently from the others in regard to total productivity. In fact, in the 1950's the highest growth shown was in textiles, clothing, and leather. (The calculations do not allow for the spread of shift work, which was particularly widespread in this industry group.)

The slow progress of total productivity in the coal industry up to 1963 is not surprising, given the contraction imposed on it. The stagnation of

TABLE 7.5
Growth Rates of Total Productivity by Sector, 1951–69
(Percent per year)

Sector	1951–1957	1957–1963	1963–1969
02. Processed foods and farm products	1.8%	1.4%	2.7%
03. Solid mineral fuels and gas	0.7	1.4	3.7
04. Electricity, water, and miscellaneous	1.6	4.2	2.6
05. Petroleum and oil products	2.3	2.1	4.5
06. Building materials and glass	4.3	2.8	4.4
07. Iron mining and metallurgy	3.9	0.2	7.2
08. Nonferrous minerals and metals	4.9	2.9	4.7
09. Mechanical and electrical industries	2.7	2.6	3.1
10. Chemicals and rubber	4.3	3.5	4.5
11. Textiles, clothing, and leather	6.3	4.5	2.1
12. Wood, paper, and misc. industries	3.9	3.0	1.1
13. Building and public works	0.3	3.0	4.0
14. Transportation and communications[a]	4.1	2.7	1.9
16. Services other than housing	2.6	2.5	1.3
19. Trade	4.0	2.1	0.5

[a]In the transportation sector, capital "excluding infrastructure" has been used for the calculation of total productivity.

total productivity in iron mining and metallurgy between 1957 and 1963, and its rapid increase from 1963 to 1969, are due to the poor results achieved by that industry in 1963. Some industries often regarded as progressive show relatively low rates: petroleum and oil products, iron mining and metallurgy, the mechanical and electrical industries. This is because their fast growth in output was accompanied by a considerable increase in factor inputs.

From the first to the third cycle retardation in the rate of increase can be observed in transportation, trade, services, textiles and clothing, and the wood, paper, and miscellaneous industries. Their high rates of growth in productivity in the 1950's can be explained largely by the disappearance of craftsmen and small businesses with very low output. This "reserve," which helped to raise productivity, grew smaller thereafter. The other industries, on the contrary, show some quickening in the rate of increase of productivity. Despite the acceleration in capital accumulation, the movement observed earlier in relation to output per man-hour applies also in the case of total productivity.

A Production Function for Industry

We have applied a somewhat different approach to Industry as a whole, and have attempted to fit a production function directly to the labor, capital, and output series. Let us suppose for the purpose of this regression that factor q_t had grown at a constant rate. This gives a first form of the production function as

$$(6) \qquad\qquad Q_t = q_0 N_t{}^a K_t{}^{1-a} e^{\gamma t}$$

where e represents the natural logarithmic base. We have considered it necessary, however, to allow explicitly for varying intensity in the use of the factors of production in the various years. According to the pressure of demand, firms use manpower and capital to a greater or lesser extent on immediate production. To bring the effect of this element to bear, we have introduced as an index of the pressure of demand the ratio (referred to as u_t) between unsatisfied demand for employment and unfilled job vacancies. (This ratio is high when the pressure of demand is low.) We have therefore written the production function as

$$(7) \qquad\qquad Q_t = q_0 N_t{}^a K_t{}^{1-a} u_t{}^\delta e^{\gamma t}$$

This equation can be written in logarithmic form as

$$(8) \qquad \log \frac{Q_t}{N_t} = (1-a)\log \frac{K_t}{N_t} + \delta \log u_t + \gamma t + \log q_0$$

To determine $(1-a)$, δ, γ, and $\log q_0$, we have made a multiple regression of $\log Q_t/N_t$ on $\log K_t/N_t$, on $\log u_t$, and on t. Using a series applying to Industry as a whole for the years 1949 and 1963,[14] we have obtained the following result:

$$(9) \quad \log \frac{Q_t}{N_t} = \underset{(0.24)}{0.36} \ \log \frac{K_t}{N_t} - \underset{(0.010)}{0.018} \ \log u_t + \underset{(0.013)}{0.030} \ t - 0.014$$

(The symbol "log" refers to the natural logarithm with base e. The values Q_t, K_t, and N_t are expressed in index numbers with $1956 = 100$. Value t designates the date of the year in question *minus* 1956.) The results are rather imprecise, as can be seen from the standard errors shown in parentheses below each coefficient. Nevertheless, the resulting value of a, 0.64, is close to that calculated as the share of labor remuneration; the estimate of the growth rate γ of total productivity is 3.0 percent per year.

To see how much the growth of total productivity might have slowed down over the period 1949–69, we have calculated the annual residuals with respect to regression (9). The results are as follows (the figures represent the percent excess of actual output per man-hour over that which would have resulted from equation [9]):

---

[14] For 1963 the figures were provisional estimates that have since been substantially revised. However, this does not affect the conclusions reported.

1949	−1.8	1955	0.2	1960	1.8	1965	−0.3
1950	0.4	1956	1.9	1961	−0.1	1966	1.0
1951	1.0	1957	−0.2	1962	−0.6	1967	0.7
1952	−0.4	1958	0.0	1963	−1.5	1968	2.1
1953	−0.2	1959	0.2	1964	−1.0	1969	3.5
1954	−0.3						

It can be seen that the real growth of productivity in industry was much faster from 1949 to 1951 than over the period as a whole. The figures thereafter fluctuated around the trend, with especially favorable years in 1956 and 1960. The years 1962–64 were below trend, but this slow-down was not maintained. As far as we can judge, total productivity growth in fact accelerated markedly in the second half of the 1960's.[15]

QUALITY OF LABOR AND CAPITAL

Measures of total productivity that we have considered treat as equivalent two separate hours worked by the labor force on two different dates, or two separate units of capital used at two different periods, and embodying the same quantity of resources. In fact, the quality of labor supplied by the work force and the nature of capital equipment have changed substantially over time; this justifies a search for correcting factors to apply to the indexes of productivity.

Quality of Labor

The third part of Chapter 2 (p. 67) measures the quality of the labor force, setting forth the principles followed, which are compatible with those underlying the indexes of productivity. We shall recall here the conclusions reached.

Changes in structure of the labor force according to age and schooling have led to gradual improvement in the quality of work supplied. Age modifications of the structure played only a small part over the long term, but in the postwar period their influence cannot be ignored. The rise in level of education had an important effect both in the first third of the century (with the introduction of universal primary education) and after World War II (with the development of secondary and higher education). All in all, we estimated that the improvement in the

[15] The fact that the 1957–63 slowdown is less apparent in this adjusted calculation than in Table 7.5 is partly due to our having allowed here for the variable u_t, which was very low in 1963 and still more so in 1957, whereas in 1951 it was at an average level. The fast growth of total productivity from 1951 to 1957 can thus be explained partly as due to intensification in the use of factors of production. Such a conclusion, however, depends on indirect measure of the intensity of factor use, i.e. the ratio between the demand and supply of employment.

quality of labor was equivalent to an increase in the volume of work input averaging 0.45 percent per year, and was fairly regular in pace since the beginning of the century.

Calculations of total productivity can allow for correction in quality. The index N_t/N_0 measuring labor input needs to be amended in accordance with the results just mentioned. Its effect on total input depends on the exponent α, here taken as equal to 0.72 for the productive system as a whole. The index of total input must therefore be corrected upward by 0.32 per year. The index of total productivity must be corrected downward by the same amount. For the economy as a whole, the annual increase in productivity would thus change from 1.1 to 0.8 percent for the period 1913–49, and from 4.0 to 3.7 percent for 1949–69.

This correction concerns the productive quality of working persons. We can also investigate the comparative intensity and quality of the work supplied in one hour in two different periods by two persons of the same sex, age, and level of education. The concept of intensity of work cannot of course be measured. Some specialists in growth studies, however, have pointed out that for long-term comparisons it must be remembered that a reduction in the time spent at work almost certainly has led to an increase in productivity in each hour worked (with lower fatigue reducing the number of mistakes, a self-generated intensification of effort and attention, shorter rest time, etc.). We have already mentioned this point at the beginning of Chapter 3, where we considered two ways of measuring labor productivity: output per man-year and output per man-hour. We shall discuss the point again here from a different position.

We should note, however, that it has no practical importance in studying the postwar period, since the length of time spent at work remained practically unchanged, with the slight increase in hours worked compensating for longer vacations. The matter is relevant only for the earlier periods. Denison, who has studied the matter exhaustively, recognizes that a precise measurement of this phenomenon is subejct to uncertainty.[16] He assumes, however, that when more than 48 hours a week are worked on the average, a small reduction in time worked is entirely compensated by an increase in hourly productivity. At 40 hours per week, a small reduction is compensated only to the extent of 40 percent. If we follow this rule, we must deduce that from 1913 to 1949 most of the reduction in time worked was compensated for by an increase in hourly productivity. The average work week fell from 53 to 43 hours, a drop of 19 percent. But simultaneously the quality of each hour

[16] *Why Growth Rates Differ*, pp. 59–62.

worked would have risen by about 17 percent simply as a result of the shortened work day.

As an average annual rate, the quality of each hour worked would therefore have increased by 0.51 percent. The necessary correction to the growth rate of total productivity from 1913 to 1949 would be 0.37 percent, bringing it to 0.4 percent. For the period 1949–69 the growth rate would be corrected from 3.7 percent to 3.6 percent per year: time worked fell by 3 percent, but according to Denison's law, up to 70 percent of this was compensated by an increase in hourly productivity. The correction required to total input is thus $3 \times 0.7 \times 0.72 = 1.5$ percent over this 20-year period.

Measuring the Effect of the Shortening Age of Capital

Can we also allow for the quality of capital? This is a difficult matter, but we shall make the attempt. The estimates of capital in Chapter 5 for France and other countries are based on investment series. They therefore measure the volume of resources embodied in capital. But because of technological progress capital equipment can be manufactured that is capable of ever greater productivity. The later the investment, the higher the technological efficiency of a given volume of resources invested in capital. This phenomenon is referred to as the "embodiment" of technological progress in investments.

Our estimates, shown above, treat as equivalent a piece of equipment built in 1925 and another built in 1955, both costing one billion francs at 1956 prices. Nevertheless, the first uses 1925 technology, whereas the second uses the presumably more effective technology of 1955. We have of course allowed for amortization in calculating net capital assets, but this relates to physical aging. It is therefore unlikely that variations in net capital correctly measure changes in the technical efficiency of capital equipment.

To this purely technological aspect should be added the fact that old equipment is often no longer suitable for the conditions of present-day production. It is not situated in the most suitable places. It was not designed to use the raw materials now found most profitable or to manufacture the products with the highest present demand. All these factors, which are particularly important when economic progress is fast, help to create what is commonly called the obsolescence of capital equipment. It is especially important to consider this aspect, since France ended the war with old and in many cases outdated capital equipment, and its renewal or replacement (*rajeunissement*) has undoubtedly been one of the factors explaining productivity growth. To allow for this factor, we have followed a method suggested by Solow and studied by various researchers.[17] We have assumed that the manufacture of productive equipment is subject to technological progress growing at a constant rate γ, so that a piece of equipment costing one billion 1956 francs and built in year t has the same productivity as one costing $(1 + \gamma)^{t-\theta}$ billion 1956 francs in year θ. On this hypothesis we have established a new capital series intended to measure the productive value of capital against the volume of invested resources. Then from this new series we have made new estimates of total productivity.

Our knowledge of the likely rate of technological progress incorporated in capital assets is limited. Our estimates therefore cannot aim at any real precision, but rather must attempt to define an order of magnitude of the effect of capital renewal—an effect difficult to appreciate beforehand. We have distinguished two kinds of assets—buildings and infrastructure, where incorporated technological progress must have been slow; and equipment, where progress must have been rapid. We have assumed that, if used with a constant quantity of labor, the former would have yielded an output rising about 0.3 percent per year according to the year of construction. In like manner, we have assumed that, if used in similar circumstances, the latter would have yielded output growing at about 1.3 percent per year according to the year of manufacture.

The method followed and the detailed calculations are shown in Appendix E. Table 7.6 shows that the effect of capital rejuvenation has been considerable and is apparently increasing. The latter feature was the result of redirection of investment, which after 1953 grew faster in implements and light equipment than in infrastructure and heavy equipment.

The estimates for 1951, 1956, 1961, and 1966 lead to an interesting conclusion: because of the acceleration of capital renewal and the increased importance of equipment in capital as a whole, the direct and indirect effects of the technological progress embodied in capital assets account for an increasing proportion of the growth of output. Contrary to what we stated earlier, this would suggest a slight slowing down in the growth rate of the residual factor that measures total productivity.

For long-term comparisons, we assume that the age structure of capi-

[17] See in particular R. M. Solow, "Investment and Technical Progress," in K. Arrow, S. Karlin, and P. Suppes, eds., *Mathematical Methods in the Social Sciences, 1959* (Stanford, Calif., 1960); R. M. Solow, "Technical Progress, Capital Formation and Economic Growth," *American Economic Review*, May 1962; O. Dumas, "Progrès technique et fonction de production macroéconomique," *Bulletin du CEPREL* (Paris), no. 1, December 1963.

TABLE 7.6
Various Calculations of Increases in Total Productivity and the
Effect of Capital Renewal, 1951–66
(Percent per year)

Category	1951–56	1956–61	1961–66
1. Net Capital	2.3%	3.4%	4.4%
2. Corresponding total productivity	4.0	4.0	4.0
3. Gross capital, cost of construction basis	2.2	2.8	3.9
4. Corresponding total productivity	4.1	4.2	4.2
5. Gross capital, technical efficiency basis	4.7	6.0	7.6
6. Corresponding total productivity	3.4	3.3	3.1
Some Explanatory Factors of the Growth of Production			
7. Effect of growth of gross capital	0.6	0.8	1.1
8. Direct effect of embodied technical progress	0.5	0.6	0.7
9. Effect of capital renewal (calculated as line 4 minus lines [6+8])	0.2	0.3	0.4

tal in 1963 was approximately the same as in 1913. This is not unbelievable, since each of these years came at the end of an investment boom that had followed a long stagnation. The effect of capital renewal will therefore be nil for 1963 in relation to 1913, and negative (−0.1 percent per year) for 1949 in relation to 1913 (i.e. representing an aging of capital).

Time Required Between Building and Utilization;
Amortization; Shift Work

It is perhaps pertinent to give attention to another feature in capital accumulation since World War II. The series in Chapter 4 have shown that heavy investments were relatively far higher in the early postwar years than later. This can affect the results of our calculations in two ways.

First, we have assumed that investment in a given year becomes a productive asset the following year. This hypothesis is not correct for large investments, which may require many years before they can be put to use. Since the proportion of heavy investment has fallen, the average time between construction and use of assets must have decreased. Up to this point we have ignored this factor. To assess its importance, we have carried out an approximate calculation starting from the hypothesis that the average lapse of time before coming into service is six months for light investment and two years for heavy investment. The results suggest that the growth of capital actually in use was little different from the growth of net capital after 1952: some 0.2 percent per year higher between 1952 and 1954, 0.2 percent lower between 1955 and 1962, and almost identical from 1962 to 1966. These differences are too low to significantly affect movements in total productivity or the conclusions we have drawn. From 1949 to 1952, on the contrary, the growth of capital in use exceeded that of net capital by about 0.6 percent per year, and the growth of total productivity shown in Table 7.1 should be reduced by about 0.2 percent per year. This would account for a small part of the fast rate of productivity growth we reported earlier for the immediate postwar period.

The second point is that heavy investment generally has a longer life than light investment. For at an equal net marginal productivity, it has a lower gross marginal productivity.[18] In other words, the increase in gross output that it allows each year is lower. To allow for this properly, we should have taken net productivity as a reference point in our calculations, but this would have entailed a precise analysis of amortization, for which insufficient data are available. For this reason we merely suggest the direction in which the influence of this factor was exerted.

Because of the predominance of heavy investment in the early postwar period, the rate of amortization in industry must have dropped, if we assume that it was based on a fixed life assumption for each type of equipment. Conversely, the predominance of light investment in recent years must have led to an increase in the country's overall amortization rate. In these circumstances an apparently steady growth in gross output over the whole period would be consistent with a faster rise in net output in the earlier years and a slower rise thereafter. If we had studied net output, we would therefore have observed a slowing down in the growth of productivity, although doubtless on a very small scale.

To the above special points we should probably add the fact that in recent years capital equipment has been more intensively used as a result of the spread of shift work. According to surveys by the Ministry of Labor, the proportion of establishments with over ten employees that applied shift work rose from 6 percent in January 1957 to 9 percent in April 1959 and to 11 percent in July 1963. The proportion of the industrial work force as a whole engaged in shift work increased from 16.5 percent in 1959 to 21.4 percent in 1963.[19] In textiles, where shift work today covers half the labor force, industry statistics trace developments since 1954. Since that year, the increase in the practice was continuous, apart from a slight slowdown in 1958. It has been estimated that the

[18] Without drawing any exact conclusions, we shall see later (p. 198) that even net marginal productivity is probably lower for heavy than for light investment.
[19] See *Revue française du travail*, April–June, 1965, pp. 87–93.

spread of shift work had the same effect in the wool and cotton industries as if capital had grown between 1954 and 1958 by 15 and 11 percent, respectively.[20] Between 1958 and 1962 the corresponding figures
would have been 20 and 10 percent. In brief, we see that taking
into account the quality of capital and its intensity of use points to a
slight slowing down, on four different counts, in the growth of total
residual productivity in the later postwar years.

EFFECTS OF INTERSECTOR TRANSFERS

Problems Involved

Chapters 2 and 6 mentioned large movements of the working population from one sector to another. It is tempting to attribute to this
phenomenon some of the progress registered by the indexes of overall
productivity, since these movements were from low-productivity to
high-productivity occupations. By increasing the size of the latter, these
job movements almost automatically raised national productivity.

Nevertheless we should examine the matter more closely before attempting to measure the incidence of these movements. High-productivity occupations demand the highest labor qualifications and capital
equipment. Migrations of workers between sectors were therefore accompanied by developments in investment and improvements in quality of the labor force already dealt with. If the differences in productivity were entirely explained by differences in the scale of capital
equipment or in employees' qualifications, the movement of a given
worker from one type of work to another would in itself imply no increase in overall production. We conclude, therefore, that job migration
has an effect of its own in cases where the marginal productivity of
labor of a given quality is not the same in two types of work. The
movement of a worker of a given quality from a job where his marginal productivity is low to one where it is higher has a positive effect
on overall production.

A similar phenomenon can arise in movements of capital. If it were
found that marginal capital productivity was particularly high in sectors with fast growth, then some of the rise in national output could be
explained by differences in rates of capital increase in various sectors.

We have studied this question more closely with the help of a formal
model in order to grasp fully the calculations required to measure the
effects of these types of transfer. This model is described in Appendix F.
It takes the case of two economic sectors, and assumes that the margi-

[20] Calculations are based on an unpublished study, "Les Conditions de la production textile en France de 1949 à 1963," INSEE.

nal productivity of capital is the same in each but that the marginal
productivity of labor is a times greater in the first than in the second.
The model then evaluates the variation ΔR in total productivity R resulting from variation ΔN_1, and ΔN_2 in the quantities of labor employed in the two sectors. It leads to the formula

$$(10) \qquad \frac{\Delta R}{R} = \alpha \left[\frac{a\Delta N_1 + \Delta N_2}{aN_1 + N_2} - \frac{\Delta N_1 + \Delta N_2}{N_1 + N_2} \right]$$

where α is the coefficient representing labor's share used in the calculation of total productivity (see formula (3), p. 180).

To calculate the influence of transfers of the working population between sectors, we must first measure the differences between the marginal outputs of labor in each use (that is, we must determine coefficients such as a). On this basis, we shall calculate two indexes of variation of work put out in the economy. One index, corresponding to the
second term in brackets of formula (10), is the usual index. The other,
corresponding to the first term, is a corrected index, which weights the
quantity of work supplied in each activity by its marginal productivity.
The effect of transfers between sectors is then equal to the difference
between these two indexes multiplied by α.

Marginal Productivities and Rates of Sector Remuneration

We must therefore first obtain a broad picture of the differences in
marginal productivity of labor as between industry groups and types of
occupation. Similar information will be sought about capital. To this
end we shall begin by examining differences between the rates of remuneration of each factor in the different activities. We shall then inquire whether these reflect differences in marginal productivity.

Table 7.7, drawn up on the basis of the estimates in the section on
results of productivity by industry group (p. 185), shows average rates
of remuneration of labor and capital in each industry in 1956. Its accuracy is rather poor, since the figures were obtained by bringing together
results from widely different sources, themselves in some cases not very
accurate. These results include an analysis of value added by sectors
converted to an industry-group basis, a breakdown of the working population, and an estimate of capital assets by industry groups. However,
we shall examine in turn the results pertaining to each of the two kinds
of income.[21]

[21] A study of the same topics for 1962 has been the occasion of considerable statistical research; see J. Mairesse, *L'Evaluation du capital fixe productif; méthode et
résultat* (Collections de l'INSEE, série C, no. 18–19, comptes et planification; Paris,
1972).

TABLE 7.7

Earnings of Labor and Capital by Sector, 1956 and 1962

Sector	Return on labor[a]	Length of time worked[b]	Weight given to Women[c]	Weight given to Management[d]	Return on capital[e]
Agriculture and forestry	3.2		33%		7
Processed foods and farm products	10.7	100	32	10%	24
Solid mineral fuels and gas	9.5	103	4		3
Electricity and water	12.2	105	16		5
Petroleum and oil products	14.1	103	16	24	29
Building materials and glass	6.5	102	17	7	18
Metallurgy	7.9	107	9	8	8
Mechanical and electrical industries	7.9	103	21	14	16
Chemicals and rubber	8.7	99	30	14	17
Textiles, clothing, and leather	4.9	93	68	6	13
Wood, paper, and misc. industries	5.9	99	31	10	16
Building and public works	5.8	107	4	7	25
Transportation and communications[f]	9.2	104	20		3
Services other than housing	6.2	95	55	27	25
Trade	6.7	96	45	15	21

[a] Thousand new francs per member of the labor force in 1956 (including both direct and indirect return).
[b] Index base, all industrial and commercial sectors, 1956 = 100 (from 3-month surveys by the Ministry of Labor).
[c] Proportion of women in the total labor force in 1962.
[d] Proportion of top and middle managers in the wage-earning labor force in 1962.
[e] Percentage ratio between net capital return (after taxes) and estimate of total value of net fixed capital assets and stocks, 1956.
[f] For this sector, return on capital has been related to productive assets only (excluding infrastructure).

The rates of return on labor, calculated as the average annual remuneration per member of the labor force in 1956, cover a fairly wide range, exceeding a ratio of 1 : 4 between the extreme industry groups. If agriculture, on the one hand, and industries with a low work force, on the other, are omitted, this still leaves a range of 5,000 to 10,000 francs per worker.[22] These divergences, however, are at least partly the result of differences between industries in the length and average quality of work. As a check, we have included three other complementary indicators in Table 7.7. The first relates to length of time worked, and is based on the Ministry of Labor surveys; it covers official weekly hours of work in establishments of over ten employees. It does not therefore allow for differences between industries arising from absenteeism or vacations, or from the length of time worked in small establishments. The second indicator shows the proportion of female workers in the labor force of the various industries at the 1962 census. The third index

[22] More reliable figures for the year 1962 (Mairesse, *ibid.*) show a narrower dispersion of the rates of return on labor. The rates for petroleum and electricity are relatively far lower. That for processed foods and food products is closer to the average, and therefore below the figure for mechanical and electrical industries. In the other industries the ranking of the results is not greatly affected.

gives the proportion of top and middle management to all employees at the 1962 census.

Apart from the important case of agriculture, most of the differences observed between the annual rates of labor remuneration can be explained fairly satisfactorily. Let us compare, for example, textiles, clothing, and leather with mechanical and electrical industries. In the former the rate of remuneration was low, 4.9, and in the latter fairly high, 7.9. Part of the difference seems due to differences in length of time worked. If hourly earnings in the textile industries had remained unchanged but the length of time worked had been raised to that of the mechanical industries, the annual rate in textiles would have risen by 10 percent, to 5.4. Another part of the difference can be explained by the size of the female work force. If the average rate of female remuneration is 80 percent of the male rate, the average rate of remuneration in the textile industries has to be increased by 11 percent, to 6.0, in order to eliminate that portion of the differential compared with the mechanical industries that is due to the sex distribution of the work force. The remaining difference then is that between 6.0 and 7.9. Now the average level of qualifications is far higher in the mechanical than the textile industries, as shown by the fact that management accounts for 14 percent of the work force in the former and for only 6 percent in the latter. We have not carried out detailed calculations to allow for this, but it is fairly clear that, if allowance is made for differences in labor quality, the residual difference is no longer of much consequence.

When these three causes of divergence are taken into consideration, most of the differences between rates of pay for labor in nonagricultural industries can be accounted for. It is difficult to say whether substantial and consistent differences remain between the marginal labor productivities of the various industries. It can be assumed, however, that, except in shops and small businesses, firms are sufficiently intent on profit to employ workers to the point where marginal productivity would fall below the rate of return. Ignoring for the moment the case of workers in small businesses and shops, we assume that labor movements among nonagricultural industries have not of themselves led to a growth in overall output.

Before looking in greater detail at agriculture, let us examine the rates of return on capital. These are shown in the last column of Table 7.7, which gives the ratio between the excess of net value added at factor cost over labor remuneration and net total capital assets (including stocks). It cannot be stressed too much that these estimates have a low statistical value, since they are the result of comparison between two poorly documented figures. In addition, the gap between net value added and labor return, here labeled "return on capital," can differ from the marginal productivity of capital by reason of rents and monopoly profits, which we have no means of measuring. The first impression given by a reading of the last column of Table 7.7 is of a wide dispersion. Nevertheless, we can immediately distinguish two categories in the nonagricultural industry groups:[23] basic industries under government control enjoying a large measure of official financing, and all other industries. In the industries not under government control, the rate of return on capital ranged from 13 to 25 percent. Classifying the industries by rate of return reveals no clear pattern, and we therefore find no reason to abandon the convenient hypothesis of equal marginal productivity of capital in them.

The rate of return on capital is very low in government-controlled industries, but, as we have mentioned, it is a poor index of marginal capital productivity. More often than not, the government fixes both product prices and size of investment for these industries. The investments are financed by funds obtained at rates generally below the market. Finally, in some of these industries the profit on production rises markedly with the volume of output. For all these reasons, the marginal productivity of capital differs from its rate of return. We do not have direct estimates of this marginal productivity for our calculations.[24] In the absence of objective data, we shall extend to all industry groups the hypothesis that the marginal productivity of capital is identical in every case.

Effects of Migration of Farm Workers

Let us now look at the case of agriculture, which we had temporarily excluded but which deserves special attention because of the large-scale exodus of workers. We shall consider first its marginal productivity of labor. We must evaluate the size of the average difference between the marginal productivities of the work of a given job-migrant in two jobs, one in agriculture and one not. Before making an estimate, however, we shall consider two possible methods of approach for assess-

[23] We shall omit petroleum and oil products, where the rate of return on capital in 1956 was exceptional. According to the accounting methods used, gross output in that sector in 1956 was much higher than in the years on either side of it.

[24] Data from investment appraisals for projects in the public sector suggest that the marginal return in different industries lies between 8 and 15 percent. This result, however, cannot be compared with rates of return in the other industries, since there is no empirical study measuring the gap between rates of return on capital and rates of marginal return on investment.

ing the difference betwen the worker's two rates of pay in these jobs. We shall then investigate any differences between these remunerations and the marginal productivities of the man's work in each case.

The first approach in establishing the rates of pay, in essence a macroeconomic one, is to take for the farming job the labor remuneration figure for farming as a whole (3,200 francs a year) and for the nonfarming job to make certain corrections to the average for nonfarming sectors (7,100 francs). These corrections make allowance for the lower quality of job-migrants' labor compared with the average.

In order to determine the correction factor, we can start from the assumption that workers transferring from agriculture to other sectors have the same characteristics as those staying in agriculture. Making use of scales shown in Chapter 2 on age and sex structure (pp. 70–72), we observe that the differences in age and sex structure between the farming and nonfarming populations do not seem to imply a significant difference in the quality of labor.[25] On the other hand, the fact that the agricultural population has on the average a lower level of education than other sectors in France points to a substantial gap in the quality of labor. If the scales shown in Chapter 2 on educational standards (p. 73) are applied to the 1954 census figures, they suggest a ratio of 0.92 between the farming and nonfarming working population to take account of the effect of schooling on labor quality.[26]

We can also examine the results of the recent INSEE survey on job qualification and employment. For a presentation of the main results of this survey, see "Une Enquête sur la formation et la qualification des Français," Etudes et conjoncture, February 1967. A breakdown of its results segregates persons working outside agriculture in January 1964 but within it in January 1959. Although the number involved is low (a little under 500), it is sufficient to establish the approximate order of the differences we are concerned with here. Three-quarters of these migrants were under the age of 30 in 1964. We shall compare them with the remainder of workers aged 20–29, since that group contains the great majority of migrants between jobs.

It can be observed that very few migrants in the 20–29 age-group had extended their schooling beyond the minimum legal age of 14 years.

[25] Exact calculation shows a ratio of 99 percent for the farm labor force compared with the total labor force. Differences in the proportion of women and old people are offset by an opposite difference in the proportion of young workers.

[26] In fact, it can be maintained, not without reason, that 0.92 is too high a ratio, since the quality of schooling is lower in rural than in urban schools. One teacher in the country frequently must teach children of widely varying ages, with the result that each child's pace of work is less even.

Their average school-leaving age was in fact 14.2 years, almost identical with the average for the whole farming population in that age-group.[27] Yet in the working population as a whole in that age-group, average school-leaving age was 15.7 years. On the basis of schooling received, therefore, former farm workers are among the least well-qualified group of workers, apart of course from illiterate or barely educated foreign immigrants. Applying the scales relating quality of labor to schooling received gives a ratio of about 0.85 to describe the average quality of labor of a migrant from farming aged under 30 in relation to the non-farming worker of the same age.

A more direct measure can be obtained of the divergence between the earnings of migrants in nonfarm work and the average for that work. It is sufficient to compare the average wages of former farm workers and those of all employees. For the 20–29 age-group, the ratio is 0.73, and it would be lower for higher age-groups. It can be objected that some of the migrants had only recently started nonfarm employment and that their wages were below average for that reason. All in all, it would seem that, on the basis of this type of data, a ratio of 3 : 4 can be accepted as a fair measure of the proportionate remuneration in non-farm work of workers originating, respectively, in agriculture and in nonagriculture.

The three comparisons above led in turn to ratios that are not widely separated: 0.92, 0.85, and 0.75. The two extreme figures, if applied to the estimate of 7,100 francs, suggest 6,500 and 5,300 francs, respectively, as the average remuneration of a migrant going from agriculture into nonfarming work. His remuneration in farming (3,200 francs) would have represented, respectively, 49 and 60 percent of these figures.

These results can be compared with those obtained by a microeconomic approach based on direct observation of a number of significant local situations.[28] Farm earnings (including payments in kind and own produce consumed) were compared with earnings in certain unskilled jobs particularly available to Breton farm workers. The ratios of the former to the latter were as follows: 64–76 percent for moves into building, 80 percent for moves to automobile factory work, and 80 percent for moves to a pork products factory. The true ratio, however, must be

[27] This agreement lends some justification to the hypothesis in the macroeconomic approach, according to which the average remuneration of migrant farm workers was the same as that of nonmigrants.

[28] We owe the results quoted here to the kindness of P. Daucé and G. Jégouzo of the Ecole Nationale Supérieure Agronomique at Rennes. Some of the results were submitted in "Les Disparités régionales de la mobilité professionnelle des agriculteurs," thesis, Rennes, December 1968.

lower: some migrants from agriculture who were not wage earners had earnings below the figure considered; some migrants acquired a level of qualification higher after their move than that assumed in the example; some migrants left their home area to work in cities where earnings were higher (particularly in the Paris region).

Taking account of all these factors, *it would seem that a figure of some 60 percent is a fair assessment of the average proportion between the two rates of remuneration obtained by a job migrant before and after migration* (the rate of remuneration in farming divided by the rate in nonfarm employment). Does this proportion correctly measure the divergence between the marginal productivities of labor in the two different employments? We assumed earlier that the desire for profit was sufficiently high in firms to equate labor's rate of remuneration broadly with its marginal productivity. But such an explanation can hardly be applied to the work of small business entrepreneurs who employ few or no wage earners. Since they are self-employed, these persons do not refer to wage rates when deciding what amount of work they will themselves put forth. In many cases they may decide to contribute any work that may increase output, by however little. Their marginal labor productivity may then fall well below their average rate of remuneration.

This comment applies particularly to farming, a sector in which owners and their family helpers represent the great majority of workers. Studies in other countries seem indeed to have established that marginal labor productivity in agriculture is below agricultural earnings.[29] Since job migrants nearly always take employment in firms where remuneration and productivity are likely to be equal, their productivity growth must often be significantly higher than the increase in their remuneration.

We must therefore correct the ratio of 60 percent found earlier. To do this would require correct determination of the average divergence between productivity and rates of remuneration in the migrants' original farming occupations. However, we do not have any reliable basis for determining this. On the one hand, we might take into account the low physical output of many of the small holdings that the migrants had left.

---

[29] See, for example, the findings for American and Swedish farms in I. Hoch, "Estimation of Production Function Parameters Combining Time-Series and Cross-Section Data," *Econometrica*, January 1962; and L. Hjelm and E. Sandqvist, "Productivity Studies in Swedish Agriculture," in H. Wold, ed., *Econometric Model Building* (Amsterdam, 1964).

Since seasonal work peaks are no longer very sharp in mixed farming and cattle-breeding, the departure of farm workers would in many cases be compensated for almost entirely by a low incremental effort of those remaining. On the other hand, evidence is not lacking of land left to waste, extensive cultivation replacing more intensive farming, shortages of manpower, etc.

Since we do not have objective data, we shall make two estimates using divergences of 50 percent and 25 percent, respectively, between the marginal productivity and the remuneration of labor in agriculture. The average proportion between the marginal productivities of a job-migrant will thus become, respectively, 30 percent and 45 percent (productivity in farm labor divided by productivity in nonfarm labor). This proportion is the value of a in equation (10), with industry group 1 representing farming and industry group 2 representing the remainder of the productive system.

If we now consider the rate of remuneration of capital in farming, we see from Table 7.7 that it is substantially lower than in the other industries not under government control. Yet our rate is probably over-estimated, since the denominator comprises only reproducible capital excluding land. Since there is no reason to believe that the marginal productivity of capital in farming exceeds its rate of remuneration, we must conclude that this marginal productivity is probably lower there than in other industries. However, we shall not allow for this difference. It would be very difficult to measure and it can have only a minimal effect on calculations of total productivity between 1949 and 1969, since in the post–World War II period reproducible capital in agriculture grew broadly at the same rate as in other industries. (Equation (10) indeed shows that the correction cancels out when the quantities of factors N_1 and N_2, employed respectively in the two sectors, grow at a common rate.) This has probably not been true over the long term. The estimates in Chapter 5 show figures of capital assets in farming little higher in 1954 than in 1913, whereas other capital assets almost doubled. But to calculate figures for a comparison between 1913 and 1963 would be so conjectural that we prefer merely to draw attention to the phenomenon and allow for it very roughly at the end of our calculations.

After this long analysis, we can now measure the effect of migrations of farm workers on the rate of growth of total productivity. For this, we need only go back to equation (10), using two figures for coefficient a: a high assumption of 45 percent and a low assumption of 30 percent.

TABLE 7.8

Corrections for the Index of Total Productivity Resulting from Labor Movements Out of Agriculture, 1963

Category	1949 = 100	1913 = 100
Work force of the productive economy (index numbers)	98.0	92.3
Corrected work force (index numbers):		
High assumption	105.3	105.4
Low assumption	108.0	110.6
Correction to work force and labor input (percent):		
High assumption	7.4%	14.2%
Low assumption	10.2%	19.8%
Correction to total productivity (percent):		
Entire period, high assumption	−5.3%	−10.2%
Entire period, low assumption	−7.3%	−14.2%
Annual rate, high assumption	−0.39%	−0.22%
Annual rate, low assumption	−0.54%	−0.31%

We have already mentioned some objective justifications of these assumptions based on study of the recent past, and for want of a better, we shall apply them also to the long term (for 1963 compared with 1913).

The main elements of the calculation are shown in Table 7.8. If every worker in farming counts as 0.45 or 0.30 according to the assumption adopted, the work force corrected on this basis ($aN_1 + N_2$ in equation (10); see p. 197) increases, whereas the gross work force ($N_1 + N_2 = N$) decreases. For the 14 years 1949–63 the correction is 7 percent for the high assumption and 10 percent for the low assumption. Although calculated for the work force, this correction applies just as well to employment. Since coefficient a, the elasticity of production to labor input, has been taken as 0.72, the effect on total productivity is 5.3 percent or 7.3 percent, according to the assumption adopted, or a yearly average rate of 0.34 percent or 0.5 percent. An analogous calculation for the period 1913–63 gives 0.22 percent or 0.31 percent per year.

We should note, moreover, that in the postwar period the effect studied here seems at first to have accelerated and then to have slowed down in recent years. On the basis of our estimates for 1949 and the figures for the 1954, 1962, and 1968 census years, our measure of this effect is as follows, on the low assumption, where $a = 0.30$: 0.39 percent yearly from 1949 to 1954, 0.58 percent from 1954 to 1962, and 0.55 percent from 1962 to 1968. Although the rate of migration from farming was higher in the last period than in the previous one, it applied to a lower agricultural population.

Other Factor Movements

We have calculated an adjustment coefficient to allow for increases in total productivity arising "automatically" from the fact that rates of change in the growth of the low-productivity farming population were different from those of the total labor force. This correction is substantial. We must therefore ask whether other job migrations may have played an analogous role.

We concluded in the section on quality of labor and capital (see p. 198) that movements affecting the breakdown of the labor force by nonfarming industry groups must have had only weak effects, since differences between rates of remuneration can be explained mainly by differences in the quality of manpower. Nevertheless, we excepted the case of self-employed workers and artisans, small businessmen, and their family helpers, for whom average rates of remuneration are a poor measure of marginal productivity. The example of farming suggests that we should briefly reexamine this category.

The number of workers in the social employment categories of artisan, self-employed fisherman, and small businessman fell by 240,000 between 1954 and 1962, and by 120,000 between 1962 and 1968. To gauge the effect that this movement toward more productive jobs may have had, we have made a calculation similar to that in the preceding section. We assumed tentatively that the marginal productivity of work doubles upon movement from one job sector to another ($a = 0.50$). The effect is in the area of 0.07 percent per year in 1954–62 and 0.04 percent in 1962–68 (the calculation was carried out with labor force figures already corrected for differences in productivity between farming and the other industry groups).

Over the long term, for example from 1913 to 1963, a similar effect probably existed. Although the number of small businessmen was about the same in the first and last of these years, the relative number of wage earners rose, and the work force in trade and services also increased. But the number of self-employed artisans fell sharply by about 1.5 million. If the same basis for calculation is followed as in the previous paragraph, the migration effect would be on the average about 0.1 percent per year. This figure is of course very uncertain, given the numerous assumptions that would have to be stipulated to justify it.

To conclude this study of the influence that intersector transfers may have had on aggregative productivity, we present an overall result of 0.3 to 0.4 percent per year on the average from 1913 to 1963 and 0.5 to 0.7 percent since World War II. This influence has tended to increase in the 1950's and to decrease slightly thereafter.

THE RESIDUAL AND TECHNOLOGICAL PROGRESS

The Residual

At this point we can bring together the numerical results reached so far of the effect of various factors on the growth of output. Table 7.9 groups six components previously identified, a new component denoting "intensity of demand" whose method of calculation we shall indicate in Chapter 8, and a residual obtained by difference (the new component takes account of variations in the term u_t shown in the production function; see p. 189). Four of the components concern labor and two concern capital. The table shows, first, average rates of increase between 1951 and 1969, the most characteristic period of French expansion since World War II, and then those between 1913 and 1963, which would seem to provide the best indication of long-term trends. (If it is granted that the ground lost because of the depression and the war was made up before 1963, as seems logical, the comparison betwen 1951–69 and 1913–63 somewhat underestimates the differences between the postwar period and the long-term trends. The period 1951–69 is divided into three subperiods corresponding to the postwar "cycles" (the calculations were made to two decimal places, then rounded).

It is unnecessary to stress the somewhat arbitrary character of some of these estimates. Thus, for migrations between industries, we have shown a midpoint estimate between those for the two hypotheses, high and low, defined in the previous section. For postwar capital renewal, we had to start from an assumption on the rate of embodied technological progress. For the long-term reduction of time at work, we have used a doubtful measure of the offset arising from the intensification of work. In other words, the accuracy of the residual is low.

Over the long term it can be seen that factors relating to labor had contradictory effects. The increase in education and of labor migrations nevertheless proved stronger than the fall in employment; according to our assumptions, the reduction of time at work had but very slight influence. In the last 20 years, although labor input remained almost constant, improvement in the quality of labor and of its occupational makeup contributed substantially to the rate of growth of output.

The quantitative increase in productive capital seems to explain

TABLE 7.9

Contributions of Sources to the Growth of French Production, 1951–69

(Percent per year)

Component	Period 1951–69	Subperiods			Long-term period 1913–63
		1951–57	1957–63	1963–69	
Gross domestic production	5.0%	4.7%	5.1%	5.1%	2.1%
Employment in the productive economy (man-years)	–	–0.2	–	0.3	–0.1
Length of time worked	–0.1	–	–	–0.3	–0.3
Quality of labor (age, education, and intensity of work)	0.4	0.4	0.4	0.5	0.6
Labor migrations between sectors	0.6	0.5	0.6	0.5	0.3
Volume of net capital	1.1	0.8	1.1	1.3	0.5
Fall in age of capital assets	0.4	0.3	0.4	0.4	–
Intensity of demand	0.1	0.3	–0.1	0.1	–
Residual	2.5	2.6	2.7	2.3	1.1

slightly less than one-quarter of this rate between 1913 and 1963, and slightly over one-fifth between 1951 and 1963. But the effect of the drop in the age of capital was a substantial additional factor after the war. The residual has accordingly amounted to about 1 percent per year over the long term, but 2.5 percent since 1951. This magnitude should not be surprising. We have allowed only in part for several important growth factors, which should be included in any complete analysis on the lines of the one we have attempted. We shall examine some of these factors below, without, however, trying to measure their effects.

First we shall compare our results with those of Denison, whose estimate of the residual is patently far lower. Complete correlation of figures is of course impossible. In the book he edited with the help of J. P. Poullier, Denison examines postwar growth in nine Western countries including France.[30] But, for one thing, his calculations refer to the period 1950–62, whereas our Table 7.9 refers to 1951–69. For another thing, he analyzes aggregates of production, working population, and capital that cover not only the "productive economy" but also the remaining activities that enter into gross national product (services of domestic servants, financial institutions, and government). However, the orders of magnitude are not affected by these differences.

A detailed comparison reveals two significant discrepancies between the two sets of estimates. It shows also that Denison has estimated the effect of certain factors, in particular economies of scale, which we have

[30] *Why Growth Rates Differ.*

not felt able to measure. The first discrepancy concerns the fall in the age of capital assets, to which Denison ascribes no role.[31] We believe he has failed to recognize the obsolescent state in which French productive capital stood after the war, and even as late as 1955 before the "light investment" boom began. The estimates we have presented of the reduction in age of assets are very uncertain, but they show a sufficiently strong trend to reflect a real phenomenon.

The second difference concerns the effect of changes in the occupational structure of the labor force, which Denison assesses at 0.9 percent per year, on the average, whereas we have used 0.6 percent. The discrepancy arises partly from a difference in methods of calculation[32] and partly from his higher estimate of gains in productivity due to each labor migration. Thus the departure of a farm worker is regarded as reducing agricultural production by only a quarter of the average output per farm worker, whereas it increases the output of other industries by an amount equal to 80 percent of output per worker in those industries. Our hypotheses are not framed in that way, but they imply approximately—for that example—a fall in agriculture not of one-quarter but of 45 percent of output per farm worker, and an increase elsewhere not of 80 percent but of 60 percent of output per worker in the other industries.[33]

These two differences offset each other exactly. The reason Denison's residual is lower than ours (apart from some details of presentation) is that he attributes an important role to economies of scale (1.0 percent per year in all). We shall therefore consider briefly the part they may have played. First, however, let us notice that if we roughly modify Denison's results[34] to produce estimates comparable with those in Table 7.9, we obtain residuals for 1955–62 of 2.7 percent per year for France, 2.2 percent for Germany, 1.3 percent for Britain, 1.0 percent for the United States, and 2.9 percent for Italy.

And last, Table 7.9 shows a slowing down of the growth of residual productivity over the 1960's. This slowing down is sharper than in the case of total productivity (from 2.7 to 2.3 percent per year instead of

[31] See his comments, *ibid.*, pp. 144–50.

[32] Denison makes use, in an apparently reasonable way, of the differences between certain proportions observed at the various dates, but he has not shown a model fully justifying his calculation, as we have tried to do on p. 197. By comparison with ours, his calculation seems to exhibit a bias toward rather high estimates.

[33] Readers wishing to have a more precise view of the differences between the two calculations may compare our section on p. 201 with Denison's pp. 209–16.

[34] Starting with the results in Table 7.3, we used Denison's estimate of the quality of labor and two-thirds of his estimate for labor migration, and introduced an estimate for the drop in age of capital assets in Germany and Italy.

from 4.0 to 3.8 percent), as a result of allowing for two new factors: the intensification of work effort accompanying a drop in time at work; and the pressure of demand, which although comparable in 1969 to what it had been in 1957, was substantially higher than in 1963.

Economies of Scale and Specialization

There are said to be "economies of scale" if the technical constraints on production are such that the volume produced would have been more than 1 percent higher in a hypothetical situation where the input of each factor was exactly 1 percent higher, the basis of comparison being the particular situation under examination. Although we cannot reach any factual conclusions on this point, we discuss below the methodology, which at least should show the nature and size of the problem.

If there are economies of scale, the production function should in principle reveal them, since it is supposed to represent the conditions of production. Now the function we have used to justify the calculations of total productivity excludes such economies. If in equation (1) (p. 179) the two values N_t and K_t representing the inputs were raised by 1 percent without changing q_t, then Q_t representing output would rise by exactly 1 percent.

A slightly more general formula would accommodate economies of scale, i.e.

$$(11) \qquad Q_t = A_t N_t^\lambda K_t^\mu$$

where λ and μ are two constants, and A_t is a number independent of the inputs used, and represents the real level of productivity in the economy. A hypothetical variation of 1 percent in N_t and K_t in year t would then be reflected by a variation of $(\lambda + \mu)$ percent in Q_t.

If we suppose that the technical constraints on production are adequately represented by equation (11), the indexes of total productivity as defined on p. 180 would not correctly measure changes in A_t. From equations (3), (4), and (11) we can easily establish that

$$(12) \qquad \frac{q_t}{q_0} = \frac{A_t}{A_0} \times \left[\frac{N_t}{N_0}\right]^{\lambda - a} \times \left[\frac{K_t}{K_0}\right]^{\mu - (1-a)}$$

The index of total productivity is therefore the product of three terms: A_t/A_0, measuring technical progress, and two terms introducing changes in the inputs. In the particular case where the two indexes N_t/N_0 and K_t/K_0 are equal to one another and therefore equal to the index F_t/F_0 defined by equation (3) for total inputs, then equation (12) can be simplified somewhat and written as

(13)
$$\frac{q_t}{q_0} = \frac{A_t}{A_0} \left[\frac{F_t}{F_0}\right]^{\lambda+\mu-1}$$

If economies of scale could be adequately measured—for example, if the values of exponents λ and μ in equation (11) were known and the equation were regarded as a good production function—it would probably be useful to calculate productivity indexes with the help of equations that integrated the effect of these economies. But in the present state of knowledge it is preferable to determine q_t/q_0 first, as we have done, and then simply to investigate the value of the corrective factors, which in equations (12) and (13) establish the relationship between q_t/q_0 and A_t/A_0.

It is then customary to seek the sum $\lambda + \mu$ that characterizes economies of scale, and next to calculate the corrective term in equation (13). On this basis Denison gives a value of 1.11 for $\lambda + \mu$ in France.[35] This estimate is highly conjectural, but would seem reasonable. If we accept it, and take for F_t/F_0 an index that integrates all the effects identified in Table 7.9, we get an adjustment term of 0.26 percent per year on the average for the period 1951–69 (0.11 multiplied by the rate of growth of total inputs F_t allowing for quality effects, i.e. 2.4 percent per year).

Even if $\lambda + \mu$ in fact has a value of 1.11, the above calculation is not very satisfactory because growth of capital inputs has been much higher in France than that of labor inputs (4.8 and 1.3 percent per year, respectively). It seems that one cannot do without a direct hypothesis concerning λ and μ as well as the position of these parameters in relation to the value already established for α. That is, the corrective term in equation (12) does not depend solely on $\lambda + \mu$. It would have grown at 0.53 percent per year if $\lambda = 0.72 = \alpha$ and $\mu = 0.39$, but only at 0.14 percent if $\lambda = 0.83$ and $\mu = 0.28 = 1 - \alpha$. A closer examination of the economies of scale cannot therefore be avoided.

At the microeconomic level two kinds of such economies should be distinguished—those internal to the firm and those external. The internal flow from the nature of manufacturing techniques, as well as from

---

[35] See Denison, p. 233. Denison in fact uses a different formula from ours, applying economies of scale not only to the inputs but also to the residual, which does not seem sensible, and obviously raises the term. In addition, he regards as reflecting economies of scale another effect that it is natural to calculate if aiming at precision in international comparisons—the effect on aggregated growth rates of differences in the price structures of the different countries. On this account he introduces an effect that in the case of France amounts to an average of 0.5 percent per year. But apart from his insubstantial statistical bases, the reasoning that this effect measures economies of scale has little cogency.

the scope for greater specialization and organization enjoyed by the larger production units. Their effect is to make large units more profitable than small ones. These are the economies of scale that one might hope to measure by statistical observation of firms. The second kind of economies of scale are felt outside the firm in which they originated. They can result from the diffused effects of increases in market size (better product diversification, lower relative burden of fixed social costs of market information and organization, etc.), or to much more localized phenomena, particularly training received by a firm's workers, often by the simple fact of their taking part in production—training that can be put to use in a different firm (the larger the industry group, the more easily can training received in one firm be put to use in another, and the greater the social benefit that is derived from this training).

It would be important to know how to measure these two types of economies of scale as well as to know their effect on the relationship between the remuneration and the marginal productivity of labor. We treated these latter values as identical earlier when deciding that α should equal labor remuneration's share of the value of production. We should therefore now inquire what light that share may throw on the exponents λ and μ of a production function that integrates all the effects of economies of scale.

Information on all these points is very limited. Data on profitability rates by size of firm show no clear trend, other than a tendency for profitability to be low in the smallest firms; medium-sized firms, however, frequently have higher rates of return than larger ones. This result can be interpreted as meaning that internal economies of scale are not important; it can also be attributed, logically enough, to the different degrees of specialization in firms of different sizes. As to external economies, no more than conjectures are feasible.

The presence of economies of scale must have the effect of bringing labor remuneration's share somewhat below the exponent λ of the production function (e.g. as a result of monopoly positions of firms with internal economies, and as a result of differences between the labor productivity within the firm and the labor productivity at the national level in the case of external economies). This difference, however, must be fairly small, and the divergence between μ and capital's share of income must be higher (one of the brakes on the growth of firms is the high uncertainty about return on investment, and the caution of firms and those providing the finance alike; as a result, the share of income accruing to capital should be below μ).

Altogether, it does seem that a corrective term should be applied on account of economies of scale, and that it could have an appreciable effect on the residual. A top boundary to this corrective term can probably be defined by taking $\lambda = 0.80 = \alpha + 0.08$ and $\mu = 0.40 = (1 - \alpha) + 0.12$; since after correction by these values the residual would be less than 0.8 percent per year in the long-term period 1913–63. This residual value would seem a minimum to allow for the effect of technical progress proper (moreover, on reflection a value of $\lambda + \mu$ equal to 1.2 for gross domestic production as a whole seems, if anything, on the high side).[36] Accordingly, these values would suggest an adjustment factor of 0.7 percent per year for the period 1951–69.

A different light can be thrown on these questions by examining progress in specialization over the postwar period. We have seen that there was not much change in the structure of the productive system, but that some specialization must have taken place in the organization within particular firms. This phenomenon could be far more important if accompanied by specialization as between firms. However, historical statistics on this point are totally lacking. Specialization is, moreover, increasingly linked to the opening of international borders. We shall therefore reserve this topic for later analysis of the possible impact of developments in foreign trade (Chapter 12). We shall then present from a different angle the matters we have been dealing with here.

Technical Development

Whatever the part played by economies of scale, they cannot explain the important divergence between the residual in the postwar period and that revealed by long-term comparisons. After taking into account all the quality effects and factor movements, the term A_t of a production function as in equation (11) has tended to grow much faster in the last 20 years than previously. Can direct evidence be found of particularly rapid technical development in that period? We shall seek it in two directions: first, by examining changes in the composition of the working population by qualification, and, second, by assessing the scale of attempts to adopt new techniques.

There is little doubt that the role of technical qualifications in the labor force has rapidly assumed increased importance since the mid-1950's (see Table 7.10). This can be seen clearly in the results of the demographic censuses of 1954, 1962, and 1968, although changes in nomenclature make detailed comparisons difficult between 1954 and

---

[36] See Denison's discussion in *Why Growth Rates Differ*, pp. 228–31.

TABLE 7.10
The Growth of the Labor Force in Certain
Socio-occupational Categories, 1954–68
(Percent per year)

Category	1954–62	1962–68
Professional classes and top management	5.2%	4.8%
Engineers		(5.5)
Middle management	5.0	4.8
Technicians		(7.6)
White-collar workers	1.9	4.0
Blue-collar workers	1.1	1.4

TABLE 7.11
Engineers and Technicians in the Manufacturing Industries
in Selected Countries, 1960–62
(Percent)

Labor force	France 1962	Germany 1961	United States 1960	United Kingdom 1961
Engineers	1.2%	3.3%	2.7%	1.5%
Technicians	2.3	0.5	1.2	1.1
Total	3.5%	3.8%	3.9%	2.6%

Source: OECD, *Statistiques relatives à la structure de la main-d'oeuvre par profession et par niveau d'éducation dans 53 pays* (Paris, 1969). Engineers are category 0-02 and technicians are category 0-X9 of the OECD nomenclature.

the two later years. Growth was fastest in top-management and middle-management socio-occupational groups, where the numbers employed doubled in 14 years. To be sure, these included teachers and qualified medical and social workers, where the increase was very large. But a more detailed breakdown shows that growth was also outstandingly fast for engineers and technicians, categories of greater interest here. There are no historical statistics to document precisely recent developments compared with earlier trends. But clearly we are witnessing a change to an entirely new order of technical emphasis in the industrial labor force.

   In this field as in others, international comparisons are uncertain. Nevertheless, statistics recently assembled and published by the OECD have enabled us to draw up Table 7.11, which shows the proportion of engineers and technicians in the industrial labor force of France, Germany, Britain, and the United States around 1960. If one looks at the total of the two occupational classes—thus eliminating national differences in meaning of the terms "engineer" and "technician"—it can be seen that France at this period had reached a level little below that of Germany and the United States, and markedly higher than that of Britain. Statistics in the same document show a change in the United States in 1950 also in the proportion of technically qualified persons in industry (the figure for the total in Table 7.11 rose from 2.0 to 3.9 percent between 1950 and 1960). The movement therefore seems not only French, but probably worldwide.

Another worldwide phenomenon is the increased favor accorded to research and development. According to estimates by the General Commission on Scientific and Technical Research,[37] gross expenditure on this activity as a proportion of gross domestic production rose from 1.12 percent in 1958 to 2.44 percent in 1966. In the same period the number of researchers increased from 18,000 to 47,000 (full-time equivalent in the case of those engaged only part-time in research). In Industry proper there was a similar trend.[38] Although progress made is probably exaggerated by the difficulties of setting up new statistics in an imprecisely defined field, there is little doubt of the increase in research effort in France.

The OECD has tried to present comparable estimates for a number of countries for 1963 or 1964. Gross expenditure on research and development as a percentage of gross national product, according to those figures, was 1.6 percent in France, 1.4 percent in Germany, 3.4 percent in the United States, and 2.3 percent in the United Kingdom. On this basis, and on the basis of researchers per 10,000 inhabitants, France ranks after the United States, Britain, and the Netherlands, broadly even with Sweden, Germany, and Japan, and well ahead of the other OECD countries.[39]

But these investments in research are not closely linked to the rate of technical development. For one thing, they reached a high level too recently to have produced their most significant results in the period we are examining. Second, every country except the most advanced in a particular field improves its productivity—at least in the short term— by adopting techniques developed elsewhere rather than by striving to initiate entirely new processes itself. The example of Britain suggests,

[37] Délégation Générale à la Recherche Scientifique et Technique (DGRST), *Les Moyens consacrés par l'état à la recherche et au développement en 1966* (Paris, 1969).

[38] DGRST, *Les Moyens consacrés à la recherche et au développement dans l'industrie française en 1966* (Paris, 1969).

[39] Organization for Economic Cooperation and Development, *Ampleur et structure de l'effort global de la RD dans les pays membres de l'OCDE* (Paris, 1967).

moreover, that a high level of research can coexist with a slow rate of technical development. France has made recognized efforts to encourage original technological research at home, but has its industry at the same time suceceded in assimilating progress achieved elsewhere?

To answer this question we can use a thoroughly documented study by M. Couturier, who has analyzed the development of expenditure and receipts for patents and licenses in the balance of payments.[40] Most of the commentators who have considered the same data have stressed the deficit apparent in them. The proportion of French expenditure abroad covered by receipts in respect to both patents and licenses moved from one-third in the early 1950's to one-half in 1960, falling slightly thereafter and fluctuating around 45 percent. France's deficit is particularly high in relation to the United States and Switzerland. According to some authors, this low rate of coverage shows an inability of French technological research to press through to truly operational solutions. In fact, however, the problem is longstanding and probably reflects the ground lost by France in the nineteenth century.

If we look at the statistics of patent applications filed in France, we see that at the peaks in 1913 (17,000 applicants) and 1930 (24,000 applications), 55 percent came from abroad.[41] Over the same years the corresponding proportions for Germany were only 25 and 20 percent. After the war, in the intermediate plateau years 1955–57 (29,000 applications per year in France), the proportion of patents from abroad was a little below 55 percent. Thereafter applications increased rapidly, reaching nearly 50,000 in 1966, and so did the proportion from abroad, which rose to 64 percent in 1966. But recent developments seem due chiefly to the increase in international transactions of all kinds, since from 1955 to 1966 the net balance of sales and purchases of patents in the French balance of payments tended to improve.

The rapid increase in patent applications is new evidence of the vigor of technical development and the acceleration of the research and development effort. This consideration of France's balance-of-payments deficit on patents and licenses has diverted us from the question raised: has France's productive system benefited from progress abroad as well as from its own technical advance? It seems to have benefited increasingly

---

[40] M. Couturier, "Les Revenus de la recherche scientifique et technique dans la balance des comptes," *Economies et sociétés*, vol. III, no. 4, April 1969.

[41] Ministry of Industry, "La Protection des inventions en France et à l'étranger," *Etudes statistiques* (Paris, 1960). We should note, however, that in the post–World War II period Germany's rate of coverage of expenditure for patents and licenses was no better than France's (37 percent in 1963, 45 percent in 1965). Large deficits appear, as in the case of France, in relation to the United States and Switzerland.

during the postwar period. Expenditure for license concessions rose from 138 million new francs in 1953 to 377 million in 1959, and to 705 million in 1965, three years with similar short-term economic conditions. In terms of dollars at the current rates of exchange, these figures come to 39 million, 76 million, and 141 million, respectively, for the three years —that is, an average annual rate of 11 percent, which seems to have been sustained to the present.

However, we should note again that this drive to assimilate foreign technology is not peculiar to France. The German balance of payments also shows high and fast-growing figures.[42] Whereas in the early 1950's German expenditure under this head was below that of France, it grew at a faster rate even than the French (at some 15 percent per year), and today it is at a similar level (although we should perhaps recall that the overall output of German industry is considerably higher than that of French industry).

We have just considered various aspects of France's technological development over the past 15 years, with no difficulty discovering evidence of it. Surprisingly, we found that its acceleration has not been peculiar to France, but has been demonstrated in a comparable manner in other industrial countries.

We should perhaps have completed this research by examining progress in methods of management. Not only are statistical data on this subject lacking, however, but this would have been too great a broadening of the concept of "physical factors," which distinguishes the first part of this work from the second. We shall therefore reserve what we have to say on the subject to Chapters 13 and 14.

Technological development, probably accompanied by progressive reform of management methods, accounts for the large weight that the postwar residual in Table 7.9 would retain if we have correctly estimated the effects of economies of scale (the residual is probably close to 2 percent per year). Without attempting an illusory degree of precision, we should note in addition that over the period 1955–62, taken as typical, the French residual thus corrected is comparable with that in Italy, but considerably higher than in Germany, Britain, and the United States. That is, the effects of economies of scale should be subtracted from the estimates on pp. 213–14; i.e. because of the growth of inputs, these economies must have been greater outside France, and particularly in Germany. There remains, therefore, a presumption that France and Italy have benefited from growth factors of a particular order.

[42] See M. Couturier, "Les Revenus de la recherche scientifique et technique," p. 865.

PROVISIONAL CONCLUSIONS

At the end of this first part of our study, in which we have attempted to examine systematically the physical sources of growth, we should pause briefly to assemble the main conclusions of our analyses so far. Since the end of World War II, the French economy has enjoyed a dynamism that contrasts with the stagnation of the previous 15 years. Our contemporaries are conscious enough of this: they frequently associate economic expansion with the recovery of the birthrate that began in 1942, and see in this recent progress a sign of national renewal.

The analyses made above lead to a less black-and-white assessment. Although French output stagnated between 1930 and 1940, productivity continued to grow significantly. Examining long-term developments, we have seen that in most industrial sectors the progress achieved in recent years in production and productivity does not seem exceptional, since it has led to levels comparable with those that would have been reached had the depression and the war not interrupted the trends prevailing since the beginning of the century. In fact, a historian trying to detect the start of secular acceleration in the French growth rate could probably place it just as validly around 1900 as around 1950.

Nevertheless, the postwar expansion has two noteworthy characteristics that are evidence of its vigor and are good indications of its continuation. First, it can be seen as a general phenomenon that affects not only Industry but also industry groups where progress had previously remained slow. The fast rate of change in agriculture and trade has greatly amplified a development whose takeoff was still tentative between the wars.

Second, if the only reason for the revival of the 1950's was a reaction to the ground lost in the depression and the war, we should be able to note some slowing down in growth, once the levels consistent with long-term trends had been regained. At several points in our study, using a variety of approaches, we have given particular attention to observing whether such a slowing down did take place. Our conclusions were mixed: we found an acceleration in the growth of labor productivity—and even of total productivity—in Industry, but a slowing down in trade and services, and a slightly falling growth rate in the residual for the economy as a whole. The differences were in every case so slight that they could be explained by the inaccuracy of our data. It must not be forgotten in this context that methods of statistical observation have significantly improved since 1949, and this alone makes it necessary to treat with caution any difference of 0.3 percent or even 0.5 percent between annual growth rates at the beginning and end of the period studied. All in all, the rapid growth of the past 20 years is being prolonged well beyond a simple return to a reference situation.

Although improvement in the scale of productivity in agriculture and trade is not peculiar to France, the absence of any significant slackening in the pace distinguishes this country from most of those that have experienced faster expansion, or as fast, in the immediate postwar period. By comparison with that of other nations, France's growth in this field therefore appears vigorous, although its pace was not exceptional: whether examined over the postwar years or over the long term, the rates of growth of output and productivity in France are comparable with those of other prosperous countries.

From an analysis of work performed by the labor force, we felt that two factors should be regarded as of some importance. First, the development of primary and later of secondary and higher education has led since the beginning of the century to continual improvement in worker qualifications. This course of events was the result of political decisions, many of which date to the distant past, as well as of free-acting trends in French family decisions. It played a considerable role in the postwar period, but no more so than in the first half of the century.

Second, migrations of workers from low- to high-productivity jobs accelerated markedly. The French labor force therefore has been more and more usefully employed. Part of this development was due to an autonomous speeding up in the improvement of farming techniques; part was the result of general economic prosperity. It is evidence, nevertheless, of the disappearance of the sociological or judicial forces of resistance that had slowed down French industrialization in the nineteenth century.

A positive role was also played by maintaining working time at a high level. Since a rise in living standards is generally accompanied by a decrease in hours worked and since the French people had experienced short working days during the war, a gradual reduction of time at work might have been expected. Despite an increase in paid vacations, however, working hours were kept at a level that today is still one of the highest in the world. This phenomenon seems due less to the tightness of the labor market than to the free choice of both employees and employers.

Over the postwar period as a whole, and more particularly in the first half of the 1950's, the French investment effort was only moderate in scale. Nevertheless, the development and modernization of productive capital had a clear influence on the country's growth, and seem to have progressed at a pace at least comparable with that of other countries. This contradiction between moderate investment effort and rapid growth of productive capital can be explained by several factors. First, the proportion of productive investment in capital formation was particularly high, especially in the immediate postwar years. In addition, the labor force was stationary, whereas in most other countries it was growing more or less rapidly. A given investment effort in France was concentrated less on enlarging existing capacity and more on productivity than in other countries. Finally, no country had experienced such a profound interruption in the formation of productive capital than had France between 1931 and 1945. Capital equipment, which had been considerably developed before World War I and in the 1920's, had aged and was outdated by 1946. Setting up new plant and machinery was one way to make up for much of the technological lag in production methods. In postwar investment we observed two rather distinct phases. Up to about 1955, the basic sectors managed or controlled by the state were predominant. Thereafter, capital formation was better balanced between industry groups, involving the lighter industries as well. The renewal and modernization of capital equipment accordingly took place rather late in some sectors. Chapters 9 and 10 will be devoted to studying the factors that may explain the scale of investment achieved; they therefore are an extension of this first part of the study.

The detailed examination of productivity trends by industry group and of structural changes in the productive system suggests that the greatest acceleration frequently took place in small and medium units of production rather than in the largest. For one thing, the rise in long-term productivity growth rates chiefly affected sectors where small firms predominated: clothing, trade, and agriculture. For another thing, trends toward concentration were more marked in small or medium firms and establishments than in larger ones. The improvement of French productivity was thus a phenomenon that reflected efforts or behavioral changes in many areas. Immediate responsibility for this cannot be attributed to just a few men directing or controlling the basic economic sectors.

All these conclusions of course are partial and provisional, expressing the main results of this first part, and to which we shall revert at the end of the study.

PART TWO

A Search for Causes

CHAPTER EIGHT

Aggregate Demand

In the first part of the study, we analyzed growth in France, directing our attention to the factors influencing the supply of goods and services. We studied in turn quantitative and qualitative changes in the primary factors of production. We then attempted to measure what proportion of the French growth rate should be ascribed to each.

According to a thesis maintained by some theoreticians of economic development, such an analysis of supply would be sufficient for research into the causes of growth. The potential production of a given country at a given period depends, in their view, only on the factors that the country can put to work. Actual production follows this level closely, and any underutilization of capacity in periods of recession has no lasting effects on growth. In other words, supply creates its own demand.

According to an opposite theory a necessary, and often even a sufficient, condition of economic development is the existence of a high level of demand. In the twentieth century, there is wide scope for raising productivity in nearly every country. This takes concrete form when firms are confronted with markets in the course of rapid expansion. The intensity of demand explains the development of production both over the long term and in short-term fluctuations.

The approach adopted in our study shows that we would a priori regard this second theory as exaggerated. It may have some validity, however, especially in the case we are concerned with, since the ground lost by France between 1930 and 1945 probably increased substantially the margin of potential growth of supply.

We must therefore ask the following question: to what extent can the fast rate of postwar growth in France be explained by the intensity of the demand to be met by the productivity system? An objective reply is a difficult matter. The fact that the growth of output was accompanied by an increase in demand is a logical necessity, which has no significance. Consequently, observation of overall stability does not enable us to distinguish cause from effect, to determine what role was played by the expansion, respectively, of supply and demand, or to ascertain where the first impetus arose.

For these reasons the part to be ascribed to demand can be revealed only by a more indirect analysis. It can be accepted a priori that a lively and sustained demand over a relatively long period is reflected in an intensified use of productive capacity, the development of investment, and acceleration of labor migrations from traditional occupations to more productive employment. The study of the various factors of production must therefore be taken up here again in order to determine what role was played in each by demand. The third part of this chapter is devoted to this topic.

First, however, it seems necessary to assess the scale of the phenomenon whose effects are to be studied, and to analyze its origins. The first part of this chapter therefore will deal with the following questions. Has the pressure of demand been greater since the war than previously? Has it grown more steadily since 1949 than in the past? Has it shown an upward or downward trend in the postwar period? What has been the postwar discrepancy between potential and actual production? The second part of the chapter examines what factors can explain the level of overall demand in the last 20 years.

MEASUREMENT OF THE PRESSURE OF DEMAND

*Has the Pressure of Demand Been Greater
Since the War than Previously?*

We shall be concerned here not with the overall level of effective demand for goods and services, which is necessarily equal to supply, but with the stimulus exerted by demand on growth. In other words, we hope to assess in broad terms the positive or negative margin between the *ex ante* demand that tended to be felt in the different markets and the *ex ante* supply that would have resulted from a normal use of productive capacity. A large positive margin could lead to overutilization of capacity and an increase in the latter's size; a negative margin could have the opposite effect. We shall call this margin between *ex ante* demand and *ex ante* supply the "pressure of demand." This, as so defined, is not measurable directly, since the differentials that may exist *ex ante* are necessarily canceled out *ex post*. But the pressure of demand is nevertheless felt in various ways, so that indirect means of measuring it are conceivable. We shall examine several.

Such indirect standards of measurement are, however, to some extent ambiguous. They relate to phenomena arising not only from gaps between *ex ante* demand and *ex ante* supply but from other factors as well. The findings would be fully conclusive only if these other factors had exerted a constant effect over the whole of the periods studied; but this has never rigorously been the case, particularly when we must make comparisons between periods widely separated in time.

In addition to this basic difficulty, there is the problem, once again, of gaps and imperfections in the available statistics. A verdict is therefore difficult to establish with authority, but a fairly clear conclusion seems to emerge, nevertheless, from the five indicators we shall now examine.

Rate of price increases. It is often maintained that high pressure of demand is accompanied by price rises, since all markets then become favorable to suppliers, who have no difficulty in gaining acceptance for increases in price. The pressure of demand could therefore be measured by a general price index. We cannot have much confidence in this indicator, however, since price variations are not determined solely by excess demand, which is what we are interested in here, but by autonomous changes in production costs as well. Developments affecting prices of imported raw materials and—even more—institutional changes in wage determination procedures can lead to price increases at a time when the pressure of demand is weak.

While keeping this comment in mind, let us nevertheless examine what movements have taken place in the wholesale price index of industrial products.[1] Of course this index concerns only raw materials and semifinished products, but it is nevertheless the best indicator available for comparisons with the distant past.

Even if the rapid increase up to 1951 is set aside, some irregularity can be observed in price movements in the period after World War II. We can nevertheless consider typical the growth rate of 2.5 percent per year, which is the average for 1951–69, a period of 18 years linking two similar short-term economic situations. Prices of imported raw materials, however, were untypically high in 1951, and for historic comparisons a slightly higher rate, on the order of 3 percent, probably represents more accurately the rise in prices of basic industrial products over the past 15 years.

The period between the wars saw such wide price movements, whose causes are various and well known, that it cannot provide any useful

[1] We have used the appropriate group in the SGF index covering 45 commodities for the years 1896–1938 and the INSEE wholesale price index of industrial products for recent years. The record index covers a much larger number of products than the first, but this does not seem to introduce any systematic error in a comparison of price trends before 1938 and after.

benchmarks. After a long period of slowly falling prices, a clear upward trend became established between 1897 and 1913. Precise measurement of the growth rate is difficult to determine, especially because of changes between 1905 and 1908 that seem to have been due to the boom, followed by a short slump (this movement, however, affected the other leading industrial nations more than France). If we take the period 1908–13 as typical of the economic expansion that preceded World War I, we get a growth rate of 3 percent for the price of industrial commodities.

It should be noted that between 1896 and 1913 wholesale food prices grew at a much more regular rate, at first averaging 1.7 percent per year, with an acceleration in 1906 (to a rate of 2.4 percent up to 1913). From 1951 to 1969, the rise in wholesale prices of food products averaged 3.7 percent per year.

To sum up, on the evidence of price increases—a somewhat doubtful measure—the pressure of demand seems to have been roughly comparable from 1951 to 1969 to that in the years immediately before World War I, and even perhaps slightly higher.

Bankruptcies and official liquidations. The higher the pressure of demand, the less onerous is competition between producers, and the smaller is the number of firms forced to close. One might therefore consider measuring the pressure of demand in terms of the frequency of bankruptcies and official liquidations. It can be observed that the average number of cases under this head was 8,700 per year from 1896 to 1913, 7,800 from 1922 to 1930, 12,100 from 1931 to 1938, 6,500 from 1950 to 1963, and about 10,000 from 1964 to 1968.[2] The postwar period is thus characterized by higher financial security in industrial and commercial affairs than in earlier periods, at least until the last few years.

This comparison, however, must be treated with caution. We took the absolute number of cases opened without allowing either for the size of the firms involved or for any differences in their total number or for the distribution by company size and legal status. We were not able to go into the figures more deeply for lack of suitable data. But is this sufficient for long-term comparisons?

In addition, we have not taken into account changes in commercial legislation and practice. A significant change in the law was introduced in the 1955 reform, which substituted a court verdict for official liquidation, and made bankruptcy more serious for the debtor. Perhaps even more important has been the change in attitudes of creditors and debtors

---

[2] *Annuaire statistique de la France,* particularly the *Annuaire rétrospectif,* 1961 edition.

in the event of financial difficulties for the latter. We have no means, however, of allowing for this factor objectively. For these reasons the statistical indicator considered in this section probably has only limited significance for the topic we are exploring.

Growth rate of imports of manufactured industrial products. As a measure of the pressure of demand on the domestic market we could use the growth rate of imports of manufactured products. When demand tends to exceed national production, purchasers naturally turn toward foreign producers, so that a high level and rapid increase in imported manufactures can point to high pressure of demand.

This measure, however, is rather ambiguous, for an increase of this kind depends also on demand conditions in other countries, movements in relative prices, and changes in the regulations governing foreign trade. The paucity of available information nevertheless requires us not to ignore any index that might throw light on the phenomenon under consideration.

In fact, from 1951 to 1957 the volume of imports of manufactures remained practically constant, owing, however, to a quota system. Beginning in 1958, on the contrary, it grew at a smart rate, unprecedented in the country's history (30 and 15 percent on the average from 1958 to 1968 for consumption goods and capital goods, respectively). But this result can be explained by the freeing of trade and setting up of the Common Market just as much as by the pressure of demand. We cannot therefore use this factor in comparisons with earlier periods to throw light on the topic under study.

Immigration of foreign workers. High pressure of demand is related to an unusually intense use of productive capacity, and particularly to some overemployment of the labor force. The excess of demand over supply should therefore become apparent simultaneously on the market for goods and on the labor market. It is reflected both by a rising demand for imports and by an increased call on foreign labor. For this reason we must examine the development of immigration of foreign workers.

This element is affected by three facts that make its interpretation more difficult. First, some migratory movements were sparked by purely political events: from 1920 to 1940, France welcomed a large number of political refugees; and since 1955, there has been a high rate of repatriation of French people living overseas. Second, immigration by North African workers, which is fairly difficult to identify in the statistics, negligible before World War II, after the war accounted for a large part of the flow within the labor force as a whole. Finally, in comparisons covering long periods, it must not be forgotten that the development of international communications makes migration easier, so that the response to demands for labor is likely to be increasingly fast and increasingly great.

We can nevertheless assess fairly precisely how intense the demand for foreign labor has been by examining two sources of information. By a method developed by H. Bunle, we can measure net immigration of foreigners between two successive population censuses by taking the increase in census figures of foreigners and North Africans, and making a number of adjustments to allow in particular for the acquisition of French nationality.[3] This net immigration grew at an average rate of around 20,000 persons a year from 1896 to 1906, and rose to 45,000 from 1906 to 1911. It reached 225,000 from 1921 to 1926, and 165,000 between 1926 and 1931, but became negative from 1931 to 1936 (−20,000), a period when French regulations deliberately opposed the entry of foreign workers. From 1946 to 1962, the net figure was close to 100,000. Thus, immigration of foreigners and North Africans seems to have been lower since World War II than between 1920 and 1930, although higher than in the boom years 1906 to 1912. The difference cannot be explained by the net immigration of political refugees, which certainly did not exceed an average of 20,000 persons a year between 1921 and 1931.

These results are confirmed by the Ministry of Labor statistics of regulated immigration of foreign workers. This reached 190,000 per year on the average in 1921–25, and 140,000 in 1926–30. It was only 35,000 in 1947–54, and then rose to 75,000 in 1955–63, reaching 130,000 in 1964–68. In the period after World War II, France benefited from a considerable net inflow of North African workers (20,000 to 30,000 a year on the average from 1949 to 1964, but very few thereafter) and between 1955 and 1963 from a large-scale repatriation (amounting to 65,000 persons a year in all, i.e. counting both members and nonmembers of the labor force, before the massive homecomings of 1962). But although the entry of North African workers may have been due to the demand for labor on the French market, the repatriations had a very different cause. To sum up, on the basis of the indicator considered here, the pressure of demand in France seems to have been slightly lower in the period after World War II than between 1920 and 1930, but probably higher than in the boom that preceded 1913.

Unemployment at census dates. Since the same imbalances simultaneously affect the market for goods and the labor market, the best way

[3] H. Bunle, "Mouvements migratoires entre la France et l'étranger," *Etudes démographiques*, no. 4, 1943, particularly pp. 67, 69, 94, 95.

TABLE 8.1
Number of Unemployed per 1,000 Employees, 1896–1968

Census year (March)	Proportion of unemployed	Economic situation	Census year (March)	Proportion of unemployed	Economic situation
1896	30	Beginning of upturn	1931	40	Slump
1901	35	Slowdown	1936	85	Prolonged depression
1906	26	Moderate expansion			
1911	18	Boom	1954	27	Recovery
1921	51	Slump	1962	15	Boom
1926	22	Inflationary boom	1968	29	Recovery

Source: Mme Cahen, "Evolution de la population active en France depuis cent ans d'après les recensements quinquennaux," *Etudes et conjoncture,* May-June, 1962, and the 1962 and 1968 census results.

of measuring the pressure exerted by demand on productive capacities would be to refer to statistics of employment. Unfortunately, data compiled at relatively short intervals exist only for the interwar years onward, and in any case they are of real use only from the 1930's. To measure the degree of employment in the labor force, we therefore have available merely the numbers of unemployed at the demographic census dates.

Table 8.1 shows the number of workers without jobs per 1,000 persons of the wage-earning labor force. A correct interpretation of it must obviously take account of the short-term economic situation at the periods in which each census took place. That information is therefore shown in the last column. The findings for 1954, 1962, and 1968 appear low but not exceptional. It must be remembered that the 1954 and 1968 censuses took place at the moments of lowest postwar strain in the labor market. Higher unemployed percentages were recorded at the beginning of the century and at the 1921, 1931, and 1936 census years, although these were periods when the economic situation was poor. From the clearly very limited figures in Table 8.1, it would seem that the pressure of demand in the past 20 years was comparable with that in the seven or eight years of expansion before World War I.

To reach any conclusions on the basis of the five indicators just considered is clearly no easy matter, particularly since their indicative value is not the same in each case. Nevertheless we have seen that 1951–68 appears with some consistency as the period in which demand was highest. This overall impression is strengthened by the fact that an examination of the unemployment rate, probably the most significant of the five indicators, leads individually to the same conclusion. The situation in the period after World War II was of course only slightly different from that recorded in other periods, particularly in the seven or eight years of expansion before World War I and in the years 1922–30. But the period of the last 20 years stands out in two ways: it seems to have had extremely high pressure of demand, and for a far longer time than in comparable periods of the past.

Has Demand Grown More Steadily Since World War II than in the Past?

A particularly steady demand, just as a particularly strong demand, seems likely to exert a favorable effect on growth, since it helps those who run the economy to make good forecasts and therefore would appear able to raise the efficiency of production to particularly high levels. It also has the effect of reducing uncertainties as to future economic growth, and thereby encourages a spirit of enterprise in those making decisions.

It should be far easier in principle to observe regularity of demand than its intensity. In the short term, changes in demand determine those in output, since each firm adapts its output rates to the level of demand for its products. The regularity of increases in production therefore directly measures regularity of demand. Nevertheless, the poor quality of estimates available for earlier periods makes this a difficult subject to study. Even a quick examination of the annual series of gross domestic production since 1896 shows a contrast between marked fluctuations up to 1939 and a far steadier growth after World War II (see for example Table 1.3 and Figure 1.1, pp. 24, 25). It is tempting to conclude that the growth of production has been steadier of late than in the past and stimulated by a much steadier demand.

And yet the contrast between the later and earlier parts of the series might well be the result of a statistical illusion. The estimates for the more distant years are based on a few figures only relating to basic sectors whose output is well known to be irregular. By contrast, gross domestic production as shown in the present-day National Accounts is based chiefly on more direct estimates of end use by classes of goods and services: for example, consumption by households, by government agencies, or for investment. It is therefore almost certain that the fluctuations of the series considered are too wide for the years before World War II.

For an unbiased comparison of the steadiness of growth at different periods, our only course must be to use series of raw figures whose accuracy cannot be contested, but the number of series of this kind is very small. Figure 8.1, for example, shows on a semilogarithmic scale the growth of output of cast iron. To help comparison, we have superim-

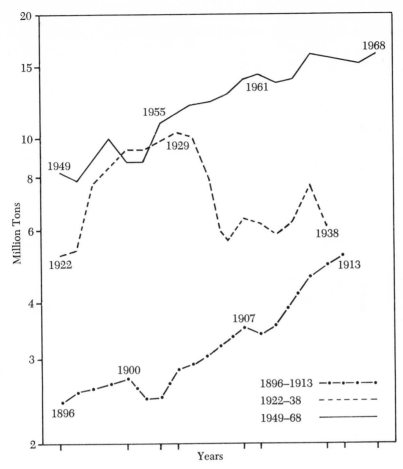

Fig. 8.1. Total output of cast iron, 1896–1968.

posed the curves for three periods: 1896–1913, 1922–38, and 1949–68. The figure shows up the well-known effect of the 1930's depression. It also reveals, however, that growth was not significantly steadier from 1949 to 1968 than in the earlier periods free of deep depressions. The same impression emerges from graphs drawn in a similar way from other raw data series.[4] The slowing down of aggregate growth that occurred in 1952, 1958, and 1964 seems to have been comparable in scale to that

[4] We have considered in this way apparent coal consumption, electricity consumption, output of manufactured gas in Paris, apparent cotton consumption, output of cement, slaked lime and mortar, railroad goods traffic, and traffic by inland waterways.

observed in 1901 and 1927; the recessions in 1921 and 1930 were obviously more marked. An examination of the 20 years before 1896 confirms the impression that growth in France after 1949 was no steadier than in earlier periods not affected by large-scale depressions.

It is probably reasonable to counter this conclusion, based on a study of a few output series, by the argument that production is increasingly becoming more highly developed and services are playing an evergrowing part, and that consequently the output of the basic sectors is taking up a smaller proportion of the whole. Moreover, output in these basic sectors grows less steadily than the rest of gross domestic production. A given irregularity in the output of the basic sectors should therefore be accompanied by a lesser irregularity in production as a whole. This argument is of course true, but its importance should not be overestimated. Perhaps, in fact, it should be interpreted as meaning that a given irregularity of demand now means a lower irregularity in output than it did previously.

Has the Pressure of Demand Shown an Upward Trend Since the War?

To answer this question we could examine year-by-year changes in the indicators we considered in the first section, and in other indicators that might be added, since statistical data today are far more complete than in the past. Such a detailed study, however, would be too lengthy; the relevant conclusions can be drawn more simply without much danger of error. We shall accordingly limit our attention to a few indicators and attempt to measure the discrepancy between potential and actual production.

Examination of selected indicators. Prices, which had grown very fast up to the end of 1951, thereafter remained more or less stable for four years. In 1956 and 1957 inflation developed, at first contained by various measures but later degenerating into somewhat disorderly increases. A new balance was not reached before about the end of 1959, when the effects of the December 1958 devaluation were being felt. Nevertheless, prices continued to rise fairly regularly thereafter (the average increase was 6.7 percent per year from 1956 to 1959, and 3.2 percent from 1959 to 1967, if we follow the evidence of the price index of gross domestic production).

We shall analyze price movements in greater detail in Chapter 11, where we shall see that the role played by the pressure of demand was especially evident in 1956–57 and 1963–64. But, on the other hand, the difference between the stability of 1952–55 and the price rises of the

1960's (except for 1963 and 1964) was due mainly to different changes in costs (prices of imported products and fiscal or parafiscal charges on firms). Here again it is difficult for us to draw conclusions from variations in imports of manufactured products. Because these were controlled before 1958, it is impossible to make a meaningful comparison between their slow growth in the 1950's and the very fast expansion in the 1960's.

A study of the labor market is likely to be much more fruitful. The years 1952–68 were characterized on the whole by a high utilization of the labor force, although there were some fluctuations. The periods of recession and recovery were of course marked by an increase in unemployment, by some reduction in weekly hours worked, and, as far as can be ascertained from the statistics, by a somewhat lessened participation of the labor force. But for the purposes of our study, rather than analyze these phenomena, it is more useful to examine labor force utilization in the expansionary periods 1953–57 and 1959–63.

The first of these must be divided from this viewpoint into two subperiods. In the years 1953, 1954, and 1955, there was a fairly high rate of unemployment by comparison with the period 1952–68 as a whole: 300,000 unemployed, on the average, in each of these years, according to the estimates in Chapter 2. Average hours worked per week were 45.2, a fairly low level in relation to the averages in the following years. By contrast, in the years 1956 and 1957 the level of utilization of the labor force was exceptionally high: the number of unemployed, which had dropped in 1955, shot downward in 1956 and reached a low for the period in 1957 (the average for the two years together was only 185,000). Weekly hours worked were 46.0. Immigration of foreign workers, which had been negligible from 1953 to 1955, increased in 1956 and even more in 1957. The activity rates of the labor force were particularly high.

The distinguishing features of the years 1959–63 seem to have been halfway between those of 1953–55 and 1956–57, and the various indicators of pressure in the labor market diverged somewhat among themselves. On the one hand, job openings increased rapidly from 1959 and in 1962–63 reached a level comparable with the 1957 high point. Simultaneously immigration of foreign workers and the positive balance of native North African immigration exceeded those recorded earlier, despite very large-scale repatriation in the same period. By 1960, hours worked per week had virtually regained the top 1957 level. On the other hand, unemployment was slightly lower in 1959 than in 1954 and then dropped after a shorter interval, but it did not reach the 1957 low point.

The numbers of unemployed on relief and those looking for jobs provide supporting evidence, even if figures concerning repatriates are excluded from the data.

After the 1964 stabilization, the labor market was considerably less tight. In 1956, supply and demand in employment regained levels comparable with those of 1960. Developments starting in early 1966 resembled those of 1961, but reversed course toward the end of the year. The 12 months preceding the events of May 1968 are distinguished by an unmet demand for jobs even higher than at the 1954 high point. Nevertheless, the pressure of demand for labor certainly remained higher in 1967–68 than it had been in 1953–54. The numbers of job vacancies were three times higher. In spite of the rise in real incomes, weekly hours worked were considerably longer. Immigration of foreign workers was much larger (100,000 a year instead of around 15,000).

This analysis clearly enables us to classify the periods studied with some objectivity. The years of recession and recovery were marked in 1952 and 1953 by a lower pressure of overall demand than in 1958 and 1959. In the expansionary periods, this pressure was strongest in 1956 and 1957, followed by 1962 and 1964, and finally by 1954 and 1955, when manpower resources were mobilized at a relatively low rate. The period 1965–68 occupies an intermediate position between the expansionary and recessionary periods.

All in all, it does not seem possible to establish a general trend toward an increase or decrease in the intensity of demand in the period from the end of the postwar reconstruction stage up to the present.

Potential and actual production. To develop a measure of the pressure of demand, American economists have in recent years been measuring the difference between actual and potential production.[5] This difference was particularly highlighted by the Kennedy Administration in trying to spread the message of the high potential for growth in the United States in 1960.

Like all abstract magnitudes, the concept of potential production can be the subject of much discussion. Applying it to France in 1950, we could for example contend that with so much ground lost in the depression and the war, potential production was considerably higher than actual production. In fact, however, those who applied this con-

[5] See, for example, *Economic Report of the President* (Washington, D.C., January 1962); M. Levy, *Fiscal Policy, Cycles and Growth* (Studies in Business Economics, no. 81, National Industrial Conference Board, 1963); B. Hickman, *Investment Demand and U.S. Economic Growth*, Washington, D.C., 1965), particularly chap. 7.

cept did so with reference to a somewhat restrictive notion of it, which we can define more or less as follows: potential production at a given period is that which would have been obtained with the existing capital and population of the country if, all other things being equal, the pressure of demand had brought about full utilization of capacity. The discrepancy between potential and actual production is then due solely to the overall underemployment of productive capacity and manpower. The possible effects of varying intensities of demand on investment and immigration are not taken into account.

A qualitative but direct measure of excess productive capacity is provided by the replies of heads of firms in periodic INSEE surveys. The lower this excess capacity, the higher the proportion of firms reporting themselves physically unable to increase output. From 1953 to 1968 this proportion fluctuated without any clear trend:[6] from 10 percent at the beginning of 1953, it rose progressively to 45 percent at the end of 1957. It then reached a low point of 10 percent at the beginning of 1959, and a high point of 38 percent at the beginning of 1964. Thereafter the lowest figures were 21 percent in 1965 and 16 percent in 1968, and the highest figure was 35 percent in 1966.

A more detailed examination of the survey replies throws useful light on the conclusions we reached earlier when considering the labor market. The proportion of firms unable to raise output for lack of manpower was highest, as might be expected, in 1957 (29 percent as against 15 percent in 1961, 13 percent in 1963 after the inflow of repatriates, and 16 percent in 1966). The proportion of firms unable to raise output for lack of capital equipment, however, was greatest at the beginning of 1964 (27 percent as against 23 percent in 1957). The pressure of demand was therefore probably stronger in 1963–64 than would appear simply from our examination of the labor market.

Various indirect measures of the difference between potential and actual production can be found.[7] We shall discuss two. In Chapter 7 we presented a production function for French industry. This function, as set up for postwar data, contained a term denoted u_t, being the ratio between unsatisfied demand and unfilled openings. This term allowed for the fact that the intensity of use of capital equipment and manpower

[6] INSEE, *Tendances de la conjoncture*, Note de synthèse (Paris, June 1969), p. 8.
[7] It is tempting to consider using as a direct measure the ratio between electricity consumed by industry and the level of power load contracted for by industrial consumers, since this ratio has been subject to fluctuation, with low points in 1953 and 1959 and no clear trend. It appears on examination, however, to be insufficiently sensitive as an indicator for our needs.

was least high in firms when the labor market was least stretched. It is interesting to examine the contribution of this term in the regression to explain the level of industrial production.

Assuming that the intensity of factor use was near its physical limit in 1957 and 1963, we find that the low levels of demand were reflected in a shortfall of production of 4.7 percent in 1953, and of 3.3 percent in 1959 and again at the beginning of 1968. Since the ratio u_t showed no marked trend, this shortfall similarly does not exhibit any trend over the period examined. The measure just considered is not of course quite appropriate for the difference between potential and actual production, since it relates only to industry. In addition, even if for want of a better hypothesis we assume that the result can be applied to the economy as a whole, we must allow not only for the intensity of factor use within production units but also for underemployment in the population.

As we shall see in the third section of this chapter, on the effect of demand on growth, a rise in male underemployment is shown in three ways: an increase in the numbers of unemployed, that is, of persons actually seeking work; a drop in the activity rates (i.e. a reduction in the number of persons expecting to join the labor force); and last a shortening of time worked by employed persons. It appears that the first two effects develop together, and are roughly equal in magnitude.[8] After the war, unemployment in France fluctuated between a minimum of some 160,000 persons in 1957 and a maximum of 435,000 in the spring of 1968 (320,000 in spring 1954). The greatest amplitude of these fluctuations was therefore 275,000 persons. If we double this number to allow for variations in the activity rate, we reach a figure slightly below 3 percent of the working population. To estimate production lost as a result of unemployment, we must allow for the marginal productivity of labor in production units. This leads to an assessment of the loss due to underemployment as about 2 percent in 1968 and 1.3 percent in 1953. The figure for 1968, however, is probably too high, since, as a result of large numbers of young people entering the labor market, the last few years have seen an increase in structural unemployment, with demand for jobs in many cases growing at the same time as vacancies.

Leaving out of account a rising trend between 1946 and 1958, hours worked seem to have fluctuated by around 1.5 percent (that is, 0.6 to 0.7 hours per week between the fall of 1951 and the spring of 1953, or

---

[8] See the study by R. Salais, "L'Adaptation à court terme de l'offre à la demande de travail; essai de mesure globale," paper submitted to the International Institute of Statistics, 1969.

between the fall of 1957 and the spring of 1959, and 0.5 hours between 1963 and the low point in 1964). Given a marginal productivity of two-thirds for labor, these fluctuations seem to account for about 1 percent of variations in the volume of output.

In all, the difference between potential and actual production appears therefore to have been about 7 percent in 1953, 6 percent in 1959, and something in between at the beginning of 1968. This calculation has the advantage of depending on a fairly detailed analysis of the problem. However, we must not forget that the data on which it is based concern only the labor market, i.e. unsatisfied supply and demand for jobs, and unemployment recorded outside production units. Later in this chapter we shall take up similar but more complete calculations.

Another approach suggested for determining the difference between potential and actual production makes use, in a purely mechanical way, of statistics relating only to production. This idea, proposed by the economist L. Klein, has been applied systematically by the group he heads at the Wharton School, University of Pennsylvania.[9] It is based on the observation that output capacities and manpower resources grow in a regular manner. Potential production therefore also has steady growth. The oscillations shown by output statistics can be interpreted accordingly as due to variations in the differential we are examining.

Rather than define the operational procedure in abstract terms, let us consider directly its application to French industry in Figure 8.2. The unbroken line on the graph (on a semilogarithmic scale) shows the growth of gross value added according to the index given in Chapter 1. Although the curve is fairly regular, some slight oscillations around the trend can be seen, with high points in 1951, 1956–57, and 1962–64. This suggests that one might draw a broken line of segments joining successive high points, and regard this new line as tracing the growth of productive potential. In the example considered here, the broken line appears almost as a straight line. Whatever the real shape, the differential between this fictitious growth and real growth can be considered a measure of the shortfall of actual output below potential output. On this basis we find a shortfall of 5.8 percent in 1954, 4.6 percent in 1959, and 1.2 percent in 1965.

This calculation, although extremely sketchy, can be improved in two ways. On the one hand, the use of annual series often underestimates the real shortfall, since annual averages conceal the amplitude of short-

[9] See, for example, L. Klein and R. Summers, "The Wharton Index of Capacity Utilization," University of Pennsylvania, Philadelphia, 1966.

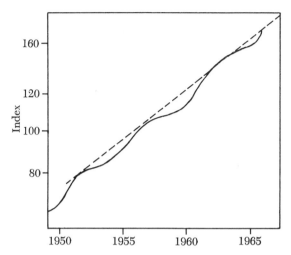

Fig. 8.2. Gross value added in industry, 1949–69.

term fluctuations. It is therefore preferable to repeat the calculation on the basis of quarterly series seasonally adjusted (a quarter is a sufficiently long period to eliminate most of the erratic variations in monthly statistics). On the other hand, to cover directly industry as a whole in the calculation amounts to assuming that productive capacities are fully employed in every sector at the peaks, which is never entirely true. One can hope therefore to get closer to reality by operating as we have done above, but for each sector taken separately. The aggregative shortfall is then calculated as the weighted average of the shortfalls in the different sectors.

Adams has carried out a calculation on this basis for 1955–67 for several countries including France, using seasonally adjusted quarterly series and a breakdown of industry into eight sectors.[10] His index of capacity utilization shows, as might be expected, a bigger differential than that suggested by our sketchy calculation. The index stood at 99 percent in the first quarter of 1958, and 98 percent in the first quarter of 1964. In the period covered, the low points were 88 percent in the first quarters of 1955 and 1959, 93 percent in the first half of 1965, and 91 percent in the second half of 1967. It would certainly have been below 88 percent at the beginning of 1954 if the calculation had covered that period.

[10] G. Adams, "Capacity Utilization in Europe," *Wharton Quarterly*, Summer, 1968.

These calculations applying the mechanical method of the Wharton School confirm the results we had reached earlier on the relative position of the various periods. Of all the slowdown periods, 1953–54 had the lowest-capacity utilization; then came early 1959, then the 12 months preceding the spring of 1968, and finally early 1956. In brief, over the period 1949–69, the pressure of demand seems to have been on an upward trend, but this trend remained fairly shallow.

The Adams article also affords comparison between a number of countries. Over the period 1953–67, the average level of the index of capacity utilization was close to 95 percent in France, Britain, Germany, and the Netherlands, but about 91 percent in Belgium and Italy, and only 85 percent in the United States. The comparison between the French and American positions can also be made on the basis of more elaborate measures of the differential between actual and potential production, however imprecise and imperfectly comparable these measures are. We have estimated this differential at 5 or 6 percent at its highest periods (1953, 1959, and 1968) on the assumption that it was virtually nil in 1957. The average estimate for the years 1953–63 is about 2.5 percent. Assuming similarly that the differential was nil in the United States in 1953, we have deduced from the calculations of the Economic Advisers to the President that the biggest gap was 12 percent in 1958 and early 1961.[11] Over the period 1953–63 the average differential was about 6 percent.

These comparisons, although obviously approximate, suggest that demand in France was at a consistently high level, roughly equal with that observed in other European countries but substantially above that in the United States.

THE GENERATION OF DEMAND

What factors account for the strength of French postwar demand? To study this question, we shall first examine briefly the end uses of production as recorded in the French National Accounts, and then consider changes in the composition of final demand. This examination will act as background to the subsequent discussion; indeed, it seems likely that the pressure of demand originated principally in the end uses of production whose growth was fastest.

We must nevertheless make a distinction. The growth of some forms of demand can be regarded as naturally induced by the growth of production, which has no particular significance for explanatory analysis.

[11] *Economic Report of the President* (Washington, D.C., January 1964).

We shall therefore try to isolate those autonomous factors that may have exerted a motive force by studying certain particular forms of demand, and thereafter by using a fairly simple model, which no doubt adequately reflects currently accepted views on the subject. Finally, we shall anticipate some of the results of subsequent chapters and give a causal description of the factors of demand.

Changes in the Composition of Demand in the Postwar Period

A quick examination of the French National Accounts suggests that all the different end uses of production grew at a broadly similar rate. The proportion taken by each stayed at a more or less constant order of magnitude. As a percentage of gross domestic production, the proportions were as follows: household consumption, 70–75 percent; government consumption, about 5 percent; investment, 20–25 percent. Imports and exports each stood at about 13 percent of production. The composition of final demand did not therefore experience changes after the war comparable in scale to those occurring between 1930 and 1938, a period when the share of consumption rose considerably at the expense of investment.

Nevertheless, a less superficial examination shows significant differences. We do not of course intend to consider here short-term movements brought about by the slowing down of activity in 1952, 1958, 1965, and 1968. We are interested only in longer-term trends likely to have affected growth. These stand out fairly clearly from a comparison of the boom years 1951, 1957, 1963, and 1969.

If foreign trade is excepted, this comparison is not significantly affected by changes in relative prices. The growth rate of each type of demand is approximately the same, whether estimated at constant prices or in current prices deflated by the gross domestic production price index. Table 8.2 shows detailed data useful for the comparison.

Between 1951 and 1957, demand by central and local government agencies grew particularly fast. Its share of gross domestic production at constant prices rose from 5.8 percent to 7.7 percent. (As a component of gross domestic *production*, government consumption does not contain compensation of government employees.) This change, which seems to have been the prime mover in this period, was itself caused both by a substantial rise in military consumption and by a rapid increase in government investment, which started from a low level and almost doubled in six years. Investment in household dwellings also grew, rising from 3.0 percent to 4.1 percent of gross domestic produc-

TABLE 8.2

Growth Rates of the Various Components of Demand, 1938–63

(Percent per year)

Component	At constant prices					In real values[a]			Gross domestic production, 1963
	1951–1963	1951–1957	1957–1963	1963–1969	1938–1951	1951–1963	1951–1957	1957–1963	
Household consumption	4.5%	4.5%	4.6%	4.6%	1%	4.5%	4.2%	4.8%	71.0
Consumption by central and local government[b]	6.6	9.5	3.7	5.4	0	5.3	8.2	2.4	4.4
Gross fixed capital formation:									
Firms	5.3	4.7	6.8	6.6	6	5.3	5.1	5.5	(15.5)
Households	6.9	10.0	3.9	8.2	2	7.9	12.4	3.6	(3.8)
Government	9.5	10.5	8.5	7.9	5	9.2	11.2	7.1	(2.8)
Total	6.3	6.2	6.4	7.0	5	6.1	7.0	5.4	22.2
Total domestic demand[c]	4.9	5.1	4.8	5.3	2	4.9	5.0	4.8	99.3
Exports	5.3	1.4	9.4	9.3	5	3.3	-0.1	5.0	13.2
Imports	6.8	5.6	8.0	10.7	2	3.4	1.8	5.0	12.5
Gross domestic production	4.8	4.6	4.9	5.2	2	4.8	4.6	4.9	100.0

Note: The official figures have been corrected to eliminate distortions due to changes in methods of evaluation (new bases in 1959 and 1962).

[a]Values in current prices divided by gross domestic production price index.

[b]This item (*consommation des administrations*) also contains consumption by a few private institutions. But it does not contain compensation of government employees (this is the origin of the main difference between gross domestic production and gross domestic product).

[c]In addition to the items in this table, gross domestic production comprises consumption and investment by financial institutions and stock formation.

tion. Exports, however, were sluggish, since the pressure of domestic demand and high prices in France prevented them from growing at the same rate as production.

Between 1957 and 1963, aggregate demand by the government sector played a smaller part than in the previous six years. Expressed in constant prices, demand grew at an average of 5.5 percent per year, or just ahead of gross domestic production, but in current prices it lagged behind gross domestic production. Whereas consumption by civilian offices was rising at the same pace as aggregate demand, consumption by military departments was sluggish and public investment grew rapidly. This change in the composition of government sector demand may have had a stimulating effect on current output, since it favored the sectors producing investment goods. It seems difficult, however, to assess the scale of this effect, or even whether it occurred.

The most marked stimulating effect in this period seems to have been exerted by investment and exports of firms. This can be seen far more clearly in the accounts shown by volume than in those expressed by value. In the former, investments by firms in fixed capital goods grew from 14.6 to 16.7 percent of gross domestic production between 1957 and 1963, and exports grew from 11.6 to 14.9 percent (after removing the effects of a changed base in 1959).

In the following years, growth of investment remained the prime mover in demand, but it flowed more from households and government agencies than from firms. Although exports were still highly dynamic, their increase was accompanied by a rapid growth of imports, and therefore no longer had the same stimulating effect on aggregate demand as it did during a few years after 1958.

It would be interesting to compare trends since the war with those before it. Unfortunately, we have available for this purpose only the accounts for 1938, when the economic situation is well known to have been unrepresentative of the periods before the Great Depression. Table 8.2 presents data comparing 1938 and 1951. Whereas consumption in 1951 was at a level scarcely higher than in 1938, investment and exports had almost doubled. It seems likely, however, that the structure of final demand in 1951 was fairly similar to what it had been in the years immediately before the depression.

Autonomous Factors of Demand

The examination above shows the important part played by government demand and by the building of dwellings between 1951 and 1957, and again after 1963; by exports between 1957 and 1963; and finally by the investment of firms since 1957. For short-term analysis, there are four kinds of demand often regarded as autonomous—that is, as predetermined in the short term and as the result of factors extraneous to the current equilibrium. These same kinds of demand are also often irregular in movement, and therefore influence, more than others, the fluctuations of economic activity as a whole. Short-term equilibria are affected not only by the movements of autonomous demand, but also by changes in behavior and by decisions relating to public transfer payments. We shall try in this section to identify the effects of each of these.

Prewar. Although we do not have available complete National Accounts for periods before 1938, we can form a view of certain factors explaining the level of demand since the beginning of the century, for we can construct indicators that, although imperfect, are probably adequate for describing changes in government consumption, investment, and exports. We are thus in a position to form a picture of the motive forces behind aggregate demand from 1896 to 1938, which is less reliable than the picture for more recent years, but nevertheless need not be treated with too much reserve.

The indicators in question are shown in Table 8.3; the bases for their calculation are explained at length in the table note. Our greatest difficulties have been in estimating government demand. We have had to confine ourselves to calculating an index of government expenditure, and have been unable to isolate figures for the consumption of goods and services. The series obtained is therefore unfortunately influenced by its transfer payment content. In consequence, the results have little significance for the years 1922–24, when very large sums of war damage compensation were paid out. For the same reason, the growth of government consumption is probably underestimated by about 10 percent for 1896–1913, and overestimated by about 10 percent for 1913–29 and by some percentage points for 1929–38. Nevertheless, the results obtained are sufficiently good to define broadly autonomous demands affecting growth from the beginning of the century.

The acceleration of the economy just before 1900 seems to have been due to the recovery first of investment and then of exports. Both of these kinds of demand grew on the average at 3 percent a year between 1896 and 1913, when aggregate production was increasing by less than 2 percent. Government demand remained almost static from 1896 to 1903, then grew steadily by 2 percent a year from 1903 to 1912. It did not rise fast until just before World War I.[12]

The most dynamic role in growth during the 1920's was again played by exports and investment. The former reached a peak in 1928, and the latter in 1930, whereas government expenditure, which of course had grown considerably during the war, was sluggish. By comparison with 1913, the situation in 1929 probably provides a good illustration of the role of prime mover played by the autonomous forms of demand. Whereas aggregate output had grown by around 30 percent, exports and investment had both increased by 44 percent; apart from transfer payments, the real value of government expenditure had simultaneously risen by the same proportion.

In the 1930's, exports and investment dropped steeply and then stagnated at a low level. In this period, the real value of public expenditure

[12] The prosperity of the years 1907–12 has often been attributed to the "armaments race." Budget expenditure for national defense certainly grew by 50 percent between 1905 and 1912, but prices rose simultaneously by 10 percent. The increase in volume of public expenditure due to the growth of military expenditure seems to have been secondary to the rise in investment, and even to have been less than the increase in exports.

TABLE 8.3
Estimates of Autonomous Demand, 1896–1938
(Billion francs)

| Year | Value in current prices | | Value in average prices, 1901–10 | | | |
	Government expenditure	Exports	Government expenditure	Exports	Investments	Total
1896	4.43	3.40	4.7	3.9	4.8	13.4
1897	4.33	3.60	4.8	4.1	4.9	13.8
1898	4.56	3.51	4.8	3.9	5.1	13.8
1899	4.61	4.15	4.7	4.5	5.0	14.2
1900	4.81	4.11	4.8	4.3	5.8	14.9
1901	4.85	4.01	4.9	4.4	5.5	14.8
1902	4.80	4.25	4.9	4.6	5.4	14.9
1903	4.73	4.25	4.7	4.5	5.3	14.5
1904	4.80	4.45	4.8	4.7	5.4	14.9
1905	4.89	4.87	4.9	5.0	5.5	15.4
1906	5.10	5.26	5.1	5.1	5.6	15.8
1907	5.22	5.60	5.2	5.3	6.1	16.6
1908	5.41	5.05	5.3	5.0	6.1	16.4
1909	5.65	5.73	5.5	5.4	6.4	17.3
1910	5.82	6.23	5.5	5.7	6.9	18.1
1911	5.99	6.08	5.6	5.6	7.5	18.7
1912	6.24	6.71	5.7	6.1	8.0	19.8
1913	6.72	6.88	6.1	6.3	8.1	20.5
1922	53.4	21.4	14.8	5.4	6.6	26.8
1923	46.9	30.9	12.0	6.5	7.0	25.5
1924	52.3	42.4	11.9	7.5	9.2	28.6
1925	46.9	45.8	9.8	7.8	8.5	26.1
1926	54.2	59.7	8.6	8.5	9.8	26.9
1927	60.9	54.9	9.1	9.2	8.0	26.3
1928	61.2	51.4	9.4	9.3	10.6	29.3
1929	66.0	50.1	9.4	9.2	11.7	30.3
1930	79.3	42.8	11.3	8.3	13.0	32.6
1931	77.4	30.4	11.3	7.1	11.5	29.9
1932	77.0	19.7	12.2	5.4	9.4	27.0
1933	78.5	18.5	12.7	5.5	9.3	27.5
1934	73.1	17.9	12.2	5.7	8.7	26.6
1935	72.9	15.5	13.0	5.2	8.5	26.7
1936	79.3	15.5	13.4	4.9	8.9	27.2
1937	97.8	23.9	14.3	5.3	9.6	29.2
1938	108.8	30.6	13.6	5.8	8.7	28.1

Note on bases for Table 8.3
  1. *Government expenditure in current prices.* We have shown total reported expenditure in the budget of the central government, *départements,* and *communes,* as given by the *Annuaire statistique rétrospectif,* 1961 (interpolations have been made for expenditures by *départements* and *communes* in certain interwar years for which the figures were not available). The homogeneity of the published series must be viewed with some doubt; only a historic study of the budgetary documents themselves could eventually enable these series to be improved. We have safeguarded ourselves against the worst errors by comparing the figures used with the analysis of central government budgets for a selected number of years as shown in J. Edmond-Grangé, *Le Budget fonctionnel en France* (Paris, 1963).
  It is relevant to note that expenditures by government agencies defined as above are different from the total of "Consumption and investment by government agencies" in the National Accounts. Our figures

trended sharply upward, which no doubt explains why the depression in France, although long-lasting, was not deeper.

Against this historic background, growth in the years 1951–57 seems to have been somewhat unusual on the demand side, whereas in the years 1957–69 the stimulus to growth was very similar to that in earlier periods of expansion, at the beginning of the century and in the 1920's.

Postwar. The preceding analysis is still incomplete in that it analyzes only partially the autonomous causes of variations in demand. Changes in fiscal pressure or in households' propensity to consume may have affected aggregate demand quite as much as intensified investment by firms. In the absence of National Accounts figures, we must make do with this partial study for the prewar periods. But we can give the subject a fuller examination for the last 20 years.

For this purpose we shall define a simplified model of demand formation, and then interpret observed development as due to changes in the exogenous variables and the parameters of the model. Let Q be the

---

Note on bases for Table 8.3 (cont.)

include, in addition to purchases of goods and services, expenditures on staff and even transfer payments. The latter, which could affect the validity of the interpretations shown here, seem to have represented roughly the following share of government agencies' expenditures: 30 percent in 1902, 25 percent in 1912, 50 percent in 1922, 33 percent in 1931, and 35 percent in 1938.

2. *Exports in current prices.* Figures from customs statistics relate to direct trade (*commerce spécial*) of France with foreign countries and French-connected areas overseas.

3. *Government expenditure in 1901–10 prices.* We have divided expenditure in current prices by a price index calculated on the following basis. We can obtain an approximate estimate of price movements by considering the ratio between an index of wages and an index of labor productivity, for if labor remuneration's share of the value of production had remained constant, this ratio would have moved exactly as a general index of national output prices. Trends observed in certain countries suggest that labor remuneration has maintained its share at a constant or only slightly rising figure. We can probably assume that it was broadly static in France from 1896 to 1920, and thereafter grew slightly up to 1938.

If we take as an index of wages the index resulting from the survey of Conciliation Boards (see *Annuaire statistique*, 1961, p. 254) and as an index of productivity the index calculated in the first part of our study for output per man-hour (both inside and outside of the productive sectors), we can make the following observations: From 1896 to 1913, the ratio under consideration rose by 18 percent, i.e. by far less than did the index of wholesale prices of 45 goods, which increased by 42 percent. We have taken a price index number of 118 for 1913, with 1896 = 100. From 1913 to 1929, the ratio grew by a factor of 6.3, the same as the retail price index of 34 goods, and slightly more than the wholesale price index. We have taken this result as our index number. From 1929 to 1938, the ratio rose by 25 percent, whereas the index of 34 goods increased by 14 percent and the wholesale price index by only 4 percent. We have taken the index of 34 goods for this period, thus assuming that labor remuneration's share of the value of production had grown by 10 percent between 1929 and 1938. For the intervening years we have interpolated to the best of our ability from the indexes available.

The price index thus obtained moves along a path similar to that of the cost of living index shown in "L'Intérêt réel du capital" (Special Study no. 1, Institut de Conjoncture, Paris 1942). The most outstanding differences concern movements from 1896 to 1900 (when, according to the study mentioned, the cost of living was static) and the 1929 level in relation to that in 1913 (which the study shows as 10 percent below our estimate).

4. *Exports at 1901–10 prices.* For the period 1896–1913, we have divided the value of exports by the index of average values covering both exports and imports (based on the index of the volume of foreign trade in this period as given in *Annuaire statistique*, 1961, p. 205). For subsequent years we have used direct the index of export volume.

5. *Investments.* We have made use of our index of the relative values of total gross fixed investment (see Table D.3, p. 528). In order to show an estimate that can be interpreted as expressed in billion francs of the period 1901–10, we have multiplied the series by a number such that for 1938 the ratio between the volume of investment and the volume of exports was the same as that in the National Accounts for that year.

demand facing production, and necessarily equal *ex post* to gross domestic production. We can describe it as follows to show its various
components:

(1) $$Q = C + G + If + Ih + Ig + Ex - Imp$$

with the following definitions:

C   Household consumption
G   Consumption by government
If   Investment by firms
Ih   Investment by households
Ig   Investment by government
Ex   Exports
Imp Imports

These forms of demand will be divided into two classes: those regarded as purely exogenous or autonomous, and those linked to other
specific factors in the equilibrium. This dichotomy is to some extent
arbitrary; it exaggerates the true differences, but it is not unmeaning-
ful.[13] We have taken as exogenous variables G, Ih, Ig, and Ex.

Investment by firms and imports will be linked to the volume of production:

(2) $$If = aQ \qquad Imp = bQ$$

where a is the propensity of firms to invest and b is the propensity to
import. (A small part of gross domestic production is made up of household production, but we shall not take this into account.) Household
consumption will be linked to household disposable revenue or income,
R:

(3) $$C = cR$$

where c is the propensity to consume.

Finally, household disposable income will be linked to the value of
production by a relationship allowing for both net transfer payments
to government agencies and nondistributed profits of firms. More precisely, we shall express this as

[13] We have hesitated over the treatment of imports and investment by firms. We
might have considered these two values as exogenous, the former by correspondence
with exports and the latter because of the great need for capital goods in the French
postwar economy. However, we have thought it best to use the model to the fullest
extent possible, since its relationships make it complementary to a direct examination
of the National Accounts. For this reason we have settled for a fairly short list of
exogenous variables.

(4) $$R = (1 - er)(Q - T)$$

where T represents net transfers to government agencies, r the share of firms' profits in disposable income, and e firms' propensity to save (the ratio between firms' savings and disposable profits). Value T will be considered as exogenous.

When referred back to (1), equations (2), (3), and (4) imply

(5) $\quad [1 - c(1 - er) - a + b]Q = G + Ih + Ig + Ex - c(1 - er)T$

This relationship can be considered as determining aggregate demand Q as a function of the exogenous variables (G, Ih, Ig, Ex, and T) and the propensities (a, b, c, e, r).

With this relationship, changes in aggregate demand between two periods can be analyzed into a sum of terms, each related to the effect of changes in an exogenous variable or propensity. If dQ, dG, dIh, ..., da, db ... represent changes in these variables and these propensities, relationship (5) implies approximately the following:

(6) $\quad [1 - c(1 - er) - a + b]dQ$
$$= [dG + dIh + dIg + dEx - c(1 - er)dT]$$
$$+ [Qda + (1 - er)(Q - T)dc - cr(Q - T)de - ce(Q - T)dr - Qdb]$$

Each term of the second side of the equation has a particular significance. Thus, save only for the effect of the "multiplier" $1/[1 - c(1 - er) - a + b]$, dG represents the effect of changes in consumption by government, minus $c(1 - er)dT$ that of variations in net transfers to government, Qda that of modifications in firms' propensity to invest, etc. We know the values for the different variables from the National Accounts, and are able to calculate the propensities for each period considered. We can then calculate each term in the right side of equation (6).

This calculation has been carried out for comparisons between 1938 and 1951, 1951 and 1957, and 1957 and 1963. Table 8.4 shows the results both for changes in exogenous demands (first square bracket of right-hand side of equation (6)), and for changes in the propensities (second square bracket).[14] We felt it appropriate to group the results in this way,

---

[14] In calculating firms' propensity to invest, we have included only investment in fixed capital, since stock formation is subject to erratic movements of little significance for a study of growth. In calculating T, we have taken the net balance of transfer transactions in the government account (the balance shown in the revenue account of the government), and have added the balance of external expenditure by government and the balance of subsidies for capital equipment and war damages (considered here as capital transactions). To express T in 1959 prices, we have

TABLE 8.4

External Causes of Changes in Demand, 1938–63

(1959 prices, *billion francs*)

	Category	1938–1951	1951–1957	1957–1963
Exogenous demand:				
dG	Consumption by government	−0.5	4.9	3.3
dIg	Investment by government	1.4	2.4	3.3
$c(1 - er)d$T	Effect on demand of net transfers to government	−17.8	−1.0	−5.0
	Effect on demand of transactions by government	−16.9	6.3	1.6
dIh	Investment by households	1.3	4.0	2.4
dEx	Exports and net services sold abroad	11.5	2.1	18.7
	Total	−4.1	12.4	22.7
Effect of exogenous changes in propensities:				
Qda	Firms' propensity to invest[a]	8.5	0.4	4.2
$(1 - er)$ (Q − T)dc	Households' propensity to consume[a]	0.3	−4.6	−5.6
$-cr$(Q − T)de	Companies' propensity to save[b]	−0.9	−1.0	−0.2
$-ce$(Q − T)dr	Share of profits in disposable income[a]	1.2	1.2	0.7
Qdb	Propensity to import[b]	−0.1	−1.4	−6.0
	Total	9.0	−5.4	−6.9

[a] A positive sign (inflationary effect) represents a rise in the propensity.
[b] A negative sign (deflationary effect) represents a drop in the propensity.

since, in a growing economy, to regard a variable as purely exogenous means ignoring the fact that in the long term it must follow the general path and itself grow. For this reason, the results shown in the first part of Table 8.4 are not truly comparable in order of magnitude with those in the second part.

Moreover, comparability between columns would not have been significantly improved if we had divided the results by the volume of gross domestic production in the initial year of each column; findings expressed in francs at constant prices are more readily intelligible. We should bear in mind, however, that gross domestic production was 32 percent higher in 1957 than in 1951, when in turn it was 27 percent above the level of 1938.

The results in Table 8.4 confirm the indications given earlier: they show clearly the importance of growth in government demand from 1951 to 1957, and of exports and an increased propensity to invest by

applied the gross domestic production price index. In calculating gross disposable income of firms, we have subtracted direct taxes, subsidies for capital equipment, and war damage from gross income in the accounts. The two latter items have also been subtracted from company savings. Movements from 1957 to 1963 have been corrected so as to eliminate the effect of the 1959 change of base.

firms in the 1957–63 expansion. They also reveal other factors that are important. The column for comparisons between 1938 and 1951 brings out clearly the unrepresentative nature of the equilibrium in 1938. Growth of demand between the two years shown was due to a return from untypically low values for exports and for the propensity of firms to invest. Growth was held back by the reestablishment of a balanced national budget, and the resulting increase in net fiscal pressure.

In the two periods following the war, the propensity of households to consume fell (the propensity to save rose), with the result that the growth of aggregate demand was substantially slowed down. We should note, however, that in our study of savings we attribute this phenomenon partly to inflation caused by too high demand; this inflation led households to rebuild their cash positions, whose purchasing power had fallen considerably by 1951 and again between 1956 and 1960 (cf. Chapter 9). The drop in households' propensity to consume thus seems partly due to pressure from exogenous demands. However, the outcome cannot be wholly explained in this way; it was also partly the result of an autonomous change in behavior.

The increase in net taxation (tax receipts less government transfers to firms and households) similarly played a moderating role between 1957 and 1963. In this period the overall effect of government transactions on demand was practically nil. This reinforces the conclusion reached earlier on this topic.

From 1951 to 1963, the impact on aggregate demand of company self-financing was almost constant, with a drop in profits' share of disposable income more or less offset by an increase in companies' propensity to save.

Last, between 1957 and 1963 a marked rise in the propensity to import lowered the pressure of demand on domestic producers. One cannot avoid comparing this fact with the growth of exports. It would be perfectly justifiable to calculate a difference between the two sets of estimates in Table 8.4 (18.7 for exports and 6.0 for the effect of the propensity to import) if the assumptions underlying our model were perfect also—that is, if the exports had been the direct result of decisions external to the French economy, and if the volume of imports were mechanically linked to that of production. But such a view is obviously too extreme, especially when applied to a period in which the opening up of the Common Market led to increased specialization among the different national economies. To take the opposite extreme, we could have considered the balance of trade ($Ex - Imp$) as an exogenous variable instead of exports, and no longer paid attention to the propensity to import. We should then have shown 2.6 instead of 18.7 in Table 8.4 for the period 1957–63 (and 5.5 instead of 2.1 for the period 1951–57). The stimulating effect of changes affecting foreign trade would then have appeared very much lower than we have indicated.

It will be interesting to extend the calculations, when a homogeneous series of accounts in constant prices is published, so as to compare the two boom years 1963 and 1969. Without too great a risk of error, we can anticipate the results. There will be a very slight net impact on aggregate demand from government transactions, since the rapid growth of their investment and the more regular pace of their consumption have been offset by a very substantial increase in net transfers to the state. As a result of the boom in house building in 1964 and 1965, the growth of investment by households in the period 1963–69 will show up as high. Measured as in Table 8.4, however, its impact will still be less than that of increases in exports.

In regard to the propensities, an expansionary effect will certainly result from a rise in the investment rate of firms, as well as a deflationary effect due to an increase in the propensity to import. Probably a slightly deflationary effect will be observed, brought about by a small increase in households' and companies' propensities to save, and probably also a weak inflationary effect resulting from a slight drop in profits.

In brief, this study of autonomous factors in demand leads us to distinguish quite clearly two periods in postwar growth. The first, prior to 1958, was marked chiefly by the impetus provided by government expenditure. The second recalled in many respects the periods of expansion at the beginning of the century and in the 1920's, since its main motive forces were investment by firms and exports.

Why Was Demand So Sustained?

The last 20 years are distinguished chiefly by the length of the expansion experienced, which is still under way with no sign of faltering. In explaining this phenomenon, it is appropriate to attribute a distinctive role to the pressure exerted by aggregate demand; this indeed was not absolutely constant, but its slacker periods were not pronounced and were fairly brief. Before turning to an analysis of the stimulating effects of demand, we shall describe the reasons for this high pressure.

At this point, therefore, we must anticipate the detailed studies in the following chapters, which will provide justification for the broad picture we are about to describe. The individual features of postwar demand can be identified only by examining the demand for investment, the formation of savings, the financing of firms, or policies for short-term regulation of the economy.

Our explanation must probably concern not so much the first ten years of growth, when in the nature of things demand was strongly stimulated by the immediate requirements for getting the economy under way again, but rather the following period, when other factors took over. Now we have seen that, in fact from 1958 onward, demand chiefly took the form of an increase in exports and investment. This fact must engage our attention.

In short, the pressure of demand on the French productive system over the past 20 years seems to have been due to a conjunction of four main causes: world economic expansion, the urgency of old or newly felt wants, a profound change in the frame of reference for firms' investment decisions, and last a deliberate choice in economic policy.

The recent world expansion is quite as remarkable as expansion in France. Not only has every major industrial country benefited from a growth rate markedly higher than in the past, but also since the war none of them has experienced a serious economic crisis. This context was eminently favorable to economic activity the world over, and in France in particular.

Demand was stimulated by this in two ways. First, in a period of lively international contact, economic development in neighboring areas could not help having favorable effects on the spirit of enterprise and investment. The example of other countries clearly was an important factor in the big change of attitude of investors toward a confident and optimistic assessment of French economic prospects. We can date this change in attitude to around 1957, that is, to the time when the stimulating effect of immediate postwar needs was played out (cf. Chapter 9, p. 276).

Second, world expansion explains the high level of foreign demand on French exporters. This was already being felt before the 1958 devaluation. At that time, when France maintained exchange controls and French currency was overvalued even allowing for certain aids to exports, sales of finished products abroad were growing rapidly in volume: by 12 and 15 percent per year on the average from 1953 to 1957 for investment goods and consumption goods, respectively (cf. Chapter 11, p. 370).

In the 1950's, substantial unsatisfied needs for investment were still to be found in firms, households, and government. There had been little renewal of productive equipment in the ten years of economic ill-health that followed the 1929 depression, and during the war it was almost totally suspended. In 1946, therefore, requirements were considerable. The priority given in that period to investment in basic sectors had the effect of putting off once again the satisfaction of demand in other sectors. As we saw in Chapter 3, it was only from 1955 that "light invest-ment" became significant, and that industry as a whole was able to re-place old with new productive equipment.

The considerable need for housing was compounded by the fact that market disorganization led to an irrational employment of the existing facilities. It is true that the French population scarcely increased be-tween 1930 and 1950 and that wartime destruction actually had affected only a small proportion of buildings. But there were still unsatisfied needs left over from the period between the wars, when building had been substantially held back by the freezing of rents beginning in 1914. But above all, the rise in the birthrate and large-scale migration toward the cities created imbalances that were particularly marked in the large urban centers. House construction was not considered a priority at the end of the war, and a figure of 300,000 dwelling completions per year was not reached before 1959, although this is a modest enough figure since it represents only some 2 percent of the housing stock. Similarly, the rise in birthrate and in the proportion of young people at school made enlargement of school and university buildings urgently neces-sary; progress in medicine required investment in hospitals, etc.

Considerable unsatisfied needs, therefore, persisted throughout the 1950's. It may even be surprising that these were not more strongly evi-dent, particularly in the short-term recession of the years 1952–53. The reason is that available finance was at that time very limited, as we shall see in Chapters 9 and 10. Firms were forced to rely chiefly on their profits, individuals needing housing first had to accumulate substantial savings, and finally the state itself aimed at reaching a surplus in order to stabilize prices (in 1952–54), or at supporting other types of expen-diture (in 1956–57).

To the more longstanding needs at war's end came others resulting from the rise in living standards, urbanization, and social progress. There is no need to dwell on the growth of private consumption and manu-facturing capital; to the extent that it accompanies an expansion of production, growth of this kind is entirely normal and cannot be re-garded as a cause of demand *pressure*. But the new needs born of growth often took the form of demand for capital equipment or public services, the financing for which is notoriously difficult. For the pressure of ag-gregate demand not to be affected by this, the public would have had to accept more readily a parallel increase of taxation. Yet, as soon as the domestic balance ceased to be bothersome, taxation tended to lag be-hind the accelerated growth of public services.

Investment demand by firms, moreover, grew far more than was re-quired merely by the enlargement of output capacities. It was due largely to investments designed to raise productivity and to reduce manpower requirements or improve the quality of manufacture, and was the consequence of a change in firms' decision-making frame of reference.

Three factors seem to have played an important part in this respect, as we shall see in Chapter 9. First, the cost of capital equipment in relation to that of labor dropped very fast, not only as a result of changes brought about by growth, such as wage increases or a drop in the real price of modern machinery, but also because of several substantial changes in taxation. Second, as the dynamic nature of world expansion came to be appreciated, and probably also in the larger firms as some confidence developed in the outlook defined by the National Plan, feelings of uncertainty about the future tended to weaken. This encouraged modernization schemes from which returns could be expected only over a time scale longer than a few years ahead. Last, competition at home, and still more competition from abroad on French and foreign markets, accelerated capital obsolescence and forced firms to find the tools for meeting a demand that was constantly changing.

An awareness of these three factors was not of course limited to business firms; it was fully taken into account in nationally owned undertakings. More widely, this awareness can be said to have been at the heart of policies for national development. Government decisions about major enterprises or industrial projects with a long pay-off period (e.g. in aeronautics, atomic energy, etc.) and that—whether right or not—did stimulate demand were made in the double context of confidence in future growth and increased international competition.

Finally, in addition to the reasons just given to explain the pressure of demand (world expansion, large unfilled needs, the attitude of investors), there was another factor that must not be overlooked—deliberate decisions of economic policy. In the fine choice between the two objectives, growth and price stability, which usually appear mutually exclusive in the short term, governments in most cases selected the former. This does not mean, obviously, that inflation was deliberately sought, but the risk that it might develop seemed in most cases less serious than the risk of slowing down growth prematurely.

We shall consider in Chapter 11 the circumstances and results of short-term economic management. We shall contend that this was not particularly easy to carry out in postwar France, for two reasons. The economy was affected by perturbations from outside (military policy in 1952–53 and 1956–57, massive repatriation in 1962, social crisis in 1968). Automatic stabilizers, often regarded as important in certain foreign countries and particularly in the United States, were still weak in France.

In these rather unfavorable circumstances, economic management can be seen to have had some success. It was not, however, entirely free of error in its appreciation of the relative strengths of trends, often contradictory, operating at particular times. Even had this been the case, it could not have aspired to certainty; the choice of economic policies always takes place in a context strongly influenced by chance.

The risk that supply might develop in excess of demand and that growth might therefore go into a long decline led to policy choices that by hindsight seem to have been the cause of an excess of demand, and consequently of rising prices. A case in point is the policy of wage increases in 1955, followed by the ill-controlled inflation of 1956–57. Another case is the somewhat too sharp push given to the economy in 1960 after the 1958–59 stabilization. Yet another case is the 1963 budget, drafted in the fall of 1962, when there were fears of unemployment among repatriated nationals. Finally, there was the policy of expansion in the summer and fall of 1968, for fear that too many businesses in difficulties would go bankrupt. In none of these different cases did the government of the day aim mainly at avoiding the risk of stimulating too high a pressure of demand.

THE EFFECT OF DEMAND ON GROWTH

We have as yet formed only tentative views on the question we must now deal with: how far can French growth be accounted for by the pressure and steadiness of growth? The influence of demand on growth is still poorly understood by economists. Objective studies are lacking, with the result that contradictory hypotheses can still be maintained with equal authority. This can be seen clearly in Britain, where attempts to achieve a short-term equilibrium have from time to time made it necessary to impose measures temporarily slowing down growth. Most commentators presume that higher and more sustained pressure of demand in Britain would have promoted more rapid growth. Professor Paish, however, holds the opposite view, that the rate of expansion would have been faster if average demand had been less strong, for prices and foreign trade would then have developed in a more balanced way.[15]

Nevertheless, the method adopted in the first part of our book can serve as a guideline for an analytical study of this topic: we can examine in turn what influence has been exerted by the level and regularity of demand on labor input, capital input, and the residual. This approach makes it possible to handle in a coherent manner the different factors involved. It should lead to answers that may be only partial but that will be objective.

[15] F. W. Paish, *Studies in an Inflationary Economy* (New York, 1962).

Work Supplied

The postwar situation of sustained demand for goods stimulated a particularly strong demand for labor by the productive system. This led to substantial immigration of foreign workers, a consistently high rate of employment in the French population, and the persistence of rather long hours of work. Let us examine each of these factors in turn and try to measure them as far as is feasible.

1. The pressure of demand influences migratory movements by foreign or North African workers. On the average, the annual inflow into the labor market was 60,000 persons between 1947 and 1954, 100,000 between 1954 and 1963, and 130,000 between 1964 and 1968. This meant an increase of the French labor force in these three periods of 0.3 percent, 0.5 percent, and 0.7 percent a year. The inflow would doubtless have been slightly bigger still, had French growth been entirely regular, since a drop in immigration can be observed after the slackening of growth in 1952, 1958, and 1965 (the inflow was low in 1953–55, in 1959–60, and after 1966). Immigration might well in such a case have raised the French labor force by an annual average of 0.6 percent over the years 1949–69.

But France has been a host country to immigrants for a long time. The net inflow was reversed only in the depression years 1931–36. Even if demand had been only moderate in the period after World War II, the labor force would have been swelled by the arrival of foreign workers, say at some 0.2 percent per year.

2. There can be little doubt that the adult population's activity rate is to some extent a response to the productive system's call on manpower. We observed this in Chapter 2 when we calculated a corrected activity rate, eliminating the effect of changes in the sex and age structure of the working population (see p. 72). At a time when the overall trend was downward, the activity rate was particularly high in 1911, a year of rapid growth, and immediately after World War I, when part of the female population and older people had to replace male losses in the labor market. On the other hand, the rate was low in 1901 and 1936, both depression years. It was also observed that the scale of female employment varied considerably from one *département* to another, and that it was high where demand from firms was high.

This phenomenon is difficult to measure, because the activity rates are known only for census years, and these were too widely spaced for the influence of demand pressure to be distinguished clearly from all the factors, sociological or other, that affect long-term changes in the quantity of labor.

We should note, however, that the activity rate shown for the spring of 1936 was 1.5 points too low in relation to the long-term linear trend fitted to the years 1911, 1931, and 1954. Thus, in that year of quite pronounced stagnation, the labor force seems to have contained 600,000 persons fewer than if the pressure of demand had been more normal.

For the postwar period, we can obtain a picture of the aggregate effect of changes in the quantity of labor by comparing annual estimates of the labor force with a series representing what it would have been year by year if the activity rates by sex and age had moved steadily in line with long-term trends.[16] From the 1954 census, which took place at the time of recovery, to 1957, when demand for labor was particularly vigorous, the surplus observed in the first series over the second was 380,000 workers. But between the years 1957 and 1959 there was a deficit of only 160,000 persons; subsequently the series based on annual estimates grew considerably less fast than would be suggested by the figures calculated from trend activity rates. A recent study by Salais enables us to investigate the problem from a different viewpoint.[17] From a study of French growth between 1951 and 1968, he has shown that short-term economic fluctuations led to variations in activity rates whose effect on the size of the employed labor force was about double that revealed by an estimate of numbers unemployed (persons seeking work). But a permanently low level of demand over a long period would probably have an even more marked effect on activity rates.

Given these observations, we consider it likely that the French labor force would have been some 240,000 persons smaller in the postwar period if demand had been only moderate. This factor would certainly have reduced the level of output. To the extent that the level of demand observed in 1950 was inevitable after the war, the rate of growth would also have been lower.

3. Similar conclusions apply to the effect of changes in the employment rate of the labor force. From 1949 to 1966 the average number unemployed was 250,000, that is, approximately the same as the number registered in each of those two end years. Referring to Table 8.1 (p. 231), we can assume that the proportion of wage earners unemployed would have stood at about 3 percent if demand had been only moderate; the number unemployed would have reached approximately 370,000—that is, 120,000 more than in fact was observed.

---

[16] M. Praderie, "La population active employée par branche entre 1954 et 1962," *Etudes et conjoncture*, March 1964, p. 18. See also the report on the National Accounts for the year 1967, *Etudes et conjoncture*, May–June 1968, p. 73.

[17] R. Salais, "L'Adaptation à court terme de l'offre à la demande de travail; essai de mesure globale."

4. It would also seem that the pressure of demand in the postwar period must have been the cause of the long hours worked. On examination, however, this effect appears too weak to be estimated with precision. First, the length of time spent at work in France was not exceptional in the 1950's. Chapter 2 showed, it is true, that the figure then was considerably above the 1938 level (12 percent higher for industrial workers, and 6 percent for the labor force as a whole). But what was exceptional was the situation in 1938.

In relation to 1929, annual hours worked had dropped by 6 percent, both in industry and in the economy as a whole. Denison has carefully compared the number of hours worked by full-time male wage earners employed outside agriculture in a number of different countries.[18] He concludes that the figure in 1962 was slightly lower in France than in Britain, slightly higher than in Italy, and higher by 5 percent and 7 percent than in the United States and Germany. According to Denison, length of time at work hardly changed from 1950 to 1962 in three countries—France, Britain, and Italy.

A downward trend in the length of time worked has been observed in most countries. It may be due to the pressure of demand that this trend appears in France later than elsewhere, and that time spent at work was thus particularly high in the late 1960's.[19] But this seems a difficult phenomenon to analyze.

Second, we cannot easily form an opinion on the influence of pressure of demand on time worked. In the short term we can observe that working hours fall when the economy slows down, but this may be due to a passing reaction of firms that may prefer to operate in this way rather than cut down their work force too drastically. If demand remained sluggish, hours might lengthen again.

To illustrate this comment, let us consider what happened in France in the years 1930–36. According to the Ministry of Labor survey of establishments with over 100 employees, weekly hours worked dropped by 11 percent from March 1930 to March 1932, whereas numbers employed fell by 19 percent. Subsequently, hours worked partly caught up again, while numbers employed continued to fall (from March 1932 to March 1936 the variation was +6 percent for working hours and −9 percent for numbers employed). All in all, of the 30 percent drop in the quantity of labor between March 1930 and March 1936, 5 percent was accounted for by working hours and 25 percent by numbers employed.

[18] E. F. Denison, *Why Growth Rates Differ: Postwar Experience in Nine Western Countries* (Washington, D.C., 1967), chap. 6.

[19] See Chapter 2; also B. Durieux, "La Baisse de la durée du travail," *Economie et statistique*, September 1970.

TABLE 8.5
Influence of Demand Pressure on Labor Supply, 1949–66
(Percent)

Source of labor increase	Annual rate of increase, 1949–66	Total increase as of 1966[a]
Immigration	0.26%	4.6%
Increase in work performed per unit of time	0.06	1.0
Increase in number of non-immigrants employed	0.03	0.6
Increase in length of time worked per worker	0.12	2.0
Total	0.46%	8.2%

[a]The figures in this column represent the supplementary amount of labor mobilized by the effect of demand over what would have been mobilized at a demand level corresponding to a constant unemployment rate of 3 percent of the wage-earning population.

These considerations lead us to think that the pressure of demand has probably acted on labor input through the level of employment rather than through a lengthening of hours worked. If an estimate is to be attempted, the most credible would seem to be that if demand had been uniformly at a moderate level, it would have been accompanied by working hours lower by 2 percent in 1966 than were in fact observed.

5. We can now try to bring together all the estimates just made, however uncertain. This is done in Table 8.5, which shows the excess of work supplied over what its level would have been in the postwar period if a merely moderate pressure of demand had entailed a constant rate of underemployment from 1954 at 3 percent of wage earners (a better situation than in 1901 or 1931, only slightly worse than in 1906 or 1954, and comparable with those in 1896 and 1968).

According to these estimates, the additional quantity of work thus mobilized by pressure of demand was 8.2 percent of that supplied in 1966. This increase is substantial although marginal. If we assume an elasticity of production to labor input of 0.7, we can estimate that the impact on the 1966 gross domestic production was about 6 percent, or approximately one year's growth at present rates.

Can we form a picture of the benefits that might have been obtained if the pressure of demand had been more regular? We suggested an estimate earlier for immigration. We know of course that the estimate is nil for the rate of employment and for hours worked, two variables that obviously were affected when the economy slowed down but that apparently thereafter regained the levels they would have attained if growth had not been interrupted. This would leave as a question whether a steadier demand would have led to favorable effects on the behavior of labor supply. Although this seems likely, we have no idea of the order of magnitude involved, and have found no way of measuring it. In all, the effects on labor input of a steadier demand must have been small.

Capital Used

In relation to capital, the pressure of demand can act in two ways: by setting off changes in the way existing capital equipment is used, or by stimulating a greater or lesser degree of investment, that is, a faster or slower growth of the volume of capital available to firms. Unfortunately, no general study exists of the ways in which existing capital equipment is used. An analysis of the circumstances of production in textiles provides some interesting pointers about this sector.[20] It shows a growing use of capital from 1952 to 1963. The ratio between equipment in use and equipment capable of use has grown particularly clearly in spinning, from 62 to 96 percent for wool and from 72 to 90 percent for cotton. At the same time, shift work spread considerably between 1954 and 1962 (the proportion of work carried out in this way moved from 23 to 53 percent in wool spinning and from 54 to 79 percent in cotton spinning).

This development is difficult to interpret. First, it was fairly regular over the postwar period, and was not very sensitive to short-term variations of demand; it seems to have been the result of attempts at rationalization rather than of a need to satisfy a strong demand. Second, it might be no more than a return to methods of operation that seem to be standard for this sector. At the end of the war, the French textile industry was notoriously oversupplied with outdated capital equipment, whose rate of utilization obviously must have been low.

In brief, it seems to be true that high pressure of demand is reflected in a particularly intense use of existing capital. But this fact seems not too important in a comparison between the period since the war and those periods before the Great Depression, or in a study of what recent growth would have been if demand had been less sustained.

It is nevertheless true that the pressure of demand stimulates capital formation. Numerous econometric studies have shown that investment was particularly high when capacity utilization was also high. In this connection, in the chapter on factors explaining the level of investment and its variations, we conclude that requirements for capital equipment formed one of the determining factors in the boom of 1956–63.

Since our aim is to study growth and not short-term fluctuations, we cannot isolate quantitatively the influence of variations in demand, since this is exerted in many different ways, which often are indirect (for ex-

[20] Study by J. Houot in the INSEE Département des Entreprises.

ample, when it changes the outlook for firms' profits). We can, however, carry out a simple calculation that should suggest an order of magnitude of the possible effect on the volume of productive capital in existence in 1966.

Let us suppose that after 1955 the ratio of gross productive investment to gross domestic production in 1956 prices remained at its 1952 level of 12 percent. Such a hypothesis probably represents in broad terms what would have happened if demand had been only moderate. For one thing, investment before 1952 was the result of a determination to reconstruct that was independent of the short-term economic situation. For another thing, it seems difficult to imagine that, over the years 1952–66 as a whole, the rate of productive investment could have been less than 12 percent on account of demand alone. Among the four factors that explain the changes observed from 1956 to 1966, two are indeed positively linked to demand (requirements for capital equipment and forecasts of the outlook for profit). However, one is linked negatively (existence of opportunities for external financing), and the fourth (changes in price structure) would have exerted a favorable effect in any case. Had demand been less powerful, the real cost of labor would have risen more slowly, but the fiscal reforms and the reestablishment of the money market would have brought about at least as significant a drop in the real cost of capital.

Reverting to the calculations reported in Chapter 3, we can estimate that in 1966 net productive capital would have been 8 percent smaller (and net total capital 5 percent smaller) if the rate of productive investment had stabilized after 1955 at 12 percent. The delay in productive capital accumulation would have been on the order of two years.

Would a steadier demand have stimulated larger capital formation? This might be thought to be the case, since capital accumulation slowed at each of the recessions of 1952, 1958, and 1965. But to justify an affirmative reply, the fact would have to be established that investment was not then simply deferred by two or three years. The key question, after all, is what repercussions did short-term economic fluctuations have on the various factors that help to determine the scale of investment. The most important of these seems to be the attitude of firms to their own long-term forecasts. On this subject, it is appropriate to distinguish between the two periods of economic deceleration of 1952 and 1958.

As we shall see in Chapter 9, an analysis of the economic press shows that, from the fall of 1951 to the end of 1954, business circles were rather cautious and mostly did not expect the expansion that followed. By contrast, in 1958 and 1959, the slowdown was regarded by everyone as temporary. The creation of the Common Market and the popularity at that time of the attempts to plan the French economy led heads of firms to plan their operations within a framework that deliberately ignored the pause in growth then in evidence.

It seems likely, then, that the stagnation of 1952 and 1953 caused a considerable delay in the development of productive capacity and in modernizing the productive system. This delay was partly responsible for the pressure in 1956 and 1957, and sufficiently substantial to have somewhat reduced later growth. Conversely, the stabilization of 1958 and 1959 probably had no lasting effect on provision of capital equipment. It is still too early to form a view about the effects of the two successive decelerations of 1965 and 1967.

Productivity and Other Residual Factors

How would productivity have developed after the war if demand had been weak? The two traditional and opposite theories are well known. According to some authorities, high demand powers the takeoff of productivity, since it encourages mobility both in people and in firms; it is accompanied by a faster replacement of capital equipment and consequently by an earlier adoption of new techniques; it stimulates invention by exhibiting the markets to be satisfied, and, finally, it makes restrictive practices obsolete. According to others, a poor level of demand helps productivity to rise by making business more difficult; it eliminates the marginal firms that slow down modernization, and it forces all those acting in the economy to increase their efforts and adapt to the new conditions created by technical progress.

On this point what we can contribute here must be incomplete, but we shall attempt to define the magnitude of some of the factors suggested in one or other of the two contending theories.

1. If a less lively demand had led to a lower rate of investment, productive capital in existence in 1966 would have been not only lower in level but also on the average somewhat less up to date. The calculation in the previous section provides an estimate of what the volume of capital would have been if the rate of productive investment had stabilized at 12 percent after 1955. Following the assumptions made in Chapter 7 (p. 193) on the variation with age of the productive capacity of equipment, we can present an estimate of what in these circumstances would have been the productive potential of equipment in existence in 1966. The differential in the actual volume of gross productive capital (K in Appendix E) would have been 5 percent; it would have been 7 percent in the figure for its productive potential (J in Appendix E). If we assume

that lowering the age of capital equipment affects net capital in the same way as it does gross capital, then had the scale of investment been smaller, the differential in the efficiency of capital would have been only 2 percent.

2. Job migration was one of the key factors in French postwar growth, and there is little doubt that it was stimulated by the pressure of demand. This topic has been studied in great depth in relation to migration from agriculture to other sectors of the economy. Febvay, for example, has shown that migrations were particularly large from 1906 to 1911, from 1921 to 1931, and after 1946, all periods of high demand.[21] Between 1931 and 1936 they almost ceased. Similarly, Echard has established that between 1954 and 1962 regions where the farm labor force had fallen fastest were also those where the pressure of demand, measured by the immigration of foreign workers, was strongest.[22]

However subject to chance any measurement of this phenomenon may be, we can presumably proceed by applying a rule of simple proportion in relation to the rate of underemployment of the aggregate labor force and stipulating that migration from agriculture would have been zero if this rate had averaged 7.0 percent (i.e. in a case of severe depression comparable to that of 1933–36). The rate of underemployment in fact averaged about 2.0 percent. A moderate level of demand leading to an underemployment rate of 3.0 percent would then have slowed down job migration by farm workers by 20 percent. In Chapter 7 (p. 201) we have suggested that this migration of itself might account for a growth rate of national productivity on the order of 0.5 percent per year. Had the pressure of demand been weaker, this contribution would have dropped approximately by 0.1 percent, that is, in all by some 2 percentage points between 1949 and 1966.

3. A similar phenomenon may have affected changes in the structures of the productive system, and particularly the gradual disappearance of very small establishments unsuited to take advantage of technological progress. As did farm workers, the self-employed artisans and small businessmen could see that the labor market was favorable to a change of jobs. Nevertheless it seems at least as likely that the high level of demand, which kept trade in a state relatively favorable to sellers, acted as a brake on developments that otherwise growth would have dictated. An examination of the figures shows in any event that changes in the

[21] M. Febvay, "La Population agricole française. Structure actuelle et évolution," *Etudes et conjoncture*, August 1956.

[22] P. Echard, "Quelques aspects de l'évolution de la population active masculine agricole de 1946 à 1962," *Cahiers de l'ISEA*, no. AG-4, November 1964.

pace of job migration are most likely to have affected the small business-men rather than others in the group.

The proportion of the industrial and crafts labor force employed in establishments with under five employees changed broadly in line with its long-term trend: 53 percent in 1906, and 28 percent in 1931. Despite the depression and the war, it was only 19 percent in 1954, and fell fur-ther, to 14 percent in 1966. By contrast, small businesses, whose share of all business had diminished in the first 30 years of the century, still hold the major position, although it is getting smaller. The proportion of the small business work force employed in establishments of under six employees had fallen from 81 percent in 1906 to 65 percent in 1931. In 1954 it was still 66 percent, and by 1966 had dropped no lower than 54 percent. It seems unlikely that a less powerful demand would have slowed down this very moderate process of concentration.

4. A change in the intensity of demand would have had a quasi-me-chanical effect on residual productivity, since within each production unit the utilization of equipment and manpower would have been lower at the end of the postwar period than at the beginning. The calculations reported early in this chapter (p. 234) lead us to estimate that low pres-sure of demand in 1966 would have led to a shortfall of about 3 percent below the actual level in that year.

5. Among the other factors that may have caused a demand effect on residual productivity, we can comment only on restrictive practices and the degree of competitiveness in the French economy. In our chapter on internal competition, we have established that expansion has had healthy effects by reducing the relative weight of forms of industrial production subject to cartel agreements, and even by making some of these agreements obsolete.

But has not the pressure of demand made business too easy, and hin-dered the thorough structural changes needed by the productive mech-anism? On this subject, it is probably necessary to distinguish two pe-riods since the war, before and after 1958.

In the reconstruction period up to the end of 1951, a too lively demand was the prime cause of the serious inflation then experienced. Firms' profit margins were very high. The rise in prices made precise economic calculation difficult. There can be little doubt that lower pressure of demand then would have been salutary both for the improvement of productivity in firms and for the elimination of those forms of business least likely to carry growth forward. The stabilization of 1952–55 for the first time made it possible to put matters into some order again, within the limits set by measures intended to protect the French economy from foreign competition. The years 1956 and 1957 once again experienced inflation and very easy business conditions, despite the price freeze attempted by the government.

After the 1958–59 stabilization, the expansion of 1960–63 took place in an entirely new climate because of the organization of the Common Market and the freeing of trade. As they found themselves becoming part of an increasingly wide and competitive market, French industrial firms had to make the same attempts at rationalization as if the domestic economic situation had been poor. This point does not apply, however, to small business, building, or some services.

In brief, it does seem that on the whole the pressure of demand exerted favorable influence on residual productivity, particularly in the second half of the period considered. Greater short-term stability would probably not have been of much benefit in this respect, unless its chief effect had been to prevent the rise in prices. Had the 1952 and 1958 decelerations not taken place, migrations of farm workers would probably have been a little faster; on the other hand, however, the necessary disappearance of marginal firms might well have slowed down.

To conclude this chapter, we can say that in the postwar period, demand (stimulated first by the needs of reconstruction, then by the growth of public consumption, and last by the development of investment and exports) exerted on the French productive system a pressure that was sustained although slightly irregular, and comparable to that in some earlier but much shorter periods (particularly in the eight years before World War I).

Among the explanatory factors in the country's growth, demand seems to have played a clearly positive role, particularly since 1958. This factor of course is difficult to isolate. Nevertheless the calculations we have carried out seem to imply that gross domestic production in 1966 would have been some 15 percent lower than the actual figure if the pressure of demand had been uniformly moderate since 1952.[23] In 14 years, in other words, it would have fallen some three years behind the level it in fact reached.

[23] The calculation comprises the following elements: 6 percent due to the quantity of work supplied; 2 percent due to capital equipment in use (7 percent with a marginal productivity of 0.3); 2 percent due to job migration; and 3 percent due to less intense factor use in production units, to which should be added a less favorable scope for economies of scale and various elements mentioned but not measured above.

CHAPTER NINE

Investment and Savings

In the first part of our study we assessed the influence of capital accumulation on the growth rate. Going further back up the causal chain, we must now investigate the reasons for the scale of investment observed, and determine what factors played a positive or negative role in this respect.

A study of this topic is probably more significant than might be suggested by the first part of our work, where investment was considered as the development of a factor of production. Nevertheless, in Chapter 8 its impact on the volume of aggregate demand made apparent a different kind of influence on growth. Above all, it must be regarded as intimately linked to the degree of dynamism in the economy. Investment cannot be said, as can the increase in the labor force, to stem from causes that are chiefly non-economic. It is motivated by the needs of future production, and therefore reflects more or less deliberate action to encourage growth. If one knows who is investing most at a given period, one also knows who is taking the risk of promoting expansion. This chapter will therefore go beyond the somewhat narrow context implicit in the first part of the study.

In order to discover what factors account for the scale of investment achieved, it is convenient to examine separately the two faces of the phenomenon: demand, that is, the reasons that led different decision makers to increase their physical capital; and supply, that is, the causes that underlie the building up of sufficient savings to finance this investment.

According to one extreme theory, only the study of demand has significance. Savings, in this view, have merely a passive role: they necessarily adjust to the level of investment, which is determined by exogenous factors. If spontaneous or *ex ante* savings tend to fall below investment, a rise in prices will cause "forced savings," which will restore equality between demand and supply. Conversely, if savings *ex ante* are too high, activity will slow down, shrink incomes, and ultimately bring savings back to the level of investment.

This theory doubtless contains a good deal of truth. It does not, however, remove the necessity of making a serious study of savings, for two reasons. Even if the theory were correct for the short and medium terms, it would be appropriate for us to examine the formation of savings in order to understand how the regulation of economic activity takes place in practice. The study of savings, then, is linked with that of overall short-term equilibrium and of economic fluctuations. In a long-term context, the degree of regularity of growth and the movements of prices affect decision makers' forecasts, their management efficiency, and their level of profits. They also no doubt affect the level of investment. Moreover, it would be an exaggeration to say that even in the short and medium terms the formation of savings has no effect on the level of investment.

First, in the present institutional situation, every agent in the economy must finance at least some of its own investment. Without sufficient savings, firms and households must restrict increases in their physical capital. A suitable level of available savings is therefore essential for the achievement of large-scale investment. True, if they feel a strong need to increase their capital equipment, decision makers will feel constrained to borrow sufficiently to finance a demand for investment that they regard as having priority. But the possibility of some indirect reaction of factors affecting savings on the volume of capital formation should not a priori be excluded. Second, the higher the level of national savings *ex ante*, the easier is credit, whether because interest rates are adjusted downward or because financial institutions have a more liberal attitude toward the granting of loans. Outside financing of investment accordingly becomes less expensive, or is subject to less strict quantity limitations.

These considerations justify the structure of this chapter: its two parts deal, respectively, with demand for investment and the supply of savings. This examination of the two aspects in which capital formation appears at the aggregate level will need to be completed by a more direct study of investment financing. The reaction of savings on investment is through the creation of more or less favorable financial terms: direct analysis of investment financing may therefore reveal causal dependences more clearly than an overall comparison between capital supply and demand. This chapter should, in principle, have a third part on finance. Since this would have led us into a somewhat lengthy discussion, we consider that, on balance, it is better dealt with as a separate chapter immediately after this one.

DEMAND FOR INVESTMENT

Why did the different decision makers seek to increase their productive equipment as they did? A precise reply to this question would require the analysis to consider in turn fairly homogeneous groups of decision makers. But here we shall confine ourselves to a preliminary study intended merely to highlight the topic's main features. We shall look first at the public sector and then at private-enterprise firms. Since we are concerned with productive investment, we shall not deal with households' demand for dwellings or with social investments, two elements in French growth that for lack of time we must to a certain extent neglect.[1]

With the existing data, a reasonably precise examination can be made only for the postwar period. Nevertheless, the question arises why investment by firms over the past 20 years has been much higher than in the past. However tentative our reply, we must devote some attention to this question, and will start with it.

The Postwar Period Contrasted to the Distant Past

The estimates in Chapter 4 provide a series showing the ratio between gross fixed capital formation and gross domestic production. This ratio apparently rose from around 15 percent at the beginning of the century to 18 percent in 1949–54, and to 24 percent in 1965–66. If we could work out a similar ratio with the numerator covering only fixed investment by firms, we should certainly get a sharper rise from the beginning of the century to the first part of the postwar period, when residential building and social capital information were at very low levels.

According to certain specialists in French economic history, however, capital formation was already higher at the start of the twentieth century than it had been in the nineteenth century. It is a fact that imports of manufactured goods, which in France largely consisted of capital goods, amounted to some 0.5 percent of gross domestic product around 1840, 0.3 percent around 1850, and 2.8 percent around 1880 (when they reached a peak), 2.4 percent around 1890, 2.8 percent around 1900, and 3.8 percent around 1910. Similarly, according to estimates by Markovitch, the output of metal-processing industries grew at an average rate

---

[1] We should stress once again that our object is to explain the growth of production, not to assess what benefits the French people obtained from this growth.

TABLE 9.1
Weighted Index of British Industrial Wages, 1831–1907
(French industrial wages = 100)

Weights used	1831	1861	1881	1891	1901	1906–7
French weights	81	87	89	97	100	98
English weights	80	102	115	128	122	115

Source: J. Marczewski, *Introduction à l'histoire quantitative* (Geneva, 1965), p. 117.
Note: Price parities calculated on a weighted basis.

of 3.3 percent per year from 1830 to 1890, but achieved 5.3 percent on the average between the two ten-year periods centered on 1890 and 1909, respectively.[2]

Increase in the rate of investment in France is therefore apparently part of a long-term picture. After the technically backward position they had fallen into in the nineteenth century, French firms seem to have gradually become more aware of the requirements of modern technology. This change, therefore, had its origins in the fairly distant past and has been in progress a long time. The weakness of French domestic investment over the course of the nineteenth century has drawn the attention of economic historians, who have developed a relatively convincing and well-argued explanation for it.[3] The reasons presented also throw light in the opposite direction, on the revival observed in the twentieth century.

Briefly, the low level of capital accumulation in France was apparently due to the indifferent condition of industrial profit. Costs in French industry seem to have been high, with demand relatively unfavorable to rapid expansion. But these special features apparently disappeared toward the end of the nineteenth century and the beginning of the twentieth.

In the first place, industrial wage levels were high in relation to those elsewhere, particularly compared with Britain. According to estimates shown in Table 9.1, industrial wages in Britain were indeed lower than in France until around 1880. This feature can be explained by the very different scale of labor migration in the two countries. In Britain, there was great movement of the labor force from agriculture to industry from the beginning of the nineteenth century, whereas in France it was slight up to 1880. At the same time, the difference between industrial and agricultural wages was small in Britain and large in France.

[2] T. J. Markovitch, "L'Industrie française de 1789 à 1964," *Cahiers de l'ISEA,* series AF, nos. 4, 5, 6, 1965 and 1966.

[3] The best presentation is that by R. E. Cameron, "Profit, croissance et stagnation en France au XIXe siècle," *Economie appliquée,* April–September, 1957.

The comparison between French and British industrial wages is particularly striking since Britain had a considerably higher level of development and of real income per capita than France during the nineteenth century (twice as high according to Cameron, 20 percent higher according to Marczewski, and 70 percent higher on the basis of a backward extrapolation from the present position). The relative cost of French industrial labor was much less unfavorable by the start of the twentieth century. No systematic study seems available comparing the cost of labor in France and in other countries in the 1920's. On the other hand, in recent years this subject has been dealt with in a number of articles, according to which the real cost of labor in industrial firms was not systematically higher in France than in other countries at a comparable stage of development.[4]

In the second place, the manufacturing and processing industries in France were affected by the high prices of new industrial products in comparison with the prices of agricultural commodities. Thus, the ratio between the prices of a ton of pig iron and a ton of wheat in 1830 was on the order of 0.80 in France and 0.22 in Britain, and in 1860 on the order of 0.34 and 0.19, respectively. In 1900, parity between these countries had virtually been reached, since the ratios were 0.46 in France and 0.42 in Britain. This comparison, of course, is somewhat simplistic and cannot be extended further. The price of wheat has become increasingly less representative of agricultural prices.

It has also been observed that, before the establishment of a complete railroad network, French industry was seriously handicapped by being far more widely dispersed over the country than was the case in other European nations. Transportation costs were high and kept profits down. This handicap almost entirely disappeared by the end of the nineteenth century.

Last, demand for industrial products was relatively low as a result of the priority given to food in the accustomed style of living, and also as a result of the high rate of savings of the middle classes, much of which was invested abroad. French exports of manufactured goods consisted mainly of products requiring considerable labor and ill-suited to incorporating technological progress. Their growth was therefore relatively slow. This structure of demand, which seems to have been unfavorable to French industry, was to continue until World War I. But between the two wars and since, these old characteristics of demand disappeared,

[4] See in particular "Comparaison des salaires français et étrangers," *Etudes et conjoncture*, May 1955; Statistical Office of the European Community, "Salaires CEE," *Statistiques sociales*, 1966, no. 5; and J. J. Branchu, "Les Charges des entreprises françaises: essai de comparaison internationale," *Economie et statistique*, September 1969, no. 4.

and substantial outlets became available to industry, comparable in nature to those in other developed countries.

In brief, some credence may be given to the hypothesis that changes in the outlook for industrial profits may explain both the low volume of French productive investment in the nineteenth century and its recovery thereafter. We shall see whether data are available to check this hypothesis directly, or even just to provide an index of change in profit rates. The statistics of stock exchange quotations would seem likely to supply some useful hints. In principle the yield on industrial bonds should correctly measure the interest on capital—that is, its scarcity value. A high rate should reveal a high demand, corresponding to a favorable outlook for profits. In a market where uncertainties about the future would have been eliminated, the yield (after tax) of variable-income stock should equal that of bonds, it being of course clearly appreciated that the yield takes account not only of distributed interest or dividends but also of changes in the stock market price. A large positive difference between the average yield of variable-income stock and that of bonds should therefore reflect the overtaking of expected profits by actual profits.[5] If such a gap persists over a relatively long period, the explanation probably lies in a favorable but not yet perceived change in circumstances in which firms carry out their activities.

The yield levels and the average gap between the yields of variable-income and fixed-income stock should therefore represent two useful indicators. Their interpretation, however, is hampered by stock exchange speculation. As J. M. Keynes has vividly explained, changes in the market price of a share do not necessarily reflect changes in the effective value of the firm in question, but rather those of the prices that each stock market operator estimates the other operators are prepared to give it. Postwar experience has recently shown how speculation can set off artificial movements in stock prices lasting several years, whether up or down. These movements obscure to a considerable extent the indications available from the stock market statistics concerning the real business situation. Furthermore, the level of interest rates is not as simple to interpret as suggested above, since these rates depend on the factors affecting supply as well as demand for savings. And last, a given level of interest rates probably does not represent the same scarcity of capital when prices are rising as when they are falling.

Bearing in mind these very important reservations, we can now look at yield rates since the end of the nineteenth century. The paucity of

---

[5] A positive but small difference may simply reflect the risk premium applied to variable income stock in relation to bonds.

our statistical information suggests that all indicators, however poor, should be examined.[6] From 1860 to 1896, interest rates of government bonds showed a downward trend, falling from around 4.5 to 3 percent. The ratio of net dividends to market value of shares, known as the capitalization rate, fluctuated widely but showed a trend similar to that above, changing from 5.0 to 3.5 percent. Over the entire period, prices of bonds increased by almost 60 percent, i.e. by an average of 1.3 percent per year. By the end of the period, prices of industrial shares had practically recovered their levels at the start. This period is thus marked by low and falling interest rates and by a bond yield slightly higher than that of variable-income industrial stock. Although the low interest level is partly accounted for by a drop in the prices of raw materials, Table 9.1 shows fairly clearly that conditions at the time were by no means favorable to industrial profits.

From 1896 to 1913, interest rates of government bonds rose somewhat, from around 3.0 to 3.5 percent. The capitalization rate of shares fluctuated between 3.5 and 4.0 percent. But industrial variable-income stock experienced a sharp price increase, averaging 4.5 percent per year. The yield of this stock therefore greatly exceeded that of bonds. Industry seems to have enjoyed circumstances far more favorable to growth than in the previous period.

The decade from World War I to the 1929 depression was too short and too complex a period to show significant trends. Prices rose rapidly up to 1927, and it is therefore not surprising that the interest rates on government bonds were high: they stood at 5.0 percent as late as 1929. The capitalization rate of shares was 4 percent until 1927, and fell to about 3 percent in 1929, but distributed dividends and stock prices rose fast: from 1913 to 1929 dividends grew by a factor of 6 in the industrial sectors, and stock market prices grew tenfold. In the same period the price of large industrials grew sixfold. On the basis of the indicators considered here, the 1920's seem to have been as favorable to industrial profits as were the years before World War I.

From 1952 to 1967, interest rates of government bonds fluctuated between 5 and 5.5 percent, apart from a temporary upsurge in 1957. The

[6] We have drawn here principally on two studies: M. Lenoir, "Le Mouvement des cours des valeurs mobilières françaises depuis 1856," *Bulletin de la statistique générale de la France*, October 1919; and J. Denuc, "Dividendes, valeur boursière et taux de capitalisation des valeurs mobilières françaises de 1857 à 1932," *Bulletin de la statistique générale de la France*, July–September, 1934. The summary given above does not refer to the aggregate indexes; those are strongly influenced by railroad company shares, which had very special features. We have used subgroups relating to industry in the broad sense.

share capitalization rate at first was close to 5 percent, fell to 1.6 percent in the 1960–62 wave of speculation, then climbed again above 3 percent in 1967. Stock prices rose rapidly until 1962, then fell again, but from 1952 to 1966 the average annual increase was about 10 percent, giving rise to a high yield for variable-income stock.

In summary, then, stock market statistics, although they must be treated with caution, seem to confirm the hypothesis made at the beginning of this section about the causes of the rise in rate of investment since the beginning of the century.

Nationally Owned Enterprises

In a study of growth in France over the past 20 years, some mention must be made of productive public investment.[7] Its volume alone would justify this, since it accounted for over one-third of total productive investment in each of the years since World War II. In addition, it may—at least in certain periods—have played a strategic role as prime mover, stimulating growth in every sector of the economy.[8] Available estimates show clearly, despite gaps in the data, that productive public investment grew rapidly in these successive waves: 1946–50, 1956–59, and finally 1962–66. The first of these periods coincided with that of the first National Plan, and deserves particular discussion.

If we simplify to the extreme, we can say that the first National Plan gave absolute priority to developing productive capacity in the basic sectors, and particularly in energy and transportation, where nationally owned undertakings predominate. There can be little doubt that the Plan had a decisive influence on the volume of public investment, as we shall see in Chapter 14. Can we judge today what the effect was of this investment policy on France's growth? We did of course attempt to do so when considering the contribution of capital accumulation to the rate of growth. But the yardstick we used depends on a marginal calculation that is not very appropriate to conditions immediately after the war.

Capital maintenance and replacement had been considerably neglected for 15 years. Without a massive investment drive in the basic industries, productive capacity would not have been sufficient for rapid expansion beyond the first few years, and serious physical bottlenecks would have developed. The first Plan's policy was based on the con-

[7] The term "public investment" has been used for brevity to translate the French *investissements publics*, which relates to nationally owned enterprises only, excluding investment by government *départements*, etc. TRANS.

[8] The case for this is made, in particular, by A. Cotta in "La Croissance de l'économie française, 1945–1975," *Analyse et prévision*, July–August, 1966.

cept that growth in France should continue well beyond the recovery that the return to peace necessarily brought with it. The outcome showed how right that concept had been. The energetic expansion that followed the years of indecision, 1952 and 1953, could not have reached the scale it did if energy and transportation shortages had paralyzed the attempts of industrial firms to nationalize, or if France, which was balancing its foreign trade with difficulty, had had to buy abroad raw materials such as steel and cement.

The absolute priority given by the first Plan to heavy investment had of course been criticized.[9] Housing and social investment suffered from relatively low-priority ranking, as might be expected at that period. Capital equipment in nonpriority industries suffered also: they had difficulty in obtaining import licenses for foreign-made equipment, and could get no outside financing other than short-term credits. In the same period, basic industries were not merely expanding their capacity but also actively modernizing. Highly mechanized and costly equipment was installed in undertakings that could take advantage of this. At a time when capital was scarce, the question might well be raised whether it might preferably have been shared in a more balanced way, so that investment in manufacturing industry might take place, at least where early and high returns could be gained.

This question deserves serious study. In particular, two aspects of it might well be considered with care. First, the policy of rapid development and modernization of public-enterprise capital equipment may have had the effect of raising the rate of investment above the level it could otherwise attain. Second, it was of course important to take advantage of technical progress and develop modern equipment suited to the economic conditions to be expected throughout its useful life. Was the degree of mechanization then adopted too high? The answer is not self-evident.

The development of investment in public undertakings after 1952, and particularly in the phases 1956–59 and 1962–66, was, it is true, carried out under government control, but it was less directly the result of a major option than in the immediate postwar period. The different governments did, of course, accept the expanding outlook of successive national Plans. But this outlook, which provided the setting for the programs of the various undertakings, was an extrapolation of earlier growth, and therefore seemed more to be expected than it would have been immediately after the war. Moreover, the detailed content

[9] We make no comment here on certain errors in the long-term forecasts of technological development, particularly those affecting the consumption of coal.

of these programs was also the result of profitability considerations very similar to those influencing investment in private firms. The high level of capital accumulation in public enterprises can therefore be explained by the high long-term rate adopted for national growth as well as by a drop in the cost of capital in relation to the cost of labor, which we shall examine more fully later.

It should be noted that throughout the 1950's public undertakings continued to enjoy especially favorable financial terms. Their loans carried reduced interest rates, and the volume of credit granted to them seems to have been larger than that consistent with the optimum allocation of resources between the public and private sectors. Indeed, the public undertakings frequently adopted policies that took insufficient account of the scarcity of capital: in the railroads, replacement of rolling stock and electrification were rapidly pushed; in electricity supply, hydroelectric schemes were developed earlier than was justified by demand, etc. This situation, which obviously led to some economic loss, also partly explains the high level of public investment at the end of the 1950's.

Private Firms

The increase in the pace of investment in private firms dates from 1955. Separate estimates for this category are not available before 1956, but there can be no doubt about the facts. Thus, in Chapter 4 we made a distinction between light investment and heavy investment, the latter relating particularly to industries where public undertakings predominate (energy, transportation, metals, and building materials). We observed then that as a proportion of gross domestic production light investment in 1956 prices amounted to 6.2 percent in 1949, 5.9 percent in 1952, 6.2 percent in 1954, 8.4 percent in 1961, and 9.0 percent in 1963 and 1964. It is perhaps even more striking to note that the volume of light investment grew by less than 1.3 times from 1949 to 1954, but by 2.5 times from 1954 to 1964. It would be necessary to examine many factors to explain fully this wave of investment, which was only temporarily interrupted by the stagnation of 1958 and 1959. But we shall confine ourselves here to finding the main features.

For this purpose we can take advantage of a large number of econometric analyses carried out with the aim of isolating the different influences on the growth of firms' investments. True, most of these studies relate to the United States; moreover, they were devised to explain short-term fluctuations rather than growth. Nevertheless, it should be possible to generalize their results to apply, at least in part, to the situation that concerns us here. All things considered, they confirm the conclusions to be reached by a theoretical analysis from first principles.

Three main factors seem to affect the scale of investment by firms: the need for higher output capacity, the relative costs of capital and labor, and the availability of financial resources. Increases in capital equipment are encouraged in the first place by a firm's desire to increase output capacity. This desire may result from observing that the rate of use of existing equipment has risen above the optimum and that profits are being affected. It may stem from a forecast that increases in outlets or changes in customers' tastes will make it profitable to increase production of certain lines and will require new equipment to be installed. Second, variations in the relative costs of capital and labor affect the optimum level of mechanization sought by a firm. When the cost of labor rises and that of capital falls, it becomes increasingly advantageous to mechanize a large number of operations. "Productivity investment," which is sometimes contrasted with "capacity investment," is favored. And last, the greater or lesser availability of financing frequently decides how far a firm's wish to invest can be satisfied. A firm that can borrow easily, and has large internal resources from profits and amortization, naturally tends to increase the pace of development and modernization of its capital equipment. A firm with financial difficulties has the opposite approach.

Of these three factors, we shall for the present examine only the first two, since Chapter 10 is devoted to financing, a subject dealt with in some depth. Very briefly, Chapter 10 concludes that greater ease of access to external financial resources in the medium and long term has been counterbalanced by a relative drop in volume of internal resources. Apart from short-term fluctuations, the overall availability of financing does not seem to have altered substantially between the beginning and the end of the postwar period.

Output capacity. There is little doubt that output capacity requirements have been high since 1955, and that this partly explains the observed increase in investment in many sectors of industry. The estimates in Chapter 5 show that in several industries the capital coefficient—that is, the ratio between capital and output—fell substantially from 1949 to 1956 (the estimates relate to net capital, but similar results would have been obtained by using gross capital). The coefficient dropped as follows: petroleum industry from 0.94 to 0.60, building materials from 1.33 to 1.12, nonferrous metals from 1.33 to 0.94, mechanical and electrical industries from 0.85 to 0.72, chemicals and rubber from 1.15 to 1.06, textiles and clothing from 1.12 to 0.70, wood, paper, and miscellaneous industries from 1.02 to 0.76. The only divisions of private industry where an opposite tendency can be observed are iron mining and metallurgy (from 1.88 to 1.94) and processed foods and farm products (from 0.49 to 0.56). We should also quote a figure from the periodic INSEE surveys of heads of firms. The proportion of firms reporting themselves "unable to increase production for lack of capital equipment" reached or topped 20 percent at the end of 1957, from 1962 to 1964, in the spring of 1966, and in 1969.[10]

Expectations of heads of firms. About the mid-1950's, not only did firms observe that their capacity margins were too low, but it seems likely they raised their sights on growth. A significant change in expectations appears to have occurred between 1952 and 1960. The decline of the 1930's and the disorganization created by the war had made managers cautious about the future. The 1946–51 reconstruction did not seem to change this attitude. The concept of a possible continuous industrial expansion in Europe, and specifically in France, which arose among a few industrialists and senior civil servants and was encouraged by missions to the United States between 1949 and 1954, began to spread in the mid-1950's. Its progress was checked by the standstill of 1952 and 1953, which was seen at the time as a slowdown in growth, or even a return to stagnation, rather than as an accident of the short-term economic situation. By contrast, the opening up of the Common Market helped to spread a deliberately expansionist frame of mind. A long, documented study would be required to reverse or discredit this view of events. We have had to restrict ourselves here to a fairly incomplete review of the economic press. It seems undeniable, however, that a turnabout in attitude has taken place.

Up to 1955 the expansionist exhortations by men closely linked to national planning were counterbalanced by far more reserved opinions on the prospects for growth. Thus, in November 1949 Charles Rist wrote: "The main danger today would be to multiply investments at a time when they might well aggravate the overproduction that now threatens."[11] This eminent economist at the same time recalled the vast capital sums lost after the investment drive of the years 1927–30. In September 1953 the review *Réalités* published a long article with the heading, "The great sleep of the French economy," and stated in particular, "Faced by the slow withering away of a great nation, an observer can

---

[10] The full series is published in "Situation et perspectives de l'économie française au début de juin 1969," *Tendances de la conjoncture,* supplement to no. 3, 1969.

[11] Charles Rist, "Plan Monnet contre l'équilibre monétaire," *La Vie française,* November 24, 1949.

only worry and wonder what the origin was of its sickness. Is French capitalism inescapably on the way down? . . . or is it merely suffering from the pangs of adapting to the twentieth century, and will farsightedness and courage enable it to recover?" In May 1954, a time of rapid economic revival, René Sédillot wrote, "Just because France manages to live along from one day to another does not mean that the next day is guaranteed."[12]

An exact study of the position in the different industries and firms would probably show very positive factors, even during the slowdown in 1952 and 1953. At the end of a detailed review of the subject, J. Choffel concluded in *La Vie française* of November 14, 1952: "No, France is not on the eve of a general industrial crisis." He added nevertheless, "There remains of course the possibility of an international crisis that could reach our country by contagion. Numerous indicators, and particularly the coming to power in the United States of a team with deflationist attitudes, make considerable fears on the subject only too appropriate." For its part, the report presented by the Banque Nationale pour le Commerce et l'Industrie in the spring of 1953 for the year 1952 considered that "for the first time there have been difficulties in selling. They surprised some people, and there has been talk of a crisis, but this word is too strong, at least for most industries: what has happened is merely a necessary phase of adaption to a more normal market situation."

In contrast to the uncertainties shown by the extracts we have quoted, the economic press seems to have been more or less unanimous between 1958 and 1963 in forecasting a lengthy expansion. The slowdown in 1958 does not seem to have lessened this fundamental optimism. On January 17, 1958, René Sédillot, whose earlier reservations we have noted, entitled his article in *La Vie française* "Les Perspectives françaises s'améliorent." After an examination of the financial recovery undertaken, he added: "In the longer term, the prospects ahead for France are even brighter." At the same time J. Choffel considered that the official forecasts were too low. He wrote: "Expansion nourishes expansion," and did not seem worried by the recession then rampant in the United States.[13]

The rapid increase in firms' output capacity from 1956 therefore took place in the context of forecasts that were considerably expansionist. Another influence was the gradual setting up of the Common Market. Since firms were constrained to sell on increasingly competitive mar-

---

[12] René Sédillot: "Situation brillante mais fragile," *La Vie française*, May 21, 1954.
[13] *La Vie française*, January 3, 1958.

kets, whether in France or abroad, they were forced to update their production and modify it to suit the tastes of increasingly demanding customers.

Relative costs. The growth of investment from 1954 can also be accounted for by changes in the relative costs of capital and labor. These moved very differently between 1953 and 1964. The introduction of the value-added tax in 1954 had the effect of removing the double burden previously imposed by the production tax (the tax paid on capital goods was not deductible from the tax payable on goods manufactured with that equipment). From 1960 on, declining-rate depreciation was authorized in place of straight-line depreciation. This had the effect of increasing annual depreciation deductions in the early years of the life of an item of equipment, and to reduce by an equal amount the taxable profit on which the industrial and commercial profit tax is calculated. Depreciation is of course correspondingly reduced, and taxable profit increased, at the end of the useful life of the equipment. But delaying part of the profit tax to a later date is obviously equivalent to a cost reduction, since the sum in question can meanwhile be profitably used.

While the tax laws were changed twice to lower substantially the cost of capital equipment, increases in employers' rates of social security contributions and a gradual lengthening of paid vacations made the use of labor increasingly burdensome. In addition to these factors, a continued rise in wages made mechanization and automation increasingly profitable. We believe this development is sufficiently important to attempt to measure it. The results of our calculations are shown in Table 9.2.[14] Since our aim is to show what order of magnitude of relative costs is likely to have brought about a substitution of capital for labor, we must consider in turn the marginal costs of capital and labor.

The marginal costs of capital, which we shall call c_k, is affected by the purchase price of the item of equipment in question, which we shall call p_k, by the interest rate applying to the financial capital tied up in it, which we shall call ρ, and last by the direct repercussions of this particular investment on other costs of the firm—and in particular on the taxes it must pay. Let us assume that the present value of the cost increases due to these direct repercussions has been calculated, and is equal to t for each frame of investment. We can then write[15]

[14] The series shown here ends in 1966. For complementary and slightly different estimates, the reader is referred to E. Malinvaud, "Peut-on mesurer le coût d'usage du capital?" *Economie et statistique*, April 1971.

[15] This of course is a very contracted formula, not easily applied to a real situation of any complexity. But it would be inappropriate here to seek a more precise formu-

(1) $$c_k = \rho \, p_k (1+t)$$

Instead of considering c_k itself, it is probably preferable to relate this cost to the price p_q of the items produced:

(2) $$\frac{c_k}{p_q} = \rho \, \frac{p_k}{p_q} \, (1+t)$$

An index of changes in c_k/p_q can thus be obtained by multiplying three indexes relating respectively to the rate of interest, the relative price of capital goods, and the factor $(1+t)$ measuring the incidence of investment on certain other costs.

We have been unable to find an index that seems satisfactory to represent movements of the rate ρ in our formula. This is in fact the *real interest* rate that firms expect to pay for a loan granted at the date of the investment (or the real rate of interest that they estimate might have been earned from an alternative investment). This rate allows for expected variations in prices, which can be expected to have had particular importance in postwar France.

There are, of course, statistics on the rates obtained on loans. Thus the rate at issue of privately owned companies' bonds became stabilized at 5.7 percent from 1960 to 1964. It had previously been somewhat higher (some 7 percent in 1952, falling to 6.3 percent in 1955–56, up again in 1957–58, when index formulas were much employed, and 6.4 percent in 1959). The rate rose after 1964 (from 6.5 percent in 1965 to 8.5 in 1969). This, however, is the nominal rate. What were the changes in the real interest rate that firms expected to pay for a loan effected at this nominal rate? In other words, what were their forecasts of future price movements? We appear to have no indicator that would throw light on this phenomenon, even indirectly.[16] Those available refer simply to forecasts for a short-term period considerably shorter than the life of assets, or even than the period of the loans obtained to finance them.

Broadly speaking, for want of more precise data it can probably be assumed that the real rate of interest remained constant at least until 1964. A slightly higher nominal rate between 1952 and 1956 seems to have been accompanied by recall of the heavy postwar inflation and consequently by an expected rise in prices also higher than in the rest of the period. The only alternative assumption possible seems to be that

---

lation. On this subject see, for example, D. Jorgenson, "Capital Theory and Investment Behavior," *American Economic Review*, May 1963.

[16] See, however, Malinvaud, "Peut-on mesurer le coût d'usage du capital?"

the long-term forecast of the rate of inflation tends to follow the rate observed over the three or four latest years. According to this alternative, the real interest rate was far higher around 1955–56 than around 1960, as a result of a higher nominal rate being accompanied by a lower growth of prices (prices remained stable from 1952 to 1955 in relation to value added in industry, moving by −0.3 percent per year; from 1955 to 1959 they increased by 6.3 percent; from 1959 to 1962 by 1.9 percent, and from 1962 to 1964 by 4.5 percent). The index relating to factor ρ of formula (2) would then have been falling; this would reinforce further the conclusions reached below. But econometric research available at present seems on the whole to exclude this alternative. It shows that price expectations entering into interest rate formation react only slowly to variations in the inflation rate.[17]

We have therefore assumed that factor ρ of formula (2) remained constant and equal to 1 until 1964. We have, however, taken account of the rise in rates in 1965 and 1966, giving to ρ the value of 1.15 and 1.20, respectively, for those years. We then estimated the value of the two other factors by reference to the case of investment in capital equipment in industry. This, indeed, is the type of asset where substitutions between capital and labor are most likely to take place.

For p_k and p_q we have used the results of the National Accounts, or more precisely the implicit price indexes applying, on the one hand, to the gross fixed capital formation of products of the mechanical and electrical industries and, on the other hand, to the gross value added in industry (industry groups 02 to 12). The ratio p_k/p_q measured in this way grew by over 10 percent from 1949 to 1952, and thereafter showed minor fluctuations. Its statistical accuracy is clearly low, in particular for the early years. Moreover, capital goods are in many cases highly specific, so that the measurement of volume indexes and the related measurement of price indexes refer essentially to the production costs of the goods in question, and largely ignore improvements in their performance and in their quality for the user. This point, which we have already stressed in Chapters 5–7, obviously affects the significance of the indexes in Table 9.2.

For the index relating to factor $(1 + t)$ we have taken account of two important tax changes: the replacement of the tax on output by the value-added tax on April 10, 1954, and the introduction of declining-rate depreciation on January 1, 1960. The first change led to a tax reduction of 15.35 percent for industrial undertakings, which had previ-

[17] See T. J. Sargent, "Commodity Price Expectations and the Interest Rate," *Quarterly Journal of Economics*, February 1969.

TABLE 9.2

Costs of Capital Equipment and Labor Compared, 1949–66

(1956 = 100)

Year	Real cost of capital equipment (1)	Real cost of labor (2)	Ratio between these two costs (1)/(2)	Year	Real cost of capital equipment (1)	Real cost of labor (2)	Ratio between these two costs (1)/(2)
1949	108	66	164	1958	98	109	90
1950	106	71	150	1959	99	110	90
1951	115	79	146	1960	95	118	80
1952	120	77	156	1961	95	125	76
1953	120	79	152	1962	95	132	72
1954	106	85	125	1963	93	137	68
1955	100	92	110	1964	92	143	64
1956	100	100	100	1965	108	151	72
1957	100	104	96	1966	114	159	72

ously been liable for the full rate of the tax on output. The effect of declining-rate depreciation is more difficult to evaluate. We have assumed a drop of 5 percent for $(1 + t)$, on basis of the following argument.

The introduction of declining-rate depreciation is advantageous to firms, since it permits part of the tax on profits to be postponed. But the assessment of the benefit obviously will depend on the discount rate used in discounted cash-flow calculations and with the tax rate applicable to a particular firm. Let us assume, as an example, a discount rate of 8 percent, and let us consider the case of a company whose tax rate is 50 percent. The key factor is then the life of assets and the amortization concessions allowed to the company under the pre-1960 rules. If the company previously enjoyed no particular concession, the net present value of the reductions and increases in taxation resulting from the change in rules for an investment in capital equipment on July 1, for example, was 3.4 percent of the purchase price of the equipment if this had a life of five years, and 5.9 percent or 6.8 percent, respectively, if the life was 10 or 15 years. In many cases industrial firms had been allowed since 1951 to practice double-amortization in the first year of an asset's life. The net present value of the benefit gained from the 1959 reform for an asset with a ten-year life was in such cases not 5.9 percent of the asset's purchase price but 4.8 percent. There is no need to take these estimates further. The few figures already reached show that 5 percent is an acceptable order of magnitude for calculating an index that in any case cannot itself claim any great precision.

The first column of Table 9.2 shows under "real cost of capital equipment" the index obtained from the product of the two terms p_k/p_q and $(1+t)$, both measured as explained above. The drop in the index from 1953 to 1964 is 23 percent, despite the fact that improvements in the quality of equipment on the market have not truly been taken into account. The rise in interest rates at the end of the period produced a substantial reversal in real cost movements. To correspond with formula (2) we can develop an analogous formula for the marginal cost of labor c_n , i.e.

$$(3) \qquad\qquad \frac{c_n}{p_q} = \frac{p_n}{p_q}(1+s)$$

where p_n is an index of wage rates and s is the rate of related costs.

We have taken the same value for p_q as used earlier, and have calculated p_n from the increase in wage rates of blue-collar workers shown in the September survey of the Ministry of Labor. The rate has been taken from the series relating to metalworking industries of the Paris region. The index c_n/p_q thus obtained is given in the second column of Table 9.2. This shows three successive phases, 1949–53, 1953–59, and 1959–64, with an especially high growth rate in the first half of each phase. The fastest rate was realized between 1953 and 1956 (8.3 percent per year). The average annual rate in each of the three phases was, respectively, 4.6, 5.7, and 5.4 percent.

The last column in Table 9.2 shows the index of the ratio c_k/c_n between the marginal costs, obtained from the two previous columns. The index fell particularly fast from 1953 to 1964—a drop of 58 percent, or 7.6 percent per year on the average. This provides a clear explanation of why firms tried to increase their productivity investments, in order to reduce the demand for labor. The rise in the index in the last two years might in part explain the pause in investment growth experienced from 1965 to 1968.

To sum up, among the factors that brought about the increase in the rate of investment by firms, some were the result of the balance between economic factors and of its previous development (a low capital coefficient in 1956, and a rapid rise in wage rates). But three not strictly economic causes seem to have played a determining role: (1) the increased optimism in firms' expectations that developed in about the mid-1950's; (2) the effect of fiscal and related policy that deliberately led to a change in relative costs, making capital increasingly profitable to use; and (3) the setting up of the Common Market, which forced firms to switch to new lines of output and therefore also to new capital equipment.

THE SUPPLY OF SAVINGS

An analysis of growth must necessarily include a study of savings. We shall therefore examine the volume and composition of total domestic savings, in order to establish their salient features. We shall then inquire what the chief determining factors were of savings, first by households and second by companies other than financial institutions, since these are the two chief autonomous components.

Special Features of Postwar Savings

Savings effected in France since World War II have been significantly higher than previously. As an attempt to measure this change, we have presented Table 9.3, which shows three rates of savings for selected periods of the country's economic history. Needless to say, these estimates are only very approximate for periods before World War II.[18]

The first of these rates refers to gross fixed capital formation, the second to gross domestic savings, and the third, somewhat incorrectly called "rate of gross private savings," to gross savings by bodies other than government agencies. This third rate is of particular interest here, since it affects savings made by decision makers whose behavior is not subject to direct control. The rate in question displays a growth trend the regularity of which is both surprising and, doubtless, somewhat misleading. According to our calculations, it rose from 17 percent at the beginning of the century and on the eve of the Great Depression, to 20 percent in 1938 and around 1950, and to 22 percent around 1960. It can be maintained, however, that this rising trend is artificial for two reasons. For one thing, the growth of gross savings has probably been faster than that of net savings. As machines and equipment developed, the average life of capital assets fell substantially; as a result, the ratio

---

[18] The first rate, relating to gross fixed capital formation, has been taken from our study of investment. From it we have derived a "rate of gross domestic savings" by adding an arbitrary figure for stock formation (based on the assumption of a ratio of 0.5 between the volume of stocks and gross domestic production) and an estimate of the surplus from foreign transactions in goods and services (for which we have used customs statistics directly and assumed after examining the balance of payments that the rate of cover consistent with a balance in current transactions as a whole was 70 percent before 1913, 85 percent from 1925 to 1930, 75 percent from 1931 to 1935, and 70 percent from 1936 to 1938). To derive a "rate of gross private savings," we have estimated government savings by assuming that government capital formation was about 2 percent of gross domestic production and by assessing financing requirements as the sum of the central government budget deficit and the issue of bonds by local government bodies (although there are gaps in the statistics of these bond issues). From this sum we have subtracted national debt repayments.

TABLE 9.3
Savings Rates in Selected Periods, 1896–1969
(Percent of gross domestic production)

Period	Gross fixed capital formation	Gross domestic savings	Gross private savings[a]
1896–1913	14%	18%	17%
1925–30	17	20	17
1931–35	16	14	18
1936–38	15	13	19
1949–51	18	22	20
1952–57	19	22	21
1958–63	22	25	22
1964–69[b]	25	25	21

[a]Gross savings of public and private sector undertakings, households, and financial institutions.
[b]An arbitrary downward adjustment has been made to the most recent estimates to eliminate the effect of the change in base.

of depreciation to gross domestic production must have risen significantly. For another thing, the accounting rules followed in France in the postwar period treat all transfers as current transactions. For the study of spontaneous capital formation by those other than government agencies, it is perhaps more significant to treat in a different way certain transfers received by households and firms for the purpose of specified investments: compensation for war damage to finance the reconstruction of destroyed buildings, capital investment subsidies paid either to households for building operations or to public undertakings to finance certain capital equipment. On present-day accounting conventions these transfers are included in the income of those to whose benefit they are made, and are therefore part of their savings. For our purposes it is better to include them directly in the capital accounts rather than through the route of firms' or households' savings. This is because those receiving the transfers must in reality regard them as linked to investment operations and not as part of the income total out of which are levied household consumption and firms' distributed profits. These "capital transfers" received by firms and households amounted to about 4 percent and 2 percent, respectively, of gross domestic production around 1950 and 1960. Before World War I they did not exist. They do not seem to have been as high between the two wars as recently.[19]

[19] According to J. Edmond-Grange (*Le Budget fonctionel en France,* Paris, 1963), central government expenditure for housing and reconstruction, which was negligible before World War I, amounted to the following proportion of national income: 0.8 percent in 1922, 0.6 percent in 1931–32, 0.7 percent in 1938, and 4.0 percent in 1952.

TABLE 9.4

Net Domestic Savings Rates in Selected Countries, 1956–64

(Percent of gross domestic product)

Category	France	Germany	United States	United Kingdom
1956				
Government agencies	1.9%	7.9%	} 3.3% {	0.9%
Public undertakings		1.9		−0.7
Private enterprise corporations[a]	} 2.2		3.7	7.0
Households and nonprofit institutions	4.9	8.8	5.9	2.4
Total	9.0%	18.6%	12.9%	9.6%
1960				
Government agencies	3.6%	7.7%	} 3.1% {	0.2%
Public undertakings		2.1		0.5
Private enterprise corporations	} 3.3		3.3	8.4
Households and nonprofit institutions	5.9	9.6	4.1	3.7
Total	12.8%	19.4%.	10.5%	11.8%
1964				
Government agencies	4.5%	7.4%	} 1.7% {	1.7%
Public undertakings		1.3		−0.2
Private enterprise corporations[a]	} 1.9		3.8	6.9
Households and nonprofit institutions	5.9	8.9	5.1	4.5
Total	12.3%	17.6%	10.6%	12.9%

Source: United Nations, *Annuaire statistique des comptabilités nationales,* 1965.

[a]Including amortization by private firms.

Without attempting to measure more exactly, we can thus conclude that the rate of private savings net of amortization has remained broadly constant since the beginning of the century. If allowance is made for capital transfers, it fell abnormally low around 1950, but regained its earlier level around 1960. A comparison with other countries is of interest, although there is no guarantee that statistical and accounting methods are sufficiently comparable. As Table 9.4 shows, the ratio of French household savings to total output seems to have been close to that in the United States, lower than in Germany, and higher than in Britain. On the other hand, savings by firms seem to have been significantly higher in the two Anglo-Saxon countries than in France or Germany.

Savings by government agencies were particularly high in France in the postwar period, when they stood at a relative level comparable with that in the years 1925–29. Although the figure was low before World War I and strongly negative in the 1930's, over the postwar period as a whole it represented a significant contribution to national savings, amounting after allowance for capital transfers to about 4 percent of

TABLE 9.5
The Structure of Savings, 1949–66
(Percent of gross domestic production)

	Gross savings, National Accounts						Net savings excluding capital transfers [a]				
	House-holds	Corporations		Government agencies	Financial institutions	Total	House-holds	Corpo-rations	Government agencies	Financial institutions	Total
Year		Private enterprise	Total								
Old Base											
1949	10.7%		12.3%	2.0%	0.5%	25.5%	3.5%	2.9%	3.5%	0.5%	10.4%
1950	10.3		11.2	1.9	0.5	23.9	4.3	2.8	4.0	0.6	11.7
1951	9.1		9.9	1.7	0.4	21.1	3.5	1.6	3.6	0.5	9.2
1952	9.1		10.1	-0.4	0.6	19.4	3.8	1.9	1.5	0.7	7.9
1953	7.5		10.7	-0.2	0.7	18.7	2.4	2.6	1.9	0.8	7.7
1954	10.0		9.8	0.8	0.6	21.2	4.6	2.1	3.1	0.7	10.5
1955	11.1		9.8	0.2	0.6	21.7	5.7	2.6	2.8	0.7	11.8
1956	10.4	(6.5)%	9.5	-1.0	0.8	19.7	5.8	2.3	1.5	0.9	10.5
1957	10.9	(6.4)	9.0	-0.2	0.8	20.5	5.5	2.1	2.0	1.0	10.6
1958	10.1	(5.7)	8.5	2.2	1.0	21.8	5.4	1.9	4.0	1.1	12.4
1959	9.6	(5.8)	9.1	2.6	0.9	22.2					
1959 Base											
1959	8.8	(5.7)	9.0	3.0	1.1	21.9	4.4	2.0	4.5	1.1	12.0
1960	10.2	(5.9)	9.4	2.8	1.2	23.6	6.3	2.5	4.1	1.2	14.1
1961	9.4	(5.5)	9.2	3.2	1.2	23.0	5.4	2.0	4.5	1.2	13.1
1962	11.2	(5.6)	9.2	2.1	1.1	23.6	7.3	1.9	3.6	1.1	13.9
1963	10.5	(5.3)	8.9	2.6	1.0	23.0	6.6	1.1	4.1	1.0	12.8
1964	10.4	(5.2)	9.2	3.4	1.1	24.1	6.6	1.1	5.1	1.1	13.9
1965	10.8	(5.0)	9.2	3.6	1.0	24.6	7.0	0.9	5.2	1.0	14.1
1966	10.7	(4.9)	9.2	3.6	1.0	24.5	6.9	0.8	5.5	1.0	14.2

[a] Figures for each year are calculated on the new 1959 base. Capital transfers taken into account are war damages, capital investment subsidies, and for 1949–54 that share of international cooperation which is represented by Marshall Plan aid.

the gross domestic production. The degree of direct or indirect financing by government is probably one of the outstanding features of the French economy in the last 20 years in relation to earlier periods. It also differentiates France from Britain and the United States. (The year 1956 shown in Table 9.4 is atypical from this viewpoint, as can be confirmed by Table 9.5.) Nevertheless, in postwar Germany, savings by government agencies provided an even higher share of the total.

Let us now examine in greater detail changes observed in the last 20 years. Expressed in real terms, French domestic savings remained practically constant from 1949 to 1953. They then grew fast and fairly regularly at an average annual rate of 7.2 percent from 1953 to 1964. The ratio of these savings to gross domestic production fell from 25.5 percent in 1949 to 18.7 percent in 1953; it reached 23.6 percent in 1960 and rose again very slightly thereafter.

The various components of savings can be described in widely different terms according to the concept followed: that of gross savings used in the National Accounts, or that of net savings with investment subsidies, war damage payments, and Marshall Plan aid treated as capital transfers. Table 9.5 gives the two relevant series of estimates. The breakdown based on the National Accounts is characterized by great stability. Households appear to have provided about 45 percent of gross savings in most years, with a peak exceeding 50 percent between 1955 and 1957. The proportion provided by corporations seems to have been especially high in 1952 and 1953, and to have moved between 45 and 50 percent in the other years of the period 1949–56. Since 1958 it has fallen to about 40 percent. The proportion from government agencies was apparently almost negligible from 1952 to 1957, reached 10 percent before and after this halfway period, until 1963, and significantly exceeded this proportion between 1964 and 1966.

The description takes on a different character if net savings are considered, and if certain transactions are treated as capital transfers. To estimate the contribution of household savings to gross domestic production, it is helpful to remove the effect of short-term economic movements between 1953 and 1959. A rising trend can then be seen, with the ratios for 1955, 1956, and 1962 particularly high above it. The growth of the aggregate rate of savings would therefore seem due in greater part to the increase in households' propensity to save. In contrast, the proportion of gross domestic production taken by the net savings of all nonfinancial corporations taken together showed a slightly downward trend up to 1962. The low levels reached between 1963 and 1966 were due almost wholly to the public undertakings. This trend will be studied in detail in the last section, on accumulation of savings by nonfinancial corporations.

As soon as certain transactions are treated as capital transfers, it can be seen that savings by government agencies played an important part over the whole postwar period. Their share of gross domestic production had fallen to about 2 percent between 1952 and 1957, but since 1958 it has amounted to over 4 percent. The high level of this type of savings in the early 1960's ushered in the second phase of the investment boom by making possible a large scale of investment by public undertakings.

Before going on to a more precise study of the behavior of households and private-enterprise corporations, it is advisable to dwell briefly on the flow of net finance from abroad. If Marshall Aid is included, this flow was positive in every year except 1954, 1955, and 1960. It reached 2 percent of gross domestic production in 1952, and also between 1956 and 1958. In the other years it played only a minor role, since Marshall Aid, which was very large in 1949 and 1950, was offset in those years by high transfers to French overseas territories.

Factors Explaining Household Savings

A feature of the postwar period was a rising trend in household savings[20]—if, that is, our viewpoint is adopted that war-damage payments and investment subsidies should be treated as capital transfers. This result, which can be seen in the second part of Table 9.5, is confirmed by a series of household savings rates as a ratio of all resources attributed to their account. This rate rose from about 8.5 percent around 1951 to 10.5 percent around 1957. It would have stood at about 12 percent after 1963 had not the change of base made in 1959 reduced it by some 0.7 percent.

On the other hand, although no precise figure except for 1938 can be used in support, it does seem that the rate of household savings was lower immediately after the war than previously (in 1938 it had reached 10.8 percent). The same feature has been observed in other countries— in some cases to an even more marked degree. In France it was shown in the low figures of financial investments and fixed capital formation by households around 1950 by comparison with earlier years. How can these features of household savings be accounted for?

---

[20] We shall use here the usual accounting convention by which direct financing by individual entrepreneurs of their own investment is considered part of the households' capital account, and therefore is shown as part of the income of individual entrepreneurs and of their savings. Adopting the opposite convention would not, in any case, change the conclusions reached.

The immediate postwar period. The low level in the immediate post-war years should not seem surprising. French people were then likely to be rebuilding their stocks of durable goods, which they had not been in a position to replace in the normal way during the war (e.g. clothing and household capital goods). The introduction of the universal social security system considerably broadened the help available to wage earners when sick or having to quit work, and thereby gave a lower priority to building up cash reserves against the unexpected. The rate of savings would probably have been lower still if credit facilities for consumption had been more extensive and if the earlier inflation had not reduced the financial wealth of households and substantially exhausted the real value of their cash nest eggs.

Immediately after the war, credit facilities for consumption were very restricted. They did not begin to develop until the slowdown of 1952-53. But at the end of 1955, outstanding credit on goods for private use still did not amount to more than 0.4 percent of gross national production (1.1 percent at the end of 1967—a far lower proportion, it should be noted, than in other countries). From the outbreak of World War II to 1948, the general level of prices grew by a factor of 18. In the three following years, prices rose by another 40 percent. It can be estimated that households at the time held some two-thirds of the total cash supply. The "forced savings" they had to make merely to keep constant the purchasing power of their nest eggs (already much reduced by long inflation) amounted to about 2.5 percent of their resources in this period. Moreover, the fall in purchasing power of interest-bearing financial assets also limited the wealth of households and consequently their demand for goods and services. It is of course sometimes asserted that inflation simultaneously discouraged savings by reducing the yield on financial investments whose nominal value was in terms of rapidly depreciating currency. Yet in the situation immediately after the war, this effect was without doubt less important than that mentioned earlier in relation to the forced accumulation of cash savings.

The revival of household savings after 1953 can clearly be explained by the return to more normal conditions. Stocks of durable goods, such as clothing and furniture, had to a large extent been replenished. The trade-off between consumption and savings could be seen as comparable to that before the war. This seems sufficient to explain much of the rise in the rate of savings from 1951 to 1957. But other factors also seem to have played an important part in the changes observed.[21]

[21] In what follows we do not allow for changes in the age structure of the population. If we took these into account, the following approach would seem to be required. Other things being equal, the savings rate of an average household is low when the

Income distribution. It is helpful to consider, first of all, what changes have taken place in income distribution. If this is altered in favor of the better-off classes, savings are thereby stimulated. This phenomenon is not easy to analyze because there are so many aspects to it. Some detailed studies are available, however, with the help of which we can reach a fairly exact view. Very briefly, we can say that income distribution changed little in the postwar period.

If we start by examining income distribution by main category, we see that average income per employed person grew in practically the same proportion for employees and wage earners, independent farmers and independent nonfarm entrepreneurs. The composition of the labor force was affected by a rapid increase in the proportion of wage earners, but this does not seem to have altered income distribution much, since the increase was at the expense of farmers, whose average income is low, and of other individual entrepreneurs, whose income is most often high. On the other hand, social security and welfare payments increased after the war faster than did incomes as a whole. This trend, which naturally helped the least privileged classes, far more than offset the slight and moreover irregular rise in investment income (dividends, interest, farm rents, and income from households' real estate property).

Among salary and wage earners, a slight expanding of inequalities seems to have occurred.[22] Average earnings of management grew faster than did those of other employees, and the number of white-collar workers in higher categories greatly increased. The index of monthly earnings for this group was ahead of that for white-collar workers in lower categories, or of the index of hourly wages of workers, by 12 percent in 1951, 16 percent in 1957, 25 percent around 1961, and 30 percent in 1967. But this widening of the range of primary incomes was offset by an upward shift in job structure of the working population. Over the unfortunately short period of 1956–65, the results of household surveys

---

chief breadwinner is under 30 years of age. It then rises to a peak at an age close to 55 years, and drops at higher ages. The absence of precise data on savings rates by age prevents measurement. We note, however, that savings were probably encouraged in 1949 by the high proportion of medium age-groups in the French age pyramid. Changes in the age structure had a downward effect between 1949 and 1955, since the birth deficit due to World War I was reducing numbers in the age-groups with progressively higher savings rates. By contrast, from 1955 to 1963 the continuation of this trend was at least partly offset by the fact that the 1932–45 birth deficit gradually reduced the proportion of young households, whose savings rate is low. The aggregate impact of these changes in the age structure, however, does not seem to have been great.

[22] See in particular "Données statistiques sur l'évolution des rémunérations salariales de 1938 à 1963," *Etudes et conjoncture*, August 1965.

and the breakdown of tax receipts indicate that the distribution of household incomes changed little, while tending toward a very slight lessening of inequalities.[23]

Finance for building. In the second place, the continuing shortage of housing in France at a time when the standard of living was rising led to an increasing share of incomes being set aside up to the mid-1960's to finance building. In the immediate postwar period, house building had been on a small scale, and financed largely by war-damage compensation payments to households (to the extent of four-fifths in 1949 and half in 1951). From 1952 special loans were available, in addition, from the Crédit Foncier (real estate credit institution). These two sources of public financing provided for a good half of the housing built by households between 1952 and 1956. But from 1957 house building accelerated rapidly at a time when war-damage compensation was tailing off and the volume of financing by special loans from the Crédit Foncier was reaching a constant level in real terms. Households were therefore led to allocate an increasing share of their incomes to house building.[24] (This was 1.4 percent in 1951, 2.5 percent in 1957, 3.1 percent in 1963, and 4.6 percent in 1966, according to calculations with the 1959 base of National Accounts.)

It seems likely that the urgent need faced by many households to finance their own home building partly explains the rise in rates of saving. If the real estate market had been more competitive, more housing would have been built by firms to rent. This reasoning may underestimate the stimulus given to savings by a competitive real estate market, where private persons would have found a remunerative field for investment. However, this does not seem to be an influence comparable in strength to a man's need to house his family.

The results of the household surveys show clearly this forced swing to home ownership. Between 1955 and 1967 the proportion of heads of

[23] See G. Vangrevelinghe, "Les Niveaux de vie en France en 1956 et 1965," *Economie et statistique*, no. 1, May 1969; and G. Banderier, "Répartition et évolution des revenus fiscaux des ménages, 1956–1965," *Economie et statistique*, no. 16, October 1970. See also C. Seibel and J. P. Ruault, "La Participation aux bénéfices," in Darras, *Le Partage des bénéfices* (Paris, 1966).

[24] The results are shown in Table 9.6. The basis for the calculation could be challenged. For one thing, building operations and the payment of war compensation or other benefits are not necessarily simultaneous. Then again we have reduced long-term loans by the amount of repayments of loans made for building operations carried out earlier. If calculations were made on different bases, the results would still be close to those obtained. Thus, if war-damage payments and building subsidies are treated as household current income not under any particular heading, own financing of building would represent, as a proportion of household incomes, 2.7 percent in 1951, 3.4 percent in 1957, 3.5 percent in 1963, and 4.9 percent in 1966.

household aged 40 who owned their own homes rose from 23 to 48 percent (these figures relate to the nonfarm population).[25] The scale of savings implied by such an increase is easily apparent.

Forced savings. Third, the rise in prices that took place at several periods since the war forced households to continually increase their cash savings in order to maintain their level of purchasing power. As an offset to these forced savings, it would be appropriate to allow for the pressure to consume and spend implied in an outlook of continually rising prices, if that were possible. However, we have not found any objective way of measuring this feature, and we believe it was on a smaller scale than the feature now being examined.[26]

To appreciate more fully the part played by forced savings, we note that the total volume of cash savings held by households was equivalent to about 2.5 months' income in early 1949 and 1952. Cash accumulation from 1949 to 1951 was therefore in the main a necessary counterpart of inflation. At the beginning of 1957, households' volume of cash was the equivalent of 3.2 months' income, whereas prices had increased only slightly since the beginning of 1952 (the index of prices relevant to total household expenditure rose by an average of 1.5 percent per year). At the beginning of 1964, households' cash savings were worth 3.8 months' income, while consumer prices had grown at approximately 5.5 percent per year since the end of 1956. Forced savings, defined as those necessary to maintain the purchasing power of cash put by, represented about 2.5 percent of household incomes in 1949–51, 0.3 percent in 1952–56, and 1.5 percent in 1957–63. In the first two of these periods, effective cash accumulation was 3.7 and 3.2 percent, respectively, of incomes. In 1957–59 it accounted for 2.5 percent of incomes, in 1960–63 for 4.9 percent, in 1964–66 for 2.4 percent, and in 1967–69 for about 1 percent.

It seems, therefore, that savings preserved as cash were substantial up to the mid-1960's and consistently in excess of forced savings that resulted from price increases. Total cash savings were particularly high in the early 1960's. This can be accounted for to only a very small extent by changes in methods of wage payment (with monthly payments replacing weekly payments) and by the increased proportion in family

---

[25] See P. Durif, "Propriétaires et locataires en 1967," *Economie et statistique*, no. 3, July–August, 1969, in particular fig. II, p. 45.

[26] Households clearly increase their purchases when they know that a rise in prices will shortly occur for particular reasons (tax increases, devaluation, etc.). But the topic relevant here is different: are savings lower in a situation of continually and steadily rising prices than in a situation of price stability? Econometric studies carried out from annual series covering roughly 20-year periods have not given a clear answer to this question.

budgets of purchases of high-cost durable goods. We believe this cash accumulation can be explained chiefly by the untypically low level of households' real cash balances around 1950. The rapid inflation experienced between 1945 and 1948 had sharply reduced the real value of the total volume of cash. Individuals had to build up their liquid reserves again; instead of doing so at one stroke, as the above calculation of forced savings supposes, they had done this gradually over the last 15 years as the rate of inflation they were providing against in fact dropped.[27] Cash savings held by households in 1938 were about 4.2 months of income, that is, relatively much larger than in 1950 and comparable to those in 1966.

In brief, the need felt by individuals to rebuild their cash reserves partly explains the postwar rate of savings. It does not seem enough, however, to account for the rise in this rate; on the contrary, the accumulation of liquid reserves was particularly large from 1960 to 1963, at a time when the rate of savings was growing more slowly than in the 1950's.[28]

Financial investments. The study of finance for house building and of forced savings has led us to examine two of the main items in households' capital account. It will be useful now to consider briefly the other items in Table 9.6. The item "Other deposits" concerns chiefly deposits in savings accounts. This took a substantial and on the whole fairly steady share of household income: 1.8 percent in 1953–56, 1.7 percent in 1957–59, 2.1 percent in 1960–63, 2.7 percent in 1964–66, and about 4 percent in 1967–69. Starting from the principle that individuals seek to hold in savings accounts a reserve with a given purchasing power, we could repeat for these the analysis of forced savings made earlier for cash holdings. In short, the conclusions would be closely similar. Sums held in savings accounts represented 2.0 months of income in 1938; 0.7 month in early 1949, 0.8 month in early 1952, 1.3 months in 1957, 1.6 months in early 1964, and 2.1 months in early 1968.[29]

Broadly speaking, net investment by households in securities was low over the whole period studied. Immediately after the war, it seems to

[27] The econometric studies by Professor M. Allais show that this was a very widespread development.

[28] It could of course be maintained that the rise in households' standard of living accounts for an upward shift in the equilibrium ratio between cash reserves and incomes, and that as a result this ratio is substantially higher than it was in 1938. But the acceleration observed between 1960 and 1963 would not be any better accounted for by this approach.

[29] At the same periods maximum amounts authorized per account were, as a proportion of households' average annual income, 0.65 in 1938, 0.37 in 1949, 0.36 in 1952, 0.60 in 1957, and 0.61 in 1964.

TABLE 9.6

Capital Transactions of Households, 1951–69

(Percent of total household income)

Category	1951[a]	1953	1957	1959[b]	1959[c]	1963	1966	1966[d]	1969
Sources:									
Gross savings by households	8.2%	7.0%	10.8%	9.7%	9.0%	11.0%	11.4%	13.8%	13.1%
Adjustment[e]	–	1.2	0.9	1.4	1.9	1.6	1.3	1.4	0.9
Total	8.2%	8.2%	11.7%	11.1%	10.9%	12.6%	12.7%	15.2%	14.0%
Uses:									
Own financing of housing[f]	1.4%	1.9%	2.5%	2.9%	2.9%	3.1%	4.6%	3.2%	1.9%
Financing of individually owned firms[g]	1.6	1.3	2.2	2.5	2.0	1.4	1.3	3.7	3.7
Increase in cash reserves	(4.0)	2.5	2.8	2.4	2.6	4.3	1.8	2.6	-0.4
Other deposits[h]	(0.9)	2.0	1.1	2.3	2.0	2.0	3.1	3.3	6.4
Net investment in stocks and bonds	(-1.0)	-0.2	2.5	0.9	1.3	1.7	1.7	2.0	2.2
Balance of other capital transactions[i]	(1.3)	0.7	0.6	0.1	0.1	0.1	0.2	0.4	0.2
Total	8.2%	8.2%	11.7%	11.1%	10.9%	12.6%	12.7%	15.2%	14.0%

[a]In the absence of capital accounts for the year 1951, the figures in parentheses are rough estimates.
[b]Base 1956.   [c]Base 1959.   [d]Base 1962.
[e]Generally interpreted as representing chiefly private capital returned from French overseas territories.
[f]Excess of gross household capital formation over war-damage compensation, capital investment subsidies (building bonuses), and net long-term loans to households.

[g]Item of the National Accounts *less* capital transfers received by individually owned firms.
[h]Chiefly deposits in savings banks.
[i]Excess of life insurance premiums over benefits, short-term loans, balance of gold and currency transactions, *less* sales of buildings by households to third parties, etc.

have been positive or negative according to whether or not a large public loan was floated in that year (loans were raised in 1949 and 1950). The stock market boomed from 1954 onward, and encouraged stock issues. Net investment in stocks and bonds was particularly high in 1956, 1957, and 1958, standing at 3.6, 2.5, and 2.1 percent, respectively, of household incomes. The year 1956 was in any case untypical because of the Ramadier loan. In none of the other years did the proportion reach 2 percent.

Even during these three exceptional years 1956–58, stock issues were far lower than they had previously been in France. The stock market had been active before World War I and in the 1920's. It had been cut down considerably by the depression, and then by the lack of confidence of business circles in the direction taken by French politics in 1936. The last 15 years' expansion does not seem to have been enough to restore to the stock market its earlier role as the chief collector of savings. The ratio between stock issues and gross domestic production in the years immediately before World War I can be estimated as about 10 percent. The ratio was 9 percent in the three years 1928, 1929, and 1930. In 1938 it was only 3.1 percent. Even in the three best postwar years, 1956–58, it did not exceed 3.9 percent.

Compared with the situation in other countries, that in France today does not seem exceptional. It would appear, rather, that what was unusual was the size of the French financial market at the beginning of the century. The report for 1964 of the Bank for International Settlements gives the following estimates for the ratio between issues by corporations and gross national product for the period 1956–63: France 2.5 percent, Germany 3.0 percent, Great Britain 1.7 percent, United States 2.8 percent, Italy 6.3 percent, Netherlands 2.7 percent, and Belgium 6.0 percent. Other financial transactions by households do not call for comment except in the case of capital movements abroad and life insurance. Immediately after the war, households' investments in gold and foreign exchange seem to have exceeded capital transfers from overseas territories. But there is little doubt that since 1953 repatriated capital systematically overshadowed the increase in gold and foreign exchange. It seems to have been particularly high in 1956, and even higher in 1961 and 1962.

The growth of life insurance after the war provided an increasingly popular outlet for household savings, but it still accounts for only a small proportion. The excess of premiums over benefits received by individuals amounted to 0.4 percent of household incomes in 1949–56, and to 0.5 percent in 1957–59. The increase in actuarial reserves of life insurance was 0.33 percent of household incomes in 1959, and 0.35 percent after 1963. Despite the difficulty inherent in any explanatory analysis, we can conclude with little risk of error that household savings in the postwar period were stimulated not so much by expectation of profitable financial investment as, far more, by the need of individuals for housing and for rebuilding money reserves. They do not seem to have been motivated to save from a desire to develop productive capital, or even to have directly aimed at uses that would conveniently finance business investment.

Accumulation of Savings by Nonfinancial Corporations

The most obvious feature in estimates of savings by nonfinancial corporations is their relatively slow increase in the postwar period. When deflated by the gross domestic production price index, the relevant series in the French National Accounts shows a growth rate of 1.7 percent per

TABLE 9.7
Data for the Study of Savings by French Corporations, 1949–66
(1962 prices, *billion francs*)

Year	Total nonfinancial corporations		Private-enterprise nonfinancial corporations		
	Gross savings of National Accounts	Net savings excluding capital transfers[a]	Gross savings	Net distributed profits[b]	Rate of gross savings[c]
1949	19.2	4.6		2.5	
1950	19.4	4.7		3.0	
1951	18.4	3.0		3.5	
1952	19.0	3.5		3.7	
1953	21.0	5.0		3.8	
1954	20.3	4.4		4.1	
1955	21.5	5.6		4.0	
1956	21.6	5.4	14.9	3.9	79
1957	21.9	5.2	15.3	3.9	80
1958	21.0	4.8	14.1	3.2	82
1959[d]	23.4		14.6	3.2	82
1959[e]	24.0	5.3	15.0	3.2	82
1960	26.7	7.3	17.1	3.2	84
1961	27.4	5.9	16.5	3.1	84
1962	29.3	6.1	18.1	3.0	86
1963	30.0	3.8	17.6	3.1	85
1964	32.6	3.8	18.5	3.1	86
1965	34.0	3.4	18.6	3.1	86
1966	36.1	3.1	19.2	3.0	87

[a]Estimates consistent with the 1959 base for each year.
[b]Dividends and preference payments *less* interest and dividends received on corporations' own investments.
[c]Percent share of gross savings in total of gross savings and net distributed profits.
[d]1956 base.   [e]1959 base.

year from 1949 to 1957 (2.9 percent from 1951 to 1957, but the year 1951 was not typical). The rate was 5.4 percent from 1957 to 1966 (see Table 9.7, col. 2, where the growth rate has been corrected to eliminate the effect of the 1959 change of base). Over the period 1957–66, growth of savings was lower in the private-enterprise corporations taken separately (2.3 percent per year on the average).

The same picture is gained, even more strongly, from considering net savings, and treating war-damage compensation and investment subsidies as capital transfers (see Table 9.7, col. 3). The series shows marked irregularities, with low points at the end of booms and the beginning of periods of stagnation. If we take as benchmarks the averages for 1949–51, 1955–57, and 1960–62, a growth rate of 4.7 percent per year can be derived for the first subperiod and 3.6 percent for the second. The low figures between 1963 and 1966 are not significant: they are the result of strongly negative savings of publicly owned corporations, which were offset by capital subsidies.

In brief, the ratio of growth of corporate savings seems to have been consistently lower than the growth of output. The ratio between these two values, therefore, shows a downward trend in the postwar period. Clearly this drop was not due to increased liberality of companies in distributing profits. These distributions had grown, in fact. at a rapid rate in the early 1950's, but thereafter remained static in real terms from 1954 to 1957, dropped sharply in 1958, and then remained static again at this lower level. From 1956 to 1966 the proportion of gross disposable income saved in all private-enterprise nonfinancial corporations as a whole grew from 79 to 87 percent. The fact that company savings grew so slowly accordingly stemmed from a drop in the ratio between profits and the value of output. This factor is important both for the formation of savings and for other aspects of growth. We must therefore first measure it and then explain it.[30]

Drop in the rate of profits. The best statistical source on this subject is provided by a breakdown of yearly declarations by firms to the direct taxation officials. These, known as "industrial and commercial profits" declarations, cover various accounting items relating to business in a given year. Breakdowns are available from 1950, and make possible interesting comparisons insofar as no substantial changes have taken place in the definitions of the values covered. We mention here the ratio be-

[30] The accounting series from which Table 9.7 is extracted seems to present an exaggerated picture, at least for the period 1959–66. The new series established in 1968 shows a faster growth of corporation profits and savings. Nevertheless, the feature in question seems to persist. More particularly, the recent revision of the National Accounts does not affect the comparisons we are about to make.

TABLE 9.8
Profit Margins in French Firms, 1951–64
(Percent)

Year	Joint-stock corporations[a]	Limited liability corporations[b]	Publicly owned corporations[c]	Personal tax-basis firms[b]	All firms
1951	9.0%	5.2%	15.3%	6.8%	8.9%
1952	8.7	4.6	15.4	7.0	8.0
1953	9.1	4.2	16.6	7.1	7.9
1954	8.9	3.9	29.8	7.0	7.8
1955	8.7	4.6	15.5	8.6	7.9
1956	8.0	4.5	16.0	8.0	7.3
1957	8.1	4.7	20.1	8.0	7.9
1958	7.9	4.5	22.4	7.4	7.7
1959	8.0	4.5	22.0	7.5	7.8
1960	8.0	4.7	13.5	7.7	7.8
1961	7.3	4.3	13.7	7.7	7.4
1962	6.8	4.3	13.1	7.8	7.2
1963	6.5	4.3	12.8	7.9	6.9
1964	6.7	4.3	13.4	8.0	7.0

Note: The profit margin is the ratio of revenue surplus to turnover (before deduction of amortization and other provisions). This is derived from statistics of industrial and commercial profits–"real profits" tax basis.
[a]This includes limited partnerships by shares.
[b]The tax statistics segregate as "corporations" firms subject to corporation tax. A variable number, difficult to estimate, of small, limited-liability companies have opted to be taxed as private individuals, and are therefore here considered personally owned firms.
[c]This includes joint public/private enterprise companies.

tween turnover and gross surplus before deduction of any provisions or special deductions. This ratio, which we shall call "profit margin," seems to have been defined consistently over the whole period.[31] Estimates are shown in Table 9.8.

Over the long term, the most significant results are probably those for the joint-stock companies, which accounted in 1950 and 1963, respectively, for 43 and 62 percent of total turnover of private enterprises, and for 51 and 74 percent of private corporations. If we take as a reference point years with an end-of-boom inflationary situation, we find profit margins of 9.0 percent in 1951, 8.1 percent in 1957, and 6.5 percent in 1963. For all private corporations together, the figures for the same years are 7.4, 7.0, and 6.0 percent. This is an undeniable drop. In both cases, it occurred during a boom period—that is, 1956–57 and 1961–63; the drop was sharper in the latter period than in the former. The results for years after 1964 are not yet available for joint-stock companies taken

[31] Of course, the results may be affected by tax avoidance. This is likely to be on a smaller scale in joint-stock companies than for all firms taken together. Moreover, its relative scale seems to have varied little from 1950 to 1968. If, as seems to be suggested by the results for individual firms, tax avoidance has become less, the real drop in margin was probably bigger than our figures suggest.

TABLE 9.9
*Average Profit Margins of all Firms in Selected
Sectors, 1956–57 and 1962–63*
(Percent)

Sector	1956–57	1962–63
Processed foods and farm products	5.3%	5.0%
Iron mining and metallurgy	12.0	9.0
Primary metal-processing	7.6	6.5
Mechanical industries	7.7	7.3
Electrical industries	6.2	7.3
Automobiles	7.5	6.5
Chemicals	9.3	8.5
Textiles	7.1	6.1
Paper and cardboard	8.6	7.9
Building materials	10.7	11.3
Building and public works	5.8	5.7
Hotels, cafes, and restaurants	7.2	7.2

separately. If we consider all public and private-enterprise corporations as a whole, the rate in Table 9.8 becomes 6.8, 7.5, 6.9, and 6.9 percent for each year from 1964 to 1967. It seems therefore that the drop in profit margin stopped in the mid-1960's.

A statistical breakdown by individual sectors does not enable the profit margin to be calculated before 1955. A comparison between the two-year averages in 1956–57 and 1962–63 shows that it fell somewhat unevenly across the sectors (see Table 9.9). The drop was particularly sharp in metallurgy, automobiles, and textiles, whereas there was a rise in electrical appliance manufacturing and in building materials.

We have been referring up to this point to gross margins, in order to eliminate the effect of changes in the rules for calculating depreciation (e.g. revaluation of assets, reducing depreciation since 1960, option of partial depreciation when operating income is too low). It would have been more significant to consider net profits after deduction of exact depreciation calculated by a constant method. However, we have confirmed by tests that this would not have produced significantly different results. Three calculations were made on the basis of annual investment series for nonfinancial private enterprises, and on assumptions of asset life. Two show a practically constant ratio of depreciation to turnover (2.5 percent in one case and 3.4 percent in the other). The third calculation produces a slightly falling ratio (3.0 percent in 1957 and 1960, 2.8 percent in 1963). According to this calculation, the net profit margin fell between 1960 and 1963 slightly faster than did the gross margin.

Explanatory factors. How can this downward tendency in profit margins be explained? The question can be approached in two ways. On the one hand, a study of firms' cost items shows which entries rose as a counterpart to the fall in disposable gross income. On the other hand, the explanation needs to be completed by a search for more fundamental causes. Each of these approaches will be adopted in turn.

It is, in fact, quite difficult to make a precise analysis of firms' cost items, particularly when trying to account for fairly slight changes in a rate of profit that itself is shown as residual. We have had to confine ourselves to a somewhat sketchy study, using mainly the National Accounts, which are not really detailed enough for our purpose. We shall therefore not show any quantitative results. Our conclusion, however, leaves little room for doubt: the drop in profit margins was accompanied by a more or less equal increase in tax and related debits. (There was also a sharp increase in interest charges, brought about by the rise in firms' indebtedness, but they accounted for only a small proportion of all costs.) Firms' accounts thus reflect the rapid increase in public consumption and investment in the postwar period.

But this increase in tax and related debits is not enough to explain completely the feature in question, since it could have been offset by a slower increase in wages. The reason why profit margins fell so low lies in the circumstances of competition between firms, particularly in the labor market. Employers' organizations have attached great importance in their studies to government control over industrial prices. But this factor does not account for the observed trend, since the price freeze was not imposed before the end of 1963. Moreover, the controls were far stricter in most industries in 1956 and 1957 than in 1962 and 1963. The drop in profit margins in metallurgy seems to have been the only direct result of the government measures.

Over most of the postwar period, the French labor market was fairly tight. This fact undoubtedly influenced the downward trend in profit margins, which had been very high in 1950. But it is not responsible for the acceleration of the trend observed in 1960–63, since the labor market was then no tighter than in 1954–57 and the profit margins had already returned to what might be considered normal levels. The ratio of unfilled job vacancies to jobs sought averaged 0.29 in the four years 1954–57 and 0.31 in 1960–63. It was growing much faster over the first period, when it roughly doubled each year, than in the second period: the ratio doubled in the two years from 1960 to 1962, but fell thereafter. The chief cause of the drop in profit margins seems to lie in two factors operating simultaneously. First, high investment in industry from the mid-1950's pulled down both the marginal productivity of capital and the competitive profit rate. Second, the opening of the French market to foreign trade was reflected by a revival of competition, which probably wiped out some above-normal profits in certain protected industries and, above all, led most firms to figure their prices more closely.

Let us call profits, output, and capital, respectively, B, Q, and K. We can then say that the profit margin B/Q is equal to the product of the capital-output ratio K/Q by the "rate of return" B/K. When there is perfect competition in a sector of production, the rate of return must be close to the marginal productivity of capital. Therefore, if imperfections in competition had not increased over the period under study, the heavy investment made since 1956 would account for a fall in the rate of return, since presumably it pulled down the marginal productivity of capital. A drop in the profit margin would have resulted, at least if the fall in B/K were greater than the rise in K/Q.

To discuss this point more exactly, we must necessarily examine more closely the production function that expresses for a particular sector the relationship between output and the factors of production used. Let us first assume that a Cobb-Douglas function is relevant, of the form $Q = qN^\alpha K^\beta$, where N is labor input, and q, α, and β are three constants. The marginal productivity of capital, a partial derivative of Q in relation to K, is equal to $\beta Q/K$. This is indeed a decreasing function of the capital-output ratio K/Q, but the profit margin is constant and equal to β if we ignore intermediate consumption, which, as we have seen, did not change.

It is generally accepted nowadays, however, that the elasticity of substitution between capital and labor is lower than assumed in the Cobb-Douglas function.[32] For functions with a constant elasticity of substitutions, the following formula establishes the value of the marginal productivity of capital, and of the rate of return, which under perfect competition is equal to it:

$$\frac{B}{K} = a \left(\frac{Q}{K} \right)^{1/\varepsilon} Q^\phi$$

where a is a constant, independent of the period considered, assuming technical progress to be neutral, where ε is the elasticity of substitution (equal to 1 in a Cobb-Douglas function), and ϕ is the constant:

$$\phi = \left(\frac{1}{\varepsilon} - 1 \right) \left(\frac{1}{\lambda} - 1 \right)$$

[32] L. Stoleru, *L'Equilibre et la croissance économique* (Paris, 1969), chap. xv.

λ is the coefficient of increase of returns to scale (equal to 1 where returns to scale are constant). The profit margin is then expressed by

$$\frac{B}{Q} = a \left(\frac{K}{Q} \right)^{1-1/\epsilon} \times Q^{\phi}$$

The rate of change of B/Q is then equal to the sum of the rate of change of K/Q multiplied by $1 - 1/\epsilon$ and the rate of growth of Q multiplied by ϕ.

In the present state of econometric studies on the factors governing output in France, we are of course not in a position to state what numerical values of the constants ϵ and ϕ would best describe the situation now prevailing in French industry. As an extreme hypothesis, opposite that underlying a Cobb-Douglas function, we can assume $\epsilon = \frac{1}{2}$ and $\lambda = \frac{5}{4}$ (when an increase of 10 percent in the inputs of labor and capital raises output by 12.5 percent). The constant ϕ would then be equal to $-\frac{1}{5}$. How did the capital-output ratio change? We established in the first part of our study that for industry as a whole the ratio of fixed reproducible capital to value added, both at 1956 prices, was 1.13 in 1951, 1.11 in 1957, and 1.18 in 1963. Let us assume that since 1956 the capital-output ratio has risen at around 1 percent per year. Given that output grew at the same time by 5 percent per year, our hypothesis on ϵ and λ leads to the conclusion that the competitive profit margin dropped at a rate of 2 percent per year and the marginal productivity of capital by 3 percent per year.

This calculation of course has value only as an illustration. But it shows that the scale of capital accumulation since 1956 would account for a considerable proportion of the drop in profit margins observed over the past ten years. A gradual sharpening of competition since 1958, leading firms to accept lower profit margins, would seem a natural consequence of the gradual setting up of the Common Market. We shall examine this question in Chapters 12 and 13. We might note at this point, however, that the results shown in Table 9.9 provide some confirmation of this view: apart from electrical appliance manufacture, the only industries to maintain their profit margins were those not much subject to international competition.

This examination of the relative drop in company profits has led us away from the subject matter of this part of the chapter, i.e. savings since the war in their explanatory factors. However, a conclusion seems to emerge. Both in households and in private enterprise corporations, the steep rise observed in capital accumulation is probably not to be accounted for by a high propensity to save. Quite the contrary: the need to make physical investments—housing in the case of households and productive equipment in the case of corporations—stimulated relatively high savings. This conclusion, basically, is consistent with the observed chronic excess of demand during the whole postwar period in France, and the need to fight against inflation and against a lack of national savings.

CHAPTER TEN

The Role of Finance

To appreciate how far the supply of savings may have helped investment and thereby growth after World War II, it is not enough, as in the previous chapter, to study the formation of savings. We must also examine under what conditions the supply of savings was made available to investors. More precisely, we must assess how the rate of capital accumulation and the investment structure were influenced by the nature of the sources of finance, by the size of internal funds, and by the suitability of various outside sources—that is, of financial channels and markets—to the needs of investors.

The study of investment financing will be centered on productive capital, which plays a particularly important part in development and which, being a physical growth factor, has a more direct effect on expansion than does other investment. Nevertheless, in the following pages we have mostly been obliged to regard as productive investment the total investment of all undertakings, which includes some investment in housing. This is because available statistics have not enabled us to separate residential building from the overall capital and financial accounts of all business ventures taken together. In all cases, however, where the disadvantages of this approach were more than minor for our purpose, we have made corrective estimates to allow for the fact that investment by all undertakings has comprised a growing proportion of housing[1] and that the financing of this investment has a very different structure from that in productive capital.

Our analysis concerns chiefly the postwar period, for lack of adequate data on investment and the nature of its financing before World War II.

---

[1] At current prices, 3.6 percent in 1949, 6.5 percent in 1954, 9.3 percent in 1959, and 12.2 percent in 1964. Investment chiefly involved is by the public HLM (*habitations à loyers modérés*) offices and by private-enterprise real estate companies.

As we saw in Chapter 4, apart from the immediate postwar reconstruction period, the growth of productive assets was particularly fast between 1954 and 1962 or, more precisely, from 1954 to 1957, and then, after a pause in 1958–59, again from 1959 to 1962. Our analysis of the financial factors underlying the productive investment carried out therefore will be centered chiefly on the periods 1954–57 and 1959–62. It seems necessary, however, to analyze the reasons for the slowing down of productive investment growth in private enterprises in 1963 and 1964. Accordingly, we shall also treat 1964 as a key year for the periods to be studied.

We shall examine in turn how business ventures financed investment from their own and from outside resources. We shall consider all enterprises as a whole, since most National Accounts statistics available when our study was carried out, especially for financing on a large scale, were not broken down by categories of enterprise. Nevertheless, in a third section we shall single out a few major categories, since the financing of investment took very different forms according to whether it concerned public enterprises, private corporations, or individually owned firms in agriculture or other fields.

INTERNAL SOURCES

Self-financing built up by enterprises affects the level of their investment for a number of reasons. First, the volume of these resources is closely linked to that of profits, which accounted for the greater part of the investment in the period examined. Thus, the ratio of gross savings in private corporations to gross profits (i.e. gross savings plus net distributed dividends) was 75 percent in 1956, 76 percent in 1959, and 80 percent in 1964. Since obtaining a return on their own funds is one of the chief motives of firms' activity, and since expectations are largely determined by the growth of profits observed, the rate of increase of self-financing has a marked effect on the growth of investment.

Second, the proportion of investment financed from outside sources is necessarily limited. Apart from the fact that many firms, especially those of small or average size, find it difficult or impossible to tap certain sources of outside financing (more will be said on this later), several security constraints have the effect of limiting the use of these sources even when access to them is easy. In the first place, borrowing mortgages the future because of the interest and repayment charges necessarily involved. (In this respect, a minimum level of savings is necessary if enterprises are to make repayments as they fall due without further borrowing.) The same applies, although far less rigidly, to increases in share capital, which eventually must be rewarded by the payment of dividends. Furthermore, too great recourse to external finance, whether through loan or share issues, can jeopardize a firm's autonomy and lead to a change of control. And last, whether outside funds can be used at all depends on whether profit margins are high enough: a firm too heavily in debt or unable to make adequate remuneration to its shareholders finds it difficult to obtain new outside financing.

To assess the effect on investment of different modes of financing, it would be desirable to study changes in the structure of firms' balance sheets, which are more significant than changes in annual profit and loss accounts and in financial flows, since this approach makes it possible to take rigorously into account the effect of price changes on the structure of assets and liabilities. Nevertheless, available statistical data have led us to concentrate in most of the chapter on a study of financial flows, since balance sheets are not reported in present-day National Accounts. We shall therefore first analyze changes in firms' self-financing ratios. Then, however, we shall present and interpret the results of estimates we have made to allow for changes in the value of assets.

The Fall in the Self-Financing Ratio

We shall assess the role played by self-financing in the demand for investment quite simply: we shall assume that the stimulus to businesses to invest (which is determined by a number of variables, such as financial resources, the relative costs of capital and labor, and the outlook for demand growth) is, for given values of the other variables, a rising monotone function of the self-financing ratio. We assume in this way that if savings output is below savings aimed at in order to undertake the desired investment, actual investment will be below desired investment (the desired self-financing ratio can of course also fall, since the respective reductions in it and in investment depend on the various other factors leading to the investment). We therefore assume here that firms cannot adjust their actual savings to their desired savings (by cost reductions or price increases) except within certain limits. In other words, savings formation in firms is taken as bound by constraints (such as domestic and foreign competition, or a rise in wage costs per unit of output) over which they have only limited control. Since a number of variables help determine demand for investment, an increase in this demand may well be accompanied by a drop in the self-financing ratio. We must then, however, admit that this drop tends to hold back demand for investment, which therefore must be accounted for other than by the development of firms' savings.[2]

Different concepts of self-financing can be used, which can lead to different assessments of changes in firms' financial position. The ratio's numerator can be either gross savings or net savings, obtained by deducting amortization from gross savings, and including or excluding loan repayments, which are in the nature of mandatory charges. Both gross and net savings can be calculated including or excluding capital-equipment subsidies and war damage benefits, according to whether these are treated as receipts in the firms' current account, contributing to their savings formation, or, on the contrary, as external capital funds in addition to their own savings. The ratio's denominator may be gross or net investment, including or excluding stock formation, and including or excluding increases in financial assets (such as working capital and shareholdings).

We have chosen three definitions of the self-financing ratio: (1) The usual definition, i.e. the ratio between gross savings by enterprises (including financing of capital formation by individual entrepreneurs) and their gross capital formation (including stock formation). (2) The ratio between the same savings and the sum of increases in physical assets (gross capital formation) and financial assets.[3] (3) Last, the ratio between "disposable" savings (gross savings after deduction of funds mandatorily earmarked for repayment of loans already received) and the increases in all assets as in definition (2).

We have chosen to use gross rather than net values because this seemed the least unsatisfactory way, in the broad context of our analysis, of reflecting the behavior of businesses. We believe that business decisions relate to overall investment programs rather than programs concerning only net investment, it being then assumed that provision for keeping prior productive potential will be made independently. In our view one of the important parameters in decisions taken was the total of own available funds, i.e. apart from recourse to credit or to shareholders, whatever the origin of these funds, public or private. Nevertheless, the last definition above of self-financing allows for the fact that part of the available funds of firms must necessarily be allotted to the repayment of earlier borrowings. By using gross values, we are

[2] This reasoning is not entirely rigorous, since it does not allow for the effect of price changes on the real makeup of the balance sheet. If price rises are sufficiently high, a drop in the self-financing ratio may not mean any balance-sheet worsening. On this topic, see the next section.

[3] Excluding credit given by one firm to another.

able, moreover, to avoid taking account in our calculations of estimates of amortization, which are well known to be statistically unreliable.

We have added stock formation to gross fixed capital formation because, like investment, it is linked to output increases in the medium term, the period we are considering here. In the series of ratios covered by the latter two of our definitions, we have also added to gross fixed capital formation the increases in firms' financial assets, which similarly are linked in the medium and long term to the growth of output.

It is appropriate, moreover, to compare self-financing ratios with investment ratios. The significance of a given self-financing ratio clearly differs according to whether the ratio between investment and gross

TABLE 10.1
*Changes in Self-Financing Ratios of Firms by Three
Definitions, 1949–67*

Year	Savings ÷ investment (def. 1)	Investment ÷ output	Savings ÷ output	Savings ÷ growth of assets (def. 2)	Savings "not allotted" ÷ growth of assets (def. 3)
			1959 base		1956 base
1949	74	19.2	14.2 ⎫ 13.7		
1950	73	18.3	13.3 ⎭		
1951	68.5	17.3	11.8 ⎫		
1952	75	16.0	12.0 ⎪ 12.0		
1953	87.5	14.2	12.4 ⎬	68	66
1954	80	14.6	11.7 ⎭	67	64
1955	78	14.7	11.5	68	64
1956	68.5	17.2	11.8	60	57
1957	63.5	17.5	11.1 ⎫ 11.5	59	56
1958	63.5	18.0	11.5 ⎬	61	58
1959	72.5	16.0	11.6 ⎭	59	55
					1959 base
1959				59	55
1960	69	17.9	12.4	59	54
1961	63.5	17.2	10.9 ⎫	53	47
1962	64.5	18.2	11.8 ⎪ 11.0	54	47
1963	60.5	17.8	10.8 ⎬	51	43
1964	58	18.7	10.8 ⎭	52	44
1965	66.5	16.8	11.1	55	46
1966	63	17.8	11.1	53	43
1967	64.5	17.8	11.5	52	42

Note: All types of firms are included: public enterprises, private corporations, individually owned firms, and real estate companies.

   Savings: Savings by corporations plus financing of capital formation by independent entrepreneurs.

   Investment: Gross fixed capital formation by firms plus inventory changes.

   Output: Gross domestic production of firms.

   Growth of assets: Gross fixed capital formation by firms plus inventory changes plus net increase in financial assets of firms.

   Savings "not allotted": Savings minus loan repayments by firms.

domestic production is low or high. A further ratio worth examining arises from this comparison, the savings ratio of firms—that is, the relationship between savings and value added. Estimates of all these different ratios are shown in Table 10.1. Col. 1 shows the *cyclical character* over the period considered of the self-financing ratio measured by the first, or usual, definition. The ratio reached peaks in upward-turning-point years—1953, 1959, and 1965; it fell gradually as expansion progressed, and fell to troughs at the end of expansionary periods and during recessions—1951, 1957–58, and 1963–64. Cols. 2 and 3 show that this cyclical movement was due to two factors: first, variations in the demand for investment and for stocks (the investment ratio rises in the upward phase of the cycle and has troughs in the years of first recovery); second, changes in firms' savings ratio, which tends to drop in the upward phase of the cycle. The cyclical movement of this latter ratio can be accounted for by changes occurring in assigning shares to profits and wages; these changes are linked to variations in the tightness of the labor market over each cycle[4] and probably also to the drop in profit ratios consequent upon a phase of quickened capital accumulation.

Table 10.1 also demonstrates a *long-term downward trend in self-financing ratios.* Before 1956 total firms' savings were in almost every year more than 70 percent of their investment; after 1961 the ratios stood broadly between 60 and 65 percent. Comparisons between periods with a similar position in the different cycles show the drop clearly: the ratios averaged 75 percent in 1954–56, as against 66 percent in 1960–62, 68.5 percent in 1951, 63.5 percent in 1957, and 58.0 percent in 1964, all end-of-production-boom years.[5] This development was due to two factors. First, the profits analyzed in the previous chapter fell relatively. Table 10.1, col. 3, shows that firms' savings ratios fell gradually from 13.7 percent in 1949–50 to 12 percent in 1951–54, to 11.5 percent in

[4] In 1953, an upward turning-point, characterized also by a marked slackening of the labor market, the ratio between the relative increases, with respect to 1952, of wages paid by firms and gross domestic production was only 0.9, whereas the corresponding ratio concerning changes in firms' savings and gross domestic production gave a figure of 2.8. In 1959–60, the figures were, respectively, 0.95 and 1.45. By contrast, over the upward phase of the cycle, paid-out wages grew faster, and firms' savings grew more slowly, than did output.

[5] The new estimates in the National Accounts, on a 1962 basis, show the drop in the self-financing ratio after 1959 to be less substantial than would appear from the figures given here, and that the reversal of the downward trend occurred in 1964 and not in 1965. According to these estimates, the rate moved as follows (in percent):

1959	1960	1961	1962	1963	1964	1965	1966	1967
72.1	70.2	68.3	67.8	66.8	68.7	72.7	73.2	72.1

But these new estimates do not alter the direction of the changes observed in the medium term, and the qualitative conclusions that can be drawn from them.

1955–59, and to 11 percent in 1961–67. Second, there was an upward movement in the rate of gross fixed capital formation: 14.6 percent in 1954–55 and 17.5 percent in 1960–61, two pairs of years in comparable positions in their cycles. The ratio used in col. 4 of Table 10.1 brings out more clearly the long-term changes in the financial situation of enterprises than does the more usual definition used in col. 1, since the sum of stock changes and increases in their financial funds moves far more steadily than either of these two values separately. The proportion of firms' own funds in annual increases of physical and financial assets was very stable at 68 percent from 1953 to 1956, and fell sharply in 1956, to remain very stable at between 59 and 61 percent from 1956 to 1960. It fell significantly again in 1961, and averaged 53 percent from 1961 to 1966. The downward trend was at a rate of about 1.5 points per year. The ratio between savings "not allotted" to loan repayments and asset growth in col. 5 fell even more rapidly, since charges for loan repayments increase substantially as firms' indebtedness relative to their asset growth increased. The ratio dropped from 65 percent at the beginning of the period to about 45 percent at the end; that is, an average drop of about 2 points per year.

These measures of the fall in firms' self-financing margins over the period studied, and more particularly in investment boom periods, nevertheless overstate the drop, for two reasons. First, investment by firms included an increased proportion of investment in housing. This is chiefly carried out by public and private real estate companies, which rely for a very large part of their financing on outside sources. The self-financing ratios excluding housing are therefore consistently higher than those for all firms taken together. Our estimates[6] show that the gap between the two sets of ratios widened from 1949 to 1965: from 2 points in 1949–51 it rose to about 4 points in 1953–58, to 5 points in 1962–63, and to an average of 6 points in 1964–66.

Second, in certain years firms' own resources were supplemented by transfers of capital from abroad as a result of disposal of assets in foreign or franc-area countries. These transfers are poorly reported in the statistics, but broadly correspond to the heading "Adjustment" in the table of financial transactions in the National Accounts. This item accounted for 4.7 percent of increases in firms' assets in 1956, and for an average of 3 percent between 1961 and 1965 (resulting chiefly from disposal of assets in Algeria). Although these resources cannot be treated completely as own resources, neither can they be regarded entirely as funds from outside. If it is assumed that half can be treated as firms'

[6] See Appendix Table 13.

own resources, average self-financing ratios for productive investments in the years 1962–64—the end of the investment boom for the period studied—must be increased by 1.5 to 2 points.

Overall, the ratio between firms' own resources (excluding housing) and their productive investment seems to have fallen, according to the corrected estimates, from 84 percent in 1954 to 66 percent in 1964, and not from 80 to 58 percent as shown in Table 10.1. These corrections do not alter the conclusions reached: the self-financing ratio of enterprises fell considerably over the period, and more particularly during the sub-periods of investment boom. This situation and this pattern of change were not confined to France. The self-financing ratio fell in all Western countries between 1955 and 1965. The position of French enterprises stands halfway between that of countries where the growth of output and investment was faster than in France (Japan and Italy) and that of countries where it was slower (United States and Britain).[7] In the early 1960's the self-financing ratios of undertakings, excluding housing (the ratio between gross savings and gross investment including stock changes), were close to 70 percent in France and about 75 percent in Belgium and Germany. In Britain and the United States they were on the order of 100 percent. In Japan they ranged between 50 and 60 percent, and in Italy on the order of 50 percent. These differences can probably be accounted for partly by differences in the rate of growth of investment (see Appendix G), but also by real differences in the availability of financing.

The Deterioration in the Balance-Sheet Position of Firms

Price rises in the period under study reduced the real value of the indebtedness of undertakings as a proportion of the real value of their assets as a whole. Betwen 1940 and 1952 the general price level grew by a factor of 20, which means a near-extinction of debts contracted before the war. From 1945 to 1948 the general price level grew by a factor of 6.5. This movement considerably lightened the debt charges of firms, which therefore entered the period under study only very slightly indebted. In order to examine how the depreciation of money reduced the real indebtedness of firms and thereby encouraged demand for loans for investment, we have evaluated the chief items in firms' balance sheets. Our object has been to analyze the changes over the period in the values of outstanding debt of all firms—of their own funds and of their physical and financial assets. In order to illustrate the effects of inflation, we have compared the movement in the ratio between firms'

---

[7] See, for example, the data in *Rapport général de la commission de l'économie générale et du financement (Ve Plan)*, appendix no. 10, pp. 115–43.

debt (net of all outstanding credits) and their reproducible capital with what the movement would have been had the general price level remained static since 1953, and assuming actual investment and annual indebtedness ratios. In this way it is possible to calculate what reduction of the debt burden of firms can be imputed to rise in prices.

Estimation of firms' balance sheet. We have evaluated for each of the years 1953[8] to 1965 the nominal value of the following items in the balance sheets of enterprises (excluding real estate companies): (1) fixed productive reproducible capital, (2) stocks, (3) financial assets, (4) total indebtedness (short, medium, and long term, including value of bond issues), and (5) own funds (total value of assets less total indebtedness).

1. *The nominal use value of fixed reproducible capital* of firms was estimated by applying the index of prices of productive investment[9] to the corresponding estimates of the volume of productive capital, excluding transportation infrastructure (the estimates are those given in Chapter 5).

2. The values of stocks was first assessed for a base year (1956) from the ratio between the volume of stocks and the volume of output. This ratio in turn was obtained by comparing the variations of stock and output in firms, these variations being examined for every year from 1949 to 1965. The ratio, which was 32 percent for the whole period from 1953 to 1965 (two years with a comparable economic situation), seems to have tended slightly downward between 1949 and 1965; thus between 1959 and 1965 (economically comparable years) it was 29 percent. For 1956 we have taken the value of 33 percent observed for the period between the two end-of-boom years 1951 and 1957. The annual estimate of stock volume was calculated from the figure obtained for 1956 by adding to it (or subtracting from it) the estimates of stock formation by volume shown in the National Accounts. In order to obtain a value series from this volume series, an index of wholesale prices was then applied to it.[10]

[8] This is the first year for which a table of financial transactions is available in the National Accounts data.

[9] This is not a rigorous method, since the price index to be applied to the volume of capital is equal to the index of investment only if the structure of capital by type of product is the same as the corresponding structure of the investment. There is no reason why this condition should in fact rigorously obtain, but any resulting error can be neglected.

[10] We have used this index rather than the price index for stock variations in the National Accounts because of the large differences that may exist, first, between the stocks' structure by products and, second, in their year-to-year changes. Over the medium term, the estimates for these two indexes are similar.

3. The nominal value of financial assets of undertakings[11] was calculated excluding their shareholdings. We have thus ignored, in calculating the worth of their assets, the value of shares of foreign companies or of financial institutions held by them. These assets were first evaluated for a base date (January 1, 1953) from the difference between an evaluation of the total indebtedness of undertakings and their total indebtedness net of credits on January 1, 1953. This latter figure, 20 billion new francs as of January 1, 1953, was itself obtained by adding to the total of firms' financing requirements between 1949 and 1952 (the balancing item of firms' financial account in the National Accounts) the net annual indebtedness incurred between 1945 and 1948. The latter was computed under the assumption of an indebtedness ratio of 20 percent applied to the nominal estimates of productive investment in those years (cf. Chapter 4). After allowing for price rises in the period, annual net nominal indebtedness decreases very rapidly as assets are traced back through the years, and the figures earlier than 1945 can be ignored. It has been verified that the estimates of assets so obtained are comparable with what is known of the distribution of the money supply between households and firms at that period, since money assets were a high proportion of firms' financial assets. Movements in these assets were calculated by adding the net changes recorded in the National Accounts' table of financial transactions to the estimate of the assets stock on January 1, 1953. No account was taken of changes in assets imputable to increases or decreases in the market value of bond issues.

. 4. Total indebtedness of undertakings was first evaluated as of January 1, 1953, from a number of sources: short-, medium-, and long-term outstanding credits shown in the reports of the Conseil National du Crédit; variations in these credits during the year 1953, shown in the table of financial transactions in the National Accounts; the sum of borrowing against bonds by private-enterprise and public undertakings since 1945 (here again it can be observed that their nominal value drops very fast as the dates are traced back, as a result of price rises before 1953; the nominal value of borrowings against bonds before 1945 can thus be ignored). Changes in the total indebtedness of firms on January 1 in years later than 1953 were calculated by adding to the estimate obtained in this way (40 billion new francs on January 1, 1945) the net changes in their liabilities (excluding share issues) shown in the tables of financial transactions in the National Accounts. A correction was made to eliminate variations in the net liabilities of real estate corporations (assuming that these, excluding share issues, represented 60

---

[11] Including financial assets held by individual entrepreneurs.

TABLE 10.2

Assets and Liabilities of Firms, Excluding Housing, 1953–66

(1962 prices, billion francs)

Year	Assets					Liabilities			
	Fixed reproducible productive capital	Stocks	Total physical assets	Financial assets[a]	Total assets	Indebted-ness	Own funds	Total liabilities	Indebtedness net of credits[b]
1953	235	71	306	29	335	57	278	335	28
1954	249	71	320	36	356	66	290	356	30
1955	242	71	313	42	355	74	281	355	32
1956	258	74	332	46	378	81	297	378	35
1957	274	79	353	50	403	92	311	403	42
1958	284	86	370	49	419	95	324	419	46
1959	280	89	369	49	418	101	317	418	52
1960	299	91	390	56	446	110	336	446	54
1961	311	98	409	63	472	126	346	472	63
1962	327	101	428	69	497	141	356	497	72
1963	342	105	447	76	523	156	367	523	80
1964	355	108	463	82	545	170	375	545	88
1965	375	113	488	86	574	188	386	574	102
1966	391	112	503	93	596	202	394	596	109

Note: Ratios are as of January 1 of each year.
[a] Excluding shareholdings; including assets of individual entrepreneurs.
[b] The difference between indebtedness of firms and the value of their financial assets (excluding shareholdings).

percent of investments in housing by all undertakings). However, no correction was made to allow for increases in nominal indebtedness corresponding to price fluctuations for those bonds that were subject to price escalation devices (issues of such bonds occurred between 1952 and 1957).

The results are shown in Table 10.2. Their approximate nature hardly need be stressed. The orders of magnitude, however, can be considered valid, and although the absolute figures must be treated with caution, the movements shown are significant.[12] In order to help comparisons, the results are shown in real terms in 1962 prices; these figures were obtained by deflating the nominal values by the gross domestic production price index, with 1962 = 1.

Movements in the indebtedness of enterprises. Table 10.2 shows that over the whole period of rapid increase in investment, from the beginning of 1955 to the beginning of 1963, total gross indebtedness of enterprises grew in real terms by a factor of 2.1 (which represents an average annual growth of nearly 10 percent), whereas their own funds increased by only 1.3 times (which represents an average annual growth of about 3.5 percent). The difference between their total indebtedness and total credits grew by a factor of 2.5, equivalent to an annual growth of 12 percent. The decline in the balance-sheet position was slightly faster over the second part of the period studied than over the first part. In the two economically comparable periods 1954–60 and 1960–66 (as of January 1 in each case), total indebtedness of firms grew by 9 and 10.5 percent per year, respectively, and their indebtedness net of credits grew by 10 and 12.5 percent. Their own funds increased at a similar rate in both periods, on the order of 2.5 percent per year. Similar comparisons for the periods of fast productive investment (the beginning

12 When these estimates were made, we had available only the traditional tables of financial transactions in the National Accounts, which show variations in financial assets and liabilities but not current figures. Since then, the National Accounts office has drawn up a table of assets and liabilities outstanding as of December 31, 1962 (internal note of the Financial Transactions Division, Direction de la Prévision, December 26, 1967). Comparison of these new data with our own calculations confirms their validity. Excluding company shares, the financial assets of firms as of December 31 were 67 billion francs, compared with our estimates of 79 billion (in current prices). But the financial assets in the new table do not cover all the assets of individually owned firms; the difference observed therefore seems in order. On the other hand, the indebtedness of firms would amount to 180 billion francs, as against our estimates of 162 billion. But in contrast to the estimates in the new table, our figures exclude indebtedness related to housing (i.e. that of real estate corporations), which we estimate at 16 billion francs. Adding our two estimates together, we get a total of 178 billion, which is almost identical to the figure in the table of outstanding financial assets and liabilities.

TABLE 10.3
Debt Ratios of Firms, Excluding Housing 1953–66
(Percent)

Year	Ratio between indebtedness (net of credits) and value of physical assets	Ratio between total indebtedness and total value of assets	Year	Ratio between indebtedness (net of credits) and value of physical assets	Ratio between total indebtedness and total value of assets
1953	9.4%	17.1%	1960	13.9%	24.7%
1954	9.5	18.6	1961	15.4	26.7
1955	10.2	20.7	1962	16.7	28.3
1956	10.6	21.6	1963	17.9	29.9
1957	11.9	22.8	1964	19.0	31.2
1958	12.5	22.7	1965	20.8	32.7
1959	14.1	24.2	1966	21.7	33.9

Note: Ratios are as of January 1 of the year shown.

of 1954 to the beginning of 1958, and the beginning of 1960 to the beginning of 1964) give ratios of 9.5 and 11.5 percent per year, respectively, for total indebtedness and 11 and 13 percent for indebtedness net of credit items. Own funds increased by 2.8 percent per year over both periods.

The structure of firms' balance sheets was substantially altered by the very different courses taken, respectively, by the real value of their own funds and their indebtedness. This is shown in Table 10.3, which traces the development of two particularly interesting balance-sheet ratios: the relationships between firms' total indebtedness (net of credits) and the value of their physical assets; and the relationship between firms' total indebtedness and the total value of their assets (this latter ratio's complement is the proportion of their own funds in total liabilities). It can be seen that the two ratios rose consistently between 1953 and 1966: from 9.4 to 21.7 percent for the first, and from 17.1 to 33.9 percent for the second.

As in the case of the self-financing ratio, international comparisons of balance sheets show that the decline in the financial position of firms has not been confined to France. French undertakings enjoyed an own-resources financing situation between those of the United States and Great Britain (which were more favorable) and those of Italy and Japan as well as Germany (which were less favorable). According to comparative balance-sheet statistics,[13] the ratio between corporations'

[13] As given by L. Jeorger in "Etude comparée du financement des entreprises dans six pays industrialisés," in ISEA, *Economie appliquée* (ISEA Archives, vol. XXI; Geneva, 1968), p. 584.

own funds and their medium- and long-term debt, between 1960 and 1965, was about 3 in France; 4.5 and 5, respectively, for the United States and Great Britain; and 2.25, 1.8, and 1, respectively, for Germany, Italy, and Japan. Between 1960 and 1965 (1966 for France, and 1964 for Italy) this ratio seems to have moved from 2.5 to 2.03 in Germany, from 3.18 to 3.07 in France, from 2.01 to 1.72 in Italy, from 5.41 to 4.70 in Britain, from 4.80 to 3.83 in the United States, and from 1.12 to 0.88 in Japan. These changes can be explained partly by the rapid upsurge of investment in these countries over the period, but probably they also reflect a drop in profit rates, which may have resulted both from a fall in the marginal productivity of capital due to the investment upsurge, and from the sharpening of international competition.

Effects of inflation. We have already indicated that price rises during and immediately after the war largely wiped out the indebtedness of French firms at that time. At the end of this period of very rapid inflation, that is to say, in 1952–53, French firms therefore carried only a low indebtedness (see Table 10.3). After 1952, price rises were not so fast. However, they were still substantial, and, as we shall see, helped to lighten the burden of indebtedness. We have therefore calculated how the ratio between indebtedness and value of physical assets would have moved if there had been no rise in prices, assuming unchanged annual ratios of indebtedness and investment. A comparison of the movements so calculated with those observed is shown in Table 10.4, and provides a measure of the influence of price increases on the structure of firms' balance sheets.

The relief to firms' indebtedness arising from the increase in prices was substantial. The difference between the observed ratio and the ratio calculated on the assumption of a nil increase in the general price level since 1953 widened continually from 1954 to 1966, and in a particularly noticeable way in periods when price rises were great—as, for example, from January 1, 1957, to January 1, 1960, or from January 1, 1963, to January 1, 1964. Between 1953 and 1966 the difference was 6.5 points, corresponding to a relief in indebtedness (current prices) of 37.5 billion francs on January 1, 1966, i.e. to 30 percent of their indebtedness at that date.

If it is assumed that the scale of investment undertaken was conditioned by the desire of firms to become indebted no further than they are shown to be *ex post* by their balance-sheet situation, the increase in their productive capital from 1953 to 1966 (if no price increase had led to a lightening of their real indebtedness) would have been lower than

TABLE 10.4
The Effect of Price Increases on Indebtedness Ratio, 1953–66
(Percent)

Year	Observed ratio (A)	Calculated ratio (B)[a]	Difference (B − A)	Year	Observed ratio (A)	Calculated ratio (B)[a]	Difference (B − A)
1953	9.4%	9.4%	0	1960	13.9%	17.6	3.7%
1954	9.5	9.4	−0.1%	1961	15.4	19.5	4.1
1955	10.2	10.4	0.2	1962	16.7	21.2	4.5
1956	10.6	10.9	0.3	1963	17.9	22.9	5.0
1957	11.9	12.6	0.7	1964	19.0	24.8	5.8
1958	12.5	14.6	1.9	1965	20.8	26.8	6.0
1959	14.1	16.9	2.8	1966	21.7	28.2	6.5

Note: Ratios are as of January 1 of each year.

[a]We assume no general price increases since 1953. Let I_t be the value of gross investment of firms in the year t; K_t be the value of the physical capital of firms on January 1 in year t; E_t be the increase in firms' indebtedness (net of credits) in the course of year t; and ϵ_t be the total debt of firms (net of credits) on January 1 of year t. Then,

$$\epsilon_t = \epsilon_{t-1} + E_{t-1} \text{ and } \epsilon_t = \epsilon_{53} + \sum_{T=53}^{t-1} E_T$$

Let $i_t/53$ = the gross domestic production index of prices, with 1953 = 1. Let $E_t/I_t = e_t$ (the proportion of investment financed by debt). Then, changes in the observed ratio R_t can be compared to those in the calculated ratio R_t' defined as follows:

$$R_t = \left(\epsilon_{53} + \sum_{T=53}^{t-1} e_T I_T\right) \div K_t \qquad R_t' = \left[\epsilon_{53} + \sum_{T=53}^{t-1} e_T \left(I_T/i_{T/53}\right)\right] \div K_t/i_t/53$$

The price indexes affecting I_t are those of average prices for the year as a whole. Those affecting K_t are the indexes of prices at January 1.

it actually was. Other things being equal, the growth of firms' productive capital would have been reduced by 25 billion francs between 1953 and 1966, that is, by 0.3 points per year. Since the growth of productive capital in real terms was 3.8 percent per year, close to 10 percent of this growth seems to have been made possible by the price rises that occurred. These estimates, however, ignore induced effects. For example, if the price increases had been lower, interest rates might also have been lower. These are therefore probably the maximum estimates acceptable of the effects of inflation on capital accumulation.

The conclusions arising from the examination of changes in the balance-sheet situation of firms confirm those reached by the study of changes in self-financing ratios. The reduction in the latter was accompanied by a deterioration in the balance-sheet situation. Although price rises slowed down this deterioration, they did not prevent it. The restriction in firms' own resources thus tended to hold back the pace of investment more at the end of the period than at the beginning. Nevertheless, it may be that the development observed is a return to a "normal" situation rather than the gradual establishment of an unfavorable economic situation. Sources of long-term financing were indeed seriously lacking in the early 1950's, as we shall see later. At any rate, the shrinking of self-financing margins probably led to improved allocation of financing resources. First of all, it was accompanied by increased mobility of capital, and second, the tightening of financial resources and more frequent borrowing obliged firms to calculate expected financial returns more rigorously than in the past.

THE ROLE OF OUTSIDE RESOURCES

The investment surge of undertakings corresponded with a large increase in their recourse to outside sources of finance. Between 1954 and 1964, gross fixed capital formation by enterprises grew by a factor of 2.1 in real terms, while their financing requirements in real terms grew by a factor of 4.8. Between 1954 and 1957 the corresponding figures were 1.4 and 2.9; between 1959 and 1964 they were 1.6 and 2.3. It is pertinent to examine whether this change in the use of outside capital was encouraged by changes in the capital markets (e.g. in the volume, cost, and efficiency of credit distribution networks, or in the activity of the stock market). In such a case investment would have been stimulated by the type of financing available. On the other hand, the prime mover may have been the size of investors' demand for capital. A study of this kind is of course difficult, since it requires an appreciation from *ex post* data of the direction of *ex ante* disequilibria.

In order to take into account the chief interdependencies between total resources available and the financial use made of them by the different agents in the economy, we shall first examine changes in the flow of finance as a whole and then study in greater detail changes in the different categories of outside resources used by firms.

Overall Changes in the Financial Flows

Under this heading we shall examine first changes in the supply of finance as a whole and in the resulting overall equilibrium between this supply and the demand for it; then we shall examine how financial resources were used to finance productive investment.

Changes in the supply of financing. Viewed as aggregates, certain agents in the economy save more than they invest; this applies particularly to households, but also to financial institutions and at times to government agencies. In certain years, moreover, sources from abroad can be net providers of capital to the domestic economy. The sum of

TABLE 10.5
Increases in the Supply of Financing, Gross Domestic Production,
and Gross Capital Formation, 1954–64
(Percent per year)

Category	1954–1962	1954–1964	1954–1957	1959–1962	1959–1964
Supply of financing	8.6%	9.1%	25.0%	24.5%	18.0%
Gross domestic production	5.3	5.4	5.8	6.4	6.2
Gross capital formation	7.6	8.0	11.6	9.2	9.2

net lending[14] thus made available through the medium of financial institutions and markets to the economic agents, which save less than they invest (i.e. chiefly firms), makes up what we term the supply of finance. A plentiful supply of savings obviously favors the activity of agents that require financing, and in particular activity from firms.

Table 10.5 shows changes in the supply of financing compared with those of gross domestic production and of overall gross capital formation for the chief periods of investment expansion that concern us. This table illustrates that the supply of financing grew considerably faster than output and slightly faster than gross fixed capital formation from 1954 to 1962 (or 1964). It increased at an extremely fast rate, far faster than that of output or investment, during the phases of rapid investment growth. Changes in the supply of investment were the result both of the growth of total available savings[15] and of changes in the contribution of those savings to the financial system (i.e. to financial markets and institutions).

Table 10.6 gives changes in representative savings ratios. It shows that the development of the supply of financing in the investment boom years is accounted for by the progressive rise in the ratio of available savings, and even more so by the increase in the contribution of available savings to the financial system. By contrast, over the long term (i.e. in comparison of the averages for 1953–58 and 1959–64) the ratio between the supply of financing and gross domestic production remained practically constant, whereas the ratio of available savings rose: the ratio of the supply of financing to available savings fell slightly as a result of a relative reduction in the contribution of foreign capital. Analysis of the contribution of the different main agents (i.e. foreign

[14] In the French National Accounts the balancing item of a financial account is called *besoin de financement* or *capacité de financement*, depending on its sign. These are translated respectively as "net borrowing" and "net lending."

[15] Total available savings equals total savings of domestic economic agents plus foreign net lending (or net borrowing from abroad).

TABLE 10.6
Representative Savings Ratios, 1954–64
(Percent)

Category	1956 base			1959 base			1959 base[a]	
							Average 1953–58	Average 1959–64
	1954	1957	1959	1959	1962	1964		
Finance supply ÷ GDP	5.0%	8.2%	3.9%	4.3%	6.8%	7.5%	6.5%	6.4%
Disposable savings ÷ GDP	20.0	23.5	21.9	22.0	23.8	25.5	21.7	23.7
Domestic savings ÷ GDP[b]	(21.2)	(20.5)	(22.1)	(21.9)	(23.7)	(24.1)	(20.3)	(23.2)
Finance supply ÷ disposable savings	24.8	34.8	18.0	19.4	28.7	29.4	30.0	27.0

Note: GDP is gross domestic production. Disposable savings equals domestic savings plus net borrowing from abroad.

[a]During both the 1953–58 and 1959–64 periods the contribution of domestic savings to the capital market remained roughly equal to one-fourth of domestic savings.

[b]The differences between the figures on this line and the preceding line reflect the net contribution of foreign capital.

sources, households, financial institutions, and government agencies), intended to show variations in pressure on the capital market, has led us to distinguish two main periods: 1954–57 and 1959–64. We shall, moreover, assess the roles of supply and demand of financing over the entire period 1954–64.

1. Between 1954 and 1957, the fast growth of financing resources (25 percent per year in real terms) was chiefly due to net inflows from abroad. Net lending to foreign countries in 1954 gave way to net borrowing in 1957, representing 3 percent of gross domestic production and 12.5 percent of gross capital formation in that year. The net contribution of households grew at 6.2 percent per year, but this was far slower than the growth of gross capital formation (11.6 percent per year). Various indicators show that pressures on financing developed from 1957 on, and particularly in 1958: the development of bond issues with price index clauses amounted to a rise in real interest rates paid by borrowers; firms repatriated foreign capital and placed restrictions on financial investments and on increases in their money holdings.[16] The slowing down in growth of the supply of financing from 1957 can be largely ascribed to measures taken by the authorities to limit inflation: restrictions on credit by increasing the discount rate (which rose from 3 percent at the end of 1954 to 5 percent in August 1957) and lowering the rediscount ceilings in 1957; and a general ceiling placed on current credit on December 31, 1957, fixing it at the average level for the fourth quarter of 1957.

[16] See firms' financing in Appendix Table 14.

That opportunities for access to financial capital became insufficient by comparison with the need for capital is shown clearly in the results of the surveys of industrialists.[17] Up to November 1956, only 16 to 19 percent of industrialists mentioned difficulties in obtaining funds as one of the factors limiting their firms' activities. In May 1957 the proportion was 24 percent. In November 1957, as a result of credit restrictions by monetary authorities, it was 44 percent. In June 1958 it was 43 percent. The highest figure—46 percent—was reached in November 1958. In fact, serious financing difficulties first arose in 1958, as shown by the rapid increase in that year of long-term borrowing by firms of share issues and of medium-term credit (see the next section, on external financing of firms). Moreover, as shown by the results of the surveys, the slowing down of investment from the beginning of 1958 is to be accounted for more by the slackening of demand and by fears of recession than by financing difficulties in the strict sense.

2. From 1959 to 1964, the increase in financial resources came chiefly from households and abroad. Net provision of financing by households grew in real terms by 19 percent yearly, though, to be sure, the base year, 1959, had a particularly low level (from 1959 to 1962, the increase was 37 percent per year). Financing from abroad became substantial between 1962 and 1964 (0.8 percent of gross domestic production in 1962 and 1.5 percent in 1964). It accounts fully for the 18 percent real increase in resources for financing between those years. The whole period 1959–64 should in fact be divided into subperiods 1959–62 and 1962–64. Between 1959 and 1962 a very rapid growth of investment (9.2 percent per year in real terms) was accompanied by a considerable increase in financial resources (24.5 percent per year in real terms) without producing tensions: interest rates were stable or even falling, transactions with other countries left net lending, and prices remained stable. The supply of savings stimulated the growth of investment. In 1963 and 1964, however, tensions did develop: demand for investment, although then slowing down in the case of firms, was the prime mover in relation to the supply of savings. To choke off inflationary tensions, the discount rate was raised from 3.5 to 4 percent in November 1963, and measures to regulate bank credit were taken as part of the stabilization plan. The growth of financial resources as a whole thus slowed down significantly. The proportion of industrialists who in their replies for the surveys[18] reported difficulties in obtaining funds rose from a stable percentage averaging about 24 percent in 1961–63 to 27 percent

[17] See *Etudes et conjoncture*, June 1957, February 1958, March 1958, and February 1959.
[18] See *Etudes et conjoncture*, Supplement no. 8, 1965.

in March 1964 to 29 percent in June 1964 to 30 percent in November 1964, and to 31 percent in March 1965.[19] Firms drew on foreign sources of finance in 1963 and 1964, probably by accelerating currency repatriations, pulling in short-term inflows, and selling currency resources.[20] At the same time, the scope for recourse to the capital market was shrinking (see the next section, on external financing).

3. If one examines as a whole the period 1954–64, when available finance grew at an average of 9.1 percent per year in real terms, faster than did gross capital formation (8.0 percent per year), the supply of capital seems to have increased of its own accord as fast as demand for capital. Interest rates in 1964 were close to their 1954 level. Capital transactions with foreign countries did not show any significant changes of pressure on domestic capital markets. Development of the supply of financing seems on the average to have favored the financing of investment over the entire period studied, apart from the end-of-boom years 1958 and 1963 and to a lesser extent 1964. In those years the demand for funds was greater than the supply of savings, and the investment effort could be financed only with the help of foreign capital. The increase in available finance between 1954 and 1962 (8.6 percent per year in real terms) is to be ascribed chiefly to funds from households, whose net contribution averaged two-thirds of total net available funds and grew by 8.6 percent per year. Thus, the financing of investment was helped by the behavior of households.

Use of financial resources in the financing of productive investment. Through financial institutions and markets, distribution of the supply of savings takes place among the different applicants for capital. In this section we shall assess whether the conditions that determined the allocation of savings met the needs of enterprises more fully than those of other economic agents. We have just noted the relatively large net supplies of financing made available by households over the period.[21] The high level of these supplies is partly accounted for, at least up to 1962, by the special circumstances of the French housing market. Individuals who were themselves satisfactorily housed and wished to invest their savings hardly ever did so in house building. This fact can be explained by two elements. First, the ceiling set on rents directly discouraged building by householders of housing to rent for profit. It also indirectly discouraged building of housing for householders' own use:

[19] These percentages are not directly comparable with those quoted earlier.

[20] The large "adjustment" item for 1963 and 1964 in Appendix Table 14 on firms' financing reflects these developments.

[21] The forms of financing are not only by purchases of stocks or bonds, but also by increases in demand deposits in banks and in post office accounts, by deposits in savings banks, by purchases of treasury bonds, etc.

the occupants' privilege resulting from the tight control on rent paid on old housing was so great that those renting old property had no incentive to build a home for themselves. The second element was the regulation on house financing, which restricted the issue of long-term loans to the Crédit Foncier, the official real estate credit and loan association. At the beginning of the period this limited or even prevented setting up private-enterprise channels for house financing and ultimately had the effect of rationing the total volume of loans. Both these elements became less important over the period considered because of the lack of restriction on rents for private houses built after 1948, and because of the gradual development in the 1960's of private-enterprise channels for financing house building. Nevertheless, over the period as a whole, and particularly at its beginning, the supply of savings of those individuals who were not obliged to build for their own use was consistently directed toward other purposes than house building, that is, toward investments by government and business.

TABLE 10.7
Distribution of External Funds by Category of User, 1949–67
(1962 prices, *billion francs*)

	Enterprise					
Year	Private sector	Public sector	Total	Government	Foreign	Total
1956 basis:						
1949			7.4	–	3.9	11.3
1950			7.8	–	4.2	12.0
1951			9.1	0.3	–	9.4
1952			6.5	4.8	–	11.3
1953			2.5	4.4	–	6.9
1954			4.5	3.0	2.6	10.1
1955			5.7	4.7	2.3	12.7
1956	6.0	4.8	10.8	8.0	–	18.8
1957	6.2	7.0	13.2	6.6	–	19.8
1958	6.8	7.3	14.1	0.4	–	14.5
1959	3.4	6.1	9.5	–	0.7	10.2
1959 basis:						
1959	5.0	6.2	11.2	–	–	11.2
1960	8.5	6.6	15.1	–	0.6	15.7
1961	12.5	5.4	17.9	–	–	17.9
1962	13.3	6.0	19.3	2.4	–	21.7
1963	15.8	6.6	22.4	1.5	–	23.9
1964	19.8	6.9	26.7	–	–	26.7
1965	12.7	7.3	20.0	–	–	20.0
1966	16.9	7.6	24.5	0.7	–	25.2
1967			24.5	4.8		29.3

Note: Net borrowing by all main borrowing agents according to National Accounts terminology.

We shall study the distribution of financing resources between these two categories of investors in two stages. First, we shall analyze their capital accounts from National Accounts data. This will show what changes took place in the net allocation of these resources between the different applicants for capital. Second, we shall examine how this allocation took place. The changes in distribution of the net supply of savings brought together by financial institutions and markets are marked by an important feature, shown in Table 10.7: starting in 1958 the government had a new attitude toward indebtedness. From 1952 to 1957, government agencies drew heavily on available financial resources. From 1954 to 1957, a boom period for productive investment, net borrowing by government averaged 35 percent of total financial resources. In contrast, after 1957, funds borrowed and lent by government agencies more or less balanced each other, and business firms were almost the only beneficiaries of net funds supplied to financial circuits by households, financial institutions, and foreign sources. This development substantially increased the availability of finance to enterprises over the second period of upsurge of productive investment, between 1959 and 1964.[22]

If we now consider the public sector of the economy as a whole, grouping together government agencies and publicly owned enterprises, the changing distribution of financial resources between the public sector and private corporations between 1956[23] and 1966 (see Table 10.8) shows a gradual reduction from 1958 on in the proportion taken by the public sector, and a consequent increase in that of private corporations.[24] Between 1959 and 1964 the net drawings of private corporations on available financing grew, in real terms, by a factor of 4. This figure can be accounted for both by the growth of financial resources as a whole and by the increase in the proportion taken by firms. The growth of financial resources was at the rate of 19 percent per year, as against 6 percent for gross domestic production and 9 percent for gross capital formation; this accounts for 60 percent of the increase in the financial resources of firms. The remaining 40 percent is accounted for by the rise in firms' proportion of total financing.

[22] A counterpart of this new attitude was an increase in tax burden on firms, which discouraged the development of their own financial resources (see Chapter 9, p. 302).

[23] The first year for which estimates are available distinguishing private enterprise from public undertakings.

[24] The figures for 1959 and 1965 should be interpreted in the light of the prevailing economic situation at the time. The drop in the proportion taken by private corporations in those years can be accounted for by their relatively low investment and correspondingly low demand for capital.

TABLE 10.8
*Distribution of Financial Resources Between the Public and
Private Sectors, 1956–66*

1956 base			1959 base					
Year	Public sector	Private sector	Year	Public sector	Private sector	Year	Public sector	Private sector
1956	68%	32%	1959	51%	49%	1963	33%	67%
1957	69	31	1960	40	60	1964	23	77
1958	53	47	1961	25	75	1965	35	65
1959	62	38	1962	39	61	1966	33	67

These developments were due essentially to a change in the policies of the government, whose intervention in gathering savings, redistributing them among the financial institutions and markets, and issuing credit were the real determinants of the aggregate growth of financial circuits and the flows along them. The government's action in gathering savings affected in the first place the "primary" savers. The Treasury pulled in savings directly by the issue of treasury bonds bearing progressive interest rates, by mandatory loans, and through post office checking accounts. The public credit institutions—Caisse des Dépôts et Consignations and Caisses d'Epargne (savings banks), Crédit Agricole (farmers credit office), Crédit National (national credit office), Crédit Foncier (real estate credit and loan association)—collected primary savings in the form of deposits (as in the case of the savings banks and the farmers credit office) and of subscriptions to mandatory loans. Various regulations and tax requirements favored the public collecting circuits: special tax rates and exemptions for treasury bonds and deposits in savings banks, controls over the bond market permitting privileged treatment to issues of the Treasury, public financial institutions,[25] public bodies and public undertakings, and special facilities at post office counters for the collection of private savings. These privileges, in addition to the particular confidence given by French savers to investment in official organizations, had the effect of enabling public institutions to draw off a very high proportion of available primary savings.

Further, redistribution of primary savings among the intermediary financial channels operated through various mechanisms to the advantage of the public institutions; for example, the imposition of minimum treasury bond holdings on commercial banks enabled the Treasury to have access to some of the savings collected by these banks; the regulation of investment by insurance companies and pension funds gave

[25] Every bond issue above a certain total value requires prior authorization by the Treasury.

special advantages to bonds issued by public credit institutions and enterprises. Thus, around 1960 about two-thirds of financial investments[26] were, in short, drawn off to public funds. The way credit was distributed among different users was influenced not only by this high proportion of savings drawn off by public institutions, but also by various regulations affecting the scope for rediscounting, interest rates, and the allowable length of loans, which gave the public sector a near-monopoly in the distribution of long-term credit.

All in all, the growth of financial resources and the manner in which they were apportioned have favored the external financing of enterprises, in particular, private corporations, and consequently investment by enterprises between 1954 and 1964: from 1954 to 1957 as a result of the very rapid growth of net additions to the supply of financing; from 1959 to 1964 as a result of both a continued growth in the supply of finance, although at a slower pace, and the "withdrawal" of government agencies—and to a lesser extent of public undertakings—as net applicants for financial resources.

The External Financing of Firms

In order to appreciate the part played by outside supplies of financing in the growth of productive investment, it is not enough to study the development of the total volume of these supplies. It is also necessary to see how the balance was established between supply and demand of financing in the different categories of external financing: the issue of shares and bonds, and short-, medium-, and long-term borrowing at banks, specialized credit institutions, and the Treasury. The funds of each undertaking form a unity, and consequently all financial resources must be taken into account in a study of their investment financing. Thus, increased recourse to short-term credit to finance a firm's working capital reduces the proportion of own resources that must be devoted to this item, and therefore assists the financing of investment.

In studying the changes in circumstances governing investment financing by undertakings, we shall examine, first, the nature of the external sources on which they can draw, second, changes in the relative importance of these various sources, and third, trends in the operation of the capital market since the beginning of the century. We shall then draw some conclusions about the influence exerted by the different circumstances of financing on capital accumulation.

Diversification of sources of financing after World War II. The

---

[26] Including all forms: increases in holdings of paper money and bank deposits, net subscriptions to treasury bonds and stocks and shares, increases in deposits in savings banks, etc.

TABLE 10.9

Sources and Uses of Firms' Funds, 1954–64

(Percent)

Category	1956 base			1959 base				
	1954	1957	1959	1959	1962	1964	Average 1954–55	Average 1960–61
Use of funds (net of outstanding debts):								
1. Gross fixed capital formation	71%	78%	74%	77%	75%	80%	74%	75%
2. Changes in stock	5	10	3	4	8	10	7	9
3. Increase in financial holdings	24	12	23	19	17	10	19	16
Total	100%	100%	100%	100%	100%	100%	100%	100%
Total stock changes plus increase in financial holdings (2+3)	29%	22%	26%	23%	25%	20%	26%	25%
Sources of funds (net of repayments):								
4. Long-term borrowing	12%	14%	17%	19%	16%	19%	12%	17%
Stocks and bonds:								
5. Bonds	(3)	(5)	(5)	(5)	(4)	(3)	(6)	(4)
6. Stocks	(3)	(8)	(8)	(7)	(7)	(6)	(4)	(6)
Total	6	13	13	12	11	9	10	10
7. Medium-term credit	4	4	1	1	3	4	1	2
8. Own resources[a]	68	60	58	58	54	52	68	56
9. Adjustment (partly capital transfers with other countries)	1	–	–	–	2	3	–	–
10. Short-term credit	9	9	11	10	14	13	9	15
Total	100%	100%	100%	100%	100%	100%	100%	100%
Total long-term indebtedness (4+5)	15%	19%	22%	24%	20%	22%	18%	21%
Total long-term resources (4+5+6+8)	86%	87%	88%	89%	81%	81%	90%	82%

[a]Own resources include companies' savings plus own investment financing by unincorporated enterprises.

sources of financing available to business firms became more diversified after World War II than in the earlier years. Before World War I, the capital requirements of firms were broadly satisfied by the capital market (through shares and bonds) and by banks (through short-term loans by deposit banks and long-term loans by merchant banks). Between the wars, new sources of financing developed in addition: loans by the specialized public credit institutions—the Crédit National set up in 1919, making long-term loans to industrial undertakings; the Caisse Nationale de Crédit Agricole set up in 1920, providing short-term credit to farmers[27]—and the war damage compensation paid by the government to undertakings whose capital had been partly or completely destroyed during the hostilities. These were all public sources of financing put in motion chiefly to rebuild the nation's wealth destroyed by war.

These new financing instruments became more diversified and far larger in scale after World War II: the Crédit Agricole extended its operations into the medium and long terms; the Caisse des Dépôts et Consignations broadened its field of activity by financing certain industrial investments; in addition to war damage compensation on a larger scale, capital investment subsidies were awarded, in particular to enterprises taken into public ownership. Moreover, two wholly new financing instruments were created: medium-term rediscountable credit from the Bank of France, and long-term Treasury loans (through the Fonds de Développement Economique et Social). This diversification of the source of financing after World War II encouraged the use by firms of outside capital.

Makeup of firms' external resources after the war.[28] Gaps in the statistics make it impossible to carry out a quantitative study of changes in the makeup of the external financial resources of undertakings from the beginning of the century. On the other hand, statistics prepared after World War II and in particular estimates in the National Accounts (table of financial transactions) make it possible to analyze with some precision the changes in the different forms of financing used by undertakings after 1952:[29] long-term borrowing, issues of shares and bonds, and short-term credit.

The role played in the financing of investment by *long-term borrowing* was relatively prominent over the entire period studied. As can be seen in Table 10.9, the proportion of long-term borrowing to all financ-

[27] The local funds of the Crédit Agricole were set up at the end of the nineteenth century.
[28] See also Appendix Table 14.
[29] The series in the tables on financial transactions begins in 1953.

ing resources of enterprises grew substantially and continually between 1953 and 1959; after reaching a peak in 1959, it thereafter remained constant. Measured on the 1959 base of the National Accounts, this proportion increased from about 14 percent in 1953–54 and 19 percent in 1959, to settle thereafter at around 17 percent. Between 1953 and 1959, long-term borrowing grew in real terms by a factor of 2 (a growth of 12 percent per year), whereas investment grew by a factor of 1.5 (an increase of 7 percent per year).

The issues of *stocks and bonds* increased at an extremely rapid pace up to 1957. After 1957, their trend was slightly slower than that of the total financial resources of undertakings. In 1953 they accounted for 5 percent of these resources and in 1954 for 8 percent; in 1957 the figure was 12 percent. Proportions close to this were reached in 1959 (11.5 percent), 1962 (11 percent), and 1965 (11 percent). The years in between were marked by lower percentages. Between 1954 and 1957, these issues grew in real terms by 90 percent (23 percent per year), whereas investments grew by 40 percent (12 percent per year). The development of stocks and bonds, respectively, was very different. The volume of stocks grew very considerably between 1953 and 1954, to be followed by a slower growth than that of investment between 1954 and 1961; growth after 1961, however, was substantially faster than that of investment. From 1954 to 1957 stock issues increased by 7.5 percent per year, as against 12.5 percent for investment. From 1959 to 1964 stock issues rose by 12.8 percent per year, as against 7.8 percent for investment. Bond issues, on the other hand, grew very fast up to 1957 (at a rate of 32 percent per year between 1954 and 1957). They then stabilized and even showed a significant drop between 1961 and 1964.

The development of long-term outside resources taken as a whole (long-term borrowing plus issues of stocks and bonds) was significantly faster than that of investment betwen 1954 and 1957. After reaching a peak in 1959 (with a growth of 40 percent), their ratio to gross fixed capital formation stabilized between 1961 and 1964 at the 35 percent level reached in 1957. Assessments based on *long-term resources as a whole* (long-term external resources plus own resources) differ slightly according to whether the development of these resources is compared with that of all financial resources of enterprises or with that of their chief use, that is to say, with gross fixed capital formation.

Between 1953 and 1959, changes in each of the long-term resources were such that, taken as a whole, they amounted to a more or less constant proportion of the financial resources of undertakings (but with a

TABLE 10.10
Financing Ratios of Firms, 1953–67

Year	Long-term loans ÷ GFCF	Issues of stocks & bonds ÷ GFCF	Long-term loans + issues of stocks & bonds ÷ GFCF	Long-term resources ÷ GFCF	Short-term credits ÷ inventory changes + growth of financial assets
1956 basis:					
1953	17	8	29	121	30
1954	16	13	29	123	32
1955	17	14	31	118	39
1956	18	13	31	113	57
1957	18	17	35	111	42
1958	19	14	33	111	23
1959	23	17	40	120	43
1959 basis:					
1959	25	15	40	116	43
1960	24	13	37	118	52
1961	21	14	35	102	69
1962	21	15	36	107	55
1963	22	12	34	99	67
1964	24	11	35	101	61
1965	21	15	36	98	74
1966	19	12	31	98	78
1967	21	10	31	98	77

Note: GFCF is gross fixed capital formation. The new estimates in the National Accounts on the 1962 base show levels and movements for these ratios somewhat different from those given in this table, but they do not significantly change the general direction of the movements and the qualitative conclusions that may be drawn from them. On the 1962 base, investments and self-financing ratios are higher than on a 1959 base, but the ratios for long-term borrowing and issues of stocks and bonds are lower. Broadly speaking, the ratio of long-term resources to gross fixed capital formation fluctuates very slightly around 107 between 1962 and 1966.

trough in 1957). The increase in the proportion of long-term external resources between 1954 and 1957 offset a reduction in the proportion of own resources. The proportion of long-term resources to gross fixed capital formation of undertakings dropped substantially, however, between 1954 and 1957, moving from 123 in 1954 to 111 in 1957 (see Table 10.10). These changes can be accounted for by the increase in the proportion of investment in total uses of financial resources by enterprises, an increase that was equivalent to a considerable slowing down in the growth of liquid funds between 1954 and 1957. The increase in money holdings of undertakings, which represented 20 percent of their uses in 1954, represented only 12 percent in 1957. By contrast, between 1959 and 1965, the financing position of enterprises can be seen to have worsened, whether from a consideration of the proportion of long-term resources to total resources (which dropped from 89 percent in 1959 to 80 percent in 1961–65, and to 76 percent in 1966–67), or of the relationship between

TABLE 10.11
Stock and Bond Issues, 1896–1964
(Percent of gross domestic production)

Year	Government, other official groupings, & public credit institutions	Corporations (private & public) Stocks[a]	Bonds	Foreign stocks	Total
1896	0.1%	0.9%	1.1%	1.9%	4.0%
1900	0.1	2.0	1.8	1.6	5.5
1913	0.5	2.6	2.9	3.2	9.2
1924	2.9	3.3	1.2	0.1	7.5
1929	−1.0	5.2	2.4	0.3	6.9
1930	0.6	3.4	4.4	1.2	9.6
1938	2.6	0.5	0.1	−	3.2
1949	1.5	0.6	0.3	−	2.4
1954	1.4	0.6	0.8	−	2.8
1959	0.5	1.7	1.4	−	3.6
1962	0.7	1.4	1.2	−	3.3
1964	1.5	1.2	1.0	−	3.7

[a]Stocks include holdings in partnerships with limited liability.

long-term resources and gross fixed capital formation, which dropped from 1.16 in 1959 to around 1.00 between 1961 and 1967 (see Table 10.10). This worsening can be ascribed both to the drop in the proportion of own resources and to the reduction in external long-term resources.

In these circumstances, the financing of enterprises after 1961 had to rely on large-scale use of *short-term credit*. Between 1960 and 1963, short-term credit contributed around 15 percent of the financing of undertakings, whereas between 1954 and 1957 it accounted for only 7.5 percent (except in 1956, when it was 14 percent). Its contribution reached 17 percent in 1966 and 1967.

Development of the capital market from the beginning of the century. This development of the financial market is traced in Table 10.11, which shows for a number of years the percentage of gross domestic production taken by gross issues of selected main categories of shares and bonds.[30] This table underlines the large contribution made by the capital market to financing the economy, and in particular to financing investment by undertakings before World War II—more precisely before the Great Depression. Particular attention should be given to the situa-

---

[30] The value of gross domestic production before the war has been calculated by applying to the volume indexes shown in Chapter 1 price indexes obtained by a simple arithmetic averaging of the indexes of wholesale and retail prices. The estimates of issues on the capital market are extracted from the INSEE *Annuaire statistique rétrospectif de la France* (1966).

tion in 1913 and 1929–30, when investment was very high, and that in 1954–62. Gross issues of stocks and bonds by corporations represented, respectively, 5.3 percent of gross domestic production in 1913 and 7.6 and 7.8 percent in 1929 and 1930, but they did not exceed 3 percent between 1954 and 1962.

The large volume of issues of shares and bonds before the Great Depression does not reflect a higher desire to save than today, but simply the fact that Frenchmen previously used their savings in a different way.[31] It also shows, however—and this is what matters here—that undertakings then made considerable use of external resources to finance investments. We have calculated the scale of self-financing for the years 1910–13 and 1928–30, when expansion was relatively fast and investment was high. These figures are based partly on estimates of investment made by us for the prewar period[32] and partly on statistics of issues of stock[33] and a very rough estimate of the other items in the table of firms' financing. The resulting rates are on the order of 80 percent just before World War I and 70 percent in the period preceding the Great Depression. If one allows for the roughness of the calculations and the fact that growth in value of investments was faster after World War II than before, the self-financing ratios of undertakings do not seem significantly different before and after the war.

The role of external financing in productive investment. After the war the sources of finance were more diversified than before, but the capital market was far less active; it might be assumed that the effect of these factors approximately canceled out. The differences in financing available for firms' investment in the postwar and prewar periods would not be enough to explain the investment boom that occurred between 1954 and 1962.

Our analysis of developments in the financial situation after the war suggests that the period of the investment surge—1954–62—should be divided into two subperiods. From 1954 to 1957 (or 1959), changes in the structure of supply of financial resources substantially helped the

[31] According to the estimates in Chapter 9, gross private savings represented 17 percent of gross domestic production between 1896 and 1915, 17 percent between 1925 and 1930, 21 percent between 1952 and 1957, and 22 percent between 1958 and 1963.

[32] See Chapter 4. We have assumed that investment by government agencies and households represented 2 percent in each case of gross domestic production and that increases in physical stocks represented between 30 and 50 percent of the increase in output.

[33] Corrected to give estimates of *net* flows of external finance. In particular, we have used for this purpose the estimates by M. Moreau-Neret in *Les Valeurs mobilières* (Paris, 1939), vol. II, p. 288.

investment drive, since increases in share issues, and above all in the availability of long-term loans particularly on the bond market, partly offset the reduction in self-financing margins of enterprises. After 1959, and particularly after 1961, the investment drive came sharply up against a situation not so much of an overall shortage of financial resources as a difficulty in finding long-term funds in sufficient quantity. For this reason firms had to turn, on a large scale, to short-term credit. Table 10.10, which shows the evolution of certain financing ratios of undertakings, brings out this development clearly: a fall in the ratio between firms' long-term resources and their gross fixed capital formation was accompanied by a very marked rise in the ratio between their increases of short-term credit and their increases of financial assets and inventories. Thus the development of external financing of firms between 1959 and 1967 does not seem to be a factor in accounting for the scale of investment carried out; indeed, it is the other way round.

THE FINANCING OF DIFFERENT CATEGORIES OF ENTERPRISES

In the preceding pages, study of the circumstances in which productive investment was financed concerned all undertakings together. In fact, however, these circumstances varied considerably in the different undertakings, and it is advisable to make a distinction at least between public enterprises, private corporations, farming enterprises, and unincorporated enterprises outside agriculture. We shall complete this study by examining briefly the circumstances of investment financing in these categories of enterprises, and shall consider in doing so to what extent the financial policy of the authorities may have encouraged a satisfactory allocation of investment in the economy.

Table 10.12 shows the distribution, according to the National Accounts, of the financing of gross fixed capital formation between own resources and net inflows of outside capital since 1956 for each of the main categories of enterprises.[34] According to these estimates, the rate of indebtedness of incorporated nonfarm enterprises fluctuated considerably over time and, on the average, were higher than those of private corporations. Such facts are difficult to account for other than by the unreliability of statistical estimates relating to these enterprises. The availability of outside financial resources to small and medium-sized enterprises is virtually limited to short- and medium-term credits. Although after the war the development of rediscountable medium-term credit at the Bank of France created more favorable conditions than

[34] There are no data for years earlier than 1956.

TABLE 10.12

Proportion of Gross Saving and External Finance, by Category of Enterprise, 1956–66

(Percent of capital invested)

Year	Public enterprises		Private corporations		Unincorporated non-farm enterprises		Farming enterprises	
	Gross savings[a]	External finance	Gross savings	External finance	Gross savings	External finance	Gross savings	External finance
1956 base:								
1956	56% (13)	44%	85%	15%	52%	48%	59%	41%
1957	48 (12)	52	84	16	67	33	57	43
1958	49 (10)	51	73	27	99	1	71	29
1959	59 (11)	41	92	8	89	11	64	36
1959 base:								
1959	59 (11)	41	86	14	69	31	65	35
1960	59 (10)	41	74	26	86	14	60	40
1961	66 (12)	34	68	32	57	43	25	75
1962	65 (15)	35	68	32	58	42	56	44
1963	66 (18)	34	66	34	55	45	29	71
1964	67 (21)	33	59	41	47	53	32	68
1965	68 (20)	32	73	27	63	37	32	68
1966	69 (25)	31	65	35	63	37	20	80

[a]Figures in parentheses are the portion of gross savings comprising capital investment subsidies and war damage compensation.

previously for financing investment, there can be no doubt that these enterprises remain in a less favorable position than large corporations for the provision of outside financing.

Table 10.12 shows that the efforts of farming enterprises to increase capital equipment, which were on a very large scale after the war, were accompanied by growing and very high indebtedness during the last few years. Between 1954 and 1962, current medium-term and long-term credit in agriculture grew in nominal terms by a factor of 4, whereas the nominal value of its fixed reproducible capital grew only twofold. Although this credit represented 13 percent of the value of its capital in 1954, it represented 20 percent in 1960, 26 percent in 1962 and 35 percent in 1964. The widening of the field of activity of the Crédit Agricole by comparison with the prewar period,[35] its large volume of funds, and the relatively low rates of interest charged have considerably increased the availability of credits to farmers; this undoubtedly is one explanation of its large scale of investment. The circumstances of the financing of public enterprises and private corporations deserve somewhat longer study.

[35] Previously, it had mostly granted only short-term loans.

The Financing of Public Enterprises

Public undertakings have a great need for financing, which was on the order of 40–50 percent of gross capital formation between 1956 and 1960 and 33–35 percent between 1961 and 1965. If capital investment subsidies were shown in the National Accounts as a capital transfer rather than as a resource in their current account, the requirements of public undertakings for outside capital would seem even larger—on the order of 60 percent between 1956 and 1958 and 50 percent between 1959 and 1965. The fall in their financing requirement's share of the national total after 1960—which changed from 41 to 33 percent—can be ascribed to the increase in capital investment subsidies they received.[36]

In spite of this financial situation, investment by public enterprises, which accounted for about 35 percent of total investment by all enterprises, has grown at a relatively fast pace: in real terms, by 8.8 percent per year from 1956 to 1959, by 5.9 percent from 1959 to 1965, and by 6.9 percent from 1956 to 1965. This contrast between fast investment growth in public undertakings and their financial situation can be explained by two lines of reasoning.

First, the figures shown concern all public enterprises as a whole, and include the public housing offices and the Atomic Energy Commission, whose investments are in the main financed by investment subsidies or loans. After deducting these two kinds of transactions, the proportions of public-enterprise financing provided by investment subsidies, savings excluding subsidies, and net indebtedness in 1962 were, respectively, 7, 57, and 36 percent, as against 15, 50, and 35 percent for all public enterprises together. The financial situation of public enterprises excluding the two is therefore better than would appear from the overall figures shown.

Second, the high level of investment subsidies and of use of outside capital in financing public-enterprise investment was the corollary of tariff and investment policies along lines laid down not by the public enterprises themselves but by the central government as part of overall economic policy. The counterpart of a policy of low tariffs was the grant of financing facilities and a shift in the flow of savings in favor of public undertakings. More specifically, this included low interest loans or capital grants from the Fonds de Développement Economique et Social, privileged access to a bond market controlled by the Treasury, whose

[36] This increase can be accounted for partly by the rise in volume of investments by the Atomic Energy Commission, which was financed largely by investment subsidies.

interest rates were kept artificially below the market level, and the obligation of insurance companies to invest part of their funds in bonds of public enterprises.

These financing privileges did not lead to the same pattern of investment as would have resulted from greater autonomy for public enterprises in determining their tariffs and investment, and from greater competition between all undertakings as a whole on the capital market. The drawing off of very substantial financial resources toward public enterprises at the beginning of the postwar period encouraged a rapid climb of investment and fast renewal of activity in the energy and transportation sectors, and consequently helped the overall growth of the economy, which at that time depended on development in those industries. On the other hand, it can be held that continuing this policy after the reconstruction period had the effect of encouraging certain investments in energy and transportation that were unnecessarily costly in their use of capital (hydroelectric power stations and coal mines in energy, the electrification option rather than dieselization in transport).

The Financing of Private Corporations

Up to 1960, own resources of private corporations were close to or over 80 percent of gross capital formation (except in 1958). These resources, however, had tended relatively to decrease, and recourse to outside sources by private corporations increased considerably between 1950 and 1960, particularly by the issuing of stock on the capital market. The broadening of this market helped the investment surge by making possible remunerative investment that earlier could not have been financed.

In the early 1950's, private corporations had virtually no way of finding funds on the bond market (see Table 10.13). At most they could obtain certain medium- and long-term credits from the Crédit National and certain long-term bank credits for capital equipment. But financing obtained in this way was on a small scale: on December 31, 1955, total current credit of this type amounted to 680 million new francs from the Crédit National and 1,580 million rediscountable medium-term credits granted for capital equipment (this second figure excludes credits for exports or building, and those released by the Caisse Nationale des Marchés de l'Etat (national fund for state markets) or authorized by the Caisse Nationale de Crédit Agricole). In the same period, gross annual fixed capital formation by private corporations alone was close to 9 billion new francs. The only significant contribution to financing investment by private corporations between 1949 and 1953 was the issue

TABLE 10.13
Stock and Bond Issues by Private Corporations, 1950–66

Year	Stock and bond issues (*billion current francs*)	Issues (*percent of gross fixed capital formation*)[a]		
		Stock	Bond	Stock and bond
1950	0.42	8%	2%	10%
1954	1.23	11	6	17
1955	1.98	13	10	23
1956	1.94	13	8	21
1957	2.95	21	5	26
1958	2.68	13	7	20
1959	4.72	20	12	32
1960	4.04	12	11	23
1961	5.04	14	10	24
1962	5.42	15	7	22
1963	5.73	15	7	22
1964	5.80	16	5	21
1965	5.68	15	5	20
1966	4.36	9	5	14

Source: Annuaire statistique de la France and National Accounts.
[a]National Accounts, 1956 base through 1958; 1959 base from 1959. These figures are indicators only; there are slight differences of coverage between the numerator and denominator.

of shares. Even this source was on a small scale, and did not exceed 10 percent of gross fixed capital formation.

As Table 10.13 shows, between 1950 and 1955 issues on the Stock Exchange grew larger again; and in the following years they increased further. In 1955 they contributed 13 percent of gross fixed capital formation of private corporations from stock issues and 10 percent from bond issues. In 1959, when these proportions reached a peak, they were, respectively, 20 and 12 percent.

Other sources of external financing were becoming available at the same time. Rediscountable medium-term credit for capital equipment was granted liberally in 1957 and 1958. Its growth stopped in 1959, however, and thereafter resumed at a slower pace. But the availability of long-term credit or non-rediscountable medium-term credit considerably increased. The Caisse des Dépôts et Consignations and the banks granted large-scale credits, while the Crédit National was developing its operations.

In order to assess the overall volume of these sources of finance, we have calculated the sum of increases in current credit of the following kinds: rediscountable medium-term credits for capital equipment,[37] loans to enterprises by the Caisse des Dépôts et Consignations, loans

---

[37] Excluding credits to farming.

TABLE 10.14
*New Medium- and Long-Term Credits for Capital Equipment
to Private Firms, 1956–66*

Year	Increase over previous year (*billion current francs*)[a]	Percent of gross fixed investment of all private non-farm enterprises[b]	Year	Increase over previous year (*billion current francs*)[a]	Percent of gross fixed investment of all private non-farm enterprises[b]
1956	0.39	2.4%	1962	2.76	9.5%
1957	0.80	4.3	1963	1.24	4.1
1958	1.18	6.2	1964	2.94	8.6
1959	0.47	2.4	1965	3.28	9.4
1960	1.32	5.8	1966	2.52	6.6
1961	2.29	8.8			

[a]From reports of the Conseil National du Crédit.
[b]Before 1959, the base year was 1956. These figures are indicators only; consistency between the numerator and denominator is only approximate.

from the Crédit National, and long-term or non-rediscountable medium-term credits from banks to enterprises.[38] We have also compared the total with gross fixed capital formation by private nonfarm enterprises. The results are shown in Table 10.14.[39]

The increase in indebtedness of private corporations after 1961 and the drop in their self-financing ratio can be seen to reflect real financing difficulties that could not avoid restricting their investment growth after 1963. From 1961 to 1966 the situation on the Stock Exchange considerably worsened: from 1961 to 1964, issues by private corporations on the capital market scarcely grew in real value (by under 1 percent per year as against nearly 17 percent per year between 1954 and 1961); from 1964 to 1966, their nominal total fell substantially.[40] The expansion of outside funds of private corporations was possible only through a very marked increase in recourse to short-term credit, while at the same

[38] Direct loans by the Fonds de Développement Economique et Social to private enterprises and loans by the Crédit Hôtelier are not included.

[39] The estimates shown in the new series on a 1962 base in the National Accounts are as follows (billion current francs):

	1962	1963	1964	1965	1966
Medium-term credits	1.4	1.4	1.7	1.6	1.4
Net long-term loans	2.9	3.0	3.3	3.6	4.7

[40] The estimates shown in the new series on a 1962 base in the National Accounts are as follows (billion current francs):

	1962	1963	1964	1965	1966
Bonds (net)	1.2	1.0	0.6	0.4	0.3
Shares	3.9	3.8	4.4	4.7	3.4

This decline in share issues largely corresponds with increased borrowings by public undertakings, whose net issues moved as follows: 1.4 in 1962, 1.4 in 1963, 1.5 in 1964, 2.5 in 1965, and 2.5 in 1966.

time the corporations were managing their own funds more strictly. Part of the investment in the years 1962–63 was thus financed from short-term funds; after 1962, therefore, the financing situation was not very favorable for continuation of the investment surge. Financing difficulties, even more than the stabilization plan, account for the slowing down of productive investment by private corporations.

Throughout the period studied, government intervention had a significant effect on the financing of investment by private corporations. The heavy industry groups in the economy, particularly iron mining and metallurgy, were marked by direct intervention, stemming from principles similar to those pursued in the case of public enterprises—price limitations, with favored access to credit and particularly to the bond market as a counterpart. As in the case of public enterprises, this policy favored reconstruction in the heavy sectors, which held the key to overall growth in the postwar economy. In the case of the manufacturing and processing industries, direct action by the authorities to assist financing has been on a small scale throughout. It took the form chiefly of loans by the Crédit National. These, however, represented no more than 3 percent of investment by private corporations in 1961, and 3.2 percent in 1964.

By contrast, fiscal policy, policy for public-enterprise tariffs, the steering of funds on the capital market toward investments regarded by the central government as having priority—in particular, to finance the heavy industry groups—had marked influence on the financing of investment by manufacturing and processing industries. The restriction on prices of basic products was in itself favorable to these industries. But the subsidies to public undertakings had as counterpart an increase in taxation, that is to say, increased costs for private enterprises. Furthermore, the drawing away of savings toward the heavy industry groups corresponded to a drop in the volume of savings available to manufacturing and processing industries, in particular on the bond market. On the whole, however, the policies followed were beneficial, since they made possible a transfer of demand for external capital from the manufacturing and processing industries to the basic industries and public enterprises, and these restricted their investment for reasons of financial equilibrium to a lesser extent than the manufacturing and processing industries would have.

CONCLUSION

At the close of this detailed examination of the financing situation for productive investment, the various partial conclusions reached should be brought together in order to form an overall assessment of the part played by this situation in the build-up of productive investment after World War II. If the different changes that affected the financing situation for productive investment after World War II are compared as a whole with those before the war, they cannot be said to explain the postwar surge of investment. The diversification in the sources of external finance available to undertakings and the development of public financing had favorable results, the credit facilities available to agricultural enterprises improved, and public tariff policies had positive effects, but against all these must be offset the drop in size of the capital market after the war by comparison with the period before the Great Depression.

Neither does it seem that changes in the circumstances for financing productive investments taken as a whole can explain the continuation in the postwar period itself of the build-up of productive investment by enterprises. However, two periods should be distinguished in this respect.

From 1950 to 1960, firms' own financing resources grew less rapidly than did their investment. This drop in the self-financing ratio, however, was accompanied by a fast increase in the supply of external financing that can be ascribed in particular to the renewal of the capital market and the development of long-term credits. Thus, from 1953–54 to 1960, the ratio between long-term funds of firms (self-financing plus long-term borrowings plus issues of stocks and bonds) and their fixed investment remained stable despite marked reduction in the self-financing ratio. This reduction can be accounted for by the very momentum of the supply of investment capital itself and probably also by the increase in internal competition. Overall, therefore, changes in the internal and external financing situation of enterprises seem to have been broadly neutral in relation to their investment drive.

After 1960, this was no longer the case. The investment boom that marked the years 1961 and 1962 was accompanied by a drop in the self-financing ratio of enterprises. This is to be accounted for partly by the very speed of growth of investment. But the ratio between firms' long-term funds and their gross fixed capital formation also dropped, since they could not find all the long-term external resources they required. They thus had to turn more extensively toward short-term credit in order to acquire the external funds needed. In 1963 and 1964, firms' financing difficulties increased, as shown in particular by the fact that in both years they had recourse to financial resources outside France and in 1964 they very considerably slowed down the growth of their financial assets. International competition intensified after a period in which French enterprises had benefited from *de facto* protection arising from devaluation: the price rises that occurred after 1958 probably more or less offset in 1963 the competitive advantage that can be ascribed to the devaluation. Enterprises were no longer able to raise their prices as high as needed to restore their self-financing ratios. Price controls instituted as part of the stabilization plan extended this constraint to the protected sectors of the economy. At the same time, the scope for drawing on the financial market was reduced as a result of a retardation in the market's expansion: drawings on it reached a ceiling in terms of absolute value, and fell in terms of relative value, by comparison with investment. The regulation of credit and rise in the discount rate within the framework of the stabilization plan also made it more difficult in 1964 for enterprises to find short-term credit. Without doubt all these financing difficulties very largely account for the slowing down in the growth of investment by private enterprises in 1963 and 1964 (private-enterprise productive investment grew by 5.6 percent in 1963 over 1962, and by 4.3 percent in 1964, as against 12.1 percent in 1960, 14.8 percent in 1961, and 9.8 percent in 1962).

To sum up: the reduction in self-financing margins of enterprises and the gradual emergence of a structure in their financial accounts less favorable than in the early 1950's reflect (particularly up to 1960) the increased scope for enterprises to draw on more abundant external sources of finance than in the past. The development of financial flows thus itself assisted the investment drive by French enterprises between 1950 and 1960. On the other hand, changes in the circumstances of financing were unfavorable to the surge of investment after 1960 and partly account for the slowing down in growth of private-enterprise productive investments during the period 1963–67.

CHAPTER ELEVEN

Economic Stability:
Problems and Policies

Anyone who approaches the economic history of France in the twentieth century must examine the inflation that arose in successive waves and to which the public likes to ascribe central importance. The reader may be surprised that we have waited until now to make price rises the theme of a separate chapter.

We would remind him, nevertheless, that we have restricted our subject to an explanatory study of the growth of production. Inflation has considerable effects on the distribution of incomes and wealth. These effects, however, concern our topic only to the extent that they played a causal role, directly or indirectly, in the economy's productivity. The inequities probably caused by inflation, and the social changes provoked by repeated increases in prices, remain outside our field of study.

As in other chapters, we shall consider first the causes and then the effects of the phenomenon in question. We must then pay special attention to the consequences for France's balance of payments with the rest of the world. The situation in France is often contrasted with that of other countries such as Britain, which also experienced inflationary tendencies but had deliberately to slow down expansion in order to deal with a chronic external deficit. This aspect deserves to be treated in depth, and is the subject of the third part of the chapter. Last, the study of inflation and the balance of payments will lead us naturally to consider in what ways government policies tried to regulate the economic situation and how successful they were.

CAUSES OF INFLATION

The Facts

Inflation in the period after World War II, on which we shall concentrate chiefly here, was not very regular. Graphs of changes in French price indexes show four periods of fast price increases since the war:

the immediate postwar years up to the autumn of 1948, the 18 months following the outbreak of the Korean war in July 1950, the three years from the autumn of 1956 to the end of 1959, and last the years 1968 and 1969. The general wholesale price index grew fourfold between January 1, 1946, and November 30, 1948. It rose by 46 percent between the end of June 1950 and the end of December 1951. It grew by 27 percent between October 1956 and December 1959, and by 19 percent between June 1968 and January 1970.

In the intervals between the first three of these periods, the wholesale price index remained more or less stable. By contrast, it continued to rise over the six years after 1959: the average increase was 2.3 percent per year up to the beginning of 1966, with a particularly sharp rise in 1962 and 1963. From the spring of 1966 to the spring of 1968 the index stayed at a more or less constant level.

Other price indexes, for example those in Figure 11.1, give a similar picture of the different inflationary phases, although in most cases they show consistently higher rates of increase. (It is, of course, well known that the general wholesale price index, which excludes services and goods at the more finished stages, rises more slowly than most of the other indexes, at least in the long term.) Thus, the average levels of the gross domestic production price deflator, as a percentage of the preceding year in each case, were as follows:

1950	107.6%	1955	100.9%	1960	103.0%	1965	102.5%
1951	116.6	1956	104.4	1961	102.8	1966	102.5
1952	112.4	1957	105.5	1962	104.0	1967	102.6
1953	99.8	1958	111.6	1963	104.9	1968	104.2
1954	100.2	1959	106.0	1964	103.6	1969	107.0

These facts of the period after World War II must be viewed in relation to earlier developments, for the great importance attached by French people to inflation may well reflect the memory of an experience of price increases over a long period quite as much as any exact appreciation of how prices moved over the past 20 years. In fact, one has to go back to the nineteenth century to find a long period without an upward trend in prices. There was a downward trend from 1872 to 1896. Even before World War I, however, a marked upward turn can be observed. The general wholesale price index rose by 17 percent between 1900 and 1913, increased threefold during World War I, and after a sharp rise and fall was back at the 1918 level in 1922. In the four years from 1922 to 1926 it more than doubled, and after the Poincaré stabilization it stood six times higher than the 1913 level. The Great Depression pulled down the price of products: the wholesale

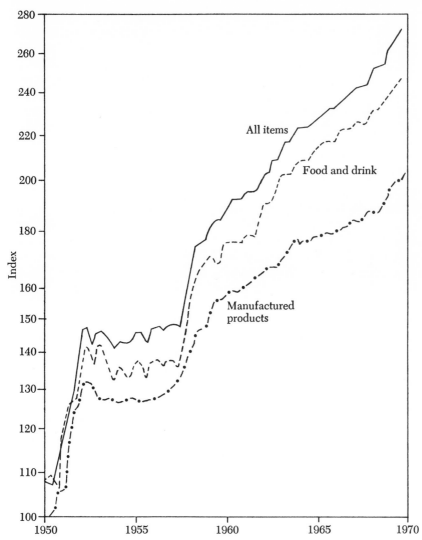

Fig. 11.1. Consumer price indexes, 1950–69 (1949 = 100).
Years are indicated as of January 1.

price index dropped by 44 percent between 1929 and 1935. The upward movement started again in 1936: the index rose by 92 percent up to August 1939, and then almost fivefold from August 1939 to December 1945.

Since our principal concern is with the period beginning in 1949, we shall dwell only briefly on the waves of inflation before that date.[1] Nor shall we discuss in detail the period after the spring of 1968. We shall thus consider chiefly the three movements of rising prices: 1950–51, 1956–59, and after 1960.

Analytical Framework

Although it is easy to write a history of inflation, it is more difficult to provide an explanatory analysis of it. General price increases are a complex phenomenon setting many interdependencies in motion. The nature of inflation cannot be understood without a fairly complete knowledge of the factors leading to economic equilibrium. It cannot be analyzed without a simple model describing the chief interdependencies and without attending to at least one important aspect of economic equilibrium. The only attitude that can avoid using an analytical framework of this type is that ascribing responsibility for inflation to a particular cause chosen a priori, or even to a particular category of citizens. This attitude seems quite unsatisfactory. It does not allow for the fact that inflation is essentially an aggregate phenomenon, and that each person experiences it without being conscious of sharing in responsibility for it.

Inflation shows to different degrees in different prices and rates of remuneration. For the sake of a simplified analysis, we shall distinguish the following four principal quantities: prices of industrial products, prices of agricultural commodities, prices of services, and wage rates. We shall examine in turn the causes of increases in these quantities in such a way as to deduce a group of external factors that seem able to account for inflation and that we shall later deal with more fully. It is not necessary for us to define the fields covered by these quantities or to verify that they leave no gaps. We shall in fact use these quantities merely as reference points for a discussion aimed at bringing out through the various interdependencies involved certain important primary factors.

---

[1] On inflation between the wars, see A. Sauvy, *Histoire économique de la France entre les deux guerres* (2 vols., Paris, 1965, 1967). On inflation immediately after the war, see C. Gruson, *Origine et espoirs de la planification française* (Paris, 1968), pp. 51–58.

Industrial prices. To analyze changes affecting industrial prices, it is probably justifiable to consider in turn costs and profits, for these two elements must be influenced by different causes. Changes in costs can be accounted for by changes in productivity, wages, and certain autonomous elements, of which we shall consider in particular prices of imported raw materials, fiscal or mandatory charges, and the rates charged by public enterprises.

In our study of inflation, we shall not return to the subject of productivity. It can be said quite correctly, of course, that increases in industrial prices reflect rigidities and routine forms of behavior that worked against a faster productivity growth than that observed. In this sense, inflation cannot be accounted for apart from development of the economy as a whole. But it would be a mistake to reexamine at this stage the productivity increases to which the bulk of the first part of the book is devoted. We shall therefore now proceed along the following lines: granted the development of productivity already observed, how is the increase in the general level of industrial prices to be explained?

The size of profit margins reflects the strength or weakness of competition between producers and of relationships between employees and employers. In a macroeconomic analysis of short-term variations, it is useful to consider three basic factors. First, demand can be strong or weak; it can lead producers to calculate their prices more or less closely and to grant smaller or larger discounts. Some guidance on this point can be obtained from changes in stocks of finished products or in order books—low demand is reflected in high stocks or in sparse order books. Second, liquid funds can be more or less tight, and can lead firms to make sales with more or less urgency, and therefore to grant terms to clients that are more or less favorable. A liberal monetary policy can therefore be a factor in inflation. And last, control over prices, which aimed not only to bring order to the market but also to influence development of the general industrial price level, has been more or less strict at different periods, and has therefore probably affected the inflation profile.

Prices of agricultural products. Two cases can be distinguished here —that of products with prices fixed by the authorities, and that of products with prices set by the market. In both cases, prices are affected by changes in industrial wages. In the first case, this situation follows from attempts to achieve parity between the growth of farm and urban incomes. In the second case, this is the result of the interplay of supply and demand on the market. But both kinds of prices also reflect autonomous factors: in the first case official decisions, and in the second case changes in weather and more generally changes in other circumstances governing supply.

Prices of services. Here again, a regulated sector and a free sector should be distinguished. Public utility tariffs and to some extent rents are the result of autonomous decisions. Prices of most other services must be influenced both by changes in labor wage rates and by more or less favorable states of demand.

Wage rates. Movements in wages are affected by three categories of factors, as shown in numerous econometric studies. First, increases in the cost of living provide justification for rises in wage rates demanded by employees. Second, variations in the pressure of demand for labor give rise to variations in the strength of competition between employers, and are sometimes more, sometimes less favorable to increases in wages. Last, pressure by trade unions, changes in negotiation practices, and particular official or contractual decisions, such as raising the minimum guaranteed wage level or concluding new national collective agreements, exert an autonomous effect at certain periods.

This brief examination indicates the interdependence between the various rates of remuneration. It also suggests, however, a list of external factors in a first-stage explanation of the general upward movement of prices. We can group these factors as follows: (1) Pressure of demand, favoring both increase in profits (demand for goods and services) and of wages (demand for labor). (2) Accidental shortfall in supply; this occurs only in the case of agricultural products. (3) Rise in certain autonomous cost elements, chiefly affecting prices of imported products. (4) Official decisions leading directly to increase in certain costs: rates charged for public services, price of controlled agricultural products, guaranteed minimum wage, rate of indirect taxes, and other mandatory charges. (5) Official decisions favoring business growth, liberal monetary policies, relaxation of price controls. (6) Agreements providing for rises in wage rates as a result of social conflict or bargaining between management and labor organizations.

This list does not, of course, attempt to trace the noneconomic causes of inflation. For example, excessive pressure of demand might be due equally to export boom or to budget deficit. The list will make it possible for the different phases of price increases to be characterized, but it is not sufficient in itself to determine where the primary responsibility for inflation lies. For example, certain economists consider that the persistent upward trend in prices can be accounted for by too fast a rate of increase in the money supply, itself said to be due to too liberal a policy overall in the creation of credit. A large supply of money is thought not only to have helped enterprises to maintain profit margins but particularly to have influenced all categories of decision makers to exert a high demand on the market. On these grounds, any responsibility for inflation attributed to demand should ultimately be attached to monetary policy.

Other economists consider that inflation is a structural characteristic of the French economy, with its origin to be found both in institutions and in attitudes. Inflation stems from institutions, according to this argument, because the structure of the French productive system is held to embody only a low level of competition: partial disequilibria on the market for goods and capital produce reactions that lead naturally to rises in the general level of prices; if supply exceeds demand, there is too little competition between sellers, who rarely choose to lower prices; if demand exceeds supply, competition between buyers works for a rise, but enterprises speed up their rate of output only slightly, so that the whole weight of correcting the disequilibrium falls on the price increase.

Inflation stems from attitudes, according to this argument, because the various categories of decision maker accept inflation without resistance: heads of firms are prepared to grant high wage increases because they can pass them on in higher prices; individuals observing price rises do not reduce their purchases correspondingly—on the contrary, they often increase them in anticipation of worse price rises later; and last, public opinion is said not to tolerate a level of unemployment that would seem acceptable in other countries; this influences governments to attach far less weight to a risk of inflation than to a risk of unemployment, and therefore to favor, on the whole, somewhat expansionist policies.

We shall accordingly attempt at the end of this section on the causes of inflation to make a judgment on the role of monetary policy and the "structural" factors of inflation. First, however, we shall try to determine in what proportion the different groups of factors listed affected the various periods of inflation experienced in France.

Inflationary Periods Before 1950

As stated earlier, we shall deal very briefly with the periods before 1950, for which we have not carried out research in depth. The different spurts in prices that took place after the 1896 downturn can be described as follows. The price increases in the last four years of the nineteenth century were the result of a rise in price of raw materials, itself due to renewed activity in the major industrial countries. Prices of food products remained stable on the whole, and wage rates grew moderately; but prices of industrial base products included in the wholesale price index of 45 commodities rose by over 30 percent. This movement, however, was reversed in 1901 and 1902. After the drop in these two years, then a rise from 1904 to 1907, and a further drop, the wholesale price index in 1909 was at a level only slightly above that in 1900, but between 1909 and 1912 it rose by 20 percent. The increase then was not only due to higher prices for certain raw materials; it seems to have been set off even more by the pressure of demand, which then grew very fast particularly as a result of the investment boom. This view is supported by a marked rise in certain retail prices (particularly for meat). There is no need to dwell on inflation in the years 1914–20. In the wartime economy, price rises due to shrinking supply and increased demand by the armed services was the means by which sacrifices required by the common effort were imposed on the nation. (In October 1916 weekly wages had risen by only 18 percent above the 1911 level, whereas many retail prices had grown twofold or even more.) When peace was restored, wage rates were reestablished at a level comparable with the rise in the cost of living, but this was before the supply of goods had recovered its previous level. Thus, inflationary pressures developed up to the outbreak of the world depression in 1920.

After falling for two years, prices climbed again from 1923 to the autumn of 1926. The cost of living index rose by 15, 9, 12 and 29 percent, respectively, in each of those four years.[2] The movements of wholesale prices were far more irregular, and there was even a substantial drop in the spring of 1924. Inflation in this period seems to have been due to a combination of two causes. First, there was high pressure of demand —the index of unemployed receiving public assistance was at a very low level. This high demand was mainly an effect of the policy for compensating war victims, which was reflected in the payment of large funds to individuals and by very high budget deficits up to 1925. Second, movements of domestic prices were influenced by variations in the exchange rate, which at that time moved freely in the course of international transactions and which was strongly affected by a consistent mistrust of French currency. Upward surges in the prices of imported products had an important effect on domestic prices, particularly in 1926, when in fact conditions necessary for stabilization had been attained inside the country. Public mistrust, however, had the effect of reducing the value of the franc in relation to the pound sterling much faster than would have been required to maintain purchasing power parity.[3]

[2] For statistical data relating to this period, see *Indices généraux du mouvement économique en France de 1901 à 1931* (Paris, 1932).

[3] This feature was very marked in 1925 and 1926, as shown by a diagram in Sauvy, *Histoire économique de la France entre les deux guerres*, vol. 1, p. 343.

The combination of measures carried out by the Poincaré government (a strict budget, a new value set for the franc in relation to gold, and maintenance of a fixed level of exchange) reestablished equilibrium in 1927. Thereafter an upward trend reappeared in retail prices, set off both by rises in costs and by pressure of demand resulting from considerable wage rate increases. But this movement did not continue beyond 1930, as a result of the collapse of the international economic situation.

The sharp rise in prices between the autumn of 1936 and the end of 1937 was undoubtedly due to the increase in costs provoked by devaluation and particularly by social policy launched too abruptly. French productive capacity was indeed partly unused, but the consistent reduction in working hours obviously led to increases in many selling prices.

The same causes that led to inflation during and after World War I pulled prices upward from 1939 to 1948. But the postwar return to norm this time was slower; it seemed that some stabilization could be achieved at the beginning of 1947, but the shortage of food products was reflected in a continuing rise in the cost of living, since rationing and price controls had ceased to be effective. Wages continued their upward trend, which became steep after the serious strikes in the autumn of 1947, when the index of hourly wage rates rose by 34 percent in three months. One year later, however, equilibrium was reached. The year 1949 was then marked by general relaxation on the markets for goods and labor.

The Rise in Costs in 1951

When the Korean war started, France was in a period of economic recovery.[4] After correction of figures for seasonal movements, the unfilled jobs and the needs for employment in the spring of 1950 had begun their characteristic seesaw movement: jobs available increased, and demand for jobs decreased. This development accelerated over the first six months of 1951, but stopped sharply by summer, when the trend reversed, particularly in the case of job offers, which fell off.

But even at its peak, the pressure of demand for workers remained moderate. The number of unemployed on relief was still 33,000, whereas it was to be only 17,000 at the end of 1957 and 20,000 at the beginning of 1963. The proportion of unfilled jobs to workers available reached exactly 25 percent, whereas it was to be as high as 70 percent in 1957

[4] The analytical approach used and the explanatory study that follows are necessarily less detailed than those of P. Herzog in "Comparaison des périodes d'inflation et de récession dans l'économie française entre 1950 et 1965," *Etudes et conjoncture,* March 1967, pp. 5–118. The reader may consult this work for many additional details and for useful information on particular points.

and 50 percent in 1962 (all figures seasonally adjusted). This situation can be accounted for in part by movements in foreign trade. Between the beginning and end of 1951, imports rose by 30 percent and exports fell by about 25 percent (according to volume index numbers). Thus the inflation, and particularly its continuation in the second half of 1951, does not seem to have been due chiefly to the pull of demand.

On the supply side, some inflationary influence should probably be ascribed to the poor farm output of 1951. Cereal, potato, vegetable, and beet crops, as well as wine production, were all at a substantially lower level than in 1950, which had been a good year. Despite an earlier regular upward trend, there was a drop in meat products as well, resulting in an increase in prices of agricultural output. Seasonally corrected, prices had grown by only 7 percent between June 1950 and February 1951; but from February to June 1951 they rose by 8 percent, and then by another 13 percent between June 1951 and January 1952. It should be noted, however, that the overall increase of 32 percent over the period as a whole was less than that of industrial wholesale prices, and close to that of the price index of gross domestic production.

The initial cause of inflation was the sharp rise in international raw material prices. The index of wholesale prices of imported raw materials almost doubled between June 1950 and the end of April 1951. This, however, ceased to be a factor from spring on in that year, since the index dropped by 28 percent up to the end of December. In most other countries the rise in prices similarly stopped in that spring and stabilized at a level comparable with that reached in France in April.[5] The principal cause of the rise in prices over the second half of 1951 seems in fact to lie in a combination of official policy decisions that had the effect of sharply raising costs. The guaranteed minimum wage for all trades was raised first by 11.5 percent in March 1951 to allow for the increase in cost of living since August 1950, and a second time in September 1951 by 15 percent to "integrate" in advance expected price increases.[6] In the provinces the regional differentials for this minimum wage below the Paris level were reduced by 25 percent in June. Prices of coal, electricity, and railroad transportation were twice substantially increased. Between 1950 and 1952, the wholesale price of coal rose by 45 percent, that of high-tension electricity by 31 percent, and that of the average ton carried by railroads by 33 percent.

[5] Between June 1951 and February 1952 the differential between retail prices in France and those in neighboring countries increased by about 15 percent (L. A. Vincent, *Le Mouvement économique en France de 1944 à 1957*; INSEE, Paris, 1958, pp. 253–55).

[6] For the history of this period, see *ibid.*, particularly pp. 260–62.

At the same time, many prices controlled by the central government were substantially raised (wheat, the price of which rose by 38.5 percent, bread, iron and steel products, newspapers, etc.). In the face of this general rise in prices, the monetary authorities acted to forestall a difficult financial situation for businesses. The overall total of items admitted for rediscounting by the Bank of France was gradually increased; the Bank of France applied a liberal policy toward the banks and frequently intervened on the open market to purchase securities. Thus, between the end of 1950 and the end of 1951, bank credits standing as counterparts to the money supply increased by over 40 percent. It was not until October and November 1951 that the discount rate was raised from 2.5 to 4 percent per year and that monetary controls were put on a stricter basis.

The Period 1952–1955

The price stability that marked these four years was due chiefly to the fact that relatively low demand faced rapidly growing potential supply. The number of unfilled jobs remained at a high level to the end of 1955. Farm output grew fast from 1952 to 1954, so that the government was able to fix lower prices for cereals, and the overall index for farm output prices fell by 9 percent between the crop years 1951/52 or 1952/53 and 1954/55.

On the cost side, prices of imported products fell sharply in 1952, and thereafter continued to show a slightly downward trend. Wages rose only slightly between January 1, 1952, and the same date in 1954: by 7 percent, according to the Ministry of Labor, an increase less than that of productivity. Thereafter, three successive increases, in February 1954, October 1954, and April 1955, raised the standard minimum Paris hourly wage by 26 percent (in the form of a bonus added to the guaranteed minimum wage). The index of hourly wages accordingly rose by 18 percent between January 1, 1954, and January 1, 1956. This considerable increase, however, was absorbed without raising the general level of prices, partly because of the stability in tax and mandatory charges of enterprises. This stability itself was the result of the drop in military expenditure (the introduction of value-added tax led to a lower burden than that of earlier taxes on turnover, and even permitted some tax reductions in the summer of 1955).

The control over prices maintained in this period was reflected in a number of decisions setting ceilings, the effect of which is difficult to evaluate. The growth of credit in the economy remained moderate, but this was chiefly because of low demand by enterprises rather than the result of policy by the banks, whose funds were plentiful. The discount rate was progressively lowered from 4 to 3 percent.

Demand Inflation in 1956 and 1957

Over the course of 1955, there was a rapid increase in demand as a result of the rise in wages and of some increase in exports due to the prosperous world economic situation. This trend accelerated in 1956 following increased military expenditure and the drafting of reservists for operations in Algeria. In 1957, the labor market was more stretched than in any other postwar period. Most productive capacity was fully employed. Imports from abroad were at a very high level, and exports were stagnant; the import coverage rate fell below 70 percent.

Despite the pressure on the labor market, costs remained fairly stable to the end of 1956, owing to severe price control. In 1956, the index of hourly wages in Paris rose by only 7 percent (as compared with 9 percent in 1954 and 1955). The regional differentials, however, were reduced by one-third, and the mandatory minimum paid vacation was extended by law to three weeks. Cost increases accelerated in the autumn of 1956, when oil products were scarce and sold at sharply increased prices as a result of the Suez crisis. The price of coal also rose. Hourly wages increased more rapidly, with the rise reaching 11 percent in Paris in 1957.

Up to the summer of 1917, credit was plentiful. The economy's bank credits standing as counterparts to the money supply rose by 22 percent in 1956. To contain inflationary tensions, the government mainly used price controls, and suspended taxes on a certain number of goods or services in such a way as to maintain the level of the overall retail price index ("the 213 items index"), which was a bench mark in many escalation clauses. Nevertheless, prices rose: industrial wholesale prices, which had dropped in the years 1952–54, grew by 4 percent in 1956. The index of retail prices of manufactured products rose to a similar extent.

Return to Normal

At the beginning of the summer of 1957, the economic situation had reached a state where fundamental measures were needed for a return to normal. Because of the pressure of domestic demand and the overvalued currency since the autumn of 1951, the foreign deficit had become very large and exchange reserves were exhausted. The central government budget also showed a high deficit. The rise in prices, which had been contained for more than a year, was making itself felt in numerous ways.

We shall not repeat the detailed history of the measures adopted by successive governments to reestablish internal and external equilibrium. Three types of action were involved. The first group of government interventions aimed at reducing the pressure of demand. They showed first through a policy of strictness toward distribution of credit. Ceilings on items admitted for rediscounting were reduced three times between July and November 1957; the overall reduction was more than 30 percent. From December 1957, direct taxes were increased, and the 1958 budget in addition was marked by a substantial reduction of expenditure. Demand fell sharply. Job vacancies dropped at the end of 1957 in a trend that accelerated in 1958. Weekly hours worked in industry were reduced on the average by one and a third hours. At the end of 1958, 85 percent of heads of firms surveyed by the INSEE reported unused productive capacity.

A second group of measures aimed at setting a new parity for the franc in relation to foreign currencies. From the end of 1951, the rate of 350 francs per dollar represented an overvaluation of French currency. Indeed, from 1952 export subsidies were instituted. In the autumn of 1957, a disguised devaluation of 20 percent was effected in the form of a new subsidy to exporters and a levy on purchases of foreign currency. A second devaluation was effected in December 1958, setting the rate at 492 francs per dollar.

Finally, abolition of tax rebates and of many subsidies, increase in social security contributions, and rise in prices of imported products made essential a thorough overhaul of prices and wages. This operation took place from the second half of 1957 well into the year 1959, if the last repercussions of the devaluation are taken into account. Between July 1957 and November 1959, the guaranteed minimum wage for all trades was raised six times, with an overall increase of 27 percent.

Inflation from 1960 to 1967

Over the years 1960–67 the rate of price increases was fairly uniform. Annual growth of the price index of gross domestic production was between 2.5 and 5.0 percent. These were accordingly years of persistent inflation, seemingly due to a progressive rise in costs on which was superimposed for a three-year period excessively strong demand pressure. The rise in costs came partly from abroad. After having dropped by about 5 percent between 1960 and 1962, the index of wholesale prices of imported raw materials rose by 12 percent between 1962 and 1967 (over these five years the general wholesale price index increased by only 9 percent). A small part of the increase in costs can also be accounted for by the rising trend of farm prices, which was indirectly a factor in raising wages. The index of farm output prices, which had grown more slowly than the general wholesale price index before 1960, rose by 24 percent between 1960 and 1967 (as against 14 percent for the general wholesale price index).

The chief cause of the rise in costs, however, was the increased revenue charges to enterprises for taxes and social security contributions: the development of public services and of social security had raised taxation and mandatory payments. Statistics of the metallurgical and mechanical industries of the Paris region indicate that these charges represented 48.4 percent of hourly wages in 1960 and 56.8 percent in 1967. According to the National Accounts, the total of taxes and social security contributions paid by nonfinancial enterprises represented 28.0 percent of their gross output in 1960 and 31.5 percent in 1967.

Apart from this, the pressure of demand had an inflationary effect between the summer of 1961 and the summer of 1964. The indicators all agree on this subject, whether one takes hours worked, the proportion of heads of firms reporting inability to produce to full capacity, or unsatisfied demand and supply of labor (after removing the temporary effect on these statistics of job-seeking repatriates). Although the situation on the various markets was not as tight as in 1957, nevertheless it made for a rise in prices. In fact, it was in this period that inflation was most rapid.

Part of the responsibility for this situation falls on the monetary authorities, who in a time of substantial balance-of-payments surpluses were unable to control the increase in available credit. This point has been demonstrated very clearly by Mme S. Guillaumont-Jeanneney.[7] From the spring of 1959 to the end of 1962, the banks consistently had substantial funds, which the Bank of France did not attempt to reduce. Thus, the money supply grew at a rate of 16 percent per year, and the credit system enjoyed an ample margin, which was to become dangerous in the winter of 1962/63, at a time when demand by repatriates from Algeria was exerting considerable force. The situation was then aggravated by an error in diagnosis that led government experts to recommend an expansionary budget for 1963. Believing that the productive system could not provide the repatriates with sufficient jobs, the experts argued for a larger volume of public demand.

From 1963, action by the government aimed at reducing the upward movement of prices. Price control was exercised with greater strictness; increases in the guaranteed minimum wage were smaller; credit was

[7] *Politique monétaire et croissance économique en France, 1960–1966* (Paris, 1969); see in particular pp. 58–73.

made more difficult. The average annual rate of growth of the money supply fell from 16 percent in 1960–63 to 7 percent in 1964–67. Nevertheless, the impact of the government's action on the rate of price increases remained weak, and an upward trend could still be observed when the events of May–June 1968 let loose a new wave of inflation due in the first place to the rise in the cost of labor and then in 1969 to the pressure of demand enabling profits to rise.

The Overall Picture

The examination above, covering the different waves of price increases experienced in France over the past 70 years, is sufficient to suggest objective reasons for each of them from an analysis of the economic situation of the time. It is not necessary to resort to a structural study of the economy to explain them.

Our review reveals a great diversity of situations. Even if one leaves aside wartime inflation and mistrust of the franc in the years before the Poincaré stabilization, the fundamental causes must be sought in some cases in the demand side (before World War I, in 1923–25, in 1956–57, and in 1963), in other cases in the cost side (in 1936, in 1951, and even in the 1960's). To look for a common explanation for such varied situations would surely be an abuse of the attempt to be systematic.

Nevertheless, those who attribute the chief role to structural factors will object that analysis of the economic situation does not provide the answer. Inflation doubtless has reflected in the economic field the many internal and external turns of fortune suffered by France since the beginning of the century, acting now in one direction and now in another. But why were price increases not offset by reductions? Why do the changes, when viewed over several decades, seem to be reflected in gradual depreciation of the purchasing power of French currency? The nineteenth century also experienced many vagaries; yet the general price level in that period did not show any marked trend.

If the matter is approached from this angle, the point should at once be made that this phenomenon is not specifically French but worldwide. In every country the purchasing power of money has fallen more or less regularly since the beginning of the twentieth century. Most of the structural factors that one might consider in order to account for the upward trend of prices in France apply just as well abroad. For this reason we must distinguish, on the one hand, between an analysis of the worldwide phenomenon and, on the other hand, a study of the structural reasons that since 1950 may have led inflation to be higher in France than elsewhere.

An explanation of worldwide inflation would take us outside our sub-

ject. Price rises are obviously helped by the inhibiting rigidities represented by mandatory pricing practices, wage negotiation procedures,
and the habit of regular and substantial increases in rates of remuneration. More fundamentally, the development of credit has brought about
rapid growth in monetary instruments, which has fed upward swells in
prices. A stricter monetary policy would have stemmed inflation, but
probably by somewhat slowing down the rate of growth. In regard to
these inflationary factors, France has been no different from the rest of
the world.

But can we find other factors to account for the fact that since 1950
the rise in prices has been higher in France than in all the other Western
industrial nations? Faster growth of productivity would probably have
acted as a brake on price rises, and failure of some of the structures of
the economy to adapt can indeed be seen as the cause of slow improvement in productivity. But such structural obstacles to progress can be
found in all countries. The direct study of productivity has shown that
France has enjoyed expansion comparable with that of its neighbors,
and failure of its industrial and commercial structures to adapt cannot
account for a sickness apparently peculiar to this country.

Similarly, it seems difficult to affirm a priori that competition is less
effective in France than in the other industrial countries of Western
Europe. We examine this question in Chapter 13 and find it impossible
to reach a firm conclusion. We consider, however, that establishment
of the Common Market has increased the scale of competition faced by
French firms. Yet the Common Market did not prevent continual rise
in French prices over the 1960's.

However, we find three distinctive features in France, compared with
other countries, that might account for particularly high inflation since
World War II: a stagnant supply of labor, brittle social cohesiveness,
and deliberate collective choice. Up to 1962, the French working population remained almost stationary, whereas it was growing rapidly in
most other countries (see Table 2.18, p. 76). Although there was active
demand for labor in France as elsewhere, the supply of labor was not
growing. The pressure of demand on the labor market was consequently
particularly high in France, which explains an atypically high average
growth rate of wages and, in turn, of prices. This reasoning is probably
too simple: even in the medium term, the pressure of demand on the
labor market is not a function merely of the growth rate of total available manpower. In France, movements of farm workers toward other
jobs and the fact that productive capacity had not been expanded at a
very rapid rate before 1960 moderated the pressure of demand. Taking

these factors into account, however, does not seem to invalidate the fact that over the 1950's the pressure of demand on the labor market was stronger in France than in most other countries. Direct measures of unemployment, although imperfect, show this clearly. This factor would explain why inflation was particularly high in France, but it cannot be applied to the period after 1962.

Our historical analysis has succeeded in showing at what dates inflation in France was higher than in other countries. One year was 1951, when the reversal of price trends on the international market made it seem impossible to stabilize prices at a level 25 percent above that in the spring of 1950. Another year was 1956, when increased military expenditure and the drafting of reservists necessarily raised prices on the market for goods and services, since the government refused any substantial increase in tax rates. Another year was 1963, as the combined result of an exaggerated inflationary monetary policy since 1960 and a deliberately expansionist budget aimed at providing sufficient jobs for the inflow of repatriates. Another period was the autumn of 1968, following the Grenelle agreements on wage increases but also under the effect of the exaggeratedly liberal financial policy maintained over the second half of that year.

The common characteristic in these four periods was the acceptance by governments of the risk of price rises. They accepted this risk deliberately in 1951, 1956, and 1968, but perhaps less consciously in 1963, since analyses of the economic situation made in the autumn of 1962, on the contrary, highlighted the risk of unemployment. Politicians in other countries, more concerned for the stability of their currency, might have acted differently in these four instances. Why did the French governments distinguish themselves in this way from those of other countries? It was surely to a great extent to avoid social unrest observed or feared. To accept high wage increases and to choose an expansionist policy that reduces the risk of unemployment often seem likely to bring back or at least temporarily maintain social harmony. It is true that unrest of this kind also happens in other countries. But it is not so serious there; contrary to what happens in France, elsewhere this unrest is not felt likely to turn into revolution. The political divisions in French society have often led to adopting inflation as a lesser-evil.

Inflation has also been the outcome of a choice consistently made in the conduct of public affairs, a choice made by governments but accepted or even desired by the majority of the people. In the delicate and uncertain adjustments made to short-term economic policies, the risk of price rises was often accepted in preference to that of a long-lasting slowdown of growth. This priority given to expansion is probably the characteristic that most clearly distinguishes French economic policy after the war from that between the wars.

The rise in prices had particularly clear repercussions on the factors governing international trade. The balance of payments is a subject requiring special examination, which we shall take up later in this chapter. For the present, therefore, we shall confine ourselves to a study of the domestic consequences of inflation. These can be grouped according to whether they relate to changes affecting the purchasing power of assets, to disorganization of markets and commercial transactions, or to the risk connected with expectations of future rates of inflation.

Erosion of Long-Standing Assets and Liabilities

Price rises automatically entail a reduction in the real value of existing financial assets and liabilities. Interest and capital owed by the debtor to the creditor represent reduced purchasing power. The real values of the wealth of each are therefore changed, and this usually has direct or indirect effects on the decisions taken by each. Let us see how this change in real wealth may have acted on French growth after the war.

In broad terms the distribution of financial assets whose value is linked with that of money can be described as follows. Households are creditors of business enterprises and government agencies. In the absence of regular evaluation of wealth held by different parties, it can be noted that from 1953, when the flow of funds was first recorded, the net increase in cash and financial claims held by households amounted each year to between 4 and 7 percent of gross domestic production (after deducting reimbursement and new debts). The net increase in liabilities of nonfinancial undertakings in most years represented about 4 percent of gross domestic production.

Inflation therefore acted consistently to reduce the wealth of households and the indebtedness of enterprises. This effect had been particularly marked during the war and in the immediate postwar period, since prices increased by a factor of about 17 from 1938 to 1949 and by a factor of about 25 from 1938 to 1952. Thus, in both 1949 and 1952 firms' indebtedness was very small, and the financial assets of households were at a relatively low level. Only stocks had kept most of their purchasing power. In subsequent years, firms' indebtedness increased and the financial wealth of households was gradually rebuilt. But the rise in prices, which was sharp from 1956 to 1959 and thereafter more moderate, had the effect of slowing down this rebuilding. The situation reached in 1967, therefore, still did not correspond to what might have been observed in French institutions if there had been a permanent situation of no price increases.

In Chapter 10 we studied the consequences of firms' indebtedness for their investments. We saw that in the 1950's firms were not inclined to restrain their capital investment drive because of reluctance to become further indebted. Fears about financial equilibrium may have affected their investment decisions from 1963, but too late to alter the economy's growth rate over the period we are considering. Wartime and postwar inflation was therefore a factor favorable to investment. This factor was not felt in the early 1950's, when the availability of long-term borrowing to private firms was very low, but it was owing to inflation that capital accumulation continued at a sustained rate after 1955 and over the first half of the 1960's.

The eased financial situation helped healthy firms to grow. It was also a survival factor for firms that were basically operating with a deficit, causing them to launch forms of activity that were not economically justified. The modernization of France's productive system and the growth of productivity were probably slowed by this fact over the whole of the 1950's. It is impossible to measure this effect, but its existence can be seen by its contrary effect, as one notes the prolonged and even apparently accelerating growth of productivity in the mid-1960's, when the eased financial situation had disappeared and competition became sharp.

In Chapter 9, when dealing with household savings, we concluded that wartime and postwar inflation had been partly responsible for the high rate of savings, particularly over the 1950's. Bringing back cash holdings and savings deposits to their 1938 relative levels accounts for a large part of household saving. To this could be added investment in securities, also intended to rebuild portfolios. These savings were a stabilizing element, since they reduced the pressure of demand. But according to the conclusions in Chapter 9, they probably had no effect on the growth of the French productive system, since the role of prime mover was played by demand for investment.

The low level of financial wealth of households in the postwar period may have tended to increase the volume of paid employment, since in a number of individual cases labor was substituted for wealth as a source of income. It seems difficult, however, to ascribe a high value to this influence, which must have affected only a small proportion of the population of working age. Nevertheless, a considerable group of older persons in 1950 found themselves deprived of savings built up before the war and kept in traditional holdings; this must have led in a number of cases to continued paid employment beyond intended retirement age. In relation to the prewar period, the reduction in real income from financial capital undoubtedly was a factor in equalizing incomes; and this, other things being equal, probably tended to reduce the average propensity to save. But this effect also seems negligible.

To sum up, the erosion of assets and liabilities caused by wartime and postwar inflation seems to have been important chiefly in its effects on firms' finances. It was probably partly responsible for the strength of the investment boom observed from 1956 to 1964. It may also explain why productivity growth was not faster during the 1950's.

Disorganization of the Market

The periods of inflation are marked not only by a general upward trend in prices but also by some lack of consistency in price changes. In response to an upward trend, some prices are adjusted almost instantaneously, whereas changes in industrial prices and wages are made in steps over relatively long periods, and the setting of new tariffs by public enterprises and utilities follows, usually after a longer delay. Until a new plateau has been reached, the factors affecting decision making in enterprises are therefore considerably disturbed. Some transactions that would normally make a profit appear temporarily as a loss, and vice versa. This interferes with the proper working of markets and the carrying out of project assessments.

We have been unable to study this feature fully or its incidence on French growth, and shall accordingly confine ourselves to presenting an opinion here, in the hope that other researchers will submit it to precise tests. It seems that disorganization of markets cannot become apparent while the rate of inflation remains below a certain threshold. A low average rate of price increase introduces temporary distortions that are too weak to affect the management of industrial and commercial affairs. In the period that interests us, we have therefore to consider only the immediate postwar period and the years 1950–52 and 1956–59.

As an example we may briefly examine energy prices, which are likely to play an important role in the choice between different modes of production. Table 11.1 shows for three particularly significant types of energy the average rate of price change from one year to another. Although calculating annual averages has the effect of reducing temporary distortions, it can be seen that over the periods of rapid price increase

TABLE 11.1
Changes in Energy Prices, 1947–67
(Percent of previous year)

Year	Coal (unwashed raw smalls)	Light fuel oil	High-tension electricity	Year	Coal (unwashed raw smalls)	Light fuel oil	High-tension electricity
1947	40.5%	−6.6%	183.2%	1958	7.7%	6.2%	4.9%
1948	86.3	140.5	21.9	1959	12.7	8.8	18.1
1949	14.6	18.9	15.7	1960	−	−3.7	−
1950	11.9	4.7	−0.5	1961	−	−0.6	−
1951	19.7	22.7	12.6	1962	−	−3.5	−
1952	13.6	5.2	22.2	1963	2.1	−	4.3
1953	4.3	−6.8	−	1964	1.4	−	−7.2
1954	1.4	−2.2	−	1965	−	3.6	2.2
1955	−	1.8	−0.5	1966	−	−0.8	1.8
1956	7.9	4.4	−0.5	1967	−	1.2	3.0
1957	10.4	12.5	0.4				

the three kinds did not change in a synchronized manner. In 1950–52 as in 1956–59, price rises for coal preceded those for fuel oil, which were larger than those for electricity tariffs.

But after 1949, the temporary differences in the rates of increase were relatively small and were never maintained for many years at a stretch. It can therefore be thought that their incidence was weak. Few inadequate decisions committing the future can have been affected by these distortions. At the most, these periods of relative price distortion may have had some transitory adverse effect on the efficiency of management.

The Risk of Inflation

Uncertainties about future price rises are likely to have played a more important part. After half a century in which years with rising price levels had been more numerous than those with falling or stable prices, when individuals and heads of firms observed a massive reduction in the purchasing power of the franc, they could not fail to make allowance in their decisions for the possibility of a further rise in prices. Moreover, whether or not such a rise would take place, and at what rate, was not known with any certainty. Thus a particular risk affected every transaction involving the future: a risk of rising costs for those who had agreed to produce at fixed prices, and a risk of price stabilization in the case of those who, in accepting certain costs, had anticipated a rise in the price of their products.

The expectation of inflation was so general that many contracts covering a long period ahead contained escalation clauses stipulating prices calculated by reference to those pertaining at the time of payment, and in this way eliminating the risk of inflation. Since World War II such clauses have become customary in many agreements concluded by public bodies and in all contracts relating to building and public works.

Between 1955 and 1958 the use of escalation clauses spread rapidly to many other types of contracts. The public authorities saw in them a threat likely to reduce substantially the effectiveness of anti-inflation machinery. Measures taken at the end of 1958 thus strictly regulated the use of escalation clauses. However, they did not eliminate them in every case where the risk of inflation would have been too serious for producers.[8] Thus official institutions themselves recognized the danger that too great uncertainty over future prices would have held back expansion of certain sectors of production. Since the regulations did not cover all cases, the question we have asked ourselves remains valid.

In order to study the effects of the risk of inflation, it is advisable to distinguish between effects resulting from the *average* expectation of continuing price rises and effects arising from *uncertainties* about future rates of inflation. It is also convenient, and sufficient as a first approximation, to adopt the assumption that households are lenders and firms are borrowers. And last, we shall not consider here the effects of inflation on the distribution of financial assets; this implies an assumption that financial intermediaries effect a satisfactory reallocation of credit.

The risk of inflation operates through the *real* price of credit. The real interest rate is by definition that which, in current market conditions, would apply to a contract in which the interest and capital to be repaid would have to be increased proportionately to the rise in prices. This rate is clearly lower, in cases of rising prices, than the nominal interest rate applying at any one time to usual contracts in which interest and capital are stipulated in money terms. We might easily show that the real interest rate is equal to the difference between the nominal rate and the expected rate of growth of the general level of prices.

We are interested here in the expected rate and not the a posteriori rate. We can therefore say that the *average* real cost of credit is equal to the difference between the interest rate and the rate of price increase that the lender or borrower expects to observe, on the average. *Uncertainty* about the real rate corresponds precisely to the uncertainty about the rate of the price increase.

---

[8] The regulations of December 30, 1958, and February 4, 1959, in principle made escalation clauses for prices or wages illegal. Nevertheless, they allowed for two important exceptions: (1) escalations on the price of goods or services with which a contract is directly concerned (for example, construction costs in the case of a new building); (2) escalations relating to the activity of the parties to a contract (for example, the turnover of the purchaser or the seller). On this subject see J. P. Doucet, *L'Indexation* (Paris, 1965).

In the case of a lending household, the average expectation of a rise in prices therefore has the same effect as a reduction in the rate of interest. It is often said that this would discourage savings; nevertheless, no convincing proof of this has been given. Economists have long known that the impact of a drop in interest rates can be broken down into two terms with opposite signs: a "substitution effect" implying an increase in present consumption (since its price falls relative to that of future consumption) and an "income effect," implying a reduction in present consumption (since real income available to a saving household for all present and future consumption has fallen). In less technical terms, the second effect reflects the following facts: a person who seeks by saving to ensure given purchasing power in the future must save more when the interest rate is lower. Econometric studies carried out so far do not a priori invalidate these points: the average expected rate of price increase seems to have no significant effect on total household savings (obviously, there is an effect on the allocation of savings between different types of investment).

Similar conclusions apply to the effect of uncertainty about the real interest rate, i.e. about the rate of future price rises. Uncertainty about the future purchasing power of invested savings probably discourages those who do not feel a pressing need to satisfy future wants by means of these savings; but on the contrary it makes necessary an increased effort by those who wish to be guaranteed against the vagaries of the future.

From the viewpoint of borrowing firms, the effects are much clearer. The average expectation of price rises and the corresponding drop in the real interest rate obviously stimulate borrowing as well as demand for investment. On the other hand, uncertainty about the rate of price increases makes the real profit from investment subject to risk; it must therefore lead to a cautious attitude by firms and hamper projects where the rate of return is not high. Nevertheless, the first effect is obviously stronger than the second if the expected rise in prices is not reflected in an increase in the nominal interest rate; for borrowing firms even an uncertain rise in prices is far preferable to a total absence of price increase.

This discussion therefore leads us to the following two conclusions: (1) If the nominal interest rate remains unchanged, an expectation of price rises stimulates investment without substantially affecting savings, even if this price increase is uncertain. (2) On the other hand, if the nominal interest rate is raised in a proportion equal to the average rate of price rises expected, the risk due to the uncertain character of the inflation depresses investment without having significant effect on savings.

In order to reach a conclusion on the effects of the risk of inflation on growth in France since the war, we must therefore examine what the nominal rate of interest was and consider what the real cost of credit may have been for firms, given their expectations of further price rises.

Undoubtedly the real cost of credit was low in France up to 1952. Although the rate for bonds had risen to 7 percent per year, private enterprises had little access to this type of financing. They used both self-financing and short-term credits for which the rate of interest was low (the discount rate was 3 percent per year and even 2.5 percent from June 1950 to October 1951). In view of the high rate of inflation, it was in the interest of firms to borrow on a large scale, and no real risk was involved.

Over the period of price stability that followed 1952, private firms increasingly raised credit through bond issues at relatively high rates, which fell from 7 percent in 1952 to 6 percent in 1955. But the discount rate, which was 4 percent at the end of 1951, was lowered to 3 percent in the course of 1954. Over this period, the vivid memory of price rises probably led many heads of firms to expect inflation again. Since interest rates remained moderate, there was only a low risk of having to carry for a long period financial charges with too high a real cost.

From 1956 to 1959 the rise in prices was so sharp and so strongly perceived by the public that the real cost of credit again became very low on the average, and enterprises had no need to fear a heavy burden of financial charges. The discount rate was raised again, but not beyond 5 percent. The rate on bond issues lost significance over this period, for the practice became general of introducing various escalation clauses in the issues, clauses that applied in some cases to the principal, and in some cases to the interest. By means of these clauses the rates offered could be kept relatively low. Moreover, when the rise in prices was fastest, firms and the public gave preference to capital raised by means of new stock issues.

From 1960 to 1967, the discount rate was kept at the moderate level of 3.5 percent per year except from the autumn of 1963 to the spring of 1965 (when it was 4 percent). Over this period, as in those preceding it, moreover, the discount rate was not a perfect indicator of the cost of short-term money. Depending on how restrictive monetary policy is, the effective cost of credit to firms can exceed the discount rate by a larger or smaller margin. The rate for bond issues remained around 5.75 percent up to 1964, and then rose to 7 percent in 1967.

The monetary stabilization of December 1958 and the setting up of the Common Market created a new climate of expectations. Because of the lack of data[9] it is impossible to compare objectively price expectations over this period with those from 1952 to 1955. It may be, however, that despite short-term price movements observed in fact in each case, heads of firms expected in the 1960's a lower medium-term rate of inflation than they had forecast during the short period of stability in the 1950's. The highest estimates of the real cost of credit by heads of firms probably therefore occurred in that period. The difference between the 1960's and previous periods, however, is small. Moreover, the spread of forecasts was probably narrower.[10]

In summary, this examination leads us to the conclusion that, taking account of expected price increases, the real cost of credit remained low over the entire postwar period. Borrowing to finance real investments or productive operations must have seemed profitable at all times, even allowing for uncertainties about the future rate of inflation. This factor accounts substantially for the high level of demand for credit.

Should it also be seen as one of the factors accounting for the heavy demand for investment? It probably played some part, but its effect was limited in two ways.

First, overall demand for credit was too high to be totally satisfied, particularly over the 1950's. Credit then was rationed in various ways. A lower demand for money would not therefore have been reflected in lower investment. Quite the contrary, a higher real cost of credit would have restored the balance between supply and demand of capital, eliminating the least justified demands. In brief, on the capital market as on other markets, inflation had the effect of introducing distortions harmful to efficiency.

Second, from 1963 on, the need to ensure equilibrium in balance sheets and to maintain the rate of indebtedness below a certain limit led firms themselves to restrict their demand for credit and consequently to control the volume of their investment (cf. Chapter 10).

Our examination of the various domestic repercussions exerted by postwar inflation on France's growth rate has led us to conclude that

[9] We have, of course, the replies by heads of firms to the regular INSEE inquiries; these show that short-term movements in prices were clearly perceived and correctly forecast. But these movements have little significance for decisions concerning long-term borrowing. What matters in that case is the average rate of price increase over the succeeding 10 or 20 years. Forecasts of this long-term movement can differ considerably from those relating to the months immediately ahead. They seem to react very slowly to variations in the observed rate of inflation. (See the reference to this subject in Chapter 9, p. 276.)

[10] An attempt to establish a series for the real rates of interest is to be found in the fourth part of "Peut-on mesurer l'évolution du coût d'usage du capital productif?" by E. Malinvaud, in *Economie et statistique*, April 1971.

little importance need be ascribed to most of them. The chief effects seem to relate to the erosion of assets and liabilities and to the easy financial circumstances that thus prevailed for firms until around 1964. This state of ease can account for some delay in productivity improvements over the 1950's and, together with the expectation of price rises, for the vigor with which investment by private enterprises grew from 1955 to 1964. The disorganization brought by inflation on the market for goods and services was also the cause of inefficiencies, particularly in the 1950's. We shall return to this subject in Chapter 13.

FOREIGN BALANCE

Prices in France and Abroad

In an open economy that has a large volume of trade with other countries, the most significant effect of inflation lies in its impact on the balance of payments. The rise of domestic prices raises the cost of exports and lessens the volume, whereas it helps foreign products to compete and therefore stimulates imports. This double movement worsens the balance of trade; to reestablish equilibrium, corrective measures are needed, which may be more or less favorable to growth. Inflation, however, will have these unfavorable effects only if it is higher within the country in question than in those countries trading with it. After the war, the rise in prices was a worldwide phenomenon. A rapid look at the data shows, however, that even if one excepts the three years immediately following 1968, inflation in France was much higher than in other countries.

The price index of the gross national product is probably the indicator most comparable internationally. The OECD National Accounts statistics estimate that this indicator rose by 143 percent in France between 1950 and 1966. Over the same period, the rise was 69 percent in Germany, 80 percent in Britain, and 68 percent in the United States. This difference was so high that it made necessary an alteration of the French rate of exchange. Only a downward readjustment of the franc in relation to foreign currencies could reestablish the competitiveness of French exports and allow the borders to be opened to foreign products. Such a readjustment was carried out in two stages in 1958, and raised the value of the dollar by 40 percent in relation to the franc.

In order to allow for the effects of alterations in exchange rates on the level of prices in France relative to those in other countries, we have calculated an index of prices applicable to the gross national product evaluated in dollars, by a simple conversion of the national currency in each case at the rate of exchange at a given time. The results obtained

TABLE 11.2

Price Indexes of Gross National Product in Six Countries, 1950–66

(Estimated in dollars at current rates of exchange; 1950 = 100)

Year	France	Germany	United States	Italy	United Kingdom	Netherlands
1950	100	100	100	100	100	100
1952	138	113	110	113	117	115
1956	151	120	117	121	135	126
1960	140	140	135	132	148	151
1966	174	186	168	162	180	196

Source: OECD National Accounts.

in this way for six countries are shown in Table 11.2, where the base year is 1950, i.e. after the various readjustments of exchange rates were carried out immediately after the war. On this base, the level of French prices expressed in dollars was comparable over the 1960's with the level of prices in the other major countries with which France traded. On the other hand, in 1951 French prices were approximately 20 percent higher, a differential that remained up to 1956 and grew larger in 1957 before the devaluation.

Table 11.2 seems to give a good picture of the differentials between French and foreign prices, although it depends on the assumption of exact parity in 1950. Before going on to other comparisons, we may make two comments on this assumption. On the one hand, it is confirmed by observation of the disequilibria in the balance of trade for the years in which parity is implied: a slight deficit in 1950, a surplus in 1960, equilibrium in 1966—after correction for the differences in the method of accounting for imports and exports. On the other hand, the direct comparison by Gilbert and Kravis for 1950 led to the conclusion that for all goods and services as a whole comprised in the gross national product, French prices converted at official rates of exchange were 30 to 35 percent higher than prices in the United States, but 5 to 10 percent lower than prices in the other three major European countries: West Germany, Britain, and Italy (geometric average of results obtained with European and American weightings).[11] Various other comparative studies have also shown that French price and cost levels expressed in dollars were substantially equal to the price and cost levels in other countries in 1950, as they were in 1960 and 1967.[12]

[11] M. Gilbert and I. Kravis, *An International Comparison of National Products and the Purchasing Power of Currencies* (OEEC; Paris, 1954).

[12] See, for example, J. Méraud, "Comparaison des prix français et étrangers," *Etudes et conjoncture,* Red Series, July–August, 1952; A. Devaux, "Quelques com-

If we wish to study more closely comparative changes in prices, we must refer to national index numbers. Those for wholesale prices seem to be difficult to compare because there is a good deal of difference in their coverage. They do not, however, give results very different from those shown in Table 11.2. For retail prices, more precise calculations were carried out in order to construct one of the "alarm-signal indicators" of the Fifth French National Plan. This indicator was intended to show quickly any incipient fall in the competitiveness of French prices in relation to those of France's chief commercial partners; it measures the difference between the annual growth rate of two index numbers: the French index of consumption prices and an average weighted index of retail prices in six countries—the United States, United Kingdom, Germany, Belgium/Luxembourg, Italy, and the Netherlands. (The national indexes are combined with weightings representing the proportion of each country in the export of manufactured products to OECD member countries.)

Calculations carried out in determining this indicator can obviously be used to define an index of the relative differential between French retail prices and foreign prices corrected for the effects of various alterations in exchange rates. On the basis of a nil differential in the first half of 1960 (i.e. after the price readjustments that followed the 1958 devaluation), French prices were 14 percent ahead in 1953 and 33 percent in the first half of 1957; this confirms clearly the results shown for the same period in Table 11.2. From 1960 to 1963 the rise in French prices seems to have been somewhat higher than that of foreign prices. Despite the reevaluation of the mark and the florin at the beginning of 1961, French prices were 5 percent ahead in the autumn of 1963. After the stabilization plan adopted at this time, the French lead was very slightly reduced: it was only 2 percent approximately between the spring of 1966 and the summer of 1967.

The slight difference between the trends in the years 1960–63 and 1964–67 can also be seen when, using the results of the National Accounts, changes in overall prices of industrial products sold on the French market are compared with those of prices of imported industrial products from the European Economic Community: +11.3 percent for the first, against +1.2 percent for the second between 1960 and 1964; +3.1 percent against +3.7 percent between 1964 and 1967.

paraisons relatives à certains niveaux de prix à la consommation dans les pays Européens," *Etudes et conjoncture*, December 1965; and A. Devaux, "Les Coûts de la main-d'oeuvre dans les industries des pays du Marché commun," *Etudes de conjoncture*, February 1968.

The significance of this comparison is somewhat obscured, however, by the setting up of the Common Market. However, setting aside the period 1952–58, we are led to the conclusion that the devaluations of French currency had the effect of maintaining the competitiveness of prices in France despite an inflation that over the past 20 years was much higher than for its partners.

The Balance of Payments

Although it is relatively easy to trace the principal features in the movements of relative prices after 1950, it is much more difficult to describe the ups and downs of the balance of payments into the black or red. It cannot be done, in fact, without going over in some detail the history of the last 20 years.[13] We shall distinguish here seven periods indicated by the annual statistics of the balance of payments (see Table 11.3).[14]

1. *Over the year preceding the Korean war*, French foreign trade had reached a credit balance. After the very large deficits of the years 1945–48, a healthy situation was reached from the autumn of 1949 on, following the readjustment of exchange rates. Slackening of the pressure of demand over the second half of 1948 set off a favorable evolution of French foreign trade. From that period on, the value of French exports was growing at a rate of about 50 percent per year, and the value of imports by only about 20 percent. In the last quarter of 1950, the rate of coverage of imports by exports reached 100 percent, which, in fact, represented a surplus.[15] France, therefore, was one of the group of European countries that were rapidly abolishing import quotas (a 75 percent free-trade level was reached in May 1951). Foreign aid then received under the Marshall Plan enabled France to rebuild its gold and currency reserves and to acquire a creditor position toward the European Payments Union set up on July 1, 1950.

2. *From the spring of 1951 to the autumn of 1952*, the situation was radically reversed. Following the downturn in world economic trends, and then the rise in French prices by comparison with those abroad,

[13] For a more complete description of changes in the balance of payments up to 1957, see Vincent, *Le Mouvement économique en France de 1954 à 1957*.

[14] Table 11.3 shows some significant balance items. The changes in 1958 in presentation of the balance-of-payments figures affect to some extent the comparison between the first and second halves of the table.

[15] It is known, of course, that the customs statistics of imports are on a CIF basis (cost, insurance, and freight), whereas exports are FOB (free on board). A rate of coverage of 92 percent therefore corresponds in France to equilibrium. This particularity of the foreign trade statistics, however, was removed beginning in 1971.

TABLE 11.3
*Principal Components of Balance of Payments Between France
and Other Countries, 1949–67*
(Million dollars)

Year	Commodities	Goods and services[a]	Capital transactions	Foreign aid and EPU[a]	Gold and currency[b]	Rate of coverage of imports by exports (percent)
1949	−468	−539	−49	1,070	330	66.8%
1950	−78	−115	23	384	170	88.1
1951	−771	−970	−24	745	−312	73.2
1952	−619	−591	102	542	21	66.4
1953	−339	282	−9	506	162	81.0
1954	−179	−20	−223	720	506	86.6
1955	86	272	−179	703	673	93.7
1956	−808	−848	−99	386	−698	72.9
1957	−950	−1,204	345	230	−716	71.3
1958	−295	−343	180	308	63	
1958	−295	−336	511		169	78.9%
1959	436	710	293		1,037	99.3
1960	92	643	−49		600	99.0
1961	417	884	−70		1,002	102.8
1962	485	773	−320		712	98.7
1963	177	384	87		726	90.9
1964	−89	−22	445		853	87.9
1965	390	442	112		1,058	96.0
1966	−38	−44	12		457	91.2
1967	150	134	122		275	90.3

[a]"Off-shore orders" have been deducted from expenditure by foreign governments and added to foreign assistance under the European Payments Union (EPU). They represent, in fact, the value in dollars of arms bought by France from the United States and reimbursed by the United States government.
[b]Increases in reserves are shown as positive.

French exports dropped by 25 percent in 18 months, whereas imports continued to grow until the winter of 1952. The rate of coverage fell to 66 percent for the year 1952 as a whole. In view of the drop in its gold and currency reserves and the size of its debtor position toward the European Payments Union, however, France abolished free trading in February 1952. In the same period, export subsidies were introduced; their modality was changed at different times, but they were kept until 1957. These subsidies took the form of lump-sum reimbursements of tax and parafiscal charges. They were maintained even after the 1954 introduction of the value-added tax, from which exports are in any case exempt. They therefore represented in reality a bonus intended to compensate exporters for the overvaluation of the French exchange rate.

3. *In the three years 1953 to 1955*, it seemed that the balance of payments was gradually being restored to equilibrium. Imports did not again reach their 1951 level until 1954 for volume, and 1955 for value.

TABLE 11.4
Indexes of Trade with Countries Outside the Franc Zone, 1953–67
(1956 = 100)

	Exports			Imports		
Year	Finished capital goods	Finished consumption goods	Total	Finished capital goods	Finished consumption goods	Total
1953	71	74	68	66	76	44
1954	86	79	80	71	72	54
1955	111	96	94	82	86	77
1956	100	100	100	100	100	100
1957	106	116	117	105	120	94
1958	105	113	138	102	118	83
1959	136	131	196	101	110	98
1960	163	176	231	123	138	146
1961	183	216	228	136	173	226
1962	202	252	274	157	214	320
1963	220	255	308	187	227	452
1964	243	273	316	215	273	544
1965	275	286	373	220	269	588
1966	296	307	416	254	312	710
1967	311	326	439	270	337	800

Exports were growing at a moderate but regular pace (see Table 11.4). In 1955 the French balance of trade was in credit. Some liberalization of imports was therefore possible from 1954, although partially offset by "special temporary taxes" added to the customs duties (7–15 percent, according to the goods in question). On January 1, 1956, the percentage of goods allowed free entry was 79 percent. Over the two years 1954 and 1955, French gold and currency reserves increased substantially as a result of the military assistance to France from the United States. Nevertheless, these results were atypical in nature, and thereby emphasized the fragile balance reached. Military assistance was to be substantially reduced in 1956 and to disappear from 1957. Import quotas were applied to the proportion of French imports, one-fifth, that was most sensitive to international competition. France's neighbors, however, had more or less completely liberalized their foreign trade, and France was entering into a policy of European economic integration that was scarcely compatible with the existence of quotas, taxes on imports, and export subsidies. Moreover, the balance of trade in 1955 had been helped by exceptionally favorable circumstances: an abundance of farm products which had reduced the need for imports, and large sales of iron and steel products as a result of abnormally high foreign demand.

4. *The demand inflation that began in 1955 and grew in 1956 and*

1957 therefore led to rapid deterioration of the balance. From the beginning of 1955 to the summer of 1957, imports grew at a very fast rate (on the order of 25 percent per year). The rising trend of exports reversed at the beginning of 1956. The balance of trade showed a large deficit, with the rate of coverage of imports sinking to a level not much above 70 percent. French gold and currency reserves shrank at a very rapid rate. In the summer of 1957 the situation demanded large-scale corrective measures. Liberalization of imports was suspended in June. A new regimen for foreign payments was adopted in October, and amounted to a devaluation of 20 percent. As we saw above, short-term economic policy was directed toward a firm restriction of demand. All these measures were kept in force until December 1958, when a new value was set for the franc and the freeing of foreign trade was resumed.

5. *The period from 1959 to 1962* is shown to be particularly favorable. Foreign trade was consistently in surplus, and the rate of coverage of imports was close to 100 percent. French exchange reserves were rapidly rebuilt.[16] The contrast with the previous period made a big impression at the time and was entirely attributed to the stabilization achieved at the end of 1958. Undoubtedly, soaring exports would not have been possible without reestablishment of economic equilibrium within the country as well as selection of an exchange rate consistent with parity between French and foreign prices. But it seems that, in addition to these necessary conditions for a return to equilibrium, other favorable factors were in operation. It can be noted in particular that, although the total volume of French exports fell by 5 percent between 1955 and 1958, the volume of exports of finished products continued to grow, by 18 percent in the case of capital goods and by 47 percent for consumption goods. Over these three difficult years for sales abroad, certain sectors of French industry seem to have made efforts to open new outlets for their products on foreign markets. These efforts enabled sales to expand rapidly after devaluation.

6. *In 1963 the French balance of payments seemed to be threatened once again.* From the autumn of 1961, the rate of growth of exports had

[16] Confirmation that these developments were not due to a change in France's favor of the structure of foreign demand for French goods can be obtained in the analysis by D. L. Phan of the period 1953–62. He determined how French exports would have moved if the proportion of French sales to world sales had remained constant on every market (by geographical area and by product). Taking the year 1953 as base, he found actual French exports to be substantially below theoretical exports in 1956–57 and substantially above in 1960–62 (see D. L. Phan, "La Position concurrentielle de la France sur le marché mondial," *Bulletin du CEPREL*, no. 5, October 1965, p. 143).

fallen as a result of the slowdown in the German economy. From January 1963 to January 1964, imports, stimulated by strong domestic demand, grew by about 35 percent. The rate of coverage fell below 90 percent. The stabilization plan of autumn 1963 had the effect of stopping the growth of imports and enabling a credit balance to be reached again at the beginning of 1965.

Nevertheless, French gold and currency reserves continued to rise in 1963 and 1964; they were fed by an influx of capital, in which two chief elements can be distinguished. First, from 1960 to 1965 private long-term loans and investments produced a net annual balance varying between 300 and 500 million dollars. This balance reached a peak in 1963 and 1964. Second, payments for goods from 1962 on showed a more favorable balance than did the customs statistics of imports and exports. This means that French exporters were confident of the strength of the franc and therefore hesitated less and less to repatriate without delay their earnings in foreign countries, whereas foreign firms selling in France were more and more willing to grant payment facilities to their customers. Thus in 1963, whereas the rate of coverage of imports had fallen to 91 percent, payments on products were still 3 percent above receipts. In 1964 the payments deficit under this heading was only 1 percent, whereas customs statistics showed a real deficit on the order of 4 percent.

7. *From 1965 to 1967 a credit position in the balance of payments seemed to have again been achieved.* Apart from short-term fluctuations, foreign trade was more or less in balance and official gold and currency reserves continued to grow. Nevertheless, some signs at the time of a less favorable long-term development may already have pointed to the violent disturbance in the autumn of 1968. A credit balance in foreign trade was achieved only by means of a slight restriction of domestic demand. It was to be feared that any attempt to reestablish a high level of employment might lead to a deficit. Since 1960 the balance of transactions in goods and services, except those relating to products in the strict sense, had worsened. An annual surplus of 500 million dollars in 1960 and 1961 had been replaced by a rough balance position since 1964. This development was probably due partly to the reduction in expenditure in France by foreign governments, particularly in connection with NATO. But another reason was the increase in transfers of labor income abroad and the disappearance of a credit balance from tourism. And last, in the second half of 1967, as a result of uncertainties about the future of reserve currencies, very large movements of short-term private capital had taken place, as French residents built up gold and currency reserves in foreign countries.

Thus, our examination of the balance of payments has led us to more reserved conclusions than on price changes. The policy of national independence and the growth of French tourism abroad made it necessary to maintain a small but positive trade balance, and therefore a somewhat sharper competitiveness than before for French products.

The Dilemma Between Growth and the Balance of Payments

This brief sketch has endeavored to show the obstacles to growth from foreign trade requirements. The dilemma many countries face from time to time is well known. With too low a rate of economic activity resulting from low demand combined with a weak balance-of-payments position, they attempt alternatively to stimulate growth by policies of expansion and to restrict demand and imports by policies of austerity, with the aim of recovering a balance in foreign trade, which any expansionist approach must endanger. This dilemma is responsible for the vicissitudes experienced over the last 20 years by economic policy in Britain. Has it had effects on growth in France?

We can, it seems, observe the presence of this feature in two periods: the 1950's and the 1960's. The deflationary policy applied from the autumn of 1951 was particularly severe because the balance of payments seemed in serious danger. Growth was therefore deliberately slowed down. Moreover, the application of quotas to imports restricted foreign competition in an uneven way and probably discouraged innovation and improvement in some sectors. Wage increases in 1954 and 1955 can be regarded as due to the pressure of rising domestic demand, but they were not reflected at once in a balance-of-payments deficit. This fact is to be accounted for not only by the protection enjoyed by French industry, but possibly also by the existence of particularly favorable factors in 1955. A balance-of-payments deficit would probably have arisen in 1956 and 1957 even if economic policy at the time had been less exaggeratedly inflationary.

After the sharp devaluation of the years 1958 and 1959, the competitive advantage enjoyed by French firms led to the disappearance of the dilemma between growth and balance of payments. Consequently, rapid economic revival was possible from the end of 1959. The stabilization plan of 1963 was probably motivated by balance-of-payments requirements, but these at that time coincided with the factors needed to reestablish the internal balance of the economy and therefore also of growth. For this reason it was not until 1966 that a contradiction again arose between the measures likely to assist growth on the one hand and the balance of foreign transactions on the other. This situation is still too recent for us to be able to judge its effects with perspective.

To sum up, owing to a sharp devaluation carried out in the middle of the period we are studying, the dilemma that is so restrictive in other countries played only a temporary role in France before 1966, although it probably somewhat slowed down growth between the years 1951 and 1956.

REGULATION OF THE ECONOMY

The dilemma we have just discussed is only one special aspect of the problems involved in choosing an economic policy. Studying how these problems were resolved will throw additional light on our analyses of inflation. We shall consider in particular the periods of slowdown, for it is then that economic policy may have had a more or less helpful effect on growth. According to what decisions were adopted at such times, the conditions necessary for growth may have been reestablished within a shorter or longer period. An examination of the slowdown periods will also enable us to complete our description of short-term developments, since in the first part of this chapter we considered the various phases of inflation. Since, in this regard, the postwar period presents a striking contrast to earlier times, we shall first examine the latter very briefly.

Short-Term Economic Policy Before World War II

Expansion in the 17 years preceding World War I can be broken down broadly into two phases of rapid growth (1896–1900 and 1906–12) on either side of a period in which progress was considerably slower. The pause at the end of 1907 resulting from a depression in the United States was too short to demand our attention, and the reaction to the cyclical swing in 1913 was too closely linked to preparations for the war. We are therefore here interested only in the years 1900–1905.

The downswing in 1900 coincided with a slowdown in investment by firms, but it was due in the first place to the effects of the depression in Germany and Russia. Exports fell in 1900 and 1901. In addition, expectations in French business circles seem to have become substantially less optimistic (the index of prices of shares on the stock exchange fell by 25 percent roughly between 1899 and 1902).

This slowdown did not give rise to any deliberate offsetting government action.[17] In real terms, expenditure by government agencies re-

---

[17] In March 1901, at the end of his speech outlining the aims of the budget bill for 1902, M. Caillaux, then Minister of Finance, spoke as follows: "[This budget] shows, we believe, the desire to restrict public expenditure as far as possible—a desire that has guided us throughout in the 1902 budget, as it did in those for 1901 and 1900." No reference was made to the economic situation of the time.

mained practically constant from 1899 to 1904. An increase of 30 percent can be observed from 1900 to 1902 in expenditure by the Minister
of Public Works, but this was due chiefly to transfers resulting from the
interest-level guarantees made by the government to the railroad companies—it had been neither intended nor even foreseen. In effect, the
slowdown of growth was accepted. The first prime mover in the acceleration experienced from 1905 on was the recovery of exports, which began in 1902.

Over the eight years following the end of World War I, the French
public was haunted by the rise in prices and the fall or fluctuations of
the value of the franc in relation to foreign currencies. It seems, however, that from 1925 on the technical conditions necessary for stabilization were combined. Transactions by government agencies then almost
balanced out—neither investment nor exports were of exceptional size.
There was in fact stagnation of industrial production in 1925.

In a climate of political uncertainty, however, the financial situation
was very unstable as a result of the high level of the short-term public
debt, repayment of which continually placed the Treasury in difficulties, and also because of the lack of control on foreign exchange operations, which made the reaction of the franc very sensitive. The fall of
the franc on the exchange markets from the end of 1924 to the summer
of 1926, as well as the rise in French prices in the second half of 1925
and the first half of 1926, seem due, as we have seen, to an absence of
confidence rather than to an excess of demand.[18]

The stabilization achieved by Poincaré in the summer of 1926 combined a psychological exercise in reestablishing confidence with relatively sharp budgetary action, which took the form chiefly of strengthening the pressure of taxation. Between October–November 1926 and
April–May 1927, the general index of industrial output dropped by 20
percent. Although the size of this drop is partly due to the fact that the
index related mainly to the output of certain basic materials, it cannot
be denied that the braking applied to the economy was considerable.

It is difficult to criticize the stabilization carried out in this way. At
most, it might be said to have been too energetic.[19] But the high rate

[18] A particularly vivid history of those years and those that followed can be seen
in A. Sauvy, *Histoire économique de la France entre les deux guerres*, vol. 1 (Paris,
1965), chaps. 3, 4.

[19] Was the slowdown sharper in 1927 than in 1952? The index of railroad companies' income at constant prices fell by 10 percent between the second quarter
of 1926 and the second quarter of 1927, and also between the fourth quarters of
1951 and 1952. But an examination of most output series seems to show clearly
that the fall was sharper in 1927 than in 1952.

of inflation just before it and the poverty of data for gauging the economy at that time fully account for the fact that the braking applied was not more delicate.

When the Great Depression broke out, France was moving forward in a period of rapid expansion. The various components of domestic demand continued to grow in 1930. Only exports of industrial products began to decline from the spring or summer of 1929. Nevertheless, although France had neither anticipated the depression nor even observed it when it came, in November 1929 the country adopted the same policy as we should recommend today. This is because the accumulation of currency reserves between 1926 and 1929 gave the public the impression that the central government had available the means for a policy of high expenditure. The Tardieu government launched a substantially increased budget for the period April 1, 1930, to March 31, 1931. There can be little doubt that such an action would have set off pronounced inflation if the "prosperity" that the Prime Minister reported had held. But in an economic situation that could be seen increasingly to be turning into depression, this budget had the effect of maintaining in France far less unfavorable conditions than in the other major industrial countries. Although involuntary, economic policy thus turned out particularly appropriate to effective regulation of the economy.

Thereafter public finance played the part of automatic stabilizer as a result of the large scale of transfer payments. Retirement pensions, war pensions, and compensation handed out by the government to large numbers of beneficiaries were set in money terms, so that the public authorities were distributing increased purchasing power as prices dropped. In the same period, a policy of social transfer payments was gradually being introduced (social insurance, unemployment benefits, and family allowances).

It is striking to realize today that the public at that time attributed responsibility for the depression to the deficit in public finance, which in fact had reduced the scale of the slump. Such an independent document as *Mouvement économique en France de 1929 à 1939*, written by the staff of the Statistique Générale de la France and published in 1941, is very revealing on this subject:[20]

The political situation (at the end of 1931) was not really suited to large-scale reforms. The fall of the pound happened at a time when all minds were already turned toward the elections. Depreciation of the British currency was not in any case assessed in France at its true value. Many people considered that this

---

[20] *Mouvement économique en France de 1929 à 1939* (Paris, 1941), p. 103.

event affected only the British economy and that it would set off in that country a rise in domestic prices.

It is therefore not surprising in these conditions that the 1932 budget did
not show any deliberate intention to adapt to circumstances. For the substantial deficit that could be observed upon a first examination of incomings and
outgoings was masked by various financial artifices, among which was the
adoption of a nine-month budget (April–December).

Confronted with the "deflation or devaluation" dilemma, the political
majority chose deflation. This was put into effect in 1933 and 1934 (by
means of an emergency tax on high earnings, reduction in public expenditure, and a drop in civil servants' salaries). Simultaneously, exports, which were hampered by an overvalued exchange rate in relation to foreign currencies, stagnated at a very low level despite the
recovery observed in various countries. In this way, the depression
reached its worst level in 1935.

The coming to power of the Popular Front government in 1936
marked a change of policy. But the new government was badly informed on the real employment situation, and decided on too large
and too widespread a reduction in the hours of work. Production costs
rose and the temporary advantages of the September 1936 devaluation
were quickly eliminated by increased prices. Reluctant to commit themselves in the face of a socialist government in power, management
circles made do with only very low investments. The recovery experienced at the beginning of 1937 gave way to a new downturn at the
end of the year. It was not before the end of 1938 that real improvement could be observed in industrial production.

This bird's-eye view of French economic movements since the beginning of the century shows mainly that the idea of regulating the economy by budgetary means virtually did not exist, or rather, that it
amounted to the simplistic view that reduction in public expenditure
is in all circumstances favorable to equilibrium. It is difficult to criticize
French politicians for this, since the same lack of understanding of the
problem was shared by most economists the world over. It was only
during the last war, and as a result of the theoretical considerations of
Keynes, that a less inadequate theory became widespread. Nevertheless, for very diverse reasons, all the major countries except France
adopted from 1933 an economic policy that was far less clumsy.

Short-Term Economic Regulation After the War

Before turning to an examination of short-term economic policy over
the last 20 years, we should form a clearer picture of the circumstances

in which it was carried out. It is clear that regulation of the economy could take place in a far less unfavorable context than between the two wars. Consequently the question arises as to how we can assess the degree of success of France's short-term policies.

The international environment was of course favorable, since none of the major industrial countries experienced any serious and prolonged crisis, and since the contractions in many cases occurred at different times in different countries. The periods of retarded activity experienced in France since World War II in fact had little to do with repercussions of downswings in the international economic situation; these played some part in 1952 and 1967, but their effects were only limited. There is nothing comparable to the world crises of 1921 and 1930.

Moreover, between 1930 and 1950, considerable progress had been made in understanding the possible scope and means available for government stabilization policies. Experience over the 1930's and the theoretical explanations that were synthesized in Keynes's fundamental work[21] had opened the way to a new concept of the role of government budgets: these should be deliberately expansive in years showing signs of a depressed situation and, on the contrary, should reduce expenditures and build up surpluses in years when the situation was inflationary. These new ideas were clearly understood by a small group of French civil servants and politicians.[22] Some circumstances were therefore present enabling a coherent policy of regulation to be followed.

Comparison between the postwar period and the years between the wars can therefore have no more than limited interest, since the difference in context between the two situations is so great. It would be more significant to compare economic regulation over the past 20 years in France and other countries. But such a comparison would be very difficult if it were to be carried out rigorously. We shall confine ourselves to two comments on this subject.

First, the economic situation was affected by the backlash of violent political and social events in France more than in other countries. The impact on the home economy of events in Algeria was particularly marked: in 1956–57 by inflationary pressure triggered by the intensification of military operations, and in 1962–63 by the special contingency of a massive inflow of repatriates.

Second, it seems to us that by comparison with other Western coun-

[21] J. M. Keynes, *The General Theory of Employment, Interest, and Money* (New York, 1942).

[22] We can take as evidence for this the book published by G. Ardant and P. Mendès-France, *La Science économique et l'action* (Paris, 1952).

tries, the "automatic stabilizers" were weak in the French economy after the war. For a given variation in autonomous demand, the variation of national output should therefore have been greater in France than elsewhere. We shall explain our meaning as follows.

Every analysis of the short-term economic situation must study the effects of variations in activity on the total income available. With the institutions existing in modern countries, these effects are not so large as is suggested by a quick examination of this feature, or for example by the multiplier theory in its simplest form. A slowing down of activity in firms of course leads to an equivalent reduction in the volume of primary income; but the changes induced in income distribution partly offset this reduction (for example, taxes are reduced, most social transfer payments are maintained and some are increased, etc.) These offsetting changes are today given the name "automatic stabilizers."

Extending social security to most of the population had the particular result of increasing automatic stabilization, not only between the prewar and postwar periods but also during the postwar period itself. We believe that France benefited less than other countries from this kind of stabilization, although we have not carried out extensive and precise studies on this question, as would be required for categoric affirmation. We base our views wholly on two facts: first, the small scope and size of progressive taxes on incomes, and second, the low volume of unemployment benefits, at least during the 1950's.

The effect of the French income tax has been clearly analyzed by Fréville.[23] The rates are approximately as progressive as in other countries. The degree of progressivity is suggested by an index of 1.68 as against 2.14 in Great Britain and 1.49 in the United States. But the French tax is not imposed at the source; it is levied—at least the main portion—more than one year on the average after the income is received. The stabilization that this tax could achieve automatically, therefore, in most cases takes place too late. Moreover, the tax affects only a fairly small proportion of households, approximately one-third in the mid-1960's and a lower proportion in earlier years. In the Anglo-Saxon or Scandinavian countries, the proportion of taxpayers is far higher.

In the 1950's, the level of official unemployment benefits was very low in France. A slowdown in the economy was therefore reflected in a drop in incomes without significant offsetting effect from assistance

[23] Y. Fréville, "L'Imposition des revenus des ménages et la conjoncture," in "L'Impôt au service de la politique conjoncturelle," *Statistiques et études financières*, April 1968.

to the unemployed. Over recent years, the official system has been complemented by many contractual insurance plans against unemployment; the situation has therefore significantly changed. But at least in the first half of the postwar period, France was clearly behind most other industrial countries in this respect. As against this, the volume of social transfer payments that are independent of the economic situation (family allowances and retirement pensions) was high.

Economic Budgets and Government Policy

Since 1954, presentation of the French government budget has been preceded by a forecast of total national activity over the period ahead—the so-called "economic budget." For the purpose of studying short-term regulation of the economy, we now ask two questions. Were the authors of the economic budgets able to forecast correctly the chief characteristics of the situation in each year? Did the political authorities adopt appropriate measures and in this way succeed in regulating economic changes in a manner favorable to growth? Let us consider each of these in turn.

The forecast is drawn up in principle in the month of September for the following year;[24] it is based on the known or foreseeable intentions of the various decision-making agents in the economy. For example, capital formation is determined as a function of approved public investment and of investment intentions by industrialists, which are known approximately by means of a survey. Similarly forecasts of expenditure and action in the market by different government agencies are studied and integrated into the forecast. The forecasts of the economic budget are not, therefore, the result of a rigid model, but are an assembly in consistent form of the information available for the year ahead. Let us see how these forecasts compare with the outcomes.

In Table 11.5 we have brought together the main data for this comparison, covering growth in volume of gross domestic production, household consumption, and investment, together with price rises affecting household consumption. We believe these are the chief values whose forecasts determine budget policy.

For the period 1954–59 we have used a report by M. Barjonet to the Economic and Social Council.[25] Although not identical with the figures in the National Accounts, those in this report are based in principle on the same data and are not very different. The divergence, however,

[24] Some budgets are, in fact, prepared at the beginning of the year in question.
[25] M. Barjonet, "Avis et rapports du Conseil économique et social," *Journal officiel*, April 19, 1961.

TABLE 11.5

Comparison of Projected and Actual Growth Rates, 1954–67

(Percent of previous year)

Year	Gross domestic production		Household consumption		Household consumption prices		Gross domestic capital formation[a]	
	Forecast	Outcome	Forecast	Outcome	Forecast	Outcome	Forecast	Outcome
1954	4.6%	5.6%	5.1%	5.2%		1.1%	8.2%	11.7%
1955	6.0	7.3	5.2	7.3		1.1	14.2	11.2
1956	5.0	4.5	5.8	5.6	0.9%	4.3	5.6	8.0
1957	4.5	6.2	5.4	5.4	0.6	4.9	4.2	10.2
1958	2.5	2.2	1.0	0	12.5	12.6	3.0	2.3
1959	0.7	2.2	−2.0	1.1	7.5	5.9	2.9	0.4
1960	5.0	6.3	4.5	4.0	3.0	3.9	7.5	5.6
1961	5.0	4.5	5.0	5.4	2.5	3.7	6.5	8.0
1962	5.5	6.3	5.5	6.7	2.3	4.3	6.5	7.5
1963	6.1	4.8	6.0	6.4	2.0	5.1	6.2	5.9
1964	4.2	5.7	4.3	4.1	3.5	3.6	4.6	8.5
1965	4.3	3.5	4.3	3.2	1.8	2.5	5.3	7.4
1966	4.5	5.0	4.1	4.6	2.0	3.0	5.4	5.8
1967	5.3	4.4	4.8	4.1	2.4	3.0	7.2	6.3

[a]Including stock variation in 1954 and 1955.

is not important enough to alter the chief conclusions to be drawn from the table.

For the years 1960 to 1970, the estimates we have used in relation to the budget forecasts are those that would have been included in the final accounts if no change had been introduced in the accounting rules. This procedure is obviously essential to ensure comparability between forecasts and outcomes, and it explains the differences between the figures in Table 11.5 and those in the other tables of this book.

Table 11.5 shows forecasts of household consumption to be fairly reliable but price forecasts to be generally far too optimistic. The forecasts of gross domestic production differ from realization more than do forecasts of household consumption, essentially as a result of large errors in foreign trade results; nevertheless forecasts of gross domestic production were fairly accurate. Similarly, forecasts of investment growth, although different from the outcomes in 1957, were nevertheless fairly close for other years. The volume forecasts were therefore more accurate than the price forecasts.

In the case of household consumption, the errors were large for 1955 and 1959. In 1955 the relationship between production and the uses to which it was put had about the same pattern as was forecast, but at a higher level and with stable prices. In particular, wage incomes of households increased by almost 10 percent over the 1954 level, compared with a forecast increase of 5 percent. For 1959, the budget forecast a revival, led by investment and without much slowdown in the pace of price rises. The fact that prices rose by a point and a half less rapidly than forecast and that investment remained stationary explains a larger increase in household consumption and in gross domestic production than forecast.

The chief differences between forecasts and results in gross domestic production can be accounted for by differences of the same order in household consumption. It can also be seen that the forecasts were more often too low than too high. This is probably an effect of the caution reflex of forecasters, who generally consider it less serious to underestimate growth and to slightly exaggerate the scale of necessary measures to redress the situation, than to err by overoptimism, which entails the risk of obscuring likely difficulties.

For investment, the forecasts were obviously difficult, and they show a tendency to underestimation. The highest error was in relation to investment by firms in 1959. Similarly, in 1960, housing construction and the effect of measures taken at the end of 1959 to reactivate investment were overstated.

And finally, price changes were in few cases satisfactorily assessed in advance. Resumption of the increase in 1956 and the relatively high growth in 1963 were not forecast. Moreover, the table should not mislead concerning the precision reached in 1958: the forecast was made at the beginning of that year, when most of the evidence of price rises was already available, and was therefore not a statement of a probable future movement but largely a recording of a movement already in the past.

To forecast changes in trend is both important and particularly difficult. From this viewpoint the slowdown in 1958 was well anticipated at a time when such an estimate seemed pessimistic. On the other hand, however, the revival of growth in 1959 was not expected as early as it occurred. Last, we have seen that accelerations in price rises could not be forecast, and this is obviously a serious difficulty. Inflation and the foreign deficit resulting from it were in fact responsible for the various slowdowns in the growth of output, since the stabilization measures inevitably resulted in a slowing down of expansion. If they had been forecast in time, these risks of price increases could have led to faster action, with results less prejudicial to growth. It can be seen also that the 1967 downturn, which was set off principally by the slowing down in exports, was not foreseen.

In brief, some aspects of short-term economic development evaded those responsible for drawing up the economic budgets. Nevertheless, the public authorities, on the whole, had before them a clear and fairly exact picture of the situation over the year ahead.

In addition to the economic budget, there were from time to time short-term analyses by which errors in the initial forecasts could be corrected fairly rapidly and appropriate measures taken in order to rectify government policy. The quality of the economic information made available in this way stands in striking contrast to the poverty of data existing before the war.

Short-Term Economic Policy Since World War II

Certain factors, linked chiefly to the vagaries of decolonization, affected the short-term stability of France's economy over the 20 years following the end of the war. In addition, the automatic stabilizers probably played a smaller part in France than in other countries. But by comparison with earlier periods, governments were far better prepared to draw up economic policies for the regulation of the economy. At the risk of some repetition, we shall now take up again the history of these 20 years in order to judge the effect of these policies.

After the rapid inflation of the immediate postwar period, stabilization was first achieved in the autumn of 1948. It remained somewhat precarious, however, since reconstruction was being carried out very fast in the basic sectors, and both private enterprise and households felt strongly the need to renew equipment and build up stocks. Consequently, the worldwide wave of price rises set off by the outbreak of the Korean war found favorable conditions in France.

Although the French authorities cannot be held responsible for the initial disequilibrium, they can be blamed for allowing inflation to develop as far as it did and for not stopping it as early as the spring of 1951, when the trend reversed on world markets. The chief positive action of the government was to refuse whenever possible to embody the impact of the rises in prices in the 1951 state budget approved at the beginning of the year. Although public sector consumption increased in volume by 15 percent between 1950 and 1951, probably in part as a result of military expenditure considered difficult to cut down, investment by government agencies increased by only 1 percent, and that by public enterprises dropped by about 10 percent.

As in 1926, objective conditions necessary for stabilization were reached; this was at the end of 1951, when M. Pinay formed a new government. Confidence was restored more easily than in 1926, since inflation had reached a more advanced stage. By hindsight, the restrictions imposed at that time now seem rather minor. Quite the reverse, however, public finances, which had shown surpluses from 1949 to 1951, had slight deficits in 1952. Although investment by public enterprises still fell in relation to the previous year, investment by government agencies increased by 15 percent, and public sector consumption grew by over 40 percent under the effect of military expenditure linked to the setting up of NATO divisions. These expenditures made necessary by events might have contributed to recovery; but this did not take place before 1953, and seems to have been neither stimulated by the government nor appreciated particularly early by forecasters: the growth of 4.6 percent in indicated production, shown for the year 1954 in Table 11.5, comes from an assessment made at the beginning of 1954; the estimate made in September 1953 expected a growth of 3.7 percent for output and 3.3 percent for household consumption.

When the socialist government came to power at the beginning of 1956, the domestic situation was healthy, since output had been growing at a rapid rate for two years and the general level of prices remained stable. Nevertheless, a positive balance of foreign trade was reached only because of import quotas and export bonuses that partially offset the overvaluation of the franc in relation to foreign currencies.

The government wished to stress social policy at home. In addition, it decided during the first weeks in office to intensify military operations in Algeria; this had the double effect of raising government expenditure and reducing available manpower through drafting certain age-groups and lengthening military service. To maintain equilibrium, it would obviously have been appropriate to take offsetting deflationary action, and in particular to raise taxes. But the government wished to believe, and wished it to be believed, that the military action in Algeria would be temporary and that the home country could easily carry the cost. It therefore allowed imbalances to appear and to grow larger.

The deficit in the balance of payments, which was very high in 1956, remained high in 1957 and caused currency reserves to be exhausted. Although prices were frozen and strictly controlled, the general whole-sale price index grew by 5 percent in 1956 and by 14 percent in 1957. Stabilization measures became essential.

Successive governments carried this out from the end of 1957. They managed to remove the budget deficit by reducing government consumption by nearly 10 percent, raising taxes directly or indirectly,[26]

---

[26] One of the most important factors in the direct rise of taxes was the maintenance of the progressive income tax schedule at a time when nominal incomes were rising substantially.

and increasing economic and transfer payments (in particular, family allowances) far less than the rise in prices would have justified. These measures enabled prices to be stabilized and made it possible to start restoring the balance of payments. The same objectives were followed in 1959. Moreover, the beginning of effective application of the Common Market obliged France to introduce a very wide freeing of foreign trade. This was made possible by the choice of a realistic exchange rate for the franc (amounting to devaluation of 15 percent). To reactivate investment, the government accelerated public ordering, in particular by nationally owned enterprises. In May it instituted an accelerated amortization rule for orders made before the end of the year. The effect of these measures was felt from 1959 on, even earlier than had been expected. From 1960, expansion continued at a sustained rate, with no large rise in prices, until 1962.

From the viewpoint of autumn 1962, the situation of the economy in 1963 appeared in a light that was quite new for France. Whereas the size of the working population had remained practically constant over the previous 15 years, a large increase was to be expected as a result of the massive return to the home country of 700,000 persons living in Algeria, and as the first large postwar age-group reached working age. The experts foretold a slowing down of the labor market and feared some underemployment. They recommended an expansionary policy.

Although no particular measures were taken, the economic situation became increasingly inflationary over the year 1963, and the labor market remained in balance. The experts had thus been mistaken: the productive system's ability to absorb labor was much greater than they had forecast; the high demand emanating from the repatriates from Algeria gave the necessary stimulus to an increase in activity and even led to pressure on prices as a result of the differential between the repatriates' demand for goods and housing and their demand for work.[27]

In order to stem the rise in prices, the government adopted in the summer of 1963 "a plan for economic and financial stabilization," which consisted chiefly of freezing prices and sharply limiting credit. At the same time it drew up a relatively hard budget for 1964, which was reflected in a large surplus and therefore in a net lending position for the government sector.

This deflationary action was less strong than that in 1958, and was

[27] In order to be complete in our analysis of the 1963 inflation, we must mention some factors that tended to reduce supply: a bad winter, strikes in the coal industry, and the award of a fourth week of paid vacation to a high proportion of wage earners.

slow to achieve effects, but it was enough to brake the rise in prices. As a result, the growth of industrial output stopped from the spring of 1964 to the spring of 1965. But the ground to be made up by output was smaller than in 1958.

Recovery began in 1965, approaching normal in early 1966. The government and the experts believed that expansion was now assured for several years. They therefore paid no attention at first to the slowdown that began in the autumn of 1966, chiefly under the effect of economic stagnation abroad, particularly in Germany. The newly acquired sensitivity of France to the economic situation in its neighbors caused surprise. Accordingly, it was not until June and September 1967 that deliberately expansionist measures were adopted (tax reductions, increased credits to building, facilities for credit sales, etc.). The winter of 1967–68 saw recovery, but apparently not strong enough, since the labor market experienced some unemployment that was not being absorbed by spring.

To sum up, three of the four economic slowdowns experienced in France since 1950 are accounted for by the need for anti-inflationary action. For each of the three relevant inflations, the government had an excuse: in 1951 the repercussion of the Korean war on prices of raw materials, and heavy foreign demand; in 1957 military operations in Algeria; in 1963 the effect of repatriation, and forecasters' mistaken appreciation of the short-term situation. These excuses are probably valid for the last period, but they do not explain why the 1951 and 1956–57 inflations went as far as they did. As for the slowdown in 1966–67, it could have been noticed—or so it seems—and stopped more quickly and energetically than it was. We cannot therefore consider short-term regulation of the economy as having been perfect since the war, even if we recognize that certain accidental events were inevitable.

Nevertheless, we may consider that by comparison with prewar periods economic regulation was on the whole favorable to growth. It attempted not only to slow inflationary movements but to resume expansion after the slowdowns in 1958 and 1964. The pause in the economy was less marked in 1958 than in 1952, and weaker in 1964 than in 1958. Although growth was inevitable in the immediate postwar period, it could have lost impetus over time and gradually slowed. From our viewpoint, the economic climate in the 1960's is more important than in the years 1950–55. A relatively regular expansion maintained from 1959 probably accounts partly for the high rate of growth of output sustained. Had it not been for the social shock in 1968, France would probably have been in danger of experiencing a slower rate of growth in the second part of the decade. With the inflation that followed, however, this danger disappeared.

A recent article by W. W. Snyder analyzes the effects of French budgetary policy between 1955 and 1965 and compares France with a number of other countries.[28] He estimates that the stabilization achieved over the whole of this period was 29 percent of the "pure cycle" that would have been experienced if, other things being equal, budgetary policy had been perfectly neutral. If this proportion is relatively low, it is because of the unduly expansionary budgets of the years 1956, 1957, 1962, and 1963. Despite this, the degree of stabilization was higher in France than in the United States and Italy, although lower than in Sweden, and comparable with that achieved in the United Kingdom.

In any economic history of development in France in the twentieth century, inflation must hold an important place. It brought a profound transformation in the structure of wealth and income in the country. The public was too well aware of the loss of prestige that inflation brought with it for this feature to be entirely neglected.

For us, who have limited our aim to an explanatory study of growth, inflation has less importance. Owing to devaluations that restored foreign competitiveness without resorting to prolonged deflations, as well as to an economic policy for the short term that despite errors achieved a certain degree of regulation, inflation had few damaging repercussions on expansion. Its chief effects can be analyzed from two aspects. First, wartime and immediate postwar inflation swallowed earlier assets and liabilities, thus creating certain favorable conditions for later growth of savings by households and of investment by firms. The change in nature of France's economic development was helped by this financial cleanup of the past. Second, unduly easy business conditions, as well as some of the measures adopted to maintain the balance of payments, probably slowed improvements in productivity in the years 1952–57.

Inflation therefore clearly had a certain impact on French growth. But in a causal analysis it cannot amount to more than one factor among others.

[28] W. W. Snyder, "La Mesure des résultats des politiques budgétaires françaises de 1955 à 1965," *Revue économique*, November 1969.

CHAPTER TWELVE

Foreign Trade and the Growth of Productivity

The rapid increase in trade between France and other countries is one of the characteristic features of growth over the past decade. This increase was stimulated by the creation of the Common Market and more generally by a policy of international trade liberalization; without doubt it assisted the progress of national productivity. Faced by a market whose geographical boundaries were receding, firms were able to specialize increasingly and to take advantage of economies of scale, which frequently were large. Thus expansion of foreign trade is one of the explanatory factors of French growth. To measure this feature we are led once again to look at the past and to relate changes in production and foreign trade from the beginning of the century. But a more exact study of the postwar period obviously is necessary.

In the first part of this chapter, which is devoted to a description of broad trends, we pay particular attention to industrial products, where the greatest effects of specialization are most likely to be felt.

The second part of the chapter concerns a number of factors relevant to explanatory analysis. Making use of studies by various authors, it will in particular exhibit the role of changes in the structure of foreign demand, and especially the impact of the creation of the Common Market.

In the third part of the chapter we shall discuss various attempts to measure the stimulating effects of the opening up of frontiers. We shall attempt to assess what part should be ascribed to them in the growth of French productivity.

THE EXPANSION OF FOREIGN TRADE

Long-Term Trends

France's foreign trade had a relatively steady growth over the nineteenth century and up to 1929. The Great Depression and World War II reversed this trend for a period of 15 years before the very sharp revival in the last 25 years. For a detailed account, the best procedure is probably to compare changes in imports and exports with changes in production. It can then be seen that over the last 20 years the growth of foreign trade was almost twice as fast as that of production. This is a feature peculiar to the postwar period, since from the beginning of the century imports and exports increased only at an average rate on the same order as that of production.

Of course, available statistics are somewhat sketchy for the earlier periods. We have already seen how production was evaluated at the different key years in our study. Statistics of foreign trade by value must be fairly well recorded by customs sources, but it is more difficult to deduce changes in volume. Indexes of volume of imports and exports exist from 1913 for three categories of products.[1] In order to go back as far as 1896, we have had to make some assumptions on the growth of prices. The index of industrial wholesale prices, which one might consider using as an indicator of export prices, is unfortunately based on raw materials to a greater extent than on finished products. From 1896 to 1901 it experienced sharp and large variations not related to the growth of wages and therefore not too significant a reflection of the prices of manufactured goods. For export prices we ultimately used an index of 105 for increases over the period 1896–1901 and the index of average values for foreign trade as a whole for increases over the period 1901–13.[2] For increases over the whole period 1896–1913, the price index is therefore 123.

For imports, we have recorded the country of origin and the nature of the products. Import prices of manufactured products have been taken as equal to export prices, and a similar assumption has been made in the case of all products from industrialized countries. The remainder of imports must consist of agricultural products (20 percent of the total including tropical products) and raw materials, whose prices may have undergone very different changes. In order to measure the discrepancy between domestic and import prices of these various goods, we have compared the general price index with that of a selected number of

[1] These indexes are for food products, materials required by industry, and manufactured goods. For the postwar period the breakdown is a little different: human foods, raw materials and semi-processed products, and manufactured products. (*Annuaire statistique de la France, rétrospectif*; Paris, 1961.)

[2] For 1896–1901 the wholesale price index is 116, and that of male wage rates is 108 in Paris and 105 in the provinces. The index of labor productivity can be assessed at approximately 107. From 1901 on, *Annuaire rétrospectif* provides a volume index of foreign trade as a whole (imports plus exports). The relationship between the value index and this volume index constitutes an "index of average values," which can be taken as a price index.

TABLE 12.1

The Growth of Foreign Trade and Production, 1896–1969

(Beginning of each period = 100)

Category	1896–1913 17 yrs.	1913–1929 16 yrs.	1929–1938 9 yrs.	1938–1949 11 yrs.	1949–1963 14 yrs.	1963–1969[a] 6 yrs.
Gross domestic production	139	134	96	111	197	135
Imports	182	133	80	101	272	193
Exports	162	147	62	118	287	170
Total foreign trade (imports plus exports)	170	139	72	108	280	181

[a]For the sake of homogeneity, the index of gross domestic production for the last period is that in the series on a 1962 basis, reduced by 0.7 percent per year.

imported commodities. This suggests that prices of imported goods rose significantly less fast than prices of domestic goods: only a small number of goods have an index higher than that of domestic prices, in the case of both industrial raw materials and agricultural products. It is particularly striking to note the very low price indexes of tropical products: 107 for sugar imported from the colonies, 103 for foreign sugar, 125 for cocoa, and 77 for coffee.

For the period 1896–1913 we adopted the export price index, that is 123, for imports from industrialized countries (50 percent of all imports), the index 130 for purchases of industrial raw materials from other countries (30 percent), and the index 115 for imports of agricultural products (20 percent). The price indexes are then 123 for manufactured products, 125 for industrial products, and 123 for imports as a whole.

Table 12.1 shows the development of foreign trade compared with that of aggregate production. Results relating to industrial products alone are shown in Table 12.2. We have also examined separately "manufactured objects" for which particular features arising out of specialization may have played a part and which we shall study in more detail for the postwar period. This group comprises products of the mechanical and electrical industries; chemicals; textiles, clothing, and leather; and wood, paper, toys, etc., known as miscellaneous products. The results are shown in the second part of Table 12.2. The periods considered are those used elsewhere in the book.

From 1896 to 1929, the volume of foreign trade grew slightly faster than that of production (the average annual rates were 2.6 and 1.9 percent, respectively, based on the results in Table 12.1). The same conclusion emerges from an examination of the results relating to manufactured products. Some international specialization was already under way

TABLE 12.2
*The Growth of Production and Foreign Trade of Industrial
Products, 1896–1963*
(Beginning of each period = 100)

Category	1896–1913	1913–1929	1929–1938	1938–1949	1949–1963
Industry:[a]					
Value added	152	155	91	109	213
Imports	189	133	78	106	289
Exports	166	153	61	120	280
Total foreign trade	172	143	70	113	285
Manufactured products:[b]					
Value added	152	149	91	106	236
Imports	212	142	58	147	334
Exports	166	169	56	137	263
Total foreign trade	175	162	57	140	290

[a]Figures for value added are from the National Accounts. Imports and exports are nonagricultural. For foreign trade, the approximate weighting is 1 for imports and 3 for exports.

[b]For value added we have considered four industry groups: mechanical and electrical industries; chemicals; textiles, clothing, and leather; and miscellaneous products. For foreign trade we have used the item "manufactured objects" up to 1938, and thereafter "manufactured products."

in that period, and this despite the fact that World War I obliged the French economy to find substitutes for some of its foreign sources of supply.[3]

The cessation of growth caused by the 1930 depression was very sharp. Under the effect first of a drop in world demand and then of exchange controls and other obstacles to international commerce, France's trade with other countries dropped between 1929 and 1938 by almost half in the case of manufactured products. This situation was made worse by the war. Nevertheless, after return to a relatively normal situation in 1949, the position seemed slightly less imbalanced than in 1938. As compared with the position in 1929, it was nevertheless marked by a degree of self-sufficiency. Whereas aggregate production and the production of manufactured products stood at levels close to those reached 20 years earlier, foreign trade was still lower by more than 20 percent. Despite a marked slowdown between 1951 and 1957, the growth of trade reached an impressive scale in the period 1949–69. Trade as a whole grew by a factor of 5, i.e. at an annual rate averaging 8.4 percent per year; trade in manufactured products grew by a factor of 6, or at an average rate

[3] The figures suggested by C. P. Kindleberger for France, insofar as they are significant, also show an increase in foreign trade faster than that of production between 1840 and 1896; see his *Foreign Trade and the National Economy* (New Haven, 1962).

of 9.4 percent. In both cases, trade grew almost twice as fast as production.[4]

A Return to Normal Conditions, or Accelerated Freeing of Trade?

This very rapid increase in the volume of trade does not represent simply a return to a situation comparable with that of 1929. True, there was still quite a lag in foreign trade behind production around 1950; any policy aimed at reestablishing earlier trade flows would have set off a sharp increase in exports and imports. But it can be said that around 1963 a situation comparable with that of 1929 had been reached once again. According to our estimates, annual production had by then grown by a factor of 2.1 since 1929; the index of volume of imports at the same time had grown by a factor of 2.2 for all items together, and by a factor of 2.9 for manufactured objects taken separately; the index of volume of exports with 1929 = 1 stood at 2.1 for all items together and at 2.0 for manufactured objects. In 1969, on the contrary, foreign trade had moved substantially ahead of production (4.2 for imports, 3.6 for exports, and 2.8 for production on the same base, 1929 = 1).

Looking at long-term trends, we note, to be sure, that the increase in foreign trade in relation to that of production over the 40 years 1929–69 was fairly comparable with that over the 33 years 1896–1929: the average growth rate of trade was about 35 percent higher than that of production in each of these two periods. This fact, however, probably cannot be interpreted as representing return to a normal manner of growth.

For one thing, what would be the significance of such a manner of growth? One might infer from it high elasticity of the French economy's demand for imported products: for a steady expansion of 10 percent in production, France would need to increase imports by about 13.5 percent; the need to maintain a balance of trade would make necessary similar growth in exports. But such high elasticity in imports can never be justified by reference to "needs." Technical progress and changes in the structure of consumption brought about by increases in real incomes, on the contrary, have the effect of reducing the ratio between imports of foreign raw materials and volume of production. The elasticity observed, in fact, results from the rapid development of imports of prod-

---

[4] This result may seem to contradict the apparent stability of the ratio of imports or exports to gross domestic production: since 1949 this ratio has remained at around 12 percent. But this is a result appearing in the National Accounts "in current prices." Average import prices have grown far less rapidly than the price index of gross domestic production (especially because prices of services and building costs are growing particularly fast).

ucts that the French economy could manufacture itself. So there is no
need to give special prominence to imports when attempting to explain
why foreign trade grows faster than production.

For another thing, the recent development would signify return to a
normal manner of growth only if over the 1960's the relationship between growth rates of trade and of production had tended to approximate the 135 percent in question. However, this was not the case. The
acceleration of trade appears, on the contrary, to be a lasting trend,
likely to continue for a long time yet.

Specialization in the Postwar Period

The absence of any slowdown appears clearly in all the statistical
data. As an example, Table 12.3 shows some indexes of volume for the
three six-year periods corresponding to "cycles" of French economic
activity. The highest indexes relate to the last period (1963–69), although differences in comparison with the previous period are in most
cases small. Short-term economic movements at the time, which we will
now briefly recall, were certainly rather diverse; but the annual fluctuations do not contradict the continuation of a rising trend at a high rate
of growth.

Between 1949 and 1951 imports increased. They remained almost
static for textiles, and increased—as did production—for mechanical
and electrical products, for miscellaneous products, and for chemicals.
This period is closer to the immediate postwar years than to the following period in regard to both foreign trade and production. In particular,
imports of "manufactured" products were twice as high in 1946 and
1947, when supplies again began to come from abroad, than in 1949;
the low growth up to 1951 may be the consequence of this starting level,
which seemed high in that period. The 1952 stabilization, as later the
1958 devaluation, led in all commodity groups to a marked drop in imports. The 1951 level was in general barely regained in 1954, whereas
the 1957 level was substantially surpassed in 1960. From 1953 to 1957,
imports increased markedly faster than did production.

Exports followed a contrary road at the beginning of the period. Starting from a level in 1946 equal to half that in 1938, they rose very rapidly until 1949 and continued to grow until 1951. Thereafter they increased only moderately. Exports in 1956 showed a very marked low
point for manufactured products as a result of the high growth of demand and of domestic prices. In 1958 and 1959, exports increased very
fast as a result of devaluation, and maintained a sustained although grad-

TABLE 12.3

The Growth of Foreign Trade, 1951–69

(Beginning of each period = 100)

Period	All trade		Manufactured products	
	Imports	Exports	Imports	Exports
1951–57	149	120	178	108
1957–63	164	170	247	173
1963–69	193	170	250	170

ually slowing rate of growth until 1963. The revival of exports from the end of 1963 on continued at a fast rate until a plateau was reached extending from the spring of 1966 to the summer of 1967, which reflected chiefly the repercussions of the drop in activity in West Germany. A new upward climb observed in the winter of 1967–68 continued, although more slowly, at the end of 1968 and in 1969.

The growth of imports in the 1960's experienced two jumps: in the year 1963 and in the period from summer 1968 to summer 1969. In both these cases the increase was on the order of 25 percent per year. By contrast, the other periods experienced a moderate increase or even a stable situation (in the years 1964 and 1967). But over the 1960's as a whole, import statistics show a rise that, as we have seen, is far greater than that of production.

This rapid growth in foreign trade can be taken as proof of increased specialization in France's productive system. In this context let us consider the following two questions. Could specialization have occurred without foreign trade growing faster than production? Could the level of trade have increased relative to that of production without specialization taking place? A negative answer to the first question clearly seems needed. Before specializing, French producers attempted themselves to manufacture all the products demanded on the domestic market as well as certain products demanded on preferential foreign markets. Since they were not internationally competitive, they sought to limit imports by obtaining the maintenance of customs duties or quotas. Similarly, exports were restricted to some products that were internationally competitive or to preferential markets. Foreign trade was then small.

Starting from a protected situation, as customs barriers dropped and the effects of international competition began to be felt, it was difficult for any national products to be competitive. Imports of those products in which France was least competitive therefore increased rapidly, restricting the domestic market of producers, who had to attempt to make their products more competitive, and to seek foreign markets for those products that could be made competitive. The phenomenon of specialization, which led some forms of production to be abandoned and others to be considerably developed, was sure to lead to faster growth of foreign trade than of production.

For the above program to be fully persuasive, a rapid increase in trade would have had to reflect real specialization. A theoretical case could be constructed to question the conclusion reached. Let us suppose that domestic and foreign products are strictly comparable in price and quality and that trade in them is at first low. If, after customs barriers have been suppressed, consumers in all the countries concerned were to buy indifferently a national or a foreign product, the share of French products in their consumption should be the same in every country, including France. To reach this situation, a rapid increase in trade would be necessary, by hypothesis starting from a low level; this phenomenon would not reflect any specialization.

It is probable that this theoretical case does not arise often, even in an approximate form. The example of automobiles, sometimes given as an illustration, seems to us on the contrary to confirm the hypothesis that specialization did occur. Of course, the number of French models offered to households has increased since 1949; but faced by the obvious variety in consumers' tastes and the very large number of models that it is possible to make, manufacturers have not tended to diversify their output very widely; they have accepted the fact that a growing share of the domestic market will evade them and at the same time have tried with varying success to increase their exports.

It must be noted, however, that specialization operates not between industry groups but at a far more refined level. Even with relatively detailed nomenclatures by products, no case is observed in which French production and exports decline while imports increase rapidly. The typical design for the industry groups is on the contrary the same as for the productive system as a whole: trade grows faster than production, but fairly similarly between exports and imports.

As an example, Table 12.4 shows results for the four industry groups that produce manufactured objects.[5] The design we have referred to can be seen particularly clearly from 1957 on; the earlier period is less

[5] The change in methods of drawing up the National Accounts means that this table cannot conveniently be continued beyond 1966. But an examination of statistics available shows that the earlier trends continued over recent years.

TABLE 12.4
The Growth of Foreign Trade and Production in Selected Industry Groups, 1951–66
(Beginning of each period = 100)

Category	09. Mechanical and electrical industries	10. Chemicals	11. Textiles	12. Miscellaneous industries
1951–57:				
Imports	116	178	130	167
Exports	114	130	99	102
Production	149	153	127	133
1957–63:				
Imports	205	176	145	208
Exports	179	217	147	154
Production	145	166	125	139
1957–66:				
Imports	295	270	181	287
Exports	234	325	166	197
Production	169	216	131	164

TABLE 12.5
Trade in Semi-Manufactured and Manufactured Products, 1959 and 1968
(Current values)

Product	Balance of trade[a] (million francs)		Index of exports, 1968 (1959=100)
	1959	1968	
Semi-manufactured products:			
Iron and steel products	2,863	1,359	127
Chemical products	1,177	1,221	301
Textile products	701	847	203
Total	4,317	2,833	198
Capital goods:			
Metal products	409	−33	196
Machine tools	−237	−413	395
Equipment for public works and the steel industry	74	117	362
Precision equipment	−102	−715	402
Other mechanical machinery	544	366	276
Electrical equipment	612	−12	298
Tractors	−113	−527	332
Aircraft and ships	134	557	382
Total	1,525	−660	309
Consumer goods:			
Automobiles	2,945	2,283	187
Textiles and leather	2,300	1,996	189
Mfd. wood products and paper	360	−710	203
Miscellaneous products	751	367	245
Total	6,356	4,936	196

[a]Exports FOB less imports CIF.

interesting as a result of the discrepancy at that time between French and foreign prices, as well as of restrictions imposed by trade control policies.

The same picture emerges from Table 12.5, where the balance of trade as shown in the customs statistics are reproduced for the two years 1959 and 1968, and for selected groups of semi-manufactured and manufactured products. This comparison raises at least three difficulties of interpretation: the results are in values, and are therefore affected by the general increase in prices; from the point of view of foreign trade, the short-term situation in the two years compared was very different (a surplus in 1959 and a deficit in 1968); and finally, the balances calculated are differences between CIF values of imports and FOB values of exports. Nevertheless, Table 12.5 shows clearly that the growth of exports was not particularly high in the 1960's for products on which the French economy had a trade surplus, and where it therefore seemed to have an advantage in specialization. On the other hand, growth was substantial for products such as machine tools and precision equipment, of which France is a net importer.

STRUCTURAL CAUSES OF THE GROWTH OF FOREIGN TRADE

The vigorous growth in foreign trade since World War II thus appears as a phenomenon that was sustained, lasting, and very widespread, since it affects most groups of industrial products. It can very naturally be ascribed to policy decisions that led to freeing of trade and to the creation of new institutional structures for transactions between the countries of the European Economic Community. Nevertheless, before testing the truth of this interpretation, we should probably examine how far changes affecting the structure by products and by countries of foreign trade are themselves responsible for part of this phenomenon.

The Structure of Foreign Trade

A good deal of the export growth would be accounted for if it could be shown that world demand grew at a particularly rapid pace either for those products that France was in the habit of exporting or from countries that are its natural customers. To determine exactly what part may have been played by this factor would require too long and detailed analytical studies; we shall therefore content ourselves with quoting some results borrowed from three studies, of which two, unfortunately, do not cover the most recent years.

D. L. Phan has studied the growth of French exports in manufactured products between 1953 and 1962.[6] He observed that they grew faster than did world exports (by 117 percent as against 85 percent over the 9 years considered). In order to isolate a residual that he then interprets as reflecting the effect of the favorable course of French prices, he has calculated two effects of changes in world demand: (1) a "structure by product effect," which he designates as $x_s - x$ equal to the difference between an index x_s, which measures the value that French exports would have reached if France's share of total world exports of each product had remained stable, and an index x representing actual world exports; and (2) a "structure effect by destination," $x_{sl} - x_s$, which introduces the index number x_{sl} measuring the value that French exports would have reached if France's share of world exports of each product toward each geographical area had remained constant.

The effects in question are −1.5 percent in the case of structure by product, and 16 percent in the case of structure by destination: French exports benefited from the country's position as supplier to its European neighbors, whose imports grew far faster than did world imports. But this accounts for only about half of the improvement in the French share of world exports. Moreover, this structure effect appears to have applied between 1953 and 1958 but to have disappeared entirely between 1958 and 1962. It cannot therefore explain the acceleration in trade observed after 1958.

Under the direction of M. Courcier, the Groupe d'Etudes Prospectives sur les Echanges Internationaux (GEPEI) studied the growth between 1954 and 1960 in imports and exports of countries of the European Economic Community, the United Kingdom, the United States, and Canada for iron and steel products, textiles, chemicals, and the products of the mechanical and electrical industries. For each country and each product, a "growth effect" for imports was first estimated, taken as equal to an index of domestic production of that product; it therefore measures the growth that imports would have reached if they had retained a constant share of the market. This hypothetical growth of imports by each country was then broken down between the various supplying countries in proportion to their share in 1954. For each country and each product, after aggregation of hypothetical sales to other countries, a "growth effect" for exports was thus obtained.

Courcier's growth effect, which is defined in a narrower manner than

---

[6] D. L. Phan, "La Position concurrentielle de la France sur le marché mondial," *Bulletin du CEPREL* (Paris), no. 5, October 1965. See also D. L. Phan, *Effets de structure et mécanisme des prix dans la demande d'exportation* (Paris, 1968).

Phan's structure effects, accounts for only a relatively small part of the improvement in French exports between 1954 and 1960 (for half in the case of chemicals, but for under a quarter for textile products and those of the mechanical and electrical industries). Similarly, French imports increased faster than the corresponding growth effects. Once again we see in the results of these calculations proof of international specialization, which was already becoming apparent in the second half of the 1950's.

Examining the period from 1958 to 1967, H. Coste has studied the growth of French exports toward a number of importing countries (Germany, Belgium, the United States, Great Britain, Italy, the Netherlands, and Switzerland).[7] He has calculated a structure effect applying to France's share in each of these markets' imports from the major industrial countries. This effect relates to a hypothetical situation in which on each market in question the French share remains constant *for each major group of products*. Because of changes in demand, the French share in aggregate imports would nevertheless have altered. It can be seen, in fact, that in most markets France on this basis would have had a slightly falling share: imports of products on which France was relatively less well placed in 1958 than its competitors have tended to grow fastest. In fact, the French proportion grew very strongly in the Netherlands (75 percent), substantially in Italy (37 percent) and in Switzerland (22 percent); it fell only in the United States (−16 percent). Thus French exporters on the whole were able to increase their penetration of foreign markets. But this result was achieved in the period 1958–61, helped by the advantage of devaluation and starting from a year in which French exports were only moderate.

On the whole, therefore, it seems that changes in the structure of foreign demand did not play an essential part in the development of France's foreign trade.

Creation of the Common Market

The changes in French foreign trade observed over the last decade seem to have been profoundly marked by the setting-up of the European Economic Community. Whereas trade with franc-zone countries was stagnating in value and falling in volume, exchanges with the Common Market partners were growing at a far faster rate than those with other trade areas. Table 12.6 shows this so clearly that no detailed analysis seems necessary.

[7] H. Coste, "Compétitivité et commerce extérieur français," *Statistiques et études financières*, quarterly, no. 3, 1971.

TABLE 12.6
The Growth of Trade by Area of Origin and Destination, 1959–68
(1959 = 100)

Area	Imports	Exports
European Economic Community	486	358
European Free Trade Area	230	233
Other countries outside the franc zone	237	247
Franc-zone countries	124	93
Total	275	226

TABLE 12.7
Trade with EEC Countries as a Proportion of French Foreign Trade, 1913–68
(Percent)

Trade	1913	1929	1949	1959	1968
Imports	24.0%	23.5%	15.2%	26.8%	47.3%
Exports	35.5	30.8	17.5	27.2	42.9

Note: Countries originally comprising the Common Market were Belgium, France, Italy, Luxembourg, the Netherlands, and West Germany.

We can make a brief comparison between recent developments and earlier trends. The changes in Germany's frontiers mean that this can be done only roughly. Table 12.7 is nevertheless interesting. It shows that in 1949 the share of France's European partners in its foreign trade was well below the norm. By 1959, however, it had recovered a level reasonably in line with what earlier trends might have foretold: roughly a quarter in the case of both imports and exports. The accelerated growth that occurred between 1959 and 1968 seems exceptional in relation not only to the distant past but also to changes observed between 1949 and 1959. The share of the Common Market countries had grown over the ten years following 1949 by 11.6 percent in the case of imports and 9.7 percent in the case of exports. Over the nine years following 1959, their share rose by 20.5 percent for imports and 15.7 for exports.[8]

These various figures are, of course, highly aggregated. They nevertheless show clearly the large scale of this feature. We are concerned here not merely with a simple reorientation of the trade flows that in-

[8] The fact that the creation of the Common Market had stimulated acceleration of trade within the Community had been established quite early in the 1960's. On this subject see the calculations made by L. Duquesne de la Vinelle on the basis of a model proposed by the Netherlands economist Verdoorn, in *Information statistique* (Office Statistique des Communautés européennes, Brussels), no. 4, 1965.

terest us, which—although helping the five other countries of the Common Market—could be thought to have harmed the rest of the world. Trade with countries outside the Common Market and the franc zone in fact grew at a sustained rate (on the order of 10 percent per year in value terms); this rate was close to what could have been foretold if the European Economic Community had not been set up. The effect of the EEC was the appearance of additional transactions between the European countries, that is to say, the creation of truly new trade flows.

This point has been established authoritatively by B. Balassa and A. Camu, who have analyzed trade between the EEC countries as well as between those countries as a whole and the rest of the world.[9] Comparing the periods 1953–58 and 1958–63, they have attempted in particular to determine what part of the acceleration of the growth of intra-Community trade after the setting-up of the Common Market could be imputed to the creation of new trade and what part was the result of a diversion of older exchanges, with some Community countries being led to change the source of their foreign supplies in favor of their Community partners.

To assess these two effects, Balassa and Camu have considered the observed elasticity of imports in relation to gross national product, for aggregate imports by both product and area (the elasticity observed over any one period is the ratio between the relative growth of imports and the growth of GDP over the same period). Absence of the creation of new trade would be shown in constant overall elasticity between one period and another; diversion of trade would show as a drop in the elasticity of imports from outside the EEC. The overall elasticity rose from 1.8 to 2.1 between the two periods 1953–58 and 1958–63. This increase was due *exclusively* to trade between Common Market countries (the elasticity rose from 2.2 to 3.0 for exchanges between these countries and stayed at 1.6 for imports from third countries).

For the products of the processing and manufacturing industries, in which we are most interested, the main results are shown in Table 12.8. A low diversion effect of trade to the detriment of third countries can be seen for chemical products, transportation equipment, and other manufactured products (which are mainly products of the textile and miscellaneous industries). This effect was offset by a contrary movement in the case of machinery. The increase in elasticity of imports from EEC countries was high in the case of all products. Overall, moderate creation of new trade can be seen in chemicals and transportation equip-

[9] B. Balassa and A. Camu, "Les effets du Marché commun sur les courants d'échanges internationaux," *Revue d'économie politique*, March–April, 1966.

TABLE 12.8

Imports of EEC Countries from Inside and Outside the EEC, 1953–63

(Percent of gross national product)

Imports.	Chemical products	Machinery	Transportation equipment	Other manufactured products	Total imports
1953–58 period:					
Intra-EEC	2.8%	2.3%	3.7%	2.7%	2.2%
Extra-EEC	2.9	1.0	1.5	2.4	1.6
Total	2.9	1.6	2.6	2.5	1.8
1958–63 period:					
Intra-EEC	3.7	3.7	4.1	3.1	3.0
Extra-EEC	2.7	3.5	1.5	2.2	1.6
Total	3.3	3.7	3.1	2.7	2.1
Difference:[a]					
Intra-EEC	0.9	1.4	0.4	0.4	0.8
Extra-EEC	-0.2	2.5	0	-0.2	0

[a] Difference between observed elasticities for the two periods.

ment, low creation in other manufactured products, and very high creation in the case of machinery.

Balassa and Camu note that the situation of full employment of the factors of production that has characterized most European countries since 1958 was in itself favorable to a sharp rise in imports from third countries; this feature seems to have been responsible for the increase observed in the case of machinery. If we should eliminate this particular feature resulting from the business cycle, a weak diversion of trade effect would appear.

Thus, contrary to the structure effects of world demand, the setting-up of the Common Market represented an important explanatory factor of the increase in French foreign trade. It is chiefly for this reason that since 1958 industrial imports and exports have been growing substantially faster than national output. The widening of the market in which activity of French firms takes place, and the increased specialization that they can and must adopt, are thus very largely the result of the political choice made by the Six European countries in the middle of the 1950's. We must now examine the effect of this choice on the growth of French productivity.

EFFECTS ON PRODUCTIVITY

The extent to which the French economy is open to the outside can affect its growth in many ways. It obviously alters the circumstances in which total demand is formed. When expansion is under way abroad, it has a stimulating effect; on the other hand, it has a depressing effect when, as in 1967, the economy of some of France's neighbors is going through a slowdown phase. Because of the fast development experienced by the economy of Europe since the end of World War II, France received additional stimulus overall from the fact that its products were offered abroad in increasingly favorable circumstances. These advantages could obviously be offset by an inflationary factor of too lively a foreign demand. But we ended Chapter 8 by asserting that the pressure of demand had on the whole been beneficial, although the rise in prices, which was faster in France than abroad, could not have resulted chiefly from the expansion of foreign trade; quite the contrary, competition from abroad most certainly acted as a brake on the rise in costs over the 1960's.

The expansion of trade was in fact one of the factors that led to the return of livelier competition in the French productive system. The protected and cartelized economy that had been set up over the 1930's and consolidated during the war was not very favorable to a rapid increase in productivity; few incentives arose on the marketplace to change methods of manufacture and marketing. Opening of the French borders was one important aspect of a structural change that we shall study in the next chapter and that in our opinion was an aspect that played a distinctly positive role.

But here we shall concentrate more narrowly on the influence that international specialization may have exerted on improved productivity. Our approach to this question is broadly as follows. Accelerating foreign trade reflected increased international specialization. This specialization is longstanding for raw materials as a result of natural conditions: mineral resources or climatic conditions enable some countries to produce commodities that others must import; colonization by the Western Powers of countries producing raw materials was partly provoked by the wish to ensure unconstrained availability of these goods. But many other circumstances peculiar to each country may play a role. Traditions, education, internal organization, or even chance circumstances make a country more or less suited to particular types of production. If every country specializes in the production of those items for which it is most suited, then productivity will rise simultaneously in all of them.

The same reasoning can be applied at the level of individual firms. Each firm must determine the sphere in which it has the greatest chance of succeeding, and must concentrate its efforts there. In this way it restricts its range of output, and allows imports to satisfy demand for products it does not manufacture. On the other hand, the market open to the products chosen is considerably widened, which makes mass production possible. Additional improvement in productivity results for all those firms that are still sufficiently small to increase their return in relation to the scale of production.

Thus two factors seem likely to play a part: (1) productivity advantages possessed by every country for certain types of production as a result of varied circumstances, and (2) economies of scale that enable firms to produce more without using additional capital or labor, by concentrating output on a smaller number of products or articles. In order to assess the effect of these two factors, we shall first examine a synthetic model borrowed from P. Carré, and we shall then attempt a more analytical treatment.

Carré's Results

Starting from the idea that a country's industrial production depends on its industrial "size," in 1960 Carré sketched the outline of a development model in which imports played an important part.[10] We have used here only that part of the model relevant to the growth of industrial production. Carré's main comment was that participation by an economy in foreign trade is equivalent to an increase in size, since large imports make possible greater specialization in domestic production. He then suggests that the industrial size of an economy can be defined by two parameters: the numbers of the working population employed in industry[11] and the volume of imports of industrial products.

More exactly, let Q be industrial production, y the manpower employed in industry, and I the imports of industrial products. It is assumed that the net effect of these imports is to provide the country with foreign labor, equivalent to a fictitious labor force y'. Industrial production would then be accounted for by the sum $(y + y')$ known as the "corrected labor force."

The relationships explaining Q as a function of $(y + y')$ and y' as a function of I are given under the form

(1) $$Q = A (y + y')^\gamma$$
(2) $$I = A (y')^\gamma$$

A and γ are constants to be determined by statistical fit.

Analyzing growth in the United States since 1869 and comparative levels of industrial production in Europe in the early 1950's, Carré finds

[10] P. Carré, *Etude empirique sur l'évolution des structures d'économies en état de croissance* (Paris, 1960), chap. 5.

[11] In his study, industry includes transportation but excludes building and public works.

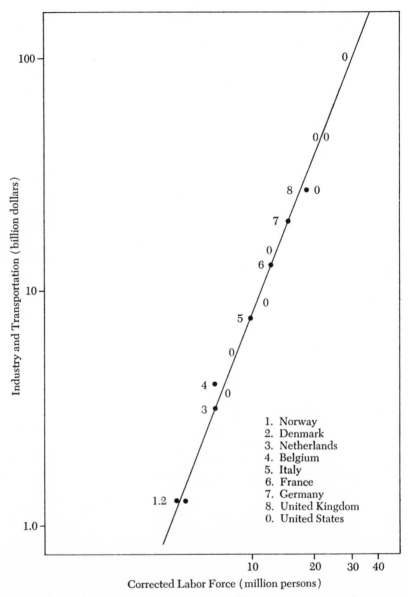

Fig. 12.1. Industrial production and transportation as a function of the "cor-rected" labor force in various countries, 1869–1955 (P. Carré, *Etude empi-rique sur l'évolution des structures d'économies en état de croissance* [Paris, 1960], chap. 5).

TABLE 12.9
*Production and the Labor Force in Industry and Transportation
in Various Countries, 1869–1955*

| Country | Billion dollars, 1952–55 prices | | Million persons | |
	Production	Nonagricul- tural imports	Labor force	Corrected labor force
United States:				
1869–73	3.7	0.8	3.3	7.0
1874–83	5.4	0.9	4.1	8.0
1884–93	8.8	1.3	6.2	10.7
1894–1903	14.5	1.3	8.4	12.9
1904–13	25.0	2.1	12.2	17.8
1919–28	43.0	2.7	15.5	21.7
1929–38	43.5	2.7	13.5	19.7
1950–55	125.0	5.8	23.1	31.8
European countries, 1952–55:				
Denmark	1.2	0.8	0.7	4.4
United Kingdom	25.0	2.7	11.5	17.7
Norway	1.2	0.8	0.55	4.3
Belgium	3.8	1.55	1.8	6.7
France	12.4	1.8	6.7	11.9
Netherlands	3.1	1.55	1.5	6.4
Germany	19.0	1.8	9.5	14.7
Italy	7.4	1.3	4.9	9.4

Source: P. Carré, *Etude empirique sur l'évolution des structures d'économies en état de croissance* (Paris, 1960).

a remarkably good fit with a value of $\gamma = 2.2$. Figure 12.1 and Table 12.9, taken from his book, show that the formulas he has used give a good account of the observed facts.

This model can be applied in another way to the development of industrial production in certain countries between 1953 and 1962. The last two columns of Table 12.10 compare the growth of industrial production observed over this period with that calculated from the model, in the case of France, Germany, Britain, and Japan. It can be seen that the differences between the two sets of figures are rather small and can probably be explained by the business cycle. In particular, the extreme years used are not very suitable to the measurement of growth in France, for which we have consistently chosen 1951 and 1963 rather than 1953 and 1962. In any case, the model can handle widely different situations. Differences between observed and calculated production seem all the smaller given that growth in France and Britain was achieved by a virtually static labor force, whereas growth in Japan was aided by an increase of 60 percent in labor employed by industry.

TABLE 12.10
The Growth of Industrial Production in Four Countries, 1953–62
(1953 = 100)

Country	Imports	Labor Force	Observed production	Calculated production
France	350	104	186	180
Germany	560	113	199	215
United Kingdom	195	101	131	130
Japan	420	160	340	320

The way the level of imports has an effect through the term y' is worth noting by reference to a comparison between France and Germany. It was calculated that German production grew by only 35 points more than French production, although Germany's imports increased more than twice as fast. The reason is that the proportion of industrial imports in production is lower in Germany than in France (9.5 percent as against 14.5 percent in 1952–55); consequently, a given rate of increase in imports is more favorable to growth in France.

The nature of the statistical adjustments just described show that Carré's law reflects at least some correlations of substantial permanence. However, this law does not make it possible to assert that imports, and imports alone, made possible the productivity growth observed.

It could be said, for example, that the model provides a means for determining imports from the level of domestic production and the "size" of a particular country measured by the numbers of its nonfarm labor force. Demand for industrial imports in a country would then obey the following law, obtained by eliminating y' from the two previous equations:

$$(3) \qquad I = A \left[\left(\frac{Q}{A} \right)^{1/\gamma} - y \right]^{\gamma}$$

It is clear that Carré adopts a causal interpretation according to which production is determined by the labor force and imports. He stresses, in particular, that increase in the fictitious labor force assumed to come from imports can be far faster than that of the real labor force, and thus permit accelerated growth of production, as in the case of Japan. He also attributes the high productivity of small European countries such as Norway or Denmark to their high imports of industrial products (almost 70 percent of production).

Following Carré, we would have to say that the growth of French industrial production between 1951 and 1963 can be accounted for as follows (average annual rates):[12]

Effect of growth of the labor force	0.3%
Effect of growth of imports	4.0
Residual	0.7
Growth of industrial output	5.0%

The residual is low in this breakdown, in accordance with the good correlations on which the model was based.

Although this model gives good representation of past changes, it is not sufficiently explanatory. At the least, it reduces the question to knowing what made possible the strong increase in imports experienced by the economy. Since average exports must grow at the same rate as imports, the internal factors that made possible the growth of foreign trade must be analyzed.

At this point in the argument, it seems difficult to assume that the essential factor in French growth had its origin in the opening of foreign trade, which of course would account at one stroke for the accumulation of capital, migrations between job sectors, and the large residual that our calculations in Chapter 7 seem to point to. Rather than using a synthetic approach to productivity improvement, however, we shall follow here the analytical approach that we have found useful up to now, restricting ourselves to a partial examination of the consequences of international specialization.

A Tentative Evaluation of the Effects of Economies of Scale

We have said there are two reasons why the specialization induced by expanding foreign trade does result in productivity improvements: economies of scale and the advantages of particular countries in certain types of production. We have not attempted to evaluate the size of the second effect because the necessary data are lacking; since specialization takes place within fairly narrowly defined industry groups, it would be necessary to have detailed statistics on the relative levels of produc-

[12] If we represent the average annual increases of the different quantities in the model by Q^*/Q, y^*/y, $y^{*\prime}/y^\prime$, and I^*/I, the first relationship enables us to write $Q^*/Q = \gamma(y^* + y^{*\prime})/(y + y^\prime)$. Taking account of the second relationship and assuming $\rho = y/(y + y^\prime)$, this is equal to

$$\frac{Q^*}{Q} = \gamma\rho\,\frac{y^*}{y} + (1-\rho)\frac{I^*}{I}$$

The first term represents the effect of the labor force and the second term that of imports. For the period 1952–55, the values of y and $y^\prime$ mean that $\rho = 56$ percent; in 1962 the value of ρ was 47 percent. We have assumed $\rho = 1/2$.

tivity in each country. On the other hand, we can make some very approximate calculations about the effects of economies of scale.

Carré has relevantly introduced the concept of a fictitious input to represent the effect that an increased use of goods manufactured abroad could have on national productivity. Adopting this concept, let us consider that the volume $Q + I$ of goods produced and imported is obtained from a "corrected" labor input $N + N'$ and a "corrected" capital input $K + K'$. The quantities N and K are the effective inputs used in the country, whereas N' and K' are fictitious inputs representing the labor and capital incorporated in the imported goods. It is natural to express the simple relationship:[13]

$$(4) \qquad \frac{N'}{N} = \frac{K'}{K} = \frac{I}{Q}$$

According to this, the fictitious inputs incorporated in I are proportional to the total inputs incorporated in $Q + I$.

We must now specify a production function allowing for economies of scale. As in Chapter 7 (p. 211), we shall write:

$$(5) \qquad Q + I = A(N + N')^\lambda (K + K')^\mu$$

Coefficient A varies with time (through technical progress); but the exponents λ and μ are considered constant. The evidence of economies of scale means that $\lambda + \mu$ is greater than 1.

Allowing for the relationships in (4), we can write the production function as

$$Q + I = AN^\lambda K^\mu \left(1 + \frac{I}{Q} \right)^{\lambda + \mu}$$

or, again,

$$(6) \qquad Q = AN^\lambda K^\mu \left(1 + \frac{I}{Q} \right)^{\lambda + \mu - 1}$$

This therefore brings us to a formula that explains national production and is analogous to those we considered in Chapter 7. The new term included is higher the higher the ratio between I and Q. Part of the growth rate of Q can be accounted for by the increase in this term: this

---

[13] The quantities N' and K' do not attempt to measure the inputs effectively used abroad for the production of imports to France. They relate rather to the inputs that would have been used if these imports had been produced in France with the degree of capitalization appropriate to that country. We should stress, moreover, that assumption (4) does not attempt to present an exact description.

part, to be exact, measures only the effect that international specialization produces through economies of scale.

The application of this formula, however, raises difficulties from the fact that international trade develops in particular products: the increase in imports has a very different composition from that of national production. The economies of scale to be allowed for in the case of imported goods must differ substantially from those relevant to production as a whole. The model indeed is too highly aggregated to make any precise estimate possible. We shall see that formula (6) leads to a rather small effect; the search for precision would therefore be irrelevant. We may content ourselves with a very approximate calculation conceived as applying to the productive system as a whole.

The last term in formula (6) grows at a rate that can be calculated by multiplying the rate of growth of I/Q by $(\lambda + \mu - 1)/(Q + I)$. In the results at constant prices, imports are shown to have grown at an average rate of 8.3 percent per year over the whole 20 years 1949–69, but at a rate of over 10 percent per year since 1959. The ratio I/Q has therefore risen at an average annual rate of 3.3 percent since 1949 and at almost 5 percent since 1959. In the middle of the period, the ratio $I/(Q + I)$ was close to 0.1. As for the coefficient $(\lambda + \mu - 1)$ measuring economies of scale, we may take a value on the order of 0.2; although too high for the economy as a whole, it is probably appropriate for taking into account the growth of chiefly industrial imports.

Allowing for the various estimates just made, we reach a result on the order of 0.1 percent per year to represent the productivity gains resulting from economies of scale through international specialization. This is not a negligible contribution, and might well be included in Table 7.9 (p. 209). It nevertheless remains limited in size.

The Spread of Technology

Along with the effects of specialization and the gains due to economies of scale, international trade raises the rate of renewal of techniques by improved knowledge of methods of production existing in the world. International trade in manufactured products makes known foreign techniques in a far more concrete way than communication by means of reviews or conferences. Machinery or products based on different concepts than comparable national products find their place on the domestic market and are often preferred. Firms obviously are led to study the reasons for the commercial success of these products, and to learn their characteristics and the circumstances in which they have been developed.

Missions abroad may complete these studies and enable people to take advantage of others' experience. Obviously, such exchanges existed before the war. In particular, certain groups in the French iron and steel area in 1850 went to Britain to study new techniques in order to apply them in their own industries. But this feature has without doubt become more important since World War II.

In particular, "productivity missions" were organized systematically over the 1950's to teach French industrialists the methods of production in the United States. It is not easy to estimate the effectiveness of these missions; it is probable, however, that without this initiative the habit of looking for information on what exists abroad would have been acquired much more slowly, and this would have made it less easy to progress through imitation as well as to make judicious use of all means already existing.

Because of deliberate action to open the country's frontiers and to create an extensive area of free trade in Europe, the rapid growth of foreign trade undoubtedly played an important role in French growth. But this role is complex, and seems still to evade quantitative measurement. In particular, the high degree of specialization of industrial products is revealed as a diffuse phenomenon, not yet sufficiently analyzed. It operated not at the level of industry groups but at the level of products and articles somewhat narrowly defined. There are no available studies showing the exact nature of this specialization and its effects on overall productivity.

Moreover, in this chapter we have not examined the influence exerted by the opening of frontiers on the reestablishment of a competitive climate. This is an important factor that develops naturally in the next chapter, where we study the various aspects of the return to a form of market economy.

CHAPTER THIRTEEN

Competition, Mobility, and the Price System

The institutional framework of French productive activity changed somewhat during the postwar period. Except for some lack of regularity in the reforms carried out, the institutional changes seem to have led toward a fairly well defined end. Over the years of poverty during the German occupation, a narrowly controlled economy had been set up. Rationing affected not only individual consumers but also firms, which had to obtain allocations of raw materials and which were subject to strict administrative control in their operations.

Abandoning this system, which at the time was called a "directed economy," France has by and large since then gradually reestablished a regime that gives the chief role to markets as regulators of the allocation of resources. In successive periods, the markets for national products, the labor market, the capital market, and the international market recovered functions close to those that had existed before the Great Depression.

Nevertheless, while a market economy was being reestablished in this way, a fairly active "indicative planning" operation[1] was kept in being. Far from contradicting the tendency toward the freeing of trade, this appeared as complementary to it. National planning quickly abandoned the aim of direct control over the economic activity of the private sector and concentrated its efforts on analyzing medium- and long-term developments—a function not performed by the market—drawing up regulatory measures designed to ensure greater efficiency for the productive system, and drafting of public decisions for the future that by their nature cannot be made by the market.

[1] A French method of trying to guide private industry by forecasting the dimensions of the economy some years ahead both in general terms and industry by industry. In arriving at the projections, business managers, labor leaders, and others are asked to cooperate in setting feasible goals consistent with projections in other sectors. The various parties so obtain a good idea of what they themselves should try to accomplish. TRANS.

To conclude our examination of French growth since the war, we shall devote the last two chapters to this institutional framework. We shall reserve a study of planning for the next chapter; here we shall consider how the price system was gradually reestablished, and shall attempt to assess the degree of competition existing in France. And last, we shall consider whether human mobility increased, as seems desirable for productivity improvement. We obviously shall not be able to attempt to measure the effects of institutional changes on the growth rate. We must content ourselves with indications based on certain general concepts of the requirements for efficiency in the organization of production and distribution. Accordingly, for proof that these changes exerted favorable influence on the country's rate of development, we shall refer to the conclusions of theoretical analyses.

More precisely, behind the statements in the present chapter lies the following argument. In a complex economy, available resources can be allotted to the various industries, undertakings, and technological processes in a manner more or less favorable in relation to the volume of final output achieved. The decisions of firms and holders of raw materials will lead to the best allocation of these resources if the following conditions are fulfilled.

1. That competition exists on the markets for the factors of production and for intermediary goods in such a way that resources are perfectly mobile and available to all potential users; that in addition all purchasers of a given good or factor pay the same price for it.

2. That there is free entry in the private sector, so that every firm can carry out any form of production with no constraint other than that of preventing its unit earnings from falling below the market selling price; that there are therefore no private monopolies or restrictive agreements.

3. That public firms acquire their inputs at market prices and sell their outputs at marginal cost.

4. That all external effects of any kind between the operations of various firms are corrected in some form, possibly even to the detriment of the entire fulfillment of conditions 1, 2, and 3 above.

On the argument in question, any departure in practice of the structure from this outline would be reflected in errors in the allocation of resources and will therefore imply losses. Moreover, for markets to function effectively, relative prices should evolve as a function of changes in needs and in the technical circumstances of production. Finally, changes in the general level of prices would matter little (but see our remarks on this subject in Chapter 11). We have taken the point of view that the argument outlined has some validity, and we shall examine how the postwar period saw in France a gradual return to "competition," that is, to a tendency for the organization of production to depart less and less from the conditions defined here.

It is appropriate to note that the somewhat ideal system defined by conditions 1–4 above is not to be identified with economic liberalism, which assumes that the state will refrain from intervening in the sphere of production. On the contrary, in order to approximate those conditions, a deliberate structural policy is necessary, which implies actions of various types: legislative or regulatory measures aimed at establishing effective competition and satisfactory organization on the markets, the institution of a tax regime that alters relative prices only to the extent required to correct external effects, the management of public enterprises, and the establishment of rates or prices for their products or services, etc.

Our guideline in this chapter is therefore not to examine whether the state has gradually limited its intervention, but rather whether it has been able to establish on the different markets circumstances favorable to efficiency.[2]

THE SITUATION IN THE EARLY 1950'S

The Great Depression of the 1930's had led to a serious disorganization of the international markets and the home market. An inevitable reaction was the setting up of controls and agreements whose aim was to stop the disorders resulting from unregulated working of the markets. During the war, the general scarcity required a system of administrative distribution that extended its effects over the whole economy. Prices, themselves also fixed by regulation, no longer played a part in the allocation of resources, which was wholly controlled by the state.

This extreme system was abandoned soon after the end of the fighting. At the beginning of 1949, most of the wartime rationing had been abolished. The sale of consumers' goods and of most intermediary goods was again carried out freely on the markets. Nevertheless, the economic system in practice was still not only far from the ideal outline we have sketched but far from the system that had existed during the 1920's. Contrary to West Germany or Belgium, France did not attempt rapid reestablishment of economic liberalism. The groups in power and public

---

[2] Let us repeat once again that our purpose in this work is not concerned with studying how just or how equitable has been the distribution of the results of growth. Measures that have ensured improved economic efficiency may have had an unfavorable effect on distribution. Far be it from us to give greater weight at the outset to efficiency than to equity. For this reason the following analyses imply no value judgments.

opinion were well aware of the disadvantages of too strict administrative controls, but for the most part they refused to allow the state to hold aloof from management of the economy. They therefore preferred to maintain in force at least provisionally, control agencies that in other countries were deliberately being eliminated.

In the early 1950's, the French economy was therefore operating in a mixed regime: certain transactions were carried out freely according to market rules; others required administrative authorization for decisions. The report of the nation's accounts for the year 1951, drafted in 1952, aimed at describing "the permanent structures of the French economy" and gave prominence to "obstacles to the play of the market."[3] It is somewhat difficult to distinguish in this document direct information from interpretations, which are always somewhat subjective; nevertheless, the indications are sufficiently precise to bring out clearly important differences by comparison with the situation in recent years.

Obstacles to foreign trade at that time were particularly great. Customs tariffs, which had been high since the end of the nineteenth century, had a smaller impact than controls over trade, and particularly than the maintenance of quotas and import licenses for those products most vulnerable to international competition. The authors of the report could speak of the "more or less complete fencing around of the French market."

On the regulation of home markets, the report quoted numerous examples relating to farm prices, a field in which the situation in France in 1951 seems in no way exceptional. But the report also shows that imported coal was sold below cost, that schemes of administrative distribution remained in force for coke, copper, aluminium, nickel, cotton, and paper, that it was still forbidden to open and develop single-price stores, and that many industrial prices were taxed. The financial market was very highly regulated in 1951. The total of private share issues and bank credits financing investment according to the classical market mechanisms represented only 8 percent of all these investments. Most financing by public credit was subject to administrative decisions.

And finally, the aftereffects of the depression and the war were apparent in the functioning of the productive sectors of the economy. Agreements covering manufacture, selling prices, or market shares played an important part in some sectors. The suppression of general rationing had

---

[3] "Rapport sur les comptes nationaux provisoires de 1951," *Statistiques et études financières*, supplément, Finances françaises, no. 18, 1953, particularly pp. 197–205.

indeed made the black market disappear. But the habit of fraud was still very widespread, even among firms of some size; it spread over into the tax sphere and thus distorted normal market relationships.

Without attempting to achieve a complete picture, we shall now see how the situation gradually changed over the 1950's and 1960's, and shall consider the various types of market.

THE LABOR MARKET

A healthy allocation of the labor force is obviously one of the first conditions for efficiency in production, since labor is the essential factor in it. Satisfactory working of the labor market therefore seems to be one of the chief elements in the price system. To study the institutional context in which growth took place since the war, we shall therefore begin by examining this market.

What a satisfactory working of it means in practice is a matter for argument. In principle the market fulfills its role if it ensures that prices paid for the use of equivalent amounts of labor are equalized, and that this common price is equalized with the marginal productivity of the labor in question. In view of the diversity of firms' situations, these conditions can in practice be fulfilled only if there is some degree of freedom on the labor market. An employer must be able to offer a high wage to ensure the services of workers who are particularly useful to him. A wage earner must be able to move from one employer to another if he finds that his services are better appreciated by the second than by the first. Such freedom does not exclude active labor unions. On the contrary, union activity can be an important element in ensuring not only humane conditions of employment but also effective equalization of incomes for equivalent outputs of labor. On the other hand, effectiveness in allocation of manpower is likely to be lessened if the whole system of remuneration is fixed at the national level by the authorities or by labor agreements. Rigidity introduced in this way opposes multiple rapid adjustments that productivity improvement requires at the local level.

Examination of institutions as they actually worked leads fairly clearly to the conclusion that from 1950 to 1968 the field open to free bargaining for wages had been growing. In 1945 a national wage system had been set up. On the basis of hourly manual wages in the Paris metalworking industry, wage commissions had worked out for each industry group a scale of different occupations with corresponding rates of remuneration. This scale had been made mandatory by official decree for all firms in the relevant industry group. In practice, this very cumbersome system pleased no one. The unions themselves demanded its abolition.

The law of February 11, 1950, gave employers and wage earners the right to fix wages in firms freely by means of collective agreements. Nevertheless, the central government defined a "guaranteed minimum all-occupations wage" (*salaire minimum interprofessionnel garanti*— SMIG), below which no wage earner's pay could fall. From that time on, a fairly complex system took shape. In some industries, like textiles and chemicals, national collective agreements were regularly adopted. In others, relationships between employers and employees were far less institutionalized.[4]

At any rate, it seems that in practice the role of the SMIG and the national collective agreements gradually diminished from 1950, or at least from 1956, to 1968. See Figure 13.1. The national minimum wage, like the minimum wages in particular collective agreements, represented a less and less constraining influence on the determination of effective wages. With October 1, 1950 = 100, the SMIG index number on April 1, 1955, was 162, whereas the general index of hourly wages was 164. This gap subsequently grew wider: the figures were 200 for the SMIG and 232 for the general index on April 1, 1959; 240 and 323, respectively, on July 1, 1963; and 284 and 425 on January 1, 1968. In brief, from 1955 to the beginning of 1968, the SMIG increased by 75 percent, and the general index of hourly wage rates by 160 percent. (Between January 1, 1968, and January 1, 1969, the SMIG rose by 39 percent and the general index of wage rates by 16 percent. The relationship between these two indicators, therefore, in early 1969 regained a level comparable with that in 1961.)

So long as the SMIG remained close to the effective minimum wage, the scale of wages was relatively rigid; any increase in the SMIG almost automatically brought with it a rise in all wage rates. But from the moment the imposed minimum was left behind by the minimum applied in practice, greater latitude was allowed for the free determination of remuneration between management and wage earners.

Can we find in a study of wage statistics any confirmation of the concept that the labor market operated with increased freedom and that, at least in the 1960's, it was fairly close in nature to the competi-

---

[4] This system does not seem to have been fully described anywhere. It is alluded to in the following study, which in any case is a good source of statistical information: M. Petrot, "Données statistiques sur l'évolution des rémunérations salariales de 1938 à 1963," *Etudes et conjoncture*, August 1965.

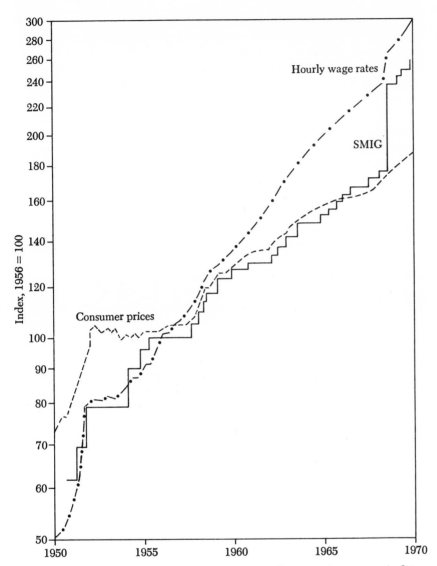

Fig. 13.1. Changes in the guaranteed minimum all-occupations wage (*salaire minimum interprofessionnel garanti*, or SMIG), the consumer price index, and the index of hourly wage rates, 1950–69. Years are indicated as of January 1.

tive market of economic theory? Before answering this question, we must ask how the competitive nature of the market could show up in the statistics. It is not easy to observe the degree to which remuneration paid by different enterprises for a *given* amount of work approximates equality. The statistics do not show precisely the nature of the contribution made by wage earners (for example, their qualifications, the intensity of effort required, etc.). Moreover, at the level of individual enterprises, wage rate differences can be observed that are difficult to explain.[5] To study the degree of equalization, one might attempt to examine those trends that affect changes in the structure of wages by skill, sex, industry group, etc. The more these trends can be explained by changes in the supply and demand of labor, the more wage equalization can be expected to take place. The difficulty of defining a rigorous statistical test for this is obvious, however.

More convincing indications may perhaps be found in short-term wage movements. A competitive market should react rapidly to disequilibria. If we can explain by precise economic causes short-term variations in relative wages, we shall have an indication that the labor market fulfills its functions. Nevertheless, the conclusions of economic analysis are frequently ambiguous, whether one is interpreting trends or short-term fluctuations. Development of wage rates is influenced by the circumstances of labor supply just as much as by those of demand for labor. On a perfect market where the supply curve does not change, price should vary all the more as demand fluctuates more strongly and as supply is less elastic. This explains why clear cases are not found in which the structure of wages can be said in advance to vary in a sharply defined manner.

Let us, for example, consider differences between female and male wage rates. The supply of female labor is certainly the more elastic of the two, since the great majority of men of working age are permanently employed (immigration by foreign workers does not seem of itself likely to alter this conclusion). One might therefore expect the difference between male and female wage rates to grow wider when demand for labor is intense, since the rise in wages is more marked for men than for women, and this would have the effect of stimulating companies to employ a higher proportion of women. But this tendency could be counteracted by the fact that demand for female labor might

---

[5] For France this conclusion emerges in particular from research carried out at Aix-en-Provence under the direction of François Sellier. See, for example, J.-P. Daubigney, F. Fizaine, and J.-J. Silvestre, "Les Différences de salaires entre entreprises; étude microéconomique," *Revue économique*, no. 2, 1971.

vary more with fluctuations in the economic situation than does demand for male labor. Now this is not impossible: since, on the average, women are less highly qualified than men, they could belong chiefly to the particular part of the labor force that becomes unwanted when production drops but indispensable when it rises (the textile and clothing industries are a particularly clear example of this situation).[6] Similarly, differences between wages of persons at different levels of qualification should widen in times of boom as a result of the inelasticity of supply of more qualified labor; on the contrary, they should narrow because demand for nonqualified labor varies more widely with the business cycle.

These uncertainties make it clear that far more detailed studies are needed. We can therefore not expect, a priori, to arrive at other than uncertain conclusions from examining the available statistical series.

Although by law female and male wage rates are equal, in practice they are, on the average, different. The difference has remained on the same order of magnitude since the war, with some variations. It has had a slightly upward trend, moving from 8 percent in the early 1950's to 10 percent since 1964. Perhaps this could be interpreted as a trend to greater freedom in wage determination, since legal parity seems to have been less and less of a constraint. In relation to this trend, variations observed on January 1 of each year show peaks at the beginning of 1950 (8 percent), 1954 (8.5 percent), 1961 (9.5 percent), and 1966 (10.5 percent). On the contrary, relatively low figures can be seen for 1955 (6.5 percent), 1962 (9 percent), and 1968 (10 percent). As can be noted, these fluctuations were small and do not seem to have been linked in any clear way with those in the state of business.

The movement of differential in relation to different levels of qualification also shows a high degree of regularity. From 1949 on, monthly salaries of management (*cadres*) have tended to grow faster than hourly wages of workers: the gap between the relative indexes reached almost 25 percent overall for the period from 1949 to the end of 1967. Since 1952, white-collar salaries have tended to grow slightly faster than blue-collar wages (approximately 7 percent from 1952 to 1967). The wages of specialists and technicians grew at the same rate as those of manual workers. The advance of management in relation to other categories took place very steadily, with interruptions in 1955, 1956, 1960, and

[6] It is often said that, to attract additional manpower, companies raise mainly women's salaries in the hope of attracting persons previously not in the labor force. This model would seem to assume that custom or institutional reasons introduce greater rigidity in male wages than in female wages.

1963, when conditions on the labor market were particularly good, since the pay of blue-collar workers tends to grow especially fast at such periods.

Direct observation seems to show clearly the existence of true competition on the management labor market. The tendency for management's pay to move increasingly ahead of manual workers' wages can be fairly well explained by considerations affecting supply and demand. Technological progress in the postwar period was reflected in a great increase in demand for management, at a time when the supply was growing slowly. The number of engineering diplomas issues each year (4,000 in the early 1950's, and 7,600 in 1966) remains low in relation to requirements (the number of persons occupying engineering posts rose from 138,000 in 1962 to 190,000 in 1968—an increase of 7,000 per year, to which should be added requirements for replacements). In the scientific disciplines, most students leaving the university were absorbed into the teaching profession.

Analyses of differences in wage rates by industry group and their changes have been the subject of numerous studies in the economic literature.[7] It is known that the various relationships observed are weak in all countries and that the interpretation to be given them has been the subject of considerable debate. However, we shall examine the French statistics in order to bring out whatever indications, no matter how uncertain, they can suggest. In conditions of perfect competition and information, and assuming each person chooses his employment essentially in terms of its remuneration, wages should tend to become equal between different industries. The only remaining disparities would arise from differences in the average qualifications required in each type of work and from the different circumstances of the work required, such as degree of hardship. To reach such equilibrium, industry groups with high manpower demand would tend to pay more than the average to attract newcomers as well as those already employed in other industries. Conversely, industries with low labor demand, or those needing to reduce employment, would be led to award only small wage increases to the point where manpower matched their needs.

In order to see whether medium-term trends conformed to this model, we have adopted the growth of the paid labor force as an indicator of manpower needs in each industry group from 1949 to 1956 and from 1956 to 1963. Clearly, the requirements of the different industries may have differed according to qualifications, but apart from the fact that

---

[7] See, for example, the OECD book *Les Salaires et la mobilité de la main-d'oeuvre* (Paris, 1965) and E. M. Hugh-Jones, ed., *Wage Structure in Theory and Practice* (Amsterdam, 1966).

TABLE 13.1
*Hourly Wage Rates and Changes in Employment by
Industry Group, 1949–63*

Sector	Wage rates at Jan. 1, 1949	1956 index of numbers (1949=100)	Wage rates at Jan. 1, 1956	1963 index of numbers (1956=100)	Wage rates at Jan. 1, 1963
02. Processed foods and farm products	65	104	138	102	2.40
06. Building materials and glass	66	108	135	104	2.40
07–08. Metal production	69	100	145	109	–
09. Mechanical and electrical industries	69	117	147	120	2.60
10. Chemicals and rubber	66	118	144	116	2.60
11. Textiles and clothing	67	87	139	94	2.50
12. Misc. industries	68	108	143	113	2.60
13. Building & public works	66	152	140	120	2.40

Note: Hourly wage rates are in francs for ordinary male manual workers (regions with zero percent abatement).

there is no long-term series giving a breakdown of employees by qualification,[8] the structure of wages by qualification remained stable over the whole period considered, apart from the remuneration of management. The strength of demand for labor is probably adequately measured by the growth of overall numbers employed.

Table 13.1 compares hourly wage rates of male manual workers with the index of numbers employed. It has not been possible to make a comparison allowing for wages of higher levels of skill, because there is no comparability between one industry group and another in terms such as skilled workers. The table shows that wage rates between industry groups had low variability, and yet there is a certain stability to the groupings one can make of them on the basis of these rates. There is only low correlation with the growth of numbers employed. Among the industry groups paying the lowest wages, to be sure, are processed foods and farm products as well as building materials and glass, in which numbers grew only little. Among those paying the highest wages are the mechanical and electrical industries, which increased greatly in size. But textile and clothing seemed to have paid average wage rates despite their sharp drop in numbers, and building and public works paid rather low wages despite their fast increase (the last case could be explained by the large supply of labor originating in French farming or abroad, which was probably more suited to work on building sites than in factories).

[8] The source used here is the series showing employed manpower in the industry groups covered by the 1954 and 1962 censuses. The definition of qualifications in these two censuses was not identical, and has not permitted detailed analysis.

In comparisons between industry groups, the most important practice is to examine not differences among wage rates at a particular time but differences among their growth rates. A certain correlation can be seen to exist between increase in numbers and rise in wages. This procedure has the advantage of greatly reducing difficulties due to the poor comparability of skills between industry groups. Indexes of wage growth are little affected by this fact, whereas wage rates themselves are considerably affected. The interpretation of the correlations between indexes, however, is ambiguous.

In fact, it would be simple if the situation at the beginning and end of each period were well known; for example, if it were known that the initial date of a comparison was a time of perfect equilibrium and the final date a time of disequilibrium. The industry groups whose numbers had grown most would also be those where labor requirements were least satisfied at the end date and where, in a market economy, there would tend to be the highest wage increases. But matters would be reversed if the period between the initial date and the final date was one of return to equilibrium.

To validate the correlations sought in the most frequent types of study, it must therefore be assumed that the industry groups whose employment figures vary most are also those in which the disequilibrium of the labor market increases (in one direction or the other). Adopting this assumption, we have examined the relevant correlations in the two periods 1949–56 and 1956–63, using an index of growth of workers' annual hourly earnings. This index seems likely to provide a good comprehensive measure of the movement of wages within each industry group, since it covers all skills and since it allows for bonuses and other additions that are part of the calculation of workers' earnings.

Table 13.2 shows that there was indeed some correlation: there was low growth of wages in the textile industries, where the labor force was decreasing, high growth from 1956 to 1963 in miscellaneous industries and in building, where labor requirements rose considerably. But, for one thing, the growth of earnings varied little between one industry and another (the extreme index numbers were 205 to 239 for the first period and 173 to 187 for the second). Moreover, the correlation was quite weak, as is demonstrated by the exceptions: the mechanical and electrical industries (which were already paying the highest remuneration), building between 1949 and 1956, and chemicals between 1956 and 1963.

We can also refer to far more complete calculations carried out for

TABLE 13.2
*Changes in Hourly Earnings and Employment by
Industry Group, 1949–63*

Sector	1956 index, 1949 = 100		1963 index, 1956 = 100	
	Earnings	Numbers employed	Earnings	Numbers employed
02. Processed foods and farm products	214	104	180	102.5
06. Building materials and glass	225	108	183	104
07–08. Metal production	227	100	178	109
09. Mechanical and electrical industries	214	117.5	173	120.5
10. Chemicals and rubber	239	118	176	116
11. Textiles	205	87	174	94.5
12. Misc. industries	217	108.5	187	113
13. Building & public works	216	152	183	120

Note: Hourly earnings are total earnings, that is, allowing for overtime, work at night, and the average hourly earnings of workers paid at piece rates. The results are taken from the inquiry by the Ministry of Social Affairs.

France and some other countries in an OECD study.[9] This considers annual indexes of workers' hourly earnings for 21 industry groups over the period 1949–62. It shows a group of correlation coefficients, each one relating to increases that have been observed across industry groups in a particular period and correlating earnings with numbers employed.

For increases observed between the average for the years 1960–62 and the average for the years 1949–51, the correlation coefficient was 0.41, a figure on the same order of magnitude as figures obtained in other countries for periods of similar length. For increases from one year to the next, two of the correlation coefficients are negative (1953–54 and 1954–55), but the 11 others are positive, with a maximum of 0.48; the four highest values relate to 1949–50, 1958–59, 1959–60, and 1960–61.

In brief, a certain relationship can be seen at the level of the industry groups between the intensity of demand for labor and the level as well as the growth rate of wages. This relationship is not strict; nevertheless, particular circumstances can easily explain some of the exceptions observed. The observations seem to indicate fairly strongly that supply and demand played an important role in the labor market.[10] They do

[9] *Les Salaires et la mobilité de la main-d'oeuvre.*

[10] In "La Dynamique des salaires nominaux en France: étude sectorielle" (*Revue économique*, no. 3, 1971), J.-J. Silvestre was led to distinguish two groups of sectors. For high-wage industries, fairly highly concentrated and unionized, the state

not, however, seem sufficient to buttress the thesis according to which market forces were more active after the 1950's than in the early years of that decade. Correlation coefficients relating to annual wage increases are indeed higher in the OECD study at the end of the period than at the beginning, but the difference cannot be regarded as significant.

Support for the view that the labor market in France was rather similar to that in other countries can be found in a recent article by Turner and Jackson.[11] Analyzing the statistics of the International Labor Office, which show year-by-year average earnings for the various branches of the manufacturing industries, the authors calculated two types of coefficients. The first are correlation coefficients for the relative wage levels in the different branches for the two years 1956 and 1965. The coefficient will be equal to 1 in cases where there is a stable structure of earnings by industry group; it will be lower the more this structure changes between the two years in question. The second coefficients measure the proportion of industry groups between which significant correlation occurred from 1956 to 1965 in earnings increases from one year to the next.

A competitive labor market is identified by Turner and Jackson as a situation in which the second coefficient is low but the first is high. The second coefficient is low because wages in each industry group are likely to react to the conditions of supply and demand peculiar to that industry. The first coefficient is likely to be high because labor mobility between industry groups will have the effect of making observed short-term differentials essentially temporary in nature.

In France the first coefficient has stood at a very high value of 0.97, and the second at 0.46. For comparison, in the 18 countries examined, which are to be regarded as "developed market economies" when taken as a whole, the first coefficient averaged 0.90 and the second 0.53. If these statistical indicators are to be believed, the French labor market seems to be relatively competitive. This impression would probably be corroborated by an institutional analysis, which would show that national collective agreements and government intervention in wage setting have played a smaller role in France than in certain other Western countries.

---

of competition on the labor market has little influence on movement of wages in the short term. It has, on the contrary, a strong influence in industries where wages are low, concentration is small, and unionization is low.

[11] H. A. Turner and D. A. S. Jackson, "On the Stability of Wage Differences and Productivity-based Wage Policies: An International Analysis," *British Journal of Industrial Relations*, vol. VII, no. 1, 1969.

LABOR MOBILITY

In order that job seekers may be directed toward the firms or the types of work in which they will be most effective, they must first have sufficient information; second, they must be able to move from one place to another easily; and last, remuneration must be in close relationship with the need of firms for labor of particular types. There has been some progress in the supply of information to the labor force, and in particular to workmen and white-collar workers; this can be seen, for example, from the increase in job advertisements in newspapers. The offices of the Ministry of Labor in each *département* were set up immediately after the war, but it is difficult to assess how effective their activity was up to 1969.

After our examination of wage determination on the labor market, a short study of labor mobility is required. Mobility is customarily measured by the size of manpower movements.[12] It consists of both geographical changes of position and changes from one economic sector, firm, or job to another. From the point of view of economics alone, it is clear that the more easily workers change jobs or residence, the more chances there are that each one will be permanently occupied in work that suits him best and in which he gives the greatest output of services. An excess of mobility would indeed be a disadvantage; if a person stays too short a time in each job, his period of adaptation to the new working situation is relatively long and reduces his overall output. But such ease of mobility is possible only if workers find more attractive circumstances elsewhere; and further, firms must also find advantage in it.

It is convenient to distinguish geographical mobility from job mobility, but these are two complementary approaches to one phenomenon. The two aspects are in fact closely interlinked: very often geographical mobility is accompanied by a change of trade; job mobility may consist in a change between firms in a given sector or even in a change from one sector to another. Since statistical information reports geographical movements far more fully than movements between jobs, it will be advantageous to consider the former as well as the latter.

We are interested in seeing whether mobility has increased, and whether by that fact it has helped to sustain growth. We shall very

---

[12] In an article in *Esprit* (April 1966) H. Bartoli commented: "Mobility is no more than readiness to move; it is not the movement itself." It would be interesting to study the extent to which people are inclined to move, but it is clear that here we are studying only the results of this mobility.

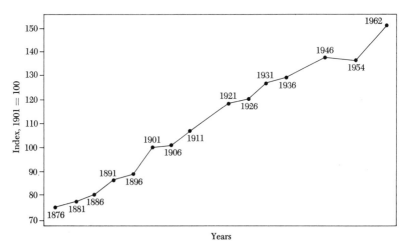

Fig. 13.2. Geographical mobility of workers, 1876–1962.

broadly situate the postwar period within a longer-term view and provide some basic data for a comparison with the United States; we shall then show that there is substantial evidence that geographical mobility has increased. On the other hand, we are unable to provide any direct indicator of an increase in job mobility within the nonagricultural sector of the economy.

The only long-term indicator available relates to geographical mobility. The series of demographic censuses gives a breakdown of the French population according to whether people are living in the *département* in which they were born. Unfortunately, it does not show how frequently they move from one *département* to another over the course of their life. Nevertheless, it seems quite clear that the scale of geographical movements has consistently increased over the past hundred years. Tugault, who has worked on this subject at the Institut National d'Etudes Démographiques (INED), has shown on a graph (Figure 13.2) the movements of an index of mobility calculated broadly on the basis of the percentage of French persons born in France and residing outside the *département* in which they were born.[13]

The rise in this index was particularly steep between 1896 and 1901,

[13] In fact, for a given mobility by age, this percentage would seem to vary slightly with changes in age structure. The index adopted has been corrected to allow for this; the correction is significant chiefly between 1954 and 1962, as a result of the drop in average age of the population. For other studies on long-term changes in geographical mobility, see Y. Tugault, "La Mesure de la mobilité," *Population*, May–June, 1973.

and fairly steady from 1906 to 1946, with some slowing down between. 1921 and 1926. This slowing down is probably the effect of the very large population movements before 1921 caused by World War I; mobility seems to have dropped from 1946 to 1954, and thereafter increased at a very rapid rate. Probably, as in 1921, the situation in 1946 was considerably distorted by the war, which had been over for only one year. Nevertheless, in relation to long-term trends, the figure for 1954 seems very low. In any case, comparisons between the two periods 1946–54 and 1954–62 must be interpreted with great care, and we shall comment on this below. However, apart from 1946, which was too close to World War II, the growth in mobility seems to have been rather low between 1936 and 1954, and high thereafter.

Geographical mobility seems nevertheless to have remained moderate in France in relation to that in certain other countries. The only comparison we can make here relates to the United States, where people move about with an ease that is well known. The significance of this comparison is therefore somewhat reduced. But the difference between the two countries is sufficiently sharp to have meaning.

The Commission on Manpower of the Fifth National Plan has carried out calculations based on the results of the demographic censuses of 1954 and 1962.[14] It assumes, by analogy to observations in the United States, that the 7 percent of the total population that had moved from one region to another (as defined in the Plan program) between the two censuses represents an annual migration of almost 2 percent; similarly, the rate of migration between *départements* was more than 10 percent between the two censuses, and is now about 2.7 percent per year.

The rate of migration is obviously higher the smaller the geographic unit considered. This complicates comparisons with the United States, where the units considered are counties, which are halfway between French *communes* and *départements*; and states, which are far bigger than regions of the Plan program. Allowing for these differences, it seems clear from Table 13.3 that geographical mobility is substantially higher in the United States than in France, by approximately an order of magnitude of 2.

Nevertheless, this wide difference between the mobilities of the two countries is not entirely to the benefit of the United States; too high mobility can have more disadvantages than advantages. Madinier stresses that "for several decades, many American employers have con-

[14] Commissariat général du Plan d'équipement et de la productivité, *Rapport général de la commission de la main-d'oeuvre, Ve Plan, 1966–1970* (Paris, 1966), pp. 306–7.

TABLE 13.3
Annual Migration Rates in France and the United States, 1963
(Percent of total population)

Migration	France	United States
Changes in residence	9%	20%
Migrations between *communes*	6.5	
Migrations between counties		6.3
Migrations between *départements*	2.7	
Migrations between regions	1.8	
Migrations between states		3.3

Source: Report of the Manpower Commission of the Fifth National Plan. The figure for French movements in residence comes from the breakdown of the housing inquiry carried out by the INSEE in 1963.

sistently attempted to slow down the rate of labor turnover, which is regarded as costly and harmful to the welfare of the firm. Economists, moreover, have urged them to do this."[15] He also draws attention to a number of practices, such as pension and retirement plans restricted to a particular firm, and hiring policies restricted to young people, which have the effect of making it costly for employees to move and make it difficult for them to find new jobs. Too great mobility between jobs probably also implies too great mobility geographically. Nevertheless, in French conditions increase in mobility seems likely to represent a growth factor and a factor in the improved working of the labor market. (It can be noted, however, that in Japan the low mobility of labor does not seem to restrict industrial growth.)

In the postwar period, geographical migrations have shown continuous growth, as can be seen from comparison between the four demographic censuses of 1946, 1954, 1962, and 1968. It is true, however, that two factors complicate an assessment of them. On the one hand, the methods adopted for the 1946 census were not the same as those used in the three following ones, and this has some effect on the results. On the other hand, in order to determine the net migration from a particular geographic unit smaller than the whole of France, it is necessary to calculate the difference between the variation in population of the local government area in question and the natural excess of births over deaths. This residual figure therefore includes both internal migration, which should be isolated as a measure of population mobility, and migration from abroad. The latter was larger between 1962 and 1968 (on account of repatriation) and smaller between 1946 and 1954. Nevertheless, a clear trend can be seen.

[15] P. Madinier, "La Mobilité du travail aux Etats-Unis et en France," *Revue économique*, no. 4, July 1959.

TABLE 13.4

Proportion of Population Moving to a Different Commune
Between 1954 and 1968

(*Percent of total population in 1968*)

Residence at preceding census	1954– 1962 (8 yrs.)	1962– 1968 (6 yrs.)
In another *commune* of the same *département*	15.3%	12.3%
In another *département* of the same region	3.5	4.3
In another French region (of the Plan program)	7.1	6.5
Outside France	3.9	4.6

Note: Figures are for the Paris *arrondissement.*

The most significant results are probably those shown in Table 13.4, since they concern not net movements between geographical units but individual movements measured direct. If the unequal length of the two periods being compared is taken into account, it can be seen that migrations from one *département* to another were more numerous between 1962 and 1968 than between 1954 and 1962. The increase, which seems to have been about 30 percent in the annual rate of migration, is particularly noticeable in the case of movements between *départements* in a given region. Similar results do not exist for the period 1946–54. But the speedup in mobility from that period on can be seen clearly in the other data available.

Thus, the net migratory balance of rural *communes* was a reduction of 760,000 persons between 1946 and 1954, but a reduction of 1,000,000 over the following eight years.[16] Similarly, the net migratory balances of *départements* containing large urban centers were far bigger between 1954 and 1962 than between 1946 and 1954 (the changes in the figures are far less significant in 1954–62 and 1962–68). For the three periods between the censuses, we have the following net migrations (thousands of persons): 53, 192, and −73 in the Seine *département*; 184, 465, and 382 in Seine-et-Oise; 38, 150, and 167 in Bouches-du-Rhône; 21, 68, and 56 in Isère; 3, 99, and 80 in the Rhône, etc.

The fact that geographical mobility of male workers as a whole was low in the immediate postwar period and that it has increased since then is consistent with what is known of the housing situation: there was a great shortage after the war, and gradual improvement from the middle or end of the 1950's. (On the basis of the results of surveys by

[16] The sources are "Premiers résultats du recensement de 1954 en matière de migrations nettes dans les communes rurales et dans les villes," *Etudes et conjoncture,* June 1955; and the results of the 1962 census, *Population légale* (*résultats statistiques*) (Paris, 1964).

the INSEE on housing, it can be calculated that the average annual rate of change of residence rose from 8.9 percent in 1962 to 9.7 percent in 1966.) It is therefore tempting to interpret the trend observed as reflecting a return to a more normal state of affairs.

As for job mobility in the strict sense, we could of course use as a measure the net increase of employment in the various industry groups. But these increases, which reflect the demand of each industry group, cannot be considered indicators of how well or how badly the labor market was functioning. Only the drop in numbers of farm workers and other independent workers is significant from our point of view, because this reduction can be interpreted as having contributed to resolving the disequilibrium in distribution of men between the different types of employment. We have seen in Chapter 2 that there was an increase in the rate of migration by farm workers to other jobs.

To measure the job mobility of nonfarm wage earners, there is only one indicator. This stems from the annual summary of wage declarations by firms, which draw up an individual schedule for each wage earner they employ in the course of the year for a period of any length. The ratio between the number of schedules and the number of wage earners still on the firms' books on December 31 of each year is a good indicator of labor mobility. The values of this ratio, seen in Table 13.5, show considerable stability from one year to another. The indicator stands at a relatively low level when there is some unemployment, and particularly if the end of the year corresponds with a period of revived hiring (1954, 1959–60, 1963–68). When there is unemployment, wage earners are obviously not highly motivated to change jobs. If these movements, due to short-term economic factors, are allowed for, the indicator is seen to have kept an almost constant level from the mid-1950's. Only in the immediate postwar years was mobility low. In addition, legislative measures introduced in the 1950's and reinforced in the 1960's set up bonus payments for workers who had to move or undergo retraining as a result of industrial changes. However, the number of beneficiaries throughout was rather modest—13,000 from 1955 to 1967.[17]

In summarizing the various institutional and statistical indicators we have brought together on the functioning of the labor market, we must first of all distinguish the situation in the immediate postwar period. Until around 1952, the structure of wages seems to have been conditioned quite strongly by national government decisions, and the mo-

[17] See, in particular, "Quatorzième rapport du Fonds de Développement Economique et Social," *Statistiques et études financières*, supplément, no. 252, December 1969.

TABLE 13.5
Mobility Coefficient of Wage Earners, 1947–68

Year	Coefficient	Year	Coefficient	Year	Coefficient
1947	1.33	1955	1.52	1962	1.53
		1956	1.54	1963	1.50
1950	1.42	1957	1.53	1964	1.51
1951	1.49	1958	1.52	1965	1.50
1952	1.50	1959	1.44	1966	1.50
		1960	1.48	1967	1.50
1954	1.49	1961	1.55	1968	1.49

bility of workers seems to have been slightly reduced. From the mid-1950's, however, the French labor market seems to have been rather sensitive to changes affecting supply and demand. From the rough analyses to which we have confined ourselves, no clear trend shows up over the period 1956–57. Nevertheless, two facts lead us to conclude that the labor market has actually been working with increasing flexibility: the gap between effective wage rates and agreed or statutory minimum rates gradually widened; and geographical mobility increased at the same time as the housing shortage became less acute.

THE CAPITAL MARKET

Too close a parallel between capital and labor is probably not justified when one is studying the role and functioning of the market. But let us now consider the second factor of production. Efficiency in the allocation of resources assumes that productive investments are made and used in those firms where they are shown to be most useful. Efficient allocation cannot be achieved without taking into account in some way the main features of future development. Indicative planning seems likely to have an important part to play in this matter. But it will always be rough-and-ready and limited to an examination of rather broad problems, since it cannot bring together the innumerable studies that would be relevant for the multiple investment decisions taken in firms.

A perfectly organized market should make possible continual confrontation between the supply and demand implied for the present and the future by the productive decisions taken at each moment. Such a confrontation is achieved to some extent, but only very partially, by the capital market. Supplies of savings and demand for investment made known on the capital market reflect some immediate consequences of decisions affecting the future. Rules for the investment of savings and the interest rates attainable for them reflect the requirements of efficiency more or less effectively. In the absence of precise data on the future prices and needs implied by present-day decisions, the risk of error is not eliminated by them. But it is somewhat reduced if the investments realized are in fact those that show the highest rates of return, as evaluated by the managers in charge of projects with the help of the partial information available to them.

When considering true efficiency in the use of newly created capital, we must therefore avoid any tendency to be dogmatic. We can illustrate the problem by distinguishing very large investments from the multitude of other investments required by the growth, renewal, and modernization of the productive system. We can then say that the former should involve centralized or concerted decisions, taken after direct analysis by special studies of their major repercussions. In the case of the latter, on the contrary, efficiency is promoted by a free capital market, which offers financing for any project with a sufficient rate of return and submitted by a solvent borrower.

On this basis, the situation has changed substantially in France over the postwar period. Up to the mid-1950's, the medium- and long-term capital market was extremely limited. Financing by means of outside long-term money was difficult for most privately owned firms; they had to rely almost entirely on self-financing. This situation was the result of a number of factors.

First, the law that immediately after the war laid the framework for the banking system limited the operations allowed to deposit banks to the issue of short-term credits. Money savings of individuals could therefore be used only for short-term loans. On a number of occasions, financing by discounting the value of commercial credits was easy; but this was obviously not suitable for investments of any size.

Second, financial institutions that could have made medium- and long-term loans confined themselves to a low overall volume of operations of this type. Merchant banks operated only in very narrow areas of the economy. Institutions such as the Crédit National or the Caisse des Dépôts et Consignations made available to firms a very low overall total of financing. That is why we saw, in Chapter 10, that even as late as 1956 the total of medium- and long-term net credits for capital investment by privately owned nonagricultural firms was only 2.4 percent of their gross investment. If estimates were available for earlier years, they would certainly show an even lower proportion.

Third, the option of direct stock issues to the public was just as difficult. In order to facilitate financing of operations that at the time seemed to deserve high priority, a law of December 1946 had required prior authorization by the Ministry of Finance for any issue exceeding

25 million old francs in value. Total resources made available through this channel to privately owned companies remained low (less than 20 percent of their gross investment); moreover, they were of help to particular sectors only, such as iron and steel.

In summary, then, the long-term capital market was available in general to only a small number of firms, and it did not permit even very productive operations to be financed in sectors of the economy not considered beforehand to have priority.

The situation changed gradually. From 1955 on, issues on the financial market became far larger. The rise in stock exchange quotations stimulated investment in industrial stock, and authorization by the Ministry of Finance became a less hampering constraint. Various regulations after 1958 embodied decisions waiving the need for this authorization for an increasing number of stock issues. In 1968 the only regulations still in force were those intended to ensure orderly progress in successive stock issues. In the same period financial institutions specializing in medium- and long-term credit made a larger volume of financing available to firms (see Table 10.14, p. 341). Increasingly numerous requests for financing therefore competed to obtain loans.

Last, the privileged condition of publicly owned enterprises, which even in the early 1960's could obtain loans at exceptionally low rates, was gradually ended. As a result, these firms were stimulated to be more economical in their capital expenditure and to eliminate investments with low returns.

Although we cannot base our remarks on any rigorous study, we believe strongly that the expanding capital market gradually transformed the factors governing distribution of financial resources from 1955 to 1965 between the different sources of demand, and that this favored increased efficiency in use of these resources. Some industrial investments with potentially high returns were not being carried out around 1950 because they did not concern sectors considered by the government to have priority and could not be self-financed. Revival of the money market made it possible to remove this cause of error in the allocation of savings.

CONTROLS OVER PRODUCTS

The efficient functioning of product markets is easy to describe in theory. But in practice it requires certain conditions more difficult to define. We shall take here the position that markets efficiency is highest when direct official controls are narrowly limited to the "policing" of transactions, when the tax system and the rates imposed by the authorities follow closely the principle that relative prices must accurately reflect the costs to the nation, and when monopolistic agreements and other restrictive practices are efficiently combated.

We shall now examine the situation in France after the war from three successive points of view. For most products, official rationing ceased before 1950. Nevertheless, import quotas existed until 1959, and carried with them a system of licensing for importers. In the winter of 1956–57 the shortage of energy products following closure of the Suez Canal had the effect of temporarily enhancing the role of these direct controls.

One should probably not exaggerate the size of the gap that may have developed between allocation by these official measures and allocation by the market. Official allocation related to a rather narrowly defined sphere, and the government officials responsible for applying it aimed at satisfying demand in terms of urgency; consequently, there were probably no very harmful effects in allocation of products. Nevertheless, it was unfavorable to those who were not listed among the traditional and large users of the products in question. The system must have slowed some technological development and some types of modernization, especially in medium and small firms. Maintenance of quotas may have resulted in delaying improvements in productivity before the early 1960's.

Although quantitative controls had by then completely disappeared, price regulation remained under changing and diverse forms. However, the repercussions on the working of the market seem difficult to trace. Let us begin with a brief historical sketch.[18]

In the period of shortages immediately after the war, prices were controlled at every stage. From the end of 1948 to the middle of 1952, the government attempted to apply a more liberal policy, and was helped in this by the end of rationing. Many prices were totally or partially freed between January 1948 and June 1949. This freedom lasted only a short time; from the summer of 1952, the government in fact resorted deliberately to a general price freeze.

Strict control remained the rule until 1957; the 1952 regulations were completed or updated in February 1954, July 1956, and August 1957. From that date on, many exceptions were made, freeing some products

---

[18] We are not concerned here with control over agricultural prices. It is well known that this control is necessary in every country both for the good of society and to regulate markets that by their nature are too unstable. For economic efficiency, agricultural price policies should favor scarce crops. This aim was not lacking in French policy, but it was probably followed too timidly, as is shown by the chronic surpluses in cereals and milk products and the chronic deficit in meat.

completely and others partially. In the latter case, price rates are reported by industrialists to the government, which may within 15 days object to them.

The agreement to institute the Common Market, and its actual setting up, made possible a gradual return to some degree of price freedom. Nevertheless, excessive price rises led the government to decide in 1963 to impose a new freeze; the decree of September 12 set production prices for industrial products at the level of August 31, 1963. Complementary decrees related to work carried out to order and to some services. This price freeze was still in force in 1966, but was relaxed gradually in an original way. Price freedom for goods produced was restored to particular firms or business organizations provided that the average price for their output as a whole did not rise. This flexibility enabled firms to offset rises on some products by reductions on others. Another procedure followed for restoring price freedom was the program contracts, by which firms committed themselves to carrying out in the medium term certain actions consistent with the general objectives of the National Plan, and in return were allowed a certain freedom in setting prices.

This rapid sketch of the ways prices were fixed shows clearly that some form of control has practically always been the rule. The various governments were anxious to combat rises in the general level of prices, and resorted from time to time to more or less systematic forms of freeze. Whether or not this approach was effective as a way of fighting inflation will not be discussed here. But were the consequences of price control entirely unfavorable to the proper functioning of markets and to the appearance of satisfactory relative prices?

For practical reasons, the government is more often in touch with business organizations than with particular firms. The former Director General of Prices stresses that "in its intervention, the government can deal only with business organizations: it is out of the question for it to discuss prices with the multitude of producers or traders involved."[19] He also mentions that the representatives of these organizations "may have a tendency to present as a typical case what is in fact an exceptional case for particular producers who are in a difficult situation; they become, without any wrong intention, the advocates of minorities whose difficulties they extend to an entire sector of the market." Moreover, many business organizations are dominated by a small number of large firms whose interest it is to see prices lined up on the costs of the least

[19] Louis Frank, in *Les Prix*, series "Que sais-je" (Paris, 1964). The information in this part of our study on price regulations comes from this book.

profitable firms. On the other side, government officials operating the controls seek to set sales prices as close as possible to production costs, and to force the marginal firms to improve productivity to an extent that will enable them to sell at those prices. But the calculation of costs is necessarily based on investigations that are difficult to carry out and update.

This description suggests the conclusion that price control must lead to results that reflect in many cases the particular features of a confrontation between business organizations and government officials rather than the real trends that, arising in changes in demand and in production methods, would find their expression on the markets. Price control, moreover, must lead to some rigidity, since in each price-setting operation, reference to prices in force earlier always has special influence. Controls are therefore likely to be harmful to the effective functioning of the market.

Nevertheless, in practice the interference with the structure of relative prices has probably been more limited than would appear at first sight, for two reasons. First, the freeze periods alternated with periods in which production prices had in fact recovered near-freedom: 1949, at the time of the first freeing of prices; 1954, when wholesale prices were trending downward; 1960–63, after price stabilization; and 1966–67, when the freeze was in practice applied with considerable flexibility. If rigid control is maintained for a relatively short period, it does not have time to be reflected in marked differentials between the effective structure of relative prices and that which would result from the operations of the market.

Second, price control has always applied to quoted price lists. But competition between firms often took the form of more or less large rebates on these prices. To the extent that these rebates become habitual, and where they did not have a discriminatory effect between buyers, market prices fell below list prices, whose role became relatively minor. We are not in a position to assess how important this second factor was; there is a complete lack of statistics on rebates of this kind. They are clearly more discreetly publicized than are list prices, and this must lead to some lack of regularity in their application. They were probably effective in periods of relative price stability, when the freeze itself was becoming less severe. The practice of having artificial price lists is, of course, not consistent with good market organization, since it has the effect of informing buyers inaccurately of the real price situation.

In summary, setting aside the administrative allocation of some products subject to quotas in the 1950's, it is difficult to form a clear picture of the functioning of markets for industrial products in the rather mixed system that prevailed, though unevenly, in France. Apart from protestations of management organizations, did the freezes affect the formation of relative prices in any marked way? Did they introduce lasting distortions in the rate of profit compared with that which would have prevailed under competition? We see no compelling reason to think so.

PRICES AND SOCIAL COSTS

In order that markets may correctly guide the allocation of resources, prices must properly reflect social costs. In the competitive equilibrium of theory, which neglects public consumption and external effects, this property would be automatically achieved. But in actual economies, which include a large public sector, to bring prices into line with social costs is not so simple. It requires deliberate acts of policy.

The state must first correct the distorting influences of the most obvious external effects. It must then correctly fix the rates for services sold by public monopolies. And last, it must act so that taxes do not lead to unjustified gaps between prices and costs. These three aims were not lacking in French economic policy after the war. Various reforms introduced in the 1950's seem to have had the effect of ensuring better consistency between prices and social costs, and therefore to improve the efficiency of the price system.

In the last section we shall discuss the policy of regional development, which was closely linked to the presence of external effects. For the moment we shall examine taxation, and then price determination for public services. Attention should be concentrated on *indirect taxation*, both because it provides French governments with two-thirds of their resources and because it is the most likely to create gaps between prices and costs. It is a general form of taxation that is practically impossible to modulate in relation to the external effects likely to arise in each particular case. The best rule here seems to be "neutrality"; indirect taxes should be set in such a way as not to affect relative prices—that is to say, the relationship between the prices of different goods and services.

It is certain that the move from taxes on business turnover and specific taxes in 1920 to the tax on production in 1936 and to the value-added tax (VAT) in 1954 represents continuous improvement in the economic neutrality of indirect taxation. The tax on business turnover was simple in principle and in method of payment, but it had the serious disadvantage that it was paid each time a product changed hands, since it was assessed on the total value of sales made by each firm. This cascade effect favored short sales links and integrated firms, although integration of this kind is not in itself in all cases economically viable. It led to too high taxation of products resulting from long manufacturing processes involving different industries. The disadvantages of this system led to the adoption in 1936 of a first form of taxation on production: this was paid once only on a product, when it moved from the industrial cycle to the trading cycle. Without modifying the principle, the 1948 reform changed the procedure for payment of this tax: it was no longer payable once only at a particular stage, but each producer had to pay on his turnover a proportional tax from which he deducted taxes paid on the raw materials *physically incorporated* in the products he was selling. This deduction effectively eliminated double taxation, but only on raw materials.

The fact that only part of the taxes on purchases was deducted led to some distortions analyzed in a book much read in that period.[20] The chief distortions resulted, on the one hand, from the fact that taxes on investments could not be deducted, so that the real cost of capital was too high, and, on the other hand, from the tax on services, which remained similar to the old tax on turnover, with all the cascade effects observed in its operation.

The tax on value added as defined in 1954 was to be levied at one rate only, and was not to have these disadvantages. All taxes on purchases and on services became deductible from taxes on sales. The value-added tax system was originally confined to industrial firms, but in 1968 it was extended to small shops, trade, and services.

In practice VAT has never been an absolutely neutral tax. Apart from the fact that it did not affect all firms before 1968, it incorporated special rates in a number of cases, which tended to increase. From the beginning, it was deliberately favorable to investment, since in most cases taxes become totally deductible as soon as capital equipment is bought, and not only in pace with amortization. Nevertheless, this tax played an undoubtedly positive role in bringing relative prices closer to costs and in improving the efficiency of the French price system. Similarly, rate policies for public services tended to bring prices paid by users closer to true costs.

At the end of the war, such rates were by no means close to what efficient organization of the productive system would have required. They were the result of rules set at more or less distant periods in the past, and in many cases set at the time of the stagnation of the 1930's. These rules were sometimes inspired by principles that today seem to us erroneous (for example, setting rates ad valorem for transport services).

[20] Maurice Lauré, *La Taxe sur la valeur ajoutée* (Paris, 1952).

At a time when inflation was pushing all prices up, rates had been updated according to rules that progressively became less and less satisfactory, less and less consistent with each other. Whatever one may think of present-day rates in relation to what they should be, it must be admitted that minimum order has been reestablished and the most obvious inconsistencies corrected.

We shall now examine more particularly price determination for different forms of energy, then rates for selling electricity, and last rates for railroad transportation. These questions are important because the scope for substitution between different types of energy and different kinds of transportation are much wider than that between raw materials in the strict sense. Firms can operate successfully using a source of energy that on grounds of national availability would not be advisable. A correct system of rates is in practice a necessary condition for the management of enterprises to be reflected in effective allocation of national resources.

Prices for different forms of energy are directly or indirectly under the control of the state. Electricity production and distribution and coal production are more or less entirely nationalized, and their rates or prices can change only by official decision. Similarly, the size of the tax on oil products enables the selling price to be controlled.

The trends of the prices of different forms of energy show no signs of marked changes in the government's policies. Table 13.6, which reproduces the wholesale price indexes of three chief forms of energy, indicates only moderate differences. Nevertheless, it reflects to some extent changes in public options in relation to energy.

In the immediate postwar reconstruction, deliberate preference was given to energy of national origin. Heavy investment was made in the coal industry and in Electricité de France. The price of coal was fixed

TABLE 13.6
Prices of Energy Products, 1949–69
(1959 = 100)

Year	Fuel oil	Coal (raw, fines)	High-tension electricity
1949	57	44	59
1952	78	68	81
1955	73	69	81
1959	100	100	100
1962	92	100	100
1965	93	104	99
1969	106	110	118

Source: Annuaire statistique de la France, résumé rétrospectif, 1966, p. 413. The 1969 figures were added subsequently by the author.

relatively low, and taxes on oil products were high. From 1955, however, the search for financial equilibrium for the coal industry introduced a gap between the price of coal and the price of fuel oil not much different from the price maintained thereafter. From 1958 it became apparent that there was a need to reduce coal output. Despite high labor costs, the rise in the price of coal was contained at the level of its "regression cost" (marginal cost for a declining industry), which was lower than the average cost of production. Over the whole postwar period, electricity prices grew roughly parallel with the prices of oil products used as a source of energy for industry.

A detailed study would be needed for rigorous comparison between prices and social costs. It can, of course, be observed that on many occasions electricity was sold at a price that did not cover operating costs, and even less financial charges. But, considered in isolation, this observation has little significance; comparison would have to be made with the situation of other forms of energy. It is not easy to reply a priori to questions such as the following: Is the cost of capital, which is obviously high in electricity production, fully taken into account in tariffs? Does taxation on oil products have the effect of ensuring some consistency between prices and social costs? In the absence of such a study, we incline to think that from 1955 the most obvious discrepancies between relative prices and costs of the different forms of energy were corrected.

For electricity, the rate structure can be more important than the particular price level of a basic consumer contract. Now the tariffs in the 1950's were not suited to a correct policy in industrial plant, as was shown brilliantly by Boiteux.[21] Those tariffs had been set in 1935 and were then probably on the right lines, but the rules of reevaluation had completely altered their effects. For one thing, the fixed charge, linked to the power taken by a high-tension subscriber, had not changed between 1935 and 1956 despite a very high increase in prices. Its real cost was therefore far too low to be a factor in limiting the level of power demanded. Second, the price per kilowatt-hour had been differentiated in 1935 according to different regions and according to the volume of consumption. The coefficients of differentiation were not subject to escalation and therefore had little weight after the war.[22] The rates were

[21] M. Boiteux, "Le Tarif vert d'Electricité de France," *Revue française de l'energie*, January 1957.

[22] The selling price was calculated by a formula of the type $p = a + b(I - I_0)$, where a was a coefficient of differentiation according to different regions and to the volume of consumption, b was an "index coefficient," and I was an index of the electricity production cost. Coefficient I was equal to 7,300, which made this corrective term preponderant.

thus in practice uniform. They penalized large consumers, who had to pay a rate higher than the cost of the energy supplied to them. They did not stimulate industrialists to set up plant where the cost of production of electricity was lowest.

The management of Electricité de France did not merely try to correct these obvious imperfections. With perseverance it was able to work out and get accepted tariff rates by means of which the price of each type of supply drew close to its marginal cost to the country as a whole. This revision took effect in 1957 for high-tension electricity and in 1965 for low-tension current.

For high-tension, which is what interests us particularly here, the new system of rates, instituted at the end of 1956, was called the "green tariff." Firms were still allowed to choose between the new tariff and the old, which however was revised by a very large increase in the fixed charge. Since the new tariff was more attractive, most of the large consumers opted for it from 1958 on. From 1961 almost all high-tension electricity was being sold under this tariff, whose main feature is to differentiate the price per kwh according to regions, hours of day, and times of year.

This system of rates must help to guide the investment decisions of large industrial consumers of electricity. Moreover, it is reflected in a rather obvious saving: since it reduces demand at peak hours, it enables certain investment projects to expand power capacity to be delayed for some months, and allows power stations required at peak but having very high generation costs to be operated for a shorter period. The annual report of Electricité de France for 1964 observes that on the day of highest demand in the year, the ratio between maximum demand at the peak hour and average demand had fallen from 1.37 in 1954 to 1.21 in 1963 and 1964. This change, which is very favorable for production costs, was attributed to the introduction of the "green tariff."

Two reforms of a similar nature were carried out in 1947 and 1962 for the rates on transportation of goods by rail. In view of the great complexity of transportation costs, it is practically impossible to work out a rate system that reflects these costs exactly. Nevertheless the two reforms in question had the effect of reducing significantly the gaps between rates and costs of production.[23]

At the end of the nineteenth century, when the railroads in practice had a monopoly on transportation, an ad valorem tariff system had been set up. Rates were low for goods regarded as of prime necessity or hav-

---

[23] For greater details see, for example, *Hommes et techniques*, no. 252, November 1965.

ing a low value; they were high for costly goods or finished products. Between the two wars, when competition from road transport began to be felt, these tariffs could be seen as quite unsuitable. Traffic was taken over by road haulage firms as soon as the cost of supply by road was significantly lower than railroad tariffs, and this applied whatever the effective supply cost of railroad transport. The result was an uneconomic distribution between road and rail.

In order to eliminate the most marked anomalies, various measures were then taken. Thus, in 1937 "ceiling price lists" simplified the tariffs of the Société Nationale des Chemins de Fer (SNCF), reducing the highest rates. In addition, complex regulations were introduced. Haulers had to obtain a license to operate. These licenses were limited in number and allocated for specified regions; they became privileges for sale to others, sometimes at high prices. Different kinds of fraud, a widening of the quotas for licenses, and the granting of nationwide licenses gradually reduced the effectiveness of these regulations in the postwar period. Moreover, the regulations were insufficient to stimulate rational allocation of traffic between the two kinds of transport.

In 1947 tariff reform was first carried out, on the principle that the rate should cover the cost of production: for each type of good, the average charge per freight car or truck and the length of the average haul were determined; these two elements were the base first for calculating the average cost of supplying the transportation for that good, and second for determining the tariffs to be charged. Various other features in the tariff attempted to translate costs accurately.

The principal criticism made of this tariff was that it did not allow for the particular features of the railroad links between the points of origin and destination. Operating conditions varied considerably between one line and another, and equalizing tariffs over all the lines of the network as a whole still led to inefficient allocation of some types of traffic. On some lines where railroad tariffs were significantly higher than costs, haulers were taking a large proportion of the market although their supply costs were higher than those of the railroads. On other lines, on the contrary, the SNCF tariffs were too low to be hit by competition from road, whereas haulers could have provided the transportation at a lower cost.

The 1947 reform was followed in 1951 by an amendment that attempted to remedy some of these defects. Indexes were applied to the different railroad stations as a function of the operating conditions of traffic leaving or arriving. For each shipment, the rate took account of the sum of indexes relating to the station of origin and the end-journey station. Nevertheless this amendment was insufficient to take directly into account differences between the supply costs on the different lines. With the accelerated increase in road haulage, examples of wrong distribution of traffic multiplied.

The reform of October 1, 1962, aimed at removing these disadvantages. It introduced the concept of a "weighted distance," which was applied to each section of the line and worked out as proportional to the cost of transportation on that section. The price for a given amount of transportation on this basis was related not to the distance actually covered but to the total weighted distance; the relationship between the latter and the former was between 0.8 and 1.4 for the great bulk of the traffic.

Thus, whether we look at indirect taxation, relative prices of different forms of energy, electricity tariffs, or tariffs for railroad transport, we find a trend toward setting prices that reflect costs with increasing accuracy. This trend is one of the features leading us to consider that the market system was gradually enabled to improve its capacity for efficient operation.

AGREEMENTS AND COMPETITION

Over the 1930's, and as a reaction against the depression, there had been a large number of agreements among French firms. During the war and immediately after it, an important role had been given to management organizations in setting up first the allocation system and then the reconstruction and modernization programs. In 1950 the French productive system was thus the setting for a complex interplay of agreements, which effectively limited the scope for competition and threatened to act as a brake on progress. However, legislation on restrictive practices, rules adopted for public purchases, and the opening of frontiers to trade led to the gradual achievement of a markedly more competitive climate.

The first measures for controlling agreements were taken in August 1953, when the Commission Technique des Ententes et Positions Dominantes was set up. Its task was to give advice on "business carried out under agreements or from dominant market positions presumed to be against the law," that is to say, business not justified by improvements in productivity and which "has as its goal or can have the effect of preventing, restricting, or distorting the play of competition." The reports of the commission are followed by administrative action and in due course by legal prosecution.

The activity and operation of this commission were considered insuf-

ficient by the committee set up by the Premier in November 1959 with
the task of studying obstacles to economic growth; this committee is
frequently called by the name of its two vice-chairmen, MM. J. Rueff
and L. Armand.[24]

Appearing before this committee, the chairman of the Commission
des Ententes admitted that its activity had only slightly affected restrictive practices. In five years, from 1955 to 1959, the commission had
studied only 20 cases, whereas in the United States the Anti-Trust Division of the Department of Justice permanently has 300 inquiries in hand
and the Federal Trade Commission considers 4,000 cases yearly. Moreover, the publicity given to the reports of the Commission des Ententes
had been very restricted.

Some strengthening of the role of the commission was thereafter carried out. It is true that the number of cases studied remained low: 6 per
year on the average between 1960 and 1968. Nevertheless the 72 cases
handled in 14 years relate to a very wide range of products, and must
have reduced the most flagrant of the restrictive practices.[25] Most of the
cases involve intermediate products sold to firms, and the agreements
were probably set up as a reaction to the policy of these firms' purchasing departments.

From 1959 on, the reports of the commission and subsequent minis-
terial decisions have been published in official journals. In most cases,
they require the restrictive practices to be abandoned. Sometimes certain practices are allowed provisionally, putting the burden of proof on
the firms in the agreement that within a predetermined time these practices have led to substantial economic benefits. Up to 1966, the official
directions sent out had not been followed by prosecution of agreements
that were against the law. After that date, some legal actions were taken
in order to encourage firms to wind up their agreements without await-
ing examination of their case by the commission.

It is difficult enough to assess the effectiveness of action taken against
restrictive practices, but the role of regulations governing public sector
purchases is even more so. To study this question, two cases should be
distinguished: public purchase of goods, articles, or services serving a
wide market, and highly specific supplies that are the subject of direct
negotiation. In the first case it is necessary only to test whether competitive conditions have been respected, and therefore in particular that

[24] *Rapport sur les obstacles à l'expansion économique* (Paris, 1960).
[25] See Information Department, Ministry of Economics and Finance, *La Commission technique des ententes et positions dominantes*, 1970.

no restrictive agreements were present. In the second case, the problem is ascertaining whether prices were correctly set, that is to say, whether the public departments purchasing were in a position to check the cost of production calculations presented by the supplier, and whether they followed a correct rule for determining margins above these production costs.

We have not been able to carry out a proper study of these matters. This would have entailed examining the rules for price decisions in public sector purchases, studying the role of price control departments in the various purchasing organizations (the Army, the Post Office and Government Communication Services, the Highways and Bridges Department, the Atomic Energy Commission, etc.). We should mention, however, that the public authorities in practice were concerned with improving the terms governing public purchases: in particular, the Commission Centrale des Marchés de l'Etat, which supplies investigators to purchasing organizations that do not have control departments, has played an increasingly important role in the 1960's.

The struggle against obstacles to efficient operation of markets may seem somewhat contradictory to the trend toward facilitating and promoting regrouping of firms, a trend that has been one of the main features of government policy from the mid-1960's. There would indeed have been a contradiction if the French market had not at the same time been opened to competition from abroad. This liberalization was without doubt the principal force behind establishment of a more competitive market.

As we saw in Chapter 12, French imports of manufactured products grew at a rapid rate from 1959 on. In some cases foreign competition became so strong that the public at large was able to see it featured in the newspapers—for example in 1962, when Italian refrigerators appeared on the French market and took over a large part of it. In most cases, the change in the market situation was less startling, but no less real. In all industrial sectors, competition increased as a result of the arrival of products and articles from abroad.

In the commercial field, it was similarly not before 1960 that competition became sufficiently strong to speed up the necessary structural changes. The shortages of the war and postwar years had generated a lack of commercial spirit, which lasted throughout the 1950's. The poor organization of distribution networks was considered in 1959 by the Rueff-Armand committee as an obstacle to growth.

Legislative and tax reforms gradually removed most of the protection enjoyed by small traders since the 1930's. This led to the setting up of supermarkets and chain stores. A number of experiments were also made aimed at lower-cost trading. One that attracted public attention may be cited here.

The Magasins Leclerc, operating in the field of mass-demand products, mainly food at the start, set out with the objective of selling practically at wholesale prices, although with a quality of service obviously lower than in other stores. There must now be around 100 such centers in France, in both the Paris region and the provinces, selling a fairly wide range of products. These centers had some difficulty in becoming established; in particular, they were forced to take advantage of legislation placing an obligation on producers to sell their products; producers, with the aim of ensuring a special position to their specialized outlets, had tended either to refuse to sell to the Leclerc stores or to sell at prices above their usual ones. The fact that these difficulties have been overcome, whereas previously they had proved insurmountable, is witness to the change in climate prevailing in relationships among firms.

To develop measures of the impact on the French productive system of the return to keener competition ought to be the task of statistical research. This is a difficult topic, however, for effects of this kind arise in the course of numerous small individual operations; their incidence at the macroeconomic level is very indirect and therefore difficult to isolate, and most often it is mixed with the effects of many other factors affecting national production. In Chapter 6, when dealing with the structure of industry, we observed that the degree of concentration has been relatively constant: it increased in some industries but decreased in others, and the most frequent trend was toward rapid growth of units of intermediate size. The point to be resolved, therefore, is what relatively "pure" signs of increased competition may have appeared at the macroeconomic level.

We thought some interesting indicators might be found in the different development of rates of profit in the various sectors. In particular, we have attempted to distinguish relatively concentrated sectors such as steel, iron foundries, automobiles, glass, and rubber from less concentrated sectors such as textiles, most of the mechanical and electrical industries, and miscellaneous industries.

For the relative movement of profit rates in these two groups of sectors to have been strongly influenced by the revival of competition, its effect must have been exercised in a different manner in each of the two groups. It may be, in particular, that the influence of oligopolies was greater in the 1950's than it is now; the concentrated sectors in such a case would have become more competitive, and this would have had the effect of lowering their profit margins. But it is also possible that the dominant role of oligopolies may have been little reduced by foreign competition and that as a result their margins have suffered little. It is also possible that foreign competition was strongest in the less concentrated sectors whose firms previously enjoyed overall protection and were ill-prepared for the opening of the French borders.

In order to see whether there were nevertheless trends to be observed, we have examined for a certain number of sectors the movements of two indicators: (1) the ratio between gross income for tax purposes (profit plus allocations to reserve funds and amortizations) and the turnover of firms subject to the real profits tax basis from 1955 on; and (2) the ratio between gross business income and turnover in the accounts of sectors for the years 1959 and 1966.[26] The changes recorded are too complex for simple trends to be easily observed. Short-term economic factors, which were different in each sector, affected margins. The long-term trend is weak both for low-concentration sectors such as textiles and for fairly highly concentrated sectors such as heavy electrical equipment or the group of chemical and rubber industries. Competition probably played a part in reducing margins in some of the concentrated sectors: iron and steel from 1960 to 1966, and automobiles from 1958 to 1961. But it had the same effect in various low-concentration sectors: primary metal processing from 1958 to 1961, the mechanical industries from 1960 to 1966, and the paper industry from 1961 to 1965. In brief, we did not extend our investigation in sufficient depth to obtain a clear picture of a fairly complex phenomenon.

ACTION ON REGIONAL DEVELOPMENT

Satisfactory functioning of the price system presupposes in particular that external effects are corrected in some manner. Economic calculations at the level of each unit of production should not neglect the benefits or costs that an increase in its activity will lead to indirectly for other units of production. A purely free-market system does not take these external effects into account. Regulations and action by the government that are in fact aimed at correcting them are many in nature and complex; they include prohibitions on certain types of output, the obligation to ensure a degree of elimination of waste, and subsidies to

[26] INSEE Collections, series C, no. 4, November 1969.

some types of activity. To study these in detail and to examine how they changed in the postwar period would have led us into a full-scale research project. Nevertheless a high proportion of these external effects is linked to the location of the activities in question. If policies for regional development are studied, a particularly important aspect of the problem is covered.

In France, regional disparities take two forms: an excessive disequilibrium between the Paris region and the rest of the country, and a contrast between the western area, where there is little employment, and the eastern area, which is more developed. From 1955 on, measures were taken to decentralize Paris and to develop the other regions; but it was chiefly from 1964 that a regional policy was fully defined and given tools for action.

If a deliberate policy of regional development represents a factor in the acceleration of growth, this is primarily for demographic reasons. In the regions that the government tried to assist, there is large net emigration, and a high proportion of the population works in agriculture. Migration is never easy: before deciding to leave, a future migrant seeks work at home even if he is not well suited to it and if wages are lower than the national average. Similarly, a peasant will change his type of work more easily if he is not at the same time forced to move to another region. For these two reasons regional development must reduce hidden unemployment. Moreover, the demand for social capital and housing created by the setting up of new economic activities is larger in the Paris region than elsewhere. It even seems that the price of social capital and all the costs of congestion are higher there than in the other regions: for example, the average cost per kilometer of urban highway or the cost of tunnels in Paris in relation to these costs in provincial cities; the average price of housing, which is 25 percent lower in the provinces; and the cost of time lost. Thus, setting up a firm in a depressed region would have favorable external effects by increasing employment. Establishing a firm or expanding it in the Paris region, on the contrary, would lead to unfavorable external effects.

The policy of assistance to regional development acted in two ways that were largely complementary: on individual firms, and on local authorities or by the creation of specialized public organizations. We shall refer here only to the effect on individual firms, which seems the most directly linked to the questions this chapter is concerned with. Moreover, it began to take effect from the mid-1950's, whereas the creation of new institutions did not become important until after 1963 through the setting up of specialized administrative bodies, and the creation of corporations for regional development or urban improvement.[27]

Public policy in this matter was made effective at the level of private firms by direct financial assistance encouraging regional development, and by the policies followed in granting building permits for industrial installations.

Since 1955, the government has granted payments and loans to firms that decentralize or convert to new types of business. Since the 1960's there have been in addition tax exemptions (increased amortization allowances, reductions in charges on transfers, exemption from patent payments). The "special capital equipment subsidies" (which became "industrial development subsidies" or "industrial improvement subsidies") are confined to firms that create or develop new types of activity in areas suffering from serious and permanent underemployment or from inadequate economic development. They can rise in particular cases as high as 25 percent of the investment they subsidize: on the average, they represent between 10 and 15 percent in different years. Loans for conversion and decentralization of firms are granted by the Fonds de Développement Economique et Social (FDES) at particularly favorable rates of interest if one takes into account the risk borne by the operations being financed. These loans are available for creating, extending, or transferring activities in areas where this is considered desirable. In 1960, for example, the loans reached 29 percent of the overall investment to the financing of which they contributed.

The total of subsidies and loans has changed substantially from one year to another according to whether or not large operations were carried out.[28] The subsidies were very low before 1959, and thereafter retained a fairly constant level (between 50 and 100 million francs at 1962 prices). The FDES loans were high between 1956 and 1958, and in 1960, 1963, 1965, 1967, and 1968. Altogether, the subsidies and loans ranged between 0.15 and 0.35 percent of total gross fixed capital formation of French firms, and the investments that were partially so financed amounted to about 1 percent of the same total.

At the same time, the building of industrial installations was subject to controls aimed at slowing development in the Paris region. Special

[27] On this subject see the appendix on the regional breakdown of the capital equipment budget in the Finance Bill for 1966 (reproduced in *Problèmes économiques*, nos. 941, 946, 947, January and February, 1966).

[28] Statistical data are given in the annual reports of the Fonds de Développement Economique et Social. See, for example, *Statistiques et études financières*, supplement, no. 252, December 1969.

approval had to be obtained for granting an industrial building permit in that region. The commission responsible for granting these approvals seems to have achieved a substantial reduction in the increase of total industrial building in Paris.[29] Considering industrial building permits for surfaces of more than 500 square meters, we see that for the period 1959–68 the total area authorized grew far more slowly in the Paris region than in France as a whole: the figures vary sharply from one year to the next, but with results for the three years 1959–61 = 100, the index for the years 1966–68 is 168 for France as a whole and only 105 for the Paris region.[30]

This double policy of encouraging development in the depressed regions and slowing expansion in Paris seems rather modest per scope. Nevertheless it may help to explain a development whose effects had been felt with increasing force over the 1960's. A study of migratory movements between the censuses of 1954 and 1962, and between those of 1962 and 1968, shows that net arrivals in the Paris region slowed (from an annual rate of 1.2 percent of the resident population to 0.7 percent). Meanwhile, departures slowed in the regions where they were largest (Western Normandy, −0.6 percent to −0.2 percent; Brittany, −0.4 percent to −0.1 percent). Similarly, the growth in industrial consumption of energy was particularly rapid in the west of France: in 1967 the index (1958 = 100) was 267 for Brittany, 263 for Aquitaine, 153 for France as a whole, and 151 for the Paris region. Last, the development of industrial employment between 1962 and 1968 shows clearly the benefit obtained by the western regions from the policy of decentralization. In 1962 these regions employed 12 percent of the labor of expanding industries; but they have since obtained 34 percent of the increase in employment of those industries. Whereas industrial employment dropped by 1 percent in the Paris region, it grew by nearly 3 percent in Brittany.[31]

Statistics cannot show clearly a measured assessment of the impact of changes in market structure on the rate of productivity growth, since this is too diffuse a phenomenon. However, pulling together our findings on the most significant changes affecting market workings leads to an overall picture as follows.

[29] See P. Durand, "Dix ans de décentralisation industrielle," *Problèmes économiques*, no. 945, February 10, 1966.

[30] See *Statistiques et indicateurs des régions françaises*, INSEE Collections, no. R2, December 1969.

[31] For further details see P. A. Muet, "L'Evolution de l'emploi industriel d'après les recensements de 1954, 1962 et 1968," *Economie et statistique*, October 1970.

A principal feature was the coexistence of public initiative and market forces. This situation altered considerably between the early 1950's and the late 1960's under the influence both of numerous legislative or regulatory decisions and the liberalization of foreign trade: obstacles to market activity more or less disappeared, the public authorities attempted to work increasingly within the context of prices reflecting true costs, and a far more competitive climate gradually came into being. Most economists are probably willing to grant these changes a role in the improvements achieved by French productivity.[32]

[32] New statistics, which became available after the French edition of this book was published, show that mobility increased substantially in the 1960's and that structural transformations accelerated. See in particular C. Thélot, "La Mobilité professionnelle," *Economie et statistique*, December 1973.

CHAPTER FOURTEEN

Planning and Economic Information

Did the system of planning set up in France beginning in 1946 contribute to the relatively fast growth in the postwar period as compared with earlier years? It is no easy task to answer this question. National planning was part of the wider whole—economic policy—from which it cannot easily be separated. Although several books have been devoted to an overall study of French planning,[1] little research has been done on the way in which it may have affected the behavior and decisions of firms and official bodies.[2] French planners themselves have not studied systematically how effective their action has been. Nevertheless a syn-

[1] We should mention in particular, among studies on the logic and philosophy of planning, François Perroux, *Le IVᵉ Plan français* (Paris, 1962); Pierre Massé, *Le Plan ou l'anti-hasard* (Paris, 1965); Claude Gruson, *Origine et espoirs de la planification française* (Paris, 1968); and, among more descriptive works, Pierre Bauchet, *L'Expérience française de planification* (Paris, 1962); John and Anne-Marie Hackett, *Economic Planning in France* (London, 1963); Atreize (a joint work organized by P. Dubois), *La Planification française en pratique* (Paris, 1971).

[2] However, some studies have been made by American researchers. Messrs. Christensen, McArthur, and Scott of the Harvard Business School carried out an inquiry in 1965 and 1966 on the mechanics through which planning affected individual firms. This was done by an in-depth study of a number of large firms; see John H. McArthur and Bruce R. Scott, *L'Industrie française face aux Plans* (Paris, 1970; see also their *Industrial Planning in France*; Boston, 1969); Douglas Keare carried out an in-depth investigation on the influence of planning (Third, Fourth, and Fifth Plans) on economic policy, but we have available only fragments of his work. Apart from these studies, we have used various official documents such as the National Plan achievement reports; the work by Jacques Lautman and J. C. Thoenig (sociologists), *Planification et administrations centrales* (Paris, 1964); the studies by CEPREL on implementing the Third Plan (*Bulletin du CEPREL*, July 1964, December 1964); the INSEE studies on implementing the Fourth Plan ("Rapport sur les comptes de la nation de l'année 1965," *Etudes et conjoncture*, June 1966); the INSEE inquiry on economic information carried out in January 1967 with the help of 2,000 heads of firms; the studies by the Institut Européen d'Administration des Entreprises (INSEAD) at Fontainebleau on firms and the Fourth Plan; the studies carried out in 1967 under the direction of J. Houssiaux at the request of the Commissariat Général of the National Plan.

thesis of the various pieces of research carried out on French national planning, an analysis of the documents on the contents of the Plans and their execution, and our own knowledge gained from personal participation in the administration of planning enable us to appraise the influence of the official plans on growth.[3]

We shall attempt to assess, first, what influence may have been exerted on the behavior of the active agents in the economy (in particular of firms) by the fact that a consistent picture of a growth economy was put before them; second, how and to what extent planning may have affected the practice of economic policy in a direction favorable to expansion; and third, what part the development of economic and technological information has played in growth.

The influences, respectively, of planning and of information must be considered together because of the close links that have existed between these two growth factors. The quality of the economic information system has conditioned the effectiveness of planning. Conversely, the progress of economic information in France since the war has been closely tied to the work of planning, and the same has been the case for information gathering and its processing or diffusion. Indeed we shall see that information has been one of the key practical instruments of the method of planning, which is based essentially on persuasion and stimulation, rather than on coercion and regulation.

NATIONAL PLAN FORECASTS AND THE BEHAVIOR OF FIRMS

Medium-term economic projections were made as part of the preparation of each National Plan, with the help of the various relevant official bodies and representatives of firms. These projections, often referred to as generalized market studies, led to the outlining of possible and coherent pictures of the economic future; the various decision-making bodies in the economy were invited to make decisions consistent with these pictures. They were invited, not constrained. The word "objectives," long used to refer to these projections, may have led to error—and may do so still. Except for the first National Plan (and only in the case of some sectors) the projections as a whole always had the character of forecasts rather than objectives. The change in terminology introduced at the time of the preparation of the Fifth Plan should not mislead: recognition of the distinction between objectives and forecasts

---

[3] At the intermediary stage of our work, we submitted our own conclusions for discussion by persons who played a central role in the French experience of planning, in particular MM. Louis-Pierre Blanc, Claude Gruson, and Jean Ripert. We thank them for their advice.

was an improvement in the definition of what French planning was about rather than a change in its nature.

Thus, projections of markets and production for particular products, made in great detail (covering several hundred products) for the Plan working groups by the industries concerned in liaison with the government, provided consistent batteries of indicators to serve as a guide for firms' decisions on production and modernization programs. Planning was thus able to contribute to growth in two ways: as an instrument for creating a climate of expansion and as a means of ensuring consistency among decisions influencing the medium-term future.

In the first place, planning may have helped growth to the extent that it led entrepreneurs and government agencies to anticipate the future in a more optimistic way than they would have done without the Plan, and also to the extent that it stimulated the work of modernization. This action of planning on behavior would have helped to raise investment rates and the degree to which productive capacity was used, as well as to stimulate productivity improvements within the various units of production.

In the second place, planning may have contributed to growth by acting as a means of ensuring consistency among decisions influencing the medium-term future: these are decisions that the play of the market can provide little light on, however effective it is in securing short-term adjustments. The National Plan, by proposing a consistent set of objectives and forecasts and acting as a generalized market study, probably makes it possible to avoid the creation of excess productive capacity or bottlenecks blocking growth or leading to external disequilibria—depending on how much weight is given the Plan by heads of firms in setting up production and investment programs for the medium term. It might even be thought that the work of preparing the Plan makes it possible to determine more efficiently the most profitable investments. It has indeed been asserted that French planning may have reduced the volume of investment necessary to ensure a given rate of economic growth.

To appreciate the role actually played by each of these two routes by which planning affects growth, it is useful to consider three categories of questions: (1) Did the projections drawn up as part of each plan represent a better guide than the forecasts that each firm would have made without them? Or at least, given that comparisons are difficult, did the National Plan outlook provide a picture of the future that, when compared with the outcome observed in practice, could be seen as correct in the case of firms that would have used it? (2) Were the projections given in the Plan known by those who prepared or made decisions?

And (3) how could these projections have been used, and how were they used, by those who knew of them?

A positive reply to the first question does not imply compellingly that, when used, the projections actually promoted growth. A priori, it is not certain that they mapped out the most effective routes for growth. If not, and if the firms had based their decisions on these projections, they might have led to a less favorable use of resources than would have been made in the absence of the Plan's forecasts. But in an economy such as the French, where the market plays an important role, it seems reasonable to assume that heads of firms did not in general make decisions contrary to the indications of the market and to the good management of their firms in order to ensure consistency with the indications provided by the National Plan.

Of course, outcomes consistent with forecasts do not necessarily mean that firms made their decisions in conformity with the Plan's forward picture. The latter was in fact largely indicative only. An outcome close to the guidelines may just as well mean that the forecasters were not wrong. This is why the two other questions must also be studied before anything can be affirmed about the effect of the projections.

Quality of the Forecasts

There are manifold difficulties in making an overall study of how the Plan's forecasts and outcomes compared.[4] First, the quantitative assessments in the Plan are not entirely standardized or made consistent with the framework of the National Accounts. This framework was in fact not available when the First Plan was prepared; it was only partially used for drawing up the Second Plan; and even in the case of the Third and Fourth Plans, which showed important improvements in statistical rigor, some slackness remained. Second, the quantitative indications in the various documents drawn up at the different stages of preparation of each plan are not entirely consistent: the report of the Plan itself, the documents of the National Accountants, the reports of commissions, and the reports of working groups. Third, changes in definition, in nomenclature, and even in numerical estimates mean that the statistical tools used for drawing up the Plan and the associated projections were, broadly speaking, not the same as the tools by which the outcome can be assessed. Fourth, revisions in the Plan and in some projections took

---

[4] There are a number of studies dealing with particular comparisons: the CEPREL study of the Third Plan (*Bulletin du CEPREL*, July 1964); INSEE reports on the Fourth Plan ("Rapport sur les comptes de la nation de l'année 1965," *Etudes et conjoncture*, June 1966, pp. 19–25, 58–91, 178–83); and references in the Plan Achievement reports.

place in certain cases while the Plan was being carried out. Chief of these revisions was the Interim National Plan drawn up while the Third Plan was being put into effect. But partial revisions also occurred in the case of other Plans; for example, forecasts for metallurgy and energy were revised while the Fourth Plan was being implemented. Finally, the projections refer to a year considered average for weather and the economic situation, whereas the outcomes relate to a particular year, marked by the special features of the moment. To carry out a rigorous comparison, the real accounts of the year studied should be replaced by fictitious trend accounts; that is, the real values for each item should be replaced by values corrected for cyclical or accidental fluctuations.

For our part, we shall merely compare with the outcomes the forecasts made at the time each plan was drawn up, since these forecasts are the most interesting from the viewpoint of our study. In most cases, the corrections necessary for a completely rigorous approach would not significantly alter the comparison. Before comparing forecasts and outcomes by industry groups, we shall consider more general values. Table 14.1 provides the basis for the comparison from National Accounts data from the Second Plan on.[5]

This table calls for several comments: (1) Significant improvements were achieved in the forward estimates from the Third Plan on; very considerable errors in fact occurred in the course of the Second Plan in relation to the different uses of output; these errors were not as great thereafter. (2) The forecast rates of growth were achieved, to an approximate order of magnitude; the slight errors incurred were upward in some cases and downward in others; they do not show any systematic over-forecasting. (3) Systematic errors were incurred in the figures for household investment (that is, investment in housing) and foreign trade; the fast rate of growth for these items was in every case underestimated, and in most cases substantially so.

The projections for investment in housing were consistently too low in all the first five plans. There are several reasons for this: underestimation of requirements,[6] which is partly explained in turn—given the ab-

---

[5] The figures relating to the First Plan are not shown, since the National Accounts system did not exist at that time. Guidelines were given only in physical terms for the output of the basic sectors (coal, steel, cement, electricity, etc.).

[6] Thus the report on the execution of the First Plan (*Cinq ans d'exécution du Plan de modernisation et d'équipement de l'Union française*, Commissariat Général du Plan, Paris, 1952, p. 349) states: "It is estimated that the rate of house building should be increased to over 200,000 dwellings per year in order to catch up with the delay incurred and to keep pace with demographic development." This order of magnitude should be compared with the estimates now commonly accepted, on the order of 500,000 dwellings.

TABLE 14.1
Forecasts and Outcomes of Four National Plans, 1952–70
(Indexes of growth)

Category	Second, 1952–57 Forecast	Outcome	Third, 1957–61 Forecast	Outcome	Fourth, 1959–65 Forecast	Outcome	Fifth, 1965–70 Forecast	Outcome
Gross domestic production	124	130	120	116	138	140	132	133
Consumption:								
By households		134	119^a	114^a	135^b	138^b	129	129
By govt. agencies		129	104	105	129	144	136	118
Total consumption	122	133			135	138	129	128
Gross fixed capital formation:								
Of firms		150	120	119	147^c	152^c	136	150
Of households	d	139^d	92	102	134^e	176^e	110	131
Of govt. agencies		143	127	129	185	176	164	142
Total capital formation	124	147	115	117	149	161	134	145
Exports	121	141	126	147	147	162	144	170
Imports	102	150	100	118	155	191	150	179

Source: Second Plan–Archives of the INSEE Programs Division. The language of the National Accounts was not yet officially in use at the time the Second Plan was drawn up. Third Plan–*Bulletin du CEPREL,* July 1964, p. 42. Fourth Plan–"Rapport sur les comptes de la nation de l'année, 1965," *Etudes et conjoncture,* June 1966, p. 19. Fifth Plan–Commissariat Général du Plan et INSEE (mimeo.), "Tableaux de bord de l'exécution du Ve Plan" (drawn up in July 1971).

Note: The periods in which the Second, Third, and Fourth National Plans were carried out were 1954–57, 1958–61, and 1962–65. But the base year for the forecasts was not necessarily that immediately preceding the first year of each plan. The figures for outcome are not entirely consistent with the latest estimates in the National Accounts; our aim has been to make the best comparisons possible.

^{a}The difference between forecast and outcome was larger in the case of consumption per capita, as a result of significant underestimate of demographic growth (between 1956 and 1961 the forecast was 1.3 million, and the outcome was 2.3 million).

^{b}As a result of the difference between the forecasts of demographic growth and the outcome between 1959 and 1965 (5.5 percent and 9.5 percent, respectively), the annual growth rate of consumption per capita achieved (3.9 percent) was lower than the forecast rate (4.2 percent).

^{c}Productive investment.

^{d}The objective was 240,000 dwellings completed in 1957; the number of dwellings in fact completed was 270,000.

^{e}Investment in housing.

sence of a true housing market—by a late appreciation of the large scale of the movement toward greater urbanization;[7] second-degree priority given to housing, explicitly in the First Plan and implicitly in the three plans following; underestimation of the pressure of demand by individuals and of the burden of saving they were ready to accept to get housing; and last, in the case of the Fourth Plan, underestimation of the size of repatriation between 1959 and 1965.

As for foreign trade, the planners made two errors in the forward projections of the first four plans. First, their statistical information was insufficient; accordingly they did not allow for the fact that by com-

[7] A change in the rate of urbanization took place after the war. Its measure could not be taken before 1962, when it became possible to compare the results of the two population censuses of 1954 and 1962.

parison with long-term movements the volume of foreign trade was extremely low in relation to production immediately after the end of World War II.[8] Second, they underestimated the influence of the General Agreement on Tariffs and Trade (GATT), and then of the Common Market. Thus, too low estimates of the growth of foreign trade were adopted in all cases in national planning. To the extent that these forecasts served as a reference point for firms, the planning led to insufficient allowance for the opening of the borders. But it seems that, if left to themselves, firms would have adopted forecast assumptions even lower than those of the National Plan, which may therefore have performed a useful role even though very inadequately. Too optimistic assumptions, on the other hand, were consistently adopted for the movement of balance of payments; this error was considerable in the Second Plan, low in the Third Plan,[9] and significant in the Fourth Plan.

Comparisons of detailed forecasts and outcomes by industry group have been possible only in the case of the Third and Fourth Plans, since statistical data relating to the Second Plan are inadequate and difficult to collect and comparison for the Fifth Plan would require precise calculations that have not yet been completed. Therefore, we shall confine ourselves to comparisons in the case of production. These are the most important for our purpose, which is to assess how realistic have been the forward assumptions most directly usable for sales forecasts. We assume, moreover, that comparison without a high degree of detail is sufficient to assess the quality of the forecasts carried out. But we must recognize that indicators of the development of production relating to groups of products in a fine breakdown studied by the Plan's working groups may have been used by firms, and that wider differences between forecasts and outcomes might well appear in a more detailed examination.

Tables 14.2 and 14.3 suggest that, in different areas of production, positive or negative differences appeared. They were not in most cases very large. For the Fourth Plan, the correlation coefficient between forecasts and outcomes was 0.82. It may therefore be thought that overall the forward views contained in the last two plans gave a relatively correct picture of the future to decision makers who used them. It should be noted, however, that some of the differences were great, as in the case of energy and metallurgy. These differences may seem all the more striking since these are very concentrated forms of activity strictly con-

---

[8] See Chapter 12, pp. 397–98.
[9] Forecast balance, 2.5 billion 1956 francs; outcome balance, 2.0 billion 1956 francs.

TABLE 14.2

Production Forecasts and Outcomes for the Third Plan, 1957–61

Products	Index of outcome[a]
01. Agriculture	96
02. Processed foods and farm products	96
03. Solid mineral fuels and gas	93
04. Electricity, water, and kindred products	102
05. Petroleum, natural gas, and oil products	96
06. Building materials and glass	104
07+08+09a. Production and first processing of metals	93
09b+09c. Mechanical and electrical industries	103
09d. Automobiles and bicycles	95
09e. Shipbuilding, aircraft, and armaments	112
10. Chemicals	117
11. Textiles, clothing, and leather	95
12. Wood, paper, and miscellaneous industries	100
13. Building and public works	99
14. Transportation and communications	100
15. Housing services	93
16. Services other than housing	93

Source: Bulletin du CEPREL, July 1964, p. 96.

[a]Ratio, multiplied by 100, between the actual level of production and the forecast level.

trolled by the government. In great part they should be seen as resulting from the fact that the National Plan forecasts stemmed from the work of commissions that were mostly, in this connection, staging grounds for confrontation between partners pursuing their own particular interests rather than as scientific forecasting instruments.

In any case, the gathering of official information made possible by the Plan studies, and the numerous exchanges of information and assessment of changes to be expected in production that took place between industrialists and experts in an organized combined effort, lead one to believe that the forecasts were better than what could have been made individually for each unit of production by means of far more fragmentary information.

Knowledge of the Forecasts

Direct participation by firms or business organizations in the preparation of the National Plan is, of course, numerically very limited (1,000 to 1,500 persons). Nevertheless the content of the National Plan report and of the reports by the commissions and working groups are widely commented on and spread through numerous channels: the economic and financial press, the general and specialist press, professional bodies and business organizations, trade publications, chambers of commerce,

TABLE 14.3
Production Forecasts and Outcomes for the Fourth Plan, 1959–65

Products	Index of increase, 1959–65		Index of actual to·forecast increase[a]
	Forecast	Outcome	
01. Agriculture and forestry	130	126	97
02. Processed foods and farm products	129	126	98
03a. Solid mineral fuels	90	90	100
04. Electricity, water, and kindred products	181	167	92
05. Petroleum, natural gas, and oil products	149	174	116
06a. Building materials and ceramics	137	160	117
06b. Glass	147	162	110
07. Iron mining and metallurgy	144	128	88
08. Nonferrous minerals and metals	156	144	92
09a. Products of first processing and manufacturing of metals	139	132	95
09b. Mechanical engines and machines	150	143	96
09c. Electrical engines and machines	180	174	97
09d. Automobiles, motorcycles, and bicycles	140	134	96
09e. Shipbuilding, aircraft, and armaments	104	134	128
10. Chemicals and rubber	157	169	107
11a. Textiles	131	128	98
11b. Clothing	137	127	92
11c. Leather	123	118	96
12a. Products of the wood industry	133	128	96
12b. Paste, paper, and card products	149	149	100
12c. Products of printing and publishing	143	140	98
12d. Products of miscellaneous industries	168	170	101
13. Building and public works	146	161	110
14a. Transportation	130	130	100
14b. Services and communications	152	156	103
15. Housing services	135	128	95
16. Services other than housing	142	143	101

Source: *Rapport sur les comptes de la nation de 1965,* pp. 68–70.
[a]Ratio, multiplied by 100, between the actual index of increase and that forecast.

specialist divisions of government agencies, and research centers. In this way, many enterprises became well informed of the projections outlined in the National Plan.

A preliminary estimate of this information can be made owing to a survey made in January 1967 by the INSEE from a sample of 2,000 firms, on the information available to the head of each firm.[10] Various questions were asked about the firm's knowledge of the forecasts in the Fourth and Fifth Plans: forecasts relating to the growth rate of the French economy, to production by the industry group of which the firm

[10] Special inquiry made as part of the preparation for a colloquium on economic information held in Paris in June 1967. Those questioned were heads of firms habitually questioned by the INSEE in monthly surveys on the situation and outlook of industry.

TABLE 14.4
Knowledge of Forecasts of the Fifth Plan by Industrial
Firms, January 1967
(Percent)

| | Number of employees in the firm | | | | | |
Category	10–99	100–499	500–999	1,000–4,999	5,000–& over	Total[a]
Firms with knowledge of forecasts relating to growth rates of the French economy	55%	72%	83%	88%	100%	79%
And simultaneously: Of production in the industry group	31	49	60	79	98	64
Of production & investment in the industry group	21	34	43	62	85	50
Of production & investment in the industry group or groups next lower in order	14	25	35	52	79	42

[a]After correcting the sample and weighting by gross value added.

was a part, to investment in that industry group, to investment and production in the next lower group or groups. The results of the replies to these questions are shown in Table 14.4.

It seems from this survey that around 80 percent of French industrial firms know the growth objective of the Fifth National Plan, two-thirds know in addition the forecasts of growth of production in their industry group, and half know the forecasts of growth in both production and investment in their industry group. The percentages are lower for small firms and higher for large firms, and the quality of information improves as the size of the firm increases.

The extent of information available to firms about the National Plan forecasts probably increased over time, particularly on the occasion of the preparation of the Fourth Plan. However, the information available was already quite substantial before this.

Utilization of the Plan Guidelines

Even when known, the National Plan assumptions are not necessarily taken into account by economic decision makers. They are, moreover, of greater or lesser relevance according to what type of forward assumption is considered and according to the situation of the possible users. It is advisable, first, to note that these assumptions, made solely for the Plan period, represent possible guides for detailed medium-term forecasts only at the beginning of each plan. For example, in 1963 the projections in the Fifth Plan up to 1970 had not yet been determined. The only projections available were those of the Fourth Plan relating to the

TABLE 14.5
The Use of Forecasts by Industrial Firms, January 1967
(Percent)

Subject matter of forecasts	Percent of firms using forecasts[a]		
	1½ to under 4 yrs.	4 yrs. & over	Total
Purchase of raw materials	15%	24%	39%
Manpower	16	30	46
Production	20	36	56
Sales	21	37	58
Financing	23	42	65
Investment	26	42	68

[a]Firms weighted by their gross value added.

period 1959–65, that is to say, relatively old ones concerning only the last two years of the Plan.

Second, firms can be led to use the Plan forecasts only if they themselves make forecasts relating to their own setting and if they take into account in their decisions the outlook for medium-term development in France as a whole. This is not the case in all firms, particularly the small and medium ones. The inquiry mentioned earlier gives some information on this point. Thus, to the question "Are your expectations for the year ahead part of longer-term forecasts?," firms gave the replies summarized in Table 14.5.

A survey was carried out in Brittany in 1964 of some 500 industrial firms employing more than ten persons each and with their legal headquarters in Brittany.[11] Almost half reported that their activity was too closely tied to the short-term economic situation, to the local or regional market, or to orders from abroad to be able to take useful account of medium-term national projections. In the same order of ideas, the studies by INSEAD (Institut Européen d'Administration des Entreprises) have showed that the usefulness of the National Plan projections for firms was tied partly to the size of their investment in relation to production, and partly to how widely their market extends in the country as a whole.

Third, it can be expected that beneficial use of the National Plan forecasts by a firm is linked to a systematic use of methods of forecasting— or at least to the existence of a controller's department (*service de contrôle de gestion*) or an economic studies department. According to investigations by Jacques Houssiaux on the use of the National Plan

[11] See *Bulletin de conjoncture régionale. Région de Bretagne*, fourth quarter, 1965.

TABLE 14.6
*Background Services for Decision Making Within Industrial
Firms, January 1967*
(Percent)

Percent of firms that reported having:	Number of employees in the firm					
	10–99	100–499	500–999	1,000–4,999	5,000–& over	Total
Controller's department	14%	26%	39%	57%	78%	43%
Economic studies department	6	9	16	31	79	29

forecasts by firms, only some 50 large undertakings in France at that time had an organization and management centered on a corporate plan. Only about 1,000 did introduce forecasting into management according to clearly defined procedures. As part of a set of questions relating to "the preparation of information necessary to decisions," the questionnaire of the INSEE inquiry on economic information asked: "Have you a distinct controller's department?" and "Have you an economic studies department?" The results of the replies are given in Table 14.6. They are surprising, and seem to contradict Houssiaux's conclusions. The sparse information available elsewhere contradicts that, showing a high proportion of firms having true controller's or economic studies departments. The replies made must therefore be interpreted. They probably mean that modern methods of management are more widespread than would seem from the investigations by Houssiaux. But they also reflect the fact that many firms confuse the terms "commercial" or "accounting departments" with the terms "controller's" and "economic studies departments." Thus, the ignorance of many French firms in regard to modern management methods is shown. All in all, the proportion of firms equipped to make proper use of the Plan's forecasts is probably not very high.

The survey included a question relating directly to the use of Plan expectations: "If a knowledge of the estimated forecasts in the Plan (Fourth or Fifth) played a part at the time some of your decisions were taken, can you indicate in which areas and to what extent these decisions were influenced?" The replies are shown in Table 14.7. They perhaps reflect some desire to be helpful to the body carrying out the inquiry, and hence may well exaggerate the true influence of the Plan forecasts on the behavior of French firms. Nevertheless they lead one to think that a large number of big firms have to a smaller or greater extent been influenced by the Plan forecasts, and that from this cause alone

TABLE 14.7

The Influence of Plan Forecasts on Industrial Firms, January 1967

(Percent)

Influence of National Plan forecasts (percent of replies)	Number of employees in the firm					
	10–99	100–499	500–999	1,000–4,999	5,000–& over	Total
On investment decisions:						
Significant	8%	11%	20%	29%	51%	24%
Slight	28	36	38	40	42	37
Nil	64	53	42	31	7	39
On production decisions:						
Significant	9	11	16	28	35	20
Slight	25	35	36	41	47	37
Nil	66	54	48	31	18	43

the influence has been spread outward through small and medium firms serving as customers or suppliers of the large enterprises. It has moreover been useful to firms to refer to the Plan when negotiating with the government. It has been observed elsewhere that consulting organizations, research departments of firms, or even groups of enterprises have been led naturally to prefer the forecasting assumptions of the Plan whenever they had to have recourse to externally provided assumptions about the future environment of their operations in order to carry out economic studies.

Influence of Projections Associated with the Plan on Growth

At this stage of our study we are in a better position to appreciate the influence on growth of the forward assumptions associated with the National Plan and to examine how they may have contributed to the creation of an expansionary climate, and also how they may have acted as an instrument for reducing inconsistencies and improving allocation of productive resources.

The forecasts have contributed to the creation of an expansionary climate. The influence of these forecasts will have been the more effective the more the expectations and spontaneous projects of firms, apart from the Plan, fell short of their expansion potential, and the more their behavior was altered by the existence of these forecasts and by a surrounding climate that was favorable to growth and in addition was stimulated by national planning.

Now there are in fact good reasons why French firms, until the middle of the 1950's at least, and particularly between the boom following the Korean war and 1954–55, had a somewhat Malthusian view of the future. Fifteen years of stagnation naturally had become the prevailing view of French society. In this respect France was an exception among Western countries: Britain and the United States had experienced strong growth during the war; Germany and Italy had known strong expansion, both before the war and in its first years, under the influence of fascism, rearmament, and the war effort.

Thus, according to the witnesses we have consulted, it seems likely that the growth expectations set forth in the Second National Plan (1954–57) were in contradiction to the conventional wisdom at the beginning of the 1950's, which expected that only low rates of growth were possible.[12] The possibility of a serious crisis after what some people called the "excesses" of the Monnet Plan was accepted by a large proportion of French management circles. Thus, it was considered that the Korean war had saved the French economy from depression. The picture of a growing economy provided by the Plan, in which production would be sure of finding sales, probably played a significant part in resumption of growth after 1952. In particular, the launching of large investment programs in the heavy sectors of the economy, such as iron and steel, must be linked with the influence of national planning. Similarly, the preparation of the Fourth National Plan seems to have played a significant part in the 1960 expansion, at a time when firms were still strongly affected by the difficulties of 1958 and 1959.

The traditional relationships in France between the public authorities and industrial firms probably explained the particularly strong influence of government actions on the firms' behavior. The drawing up of consistent growth expectations to which was attached an official label acted as a "reducer of uncertainty"[13] and as a source of collective security favorable to initiative and enterprise. The expectations of growth set forth as part of the National Plans thus contributed to the creation of a climate that exercised a positive influence on French growth. We believe that this influence was particularly strong in the case of the First and Second Plans.

The forecasts improved allocation of productive resources only slightly. On the other hand, several reasons lead us to think that the forecasts carried out as part of the Plans had rather slight influence on the consistency of decisions and the allocation of resources. In the first place, we have already seen that the quality of the detailed forecasts carried out was not always very high.

Second, the Plan sets out only the outlook for industry groups at the

[12] Some representative press extracts have already been quoted in Chapter 9, pp. 278–79.

[13] *"Réducteur d'incertitude,"* to use the expression of Pierre Massé (in *Le Plan ou l'anti-hasard*).

national level. It therefore does not provide all the information that, if it were realistic and systematically taken into account by firms, would make decisions internally consistent. Although the mean assumptions on growth for each industry group can usefully serve as a guide for firms in it, they can be led, each taken on its own, to make inconsistent assumptions about the increase or decrease of their share in the overall output of the group as a whole. For all firms with a purely regional market, the mean assumption of national growth cannot be of direct use. Even in the case of markets dominated by a monopoly or an oligopoly, where the overall expectation adopted takes into account the individual plans of large firms, the reports made of their plans must be regarded as part of the strategy of these firms rather than as an effort at objective assessment. This is true even for public undertakings. Thus the *ex ante* consistency of plans cannot be regarded as guaranteed by the national planning studies.

Third, in a growth economy, temporary excess output capacity may arise, but cannot continue for long. For this reason, the direct effect of the Plan on the full use of output capacity by eliminating partial disequilibria must have been slight.

Last, the national planning studies aimed at defining a possible picture of the medium-term economic situation far more than to attempt optimum development of the various types of production. The techniques of economic analysis used, which were chiefly those of projection, were not sufficient, moreover, for the study of problems of the optimum allocation of resources. Even in the particular case of parts of economic sectors that were in absolute or relative decline (agriculture, coal mining, iron mining, shipbuilding, or textiles), it is not certain that national planning made it possible to anticipate earlier than otherwise changes in trend and to organize a switch into other forms of output in the most favorable way for growth.

One cannot deny, however, that national planning acted positively in these areas. Although information on the outlook provided to firms did not make it possible to eliminate inconsistencies between the various medium-term production and investment programs, even on the assumption that it had been systematically taken into account, it nevertheless tended to reduce these inconsistencies. Moreover, a common approach to the problems of medium-term development has led firms to take account more quickly of the nature of some of these problems and of the solutions they require. By announcing the changes that must accompany growth, national planning has probably contributed to making them happen. Finally, the systematic effort of medium-term forecasting by the Plan's working groups and commissions contributed to developing, in an economic environment that was not at all prepared for it, a concern for medium-term forecasting itself. The development of research and forecasting functions in firms is indeed still at a low level, but it has in part been induced in large firms by studies on the outlook carried out as part of national planning or by the increasing need for large firms and business organizations to use in negotiations with the government the language of quantitative forecasting.

NATIONAL PLANNING AND ECONOMIC POLICY

To assess the effects on growth of planning of the economy's public sector, we must reply in turn to two sorts of questions: What was the influence of planning on the course of economic policy, and on the behavior and economic decisions of the government and other public bodies (public enterprises, local official agencies, etc.?[14] What effect did this influence ultimately have on growth?

To this end, it is helpful to analyze the government's economic decisions under a small number of major categories. This can be done according to various criteria: instruments of economic policy put into operation (taxation, credits, subsidies, tariff setting, old-age pensions, welfare payments, public investment, information and persuasion, regulation, institutions); areas of application of government action (different sectors of production, different categories of investment by government agencies, employment, productivity, distribution of income, savings, financing of different categories of investment, foreign trade, consumption); agencies responsible (different government bodies, local official bodies . . .), etc. It is obviously out of the question in the limited framework of this study to bring all these criteria together. We shall give preference to classification by the economic functions of the public sector, but will bear in mind the existence of other criteria.

Three economic functions of the public sector will therefore be distinguished: (1) The function as producer of goods and services, whether these are sold (for example, electricity) or supplied "free" to the users (for example, educational services); we shall examine chiefly under this head the influence of national planning on public investment. (2) The function as maintainer of overall economic equilibria and of short-term regulation of the economy; we shall study under this head how national

---

[14] On this subject see, in particular, Gilles de la Perrière, "Les Moyens d'exécution du Plan," *Bulletin des finances*, June–August, 1961, pp. 6–18; and "Les Moyens d'exécution du Plan, la situation actuelle et les critiques qui lui sont adressées," in the book *Pour une démocratie économique* (Paris, 1964), pp. 77–105.

TABLE 14.8

Effects on Economic Growth Attributable to Government Economic Planning

Category	Economic functions of the economy's public sector		
	Production of the public sector (public investment)	General economic responsibilities of the government	
		Short-term regulation of the economy (general economic equilibria)	Improvement of structures and sectoral policies
Influence of planning: (Influence of planning studies and of actions by the Commissariat Général du Plan on quantitative public decisions; changes in institutions & regulations; transformation of attitudes and behavior)	Influence on: Investment and output of public enterprises Capital equipment of govt. bodies (& services rendered by govt. bodies) Investment in housing	Influences tending to protect with increased emphasis, in short-term economic management policies, objectives for growth, and investment	Influence on: Improvements in structure enabling certain obstacles to expansion to be overcome Guiding private enterprise activity by means of credit, taxation, subsidies, etc.
Effects on growth: (Volume of investment; working population; allocation of productive resources; demand & degree of use of productive capacity)	Effect on: Volume of investments Rationality of decisions and nature of investments Quality of the working population	Effect on: Demand and degree of utilization of productive capacity	Effect on: Volume of private investment Working population Allocation of resources

planning has been reflected by increased concern for protecting in the course of short-term economic management the growth objectives and particularly the investment objective. (3) The function of reforming and improving economic structures; we shall analyze under this head whether national planning facilitated structural reforms so as to over-come certain obstacles to expansion, and whether it contributed by ac-tion in the different sectors to guiding private enterprise toward better use of productive resources.

Our classification of the economic functions of the economy's public sector does not include a redistribution-of-incomes function (or even of guidance in the formation of primary incomes). The action exercised in this field by the first five Plans was only limited[15] and its effects on growth can be ignored. Our framework for the analysis of planning of government activity can be summarized as shown in Table 14.8.

We shall study the influence of planning on the exercise of each of the economic functions shown there before offering, as the chapter's conclusion, a comprehensive assessement of its effects upon growth.

National Planning and Public Investment

For 20 years investment directly controlled by the official decision-making centers has held an important position in relation to investment as a whole: over 50 percent of "assisted" housing investment is included (see Table 14.9).[16] One might therefore think a priori that national planning played an important part in determining the country's invest-ment programs and therefore its growth. But the proportion of public investment is substantially lower if one considers only productive invest-ment, which is that most directly linked to growth: it was about 36 percent only in 1959[17] if one takes all public enterprises as a whole as defined in the National Accounts,[18] and 30–33 percent if one does not include public enterprises that were relatively autonomous in relation to the general coordination procedures exercised by the government (the Renault Corporation, aircraft building, oil, etc.). Moreover, the proper role of planning must not be confused with the role of the gov-ernment as such. To bring out the part played by planning, it is helpful to study the influence it has exercised on decisions affecting each of the

[15] Apart from policy on farm prices, which can be included under the heading "Structural Improvements and Sectoral Policies" (p. 483).

[16] The approach adopted here concerns investment directly determined by public decisions, whatever the relative weight of public and private funds in financing these investments.

[17] This percentage has not varied significantly over the whole period studied.

[18] See *Etudes et conjoncture*, March 1966, p. 195.

TABLE 14.9

The Structure of Gross Fixed Capital Formation, by Functions and Decision Centers, 1959

Category	Productive investment	Capital investment of govt. agencies[a]	Housing	Total
Government agencies:				
Central govt.	–	1.9	–	1.9
Local authorities[b]	–	3.8	–	3.8
Other	–	0.3	–	0.3
Total govt. agencies	–	6.0	–	6.0
Firms:				
Private	19.9	–	1.4	21.3
Of which metallurgy[c]	(1.6)	–		
Public enterprises	11.5	–	2.2	13.7
FDES	*(8.3)*	–	–	*(8.3)*
(Excluding FDES)	*(3.2)*	–	–	*(3.2)*
Energy	*(5.9)[d]*	–	–	*(5.9)*
Transportation	*(2.9)[e]*	–	*(0.3)*	*(3.2)*
Communications	*(0.7)*	–	–	*(0.7)*
Atomic energy	*(0.7)*	–	–	*(0.7)*
Other productive enterprises	*(1.2)*	–	–	*(1.2)*
Public housing offices	–	–	*(1.9)*	*(1.9)*
Total public & private firms	31.4	–	3.6	35.0
Households	0.1	–	9.6	9.7
Of which, assisted housing	–	–	*(6.6)[f]*	*(6.6)[f]*
Financial institutions	–	0.2	–	0.2
Grand total	31.5	6.2	13.2[g]	50.9

Source: Les Comptes de la nation (Paris, 1960).

Note: Selecting a year other than 1959 would not significantly alter these conclusions about the size of public investment in relation to investment as a whole.

[a]Includes housing of government agencies (0.1 billion francs) and investment by financial institutions.

[b]Includes semipublic bodies with economic responsibilities.

[c]In a great many ways (price fixing for metallurgy, control over share issues, etc.) the government exercises an influence on investment by metallurgy. It must be considered that this investment is, partly at least, determined by government decisions.

[d]Coal Mining, 1.1; Electricité de France, 3.4; Gaz de France, 0.7; other, 0.7.

[e]Of which the Société Nationale des Chemins de Fer (SNCF) is 2.3.

[f]Assessed at 85 percent of investment in new housing; it will be noted, moreover, that investment in major upkeep (1,777 million francs in 1959) is partly determined by policies for rent regulation.

[g]Not including housing of government agencies.

categories of investment (investment by public enterprises, investment by government agencies, and investment in housing).

Investment by public enterprises. The greater part of the total volume of investment by public enterprises (energy and transportation) is programmed in the National Plan. The major operations (for example, building dams) are even mentioned individually and are programmed in physical quantities. The annual investment programs of public enterprises are approved by the Ministry of Industry and the Ministry of Finance, after a recommendation has been reported by the FDES.[19] The Commissariat Général du Plan is directly represented on the management board of this organization and on the specialist committees that assist it.[20] At first sight, the role of the Plan in determining investment of public enterprises is therefore important.

It seems that the role of the First and Second Plans was in fact very important in this respect. The Plan laid down for public enterprises the image of an economy in course of rapid growth, and secured recognition for the need to give priority to financing the basic sectors (transportation, electricity, and coal), which then determined the extent to which the rest of the economy could develop. The size of investment by public enterprises over this period was strongly influenced by the Plan. Pierre Massé has spoken of it in these terms: "If I am allowed to refer to a personal memory, I can still recall the shock caused in Electricité de France, where I had just been appointed Director of Plant and Investment, by the announcement of an objective of 39.5 billion kwh, whereas consumption in the best prewar year had not exceeded 21 billion kwh. Without the coordinated effort announced by the Plan, this ambitious aim would have collided with a paralyzing skepticism."[21]

The impact of subsequent plans was more complex, once it had been recognized that high growth required high investment. National planning exercised positive influence on the adoption of rational criteria of economic choice and on the development of research departments in public enterprises. But the procedures of the FDES, which had become traditional, and the terms of low-interest loans probably led to the financing of some capital investment programs less profitable than investments in other sectors of the economy. This seems to have been the case for some investments in coal mining and in the Société Nationale des Chemins de Fer (SNCF).

Capital investment by government agencies[22] is comprised chiefly of investments by the government and by local public authorities. Although the central government's influence is exercised in a direct way on investments by the state itself, this is not the case for investments by local authorities. They are carried out mainly through the granting of sub-

[19] The Fonds de Développement Economique et Social in 1955 replaced a number of funds, notably the Fonds National de Modernisation et d'Equipement.

[20] The National Plan's Commissaire Général is a member of the Management Committee of the FDES.

[21] Pierre Massé, *Le Plan ou l'anti-hasard*, p. 146.

[22] By this term we mean investment carried out by government agencies as defined in the National Accounts.

sidies for particular operations, which in principle governs whether or not loans can be obtained, in particular from the Caisse des Dépôts et Consignations. But apart from the freedom of action that obviously arises from self-financing by local authorities, the all-purpose nature of their funds, and certain time lags, the actual conditions for granting loans are very liberal and not strictly laid down in advance. Local authorities therefore have fairly wide autonomy in relation to the central government and, a fortiori, in relation to decisions reached within the framework of national planning.

Programs for government investments are given in the Plan in the form of objectives for volume of works to be achieved during the final year of the Plan, and, by major investment categories, in the form of overall appropriations allotted for the operations to be started during the course of the Plan. These two assessments are not clearly coordinated. Accordingly, the lack of precision as well as the absence of itemization for a large number of broad projects gives a certain obscurity to the Plan's objectives.

For a time after 1956, investment decisions depended on programs set out in particular "program laws."[23] But their coordination with the National Plan was only imperfect. Thus, in some cases they determined future action over periods that did not coincide with the Plan period, and without preparatory studies being carried out within the Plan's commissions.[24] Moreover, the need to restore general economic equilibrium in 1957 and 1958 led to their scope being considerably reduced.

In any event, the planning procedures influenced government decisions relating to capital investment in a systematic way only beginning with the Fourth Plan, when the Ministry of Finance and the spending departments referred freely to the Plan in the course of budget discussions. Thus the following facts—that the stabilization plan put into effect from 1963 on was not reflected by a reduction in investment programs by government agencies as intended by the Fourth Plan, as well as the progressive introduction of price revisions in budget discussions as they took place in practice, and finally the high growth rate of government investment achieved between 1962 and 1965—can all be broadly imputed to the existence of national planning.

Table 14.10 shows how the investment objective for government agen-

---

[23] By the application of article 2 of the law of March 27, 1956, approving the Second Plan for modernization and investment and providing for "program laws" in certain fields of planning; such laws comprised commitments to the granting of credits for the Plan period as a whole.

[24] See the article by Gilles de la Perrière, "Les Moyens d'exécution du Plan," p. 10. See also *Bulletin du CEPREL*, no. 3, pp. 40–43.

TABLE 14.10
The Growth of Investment by Government Agencies, 1955–65
(Earlier year = 100)

Period	Index	Period	Index
1955–56	109.3	1961–62	112.9
1956–57	101.5	1962–63	110.1
1957–58	102.2[a]	1963–64	110.3
1958–59	109.8[a]	1964–65	110.6
1959–60	103.7[a]		
1960–61	112.4		
1957–61:		1961–65:[b]	
Forecast	127	Forecast	150
Achieved	129	Achieved	151.5

[a]The real differences between the growth indexes were probably lower than they seem from these figures. The assessments of capital equipment programs actually carried out are in fact based on the use made of credits for the necessary payments, and it seems likely that the developments observed in 1959 partly represent freeing of credits that made it possible to reduce the time lag between completion and payment.
[b]A more detailed analysis would show significant inconsistencies between forecasts and achievements by categories of investment: achievement was lower than objectives for public health investment, rural investment, urban investment, and school investment, but higher for roads, airfields, and harbors.

cies included in the Fourth Plan was achieved in a fairly regular way, although there were significant fluctuations in aggregate economic growth. It shows, on the contrary, that although the "objective" presented by the Third Plan was reached, this was within the framework of a fundamentally anticyclical policy.

In addition to these analyses, it should be noted that concern for faster growth of government investment appeared from the Second Plan on, particularly in relation to schools. The planning studies influenced the development of attitudes both within government managing circles and in public opinion. From the time of the Second and Third Plans, planning thus played a more important part in the development of the capital investment of government agencies than appears from an examination of the official procedures for determining public investment programs.

It would be appropriate, in addition, to assess what effect national planning has had on the nature and the degree of rationality of investment carried out, both in the distribution between major categories and in more detailed determination. For the Fourth Plan, planning contributed chiefly to securing recognition of priority for education. From the Fourth Plan on, the influence of planning was more diversified and was a factor in stimulating government agencies toward change. A sociological preliminary inquiry carried out in the Ministry of Public Works,[25] which in the French government system was a pioneer in the

25 Lautman and Thoenig, *Planification et administrations centrales.*

rational study of investment choice, has shown some of the processes by which national planning exerted its influence, particularly from the time of preparation of the Fourth Plan.

This inquiry shows that the creation in 1960 of an economic studies department (the SAEI) within the Ministry of Public Works can be imputed to the development of national planning work. The study by Lautman and Thoenig also shows how national planning tends to introduce a new intellectual attitude, characterized by concern for measuring and for economic calculation, as well as by considering objectives based on a self-consistent picture of the future. It also shows how national planning "modifies the rules of competition and of coordination between government agencies, making them stricter and more closely based on economic data." The case of the Ministry of Public Works is not the only one: in effect, national planning has accelerated the setting up of research bodies in many government agencies.

National planning has also encouraged the attempts by some ministries to reduce the cost of investment—as can be shown, for example, by the recommendations in the Second Plan (p. 83 of the Plan) on rationalization of investment in schools: adoption of norms for sizes and for standard plans, group tenders, certification of procedures, and organizing coordination of work at *département* level. Analogous recommendations are contained in the Third Plan (pp. 211–13 of the Plan). More generally it does seem that national planning has helped government agencies to set up investment services able to make better use of the credits allotted them. This was particularly true in the case of the Ministry of National Education.

Investment in housing has been determined since the war chiefly by government decisions, even though the part played by individuals and by private building loan companies has increased since 1960. Rent policy, policy for assistance to private building (subsidies and low-interest loans, or reconstruction compensation) and finally direct public investment by the public housing offices, when taken as a whole, have played a fundamental role in determining total investment in housing.

What was the overall result of government action on the volume of this investment? In relation to the situation at the start, there can be no doubt that the authorities' action had a positive effect on the building program. But in relation to what would have been achieved by a policy more strongly based on market mechanisms (such as rent freedom or less strict regulation of financial mechanisms), government intervention undoubtedly led to a certain slowing down of the building program. For one thing, house building would have been more attractive to private capital if rents had been freed and therefore higher; this applies both to capital for financing investment housing and to individual savings by householders wishing to own their own homes. For another thing, a faster creation of the mortgage market, and a faster easing of financial regulations relating to the length of loans and to interest rates, would have made possible longer-term loans to households and more dynamic behavior by financial institutions in accumulating savings intended for housing finance.

The consequences for growth of either accelerating or slowing the overall building program are difficult to assess. On the one hand, housing investment stimulates demand. It also encourages labor mobility and thus improves allocation of productive resources and limits inflationary tensions that may arise from geographical disequilibria on the labor market. In that way it encourages growth. But, on the other hand, to the extent that demand is too high and savings resources insufficient—which was generally the case over the periods studied[26]—investment in housing exercises inflationary pressure and can limit the total savings available for other investments, in particular directly productive investment. There is indeed reason to believe that an increased flow of investment in housing must be accompanied by a lower volume of savings accumulation.

Taken as a whole, the influence of planning studies on housing policies seems to have been small, at least over the period considered. The fact that the forecasts made as part of the preparation of the National Plans were in every case lower than the outcomes[27] suggests, however, that planning has not on the whole assisted investment in housing and therefore has—explicitly in the First Plan and implicitly in the Second, Third, and Fourth Plans—assisted financing of other investments.

National Planning and Short-Term Economic Management

The influence of national planning on short-term management of the economy must be analyzed from different points of view: What was the role of planning reports in the studies underlying decisions of short-term policy? What was the institutional role of the National Plan's Commissariat Général in decisions concerning short-term economic policy? How did different ideas current at the time that could be imputed to the existence of a planning apparatus possibly change behavior and decisions in those responsible for short-term policy?

Few links have been established between the Plan reports and the preparatory studies for short-term economic policy decisions over the course of the first four Plans, apart from the Interim Plan for 1959–60.

[26] See Chapter 10.
[27] See above, pp. 461–65.

For one thing, the Plan reports related exclusively to medium- and long-term periods, and no specific routes were charted between the base year and the last year of the Plan. For another thing, the preparatory studies for short-term decisions were on the whole carried out without explicit reference to the National Plan. This applied to the preparation of economic budgets that each year accompanied the finance act, which represented the most systematic group of studies attempting to provide guidance for the decisions of short-term economic policy. It was only from the Fifth Plan on that a closer link methodologically and in practice was shown clearly between the studies for the Plan and those concerning annual economic budgets.

Responsibility for concerning and carrying out short-term economic policy has always rested with the Minister of Finance and his departments. Until recently few links existed between them and the National Plan Commissariat Général in regard to the conduct of short-term economic policy, although the Plan institutionally was attached to the Ministry of Finance and National Economy between 1954 and 1962. The first institutional link between planning and short-term management of the economy was the setting up of the procedure for the so-called "flashing signals" or "warning signals" (*clignotants*) within the framework of the Fifth Plan's execution: the Plan stipulated that short-term corrective actions would have to be considered if some major economic indexes would not sufficiently conform to preassigned patterns.

However, one cannot form a conclusion from these facts. They would tend to show that over the period studied the national planning mechanism did not have a direct effect on the conduct of short-term policy, nor did the Plan. It is true that national planning did not lead to the setting up of new instruments for managing the economy, at least before the Fifth Plan. (An incomes policy set up in the middle of the 1960's can in fact be credited chiefly to the stimulus of the national planning mechanism.) But it is likely to have exerted an influence on the way those responsible for short-term economic policy used the instruments of management then existing. Priority given to the investment drive throughout the National Plans helped to diffuse the idea that this objective must be maintained despite the vagaries of the economic situation. It can thus be considered that the 1959 recovery was hastened by the influence of ideas spread by the National Plan. The growth objectives set out in the Plan, moreover, were increasing constraints on those responsible for short-term economic policy. Thus, reference to the Plan became more and more explicit and customary in political circles and in public opinion; the preparation and carrying out of the stabilization plan of 1963 were forced to take account of the requirements of the Fourth Plan and did not lead to a slowing of growth in public capital investment or in the growth of investment by public enterprises.

In the same context, the expansionary outlook defined in the Plan may have had an influence on the regularity of investment demand by private firms and consequently on the regularity of growth. The existence of the Plan, all in all, may have led government agencies and firms to adopt an investment policy that, although based chiefly on assessment of short-term developments, also rested on the desire for or anticipation of medium-term expansion. As a result, the amplitude of investment cycles seems to have diminished. Overall, we believe that the influence of national planning on demand management was moderate, but that it nevertheless took place and helped in the growth of investment.

Structural Improvement and Sectoral Policies

Various structural reforms that led to better use or allocation of resources were carried out in France over the postwar period. In this field, the influence of national planning was exerted in two ways: first, the National Plans Commissariat Général took part concurrently with other government organizations in defining the changes to be carried out; second, although Plan studies were rarely reflected in a direct way by specific decisions—for example, in the form of legislation—they did lead to defining guidelines and recommendations in many fields. National planning thus represented a stage in the process that led from recognizing certain problems and studying their possible solution to decisions. The principal means of action recommended and used were improvements in taxation, financial incentives, and finally information and persuasion.

The role of planning in structural improvement can be seen clearly only from the Second National Plan on (Plan, p. 11); this stressed the need for "basic actions," that is, reform programs.[28] Our analysis indeed will concentrate on the Second and Third Plans, which are the most important for the purposes of our study. In view of the delays in putting structural reforms into practice, it seems that the Fourth Plan is less important for the period we are considering.

[28] The report on the First Plan is built chiefly around a development program for six "basic sectors," and devotes only two and a half pages (out of 200) to structural reform. These concern the development of statistical information, tax improvements to assist investment by reducing amortization deductions and to avoid penalizing mergers or divisions by firms, and employment policy (development of labor resources, increases in hours worked, and professional training).

Administrative action by the Commissariat Général. In terms of day-to-day administrative practice, the National Plan's Commissariat Général (CGP) has almost no powers of decision. It controls almost no funds. It determines almost no major programs. Its small staff—approximately 25 administrators immediately after its creation and 40 at present—and its position in the administrative structure do not enable it to carry out direct studies of many measures proposed. It shares the function of initiating overall economic policy with other bodies: the private offices of a number of ministers and, in particular, that of the Minister of Finance, the DATAR interministerial commissions, and ad hoc study groups. But its participation in many commissions and government bodies, its official and unofficial role as an advisory body in many fields, its function as initiator and coordinator of studies, and its role as instigator of round-table discussions for the ministers as a whole, enable it to exercise a coordinating influence the importance of which is clear although its exact limits are difficult to define.

The most clearly defined intervention of the Plan into practical administration is that affecting the financing of investment. We have already noted that the National Plan Commissariat was part of the FDES. It provides, in particular, the chairmanship for Committee no. 1 of the FDES, which is responsible for preparing government intervention to help investment by industrial and commercial firms in the private sector. Although limited, the role of the FDES in financing private investment makes possible certain actions in individual sectors. The National Plan Commissariat states an official opinion on mandatory loan issues. Up to 1959 it did so also on capital increases financed in the public market; until then it was necessary to obtain Treasury authorization, subject to a prior opinion by the Commissariat. Apparently more important was the Plan's role in investigating applications for tax exemptions linked to the issue of shares by private companies (under the terms of the regulation of August 29, 1957).[29] The Plan also acts within the field of the Crédit National. By tacit and unofficial agreement, the latter submits applications to the Plan Commissariat and to the Treasury for their opinion on proposed large loans to firms (at present this covers loans of over 1 million francs for the medium term and 2.5 million for the long term). The CGP's Financial Department estimated in this context in the course of the Fourth Plan that, as a result of various procedures likely to give certain advantages to private firms, about 80 percent of investment and financing programs of the major private companies were the subject of some discussion over the past

[29] See de la Perrière, "Les Moyens d'exécution du Plan," p. 13.

few years between the Plan's Commissariat and those concerned, with the Plan playing an essentially consulting role.[30] In this way, the Plan was able to achieve some stimulation of private-enterprise investment. But we believe that taking account of the absence of decision criteria for investment through a central agency (and often even the absence of criteria for consistency of investments by particular firms with the Plan's guidelines for particular industries), this action by the Plan could not have effects markedly greater than those of traditional decision making in improving the allocation of resources.

However, the Plan did not fail to exercise some influence on the use of other official tools for action in particular sectors, such as price regulation, government purchases, orders by nationally owned enterprises, tax exemptions, investment premiums, and subsidies. But the influence of the Plan in this field was diffuse, and the rigidity of the procedures used, the uncoordinated nature of studies on particular cases, and the absence of clear criteria for government action lead one to doubt how effective these official interventions may have been.

We have shown earlier how planning was a factor in stimulating government agencies toward change and in rationalizing decisions, in particular by helping to develop research departments and capital investment departments within the various ministries.

The concerted approach and studies of Plan preparation. The chief contribution of national planning to structural improvement stemmed from coordinating views and from studies marking preparation of the Plan. Planning is a tool for debates between the various active forces in the economy; it provokes special study and reflection on development problems and makes it possible to draw up guidelines and recommendations that in structure constitute the text of the Plan. Planning is therefore an instrument by which awareness of weaknesses in the economy and flaws in its structure develops faster, by which the means to overcome difficulties brought to light are considered more fully, and by which the working out of decisions is on a broader scale.

In the limited framework of our study, we have not been able to make a systematic inventory of the recommendations on economic pol-

[30] On this matter Pierre Bauchet notes in *L'Expérience française de planificaton* (p. 102): "The influence exerted by the Plan on firms depends less on whether they are publicly owned or private-enterprise than on the type of production and their financial situation. If they belong to so-called base sectors (transportation, energy, metal production) or are large in size (chemical firms), price control and the need . . . to carry out large-scale investment often lead them to have recourse to the public authorities to obtain tax advantages, loans on special terms from the FDES, or price increases. Their dialogue with the state is closer than in the processing and manufacturing industries."

icy contained in the text of the Plans, or of reports by commissions and working groups, nor have we been able to compare these recommendations systematically with the economic policy actually carried out. For this, numerous research studies and reconstruction of documents would be necessary in order to discover how decisions affecting structural improvement were made. We shall confine ourselves to showing the results of a sketchy comparison we carried out between the guidelines and recommendations given in the texts of the Plans as a whole and the economic policy that was in fact carried out.[31] This comparison suggests that national planning helped to encourage productive investment and savings, to restore the action of both internal and external competition, and to transform the nature and modes of government intervention in the economy.

To encourage investment, the First Plan suggested reform of the amortization rules. The Second Plan (Plan, pp. 141–43) recommended introducing the value-added tax with full deduction for investment, reforming the method of levying succession duties applying to individually owned firms, and changing the rules governing taxes on firms' profits. These measures also helped to stimulate savings. The same applies to recommendations in the Third Plan, which attempted to increase self-financing of public enterprises, the government, and local authorities by changes in tariffs or a partial or total financing of some expenditures by the clients (see Third Plan, pp. 45–46). Various tax measures, moreover, were proposed to encourage the growth of savings (see Second Plan, p. 143, and Third Plan, pp. 58–59). Some of these measures in fact were put into effect.

It only seems paradoxical that stimulating competition and setting up a market economy would appear throughout the different plans as one of the chief goals of French national planning. According to the Second Plan (p. 26), "one of the essential objectives of the new Plan is to restore the free play of competition in the economy." To this end, it was held advisable to abolish some protectionist legislative and regulatory provisions (pp. 10–11, 123–24), to keep watch on agreements (p. 136), and to change taxation in the direction of economic neu-

---

[31] We have also used some fragments of the study by Douglas Keare, and the results of an investigation on the carrying out of the Third Plan. The latter, which is in some depth but limited to analyses of documents, was made by the CEPREL (see *Bulletin du CEPREL*, December 1964). The method followed by the CEPREL was (1) to reconstitute the contents of the Plan in the form of economic policy recommendations from a systematic analysis of it, of the reports by commissions, and of the statements of working groups; (2) to compare the recommendations made with the decisions taken; and (3) to assess the links between decisions and recommendations.

trality. This is another reason why the Plan recommended setting up the value-added tax (Second Plan, pp. 140–41, 143; Third Plan, pp. 60–61), to develop the financial market (Third Plan, p. 47), to restore "truth in prices" (Third Plan, pp. 45–46), and to return gradually to a market for housing (Fourth Plan). Most of these guidelines were followed by practical measures.

National planning also helped to open the French economy to foreign trade. It played a fundamental part in France in the creation of the European Coal and Steel Community, which was the first stage leading to the setting up of the Common Market. National planning played an active part during the preparation of the Third Plan in getting firms to accept freeing of foreign trade. This is shown clearly in the differences between the guidance given by the text of the Plan and the reports of the commissions. The policy of opening up frontiers was vigorously defended in the text of the Third Plan: "Our country cannot choose a policy of protectionism and withdrawal without at the same time running the risk of finding itself in a few years' time impoverished, isolated, and—as it were—rejected by history" (extract of sec. 26). In contrast, the reports of the highest commissions in general, and of the processing and manufacturing industries in particular, presented a great many demands aimed at strengthening the protection and official assistance already in existence rather than setting up a more liberal regime for foreign trade (see *Bulletin du CEPREL*, no. 3, pp. 29–30).

Finally, by tending to replace the "managed economy" (*dirigiste*) tradition, which was particularly long established in France and had been reanimated by the war, with the practice of a concerted approach, French planning introduced a new type of relationship between government agencies and firms. This relationship was directed at reaching a common awareness of the problems of development and at stimulating private enterprise by measures at a general level rather than by government intervention in particular cases of private-enterprise activity.

This philosophy for policy, which was new in France and due to Jean Monnet, can be seen in the First Plan itself, despite the fact that its preparation took place in the very midst of the period of economic *dirigisme*: "In this way, problems can be solved by a permanent exchange of ideas between the government and the country in a "concerted economy" and not in a directed economy of a bureaucratic or corporative nature" (Report on the First Plan, p. 101).

In this spirit an important tool for action by national planning was information and discussion on the problems of development—a factor in the acceptance of necessary change. Thus the confrontations to which preparation of the Plans gave rise made it easier for farm organizations to accept guidelines for agricultural change based on large-scale movement out of farming and reduction in the number of farmers. As for the means of intervention, the Plan recommended that the government use the following: tax improvements, better organization of public purchases, programs of job training and of research and development, development of information, standardization and specialization, and spreading of modern methods for the organization of production (see, for example, the text of the Second Plan, p. 27).

The Plan seems to have encouraged mergers, specialization, and the grouping of firms by gradual transformation over the period considered of tax legislation that previously discouraged regrouping.[32] The productivity campaign and in particular the productivity missions to the United States were stimulated by national planning. In addition, by initiating and obtaining the adoption of equal-tax treatment for shares and bonds, the Third Plan removed an obstacle that prevented capital increases. In general, national planning seems to have encouraged people to regard taxation as a tool of economic policy that should help savings, competition, or concentration (see the texts of the Second Plan, pp. 140, 143, and the Third Plan, pp. 57–62).

After this analysis, our overall assessment of the influence of national planning on the government's attempts to improve the structures of the French economy stands between two extremes. At one end, these attempts might be regarded as almost independent of the existence of national planning. The analysis actually shows how strong the links were between these reforms and the national planning operation. At the other end, the structural reforms could be said to be chiefly ascribable to national planning. In fact, however, certain important reforms or major plans for reform were not directly linked to the activity of national planning. The inception and carrying out of certain important projects such as the Rueff-Armand report did not stem directly from national planning activity. Although the Plan helped to obtain acceptance for the introduction and then the extension of the value-added tax, its concept and launching cannot be attributed to the Plan. More especially, neither at the level of principles nor at the level of everyday

[32] It will be noted that from the First Plan on (in which only two pages out of one hundred are devoted to specific reforms), recommendations are made in this field; see also the text of the Second Plan, pp. 140, 143, and the text of the Third Plan, sec. 64. In the same context attempts of the Plans to encourage standardization of output helped economies of scale and therefore growth.

negotiation was the Plan's Commissariat associated in a practical way with the definition of France's position with regard to the Common Market and its development. All in all, our feeling is that national planning did play a part in causing some structural reforms to occur earlier than they would have otherwise and in speeding up the evolution of certain parts of the economy's structure.

DEVELOPMENT OF ECONOMIC AND
TECHNOLOGICAL INFORMATION

The development of economic and technological information is one condition necessary to the spreading of new ideas and to improving the rationality of decisions. Thus better knowledge of internal and foreign markets and of their likely development makes it possible to determine production and investment programs that are better suited to demand. The spreading of technological information, relating to new equipment, new manufacturing methods, and new raw materials, is a necessary condition for improving production techniques. In the present state of knowledge, it seems an empty exercise to attempt to measure the effect on growth of improvements in economic and technological information. But it is important to assess, if only in a general way, the scale of this improvement by comparison with earlier years. We shall analyze in turn improvements achieved in the public and in the private information networks.

Improvement of the Public Network of Economic Information

Improvements since World War II in the total structure of general economic information, which in France is almost entirely from public sources, has been very great. First came the complete alteration in the central system of statistical information. Before the war, the central body for statistical information was the Statistique Générale de la France. This organization, which was situated entirely in Paris, consisted of only about 100 persons, of whom roughly 10 were of professional status, and had very limited budget resources. It was succeeded during the war by the national statistical service, and after the war by the Institut National de la Statistique et des Etudes Economiques (INSEE). This body was set up in 1946 and from the start had available far greater resources than had the Statistique Générale de la France. Today the INSEE consists of 4,000 persons, of whom about 400 are senior professional people; there are 18 regional directorates under the Paris office. From 1962, when M. Claude Gruson was put in charge of it, this organization has been responsible for compiling the retrospective National Accounts and the technical studies leading to short-, medium-, and long-term economic forecasts. From that time on the INSEE has directed its statistical work toward the needs of forecasting, and in particular toward the requirements linked with preparation of national plans.

A second change was the development or setting up of departments of statistical or economic studies within most of the major government departments. Among these should be mentioned the creation in 1950 within the Ministry of Finance of the Service d'Etudes Economiques et Financières (SEEF),[33] which was set up by Claude Gruson and directed by him until 1962, and which gradually built up a complete and detailed system of National Accounts in order to provide information for decisions of general policy.

The work of the modernization commissions of the Plan, which in different years brought together between 2,000 and 3,000 representatives of business organizations and trade unions, of producers and government agencies, made it possible—at a time when the overall economic information network was still very inadequately developed—to collect and give out a large volume of information.

Finally, various public or semipublic research bodies were set up after the war, particularly during the 1950's: INED, CREDOC, SEDES, BIPE, and SODIC.

The result was a large increase in general economic information that before the war had been extremely patchy in all fields, industrial statistics, statistics of prices, consumption, etc. The techniques of sample survey and national accounting, which were unknown in France before the war, were introduced soon after the war and were developed by the INSEE and SEEF, respectively. Among the most important achievements for the knowledge and forecasting of aggregate economic developments and for improving the quality of economic policy decisions should be emphasized the short-term economic studies, which made possible significant improvements in the government's economic management, and the National Accounts projections. The latter comprise short-term projections designed to provide information for the decisions of the Ministry of Finance with particular relation to the preparation of economic budgets that accompany the finance acts, and medium-term projections as part of the preparation of the National Plans.

[33] In 1965 this department became the Direction de la Prévision; it provides information for decisions in budgetary and financial policy, in particular by means of economic budgets, and it provides a starting point for attempts within government departments as a whole to rationalize budget decisions.

Development of Private Information Networks

Information available to firms improved substantially over the postwar period, both from firms' internal sources and from data on the economic and technological environment. In the first place, the economic press as well as the professional and technical press significantly developed during the period after the war. Improvements also took place in the economic content of the general press. Publications of particular interest to large firms diversified and developed through daily bulletins, new reviews of general economic information such as *Entreprise* (circulation 40,000), *Direction* (12,000), *Jeune patron* (6,000), *Vendre* (15,000), and more recently *l'Expansion* (130,000). Publications of interest to firms in general have a considerable circulation in some cases: *la Vie des métiers* (72,000), *le Courrier de la Chambre de commerce de Paris* (280,000), *la Volonté du commerce et de l'industrie* (210,000), *l'Usine nouvelle* (50,000), *la Vie française* (150,000), *les Echos* (45,-000), *l'Information* (55,000), etc. The number of technical and specialist reviews can be assessed at 800.[34]

Second, missions abroad and in particular the productivity missions organized between 1949 and 1952 to enable French industrialists to learn methods of organizing production and the technological processes used across the Atlantic, probably played a significant part in spreading advanced techniques of production. Between 1949 and 1952, 140 missions abroad involving over 1,700 persons were arranged. Conversely, foreign experts came to France to study particular problems. The lessons learned in these missions were widely disseminated in the various trades and made public in the form of reports, press conferences, publications, and meetings. This effort at information and education was followed by the setting up of specialist bodies, both public and in industry, with the aim of spreading economic and technical information and of promoting experiments in modernization.[35]

Third, the creation of research and controller's departments,[36] the use of cost accounting, in some cases the application of techniques of economic calculation, and the provision of technical documentation within many large firms are all innovations since the war. It is true that most firms, even large ones, still do not make use of modern management

[34] Figures taken from the work by R. Salmon, *L'Information économique, clé de la prospérité* (collection "Entreprise," 1963).
[35] See, for example, the report of the execution of the First National Plan, pp. 358–59.
[36] Cf. above, pp. 468–69.

techniques such as systems of management by forecasting, and are a long way behind their American counterparts. But the starting point was so low that progress in comparison with the past is considerable.

Fourth, the creation of economic consulting and research bodies, bodies for engineering studies, and organizations for research in particular business fields or groups of fields characterized the 1950's. They represented the desire of a number of firms to base their policy more systematically on market studies and analyses of the short-term economic situation as well as to make use of the techniques of operation research. In the same context should be noted the importance of the creation of "organizing committees" during World War II. The function of these committees at that time was to help distribute scarce resources among firms (chiefly raw materials). After the war, these committees became business organizations with some function in providing information and even carrying out research for the firms belonging to them: information on products and activities in the relevant sectors, on outlets and techniques, general information on economic activity, legal and tax information, finally information on trade union activities.

In the case of agriculture, there was a particularly marked blossoming of private activity in this area: a widening of the field covered by the Agricultural Bureaus, many of which set up technical and economic information services and even economic research offices (the reevaluation of the special rate in 1952 provided them with the necessary finances); the creation in 1945 of agricultural technical study centers (CETA), which are research centers serving all enterprises in general and now number about 1,500; the appearance after the liberation of a rural commentary press; the development of the JAC (Jeunesse Agricole Chrétienne), whose press (with a circulation of about 200,000) and powerful organizations have probably played an important part in spreading new forms of behavior among young farmers. To this must be linked the creation of the CNJA (Centre National des Jeunes Agriculteurs), whose 2,000 centers in the different local districts carry out studies of the means by which firms can be made viable.

Finally, we shall mention the drive for economic education launched after World War II. In 1945 virtually nothing had yet been achieved in France in this field. By and large, the teaching of economics was then confined to short, sketchy lessons in the faculties of law. The gradual evolution of economic teaching in the different faculties, the development of economics courses within a number of the major centers of higher learning, and the activity launched at the fringe of traditional university teaching in the business studies centers were complemented by a wide range of private initiatives. These took the form of lectures, one-day meetings, study sessions, and information programs, all aimed at providing a minimum of economic training for heads of firms or even managers in business organizations and trade unions. In this way, the ability of firms and government agencies to use economic information was greatly improved.

CONCLUSION: THE ROLE OF NATIONAL PLANNING
AND ECONOMIC INFORMATION IN GROWTH

The preceding pages have shown that the mechanisms by which national planning acted on the economy in France were not the same kind as those of the traditional means of government intervention. The National Plan has been a guide containing a group of recommendations, indications, forecasts, and qualitative or quantitative guidelines, rather than an interlinked group of binding objectives and measures to be applied directly. The influence of national planning has been exerted chiefly through the changes it led to in the attitude and behavior of decision makers, public and private. It has not, in the main, stemmed from the mere existence of official reference documents that the texts of the Plan represent, but far more from the concerted action, the efforts of the Plan's working groups and commissions, the studies stimulated by planning within government agencies and firms, and finally the actions of the Plan's Commissariat while each Plan was being put into effect. The role of the exchange of information and ideas, of increased awareness of the problems to be resolved, and of the need for research to provide solutions stemmed from the process of seeking concerted action, which led decision makers themselves to define the outlook for development and its necessary conditions. The importance of this role has been increased by the fact that this process has developed in numerous ways through very different channels, such as the general and specialist economic press or business organizations and trade unions. The tools for carrying out national planning have thus been closely linked to those for developing economic information.

In this way, national planning and above all economic information are not to be seen as causes of growth somehow superimposed on the causes analyzed in this second part of our study. Rather, these two factors help to explain the decisions and the behavior whose consequences have been analyzed in these chapters. For example, the existence of national planning partly explains the structural improvements whose possible consequences were examined in Chapter 13.

The part played by national planning in growth, and the role of the development of economic information, varied with the different plans. Over the ten years following the war, the first two plans substantially helped to replace the image of a stagnant economy or one threatened by depression with the image of an economy holding sure promise of long-lasting expansion. As we said earlier, the situation of France immediately after World War II was exceptional. France was the only Western country to experience 15 successive years of economic stagnation. In these circumstances the picture naturally in the minds of economic decision makers was one of stagnation or at least of return to past circumstances. National planning played an important part in changing the expectations and behavior of economic decision makers. It stimulated investment and modernization. The effect of national planning was particularly strong and direct on investment by public enterprises. In all, we believe that part of the pace of reconstruction should be ascribed to the First Plan and to the actions of the founder of French national planning, Jean Monnet, and that part of the resumption of growth after the 1952–53 recession should be ascribed to the Second Plan.

Thereafter, during the Third, Fourth, and Fifth Plans, planning continued to influence favorably the course of economic policy. But its impact on growth was more diffuse and probably smaller, at a time when the impact of improvements in economic information was growing. The role of accelerator or initiator played by national planning in the growth of investment by government agencies, particularly in education, and in a number of structural reforms, and the role of national planning as stimulator in the 1959–60 recovery, as well as the growth of public and private economic information networks, were all causes of growth. The analysis we have carried out in this chapter, and the conclusions to which we are led by previous chapters—particularly those on the role of pressure of demand, opening of foreign trade, and competition—lead us to believe that, taken separately, each of the effects of national planning or of improvement in information has been only modest. But, taken as a whole, these effects have played a part in national growth that, although limited, is nevertheless undeniable.

Conclusions

On reaching the end of this study, we are conscious of its many gaps. But readers will wish, not for a list of its limitations, but rather for a summary in which we draw conclusions about the factors that governed the economy's ability to grow. We must therefore present a synthesis of the phenomena we have analyzed, painting a general picture from their particular and often contradictory features.

France had never previously known such high growth over such a long period as that of the past 25 years. Although the growth rate of production had reached 5 percent per year in earlier boom periods and over the entire 1920's, average growth rates covering more than two decades did not exceed 2 percent per year before World War II. Similar acceleration in the long-term trend was shown in average labor productivity. For all industry groups as a whole, production per man-hour rose at an average annual rate of 2 percent before World War I and 2.5 percent between 1913 and 1929. Since 1949 the corresponding rate has been over 5 percent.

The analysis of physical factors shows that this fact is partly explained by a high investment effort, but even more by acceleration in the residual trend, often called technological progress, which reflects the rate at which effectiveness in use of the factors of production improves. Whereas capital accumulation would, to the best of our knowledge, explain an annual growth not much above 0.5 percent per year between 1913 and 1929, over the past 20 years its contribution has been more than 1 percent per year. The residual, after taking into account quantitative and qualitative changes in the factors of production, grew at an approximate annual rate of 1 percent in the first part of the century; it is now growing at about 2.5 percent per year.

A PREDOMINANT CAUSE?

There is no shortage of hypotheses to explain by a single cause most of the vigorous and lasting postwar growth. For some people, the cause is a natural and, essentially, spontaneous phenomenon of *catching up*: France was lagging behind other industrial nations; the economy had experienced a prolonged depression from 1929 to the end of World War II; hence the return to more normal conditions and the increased scale of international communication caused the French economy to close the gap first between the prevailing level and its earlier trend, and then between the new level and that of its neighbors.

Others attribute the chief responsibility for growth to certain changes in behavior. Thus the recovery of the birthrate is said to have brought about a change in attitudes toward the necessity for economic progress. A fearful and paralyzing Malthusian attitude, according to this argument, gave way to the determination to build a better future for young people; then, as the new generation grew up, the dynamic attitude that marks youth spread to society as a whole. The transformations on which growth depends were on this account accepted, whereas earlier they had been rejected.

Another simple sociological explanation is one that relies on *the shock caused by the 1940 defeat*, as well as by the occupation and resistance that followed over four years. In this difficult period, it is argued, there was a turnover of groups in power; the French questioned all traditional values and became aware of the need for fundamental changes. Like the other defeated countries (Germany, Italy, Japan), France in this way found itself in conditions that were particularly favorable to fast economic progress.

For others again, institutional reforms have been the chief cause of the success achieved. Sometimes the *nationalizations* carried out immediately after the war are referred to; they are said to have radically changed the management of basic industries and in this way to have provided the basis for harmonious industrial expansion.

The public financing of investment is also cited as having made possible a high level of national savings, ensured expansion of productive capital beyond comparison with that achieved earlier, and guided new capital investment toward those sectors best able to act as "growth poles," to use the expression of François Perroux.[1]

The French system of *national planning* is stressed, as able to ensure

---

[1] François Perroux, "Note sur la notion de pôle de croissance," *Economie appliquée*, no. 1–2, 1955.

a high degree of consistency among decisions affecting the future, to reduce uncertainty of the environment within which each firm's activity takes place, and to stimulate confidence in the likelihood of growth, a confidence that is itself favorable to growth.

All these hypotheses may contain part of the explanation, but none seems acceptable as a unique explanation of the phenomenon we are studying. Critical examination shows the weaknesses in each of these approaches and reveals their partial nature.

The catching-up hypothesis is not in fact an explanation—that is its chief fault. It does not analyze why France had earlier fallen consistently behind other countries, or why it now seems to be partly closing the gap. Therefore this hypothesis does little to answer the question raised by a search for causes.

Moreover, it seems to apply poorly to the growth observed over the 1960's. It is true that in the immediate postwar period the mere fact of recharging the productive mechanism for a time led to high growth rates. This has often been forgotten by those who have examined French postwar growth without comparing it with the past. But once the lag behind previous trends is made up, it would seem that growth should slow down, since the only gap then left is in relation to certain other countries. Now we have seen that the trend of labor productivity for the first 30 years of the century was overtaken from 1950 on in agriculture and from about 1965 in industry. Nevertheless, no slowing down in growth has appeared since then.

To uphold the catching-up hypothesis, one must link with it the idea of a universal increase in growth rates of productivity: in other industrial countries it appears that acceleration in long-term trends has also been observed. But the hypothesis then loses the simplicity that was its principal attraction.

One wishing to assess the part to be ascribed to the birthrate explanation ought to carry out a detailed examination of changes experienced in certain types of behavior. This explanation might then be seen to have some importance, but it is obviously not the chief key to the phenomenon. To accept this, one need only recall the following facts. The fastest drop in French births occurred in the 20 years preceding World War I, a period of revival of economic growth.[2] The industrial country with the fastest postwar growth, Japan, has also restricted its birthrates most. The revival in birthrates has been almost general over Western Europe;

---

[2] The most relevant index is probably that of fertility rates per 100 women aged 30–34 years. It fell from 13.3 in 1895–97 to 10.1 in 1910–12 and then to 7.9 in 1935–37. In 1953–55 it stood at 11.0.

nevertheless the rate of economic growth has varied significantly from one country to another. A notable exception is Italy, where birthrates have fallen below prewar levels, whereas growth has been very fast.

The hypothesis that stresses differences between victorious and defeated countries is less easy to refute as a whole.[3] However, this is partly due to the fact that production was very low after the war in the so-called defeated countries, whereas it was far closer to normal in the victorious countries. The growth rates achieved since the end of the war represent, then, misleading indicators that are systematically favorable to the countries that were destroyed.

More generally, the two hypotheses just considered seem to rely on an incorrect view of the changes experienced by the French economy between the 1920's and the period after World War II. They assume that the structure of the economy altered far faster in the recent past than in earlier periods. However, we have not observed such an acceleration, at least in the structural features that we have analyzed. Apart from the acceleration of migrations from farming, structural changes in the productive system do not seem to have occurred, at least up to 1966, any faster than before 1930. Although restrictive practices probably lost some of their strength between 1950 and 1970, there is no evidence that they are less severe now than during the 1920's. Comparison with the period 1930–39 of course leads to different conclusions; but it is of little interest for an understanding of present-day growth.

A comparative study of management efficiency in the public and private sectors would be very difficult. In any case, to attribute the chief responsibility for postwar growth to nationalizations it is not enough to establish that new government enterprises are better managed than the private companies they replaced; the public sector of production must also be shown to exercise a role as prime mover. In the immediate postwar reconstruction, nationalizations may have helped development of the basic sectors, to which high priority had been given. This, however, is not entirely certain, since in the private sector iron and steel, the cement industry, and chemical firms were also able to develop rapidly. But above all, nationalizations cannot be regarded as the cause of the sustained growth in productivity over the 1960's: the processing and manufacturing industries, in which the public sector has only a small part, were at that time the scene of continual and fast improvement.

The existence of public financing, which was on a large scale except in the period 1952–57, was of great assistance to the investment drive carried out in France. In a situation where savings were continuously

[3] One should note, however, that France experienced strong expansion in the 1920's, whereas German production grew only moderately in that period.

scarce, financial constraints would have been felt very strongly if the government had not provided a large part of capital formation—direct public investment, long-term loans, investment subsidies, etc. But the impact of this public financing cannot be greater than that ascribable to capital accumulation. The detailed examination in Chapter 7 has shown that this accumulation must be regarded as having played a significant part but not a preponderant one.

We have given a good deal of attention to the role of national planning, and have concluded that it did indeed have an influence on growth. It is the most visible expression of a dynamic and somewhat original concept of the role of government in running the economy, and this concept also inspires economic management in the short-term, the regulation of prices or agreements, the management of major public enterprises, etc. By attempting to clear away obstacles to economic expansion and to spread relevant information over a wide field, national planning assisted growth, diffusely but undeniably.

However, it was too limited in means and impact within the productive system to have amounted to the *deus ex machina* that some have believed it to be. It can obviously account for only a small part of the sustained growth experienced by labor productivity in firms. It would have been only an empty frame if it had not been applied to an economy that was in any case solidly on the move. We can no more accept the hypothesis that national planning was the central explanation of French growth than we can the other hypotheses examined here. If a person should single out institutional factors, nationalizations, public financing, national planning, or other such factors, he must answer the objection that growth was fast in other countries also where the institutional context was substantially different from that in France, and in particular in West Germany. Detailed comparative research would be of great interest to chart the likely influence of some of the factors. But even lacking the results of such research, we may confidently assert that no single factor can provide the chief answer to the explanation we are seeking.

On completing our studies, we have personally reached the conclusion that French postwar growth was the result of a conjunction of many favorable factors whose effects were compounded. To attribute the primary credit to one factor alone seems to us an attempt to apply rigid systematizing not justified by objective examination of the facts. In the same way as biological growth, cannot economic growth be determined by a complex combination of causes?

We may distinguish two groups of factors favoring growth. On the one hand, there were forces external to the country and independent of its actions since 1945. So far as these go, French postwar growth would have been high barring positive errors in its own economic policy. On the other hand, there were forces, resulting from the country's own efforts during the last 20 years, that help explain why the expansion was so long sustained.

FACTORS FROM EARLIER PERIODS, AND THE INTERNATIONAL ENVIRONMENT

The progress achieved today has its origin partly in a far earlier past than is usually thought. New factors that were to permit acceleration of French growth appeared in the last years of the nineteenth century and the first years of the twentieth century. This acceleration occurred even before World War I and during the 1920's, but it apparently was halted in 1930. French productive potential, however, continued to grow in such a way that production in 1946 was still at a far lower level than the country could have expected to reach in a lasting situation of balanced growth.

There can be little doubt that the French lag behind long-term trends was particularly great in 1946. In the United States production was then 75 percent higher than in 1929, and labor productivity measured as output per man-hour was 40 percent higher. In the United Kingdom, the increases over 1929 were respectively 40 percent and 10 percent. In France, on the contrary, production in 1946 was 20 percent lower than in 1929, and labor productivity about 5 percent lower. Now from 1896 to 1929, labor productivity had grown in France almost as fast as in the United States and much faster than in the United Kingdom. But this lag in production and labor productivity was not accompanied by any lasting interruption in the growth of French productive capacity. The most fundamental growth factors continued to provide the basis for progress. Two facts seem of particular importance in this context.

First, *education* of the French population continued without interruption from the end of the nineteenth century. The working population thus contained a growing proportion of men equipped to take part in modern industry. In 1896 half the work force had not been to school or had ended schooling before the age of 13, and only 13 percent had remained in school until 15 years old or over. In 1931, the corresponding proportions were 15 percent and 21 percent. In 1946 they were 6 percent and 27 percent. This better educated population was ineffectively used at the end of the war. But when directed toward modern activities, this group after a few years of experience was to reach far higher productivity than that achieved 20 years earlier.

Second, development in *industries with a future* was an increasing feature from the beginning of the century. France entered the Industrial Revolution after Britain. Over the second half of the nineteenth century, it lost ground to Germany and the United States, which experienced accelerated industrial expansion at that time. But after 1900 an opposite reaction took place, to be considerably assisted, it would seem, by World War I. This fact is particularly clear in the capital goods industries, as can be seen by examining the proportion of foreign capital equipment in investment in each year with an investment boom. It was 38 percent on the average in the two years 1899 and 1900, 40 percent during the investment booms of 1911 to 1913, but only 25 percent in 1928, 1929, and 1930. The depression and the war probably interrupted growth in the relevant industry groups. But engineers and technicians continued to work on new techniques, and were ready to develop them rapidly after the war. Significantly, the share of foreign capital goods in investment was only 15 percent in 1949 and 20 percent in 1963, despite the liberalization of foreign trade.

Thus, French productive potential, despite appearances, continued to grow after 1930 in its most fundamental features. The aging of capital equipment, the halt in migration from farming, the fall in activity rates, and the shortening of the work week then accounted for the low level of production and productivity in that period. But the return to normal economic conditions was to make these causes of slow growth gradually disappear. In brief, the productive system was ready to respond to expansion.

Now the situation left behind by the depression, the war, and the immediate postwar period carried with it in a latent state a *very substantial potential demand.* Many needs had remained unsatisfied for a long period: demand for household durable goods, whose use was not very widespread in relation to that in other countries; demand for housing for a population once again growing; demand for replacement and modernization of productive equipment, in many cases dating back from the 1920's. Individuals and firms wished to acquire massive volumes of goods. And in a manner that is only apparently paradoxical, inflation had made the financial situation healthier: old debts were virtually wiped out by the great increase in prices; the balance sheets of firms as a result had a healthy structure; lenders and borrowers could feel only slight reluctance to undertake investments financed from borrowing.

To these national circumstances were added an *international environment* that was eminently favorable. The cooperation and financial assistance given for a period by the United States made it possible to get the economy rapidly under way again, and brought to the attention of French industrialists techniques of production and organization that were customary in other countries. Among France's nearest neighbors, with whom contact is particularly frequent, labor productivity also was growing at a rapid pace, which suggested numerous opportunities for progress to the heads of French firms. And last, the vigor of demand in a once-again peaceful Europe meant a sustained stimulus to the most modern parts of French industry.

It is easy therefore to understand why French gross domestic production in 1948 had recovered its 1929 or 1939 level, and that over the following ten years it grew at a rate of 5 percent per year. But the lag at the end of the war is not enough to explain how that pace was maintained without slackening until the present day, although the expansion achieved immediately after the war probably helped to make growth the normal touchstone of expectations by decision makers in the economy. New factors came into play; we have mentioned these in the course of our detailed analyses. The chief ones can be grouped around three observations: the French kept work output at a high level, units of production invested in new equipment and were reorganized, and the economic administration of the country gave proof of a dynamic attitude.

THE FRENCH AT WORK

Although it is impossible to measure the intensity of the work effort, a number of indexes show that the French gave a degree of priority to work. The changes in activity rates, in geographical mobility, and in working hours are quite revealing.

It is likely that the increase in years at school and the sharp reduction in number of independent workers in farming and trade had the effect of lowering activity rates in the extreme age-groups. But women sought work in growing proportions: this can be seen particularly clearly in the case of activity rates at ages below 40 (at the age of 25 years this rate grew from 47 percent in 1954 to 52 percent in 1962 and to 56 percent in 1968).

Although it is still low by comparison with countries like the United States, geographical mobility seems fairly noteworthy. It has been increasing; moreover, it has reached levels that seem high if one bears in mind the great housing difficulties that prevailed over the whole postwar period in most areas of urban concentration. Many people were prepared to endure uncomfortable living conditions in order to have a better job.

Finally, the prevalence until recently of long working hours seems to have been due largely to a change in attitude of the adult population. For example, annual hours worked, which in industry had fallen by about 20 percent between 1896 and 1929 and were then sharply reduced again by the depression and the 1936 legislation, in the postwar period stood at a level little below that of 1929, since first the granting of vacations and then their lengthening had been offset by an increase in weekly hours worked. The trade unions, which immediately after the war fought for a drop in weekly hours, thereafter realized that this was not widely desired, at least until May 1968. Some opinion polls also showed that most wage earners placed the desire to increase income well ahead of reduced working hours. Thus, France around 1965 was one of the countries with the longest hours of work.

INVESTMENT AND MODERNIZATION BY FIRMS

Modernization of the productive mechanism played an important part. Probably as a result of this, productivity improvements did not slow down during the 1960's and even accelerated slightly in industry. At two periods, crucial options were taken. From the earliest postwar years, the government and those responsible for the public sector carried out an optimistic reconstruction of the infrastructure and the basic industries. At the end of the 1950's and the beginning of the 1960's, heads of firms gained an awareness of the requirements of modern production and took the decision to meet them. They understood this information to be part of the movement in favor of productivity; they accepted the consequences and did not delay the opening of the Common Market. Many were able to take advantage of the loosening of trade barriers.

It is true that earlier inflation had probably improved the financial position of firms. Various tax measures had the effect of reducing the effective cost of utilization of capital equipment, and foreign competition in many cases forced firms to carry out large-scale reorganizations. But if the heads and managers of industry had not had the will to promote expansion in their firms, modernization would have been slower.

As always happens in periods of rapid change, success was accompanied by a certain proportion of failures. These always come to public attention, but with a certain amount of perspective, which we have striven for in this book, one can see emerging a picture of modernization with an overall efficiency that cannot be denied.

A DYNAMIC ECONOMIC POLICY

At many points we have noted the role played by government authorities. This role was bound to be significant, since at the end of the war there was a publicly owned productive sector that had been substantially enlarged by the 1946 nationalizations, there were control bodies with economic aims, and there was a high-quality administrative staff. But these advantages were offset by the almost complete lack of tools for documenting the economy, by the poor economic training of management, and by the absence of a clear, widely accepted set of principles.

The fact that the economic policy that was followed seems, with hindsight, to have been endowed on the whole with dynamism and consistency can be attributed to a fundamental change in government action, which owes much to the conjunction of efforts by a few groups of men and to the progress made in economic knowledge. Each of these groups, because of either its duties or its experience, was sensitized to a particular aspect of economic development and had the will to make improvements in it. The combination of efforts of this kind produced a system that owes much to empiricism but seems marked by a certain effectiveness.

Together with Jean Monnet, a number of men who had lived through the Great Depression in management circles fought for the basic industries to be reorganized, for a National Plan to be set up outlining a forward-looking framework as a reference to medium- and long-term government action, and last for a bold policy of European union and of opening the doors to the outside world. Men like Alfred Sauvy and Claude Gruson, who were responsible both for keeping track of economic developments and for advising the government authorities, were able to show the importance of correct economic information and of analysis of the impact of public finance on short-term economic development and growth. A determining influence was also exercised by civil servants such as Maurice Lauré, who showed that reform of the tax system must be carried out with a view to its impact on the organization of production and on investment programs. With Pierre Massé, engineer-economists working in the nationalized sector, or in control bodies, put economic calculations in the forefront of their work and associated them with deliberately expansionist views of the future.

In this way was born a mixed economic system, in which markets play a great role, and competition is maintained or reestablished among national producers both at home and overseas, but in which also a system of indicative national planning fosters awareness of the requirements and characteristics of growth, while the government takes on certain direct responsibilities in economic management.

The government indeed carried out a large number of timely operations aimed at helping economic growth; this was done through management of public enterprises, through public financing of large investments, and through improving regional development or in reorganizing large firms. Not all these operations may have succeeded, as can be shown by a detailed examination.[4] Nevertheless, although the underlying concept was not fully set forth, most of these operations belong within a fairly consistent view of the public action for economic growth.

THE OUTLOOK

Thus the explanatory forces with which we emerge at the end of our study bring into play the economic agents themselves: workers, heads and managers of firms, directors of economic policy. Our economic analysis should therefore be completed by a historical and sociological analysis that would seek more basic explanations. The relevant actors in society should be identified, their role in economic change studied, and the nature of the relationships linking them should be identified.[5]

While we invite historians and sociologists to take on the next stage of the study, we should not wish to close without mentioning two kinds of question that arise from our subject: How will growth be maintained? What advantages do we receive from growth?

As time passes, the importance of positive factors resulting from earlier actions grows less, and that of new factors proper to the postwar period increases. Some measures whose effects are not yet felt will be seen as increasingly favorable to growth, but expansion may also be affected by retarding forces.

The development of education is the most certain source of future progress. Not only is the active population getting younger, but it has an increasingly high level of education. The increase in numbers in secondary and higher education over the past 20 years means that each successive generation is better trained than that before it.

Similarly, investment from the 1960's in research and development is only beginning to bear fruit. It should continue to produce effects for a long time yet.

The most profound changes resulting from international competition and the Common Market are no doubt still to come. Improvements in management methods and the restructuring of firms should represent a strong stimulus to productivity.

---

[4] See for example L. Stoleru, *L'Impératif industriel* (Paris, 1969), chap. 3.

[5] We have in our study ventured on certain questions of a sociological kind. Although these questions are not within our field, we have the feeling that answers have not yet been found to them. Each would require long research not yet carried out. In the hope that sociologists may deal with the problem of the causes of growth, we have reproduced in Appendix H a list of questions that seem to us particularly relevant.

The effects of the three factors mentioned work toward acceleration of growth. On the other hand, the exhaustion of manpower reserves represented by underemployment or inefficient employment in farming, the limitations to benefits from the increased substitution of capital for labor, and the closing of the gap in productivity between France and the most advanced countries will make further progress increasingly difficult.

Taking everything into account, it seems that the extraordinary growth experienced by France and many other countries since the war is unlikely to slow down significantly for a good many years. A rise in production and in living standards will probably be the major economic feature of the latter part of the twentieth century.

WHAT IS GROWTH FOR?

In the immediate postwar period, with memory still fresh of the misfortunes inflicted by the depression and the war, French economists naturally gave their attention to improvement in productivity. Today, seeing how strong and long-lasting growth has become, it is necessary to question more and more the benefits people get from it.

Does growth result in greater equality among the citizens of the country? Does it lead to greater international solidarity between rich and poor? Do not the production and consumption of material goods develop at the expense of the quality of life and of relationships among men? Does expansion of the economic power system that accompanies growth make men more responsible members of society and more masters of their fate? These are urgent and burning questions, which would make the subject of another book.

Appendixes

Estimation of Indexes of Production over the Long Term, 1896–1963

Tables 1.1, 1.7, 1.8, and 1.9 show the results related to production in 1896, 1913, 1929, 1938, 1949, and 1963. The bulk of these figures were taken from estimates made by L. A. Vincent.[1] Nevertheless, we have made some modifications in the indexes of production of the different industry groups. We have had to adopt our own indexes for certain services, and we have carried out a new aggregation to determine the indexes relating to production or to gross domestic product. This appendix explains the procedure we have followed and shows the indexes we have used.

Table A.1 shows the usual industry group classification of the French National Accounts,[2] with the difference that Metallurgy groups iron mining and metallurgy with nonferrous minerals and metals. Moreover, the three items Financial institutions, Domestic service, and Government do not correspond to industry groups regarded in France as productive. For international comparisons we have had to refer to an aggregate including these activities. This is why we have introduced them from the start. The indexes that relate to them reproduce indexes relating to labor input, shown in Chapter 2. Moreover, it is in agreement with international usage to identify output and labor input at least in the case of domestic service and government agencies.

The last column of Table A.1 reproduces the results of the National Accounts[3] for the indexes of production for the year 1963, with 1949 = 100. The only exception concerns the item Agriculture and forestry, for which we have

---

[1] See L. A. Vincent, "Evolution de la production intérieure brute en France de 1896 à 1938, méthode et premiers résultats," *Etudes et conjoncture*, November 1962; also his "Population active, production et productivité dans 21 branches de l'économie française, 1896–1962," *Etudes et conjoncture*, February 1965.

[2] For their definition one can refer, for example, to "Méthodes de la comptabilité nationale: cadres et définitions de la base 1959," *Etudes et conjoncture*, no. 3, March 1966, pp. 208–10, 98–143.

[3] Calculations for the figures in this appendix were carried out at the end of 1964 from the provisional results for 1963, and the results were thereafter amended slightly upward. But the correction was too small to cause recalculation of the figures. The correction was applied after the event to the various tables shown in the text.

attempted to determine an index for "normal weather conditions," which would give a better picture of the trend than an index directly obtained for each year in question. Thus it can be estimated that in 1949 the trend under normal weather conditions was higher than the observed index by about 7 percent, whereas in 1963 it was higher by 2 percent. The index of 154 from the National Accounts for 1963, with 1949 = 100, should therefore be reduced by 5 percent to 146.

The first three columns of Table A.1 were established from estimates worked out by Vincent. Our indexes for the prewar periods are therefore subject to the same uncertainties as those estimates—which, as we recall from the text of Chapter 1, depend on a somewhat restricted number of direct observations. The reader may refer to Vincent's studies for all details of the procedures followed in calculating the indexes of particular industries.

Nevertheless, we have made some modifications to Vincent's estimates, for a number of reasons. In the first place, we have retained the definition of industry groups adopted by the French National Accounts. We have therefore had to carry out a number of regroupings and even to reestimate certain indexes. Hereafter, we shall be able to refer to Vincent's results in tracing development of particular industries that he has analyzed in more detail than we.

In the second place, in line with the approach for the postwar period, we have attempted to measure output by value added at constant prices, whereas Vincent refers to overall output of each industry group.[4] This conceptual difference, nevertheless, has only slight effect on the estimates, since with the available information we must accept as a general rule the fact that value added at constant prices and overall output evolved in parallel. We have made a different hypothesis only in the case of Agriculture and forestry, where consumption of intermediate products grew faster than output. To obtain the index of value added, we have reduced the index of overall output by 4 percent between 1896 and 1913, by 3 percent between 1913 and 1929, and by 3 percent between 1929 and 1938.

In the third place, Vincent took as a base for the 1929 indexes the output in 1913 of the 90 *départements* that made up France in 1929. For our 1929 indexes, however, the base is output in 1913 in French territory as a whole in that period. This explains why our 1929 indexes are higher than his, with a difference in most cases of about 4 percent.

In the fourth place, we have corrected the index for Mechanical and electrical industries. Vincent's index for output by this industry group for the prewar period is based almost entirely on apparent consumption of metals, which is in fact a very imprecise method of estimation. Another study has

---

[4] In his 1962 article Vincent attempted to estimate production by each industry group of only those goods that entered into the final French output and no others. But this principle was followed only imperfectly in the case of Industry. In his 1965 study, which we have used, the figures shown are overall output by each industry group.

TABLE A.1

Production by Sector in Key Years, 1896–1963

Sector	1913 index (1896=100)	1929 index (1913=100)	1938 index (1929=100)	1949 index (1938=100)	1963 index (1949=100)
01. Agriculture and forestry[a]	115	102	109	108	146
02. Processed foods and farm products	126	140	103	100	164
03. Solid mineral fuels and gas	144	142	89	120	122
04. Electricity and water	425	700	134	127	376
05. Petroleum and oil products	–	–	500	181	404
06. Building materials	149	148	62	112	213
07–08. Metallurgy	290	186	66	145	210
09. Mechanical and electrical industries	210	199	77	117	236
10. Chemicals	267	316	108	134	289
11. Textiles, clothing, and leather	127	114	88	90	187
12. Miscellaneous industries	153	147	118	103	201
13. Building and public works	140	124	60	150	227
14. Transportation and communications	182	160	85	134	200
15. Housing services	132	128	107	92	163
16. Services other than housing	141	119	114	114	200
19. Trade	128	124	103	98	197
Financial institutions[b]	167	164	75	110	136
Domestic service[b]	92	79	90	78	74
Government[b]	116	74	126	139	139

[a]Production "in normal weather conditions."
[b]Indexes relating to labor input.

concluded that in Great Britain output of the mechanical and electrical industries grew faster than apparent consumption of metals, with a difference of approximately 0.8 percent per year between 1907 and 1924 and 1.7 percent between 1924 and 1935.[5] We have accordingly raised this index of production somewhat.

Previously we made a detailed study of changes in the composition of this industry group, which can be seen in the various demographic censuses from the distribution of workers by the industrial activity of the establishments where they worked. This study shows that, from 1896 to World War I, the growth of production of machinery and equipment was accompanied by stability in the production of what often were more elaborately worked articles (cutlery, watch-making, etc.) and by a drop in the relative weight of small shops (blacksmiths, locksmiths, tinsmiths, etc.). It therefore seemed inadvisable to raise the 1913 index with 1896 = 100. By contrast, between 1921 and 1936, it can be seen that the growth in output of the modern mechanical and elec-

[5] C. T. Saunders, "Consumption of Raw Material in the United Kingdom, 1851–1950," *Journal of the Royal Statistical Society*, series A, part III, 1952.

trical industries is very much higher (heating equipment, bicycles, sewing machines, automobiles, electrical machinery and appliances, optical instruments, etc.). We have therefore assumed that from 1913 to 1938 the growth in output of this group exceeded apparent consumption of metals by 1.5 percent per year.

This overall correction has had the effect of producing results that a priori are more credible than Vincent's for the growth of labor productivity in the Mechanical and electrical industries. According to Vincent, labor productivity in those industries grew only slightly from 1913 to 1929 and dropped from 1929 to 1938, but this seems highly improbable, given the substantial technological progress.

For the comparison between 1938 and 1949, shown in the penultimate column of Table A.1, we have reproduced almost without alteration the estimates assembled by Gavanier and the staff of the National Plan's Commissariat General.[6] We have regrouped them, however, in order to follow present-day nomenclature of the industry groups.

In the form shown, our estimates of indexes for the industry groups therefore contain some heterogeneity which may be the source of errors in interpretation when one attempts to compare postwar growth with earlier trends. Nevertheless, it seems difficult to make an accurate assessment of what such errors in interpretation might be. The fact that for the postwar period we have in general treated indexes of value added as identical with indexes of overall output probably leads to a slight overestimation of the growth of value added. But, on the other hand, the fact that the estimates for earlier periods take little account of highly worked outputs and improvements in quality must lead to underestimation of real growth. We therefore feel we cannot do better than leave the indexes as they are. Readers will, we hope, remember that their exactness leaves something to be desired.

WEIGHTING COEFFICIENTS FOR OVERALL INDEXES

To measure the development of overall output, we refer in principle to an aggregate at constant prices. But since our period covers in all 67 years, we cannot retain the same prices throughout the series. Changes in relative prices have been too great for recent price relationships to be suitable for calculations of the comparative magnitudes at earlier periods in the various industries. So we must consider separately the various subperiods that we have distinguished earlier and adopt appropriate prices for each.

The rest of this note will be clearer if we state the principles underlying our calculations. Let us call q_{it} the volume of production achieved by industry i in the year t, p_{it} the price of this output over the same year, and v_{it} the product $p_{it}q_{it}$.

---

[6] M. Gavanier, "Le Revenu national de la France: production et disponibilités nationales en 1938 et de 1946 à 1949," *Statistiques et études financières*, supplement, Finances françaises, no. 20, 1953.

To compare total output achieved in two years t and θ, where θ is later than t, we can in principle use either prices for year t or those for year θ. Prices for year t for a comparison of overall output in the two years result in a "Laspeyres index," equal by definition to

$$(1) \qquad I_L = \sum_i p_{it}q_{i\theta} \Big/ \sum_i p_{it}q_{it}$$

Prices for year θ result in a "Paasche index" equal to

$$(2) \qquad I_P = \sum_i p_{i\theta}q_{i\theta} \Big/ \sum_i p_{i\theta}q_{it}$$

In general, a Laspeyres index can be expected to somewhat overestimate growth of total output, whereas a Paasche index will slightly underestimate it.[7] This is why a "Fisher index" is often calculated, which is equal to the geometric mean of the Laspeyres and the Paasche indexes, i.e.,

$$(3) \qquad I_F = \sqrt{I_L I_P}$$

For total French output, we shall calculate the three indexes Laspeyres, Paasche, and Fisher for each of the subperiods, that is, for 1913 with 1896 = 100, 1929 with 1913 = 100, 1938 with 1929 = 100, 1949 with 1938 = 100, and 1963 with 1949 = 100. Finally, we shall also calculate as a control the three indexes for the period as a whole, i.e. for 1963 with 1896 = 100.

For our calculations we shall use formulas somewhat different from equations (1) and (2). I_L can in fact be written in the form

$$I_L = \sum_i \left[\left(p_{it}q_{it} \Big/ \sum_j p_{jt}q_{jt} \right) \times \left(q_{i\theta} \Big/ q_{it} \right) \right]$$

or again,

$$(4) \qquad I_L = \sum_i \frac{v_{it}}{V_t} \times \frac{q_{i\theta}}{q_{it}}$$

where V_t represents the sum of v_{it} for all industry groups. The Laspeyres index thus appears as a weighted arithmetic mean of the indexes for the different industries, i.e. $q_{i\theta}/q_{it}$, with v_{it}/V_t as weighting coefficients. In the same way, the Paasche index can be calculated with the aid of the following formula, which is equivalent to equation (2):

$$(5) \qquad \frac{1}{I_P} = \sum_i \frac{v_{i\theta}}{V_\theta} \times \frac{q_{it}}{q_{i\theta}}$$

The inverse of the Paasche index is therefore a weighted arithmetic mean of the inverses of the industry group indexes with $v_{i\theta}/V_\theta$ as the weighting

[7] For example, on this subject see INSEE, *Initiation à la comptabilité nationale* (3d ed., 1965), chap. 13.

coefficients. (The Paasche index can also be regarded as a weighted harmonic mean of the indexes for the different industry groups.)

The industry group indexes, $q_{i\theta}/q_{it}$, are shown in Table A.1. This leaves for calculation the weighting coefficients, v_{it}/V_t, representing the share of industry group i in the value of total output.

What is the best way for each of the years studied to represent the proportion of each industry group in the value of French output? It would seem that the following principle must be adopted. Each industry group should be given a weighting proportional to its share of primary productive resources. This principle stems from the fact that if two industry groups have the same weighting, overall output is not changed by decreasing the output of the first industry by 5 percent and increasing the output of the second by 5 percent, and vice versa. Such substitutions are possible, given the primary resources available to the economy in terms of manpower and capital equipment, only if the two branches use equal quantities of these resources.

Now the volume of primary resources used in an industry group can be regarded as measured by the value added in that industry. In the applications, coefficient $v_{i\theta}/V_\theta$ from the preceding formulas will then be replaced by the ratio between value added in industry i and value added in all industry groups together.[8]

The principle stated above also implies that the values added must be defined "at factor cost," that is to say, that they do not include indirect taxes paid by the industry group in question. One would also expect them to be "net," that is, that capital depreciation should be deducted from the value of output in the same way as intermediary consumption. In the long term, depreciation must indeed measure some kind of intermediary consumption, i.e. that of capital goods which help to create production over a period of several years. Nevertheless, the assessment of depreciation is in reality difficult to carry out properly. The share it represents of gross value added, although varying from one industry to the other, is never very important. We shall therefore follow the usage established in France as well as in other countries, and base our figures on gross value added. This will make comparisons easier with the results obtained in other countries.

But in order to apply this principle, while we have no direct assessments of value added in each industry in years before 1949, we must estimate them from existing statistical data. We shall accordingly adopt the hypothesis that, in current prices, value added per hour of work varies proportionately in all industry groups.

Let a_{it} and u_{it} represent, respectively, labor input—that is, the number of hours of work supplied—and value added per hour of work in industry group i over the year t. From the definition of u_{it},

$$(6) \qquad\qquad v_{it} = a_{it}u_{it}$$

[8] For a discussion in greater depth, see *ibid.*

Our hypothesis assumes identities of the type $u_{it}/u_{jt} = k_i/k_j$ for every t where k_i and k_j represent fixed numerical coefficients. It can also be written as

$$(7) \qquad\qquad u_{it} = k_i s_t$$

where s_t is a value varying from one year to another but applicable to all industry groups (the common value of the ratios u_{it}/k_i).

In these circumstances we can determine v_{it}/V_t from the values observed for these ratios over a recent year that we shall call τ. This is because (6) and (7) imply $v_{it} = a_{it} k_i s_t$. Therefore,

$$(8) \qquad\qquad \frac{v_{it}}{v_{i\tau}} = \frac{a_{it}}{a_{i\tau}} \times \frac{s_t}{s_\tau}$$

or

$$v_{it} = \frac{s_t}{s_\tau} \times \frac{a_{it}}{a_{i\tau}} v_{i\tau}$$

From the sum of the v_{it} in the different industry groups, V_t becomes

$$V_t = \frac{s_t}{s_\tau} \sum_i \frac{a_{it}}{a_{i\tau}} v_{i\tau}$$

Whence

$$(9) \qquad\qquad \frac{V_t}{V_\tau} = \frac{s_t}{s_\tau} \sum_i \frac{a_{it}}{a_{i\tau}} \times \frac{v_{i\tau}}{V_{i\tau}}$$

From a comparison between (8) and (9) we obtain

$$(10) \qquad\qquad \frac{v_{it}}{V_t} = \frac{(a_{it}/a_{i\tau}) \times (v_{i\tau}/V_\tau)}{\sum\limits_i (a_{it}/a_{i\tau}) \times (v_{i\tau}/V_\tau)}$$

In brief, by means of the hypotheses adopted, we can determine the coefficients v_{it}/V_t by multiplying the known coefficients $v_{i\tau}/V_\tau$ by the labor input indexes $a_{it}/a_{i\tau}$ for year t in relation to year τ, then increasing or decreasing the results proportionately in order to bring back the sum of the v_{it}/V_t to 1. Now we know the labor input indexes for the various industry groups for the key years already shown. These indexes are given in Chapter 2; we shall now deduce from them the weighting coefficients that we require.[9]

It is probably advisable beforehand to discuss the hypothesis we use. It has already been used by various authors. Thus, Vincent utilized it to measure differences between particular products when measuring the size of productivity gains.[10]

---

[9] The group Housing services obviously cannot be treated like the others, and is the subject of a direct estimate.

[10] L. A. Vincent, *Le Progrès technique en France depuis cent ans* (Etude spéciale no. 3, Institut de Conjoncture, Paris, 1944).

The hypothesis seems a priori quite reasonable. Under the form of equation (7) it assumes that, in each industry group, value added per hour of work moves at the rate applicable to the economy as a whole. One can, for example, consider s_t as the wage rate, or more generally as the rate of labor remuneration, and make use of the fact that this remuneration's share in value added changes little over time. The differences between the coefficients k_i relating to the various branches can be explained by the variable scale of capital equipment, by differences in the average level of qualification of those in the labor force, and by inequalities in the rates of remuneration between industry groups. The hypothesis is equivalent to assuming that these three causes of difference act in a fairly constant way over the whole period studied.

For testing this hypothesis, the best source is probably Kendrick's data, which refer to the United States for the period 1899–1953.[11] Kendrick in particular has studied the inverse correlation between the growth of product prices and the growth of productivity in the industries manufacturing those products. If p_{it} and q_{it} represent, respectively, the indexes of price and of volume relating to value added in industry i, our hypothesis implies the following equation:

$$\frac{p_{it}}{p_{i\tau}} \times \frac{q_{it}/a_{it}}{q_{i\tau}/a_{i\tau}} = \frac{p_{jt}}{p_{j\tau}} \times \frac{q_{jt}/a_{jt}}{q_{j\tau}/a_{j\tau}}$$

In each part of this equation, the first term represents a price index for year t in relation to year τ, the second term an index of labor productivity. The hypothesis therefore implies a strict inverse correlation between the price indexes relating to the different industry groups and the labor productivity indexes relating to these same industries. Taking the indexes for 1953, with $1899 = 100$, and using a breakdown of the United States economy in 33 industry groups, Kendrick in fact observed a high inverse correlation.[12] A test more appropriate to the situation in France but applying to a far shorter period is to compare for the postwar period the weightings resulting from our hypothesis with those that would stem from the values added in the National Accounts. Table A.2 gives the main data for this comparison for the years 1949 and 1963, with 1954 taken as the base year in the application of our hypothesis. The agreement is not perfect, although the variations from 1949 to 1963 are in the same direction. But it must be remembered that the calculations for the National Accounts, as well as those necessary for applying our hypothesis, make use of numerous statistical sources some of which contain gaps. The results for 1949 in particular may be affected by rather

[11] John W. Kendrick, *Productivity Trends in the United States* (Princeton, N.J., 1961).

[12] Kendrick calculated the coefficient of rank correlation between the price index for value added ("unit value added") and the index of total factor productivity defined in our Chapter 7. The coefficient was -0.74.

TABLE A.2

Proportional Distribution of Value Added at Factor Cost, 1949–63

(Percent of all sectors)

Sector	From the National Accounts[a]			From the hypothesis adopted	
	1949	1954	1963	1949	1963
Agriculture and forestry	17.6%	14.8%	11.2%	17.3%	9.7%
Industry:					
Processed foods and farm products	9.2	6.4	5.1	6.5	5.9
Solid mineral fuels and gas	2.4	2.1	1.7	2.6	1.6
Electricity and water	1.1	1.3	1.4	1.2	1.3
Petroleum and oil products	0.7	0.9	1.4	0.7	1.1
Building materials	1.5	1.7	1.7	1.6	1.7
Metallurgy	1.9	2.2	2.5	2.4	2.3
Mechanical and electrical industries	11.9	12.6	12.7	11.8	15.1
Chemicals	2.8	3.3	3.2	3.0	3.7
Textiles, clothing, and leather	8.6	7.5	5.8	8.5	5.8
Miscellaneous industries	3.0	4.5	4.7	4.6	4.5
Total industry	43.1	42.5	40.2	43.0	43.0
Other industry groups:					
Building and public works	7.5	7.4	9.1	5.9	8.8
Transportation and communications	6.8	6.9	8.2	7.8	7.1
Housing services	1.5	2.7	4.4	1.5	4.4
Services other than housing	11.1	13.2	14.9	12.6	13.5
Trade	12.4	12.5	12.0	11.9	13.5
Total of other industry groups	39.3	42.7	48.6	39.7	47.3
Total of all industry groups	100.0%	100.0%	100.0%	100.0%	100.0%

[a]To ensure comparability between 1963 and earlier years, block corrections have been made to the results on the basis of the differences between "accounts on the old base" and "accounts on the new base" for the year 1959.

large errors.[13] The comparison shown in Table A.2 may therefore reveal errors in the French National Accounts just as much as discrepancies between our hypothesis and reality.

Be that as it may, and although it is only a first rather rough approximation, our hypothesis is probably sufficient for a correct estimation of the indexes of overall production: it applies only to the calculation of weighting coefficients, for which high precision is not necessary.

[13] For Processed foods and farm products and Miscellaneous industries, the 1949 results seem rather unlikely. They imply, in fact, that value added at factor cost per member of the labor force was 9,600 francs in the former group and 2,700 in the latter, whereas in the other industry groups this value is close to 5,000 francs (for example, 5,500 in the mechanical and electrical industries and 3,600 in textiles, clothing, and leather). To be sure, the processed foods and farm products were at the time benefiting from a climate of shortage, whereas prices were not favorable to the wood and paper industries. These particular features, however, do not seem to explain such large differences as those mentioned above.

TABLE A.3
Weighting Coefficients by Sector, 1896–1963

Sector	1896	1913	1929	1938	1949	1954	1963
Agriculture and forestry	26.5	21.5	18.8	20.9	17.3	14.8	9.7
Industry:							
Processed foods and farm products	5.9	6.1	5.6	6.1	6.5	6.4	5.9
Solid mineral fuels and gas	1.4	1.8	2.3	2.2	2.6	2.1	1.6
Electricity and water	0.2	0.5	0.8	1.0	1.2	1.3	1.3
Petroleum and oil products	–	–	0.2	0.4	0.7	0.9	1.1
Building materials	1.8	1.9	1.9	1.5	1.6	1.7	1.7
Metallurgy	0.7	1.0	1.8	1.6	2.4	2.2	2.3
Mechanical and electrical industries	6.1	7.4	10.2	8.8	11.9	12.6	15.1
Chemicals	0.8	1.2	2.0	2.1	3.0	3.3	3.7
Textiles, clothing, and leather	17.3	16.0	11.5	9.4	8.5	7.5	5.8
Miscellaneous industries	4.7	4.7	4.7	4.1	4.6	4.5	4.5
Total industry	38.9	40.6	41.0	37.2	43.0	42.5	43.0
Other industry groups:							
Building and public works	5.0	5.4	5.7	4.2	5.9	7.4	8.8
Transportation and communications	5.1	5.8	7.8	7.2	7.8	6.9	7.1
Housing services	6.0	6.0	6.0	6.0	1.5	2.7	4.4
Services other than housing	9.4	10.5	10.0	12.1	12.6	13.2	13.5
Trade	9.1	10.2	10.7	12.4	11.9	12.5	13.5
Total of other industry groups	34.6	37.9	40.2	41.9	39.7	42.7	47.3
Total of all productive industry groups	100.0	100.0	100.0	100.0	100.0	100.0	100.0
Financial institutions	0.4	0.9	1.8	1.6	1.7	1.7	2.2
Domestic service	1.9	2.1	2.1	2.2	1.6	1.6	1.2
Government	3.8	5.4	5.0	7.4	9.6	10.6	12.0
Overall total	106.1	108.4	108.9	111.2	111.2	113.9	115.4

Table A.3 shows the weighting coefficients obtained for the different industry groups and the different years by applying our hypothesis to the structure of values added at factor cost in 1954.[14] The weighting would not have been very different if we had taken as a base the values added in 1963. Nevertheless, the weighting of the Mechanical and electrical industries would have been lower and that of Agriculture much higher. The overall indexes would have grown slightly faster.

AGGREGATE INDEXES

Table A.4 shows the aggregate indexes calculated from the principles just outlined. We calculated three series of indexes relating, respectively, to industry as a whole, all productive industry groups together, and all industry groups including even those considered in France as nonproductive. The last two indexes respectively correspond to the aggregates here called Gross Domestic Production and Gross National Product.

[14] For value added by housing services, we have used the estimates in the National Accounts for the postwar years and those by L. A. Vincent for the prewar years.

TABLE A.4
Aggregate Indexes of Production, 1896–1963

Index	1913 index (1896=100)	1929 index (1913=100)	1938 index (1929=100)	1949 index (1938=100)	1963 index (1949=100)
Industry as a whole:					
Laspeyres index	152	155	93	109	213
Paasche index	148	152	89	109	210
Fisher index	150	153	91	109	212
Growth rate[a]	2.4	2.6	–1.1	0.8	5.3
All productive industry groups together:					
Laspeyres index	139	134	97	111	197
Paasche index	137	130	96	111	197
Fisher index	138	132	96	111	197
Growth rate[a]	1.9	1.7	–0.4	0.9	5.0
Productive industry groups and other industries taken together:					
Laspeyres index	137	130	98	112	189
Paasche index	134	124	97	112	184
Fisher index	136	127	97	112	187
Growth rate[a]	1.8	1.5	–0.3	1.1	4.6

[a] Average annual percent growth rate of Fisher index.

The indexes in Table A.4 do not necessarily agree with those deduced for the last period from values added at constant prices shown in the National Accounts. For one thing, the same years have not been taken as base years for calculating the weightings.[15] For another thing, we have used factor costs, whereas the National Accounts are based on market prices. It can be seen, nevertheless, that there is satisfactory agreement in the comparison between 1963 and 1949: for industry as a whole, our Laspeyres and Paasche indexes are 213 and 210, respectively, whereas that from the National Accounts[16] is 213; for all productive industry groups together, our two indexes are 197, and that of the National Accounts is 201.

[15] The results taken from the National Accounts stem from two series, one for the years 1949–59 in 1956 prices, and the other for the years 1959–63 in 1959 prices.
[16] Calculations made on the basis of estimates available at the end of 1964.

The Method for Determining the Contributions of Various Factors to Change in the Aggregate Labor Force Participation Rate

Let $a(t)$, $m(t)$, $f(t)$, $m_i(t)$, $f_i(t)$ be, respectively, the overall activity rate, the overall male and female activity rates, and the male and female activity rates at age i in the year t.

Let $p(t)$ and $q(t)$ be the proportion of men and women in the total population in year t.

Let $p_i(t)$ and $q_i(t)$ be the proportion of men and of women at age i, respectively, in the total male population and in the total female population in year t. This gives

$$p(t) + q(t) = 1 \qquad \sum_i p_i(t) = 1 \qquad \sum_i q_i(t) = 1$$

where $\sum_i$ represents the sum over all age-groups.

$$a(t) - a(54) = p(t)m(t) + q(t)f(t) - p(54)m(54) - q(54)f(54)$$
$$= p(t)[m(t) - m(54)] + q(t)[f(t) - f(54)]$$
$$+ m(54)[p(t) - p(54)] + f(54)[q(t) - q(54)]$$

The sum of the third and fourth terms in the second half of this equation represents an attribution of what, in the difference between the activity rates, is accounted for by changes in structure of the total population by sex. The first two terms can be written as follows:

$$p(t)\left[\sum_i p_i(t)m_i(t) - \sum_i p_i(54)m_i(54)\right]$$
$$+ q(t)\left[\sum_i q_i(t)f_i(t) - \sum_i q_i(54)f_i(54)\right]$$

or again

$$p(t)\left[\sum_i p_i(t)m_i(t) - \sum_i p_i(t)m_i(54) + \sum_i p_i(t)m_i(54) - \sum_i p_i(54)m_i(54)\right]$$
$$+ q(t)\left[\sum_i q_i(t)f_i(t) - \sum_i q_i(t)f_i(54) + \sum_i q_i(t)f_i(54) - \sum_i q_i(54)f_i(54)\right]$$

That is to say,

$$p(t)\left[\sum_i m_i(54)\left[p_i(t) - p_i(54)\right]\right] + q(t)\left[\sum_i f_i(54)\left[q_i(t) - q_i(54)\right]\right]$$
$$+ p(t)\left[\sum_i p_i(t)\left[m_i(t) - m_i(54)\right]\right] + q(t)\left[\sum_i q_i(t)\left[f_i(t) - f_i(54)\right]\right]$$

or in simplified form

$$p(t)[\text{I}] + q(t)[\text{II}] + p(t)[\text{III}] + q(t)[\text{IV}]$$

The sum of terms I and II represents an attribution of what, in the difference between the activity rates of year t and 1954, is due to changes in the age structure of the population, and the sum of terms III and IV is an attribution of what is due to the movement of activity rates.

Estimation of Gross Fixed Capital Formation Since the War

Until publication of the series known as the "1962 new base," investment was estimated in the National Accounts by methods stemming from one principle. We shall first describe this, and then indicate how the breakdown by industry groups or by category of investment good was made. We shall explain why it has seemed necessary to revise estimates for the years 1949 to 1952. And finally, we shall give an idea of the uncertainties affecting the results shown.

In the series used for this study, overall investment has been calculated for each year by adding the values for different capital goods available on the market. For each good, this determination stemmed from statistics of production and foreign trade: availability on the market is made up of production in a given year less stock increases, to which is added algebraically the balance of foreign trade; that is, imports, plus duties and taxes borne by them, less exports, plus taxes deductible upon exports (essentially the value-added tax). For completeness, commercial margins must be restored on these products when they are not directly put on the market by the producers. The chief difficulty is distinguishing between products intended for investment and those intended for consumption. In many cases, rather detailed nomenclature for products makes it possible to avoid this difficulty almost completely. Particularly in the especially difficult case of private cars, the breakdown between those representing an investment by firms and those required by the other economic agents is obtained by an analysis of statistics of new vehicle licensing, which indicates the status of purchasers and permits approximate allocation to be made.

The breakdown of overall investment by major categories of use is based on direct information on investment in housing and investment by government. For the former, the statistics of the Ministry of Construction on housing starts and on dwellings completed have been compared with the survey of the Commissariat Général aux Entreprises, which shows the nature of work carried out by construction firms. For the latter, analyses of the public accounts provide an estimate stemming from the accounts of the various groups of government agencies. In our presentation, investment by financial institutions has been regrouped with that by government, and represents about 3 percent of investment by government.

From 1956 on, an annual survey for investment by industrial firms makes it possible to break down investment by industry groups and to check the overall figure; this check, however, is not precise because services and trade are not covered by the survey. The only overall verification available of the National Accounts is that provided by estimates of investment based on variations in capital assets in the balance sheets of firms. These statistics are available by sector and result from firms' tax declarations; they cover all private nonagricultural firms whose turnover is above a certain minimum (400,-000 francs since 1959). In particular, they make it possible to assess investment by services and trade.[1]

The breakdown of productive investment by industry group after 1956 therefore is based on a survey of industry, the accounts of certain public enterprises, and an estimate by products for farming (buildings, agricultural machinery, and vehicles, which represent the major part of agricultural investment). Before 1956, the breakdown is more approximate. It is based on accounts of the national enterprises for industry groups where they have an important place, and on the Plan annual progress reports for the other nonagricultural industries. For farming, agricultural machinery as a whole has been the chief indicator.

As a general rule, we have used overall figures of investment given by the National Accounts[2] except for the years 1949–52. We have adjusted the changes in output and value added of building and public works for 1949–52. Since for those years the determination of gross fixed capital formation was essentially based on an estimate of the products comprising it, the drop in output of building and public works is reflected in total investment and productive investment. The estimates of gross fixed capital formation in housing and by government agencies, indeed, stem from direct data that should not be affected by the reduction in output of buildings and public works.

The indexes with 1956 = 100 that we have adopted for this industry group have therefore been applied to the value of production in 1956, which has not changed, and the differences have been applied to the relevant investment figures (see Table C.1).

We can, finally, indicate the degree of accuracy of these investment series. For estimates in constant prices, the same price index has been used for all industry groups between 1949 and 1956; in the most recent series, account has been taken of the proportion of building and public works, vehicles, and other equipment in each industry group; the corresponding price indexes have been applied to each of the parts. It should be recalled also that the break-

[1] In fact, the corresponding estimate is still not very precise because of the large number of firms in these sectors that are below the minimum turnover figure and for which the estimate of investment is not direct.

[2] In particular, the December 1963 issue of *Etudes et conjoncture*, which regroups the data relating to 1949–59 and the annual reports on the nation's accounts.

TABLE C.1
Production Figures for Construction and Public Works, 1949–56

Category	1949	1950	1951	1952	1953	1956
National Accounts indexes	75.4	74.8	79.0	78.4	79.7	100
Indexes adopted	65.8	67.8	72.9	74.7	79.7	100
Value in National Accounts (million 1956 francs)	15,883	15,760	16,642	16,501	16,785	21,059
Value adopted	13,857	14,278	15,352	15,731	16,785	21,059
Difference	2,026	1,482	1,290	770	—	—
Investment figures adopted (million 1956 francs):						
Total	22,612	23,373	24,906	24,453	25,390	33,756
Productive	16,631	16,958	17,367	15,945	16,432	21,284

down of investment between industry groups is based on fragmentary evidence, so the quality of the results varies considerably in the different industry groups.

Investment by Coal, Gas, Electricity, and Transportation and communications is known with a fairly high degree of accuracy, since the figures are based on accounts of national enterprises, which make up the greater part of the relevant industry groups. The estimate of major maintenance, however, which represents half the investment in railroad transport, gives a margin of uncertainty to the estimates for transport in the earliest years.

Similarly, investments by Metallurgy, given their importance for the restored economy after the war, are the subject of precise data in the various Plan progress reports. It can therefore be considered that heavy investment is quite well documented.

Investment by Agriculture, which is known from information on the internal market in agricultural equipment, and in chemicals, mentioned in the Plan progress reports, are the best known of the other types of investment between 1949 and 1956. There are a number of indications that permit tentative assessment to be made of investment in Building and public works and in the Mechanical industries, Textiles, and Miscellaneous industries. But investment in Processed foods and farm products, services, and trade were obtained by difference. The movement of these figures is therefore not very reliable. After 1956 the survey on investment, complemented by estimates taken from balance sheets, gives figures that are statistically more reliably based. The available information, however, is insufficient for processed foods and farm products, services, and trade up to recent years.

Fixed Capital Formation, 1896–1938

In order to study objectively the development of the French economy in the first half of the century, it seems essential to construct series relating to investment. The statistical sources are, it is true, so scarce that constructing such series is a hazardous undertaking. But the little that does exist makes it possible to draw a rough picture of capital formation at different periods.

We have attempted to estimate for each year the volume of investment, on the one hand, and the rate of investment in relation to gross domestic production, on the other hand. To arrive at our results, we had to examine, in particular, investment in products of the mechanical and electrical industries, as well as the development of relative prices of capital goods in relation to other goods making up national output. We have ignored the years 1914–21, which seem too atypical to be suited to even imprecise estimates.

VOLUME OF INVESTMENT IN CAPITAL GOODS

For products of the mechanical and electrical industries, we estimated successively for each year output by this industry group, the proportion that consisted of capital goods, and foreign trade in these goods. The estimates in Chapter 1 were used for output of the mechanical and electrical industries in 1896, 1913, 1929, and 1938. Estimates by L. A. Vincent were used for the years 1924, 1928, and 1930. Finally, the annual index of metal-processing and manufacturing made possible an interpolation covering the other years as a whole. It is known that this index is based in essence on apparent consumption of metals and that it is therefore very imprecise;[1] it must, however, give a picture of the main developments. The results obtained are shown in the first column of Table D.1.

In order to determine the proportion of capital goods in the production of each industry group, we have carried out a detailed analysis of workers by type of production of the establishments in which they were employed. With the help of the demographic censuses of 1896, 1901, 1906, 1921, 1926, 1931,

[1] See *Indices généraux du mouvement économique en France de 1901 à 1931* (Paris, 1932).

TABLE D.1

*Indexes of Investment in the Mechanical and Electrical
Industries, 1896–1938*

(1913 = 100)

Year	Output of metal mfg. & processing	Proportion representing investment goods	Output of investment goods	Imports	Exports	Investment in capital equipment
1896	48	87	42	25	28	37
1897	49	88	43	27	34	37
1898	50	90	45	30	38	39
1899	52	91	47	39	41	45
1900	55	93	51	57	43	54
1901	50	94	47	45	43	47
1902	51	93	47	41	50	45
1903	52	92	48	40	46	46
1904	56	91	51	40	55	47
1905	56	91	51	47	73	46
1906	62	91	56	51	71	53
1907	67	92	62	74	78	65
1908	65	94	61	70	71	63
1909	71	96	68	66	73	66
1910	78	98	77	76	85	76
1911	87	99	86	88	91	86
1912	98	100	98	90	98	95
1913	100	100	100	100	100	100
1922	92	120	110	100	136	102
1923	107	118	126	79	204	95
1924	148	116	172	77	225	128
1925	141	114	161	69	279	110
1926	165	113	186	68	313	124
1927	145	115	166	54	343	100
1928	179	117	210	62	334	136
1929	199	118	235	101	365	166
1930	194	117	228	142	306	184
1931	164	115	188	108	239	150
1932	130	115	150	54	153	111
1933	150	115	172	46	172	122
1934	145	115	167	42	179	116
1935	144	115	166	31	142	114
1936	157	115	180	30	124	126
1937	181	115	208	42	130	151
1938	154	115	177	32	126	123

and 1936, we broke down the labor force in the metal industries into three subgroups working, respectively, on production of goods for intermediary consumption, final consumption, and investment. We then estimated the movement of the figures for these three subgroups in other years, bearing in mind what we knew of the economic history of the period. The "investment share" was assumed equal to the ratio between manpower in the third sub-

TABLE D.2
Unit Values Adopted for Indexes of the Volume of Imports and Exports

Category	Imports	Exports
Machinery, apparatus, and equipment	2	2
Steam boilers, gasholders, etc.	1	1
Machinery and equipment spare parts	2	2
Tools and metal products	0.5	0.3
Automobiles	1	2
Other vehicles	1.2	2
Aircraft	20	20
Ships and boats	0.3	0.3

group and total manpower in the metal industries. An index was then calculated for this ratio, with 1913 = 100; it is shown in the second column of Table D.1. The index of production of capital goods by the mechanical and electrical industries is obtained in the third column by dividing the product of the first two columns by 100.

To estimate foreign trade in machinery and equipment, we constructed two indexes for the volume of imports and exports of these goods. Imported and exported tonnages of eight groups of products of the mechanical industries were multiplied, respectively, by coefficients broadly proportional to the average prices of articles in these groups, since we have observed that the scale of their relative prices was approximately the same in 1913, 1929, and 1938. In this way, we obtained the coefficients shown in Table D.2, which are based on this relative price scale but have been halved in the case of two groups of products that seemed to relate to consumption as much as to investment (tools and metal products, and automobiles). These indexes are not very sensitive to the particular coefficients used, since the largest of the eight series covered moved in a similar manner. On the other hand, changes in quality affecting the products of each group represent a serious source of imperfection in the indexes.

The series relative to "investment in capital goods" was obtained from three series relating to output of investment goods, imports, and exports (see Table D.1). Analysis of resources and uses in 1938 for these products was the basis for the calculations. In 1938, output of investment goods by the mechanical and electrical industries was approximately 24.8 billion francs, imports of similar products were 2.5 billion francs, and exports were 3.3 billion francs. Consequently, French investment was $24.8 + 2.5 - 3.3 = 24.0$ billion francs. Investment in capital equipment in 1913 at 1938 prices can be calculated as $24.8 \div 1.77 + 2.5 \div 0.32 - 3.3 \div 1.46 = 19.5$ billion francs. The three results for the year 1938 were divided, respectively, by the indexes for 1938 on a 1913 base. The index of investment in capital goods for 1938, with 1913 = 100, is thus $24.0 \times 100/19.5 = 123$. A similar calculation for each year provides the series shown in the last column of Table D.1.

VOLUME OF OVERALL INVESTMENT

To evaluate fixed capital formation in 1938 prices, we simply combined the series for investment in capital goods and a series for the output of building and public works. In doing so, we ignored two facts: a small fraction of the investment is represented by products of other kinds, and the output of building and public works is not only for investment. In view of the level of precision of our estimates, we thought it unnecessary to measure output of

TABLE D.3

Indexes of Overall Investment, 1896–1938

(1913 = 100)

				Relative prices			
Year	Investment in capital equipment	Bldg. & public works	Volume of investment	Output of mechanical industries	Building	Relative value of investment	Investment ratio *(percent)*
1896	37	72	59	116	96	59	13.4
1897	37	74	61	115	96	61	14.4
1898	39	78	64	114	97	64	14.4
1899	45	80	67	113	97	68	14.4
1900	54	82	72	112	97	73	15.2
1901	47	82	69	112	97	69	14.9
1902	45	80	67	111	98	68	14.5
1903	46	78	66	110	98	67	13.9
1904	47	79	67	109	98	68	13.3
1905	46	81	68	108	98	69	11.8
1906	53	80	69	107	99	70	11.8
1907	65	79	74	106	99	75	14.5
1908	63	82	75	105	99	75	14.5
1909	66	86	78	104	99	79	14.9
1910	76	90	85	103	100	85	16.3
1911	86	95	92	102	100	92	16.7
1912	95	101	99	101	100	99	16.5
1913	100	100	100	100	100	100	16.8
1922	102	65	79	99	102	80	13.9
1923	95	80	85	98	103	86	14.0
1924	128	100	110	98	104	112	16.7
1925	110	96	101	97	105	103	15.2
1926	124	115	118	97	106	121	17.4
1927	100	93	95	96	107	98	14.7
1928	136	105	116	96	108	120	17.5
1929	166	124	140	95	109	144	18.3
1930	184	135	153	96	109	158	20.8
1931	150	125	134	97	110	140	19.1
1932	111	109	110	98	110	116	16.4
1933	122	100	108	99	111	114	15.7
1934	116	90	100	100	111	107	14.6
1935	114	85	96	101	112	103	14.7
1936	126	86	101	102	112	109	15.3
1937	151	83	102	103	113	117	15.6
1938	123	75	93	104	113	101	13.4

capital goods by haulers, upholsterers, and other trades. Any estimate of these would have been uncertain, and the contribution of these types of equipment to overall investment has always been low.

Similarly, we have not found an objective way to determine changes in the proportion of output of building and public works devoted to maintenance; it has in any case never been very high. In order to construct the annual index of output of building and public works, we used the same estimates as in Chapter 1 for the years 1896, 1913, 1929, and 1938, and the estimates by L. A. Vincent for 1924, 1928, and 1930. Results for the other years were obtained by interpolation based, from 1896 to 1901, on the output of cement, slaked lime, and other binding agents; from 1901 to 1928 they are based on the average of the building series in the index of industrial production (building permits)[2] and a series of apparent consumption of cement, slaked lime, and other binding agents; from 1928 to 1939 the figures are based on the group on building and public works of the index of industrial production.[3]

Since we knew that the contribution of the mechanical and electrical industries and that of building and public works to investment in 1938 were, respectively, 24.0 and 25.0 billion francs, we were able to combine the series shown in the first two columns of Table D.3, using calculations similar to those described at the end of the previous section. The index of volume of investment thus obtained is shown in the third column of Table D.3.

RELATIVE PRICES OF CAPITAL GOODS

In order to ascertain the scale of investment carried out at different periods, we calculated in current prices the ratio of gross fixed capital formation to gross domestic production. To do so, we estimated changes in relative prices of capital goods and goods making up total national production.

In the absence of sufficiently complete and accurate direct data, we fell back on the hypothesis by which we had estimated value added by industry groups for weighting indexes of production for these groups. (See Appendix A, p. 512.) We therefore assumed that, in current prices, value added per hour of work varied proportionately in all industry groups, so that to know relative prices it was sufficient to refer to the indexes of labor productivity of the industry groups (see Chapter 3, p. 96).

For the metal industries, which use few products of other industries, we have ignored intermediary consumption. We have therefore assumed that relative prices of their production varied in the same ratio as that between hourly labor productivity in all industry groups and hourly labor productivity in those particular industry groups. The estimates in Chapter 3 thus made it possible to calculate the index of relative prices for 1896, 1913, 1929, and 1938. The results are shown in the fourth column of Table D.3. For the intervening years, we carried out linear interpolations.

Such a simple calculation did not seem justified for prices of building and

[2] *Ibid.*
[3] See *Mouvement économique en France de 1929 à 1939* (Paris, 1941).

public works, since that industry group makes use of large-scale intermediary consumption; moreover, its labor productivity has changed in a somewhat different way from that observed in other industries. But using the table of inter-industry inputs and outputs for 1959, we calculated a breakdown of prices of products of building and public works, which shows the share of value added by the different industry groups incorporated in those products.[4] We assumed for lack of better evidence that the structure of costs thus obtained for 1959 was valid for the other years. We were then able to calculate an index of hourly productivity of labor used, directly or indirectly, in the products of building and public works. The index of relative prices for that industry was then calculated as shown above for the mechanical and electrical industries.

Against the doubts that might be felt a priori about the hypotheses underlying our calculations, our results may seem to some extent buttressed by the indexes of relative prices shown in the study on the United States. With $1913 = 100$, the index of relative prices of capital goods in the United States was 102 in 1896, 104 in 1929, and 113 in 1938 (as against 116, 95, and 104, respectively, for the same years in France). The index of relative prices for construction in the United States was 94 in 1913, 112 in 1929, and 132 in 1938 (as against 96, 109, and 113, respectively, in France).

INVESTMENT RATIO

With indexes of volume and indexes of relative prices available for investment in the two main categories, we calculated an index of the relative value of investment. It was sufficient for each category to multiply the volume index by the relative price index, and then to combine the results of the two categories, taking 1938 as a base year. The aggregate index thus obtained, and shown in the penultimate column of Table D.3, measures in principle the ratio between the investment index in current prices and the index of prices for gross domestic production.

It is interesting to compare the series obtained with a series of the real value of share issues by firms on the stock exchange. These two series are not of course identical, but it seemed a priori that their fluctuations ought to be concordant, with the second showing greater irregularities than the first. This is in fact what we do see in Figure D.1, where we have shown the lines of our index of the relative value of investment and a series of the real value of share and bond issues by companies.[5]

[4] We know that Leontief's model enables such a breakdown to be calculated (see, for example, *Initiation à la Comptabilité nationale* [Paris, 1964], chap. 14). The breakdown obtained was 55 percent for building and public works, 10 percent for building materials and glass, 12 percent for mechanical and electrical industries, 5 percent for miscellaneous industries, and 18 percent for all other industry groups together.

[5] The statistics of the Credit Lyonnais provide figures of these issues, which we expressed in 1938 francs by dividing them by the simple arithmetic mean of the index of wholesale prices and the index of retail prices.

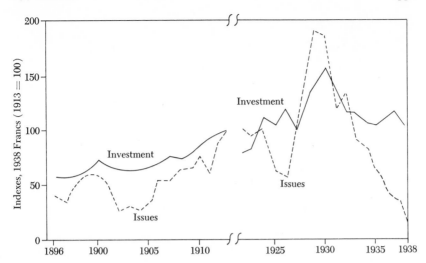

Fig. D.1. Relative value of investment and issues of corporate
securities, 1896–1938.

With the investment ratio for 1938 known from the National Accounts for
that year, and with a series of the relative value of investment available, it was
sufficient, in order to determine the investment ratio in each of the years
studied, to have an index of the volume of gross domestic production. We
used the index shown in Table 1.3 (p. 24). The investment ratios calculated
from these elements are shown in the last column of Table D.3.

RECONCILIATION WITH POSTWAR SERIES

To reconcile the series described above with those for postwar years, we
used figures relating to the investment ratio without attempting to correct
them for the rather minor differences affecting definitions and methods of
estimation. Using the results in Chapter 1 for the volume indexes of gross
domestic production, we were able to apply immediately the series relating
to the relative value of investment. For the volume indexes we used, on the
one hand, comparisons shown in the National Accounts for 1938[6] and, on the
other hand, the volume indexes of exports and imports of finished capital
goods products.

Finally, we made sure that the indexes of relative prices implied by comparison between the indexes of relative values and the volume indexes were
close to those used in the National Accounts for 1938.

[6] See *Statistiques et études financières*, no. 85, January 1956, and no. 101 (supplement), May 1957.

Effects of the Decline in the
Age of Capital

In Chapter 7 (p. 193) we indicated why part of technical progress can be considered incorporated in capital at the time it is installed. We distinguished two categories of capital equipment: first, buildings and infrastructure, where incorporated technical progress on the average was slow, and second, capital equipment, where it was rapid. We assumed that, when used with a constant quantity of labor, the former made it possible to obtain production increasing by about 0.3 percent per each successive year of construction. Similarly, we assumed that, used in similar conditions, the latter made it possible to obtain production growing by about 1.3 percent per each successive year of manufacture.

Using the Cobb-Douglas function that we adopted, in which the capital exponent is close to one-third, these assumptions imply that in a year t later than 1956, a volume of resources K invested in 1956 is equivalent to a higher volume invested in an earlier year θ, and that the ratio between these two volumes is approximately equal to $\lambda_\theta = (1.01)^{1956-\theta}$ for buildings and infrastructures and $\mu_\theta = (1.04)^{1956-\theta}$ for capital equipment.[1]

Let K_{1t}^θ and K_{2t}^θ be the quantities of capital equipment existing in year t and built during the earlier year θ, respectively, for building and infrastructures and for capital equipment. The new capital series, which allows for incorporated technical progress, will then be defined by the value J_t, as follows:

(1)
$$J_t = \sum_\theta \left[\frac{1}{\lambda_\theta} K_{1t}^\theta + \frac{1}{\mu_\theta} K_{2t}^\theta \right]$$

---

[1] If we consider, for example, capital equipment of volume K used together with a quantity of labor N, the production it makes possible is, on the one hand,

$$(1 + 4/300)^{1956} q_t N^{2/3} K^{1/3}$$

and, on the other hand,

$$(1 + 4/300)^\theta q_t N^{2/3} [K(1.04)^{1956-\theta}]^{1/3}$$

These two quantities are approximately equal (q_t represents a factor relating to the part of technical progress that is not incorporated in the capital equipment).

To obtain a feel for the credibility of the hypothesis we have adopted, we can refer to the values of the coefficients $1/\lambda_\theta$ and $1/\mu_\theta$.

By comparison with buildings and infrastructures constructed in 1956, those constructed before 1880 would have a coefficient $1/\lambda_\theta$ close to 0.4, those constructed between 1880 and 1913 a coefficient of between 0.5 and 0.6, and those constructed between 1920 and 1940 a coefficient of about 0.75. By comparison with capital equipment manufactured in 1956, the coefficients are roughly around 0.15 for equipment manufactured before World War I, between 0.25 and 0.5 for those manufactured between the wars, and 0.75 for those manufactured in 1948. In other words, the hypothesis adopted assumes fairly rapid obsolescence for capital equipment, and this seems to agree with the pace of change in industrial technology.[2]

ATTEMPTS AT APPLICATION

To apply the hypothesis specified by formula (1), we had to construct the series $K_2{}^\theta{}_t$ and $K_1{}^\theta{}_t$, that is, to break down for certain years t the gross capital in existence according to its date of manufacture θ and according to whether it consisted of buildings and infrastructures or capital equipment. We have been able to do this only roughly, making use of the investment series shown in Chapter 4, but without being able to check our estimates with other kinds of statistics. The data adopted are shown in Table E.1, which must be considered an intermediary step in a somewhat uncertain calculation and not an intrinsic source of information.

These estimates, calculated for the four years 1951, 1956, 1961, and 1966, imply a reduction in the age of capital, which in fact has been achieved at a particularly rapid rate since 1956. The average age of buildings and infrastructures seems to have been 41 years in 1951 and 1956, 40 years in 1961, and 38 years in 1966. The average age of capital equipment seems to have been 18.4 years in 1951, 16.9 years in 1956, 14.3 years in 1961, and 12.2 years in 1966. This sharp reduction in age can be compared with the British estimate relating to equipment used in the manufacturing industries. Its average age was apparently 13.8 years in 1948 and 13.2 years in 1962.[3]

The new series for capital corrected for the changes in its technical efficiency, that is, the series for value J_t defined by formula (1), shows far faster growth than the series used earlier. Whereas net capital estimated from its cost of production grew at average rates of 2.3, 2.8, and 4.4 percent per year, respectively, in each of the three five-year successive periods (and gross

---

[2] We do not have available information sources for direct measurement of technical obsolescence, which we are trying to allow for here. The only estimate we have found concerns British machine tools manufactured, respectively, in 1960 and 1950; the former apparently were more productive than the latter by about 40 percent (see "The First Census of Machine Tools in Britain," *Metalworking Production*, December 29, 1961; McGraw Hill). This obsolescence rate is slightly higher than the rate we have adopted for capital equipment.

[3] Cited by R. C. O. Matthews, C. H. Feinstein, and J. C. Odling-Smee, *Economic Growth in Great Britain* (forthcoming), chap. 3.

TABLE E.1
Age Structure of Gross Productive Capital, 1881–1965
(1956 prices, billion francs)

Construction date	Before 1881	1881–1900	1901–1910	1911–1920	1921–1930	1931–1940	1941–1945	1946–1950	1951–1955	1956–1960	1961–1965	Total
Existing capital in 1951:												
Buildings and infrastructures	42	39	32	27	37	35	10	30	–	–	–	252
Capital equipment	–	–	12	22	44	52	12	42	–	–	–	184
Total	42	39	44	49	81	87	22	72	–	–	–	436
Existing capital in 1956:												
Buildings and infrastructures	40	37	30	25	35	35	10	30	29	–	–	271
Capital equipment	–	–	7	15	40	45	10	40	57	–	–	214
Total	40	37	37	40	75	80	20	70	86	–	–	485
Existing capital in 1961:												
Buildings and infrastructures	38	35	27	22	32	33	10	30	29	36	–	292
Capital equipment	–	–	3	7	34	36	8	36	54	86	–	264
Total	38	35	30	29	66	69	18	66	83	122	–	556
Existing capital in 1966:												
Buildings and infrastructures	36	33	25	20	30	31	9	29	29	36	50	328
Capital equipment	–	–	–	3	26	28	6	30	49	81	122	345
Total	36	33	25	23	56	59	15	59	78	117	172	673

Note: Very uncertain estimates are presented here for the calculation of the effect of reduction in the age of capital.

capital grew by 2.2, 2.8, and 3.9 percent), value J_t seems to have grown over the same periods at average rates of 4.7, 6.0, and 7.6 percent.

How should the result of these calculations be used to determine the effect to be attributed to a reduction in age of capital equipment? A first approach would be merely to substitute J_t for K_t in the calculations of total productivity. Using the same coefficient $\alpha = 0.72$, we would find that total productivity would have grown at an annual rate of 3.4 percent between 1951 and 1956, 3.3 pecent between 1956 and 1961, and 3.1 percent between 1961 and 1966, whereas the results in Table 7.1 (p. 182) imply one rate of 4.0 percent per year in the three periods.

The difference between these two estimates of total productivity, however, is due quite as much to the technical progress incorporated in capital equipment as to a reduction in age of capital. If we wish to isolate this second effect, we must estimate the first. This does not present any difficulty of principle, since we can calculate directly what the growth of the technical efficiency of capital would have been if its composition and its age structure had remained the same as at the beginning of the period. We then find that this growth would have raised production figures by 0.5 percent per year between 1951 and 1956, 0.6 percent per year between 1956 and 1961, and 0.7 percent between 1961 and 1966.

To complete the comparison, account should also be taken of the fact that the calculations in Table 7.1 are based on net capital, whereas J_t was estimated from the composition of gross capital. Now gross capital grew substantially more slowly in the postwar period than net capital, and this led to a difference of 0.1 to 0.2 percent in the annual growth rate of total productivity.

The different results of these calculations are brought together in Table 7.6 (p. 195). It shows that the effect of a reduction in age of capital can be assessed at about 0.2 percent per year between 1951 and 1956, and 0.4 percent between 1961 and 1966.

Effects on Growth of Transfers of Factors from One Sector to Another

Let us consider two industries producing, respectively, quantities Q_1 and Q_2 and using, respectively, quantities N_1 and N_2 of labor and K_1 and K_2 of capital. Let us assume that the units of measurement of goods are chosen in such a way that overall production is

(1) $$Q = Q_1 + Q_2$$

Let us similarly denote by N and K the overall quantities of labor and capital:

(2) $$N = N_1 + N_2$$

(3) $$K = K_1 + K_2$$

Let us assume that production is governed in each industry by a Cobb-Douglas function:

(4) $$Q_1 = A_2 N_1^{\alpha_1} K_1^{\beta_1} \qquad Q_2 = A_2 N_2^{\alpha_2} K_2^{\beta_2}$$

We propose to study how small variations, dN_1, dN_2, dK_1, dK_2 in the quantities of factors employed affect overall productivity measured for the two industries together. To this end, we assume that the factor marginal productivities are not the same in the two industries. Let us call a the ratio between the marginal productivities of labor and b the ratio between the marginal productivities of capital:

(5) $$\frac{\alpha_1 Q_1}{N_1} = a \frac{\alpha_2 Q_2}{N_2}$$

(6) $$\frac{\beta_1 Q_1}{K_1} = b \frac{\beta_2 Q_2}{K_2}$$

The variations considered will lead to variations dQ_1, dQ_2, and dQ in production and a variation dR in total productivity R. These variations will obey the following relationships:

(7)
$$\frac{dQ_1}{Q_1} = \alpha_1 \frac{dN_1}{N_1} + \beta_1 \frac{dK_1}{K_1}$$

(8)
$$\frac{dQ_2}{Q_2} = \alpha_2 \frac{dN_2}{N_2} + \beta_2 \frac{dK_2}{K_2}$$

(9)
$$\frac{dR}{R} = \frac{dQ}{Q} - \alpha \frac{dN}{N} - \beta \frac{dK}{K}$$

If α and β denote the overall shares of labor and capital in the value of output, one can immediately calculate

$$\alpha = \frac{\alpha_1 \dfrac{Q_1}{N_1} N_1 + \alpha_2 \dfrac{Q_2}{N_2} N_2}{Q}$$

or

(10)
$$\alpha = \frac{\alpha_1 Q_1 + \alpha_2 Q_2}{Q}$$

(11)
$$\beta = \frac{\beta_1 Q_1 + \beta_2 Q_2}{Q}$$

If we denote by q_1, n_1, and k_1 the ratios Q_1/Q, N_1/N, and K_1/K, and by q_2, n_2, and k_2 the similar ratios defined for industry 2, we can then write:

(12)
$$\alpha = \alpha_1 q_1 + \alpha_2 q_2$$

(13)
$$\beta = \beta_1 q_1 + \beta_2 q_2$$

Equations (5) and (6) similarly become

(14)
$$\alpha_1 q_1 = a \frac{n_1}{n_2} \alpha_2 q_2$$

(15)
$$\beta_1 q_1 = b \frac{k_1}{k_2} \beta_2 q_2$$

Combining (12) and (14) we get

(16)
$$\alpha n_1 = \frac{\alpha_1 q_1}{a} (an_1 + n_2) \qquad \alpha n_2 = \alpha_2 q_2 (an_1 + n_2)$$

and similarly from (13) and (15) we get

(17)
$$\beta k_1 = \frac{\beta_1 q_1}{b} (bk_1 + k_2) \qquad \beta k_2 = \beta_2 q_2 (bk_1 + k_2)$$

Reverting to formula (9), we can write the relative change in overall productivity as

(18) $\dfrac{dR}{R} = q_1 \dfrac{dQ_1}{Q_1} + q_2 \dfrac{dQ_2}{Q_2} - \alpha n_1 \dfrac{dN_1}{N_1} - \alpha n_2 \dfrac{dN_2}{N_2} - \beta k_1 \dfrac{dK_1}{K_1} - \beta k_2 \dfrac{dK_2}{K_2}$

or again, taking into account (7) and (8),

(19) $\dfrac{dR}{R} = (\alpha_1 q_1 - \alpha n_1) \dfrac{dN_1}{N_1} + (\alpha_2 q_2 - \alpha n_2) \dfrac{dN_2}{N_2}$

$$+ (\beta_1 q_1 - \beta k_1) \dfrac{dK_1}{K_2} + (\beta_2 q_2 - \beta k_2) \dfrac{dK_2}{K_2}$$

Now the equations in (16) imply

$$\alpha_1 q_1 - \alpha n_1 = \alpha \dfrac{n_1 n_2}{a n_1 + n_2} (a - 1)$$

and

$$\alpha_2 q_2 - \alpha n_2 = \dfrac{\alpha n_1 n_2}{a n_1 + n_2} (1 - a)$$

Obtaining in the same way the expressions $\beta_1 q_1 - \beta k_1$ and $\beta_2 q_2 - \beta k_2$ and substituting in (19), we find

(20) $\dfrac{dR}{R} = \alpha(1 - a) \dfrac{n_1 n_2}{a n_1 + n_2} \left(\dfrac{dN_2}{N_2} - \dfrac{dN_1}{N_1} \right)$

$$+ \beta(1 - b) \dfrac{k_1 k_2}{b k_1 + k_2} \left(\dfrac{dK_2}{K_2} - \dfrac{dK_1}{K_1} \right)$$

It can be seen therefore that total productivity would not vary in two cases: (1) if factor marginal productivities were the same in the two industries ($a = b = 1$); and (2) if the relative variations of the quantities of factors used were the same ($dN_2/N_2 = dN_1/N_1$ and $dK_2/K_2 = dK_1/K_1$).

For the calculation, expression (20) is not the most convenient. As we shall show below, we can substitute for it the following equivalent expression:

(21) $\dfrac{dR}{R} = \alpha \left(\dfrac{a dN_1 + dN_2}{a N_1 + N_2} - \dfrac{dN}{N} \right) + \beta \left(\dfrac{b dK_1 + dK_2}{b K_1 + K_2} - \dfrac{dK}{K} \right)$

The first expression in parentheses, for example, represents the opposite of the difference between the relative variation of total employment and the relative variation of a new index of employment.

In this new index, employment in each industry would be weighted by the marginal productivity of labor in the industry concerned. Thus, total productivity would not have varied if it had been calculated from such weighted indexes for the quantities of labor and capital. The effect of transferring the factors of our measure of total productivity can be determined quite simply by reference to equation (21) after calculating the weighted indexes of labor and capital.

Finally, to verify that formulas (20) and (21) are equivalent, it is sufficient to establish, for example, the equation

$$(1-a)n_1n_2\left(\frac{dN_2}{N_2} - \frac{dN_1}{N_1}\right) = (an_1 + n_2)\left(\frac{adN_1 + dN_2}{aN_1 + N_2} - \frac{dN}{N}\right)$$

Now, after multiplication by N, the right and left terms can also be written

$$(1-a)(n_1dN_2 - n_2dN_1) = adN_1 + dN_2 - (an_1 + n_2)(dn_1 + dN_2)$$

It is obvious that these two terms are equal, for the multiplier of dN_1, for example, in the left term is $(a-1)n_2$, and in the right term is

$$a - (an_1 + n_2) = a(1 - n_1) - n_2 = (a-1)n_2$$

In summary, then, to calculate the influence of factor transfers, we must first seek to evaluate coefficients a and b representing the relative differences in the marginal productivities; then we must apply formula (21), which introduces between parentheses corrective terms that can be interpreted as measuring the differences between two quite separate indexes of the variations experienced by the overall quantity of a given factor.

The Self-Financing Ratio and the Growth Rate of Investment

The classical definition of the self-financing ratio (the ratio between gross savings and gross capital formation) should be used with care in comparing the financial situation in different periods or in different countries characterized by different rates of growth of the value of investment. These comparisons must indeed allow for the fact that, as we shall show by a very simple model, an inverse relationship exists between the self-financing ratio and, on the one hand, the growth rate of investment and, on the other hand, the ratio between investment and capital.

Let us consider a situation at a particular time with the following characteristics:

A growth of gross investment of value J at rate α between year $(t-1)$ and year t:

$$(1) \qquad J_t = J_{t-1}(1 + \alpha)$$

A capital K_t at the beginning of year t and a given rate a of amortization:

$$(2) \qquad A_t = aK_t$$

A given allocation of capital K_t between own funds K_t^p and indebtedness K_t^e at the beginning of year t:

$$(3) \qquad K_t = K_t^p + K_t^e \qquad \text{and} \qquad K_t^p = rK_t$$

A given allocation of gross profits P_t^b between dividends and self-financing E_t over the year t:

$$(4) \qquad E_t = kP_t^b$$

A given rate of net profit P_t^n over the year t:

$$(5) \qquad P_t^n / K_t^p = p$$

The ratio of self-financing over the year t is $\tau = E_t / J_t$. But

$$E_t = k(P_t^n + A_t) = k(pK_t^p + aK_t) = k(prK_t + aK_t)$$

from (2), (3), (4), and (5). Thus, allowing for (1),

$$\tau = \frac{K_t}{J_{t-1}} \times \frac{k(pr + a)}{1 + \alpha}$$

For a given ratio of own funds and amortization to capital, and a given distribution of profits between dividends and nondistributed profits, it can be seen that the self-financing ratio, allowing a given rate of remuneration of own funds, is an inverse function of two variables: (1) $1 + \alpha$, which is an index at a particular time of the increase in value of gross investment, and (2) J_{t-1}/K_t, which is the ratio between gross investment and capital, and is high in periods or countries marked by rapid growth of investment.

Sociological Factors in Growth

Questionnaire to Our Sociologist Colleagues

Our explanatory study of French economic growth over the past 20 years should not end without examining its sociological aspects. As in the economic part of our work, we should attempt to discover the roles that may have been played by the various factors that come to mind; we should do this in a critical manner, attempting to test each of the explanations proposed.

We have organized our study around the concept that economic growth is shown and can be measured by the development of production. To analyze the latter it is advisable to direct attention in turn to (1) the quantitative and qualitative changes in the work provided by the population, (2) the increase in physical productive capital, and (3) the residual factors that might explain why production increases even in the absence of alterations in inputs of labor and capital. This scheme will be followed in this questionnaire, although it runs the risk of appearing artificial in some cases.

INPUT FROM THE LABOR FORCE

At the overall level we have observed significant change in the activity rates of women; these rates, which were not unusual in 1954 in relation to past experience, increased between 1954 and 1968. We have also observed that up to 1965 hours worked remained at a high level despite lengthening vacations, at a time when we might have expected a drop.

Has the increase in the female activity rates been due solely to the existence of wider employment opportunities, or should it be attributed to a change in behavior? If so, does this change in behavior stem from a change in the role that the prevailing ethic gives to women in society, or was it made possible simply by the development of household equipment and certain community services (day nurseries, etc.)?

Was the high level maintained by weekly hours worked desired by the workers? If so, is this to be explained by the common aspiration to middle-class modes of consumption? Is that a reflection or a cause of reduction in class consciousness?

Or, on the contrary, is the maintenance of long working hours to be explained by the high birthrate and the expense of maintaining larger families?

Do long hours of work and a high birthrate both stem from a more confident attitude toward the future, and does such an attitude distinguish French society today from that between the two wars?

THE ACCUMULATION OF CAPITAL

Simplifying to the extreme, we can say that the accumulation of productive capital in the postwar period took place in two successive waves. From 1946 to 1951, a deliberate effort of public investment was imposed. From 1955 to 1969, private firms built up capital equipment more and more rapidly. The first wave was the result of a political act, itself imposed by the will of a small number of people and sustained by a new awareness of the need for expansion at the top levels of the civil service. Economic explanations can be found for the second wave. But can it not also be explained by renewal of the spirit of enterprise in business circles?

Does not the history of the building up of the European Community supply an interesting parallel, with the European Coal and Steel Community, as a technocratic construction and the Common Market as a journey toward a great adventure?

Is it true that awareness of the need for expansion and of French technological backwardness was particularly sharp in the top civil service at the end of World War II? Commissions of civil servants had also urged in the past that the country needed an advanced degree of industrialization. Might it be, then, that the will to move from theory to achievement had become stronger?

Can one establish the existence of a renewal of the spirit of enterprise in France between 1955 and 1960? If so, was it linked to increased confidence toward the future or to a change in the predominant ethic in favor of risk and to the detriment of security?

THE RESIDUAL FACTORS

Our study has shown that labor input and productive capital explain only partially the improvement in French production. For a growth rate of 5 percent per year, the unexplained residual of this kind reached 4 percent per year. What is more, it has not tended to drop over the past 15 years, contrary to what we might have expected. Bringing the productive system back to normal after the period from the 1930's to 1946 might explain a particularly high residual around 1950, but it can no longer be applied today.

We have, however, been able to analyze this residual and to attribute about half of it to three factors: the continual increase in the level of education of manpower effectively employed, migration of workers from low-productivity employments toward others with higher productivity, and the accelerated modernization of capital equipment that resulted from the high level of investment from 1946 on, after a long period of capital aging. The rest of the residual can be explained by intensification in the effort put into work, by better organization of production (better use of manpower, better internal organization of firms, and better division of labor between firms), by economies linked to an ever increasing volume of production, and last to technical progress.

Is there a test of the thesis that education and training given to future management, and more widely to future workers, were from about 1930 on better suited to the needs of modern production?

Did the increase in job mobility in relation to the past stem from wider employment opportunities in the expanding sectors, from better information to workers on these opportunities, or from a change in attitude that favored the adventure represented by changing jobs?

Can one conclude that there has been intensification in the work supplied by the labor force between 1950 and today? If so, is this due to stricter organization and management of the workers, or to the workers themselves deciding to put in more sustained work effort? In the latter case, is this a sign of a change in the characteristics of the class struggle?

Can it be said that the workers have progressively increased collaboration among themselves in such a way as to improve the overall efficiency of their labor? If so, is this an aspect of the disappearance of "traditional French individualism"?

Is it possible to learn whether promotion within firms to technical or managerial jobs has accelerated and has been based, more since the war than before, on personal qualities?

Is it true that family firms are less productive, assimilate progress more slowly, take less advantage of opportunities for expansion than other forms of undertakings? If so, has the proportion of family firms in the French productive system tended to shrink faster than it did previously?

Are there any objective proofs that between 1946 and 1955 businessmen became aware of falling behind? Did this lead to an attitude more favorable to innovation and to rational management?

Can it be said that heads of firms have increasingly since the war accepted that they must be subject to the constraints of domestic and foreign competition? That they have sought less than formerly to reach restrictive agreements? That they have less than before respected the "hunting preserves" of their competitors?

Certain historians have thought that influence on the economic dynamism of people should be attributed to the prevailing religion. Should one ascribe a role in recent French economic growth to the evolution that has been experienced by the Catholic Church? If so, through what mediums has this role been carried out?

Appendix Tables

Gross Value Added by Sector, 1949–66
(1956 = 100)

Sector	1949	1950	1951	1952	1953	1954	1955	1956
01. Agriculture and forestry	83.1	97.1	94.2	96.4	104.3	111.4	111.3	100.0
Industry:								
02. Processed foods and farm products	69.3	73.1	82.1	83.1	84.1	87.4	91.5	100.0
03. Solid mineral fuels and gas	89.7	89.6	92.9	96.8	92.7	95.7	100.4	100.0
04. Electricity, water, and kindred products	48.6	56.8	67.8	73.3	75.4	83.2	91.2	100.0
05. Petroleum, natural gas, and oil products	41.4	53.6	62.9	70.8	77.3	81.3	90.3	100.0
06. Building materials and glass	70.0	73.5	79.3	83.5	80.1	89.7	95.1	100.0
07. Iron mining and metallurgy	69.5	66.9	76.5	79.1	72.8	87.7	97.4	100.0
08. Nonferrous minerals and metals	56.5	63.3	69.4	70.4	74.1	82.0	88.7	100.0
09. Mechanical and electrical industries	66.0	70.9	77.5	80.9	82.0	83.4	87.7	100.0
10. Chemicals	61.3	66.3	74.4	70.9	73.8	82.9	91.4	100.0
11. Textiles, clothing, and leather	71.3	80.2	85.6	83.5	87.5	91.5	93.9	100.0
12. Wood, paper, and miscellaneous industries	71.2	81.0	83.3	82.6	85.2	88.6	94.5	100.0
Total (02–12)	66.3	72.1	79.0	80.6	82.6	86.5	91.7	100.0
Other industry groups:								
13. Building and public works	65.8	67.8	72.9	74.7	79.6	87.5	96.5	100.0
14. Transportation and communications	72.1	75.8	82.4	84.4	82.4	86.9	92.5	100.0
15. Housing services	86.0	86.2	87.6	88.9	90.1	93.4	97.4	100.0
16. Services other than housing	71.2	73.8	80.1	83.8	85.8	89.7	95.3	100.0
19. Trade	69.8	73.3	78.5	81.5	85.1	88.8	95.0	100.0
Gross domestic production	70.8	75.8	80.7	82.6	85.1	89.8	95.1	100.0
Gross national product	71.3	76.6	81.4	83.8	86.1	89.8	94.5	100.0

Note: Series on old base for 1949–59. Series on new 1959 base adjusted to series on old base for 1960–66; see *Etudes et conjoncture,* December 1963, for the years 1949–59.

APPENDIX TABLE 1 *(continued)*
Gross Value Added by Sector, 1949–66
(1956 = 100)

1957	1958	1959	1960	1961	1962	1963	1964	1965	1966	Ave. annual growth rates, 1949–66	Gross value added in 1956 *(million francs)*
108.7	109.1	114.3	127.9	120.7	132.1	128.6	130.0	137.8	136.0	2.9	17,883
99.8	101.1	100.8	102.5	106.4	109.8	113.6	117.2	118.9	127.3	3.6	13,289
103.9	107.4	108.7	107.7	104.0	109.6	105.5	114.5	115.1	117.1	1.6	2,961
107.3	ł20.4	124.2	142.3	150.2	163.1	182.8	189.4	210.0	226.2	9.5	2,193
94.5	105.4	112.6	123.7	138.9	150.5	166.9	185.1	201.6	212.3	10.1	5,846
110.2	111.8	115.6	123.0	129.8	139.2	149.8	175.7	187.7	194.8	6.2	2,678
107.8	108.7	112.3	135.7	132.6	133.0	132.3	149.8	152.3	154.3	4.8	3,686
103.9	113.4	132.5	147.5	150.1	154.4	157.3	180.6	190.8	205.6	7.9	904
108.0	114.6	117.5	128.2	138.1	147.6	156.4	162.6	168.1	179.5	6.1	20,950
112.6	121.4	131.3	143.1	150.2	165.4	177.5	193.0	207.2	224.8	8.0	5,688
108.4	106.9	104.1	114.7	116.7	122.6	133.2	136.0	129.6	139.6	4.0	11,356
107.7	108.1	110.7	123.2	129.0	136.2	142.2	149.3	155.9	147.1	5.0	7,897
105.8	109.8	112.3	122.1	128.1	135.8	143.9	152.2	157.7	167.4	5.6	77,448
105.2	110.5	118.0	120.6	131.1	141.0	151.9	173.9	184.8	191.6	6.5	12,607
108.8	112.9	115.5	122.3	129.4	137.0	144.0	152.5	156.8	164.2	5.0	10,612
105.1	110.6	116.3	121.5	127.6	134.2	139.3	144.0	149.3	154.8	3.5	4,257
106.9	109.6	112.1	120.2	127.3	133.8	142.6	151.3	159.9	168.9	5.2	19,933
106.2	104.5	108.3	114.9	121.2	130.3	137.9	144.4	137.3	154.7	4.8	20,774
106.4	109.2	112.5	121.5	127.0	135.8	143.3	152.2	158.5	166.6	5.2	166,480
105.0	107.9	110.8	119.2	124.7	132.8	139.8	148.0	154.1	161.7	4.9	

APPENDIX TABLE 2
Population of France, 1851–1968
(Millions)

Year	Population, with borders at the time[a] Total[b]	Statistical[c]	Year	Population, with borders at the time[a] Total[b]	Statistical[c]
1851	35.8	35.8	1936	41.9	41.2
1896	38.6 (40.2)	38.3	1938	42.0	
1901	39.0 (40.7)	38.5	1946	40.3	39.8
1906	39.3 (41.1)	38.8	1949	41.5	
1911	39.6 (41.5)	39.2	1951	42.2	
1913	39.8 (41.7)		1954	43.1	42.8
1921	39.2	38.8	1957	44.3	
1926	40.9	40.2	1962	47.0	46.5
1929	41.2		1963	47.8	
1931	41.9	41.2	1968	49.9	

Principal source: INSEE, *Annuaire statistique rétrospectif de la France,* 1966.

[a]Figures in parentheses are present borders. In 1851, present-day territory excluding Nice and Savoie; 1896–1913, present-day territory excluding Alsace; and 1921–68, present-day territory.

[b]Normal resident population, including military stationed temporarily outside the home country. Estimates based on data from population censuses, later corrected to allow for certain differences in definition or imperfections in censuses. Population in midyear.

[c]Figures from population censuses at census dates on which statistical breakdowns are based (breakdown by type of employment of workers, etc.). Through 1946 this series relates to the present population, which excludes in particular professional military and the draft from the home country stationed abroad. In 1954 and 1962 the series relates to the normally resident population, including the draft outside the home country and French professional military stationed in Germany but not including French professional military stationed overseas (100,000 for this last category in 1962).

APPENDIX TABLE 3
Factors of Population Change in France, 1896–1968
(Thousands)

Period[a]	Variations over the period Population increase	Births & deaths	Net immigration	Average annual variation Population increase	Births & deaths	Net immigration	Proportion of immigration in total increase (percent)
1896–1906	720	530	190	70	50	20	30%
1906–11	350	200	150	70	40	30	40
1921–26	1,630	390	1,240	330	80	250	75
1926–31	990	290	700	200	60	140	70
1931–36	50	130	–80	10	30	–20	—
1946–54	2,770	2,420	350	340	300	40	15
1954–62[b]	3,940	2,390	1,550	490	300	190	40
1962–68	2,920	1,910	1,010	490	320	170	35

Source: INSEE, *Annuaire statistique rétrospectif de la France,* 1966, pp. 66, 68, 72.

Note: Borders are as of the time.

[a]Gaps are left for 1911–21 and 1936–46, for which the following information is known:

Population in 1911	39,600	Population in 1936	41,600
From 1911 to 1921:		From 1936 to 1946:	
Births less natural deaths	(–1,150)	Births less natural deaths	(–400)
Deaths due to war	(–1,400)	Deaths due to war	(–600)
Alsace-Lorraine	(+1,700)	Net immigration	(–300)
Net immigration	(+450)	Population in 1946	40,300
Population in 1921	39,200		

[b]Variations are measured from the average annual populations (arithmetic mean of total population between two successive dates as of January 1). Therefore, variations over this period include some 350,000 "immigrants" as a result of repatriations from Algeria in 1962.

Annual Changes in Various Categories of Workers, 1949–66
(Thousands)

	Labor force				Employed workers		
Year	Total	Military·draft	Total available	Unemployed	Outside productive sectors	Within productive sectors	Total
1949	19,496	280	19,288	241	2,481	16,566	19,047
1950	19,493	208	19,285	271	2,517	16,497	19,014
1951	19,559	234	19,325	226	2,521	16,578	19,099
1952	19,630	332	19,299	245	2,543	16,509	19,052
1953	19,582	359	19,223	300	2,585	16,338	18,923
1954	19,612	307	19,305	311	2,640	16,354	18,994
1955	19,638	336	19,302	283	2,688	16,331	19,019
1956	19,792	554	19,238	212	2,715	16,311	19,026
1957	19,876	605	19,271	161	2,742	16,368	19,110
1958	19,826	567	19,239	183	2,772	16,304	19,076
1959	19,740	541	19,199	254	2,806	16,137	18,945
1960	19,723	552	19,171	240	2,839	16,092	18,931
1961	19,694	550	19,144	212	2,858	16,064	18,932
1962	19,747	510	19,237	230	2,914	16,093	19,007
1963	20,036	410	19,626	273[a]	2,971	16,382	19,353
1964	20,201	335	19,866	216	3,037	16,613	19,650
1965	20,259	300	19,959	269	3,069	16,621	19,690
1966	20,294	294	20,000	280	3,116	16,604	19,720

Note: Including professional military and the draft stationed outside the home country. Figures given are averages for the year.
[a]Including about 50,000 repatriated.

Working Population by Economic Activity, 1949–66
(Thousands)

Economic activity[a]	1949	1950	1951	1952	1953	1954	1955
01. Agriculture and forestry	5,555.0	5,438.0	5,320.0	5,204.0	5,090.0	5,007.0	4,847.0
Industry:							
02. Processed foods and farm products	640.8	636.5	655.1	646.1	645.1	642.3	638.9
03. Solid mineral fuels and gas	310.3	293.6	280.1	277.5	266.7	257.5	247.5
04. Electricity, water, and kindred products	80.4	82.6	84.3	85.0	85.3	85.6	85.7
05. Petroleum, natural gas, and oil products	38.2	41.5	45.6	47.0	46.0	47.6	49.5
06. Building materials and glass	237.8	234.2	245.8	250.7	243.4	245.9	250.9
07. Iron mining and metallurgy	229.1	226.6	229.8	233.3	226.1	219.0	222.7
08. Nonferrous minerals and metals	29.3	29.6	30.2	31.2	31.2	30.4	31.2
09. Mechanical and electrical industries	1,446.7	1,455.6	1,509.1	1,549.6	1,514.4	1,552.3	1,613.6
10. Chemicals	273.7	282.6	297.7	296.2	295.9	305.6	314.5
11. Textiles, clothing, and leather	1,588.3	1,575.1	1,576.6	1,507.5	1,467.9	1,414.4	1,348.3
12. Wood, paper, and miscellaneous industries	744.8	755.1	770.2	766.0	747.7	748.9	756.7
Total (02–12)	5,619.4	5,613.0	5,724.5	5,690.1	5,569.7	5,549.5	5,559.5
Other industry groups:							
13. Building and public works	1,043.8	1,089.9	1,146.7	1,217.5	1,265.8	1,343.6	1,410.6
14. Transportation and communications	988.9	970.2	954.4	935.6	926.2	912.2	911.4
15. Housing services	62.1	62.1	62.1	62.1	62.1	62.1	63.3
16. Services other than housing	1,728.9	1,742.9	1,755.0	1,771.0	1,786.9	1,824.1	1,845.0
19. Trade	1,568.2	1,581.1	1,614.9	1,628.8	1,637.3	1,656.0	1,694.0
Total (02–19)	11,011.3	11,059.2	11,257.6	11,305.1	11,248.0	11,347.5	11,483.8
Total (01–19)	16,566.3	16,497.2	16,577.6	16,509.1	16,338.0	16,354.5	16,330.8
Financial institutions	170.0	–	–	–	–	201.0	206.0
Domestic service	650.0	–	–	–	–	590	580.0
Government[b]	1,661.0	–	–	–	–	1,849.0	1,902.0
Total	2,481.0	2,517.0	2,521.0	2,543.0	2,585.0	2,640.0	2,688.0
Grand total	19,047.3	19,014.2	19,098.6	19,052.1	18,923.0	18,994.5	19,018.8

Source: Etudes et conjoncture, March 1964, for the years 1954–62.

Note: The apparent accuracy of the figures should not mislead. They have not been rounded for reasons of statistical convenience. Figures are averages for the year.

[a]The sectors are defined according to the concepts used in building up the economic accounts on the "new, 1959, base."

[b]Includes professional military stationed outside the home country.

Working Population by Economic Activity, 1949–66
(Thousands)

1956	1957	1958	1959	1960	1961	1962	1963	1964	1965	1966
4,668.0	4,454.0	4,284.0	4,174.0	4,029.0	3,884.0	3,745.0	3,605.0	3,472.0	3,334.0	3,290.0
643.8	656.3	667.2	671.3	666.0	650.2	640.1	645.0	653.6	656.1	656.3
240.8	241.0	238.0	232.4	220.5	207.1	200.9	197.3	189.8	178.7	171.1
87.0	88.9	91.0	93.3	95.4	97.0	97.5	99.1	101.7	103.4	106.3
51.4	53.3	55.2	57.1	58.9	60.9	62.8	63.2	63.4	64.0	64.4
253.2	256.6	259.0	254.4	254.0	255.5	256.9	264.3	271.4	278.3	280.4
222.7	234.6	237.7	236.0	241.4	246.8	245.8	246.0	248.1	244.7	234.7
32.1	33.7	35.1	35.4	36.5	37.6	37.9	37.8	39.0	40.1	39.4
1,676.5	1,755.9	1,800.5	1,778.6	1,814.6	1,870.4	1,944.0	1,999.6	2,038.9	2,034.3	2,051.3
318.7	324.1	332.7	333.9	343.3	351.6	359.3	367.8	381.5	384.6	387.3
1,318.2	1,327.4	1,290.0	1,217.5	1,206.4	1,185.3	1,162.0	1,187.3	1,207.1·	1,139.4	1,142.2
761.0	777.8	784.8	766.2	765.5	771.3	783.2	817.1	837.3	848.1	853.1
5,605.4	5,749.6	5,791.2	5,676.1	5,702.5	5,733.7	5,790.4	5,924.5	6,031.8	5,971.7	5,986.5
1,447.6	1,498.7	1,493.2	1,503.9	1,521.4	1,550.7	1,597.9	1,700.3	1,811.1	1,899.3	1,945.8
918.4	934.7	948.4	955.8	968.9	986.0	1,004.5	1,035.1	1,063.6	1,080.7	1,086.3
64.4	65.6	66.7	67.8	69.0	70.1	71.2	72.5	74.5	77.5	80.5
1,870.0	1,890.0	1,912.0	1,936.8	1,958.0	1,976.0	1,994.0	2,088.0	2,174.0	2,227.0	2,328.0
1,732.0	1,775.0	1,809.0	1,823.0	1,843.0	1,864.0	1,890.0	1,956.1	1,995.9	2,040.7	2,073.9
11,637.8	11,913.6	12,020.5	11,963.4	12,062.8	12,180.5	12,348.0	12,776.5	13,150.9	13,296.9	13,494.0
16,305.8	16,367.6	16,304.5	16,137.4	16,091.8	16,064.5	16,093.0	16,381.5	16,622.0	16,630.9	16,694.0
210.0	216.0	224.0	232.0	240.0	251.0	263.0	283.0	295.0	306.0	318.0
568.0	557.0	546.0	536.0	525.0	514.0	503.0	497.0	491.0	485.0	478.0
1,936.0	1,969.0	2,002.0	2,040.0	2,074.0	2,103.0	2,148.0	2,211.0	2,291.0	2,338.0	2,400.0
2,714.0	2,742.0	2,772.0	2,808.0	2,836.0	2,868.0	2,914.0	2,991.0	3,077.0	3,129.0	3,196.0
19,019.8	19,109.6	19,076.5	18,945.4	18,930.8	18,932.5	19,007.0	19,372.5	19,699.9	19,759.9	19,890.0

Indexes of Working Population by Economic Activity, 1949–66
(1956 = 100)

Economic activity	1949	1950	1951	1952	1953	1954	1955
01. Agriculture and forestry	119.0	116.5	114.0	111.5	109.0	107.2	103.8
Industry:							
02. Processed foods and farm products	99.5	98.9	101.8	100.4	100.2	99.8	99.2
03. Solid mineral fuels and gas	128.9	121.9	116.3	115.2	110.8	106.9	102.8
04. Electricity, water, and kindred products	92.4	94.9	96.9	97.7	98.0	98.4	98.5
05. Petroleum, natural gas, and oil products	74.3	80.7	88.7	91.4	89.5	92.6	96.3
06. Building materials and glass	93.9	92.5	97.1	99.0	96.1	97.1	99.1
07. Iron mining and metallurgy	100.6	99.5	100.9	102.5	99.3	96.2	97.8
08. Nonferrous minerals and metals	91.3	92.2	94.1	97.2	97.2	94.7	97.2
09. Mechanical and electrical industries	86.3	86.8	90.0	92.4	90.3	92.6	96.3
10. Chemicals	85.9	88.7	93.4	92.9	92.9	95.9	98.7
11. Textiles, clothing, and leather	120.5	119.5	119.6	114.4	111.4	107.3	102.3
12. Wood, paper, and miscellaneous industries	97.9	99.2	101.2	101.7	98.2	98.4	99.4
Total (02–12)	100.1	100.0	102.0	101.4	99.3	98.9	99.1
Other industry groups:							
13. Building and public works	72.1	75.3	79.2	84.1	87.4	92.8	97.4
14. Transportation and communications	107.7	105.7	103.9	101.9	100.9	99.3	99.3
15. Housing services	96.4	96.4	96.4	96.4	96.4	96.4	98.3
16. Services other than housing	92.5	93.2	93.9	94.7	95.6	97.6	98.7
19. Trade	90.5	91.3	93.2	94.0	94.5	95.6	97.8
Total (02–19)	94.6	95.0	96.7	97.1	96.6	97.5	98.6
Total (01–19)	101.6	101.1	101.6	101.2	100.2	100.3	100.1
Financial institutions	—	—	—	—	—	95.7	98.1
Domestic service	—	—	—	—	—	103.9	102.1
Government	—	—	—	—	—	99.5	98.2
Total	91.4	92.7	92.8	93.7	95.2	97.2	99.0
Grand total	100.1	99.9	100.4	100.1	99.5	99.8	100.0

Indexes of Working Population by Economic Activity, 1949–66

(1956 = 100)

1956	1957	1958	1959	1960	1961	1962	1963	1964	1965	1966
100.0	95.4	91.8	89.4	86.3	83.2	80.2	77.2	74.4	71.4	68.6
100.0	101.9	103.6	104.3	103.4	101.0	99.4	100.2	101.5	101.9	101.9
100.0	100.1	98.8	96.5	91.6	86.0	83.4	81.9	78.8	74.2	71.0
100.0	102.1	104.6	107.2	109.6	111.5	112.0	113.9	116.9	118.8	122.1
100.0	103.7	107.4	111.1	114.6	118.5	122.2	123.0	123.4	124.5	125.3
100.0	101.3	102.3	100.5	100.3	100.9	101.4	104.4	107.2	109.9	110.7
100.0	103.0	104.4	103.7	106.0	108.4	108.0	108.0	109.0	107.5	103.1
100.0	105.0	109.3	110.3	113.7	117.1	118.1	117.7	121.5	124.9	122.7
100.0	104.7	107.4	106.1	108.2	111.6	116.0	119.3	121.6	121.3	122.4
100.0	101.7	104.4	104.8	107.7	110.3	112.7	115.4	119.7	120.7	121.5
100.0	100.7	97.9	92.4	91.5	89.9	88.1	90.1	91.6	86.4	86.6
100.0	102.2	103.1	100.7	100.6	101.3	102.9	107.4	110.0	111.4	112.1
100.0	102.5	103.2	101.1	101.6	102.2	103.2	105.7	107.6	106.5	106.8
100.0	103.5	103.2	103.9	105.1	107.1	110.4	117.4	125.1	131.2	134.4
100.0	101.8	103.3	104.1	105.5	107.4	109.4	112.7	115.8	117.7	118.3
100.0	101.9	103.6	105.3	107.2	108.9	110.6	112.6	115.7	120.3	125.0
100.0	101.1	102.3	103.6	104.7	105.7	106.6	111.7	116.3	119.1	124.1
100.0	102.5	104.5	105.3	106.4	107.6	109.1	112.9	115.2	117.8	119.7
100.0	102.3	103.2	102.7	103.6	104.6	106.0	109.8	113.0	114.3	115.9
100.0	100.3	100.0	98.9	98.7	98.5	98.7	100.5	101.9	102.0	102.4
100.0	102.9	106.7	110.5	114.3	119.5	125.2	134.8	140.5	145.7	151.4
100.0	98.1	96.2	94.4	92.5	90.5	88.6	87.5	86.4	85.4	84.2
100.0	101.7	103.4	105.4	107.1	108.6	110.9	114.2	118.3	120.8	124.0
100.0	101.0	102.1	103.4	104.4	105.6	107.3	110.2	113.4	115.3	117.8
100.0	100.4	100.3	99.6	99.5	99.5	99.9	101.9	103.3	103.9	104.6

Indexes of Annual Hours Worked per Worker by Sector, 1949–66
(1956 = 100)

Sector	1949	1950	1951	1952	1953	1954	1955
Industry:							
02. Processed foods and farm products	99.8	100.7	100.9	99.5	99.8	100.4	99.5
03. Solid mineral fuels and gas	102.1	102.1	102.1	102.1	102.1	102.1	101.4
04. Electricity, water, and kindred products	101.9	101.9	101.9	101.9	101.9	101.9	101.3
05. Petroleum, natural gas, and oil products	103.5	102.4	102.4	101.1	101.9	101.9	101.9
06. Building materials and glass	99.8	100.2	100.9	99.3	99.6	100.9	100.6
07. Iron mining and metallurgy	99.0	100.2	100.4	100.4	99.0	98.3	100.4
08. Nonferrous minerals and metals	99.0	100.2	100.2	100.4	99.0	98.3	100.4
09. Mechanical and electrical industries	98.5	99.1	100.6	99.8	98.5	100.2	100.4
10. Chemicals	100.4	100.7	101.3	100.7	100.4	101.3	100.7
11. Textiles, clothing, and leather	98.1	101.0	101.0	98.1	99.5	100.5	98.8
12. Wood, paper, and miscellaneous industries	98.0	99.6	100.5	99.1	99.3	100.2	100.2
Total (02–12)	98.4	99.8	100.4	99.1	99.1	100.2	100.0
Other industry groups:							
13. Building and public works	97.5	97.9	98.3	98.3	98.7	100.2	100.2
14. Transportation and communications	101.9	101.9	101.9	101.9	101.9	101.5	101.1
16. Services other than housing	99.5	100.5	100.9	100.9	100.9	101.6	100.9
19. Trade	99.5	100.5	100.9	100.9	100.9	101.6	100.9
Total (02–19)	98.9	100.0	100.4	99.8	99.8	100.7	100.4

Indexes of Annual Hours Worked per Worker by Sector, 1949–66
(1956 = 100)

1956	1957	1958	1959	1960	1961	1962	1963	1964	1965	1966
100	100.4	99.8	100.2	100.9	102.0	102.0	100.9	100.8	100.5	100.3
100	100.0	101.4	100.2	98.1	99.3	100.9	89.8	97.0	96.0	97.5
100	100.0	100.0	100.0	100.0	100.0	100.0	93.2	92.9	92.8	92.7
100	100.4	100.6	100.6	100.2	100.6	100.2	97.2	96.0	94.8	94.0
100	100.9	100.6	99.8	101.1	101.3	101.7	100.8	100.9	100.6	99.9
100	100.0	98.7	97.9	98.7	98.7	98.3	96.8	97.0	96.7	96.1
100	99.8	98.7	97.9	98.7	98.7	98.5	96.8	97.0	96.7	96.3
100	100.4	99.6	98.5	99.8	100.0	100.6	99.3	98.2	97.4	97.3
100	100.4	100.2	99.8	100.7	100.4	100.2	98.9	98.8	98.3	97.7
100	101.7	98.3	98.3	100.5	101.0	101.4	101.7	99.8	97.6	100.0
100	100.7	99.8	99.1	100.2	100.9	101.6	99.1	98.8	98.6	98.6
100	100.7	99.5	99.1	100.4	100.9	101.3	100.0	99.5	98.7	99.1
100	100.4	100.2	99.6	100.2	101.0	101.7	101.6	101.2	100.7	100.3
100	100.2	100.2	100.2	100.4	100.6	100.2	98.3	98.3	98.3	98.3
100	100.2	100.2	100.5	100.9	101.2	101.4	101.0	101.1	101.0	100.9
100	100.2	100.2	100.5	100.9	101.2	101.4	101.0	101.1	101.0	100.9
100	100.4	100.0	99.8	100.7	101.1	101.6	100.6	100.2	99.9	100.0

Indexes of Total Annual Labor Input by Sector, 1949–66
(1956 = 100)

Sector	1949	1950	1951	1952	1953	1954	1955
Industry:							
02. Processed foods and farm products	99.3	99.6	102.7	99.9	100.0	100.2	98.7
03. Solid mineral fuels and gas	131.6	124.5	118.7	117.6	113.1	109.1	104.2
04. Electricity, water, and kindred products	92.2	96.7	98.7	99.6	99.9	100.3	99.8
05. Petroleum, natural gas, and oil products	76.9	82.6	90.8	92.4	91.2	94.4	98.1
06. Building materials and glass	93.7	92.7	98.0	98.3	95.7	98.0	99.7
07. Iron mining and metallurgy	99.6	99.7	101.3	102.9	98.3	94.6	98.2
08. Nonferrous minerals and metals	90.4	92.4	94.3	97.6	96.2	93.1	97.6
09. Mechanical and electrical industries	85.0	86.0	90.5	92.2	88.9	92.8	96.7
10. Chemicals	86.2	89.3	94.6	93.6	93.3	97.1	99.4
11. Textiles, clothing, and leather	118.2	120.7	121.8	112.2	110.8	107.8	101.1
12. Wood, paper, and miscellaneous industries	95.9	98.8	101.7	99.8	97.5	98.6	99.6
Total (02–12)	98.5	99.8	102.4	100.5	98.4	99.1	99.1
Other industry groups:							
13. Building and public works	70.3	73.7	77.9	82.7	86.3	93.0	97.6
14. Transportation and communications	109.7	107.7	105.9	103.8	102.8	100.8	100.4
16. Services other than housing	92.0	93.7	94.7	95.6	96.5	99.2	99.6
19. Trade	90.0	91.8	94.0	94.8	95.4	97.1	98.7
Total (02–19)	93.6	95.0	97.1	96.9	96.4	98.2	99.0
Total (01–19)	100.5	101.1	102.0	101.0	100.0	101.0	100.5

Note: The index of activity is the product of the index of working population by the index of annual hours worked per worker.

Indexes of Total Annual Labor Input by Sector, 1949–66

(1956 = 100)

1956	1957	1958	1959	1960	1961	1962	1963	1964	1965	1966
100.0	102.3	103.4	104.5	104.3	103.0	101.4	101.1	102.3	102.4	102.2
100.0	100.1	100.2	96.7	89.9	85.4	84.2	73.5	76.4	71.2	69.3
100.0	102.1	104.6	107.2	100.6	111.5	112.0	106.2	108.6	110.3	113.3
100.0	104.1	108.0	111.8	114.8	119.2	122.4	119.5	118.4	118.0	117.8
100.0	102.2	102.9	100.3	101.4	102.2	103.1	105.2	108.2	110.6	106.8
100.0	103.0	103.0	101.5	104.6	107.0	106.2	104.5	105.4	103.9	99.1
100.0	104.8	107.9	108.0	112.2	115.6	116.3	114.0	117.9	120.8	118.2
100.0	105.1	107.0	104.5	108.0	111.6	116.7	118.5	119.4	118.1	119.0
100.0	102.1	104.6	104.6	108.5	110.7	112.9	114.1	118.3	118.5	118.7
100.0	102.4	96.2	90.8	92.0	90.8	89.3	91.6	91.4	84.3	86.6
100.0	102.9	102.9	99.8	100.8	102.2	104.5	106.4	108.7	109.8	110.5
100.0	103.2	102.7	100.2	102.0	103.1	104.5	105.7	107.1	105.1	105.8
100.0	103.9	103.4	103.5	105.3	108.2	112.3	110.3	126.6	132.1	131.8
100.0	102.0	103.5	104.3	105.9	108.0	109.6	110.7	113.7	115.6	116.2
100.0	101.3	102.5	104.1	105.6	107.0	108.1	112.8	117.6	120.3	125.2
100.0	102.7	104.7	105.8	107.4	108.9	110.6	114.0	116.5	119.0	120.8
100.0	102.7	103.2	102.5	104.3	105.8	107.7	110.5	113.2	114.2	115.9
100.0	100.7	100.0	98.7	99.4	99.6	100.3	101.0	102.1	101.8	101.8

Indexes of Production per Worker by Sector, 1949-66
(1956 = 100)

Sector	1949	1950	1951	1952	1953	1954	1955
01. Agriculture and forestry	69.8	83.3	82.6	86.5	95.7	103.9	107.2
Industry:							
02. Processed foods and farm products[a]	69.6	73.9	80.6	82.8	83.9	87.6	92.2
03. Solid mineral fuels and gas	69.6	73.5	79.9	84.0	83.7	89.5	97.7
04. Electricity, water, and kindred products	52.6	59.9	70.0	75.0	76.9	84.6	92.6
05. Petroleum, natural gas, and oil products	55.7	66.4	70.9	77.5	86.4	87.8	93.8
06. Building materials and glass	74.5	79.5	81.7	84.3	83.4	92.4	96.0
07. Iron mining and metallurgy	69.1	67.2	75.8	77.2	73.3	91.2	99.6
08. Nonferrous minerals and metals	61.9	68.7	73.8	72.4	76.2	86.6	91.3
09. Mechanical and electrical industries	76.5	81.7	86.1	87.6	92.8	90.1	91.1
10. Chemicals	71.4	74.7	79.7	76.3	79.4	86.4	92.6
11. Textiles, clothing, and leather	59.2	67.1	71.6	73.0	78.5	85.3	91.8
12. Wood, paper, and miscellaneous industries	72.7	81.7	82.3	82.0	86.8	90.0	95.1
Total (02-12)	66.2	72.1	77.5	79.5	83.2	87.5	92.5
Other industry groups:							
13. Building and public works	—	—	—	—	—	94.3	99.1
14. Transportation and communications	66.9	71.7	79.3	82.8	81.7	87.5	93.2
15. Housing services	89.2	89.4	90.9	92.2	93.5	96.9	99.1
16. Services other than housing	77.0	79.2	85.3	88.5	89.7	91.9	96.6
19. Trade	77.1	80.3	84.2	86.7	90.1	92.9	97.1
Total (02-19)	73.5	77.6	82.4	83.9	86.3	89.8	94.6
Total (01-19)	69.9	75.4	80.0	82.2	85.4	89.9	95.2
Gross Domestic Production	69.7	75.0	79.4	81.6	84.9	89.5	95.0

Note: Output of workers obtained by division of data of Appendix Tables 1 and 6.

[a]The nature of the results shown is partly explained by the bad quality of the basic statistical data.

Indexes of Production per Worker by Sector, 1949–66
(1956 = 100)

1956	1957	1958	1959	1960	1961	1962	1963	1964	1965	1966
100.0	113.9	118.8	127.9	148.2	145.1	164.7	165.7	172.9	189.0	192.9
100.0	97.9	97.6	96.6	99.1	105.3	110.5	113.4	115.5	116.7	124.9
100.0	103.8	108.7	112.6	117.6	120.9	131.4	128.8	145.3	155.1	164.9
100.0	105.1	115.1	115.9	129.8	134.7	145.6	160.5	162.0	176.7	185.3
100.0	91.1	98.1	101.4	107.9	117.2	123.2	135.7	150.0	161.9	169.4
100.0	108.8	109.3	115.0	122.6	128.6	137.3	145.2	167.0	175.9	183.1
100.0	104.7	104.1	108.3	128.0	122.3	123.1	122.5	137.4	141.7	149.7
100.0	99.0	103.8	120.1	129.7	128.2	130.7	133.6	148.6	152.8	167.6
100.0	103.2	106.7	110.7	118.5	123.7	127.2	131.1	133.7	138.6	146.7
100.0	110.7	116.3	125.3	132.9	136.2	146.8	153.8	161.2	171.7	185.0
100.0	107.6	109.2	112.7	125.4	129.8	139.2	147.8	148.5	150.0	161.2
100.0	105.4	104.8	109.9	122.5	127.3	132.4	132.4	135.7	139.9	131.2
100.0	103.2	106.4	111.1	120.2	125.3	131.6	136.4	141.7	148.4	157.2
100.0	101.6	107.1	113.6	114.7	122.4	127.7	130.5	141.2	143.9	147.6
100.0	106.9	109.3	111.0	115.9	120.5	125.2	127.8	131.7	133.2	138.8
100.0	103.1	106.8	110.4	113.3	117.2	121.3	125.5	129.7	134.5	139.5
100.0	105.7	107.1	108.2	114.8	120.4	125.5	127.8	131.0	135.9	141.7
100.0	103.6	100.0	102.8	108.0	112.6	119.4	122.1	125.3	116.6	129.2
100.0	103.7	105.9	109.5	116.3	121.6	127.5	130.9	135.7	139.8	146.1
100.0	106.1	109.8	114.0	122.9	128.5	136.6	141.2	147.3	153.5	160.7
100.0	106.1	109.2	113.8	123.1	128.9	137.6	142.7	149.4	155.5	163.7

Indexes of Production per Man-Hour by Sector, 1949–66
(1956 = 100)

Sector	1949	1950	1951	1952	1953	1954	1955
Industry:							
02. Processed foods and farm products[a]	69.8	73.4	79.9	83.2	84.1	87.2	92.7
03. Solid mineral fuels and gas	68.2	72.0	78.3	82.3	82.0	87.7	96.4
04. Electricity, water, and kindred products	51.6	58.7	68.7	73.6	75.5	83.0	91.4
05. Petroleum, natural gas, and oil products	53.8	64.9	69.3	76.6	84.8	86.1	92.0
06. Building materials and glass	74.7	79.3	80.9	84.9	83.7	91.5	95.4
07. Iron mining and metallurgy	69.8	67.1	75.5	76.9	74.1	92.7	99.2
08. Nonferrous minerals and metals	62.5	68.5	73.6	72.1	77.0	88.1	90.9
09. Mechanical and electrical industries	77.6	82.4	85.6	87.7	94.3	89.9	90.7
10. Chemicals	71.1	74.2	78.6	75.7	79.1	85.4	92.0
11. Textiles, clothing, and leather	60.3	66.4	70.9	74.4	79.0	84.9	92.9
12. Wood, paper, and miscellaneous industries	74.2	82.0	81.9	82.8	87.4	89.9	94.9
Total (02–12)	67.3	72.2	77.1	80.2	83.9	87.3	92.5
Other industry groups:							
13. Building and public works	–	–	–	–	–	94.1	98.9
14. Transportation and communications	65.7	70.4	77.8	81.3	80.2	86.2	92.1
16. Services other than housing	77.4	78.8	84.6	87.7	88.9	90.4	95.7
19. Trade	77.6	79.8	83.5	86.0	89.2	91.5	96.3
Total (02–19)	74.3	77.6	82.1	84.1	86.5	89.2	94.2
Total (01–19)	70.6	75.4	79.7	82.4	85.6	89.3	94.8
Gross domestic production	70.4	75.0	79.1	81.8	85.1	88.9	94.6

Note: Output per working hour obtained by division of data in Appendix Tables 1 and 8.

[a]The nature of the results shown is partly explained by the bad quality of the basic statistical data.

Indexes of Production per Man-Hour by Sector, 1949–66
(1956 = 100)

1956	1957	1958	1959	1960	1961	1962	1963	1964	1965	1966
100.0	97.6	97.8	96.5	98.3	103.3	108.3	112.4	114.6	116.1	124.6
100.0	103.8	107.2	112.4	119.8	121.8	130.2	143.5	149.9	161.7	169.0
100.0	105.1	115.1	115.9	129.8	134.7	145.6	172.1	174.4	190.4	199.6
100.0	90.8	97.6	100.7	107.8	116.5	123.0	139.7	156.3	170.8	180.2
100.0	107.8	108.6	115.3	121.3	127.0	135.0	144.0	165.6	174.9	183.3
100.0	104.7	105.5	110.6	129.7	123.9	125.2	126.6	141.9	146.5	155.7
100.0	99.1	105.1	122.7	131.5	129.8	132.8	138.0	153.2	157.9	173.9
100.0	102.8	107.1	112.4	118.7	123.7	126.5	132.0	136.2	142.3	150.8
100.0	110.3	116.1	125.5	131.9	135.7	146.5	155.6	163.1	174.9	189.4
100.0	105.9	111.1	114.6	124.7	128.5	137.3	145.4	148.7	153.7	161.2
100.0	104.7	105.1	110.9	122.2	126.2	130.3	133.6	137.4	142.0	133.1
100.0	102.5	106.9	112.1	119.7	124.2	130.0	136.4	142.4	150.3	158.7
100.0	101.3	106.9	114.0	114.5	121.2	125.5	128.4	139.5	142.9	147.2
100.0	106.7	109.1	110.7	115.5	119.8	125.0	130.0	134.1	135.6	141.3
100.0	105.5	106.9	107.7	113.8	119.0	123.8	126.5	129.5	134.5	140.5
100.0	103.4	99.8	102.4	107.0	111.3	117.8	121.0	123.9	115.4	128.1
100.0	103.3	105.9	109.8	115.5	120.2	125.5	130.2	135.5	139.9	146.1
100.0	105.7	109.8	114.2	122.0	127.1	134.4	140.4	147.0	153.5	160.6
100.0	105.7	109.2	114.0	122.0	127.5	135.4	141.9	149.1	155.7	163.7

Investments by Sector, 1949–65

Sector	1949	1950	1951	1952	1953	1954	1955
01. Agriculture	1,730	1,710	1,740	1,700	1,746	1,980	2,320
02. Processed foods and farm products	555	686	1,004	840	844	748	868
03. Solid mineral fuels and gas	1,217	994	797	872	923	823	709
04. Electricity, water, and kindred products	2,674	2,663	2,543	2,140	1,831	1,817	1,970
05. Petroleum, natural gas, and oil products	369	399	491	452	415	340	460
06. Building materials and glass	329	321	288	230	304	302	349
07. Iron mining and metallurgy	748	973	858	882	920	724	755
08. Nonferrous minerals and metals	105	111	89	75	87	56	102
09. Mechanical and electrical industries	1,745	1,800	1,901	1,700	1,654	1,802	2,072
10A. Chemicals	725	814	757	690	743	773	848
10B. Atomic energy	17	13	25	25	51	70	140
11. Textiles, clothing, and leather	–	–	–	–	–	–	–
12. Wood, paper, and miscellaneous industries	592	744	892	960	971	1,108	1,285
13. Building and public works	599	624	709	608	657	719	809
14. Transportation and communications	3,605	3,362	2,857	2,898	3,151	3,314	3,484
16. Services other than housing	–	–	–	–	–	–	–
19. Trade	1,279	1,411	2,141	1,603	1,803	2,013	2,700
Total production	16,631	16,958	17,367	15,945	16,432	16,932	19,182
15. Housing services	740	800	965	945	995	1,240	1,295
Grand total (01–19)	17,371	17,758	18,332	16,890	17,427	18,172	20,477

Investments by Sector, 1949-65

1956	1957	1958	1959	1960	1961	1962	1963	1964	1965
2,620	2,924	2,900	2,619	2,594	2,945	2,881	3,100	3,437	3,468
842	1,026	905	997	1,070	1,155	1,251	1,412	1,396	1,440
697	721	731	706	727	637	581	551	595	582
2,183	351	2,631	2,950	2,829	2,839	3,013	3,213	3,514	3,649
664	758	1,040	1,007	723	907	1,126	1,288	1,428	1,432
399	472	488	477	519	643	710	789	868	962
922	1,129	1,150	1,170	1,446	2,063	2,136	1,614	1,219	981
122	112	161	211	159	196	158	90	116	142
2,533	2,763	2,711	2,700	3,042	3,619	3,986	3,980	4,299	4,202
903	1,044	1,130	1,134	1,438	1,534	1,624	1,752	1,627	1,830
260	400	461	615	628	1,045	1,295	1,656	2,104	2,528
717	910	861	770	898	985	1,090	1,205	1,336	1,141
662	788	784	748	847	896	1,150	1,193	1,166	1,112
908	1,082	1,057	974	1,079	1,193	1,291	1,541	1,720	1,611
3,476	3,721	3,844	4,033	4,788	4,797	4,786	4,978	5,581	5,836
1,368	1,415	1,451	1,440	1,781	1,977	2,324	2,603	2,658	2,737
1,610	1,639	1,760	1,740	1,998	2,305	2,660	3,052	3,349	3,439
21,284	23,681	24,675	24,889	27,031	30,162	32,479	34,438	36,864	37,630
1,520	2,019	2,304	2,551	2,736	3,019	3,347	3,938	4,341	4,533
22,804	25,700	26,979	27,440	29,767	33,181	35,826	38,376	41,205	42,163

Fixed Reproducible Capital by Sector, 1949–66
(1956 prices, *million francs*)

Sector	1949	1950	1951	1952	1953	1954	1955
01. Agriculture	15,030	15,760	16,420	17,060	17,660	18,230	18,940
Industry:							
02. Processed foods and farm products	4,540	5,100	5,800	6,600	6,880	7,130	7,260
03. Solid mineral fuels and gas	6,380	7,440	8,300	8,850	9,460	10,120	10,650
04. Electricity, water, and kindred products	8,170	10,530	12,790	14,840	16,410	17,610	18,750
05. Petroleum	2,280	2,450	2,640	2,910	3,120	3,260	3,320
06. Building materials and glass	2,490	2,600	2,700	2,750	2,760	2,850	2,900
07. Iron mining and metallurgy	4,830	5,180	5,720	6,040	6,440	6,820	6,980
08. Nonferrous minerals and metals	680	730	780	800	810	820	820
09. Mechanical and electrical industries	11,780	12,260	12,750	13,300	13,670	13,960	14,360
10. Chemicals and rubber	4,000	4,330	4,720	5,010	5,250	5,470	5,710
11. Textiles, clothing, and leather	9,030	8,640	8,360	8,180	8,110	7,980	7,940
12. Wood, paper, and miscellaneous industries	5,750	5,770	5,790	5,800	5,830	5,850	5,870
Total (02–12)	59,930	65,030	70,350	75,080	78,740	81,870	84,560
Other industry groups:							
13. Building and public works	2,230	2,510	2,770	3,080	3,330	3,510	3,720
14. Transportation and communications	134,780	136,410	137,730	138,480	139,310	140,290	141,400
Of which infrastructure	(48,140)	(49,770)	(51,090)	(51,840)	(52,670)	(53,650)	(54,760)
16. Services other than housing	3,500	3,750	4,000	4,370	4,660	4,890	5,200
19. Trade	11,680	12,200	12,780	13,820	13,430	13,060	12,830
Grand Total (01–19)	227,150	235,660	244,050	251,890	257,130	261,850	266,650

Fixed Reproducible Capital by Sector, 1949–66
(1956 prices, *million francs*)

1956	1957	1958	1959	1960	1961	1962	1963	1964	1965	1966
20,000	21,290	22,760	24,130	25,150	26,060	27,330	28,360	30,990	33,920	35,130
7,500	7,690	8,060	8,270	8,560	8,810	9,130	9,500	10,090	10,610	11,130
11,000	11,410	11,890	12,540	13,080	13,530	13,790	13,990	14,090	14,250	14,470
20,000	21,380	22,880	24,600	26,560	28,330	30,030	31,850	33,790	35,950	38,160
3,500	3,860	4,310	4,980	5,660	5,930	6,400	7,270	7,940	8,690	9,380
3,000	3,140	3,340	3,540	3,710	3,880	4,210	4,550	4,950	5,390	5,890
7,150	7,450	7,930	8,390	8,850	9,550	10,800	12,100	12,660	12,770	12,630
850	900	930	1,010	1,130	1,190	1,290	1,360	1,330	1,330	1,360
15,000	16,030	17,190	18,190	19,080	20,290	21,780	23,530	25,160	26,940	28,360
6,000	6,310	6,740	7,210	7,640	8,340	9,060	9,800	10,590	11,180	11,910
8,000	8,100	8,330	8,530	8,640	8,890	9,190	9,550	10,020	10,580	10,900
6,000	6,160	6,430	6,680	6,880	7,090	7,330	7,800	8,690	9,680	9,980
88,000	92,430	98,030	103,940	109,790	115,830	123,010	131,300	139,310	147,370	154,170
4,000	4,330	4,760	5,100	5,320	5,620	5,980	6,390	7,000	7,700	8,200
142,700	144,030	145,580	147,210	149,050	151,630	154,250	156,910	159,810	163,360	167,220
(56,000)	(57,180)	(58,560)	(60,000)	(61,570)	(63,830)	(66,010)	(68,090)	(70,280)	(72,980)	(75,820)
5,800	6,450	7,040	7,590	8,050	8,860	9,780	10,880	12,120	13,270	14,350
13,000	13,310	13,650	14,050	14,390	14,930	15,730	16,740	18,120	19,660	21,130
273,500	281,840	291,820	302,020	311,750	322,930	336,080	350,580	367,350	385,280	400,200

Financing of Firms, 1953–67
(1962 prices, *billion francs*)

				1956 base	
Category	1953	1954	1955	1956	1957
Allocations (net of recoveries):					
Gross fixed capital formation	24.6	25.4	28.5	31.4	36.2
Stock changes	1.6	3.0	2.1	5.2	4.6
Increase in money holdings	8.3	7.3	6.3	6.4	5.9
Total allocations	34.5	35.7	36.9	43.0	46.7
Of which stock changes + increase in money					
holdings	*9.9*	*10.3*	*8.4*	*11.6*	*10.5*
Assets (net of repayments):					
Long-term borrowing	4.2	4.2	4.8	5.6	6.6
Issues of bonds and stocks	2.0	3.2	4.0	4.2	6.0
Of which bonds	*(0.9)*	*(1.2)*	*(1.9)*	*(2.1)*	*(3.6)*
Of which share stocks	*(1.1)*	*(2.0)*	*(2.1)*	*(2.1)*	*(2.4)*
Medium-term credit	1.4	0.8	0.2	0.9	2.0
Own financing (companies + FFCEI)	23.6	23.8	24.9	25.8	27.5
Adjustment (in part, capital transfers abroad)	0.3	0.4	−0.3	−0.1	0.1
Short-term credit	3.0	3.2	3.3	6.6	4.4
Total assets	34.5	35.6	36.9	43.0	46.6
Of which long-term indebtedness	*5.1*	*5.4*	*6.7*	*7.7*	*10.2*
Of which long-term assets (long-term indebted-					
ness + shares + own resources	*29.8*	*31.2*	*33.7*	*35.6*	*40.1*

Source: National Accounts.

Note: This table of firms' financing relates to all the allocations and apparent assets in the capital and financial accounts of firms as shown in the National Accounts. These two accounts have been consolidated. Allocations and assets have been shown by order of growing liquidity in order to facilitate comparisons between the different items. There is of course no rigorous relationship between assets and allocations in view of the indivisible nature of firms' finances, but it can be considered that long-term assets (particularly those related to indebtedness) and medium-term credit for capital equipment are chiefly allocated to long-term uses (gross fixed capital formation), and that short-term assets (short-term credit) are allocated to short term uses (stock changes and increases in money holdings).

Some items require special comment: (1) To avoid imputations that are always somewhat arbitrary, we have not distinguished *stock* changes due to changes in the market situation from stock changes required by the increase in output, although the latter play a part in production analogous to that of investments. (2) In order to simplify, we have not distinguished (in *increases of financial holdings*) shares and long-term loans abroad from other holdings; the latter depend on the financial policy of firms; the former are substantially lower in total value and represent shareholding linked to firms' medium- or long-term policy. (3) The item *medium-term credit* includes credit for capital equipment and credit for exports. (4) The item *own assets* should not be compared solely with "gross fixed capital formation." It

Financing of Firms, 1953–67
(1962 prices, *billion francs*)

		1959 base								
1958	1959	1959	1960	1961	1962	1963	1964	1965	1966	1967
36.7	37.2	38.6	41.4	46.1	49.4	52.8	56.3	57.6	61.4	65.6
6.0	2.0	2.0	7.6	3.0	5.4	4.2	7.4	1.9	4.4	3.3
4.3	11.4	9.4	8.8	9.7	10.9	11.4	7.1	12.5	12.4	16.0
47.0	50.6	50.0	57.8	58.8	65.7	68.4	70.8	72.0	78.2	84.9
10.3	*13.4*	*11.4*	*16.4*	*12.7*	*16.3*	*15.6*	*14.5*	*14.4*	*16.8*	*19.3*
7.1	8.4	9.6	10.0	9.8	10.3	11.5	13.7	12.2	11.4	13.8
5.0	6.3	5.8	5.2	6.2	7.3	6.4	6.4	7.8	7.5	6.3
(2.4)	(3.8)	(3.5)	(2.4)	(3.6)	(2.8)	(2.4)	(2.1)	(2.5)	(2.2)	(2.5)
(2.6)	(2.5)	(2.3)	(2.8)	(2.6)	(4.5)	(4.0)	(4.3)	(5.3)	(5.3)	(3.8)
1.7	0.4	0.4	1.2	1.6	2.1	2.7	2.7	2.3	3.1	3.9
28.6	29.7	29.4	33.9	31.2	35.5	34.6	37.0	39.6	41.3	44.4
2.2	0.0	-0.1	-0.9	1.2	1.4	3.6	2.2	0.9	1.8	1.7
2.3	5.8	4.9	8.5	8.8	9.1	10.2	8.8	9.3	13.1	14.8
46.9	50.6	50.0	57.9	58.8	65.7	68.4	70.8	72.1	78.2	84.9
9.5	*12.2*	*13.1*	*12.4*	*13.4*	*13.1*	*13.9*	*15.8*	*14.7*	*13.6*	*16.3*
40.7	*44.4*	*44.8*	*49.1*	*47.2*	*53.1*	*52.5*	*57.1*	*59.6*	*60.2*	*64.5*

can be regarded as usual for a part of those assets to be allocated to increases in stocks and in money holdings. (5) Although "adjustment" partly represents statistical errors, it is also linked to capital movements abroad, representing liquidations of foreign balances of a temporary nature linked to the economic situation (for example, repatriations of current account holdings abroad), or of a structural nature (for example, repatriations of capital linked with decolonization).

To interpret the figures in this table correctly, account must be taken of the impact of the short-term economic situation on the financial accounts of firms. Thus the rate of indebtedness of firms increases in the rising phases of economic growth, at a time when prices are rising and the pressure of demand is growing; changes in money holdings by firms have a related "cyclical" character; firms increase their money holdings less rapidly when their indebtedness or their stocks are increasing rapidly. To bring out long-term trends, this influence must be eliminated, and the figures must be based on data relating to years in which the economic situation is comparable: on the one hand, 1953, 1959, and 1965 (years of economic revival) and, on the other hand, 1954–55 and 1960–61 (growth years with relative price stability). It is, moreover, particularly interesting to study changes in financing between the beginning (1954) and the end (1962) of the period of rapid investment growth (without allowing for the short-lived slowdown in 1958 and 1959) and during each of the investment boom subperiods, 1954–57 and 1959–62.

Comparative Changes in Self-Financing Ratios of Firms,
Including and Excluding Housing, 1949–66

| | Old base | | | New base, 1959 | |
Year	Including housing	Excluding housing	Year	Including housing	Excluding housing
1949	75.0	76.7	1959	72.3	78.3
1950	74.2	76.1	1960	69.1	73.9
1951	70.5	72.7	1961	63.5	68.2
1952	73.3	79.8	1962	64.7	69.6
1953	90.4	94.3	1963	60.6	65.6
1954	83.9	88.0	1964	58.0	64.0
1955	81.5	85.4	1965	66.5	73.5
1956	70.4	73.6	1966	62.8	68.8
1957	67.5	71.2			
1958	67.1	71.0			
1959	75.9	81.5			

Note: The self-financing ratio is the ratio between gross savings of firms (including financing of capital formation by individual entrepreneurs) and gross capital formation (excluding stock changes). This ratio was estimated in particular for housing corporations, both public and private, for the years 1956–59, on the one hand, and for 1962, on the other hand. It appears to be very stable: 17 percent on the average between 1956 and 1959, and 18 percent in 1962. Applying this almost constant ratio to the estimates of investment in housing by firms provides an order of magnitude of the use of own resources corresponding to "housing expenditure by firms," to be deducted from own resources of firms as a whole in order to obtain a series of own resources excluding housing. When compared with estimates of productive investments, this series makes possible an evaluation of self-financing ratios relating to productive investment taken by itself. The comparative estimates of self-financing ratios of firms, including and excluding housing, are shown above. The ratios excluding housing are consistently higher than those including housing.

Index

Index

Adams, G., "Capacity Utilization in Europe," 240–41
Age structure: of workers and labor quality, 71–72; of capital, 193–95, 196, 209, 286
Agricultural Bureau, 492
Agricultural technical study centers (CETA), 173, 492
Agriculture: production levels, 11, 12–13, 26, 509–10, 511, 516; fertilizer use, 12–13, 28; structural change, 12–13, 28, 171–73, 488; labor force, 13, 15, 90f, 94, 158, 550, 552; growth rates, 15, 22, 28; farm size, 15, 170–71; labor force participation rates, 51–52; labor productivity, 79, 96f, 100, 171–73, 199, 200–205; investment, 113, 337, 523f; capital, 126, 130, 151, 156; capital-output ratio, 152–53, 154; capital-labor substitution, 156; migration out of, 159, 161, 171–73, 270; labor force quality, 202–3; labor earnings, 203–4; rate of return, 205; in postwar economic growth, 219; prices, 349–50, 354, 357–58; imports, 394–95; National Plans forecast accuracy, 465f. *See also in tables dealing with quantities by sector*
Algeria: repatriates' effects on 1963 economy, 358, 383, 390, 463; military action and 1956–57 inflation, 383, 389
Amortization of capital, 123–24, 131–39 *passim*, 196
Anti-trust action, 449–50
Artisans, 162–63, 207, 264–65
Atomic Energy Commission investments, 338
Automobile and bicycle industry: concentration, 169, 452–53; National Plans forecast accuracy, 465f

Automobile industry profits, 301, 452–53

Balance of payments, 326, 373–79, 464
Balance of trade, 373–77 *passim*
Balance sheets of firms, 308, 313–20
Balassa, Bela, 406–8
Bank of France credit to firms, 331
Bankruptcies and aggregate demand, 228–29
Banks: government-owned, 328; credit restriction law of 1946, 438
Barjonet, M., for Economic and Social Council, 385
Basic industries reconstruction and economic growth, 221, 503
Belgium: capital per worker, 155; firm size, 166; productivity, 185; capacity utilization, 241; firm finance 297, 313
Bénéfices industriels et commerciaux (BIC) statistics on capital, 127–28, 131
Birthrate, 36–38, 41; effects, 43, 45, 496, 497–498
Boiteux, M., on electricity prices, 446
Bonds, interest and real cost of credit, 368. *See also* Stocks and bonds
Borrowing: postwar foreign, 326; long-term, by firms, 331–34. *See also* Credit; Finance; Self-financing ratio
Branche, translation of, 11
Brangeon, J. L., on agricultural labor, 172
Building and public works industry: output, 30ff, 105, 465f, 516, 523–24; labor data, 91, 95, 158, 550, 552; productivity, 96, 101; capital data, 130, 153f, 156; monopoly returns to capital, 188; wages, 427f. *See also*

in tables dealing with quantities by sector

Building materials and glass industry: output, 17, 465f, 516; productivity, 96, 100f; labor data, 96, 100, 550, 552; investment and depreciation, 112, 130; profit, 301; wages, 427. *See also in tables dealing with quantities by sector*

Buildings and infrastructure technical progress, 194, 532–33

Buildings and public works: as form of investment, 108–9, 117, 121, 528–29; relative price estimation, 528, 530

Bunle, H., on net immigration, 230

Businessmen, small, 185–86, 207, 264–65

Business organizations activities, 17, 441f, 492

Caisse des Dépôts et Consignations, 328, 331; and firm finance, 340–41, 438; and local government finance, 477–78

Caisses d'Epargne, 328

Camu, A., on Common Market and trade, 406–8

Canals, 14

Capacity utilization, 196–97, 237–38, 239–41, 261, 277–78

Capital: price of, 114, 119, 124–25; return to, by sector, 185–86, 200–201; monopoly returns, 188; intensity of use, 196–97, 237–38; productivity, 197, 201; cost of, 255, 276, 280–84 *passim*, 366–69; social aspects of accumulation, 543. *See also* Capacity utilization

Capital equipment: price, 114, 119, 124–25, 528; investment in, 117–18, 121, 528; imported, 118; technical progress in, 194

Capital formation, gross fixed, 105, 113, 285; by firms, 321, 332. *See also* Investment

Capital goods industries: prices, 114, 119, 124–25; growth, 501. *See also* Building and public works industry; Mechanical and electrical industries

Capital-investment ratio, 540–41

Capital market, 334–36; foreign capital flows, 297, 312–13, 322–23, 325, 377; funds by term, 377, 438–39

Capital-output ratios, 154, 277–78; by industry, 152–53

Capital per worker, 154–56

Capital stock: estimation, 104, 122–31, 140–43, 147–52, 195–96; gross vs. net, 124, 133; growth, 143–47, 151–52, 157, 183; age and obsolescence, 193–95, 196, 209, 286; and economic

growth, 209, 221, 274–75; effect of aggregate demand on, 262. *See also* Productive sectors

Carré, P., on effects of foreign trade, 409–13

Cattle industry, 28

Censuses, quinquennial demographic, 4

Centre National des Jeunes Agriculteurs (CNJA), 492

Centres d'Etudes Techniques Agricoles (CETA), 173, 492

Chemical products foreign trade, 398, 400, 406–7

Chemicals and rubber industry: growth rate, 30, 32; labor force, 91, 95, 550, 552; productivity, 96–102 *passim*; investment, 113; capital data, 130, 149, 152, 154, 156; concentration and competitiveness, 164, 169, 452–53; wage growth, 428; profit, 452–53; output, 465f, 516. *See also in tables with quantities by sector*

Choffel, J., on recessions, 279

Clothing industry, *see* Textiles

Coal industry: output growth, 29, 30–31; productivity, 96f, 188; investment, 112, 144–46, 477; price changes, 365, 445–46. *See also* Solid mineral fuels and gas

Cobb-Douglas production function use, 179–81, 182, 536–39

Colson, C., capital stock estimates, 147, 150

Commerce, *see* Trade

Commission Centrale des Marchés de l'Etat, increasing role, 451

Commission on Manpower estimates on mobility, 433

Commission Technique des Ententes et Positions Dominantes, 449–50, 451, 488

Common Market: effects on firms, 263, 266, 278f, 303f; and foreign trade, 390, 404–7; and National Plans, 487, 489

Communications industry, 96, 100, 466. *See also* Transportation and communications industry

Competition: and profit rates, 303; and inflation, 351, 360; removing obstacles to, 408, 449–50; growth of, 408, 452, 486–87

Concentration of firms, 15, 163–70, 176, 452–53

Consumption, 247–51; by households, 243, 250, 386–88; by public sector, 243–50 *passim*, 388f; credit for, 291

Corporations, *see* Firms; Public enterprises

Coste, H., export growth study, 404

Courcier, M., export growth study, 403–4
Coutin, P., 91
Couturier, M., on foreign technology, 217
Craftsmen, 162–63, 207, 264–65
Credit: for consumption, 291; medium-term for firms, 332, 340–41; short-term for firms, 332–36 *passim*, 340–43; availability and cost, 356, 357, 368f
Crédit Agricole, 328, 331, 337
Crédit Foncier, 326, 328
Crédit National, 328, 331, 484; funds for firms, 339–42 *passim*, 438
Currency valuation, *see* Exchange rates
Customs duties, *see* Import quotas

Death rate, 39, 41
Debt of firms, 313–20, 336–37, 362–64; debit-to-equity ratio, 317–19. *See also* Self-financing ratio
Decentralization of production and externalities, 453–56
Demand, aggregate: effect on production growth, 190, 209, 231–32, 234–41; affecting economic growth, 225f, 232–34, 501; and labor market, 235–36; composition and causes, 242–53 *passim*; effect on productivity, 263–66; and prices, 349–58 *passim*
Denison, Edward F., 2, 68n, 73, 155, 184–85, 192–93, 209–11, 212, 259
Denmark, comparisons, 155, 185, 412
Denuc, J., estimates of prewar firm size, 161, 166–67
Depreciation, declining-rate, 280, 282–83
Depressed areas, 455
Depression: effect on population, 36, 40; effects on labor force, 40, 47, 91, 163; effect on productivity, 79–81, 501; and postwar growth, 219–20, 496f; other effects, 346–47, 396, 419; government economic policy, 381–82
Depressions of 1800's, 12, 14
Devaluation of 1958, effects, 343–44, 373–79 *passim*, 398
Devaluations and inflation, 392
De Ville-Chabrolle, M., firm size estimates, 161
Directed economy of World War II, 417, 419, 487
Dirigisme, 417, 419, 487
Discount rates and real cost of credit, 368. *See also* Monetary policy
Divisia, Dupin, and Roy, capital estimates, 132, 136, 138f, 147, 150–51
Domestic service sector: labor data, 59, 91, 550, 552; output, 509, 511
Durable goods stocks and savings, 291

Earnings of labor, 185–86, 213. *See also* Wages
Easterlin, Richard A., 38
Echard, P., change in farm structure, 172
Economic budgets, 385–88
Economic consciousness and national planning, 480, 492
Economic consulting, growth of, 492
Economic data: prewar scarcity, 16; growth and use, 489–90, 491–93, 504
Economic education improvement, 492–93, 504
Economic growth: rates, 1, 12, 20–27 *passim*, 219–20, 495; miscellaneous influences on rates, 14–15, 22, 219–21, 253, 460–61, 505–6; and productivity, conclusions, 219; international growth effect on France, 253; and inflation, 361–62
Economic policies: on economic growth in 1950's, 255–56, 342; and inflation, 354–55, 361–62; government budget balance, 361–62, 389–90; prewar, 379–82; and National Plans, 481–83, 486–87. *See also* Stabilization policy; *and under* Finance
Economic stabilization, *see* Stabilization policy
Economies of scale, 212–14; by plant, 165–66, 169; in production function, 180, 211–12, 413–15
Economy, industrial size of, defined, 409
Education: employment in, 59, 94; measurement of levels of, 62–67, 202–3, 500; effects on labor force quality, 72–75, 214–16; effect on total productivity and growth, 191–92, 220, 505; investment and National Plans, 479f
Electrical and mechanical industries, *see* Mechanical and electrical industries
Electrical manufacturing industry, 169, 301, 304
Electricity, water, and kindred products industry: growth rates, 17, 30, 32; labor force, 91, 550, 552; productivity growth, 96–102 *passim*; postwar investment, 109–12, 144–46, 477; capital data, 127, 130, 144–46, 152, 154, 156; return to capital, 187; price changes, 365, 445–47; output, 465f, 516. *See also* Energy industries; *and in tables with quantities by sector*
Emigration, 40
Employment: by major categories, 57–60, 77, 94; and production growth, 209; growth, 260, 377. *See also* Labor market

Energy industries: growth rates, 30–31, 464–65; capital and finance, 142, 339; prices, 364–65, 445. *See also* Electricity, water, and kindred products industry; Heavy industries, investment; Oil industry; Solid mineral fuels and gas industry

Engineers, growth in numbers, 215

England, *see* Great Britain

Entrepreneurs, independent, 185–86

Equipment, *see* Capital equipment

Equity of firms, 316, 317–19. *See also* Stocks and bonds

Escalation clauses, 365–66, 368

Estimation methods, *see within items to be estimated*

European Coal and Steel Community, 487

European Economic Community, *see* Common Market

European Free Trade Area, trade growth with, 405

European Payments Union, 373

Exchange rates, effects of, 253, 352, 356–57, 382

Expectations, 278–79, 470–71

Exports: volume, 14f, 243–44, 246–47, 271, 373–77 *passim*, 398–99; and aggregate demand, 245, 247–49, 251–52; expansion causes, 253, 402–4; and exchange rate, 354, 374, 382, 389; subsidies, 374, 389; capital and consumption goods, 375; export growth in net import products, 402. *See also* Foreign trade

Externalities and firm location, 453–56

Extractive industries, 17

Family Code of 1938–39, 37

Family deduction in income tax, 37–38

Farm products processing, *see* Processed foods and farm products industry

Febvay, M., 37

Females, *see* Women in labor force

Finance: postwar supply, 321–22, 325–26, 334–36; and investment volume, 322, 343; government intervention in allocation, 325–26, 328–29, 331, 338–39, 342, 420; sources of, 325–26, 331–34, 343; government-business allocation of supply, 326–29; National Plan Commissariat and policy, 484; public finance as cause of economic growth, 496, 498–99

Financial assets of firms, 316

Financial institutions: employment, 59, 550, 552; savings, 288; output, 509, 511

Financial linkages of firms, 167

Fire insurance valuations of capital, 128

Firms: size data, 161–62; external finance and own savings, 288, 326, 332, 337, 362; use of economic information, 491–92. *See also* Borrowing; Debt of firms; Finance; Investment; Savings; Self-financing ratio

Fonds de Développement Economique et Social (FDES), 331, 338, 455, 477

Foods and farm products, *see* Processed foods and farm products industry

Forecasting, annual government methods, 385, 386–88, 490. *See also* National Plans

Foreign capital funds, *see under* Capital market

Foreign exchange reserves, 373–77 *passim*

Foreign trade: volume, 356, 396–98, 463–64; restrictions of 1950–58, 373–76 *passim*; trade balance, 373–77 *passim*; trade growth and output growth, 394, 397–98, 409–13; and inflation, 397–98, 408; and economies of scale and specialization, 399–400, 413–15; and spread of technology, 415–16; and competitive markets, 451. *See also* Exports; Imports

Franc-zone countries, trade growth with, 405

Freycinet Plan, 14

Full employment output, *see* Output, potential

Gas industry, 130. *See also* Oil industry; Solid mineral fuels and gas industry

Gavanier, M., 105f, 512

General Agreement on Tariffs and Trade, 464

Germany: development and growth rates, 12, 14–15, 22f, 149–50; population growth, 12, 36; labor data, 53, 61, 76, 215–16, 259; productivity, 82, 86–87, 185; capital per worker, 155–56; industrial concentration, 165f, 170; technical progress, 210, 215–16, 218; capacity utilization, 241; savings, 287–89; firm finance, 297, 313, 318–19; price levels, 370f; recession of 1966 and French exports, 399; Carré's theory applied, 411f. *See also in tables on principal Western countries*

Gilbert, M., and I. Kravis, on international price levels, 371

Glass industry, 452–53, 466. *See also* Building materials and glass industry

Government: expenditures, 14, 33, 242–52 *passim*, 509–11; data on labor

force in, 91–92, 550, 552; investment, 106–8, 109, 113, 243, 250, 388f, 522–23; assets, 138–46 *passim*; demand in aggregate demand, 242–44, 247–49; savings, 287–89, 328; net borrowing, 326; planning bodies and National Plans, 480, 485. *See also* Economic policies; Public investment; Public sector; Stabilization policy
Government-controlled industries, 201, 221. *See also* Heavy industries
Government-firms relationship, 417, 419, 487
Great Britain: economic growth, 11–12, 22f, 210, 345, 411; population growth, 12, 36; labor data, 52f, 75–76, 82, 87, 159, 215–16, 270–71, 411; hours worked, 61, 259; productivity, 82, 87, 184f, 210, 500; investment, 119–21; capital data, 149–56 *passim*; industrial concentration, 165, 170; technical progress, 215–16, 218; capacity utilization, 241; prices, 270–71, 345, 370f; savings rates, 287, 289; firm finance, 297, 313, 318–19; Carré's theory applied, 412. *See also in tables on principal Western countries*
Green tariff for electricity, 447
Gross domestic product, 21, 27, 33, 386–88. *See also* Output
Groupe d'Etudes Prospectives sur les Echanges Internationaux, export growth study, 403–4
Gruson, Claude, 4, 489f, 504
Guillaumont-Jeanneney, S., on monetary policy, 358

Heavy industries: investment, 109–10, 111–13, 144–46, 195–96, 221, 275, 524; capital measurement, 144–46, 195–96; government intervention in finance, 275, 342
Hours worked, 60–62, 260, 542–43; laws and effects, 60, 92, 353, 382; and quality coefficient, 68–75, 260; effect on productivity, 79, 192–93; effect on sector wages, 199f; and production growth, 209; and economic growth, 220, 502–3; and aggregate demand, 235–39 *passim*, 259–60; and unemployment, relationship, 238–39, 259–60
Households: investment, 243, 250, 293–94; wealth, 362–64. *See also under* Consumption; Savings
Housing investment, 106–8, 109, 113, 135–38, 338; and demand, 242–44, 252, 254; as saving stimulus, 293–94, 305; and government intervention,

326, 480; of public housing offices, 338; and National Plans, 462–63, 481; sources of data, 522f
Housing services industry: growth, 33; output, 465f, 516; labor force size, 550, 552
Housing stock, 134–38, 140, 142, 151; in total capital, 141; growth, 143f, 146, 151–52; and mobility, 435; prices Paris vs. elsewhere, 454
Houssiaux, Jacques, 166–67, 468–69

Immigration, net: amounts and causes, 39–41, 260, 548; effect on population structure, 43; and aggregate demand, 229–30, 235–36, 257
Import prices: effect on inflation, 349–57 *passim*; index, 394–95
Import quotas: postwar, 373–76 *passim*, 420; effects, 378, 389, 440
Imports: volume, 14, 243, 354, 373–77, 394–95, 398–99; by major product category, 118, 269, 375, 402, 412; and aggregate demand, 229, 235, 247–49, 251–52; changes in propensity, 250, 397–98; 1951 rise and inflation, 354; and growth of industry, 412f. *See also* Foreign trade; *and under product category name*
Income distribution, postwar, 292–93
Income tax, 37–38, 384
Indebtedness, *see* Debt of firms
Indicative planning, 417. *See also* National Plans
Indirect taxation, 443–44
Industrial Revolution, 12
Industrial size of an economy, 409
Industry: production, 11,13f,17,26, 29–32; growth and development, 13, 14–15, 31–32, 409–13; labor force, 15, 90–91, 456; productivity growth, 79, 83f; capital, 151; production function, 189–90; demand for output in 1800's, 271; price increases, 349, 354–55; and government policies, 453–56; employment growth by regions, 456. *See also* Productive sectors
Inflation: and real interest rates, 281–82, 366–69; effect on savings, 291, 294–95; and firms' debt and investment, 313–20; history of, 345–48, 351–55, 370; causes, 348–51, 359–62; and economic growth, 361–62, 387; and market disorganization, 364–70; and foreign trade, 408; and postwar demand, 501. *See also* Prices
Information, economic, *see* Economic data

Infrastructure: capital depreciation rates, 130, 194; and technical progress, 194, 532–33; postwar reconstruction and economic growth, 274–75, 503
Institut National de la Statistique et des Etudes Economiques (INSEE), 466–70, 489–90
Interest, 281–82, 366–69. *See also* Capital; Investment; Monetary policy
International comparisons, *see headings for countries to be compared*
International environment and postwar growth, 253, 501
Inventories of firms, 314, 316
Investment: volume data, 14, 105–9, 113–18, 243–44, 246–47, 269–74, 386–88, 522–24; price of, 114, 119, 366–69; international comparison, 119–21; effect on productivity, 120–21; in estimating capital stock, 128–31, 141, 195–96; and economic growth, 220–21; and aggregate demand, 243–45, 247–49, 252, 261–63; causes of, 250, 253–55, 269–74, 277–78; and profits, 302–3; and finance, 308–9, 343, 475; and indirect taxes, 444; and national planning, 460–61, 467–70, 483; share of foreign capital goods in, 501. *See also* Capital formation; Finance; *under* Government, Public enterprises, *and individual industrial sectors*
Investment-capital ratio, 540–41
Investment cycles, 483
Iron and steel industry, stock and profits, 438–39, 452–53
Iron mining and metallurgy industry: output, 31, 466; productivity growth, 101, 188–89; investment, 112; capital data, 130, 149, 152, 154; government intervention in finance, 342; labor force, 550, 552. *See also* Metallurgy industries; *and in tables with quantities by sector*
Italy: economic growth rates, 22f, 498; labor data, 61, 76, 166 ,259; productivity, 82, 185; investment, 119–20; capital data, 150, 155; industrial concentration, 165f; technical progress, 210, 218; capacity utilization, 241; firm finance, 297, 313, 318–19; prices, 371. *See also in tables on principal Western countries*

Jackson, D. A. S., on labor market competition, 430
Japan: industrial concentration, 165f,

170; labor force data, 166, 411, 434; research, 216; firm finance, 313, 318–19; Carré's theory applied, 412; birthrates and growth, 497
Jeunesse Agricole Chrétienne (JAC), 492
Job migration, *see* Migration; Mobility
Job openings, 235f

Kendrick, John W., price and productivity movements, 516–17
Keynes, John Maynard, 382f
Klein, Lawrence, index of capacity utilization, 239
Kravis, I., and M. Gilbert, on international price levels, 371

Labor: supply, sector supply, and changes, 32, 55–57, 75–76, 87–91, 93, 94–95; force participation rates, 46–57, 89, 257–58, 502; quality, 64–75, 191–92, 199f, 209; input measurement, 77–78, 514–18; intersectoral shifts, 87–91, 94–95, 158–61; input and total productivity, 182, 185; involvement in shift work, 196–97; cost of, 280, 284; supply and inflation, 360–61, 363–64; input intensity, 544. *See also* Migration; Mobility
Labor market: and aggregate demand, 235–36, 257–61; and immigration, 235–36, 257, 390; and profits, 302; competitiveness, 421–30
Labor productivity: growth, 78–84 *passim*, 95–102, 183, 495, 500; growth rates by sector, 79, 81, 83, 95–102; influences on, 79–87; and labor force size, 102; and capital, 157, 183; marginal, 198–205, 213; and aggregate demand, 263f. *See also* Productivity, total
Landry, Adolphe, 38
Lautman, J., and J. C. Thoenig, study of Plan influence, 479–80
Leather industry, output forecast accuracy, 466. *See also* Textiles, clothing, and leather industry
Liabilities of firms, *see* Debt of firms
Life insurance in household savings, 297–98
Light industry: investment, 111–13, 195–96; industrial concentration in, 168
Liquidations, official and aggregate demand, 228–29
Liquid funds of firms, postwar, 333
Local government investment, 151, 477–78

Machinery and equipment, foreign trade, 406–7, 527
Madinier, P., mobility in America, 433–34
Magasins Leclerc, 452
Mairesse, J., estimates of capital, 126, 144
Management: job growth, 215; wages, 425–26
Manpower, *see* Labor
Manufactured goods, foreign trade, 395–97, 402, 406–7
Manufacturing and processing industries: capital-output ratio, 152–53, 154; capital per worker, 156; output index and estimating investment, 525–27. *See also* Light industry
Marczewski, J., 1800's growth, 11
Market allocation: misallocation due to inflation, 364–65, 369; regulation by government, 420. *See also* Prices, controls; Resource allocation efficiency
Market studies, generalized, in National Plans, 459
Markovitch, T. J., 1800's output estimates, 11, 269–70
Marshall Plan aid, 289f, 373, 501–2
Massé, Pierre, on electricity investment, 477
Matthys, G., capital estimates, 125ff, 131f
Mechanical and electrical industries: labor force data, 91, 95, 158, 164, 550–52; productivity, 96, 100, 101, 189; investment, 112, 117; capital stock data, 130, 133, 142, 154, 156; firm size, 164, 169; labor earnings, 200, 427f; foreign trade, 398, 400, 406–7; production, 400, 510–11, 516; changes in competitiveness and profits, 452f; National Plans forecast accuracy, 465f; output vs. raw materials input growth, 510–12; output share in total investment, 525–27, 529. *See also* Electrical manufacturing industry; *and in tables dealing with quantities by sector*
Mechanical industries: concentration, 169; Plans forecasts, 466
Mechanization of industry, 149–50
Méline Law of 1892, 14
Mergers, 488
Metallurgy industries: production, 17, 32, 509, 511, 516; labor productivity, 96–102 *passim*; firm size distribution, 164; profit decline, 301, 453; Plans forecast errors, 464–65, 466. *See also* Iron mining and metallurgy industry; Nonferrous metals and minerals industry

Migration: from agriculture, 159, 161, 171–73, 270; effect on productivity, 197–98, 201–5; and economic growth, 209, 220, 454; rates by regions, 435, 454, 456. *See also* Mobility
Military: draft size, 58, 549; expenditure and state of economy, 355, 361, 388f
Minerals industry, *see* Nonferrous metals and minerals industry
Minimum wage, 354, 357, 422–23
Mining, *see* Iron mining and metallurgy industry; Nonferrous metals and minerals industry; Solid mineral fuels and gas industry
Ministry of Labor employment statistics, 87, 91, 94
Ministry of Public Works study of investment choice, 479–80
Miscellaneous industries sector: productivity, 96–102 *passim*, 189; investment, 113; capital, 130, 154; competitiveness and profits, 169, 452–53; foreign trade, 398, 400; output, 400, 465f, 516; wages, 428; labor force, 550, 552. *See also in tables with quantities by sector*
Mobility: job, 264, 436–37; geographical, 432–36; government and other incentives, 436–37, 544; and economic growth, 502; and productivity growth, 536–39. *See also* Migration
Modernization and postwar growth, 503
Monetary policy, and inflation, 349, 355–56, 358–59, 361–62. *See also* Stabilization policy
Money holdings of firms, postwar, 333
Money supply and inflation, 350–51
Monnet, Jean, 487, 494, 504
Monnet Plan, 471
Monopoly returns to capital, 188
Mouvement économique en France de 1929 à 1939, quoted, 381–82

Napoleon I and technical schools, 13
National Accounts: estimation methods and changes, 5, 17–19, 522–24; balance-sheet terms translated, 322; origin of system, 490
National income, *see* Output
Nationalizations as cause of growth, 496, 498
National Plans: effect on investment, 255, 263, 274–75, 475–81; and economic policy, 274–75, 372, 471–73; 481f; accuracy of forecasts, 461–65; use by firms, 465–70; organizational structure and roles, 481–85 *passim*;

as cause of growth, 496–97, 499;
Commissariat Général on 1938–49
output by sector, 512
Nationally owned enterprises investment, 221, 274–76, 475
Natural gas industry, *see* Oil industry
Netherlands: capital growth, 155, 297;
industrial concentration, 165f, 170;
productivity, 185; research, 216;
capacity utilization, 241; prices, 371
Neutrality of taxation, 443
New products, output underestimation
of, 18
Nominal interest rates, *see* Real interest
rates
Nonferrous metals and minerals industry: output and investment growth,
30, 466; productivity, 101f; capital
data, 130, 146, 156; labor force size,
550, 552. *See also* Metallurgy industries; *and tables dealing with quantities by sector*
North Atlantic Treaty Organization
(NATO) and balance of payments,
377. *See also* Military
Norway: capital per worker, 155; productivity, 185, 412

Obsolescence of capital, effect on productivity, 193–95
Occupational groups wage differentials,
292, 425–26
Oil industry: output, 30, 465f, 516;
labor force, 91, 550, 552; productivity, 96–102 *passim*, 189; investment, 112; capital data, 130, 152–53;
return to capital, 187n, 188; prices,
365, 445–46. *See also* Energy industries; Heavy industries; *and tables
dealing with quantities by sector*
Organization for Economic Cooperation
and Development (OECD) study of
wages, 429–30
Organizing committees, postwar roles,
492
Output: estimation methods, 4–5, 18–
19, 522–24; per unit labor, 79–81,
84–85; shares of labor and capital in,
185–86; accounting for the inputs
and residual, 208–18; potential, 236–
41; national income forecasts, 386–
88; 1929 vs. 1946, 500. *See also*
National Plans
Owner-managers, returns to factors,
185–86

Paish, F. W., effect of demand on
growth, 256

Paper industry, Plan forecast accuracy,
466. *See also* Miscellaneous industries
sector
Patent applications, 217
Peak-load pricing in electricity, 447
Perroux, François, on growth poles,
496
Petroleum, natural gas, and oil industry,
see Oil industry
Phan, D. L., on export growth, 402–3
Pinay government and 1952 stabiliza-
tion, 388–89
Planning, and efficiency of investment,
460–61. *See also* National Plans
Plant and equipment investment, 108–
10. *See also* Capital equipment
Plant size and economies of scale, 165–
66
Poincaré stabilization, 3, 353, 380–81
Popular Front government, laws on
work hours, 14, 79
Population: growth, 12, 35, 36–39,
41–42, 59, 60; structure, 13, 43–46
Press development of economic information, 491
Prices: level changes, 3, 227–28, 234–
35, 349–50, 365–70; choice of indexes over time, 19, 512–13; relative,
of output categories, 271, 512–14;
controls, 350, 356, 358–59, 440–43;
international comparison, 371–72;
forecasts, 386–88
Processed foods and farm products industry: productivity growth, 96, 100f;
investment, 113, 524; capital data,
130, 149, 154; monopoly returns to
capital, 188; wages, 427; output,
465f, 516; labor force, 550, 552. *See
also* Manufacturing and processing
industries; *and in tables with quantities by sector*
Production, *see* Output
Production function, uses of, 179, 189–
90
Production tax of 1936, features of,
443–44
Productive sectors: definition, 57; employment in, 77, 93f; investment,
106–8, 109, 113–14; capital stock,
123, 140f, 147–51; capital growth,
143f, 146; capital-output ratios, 153;
productive capital in total productivity, 182, 185
Productivity, total: effect of concentration, 168–70; measurement, 178–82
passim, 191–97, 535; growth rate,
180, 183, 188, 190–91; and intersector factor shifts, 206–7, 536–39;
and economic growth, conclusions,
219; effect of aggregate demand on,

263–66; and inflation, 360, 363, 364; and international specialization, 408–16. *See also* Labor productivity; Residual factor in growth

Productivity missions of the 1950's, 416, 488, 491

Professional labor growth, 215

Profits: rates and influences on, 213, 349, 452–53; history of, 250, 270–74, 298; causes of postwar decline, 299–304; and self-finance of investment, 307

Projections, *see* Forecasting; National Plans

Proprietorships, 185–86, 207, 264–65

Protectionist policies, *see* Import quotas

Publications, *see* Press development

Public enterprises: external finance, 326, 337, 338–39; investment, 338–39, 388f, 476–77; rates vs. true costs, 444–45

Public investment, 221, 274–76, 475

Public sector: debt as share of total, 327–29; finance sources for firms, 331; purchases and competitive prices, 450–51. *See also* Government

Public works, *see* Building and public works industry

Railroads, 14, 447–49, 477

Raw materials prices, 351–57 *passim*, 394–95

Real interest rates and postwar inflation, 366–69

Recession: of 1952–53, 254, 262–66 *passim*, 278–79; of 1900–1905, 379; postwar, 391

Regions (provinces), 172–73, 456

Rent control and housing investment, 293–94, 325–26

Research and development, 216, 480, 485, 492, 505

Residual factor in growth, 214, 218, 265, 495

Resource allocation efficiency, 418–19, 471–73. *See also* Competition; Market allocation

Restrictive practices, postwar controls on, 449–50

Retraining of workers, bonus payments, 436–37

Risk in contracts and inflation, 365–70

Rist, Charles, on overinvestment danger in 1949, 278

Rueff-Armand Commission, 449–50, 451, 488

Rural out-migration rate, 435. *See also* Migration

Salais, R., on labor force participation rates, 258

Sauvy, Alfred, 5, 23, 38, 504

Savings: postwar propensity, 248–51 *passim*; by firms, postwar, 250, 298–99; definitions of rates, 285n, 286; by government, postwar, 287–90, 328; by households, 288–98, 324f; in liquid form, 294–95; availability and supply of finance, 322–26 *passim*; housing restrictions and use of, 325–26; government policy toward use, 325–29 *passim*, 486

Schools: enrollment rates, 62–64; investment, 106, 143–44; value of buildings, 139. *See also* Education

Sédillot, René, on economic future in 1950's, 279

Self-employed workers, 185–86, 207, 264–65

Self-financing ratio, 308–13; definitions, 309, 540; effects of decline, 321, 343; prewar and postwar, 335, 341. *See also* Firms

Service d'Etudes Economiques et Financières (SEEF), 490

Services: output growth, 22, 26, 30f, 32, 465f, 516; labor force, 90–91, 95, 550, 552; productivity, 96, 100ff, 189; investment, 113, 523f; capital data, 130, 151–56 *passim*; monopoly returns to capital, 188; causes of inflation, 350. *See also in tables dealing with quantities by sector*

Shipbuilding, aircraft, and armaments industry, National Plans forecast accuracy, 465f

Snyder, W. W., stabilization and budgets, 392

Social capital costs, Paris vs. elsewhere, 454

Social cohesion, lack of, and inflation, 360f

Social security system, effects of, 291f, 358, 384

Social upheaval of 1968 and growth, 391–92

Société Nationale des Chemins de Fer, 14, 447–49, 477

Solid mineral fuels and gas industry: output, 31, 465f, 516; labor force, 91, 95, 550, 552; productivity, 96–101 *passim*; capital data, 130, 152, 154, 156, 187. *See also in tables dealing with quantities by sector*

Solow, R. M., "Investment and Technical Progress," 194

Specialization in production, 214, 399–400, 408–16, 488

Stabilization policy: Poincaré policy of

1926, 3, 353, 380–81; of 1952, 388–
89; of 1963, 377; postwar circumstances and instruments, 382–85;
postwar international comparison, 392
Statistique Générale de la France, 381–
82, 489
Stock exchange values as profit indicators, 272
Stock issues: and 1946 authorizations
law, 438–39; and investment volume,
530
Stocks and bonds: in total postwar savings, 295–97; in total firm finance,
postwar, 332–36, 339–40; new issues
and firm investment, 333, 530
Suez Canal closure and import controls,
440
Sweden, research in, 216

Tardieu government budget and Depression, 381
Tariffs, from 1881 to 1892, 14. *See also*
Import quotas
Taxation: in aggregate demand formation, 248–49, 251; effects on industrial costs, 280, 302, 358; and price
level, 355; and National Plans, 488.
See also taxes by specific names
Technical progress: and labor skills, 13,
214–16; measuring effect on growth,
177–78; embodiment in capital, 193–
95, 532–33, 535; the residual factor
in output growth, 208–11, 214, 218.
See also Technology
Technicians, growth in labor force, 215
Technology: use of foreign, 216–18,
415–16
Textiles, clothing, and leather industry:
prewar data, 15, 17; output, 31, 400,
465f, 516; labor force, 91, 95, 158,
164, 550, 552; labor productivity,
96–102 *passim*; productivity, 101,
188f, 196–97; investment, 113; capital, 130, 154, 261; concentration, 164,
169; shift work increase, 196–97, 261;
labor earnings, 200, 427f; profit drop,
301, 452–53; foreign trade, 400; competitiveness, 452–53. *See also* Manufacturing and processing industries;
*and tables dealing with quantities
by sector*
Tourism and balance of payments, 377f
Toutain, in *Cahiers de l'ISEA*, 11
Trade: output, 32, 516; employment,
95, 550, 552; productivity, 96–102
passim, 189; investment, 113, 523f;
capital, 130, 152–53; concentration,
174–76; in postwar economic growth,
219; competition and efficient struc-

ture, 451–52. *See also in tables dealing with quantities by sector*
Trade organizations, 17, 441f, 492
Transfer payments of government, macroeconomic effects, 286, 381, 385.
See also Social security system
Transportation and communications
industry: growth, 13–14, 30f, 32,
465f, 516; labor force, 91, 550, 552;
productivity, 96–102 *passim*, 189;
investment, 106–7, 109–12, 477, 524;
infrastructure, 106–7, 134, 154; capital, 126–27, 130, 134, 142, 151–57
passim, 187; concentration, 173–74;
financing privileges, 339. *See also in
tables dealing with quantities by
sector*
Transportation costs in 1800's, 271
Transportation equipment trade and
Common Market, 406–7
Transport modes, relative prices, 447–49
Tugault, Y., mobility measurement,
432–33
Turner, H. A., on labor market competition, 430
Turnover tax, features of, 443–44

Unemployment: levels, 57f, 353–54,
549; and aggregate demand, 230–31,
235f, 258; hidden or underemployment, 238, 454; and hours worked,
259–60; benefits payments and
stabilization, 384–85
Unions and competitive labor market,
421
United Kingdom, *see* Great Britain
United States: growth and development,
12, 14–15, 22f, 149–50, 500; population growth, 12, 36; labor, 52–53,
75–76, 166, 215–16; hours worked,
61, 259; productivity, 82, 86–87,
184f, 500; investment, 119–21; capital, 151–52, 155; labor mobility, 159,
433–34; concentration, 165f, 170;
technical progress, 210, 215–18;
capacity utilization, 241; savings
rates, 287, 289; firm finance, 297,
313, 318–19; inflation, 370f, Carré's
theory applied, 411; anti-trust activity, 450; and postwar French growth,
502. *See also in tables on principal
Western countries*
Urbanization, 13, 254, 454
Utilities, capital per worker, 156. *See
also* Electricity, water, and kindred
products industry

Vacations from work, 60ff, 92, 95; 1956

law and inflation, 356; and work hours offset, postwar, 503
Value-added tax, 280, 282–83, 443–44, 486ff
Vincent, L. A.: estimates, 4f, 91, 515–16, 525, 529; output estimates, 17, 23, 509–12; capital estimates, 126f, 131f

Wages: government policy, 62, 421–22; and labor quality, 65, 199f, 213; by sectors, 185–86, 199f, 426–30; male vs. female, 199f, 424–25; levels in 1800's, 270–71; by occupational group, 292, 425–26; causes of short-term increases, 350; and price level, 354f, 357; and competitive labor market, 421–30
War, effects of: on population, 36–43

passim; on labor, 46–47, 81–82; on postwar savings, 290–91; on prices, 352f; and government control of economy, 417, 419
Water industry, *see* Electricity, water, and kindred products industry
Wealth of households, 291, 294–95, 362–64
White-collar workers, 215, 425
Women in labor force: 48–54, 502; labor force quality, 70–71; wages, 199f, 424–25; social questions, 542
Wood, paper, and miscellaneous industries, *see* Miscellaneous industries sector
Workers, unpaid family, 161f, 174, 204, 207
Work hours, *see* Hours worked
World War II and economic growth, 3, 219–20, 470–71, 496, 498